Collins

# The Shanghai Maths Project

For the English National Curriculum

## Teacher's Guide 3B

**Teacher's Guide Series Editor:** Amanda Simpson

**Practice Books Series Editor:** Professor Lianghuo Fan

**Authors:** Caroline Clissold, Jane Jones, Steph King, Brian Macdonald, Richard Perring and Paul Wrangles

William Collins' dream of knowledge for all began with the publication of his first book in 1819.

A self-educated mill worker, he not only enriched millions of lives, but also founded a flourishing publishing house. Today, staying true to this spirit, Collins books are packed with inspiration, innovation and practical expertise. They place you at the centre of a world of possibility and give you exactly what you need to explore it.

Collins. Freedom to teach.

Published by Collins
An imprint of HarperCollins*Publishers*
The News Building
1 London Bridge Street
London
SE1 9GF

Browse the complete Collins catalogue at
**www.collins.co.uk**

© HarperCollins*Publishers* Limited 2017

10 9 8 7 6 5 4 3 2 1

978-0-00-822603-9

The authors assert their moral rights to be identified as the authors of this work.

Teacher's Guide Series Editor: Amanda Simpson

Practice Books Series Editor: Professor Lianghuo Fan

Authors: Caroline Clissold, Jane Jones, Steph King, Brian Macdonald, Richard Perring and Paul Wrangles

All rights reserved. No part of this publication may be reproduced, stored in a retrieval system, or transmitted in any form by any means, electronic, mechanical, photocopying, recording or otherwise, without the prior written permission of the Publisher or a licence permitting restricted copying in the United Kingdom issues by the Copyright Licensing Agency Ltd., Barnard's Inn, 86 Fetter Lane, London, EC4A 1EN.

British Library Cataloguing in Publication Data

A catalogue record for this publication is available from the British Library.

Publishing Manager: Fiona McGlade
In-house Editor: Nina Smith
In-house Editorial Assistant: August Stevens
Project Manager: Emily Hooton
Copy Editors: Catherine Dakin and Tanya Solomons
Proofreader: Helen Pettitt
Cover design: Kevin Robbins and East China Normal University Press Ltd
Internal design: 2Hoots Publishing Services Ltd
Typesetting: 2Hoots Publishing Services Ltd
Illustrations: QBS
Production: Rachel Weaver

Printed and bound by CPI Group (UK) Ltd, Croydon, CR0 4YY

**Photo acknowledgements**
The publishers wish to thank the following for permission to reproduce photographs. Every effort has been made to trace copyright holders and to obtain their permission for the use of copyright materials. The publishers will gladly receive any information enabling them to rectify any error or omission at the first opportunity.

(t = top, c = centre, b = bottom, r = right, l = left)

p329 l Mr. Luck/Shutterstock, p329 r Mascha Tace/Shutterstock, p329 cl Scanrail1/Shutterstock, p243 br Quackdesigns/Shutterstock.

# Contents

# The Shanghai Maths Project: an overview

The Shanghai Maths Project is a collaboration between Collins and East China Normal University Press Ltd., adapting their bestselling maths programme, 'One Lesson, One Exercise', for England, using an expert team of authors and reviewers. This carefully crafted programme has been continually reviewed in China over the last 24 years, meaning that the materials have been tried and tested by teachers and children alike. Some new material has been written for The Shanghai Maths Project but the structure of the original resource has been preserved and as much original material as possible has been retained.

The Shanghai Maths Project is a programme from Shanghai for Years 1–11. Teaching for mastery is at the heart of the entire programme, which, through the guidance and support found in the Teacher's Guides and Practice Books, provides complete coverage of the curriculum objectives for England. Teachers are well supported to deliver a high-quality curriculum using the best teaching methods; pupils are enabled to learn mathematics with understanding and the ability to apply knowledge fluently and flexibly in order to solve problems.

The programme consists of five components: Teacher's Guides (two per year), Practice Books (two per year), Shanghai Learning Book, Homework Guide and Collins Connect digital package.

In this guide, information and support for all teachers of primary maths is set out, unit by unit, so they are able to teach The Shanghai Maths Project coherently and confidently, and with appropriate progression through the whole mathematics curriculum.

# Practice Books

The Practice Books are designed to serve as both teaching and learning resources. With graded arithmetic exercises, plus varied practice of key concepts and summative assessments for each year, each Practice Book offers intelligent practice and consolidation to promote deep learning and develop higher order thinking.

There are two Practice Books for each year group: A and B. Pupils should have ownership of their copies of the Practice Books so they can engage with relevant exercises every day, integrated with preparatory whole-class and small group teaching, recording their answers in the books.

The Practice Books contain:

- chapters made up of units, containing small steps of progression, with practice at each stage
- a test at the end of each chapter
- an end-of-year test in Practice Book B.

Each unit in the Practice Books consists of two sections: 'Basic questions' and 'Challenge and extension questions'.

We suggest that the 'Basic questions' be used for all pupils. Many of them, directly or sometimes with a little modification, can be used as starting questions, for motivation or introduction or as examples for clear explanation. They can also be used as in-class exercise questions – most likely for reinforcement and formative assessment, but also for pupils' further exploration. Almost all questions can be given for individual or peer work, especially when used as in-class exercise questions. Some are also suitable for group work or whole-class discussion.

**1** Calculate mentally.

| | | |
|---|---|---|
| (a) 63 + 9 = ☐ | (b) 75 + 24 = ☐ | (c) 84 − 16 = ☐ |
| (d) 70 − 35 = ☐ | (e) 34 + 16 = ☐ | (f) 48 + 25 = ☐ |
| (g) 63 − 36 = ☐ | (h) 93 − 53 = ☐ | (i) 38 + 25 = ☐ |
| (j) 27 + 44 = ☐ | (k) 74 − 58 = ☐ | (l) 60 − 42 = ☐ |
| (m) 36 + 18 = ☐ | (n) 67 − 27 = ☐ | (o) 50 − 43 = ☐ |
| (p) 90 + 10 = ☐ | (q) 82 − 45 = ☐ | (r) 36 + 55 = ☐ |

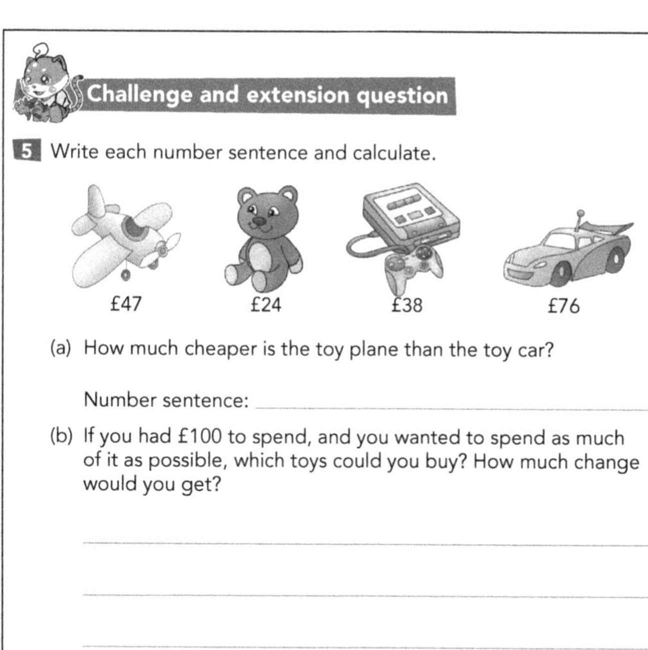
**Challenge and extension question**

**5** Write each number sentence and calculate.

£47 £24 £38 £76

(a) How much cheaper is the toy plane than the toy car?

Number sentence: ______________

(b) If you had £100 to spend, and you wanted to spend as much of it as possible, which toys could you buy? How much change would you get?

All pupils should be given the opportunity to solve some of the 'Challenge and extension questions', which are good for building confidence, but they should not always be required to solve all of them. A general suggestion is that most pupils try about 40–60 per cent of the 'Challenge and extension questions'.

Unit tests sometimes include questions that relate to content in the 'Challenge and extension questions'. This is clearly shown in the diagnostic assessment grids provided in the Teacher's Guides. Teachers should make their own judgements about how to use this information since not all pupils will have attempted the 'Challenge and extension question'.

# Teacher's Guides

## Theory underpinning the Teacher's Guides

The Teacher's Guides contain everything teachers need in order to provide the highest quality teaching in all areas of mathematics, in line with the English National Curriculum. Core mathematics topics are developed with deep understanding in every year group. Some areas are not visited every year, though curriculum coverage is in line with Key Stage statutory requirements, as set out in the National curriculum in England: mathematics programmes of study (updated 2014).

There are two Teacher's Guides for each year group: one for the first part of the year (Teacher's Guide 3A) and the other for the second (Teacher's Guide 3B).

The Shanghai Maths Project is different from other maths schemes that are available in that there is no book called a 'textbook'. Lessons are a mixture of teacher-led, peer and independent work. The Teacher's Guides set out subject knowledge that teachers might need, as well as guidance on pedagogical issues – the best ways to organise activities, to ask questions, to increase difficulty in small steps. Most importantly, the Teacher's Guides contain, threaded throughout the whole book, a strong element of professional development for teachers, focusing on the way mathematics concepts can be enabled to develop and connect with each other.

The Shanghai Maths Project Teacher's Guides are a complete reference for teachers working with the Practice Books. Each unit in the Practice Book for each year group is set out in the corresponding Teacher's Guide over a number of pages.

Most units will need to be taught over more than one lesson – some might need three lessons. In the Practice Books, units contain a great deal of learning, densely packed into a few questions. If pupils are to be able to tackle and succeed with the Practice Book questions, they need to have been guided to learn new mathematics and to connect it to their existing knowledge.

This can only be achieved when teachers are able to break down the conceptual learning that is needed and to provide relevant and high quality teaching. The Teacher's Guides show teachers how to build up pupils' knowledge and experience so they learn with understanding in small steps. This way, learning is secure, robust and not reliant on memorisation.

The small steps that are necessary must be in line with what international research tells us about conceptual growth and development. The Shanghai Maths Project embodies that knowledge about conceptual development and about teaching for mastery of mathematics concepts and skills. The way that difficulty is varied, and the same ideas are presented in different contexts, is based on the notion of 'teaching with variation'. 'Variation' in Chinese mathematics carries particular meaning as it has emerged from a great deal of research in the area of 'variation theory'. Variation theory is based on the view that, 'When a particular aspect varies whilst all other aspects of the phenomenon are kept invariant, the learner will experience variation in the varying aspect and will discern that aspect. For example, when a child is shown three balls of the same size, shape, and material, but each of a different color: red, green and yellow, then it is very likely that the child's attention will be drawn to the color of the balls because it is the only aspect that varies.' (Bowden and Marton 1998, cited in Pang & Ling 2012)

In summary, two types of variation are necessary, each with a different function; both are necessary for the development of conceptual understanding.

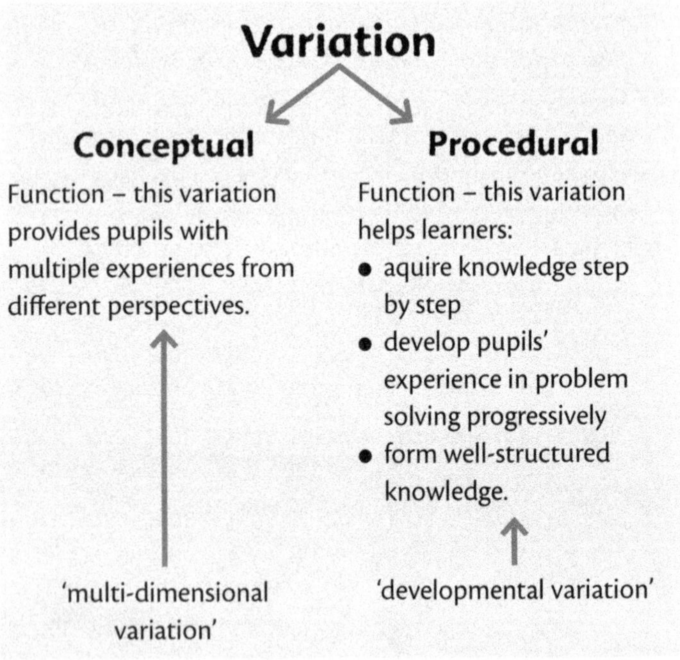

**Variation**

| **Conceptual** | **Procedural** |
| --- | --- |
| Function – this variation provides pupils with multiple experiences from different perspectives. | Function – this variation helps learners:<br>• aquire knowledge step by step<br>• develop pupils' experience in problem solving progressively<br>• form well-structured knowledge. |
| 'multi-dimensional variation' | 'developmental variation' |

Teachers who are aiming to provide conceptual variation should vary the way the problem is presented without varying the structure of the problem itself.

The problem itself doesn't change but the way it is presented (or represented) does. Incorporation of a Concrete–Pictorial–Abstract (CPA) approach to teaching activities provides conceptual variation since pupils experience the same mathematical situations in parallel concrete, pictorial and abstract ways.

CPA is integrated in the Teacher's Guides so teachers are providing questions and experiences that incorporate appropriate conceptual variation.

Procedural variation is the process of:

- forming concepts logically and/or chronologically (i.e. scaffolding, transforming)
- arriving at solutions to problems
- forming knowledge structures (generalising across contexts).

In the Practice Book there are numerous examples of procedural variation in which pupils gradually build up knowledge, step by step; often they are exposed to patterns that teachers should guide them to perceive and explore.

It is this embedded variation that means that when The Shanghai Maths Project is at the heart of mathematics teaching throughout the school, teachers can be confident that the curriculum is of the highest order and it will be delivered by teachers who are informed and confident about how to support pupils to develop strong, connected concepts.

## Teaching for mastery

There is no single definition of mathematics mastery. The term 'mastery' is used in conjunction with various aspects of education – to describe goals, attainment levels or a type of teaching. In teaching in Shanghai, mastery of concepts is characterised as 'thorough understanding' and is one of the aims of maths teaching in Shanghai.

Thorough understanding is evident in what pupils do and say. A concept can be seen to have been mastered when a pupil:

- is able to interpret and construct multiple representations of aspects of that concept
- can communicate relevant ideas and reason clearly about that concept using appropriate mathematical language
- can solve problems using the knowledge learned in familiar and new situations, collaboratively and independently.

Within The Shanghai Maths Project, mastery is a goal, achievable through high-quality teaching and learning experiences that include opportunities to explore, articulate thinking, conjecture, practise, clarify, apply and integrate new understandings piece by piece. Learning is carefully structured throughout and across the programme, with Teacher's Guides and Practice Books interwoven – chapter by chapter, unit by unit, question by question.

Since so much conceptual learning is to be achieved with each of the questions in any Practice Book unit, teachers are provided with guidance for each question, breaking down the development that will occur and how they should facilitate this – suggestions for teachers' questions, problems for pupils, activities and resources are clearly set out in an appropriate sequence.

In this way, teaching and learning are unified and consolidated. Coherence within and across components of the programme is an important aspect of The Shanghai Maths Project, in which Practice Books and Teacher's Guides, when used together, form a strong, effective teaching programme.

## Promoting pupil engagement

The digital package on Collins Connect contains a variety of resources for concept development, problem solving and practice, provided in different ways. Images can be projected and shared with the class from the Image Bank. Other resources, for pupils to work with directly, are provided as photocopiable resource sheets at the back of the Teacher's Guides, and on Collins Connect. These might be practical activities, games, puzzles or investigations, or are sometimes more straightforward practice exercises. Teachers are signposted to these as 'Resources' in the Unit guidance.

Coverage of the curriculum is comprehensive, coherent and consolidated. Ideas are developed meaningfully, through intelligent practice, incorporating skilful questioning that exposes mathematical structures and connections.

## Shanghai Year 3 Learning Book

Shanghai Year 3 Learning Books are for pupils to use. They are concise, colourful references that set out all the key ideas taught in the year, using images and explanations pupils will be familiar with from their lessons. Ideally, the books will be available to pupils during their maths lessons and at other times during the school day so they can access them easily if they need support for thinking about maths. The books are set out to correspond with each chapter* as it is taught and provide all the key images and vocabulary pupils will need in order to think things through independently or with a partner, resolving issues for themselves as much as possible. The Year 3 Learning Book might sometimes be taken home and shared with parents: this enables pupils, parents and teachers to form positive relationships around maths teaching that is of great benefit to children's learning.

* Note that because Chapter 6 in Year 3 is a Consolidation and Enhancement Chapter, there is no Chapter 6 in the Year 3 Learning Book.

# How to use the Teacher's Guides

## Teaching

Units taught in the first half of Year 3:

## Contents





Teacher's Guide 3A sets out, for each chapter and unit in Practice Book 3A, a number of things that teachers will need to know if their teaching is to be effective and their pupils are to achieve mastery of the mathematics contained in the Practice Book.

Each chapter begins with a chapter overview that summarises, in a table, how Practice Book questions and classroom activities suggested in the Teacher's Guide relate to National Curriculum statutory requirements.

### Chapter overview

| Area of mathematics | National Curriculum statutory requirements for Key Stage 2 | Shanghai Maths Project reference |
|---|---|---|
| Number – fractions | Year 3 Programme of study<br>Pupils should be taught to: | |
| | ■ count up and down in tenths; recognise that tenths arise from dividing an object into 10 equal parts and in dividing one-digit numbers or quantities by 10 | Year 3, Unit 8.1 |
| | ■ recognise, find and write fractions of a discrete set of objects: unit fractions and non-unit fractions with small denominators | Year 3, Units 8.1, 8.2, 8.3 |
| | ■ recognise and use fractions as numbers: unit fractions and non-unit fractions with small denominators | Year 3, Units 8.1, 8.4 |
| | ■ recognise and show, using diagrams, equivalent fractions with small denominators | Year 3, Units 8.2, 8.3 |
| | ■ add and subtract fractions with the same denominator within one whole (e.g. $\frac{5}{7}+\frac{1}{7}=\frac{6}{7}$) | Year 3, Unit 8.4 |
| | ■ compare and order unit fractions, and fractions with the same denominators | Year 3, Units 8.1, 8.2, 8.3 |
| | ■ solve problems that involve all of the above | Year 3, Units 8.1, 8.2, 8.3, 8.4 |

It is important to note that the National Curriculum requirements are statutory at the end of each Key Stage and that The Shanghai Maths Project does fulfil (at least) those end of Key Stage requirements. However, some aspects are not covered in the same year group as they are in the National Curriculum Programme of Study – for example, end of Key Stage 1 requirements for 'Money' are achieved in Year 2 and 'Money' is not taught again in Year 2.

All units will need to be taught over 1–3 lessons. Teachers must use their judgement as to when pupils are ready to move on to new learning within each unit – it is a principle of teaching for mastery that pupils are given opportunities to grasp the learning that is intended before moving to the next variation of the concept or to the next unit.

All units begin with a unit overview, which has four sections:

Conceptual context – a short section summarising the conceptual learning that will be brought about through Practice Book questions and related activities. Links with previous learning and future learning will be noted in this section.

**Conceptual context**

Prior to counting sets of objects, learning the numbers to 10 and comparing them, there are several skills that need to be developed. These include being able to process information presented visually and link it to known facts about objects, to understand how abstract tokens can be used to represent objects, and compare sets of different objects through subitising or counting.

At this stage, pupils need hands-on experiences – being able to handle objects as they count them adds an important physical and concrete dimension to counting. Number is an abstract concept and pupils need to experience it and see it represented in many different ways. This will help them to form meaningful number concepts that will form vital foundations for their mathematical thinking. Although the questions in the Practice Book provide necessarily pictorial representations, the experiences that you provide in your teaching should focus where possible on the 'concrete' aspect of the Concrete Pictorial Abstract approach. Pupils should be provided with opportunities to count, match and sort physical objects, both everyday objects and abstract tokens (for example, plastic counters).

It is important that, through these activities and questions, pupils have the opportunities to learn that:

a) objects do not always have to be counted – often it is possible to see how many there are without counting them individually (subitising)
b) each object that is counted is only given one number name (one-to-one correspondence)
c) numbers occur in a fixed order – the same order every time
d) it does not matter in which order objects are counted or how they are arranged (conservation of number)
e) the last number said is the total number of objects counted.

**Learning pupils will have achieved at the end of the unit**

- Pupils will have practised generating a subtraction number sentence from a story (Q1)
- Pupils will have revisited recording part–whole relationships in abstract representations such as bar models (Q1)
- Pupils will have used concrete and pictorial bar models to reinforce understanding of subtraction using addition bonds (Q1, Q2, Q3)
- Pupils will have consolidated using a variety of representations for recording subtraction, including pictures (Q1), bar models (Q1, Q2, Q3), mapping format (Q2), number sentences (Q1, Q2, Q3)
- Pupils will have linked the mapping format with the bar model (Q2)
- Pupils will have revisited and reinforced the correct language for subtraction (Q2, Q3)
- Pupils will have revisited recording addition and subtraction in a number sentence (Q3)

This list indicates how skills and concepts will have formed and developed during work on particular questions within this unit.

These are resources useful for the lesson, including photocopiable resources supplied in the Teacher's Guide. (Those listed are the ones needed for 'Basic questions' – not for 'Challenge and extension questions'.)

This is a list of vocabulary necessary for teachers and pupils to use in the lesson.

| **Resources** | **Vocabulary** |
| --- | --- |
| small world toys, e.g. domestic animals, wild animals, sea creatures, vehicles; sets of natural objects, e.g. shells, leaves, fruits, vegetables; beads; buttons; coloured counters; coins; sets of objects made from different materials, e.g. plastic/metal/wood; 2-D/3-D shapes, interlocking cubes, hoops or sorting rings<br>**Resource 1.1.2** 'Can you see...?' | sort, sets, group, similar, same, different, criteria, characteristic, odd one out |

After the unit overview, the Teacher's Guide goes on to describe how teachers might introduce and develop necessary, relevant ideas and how to integrate them with questions in the Practice Book unit. For each question in the Practice Book, teaching is set out under the following headings:

**What learning will pupils have achieved at the conclusion of Question X?**

This list responds to the following questions: Why is this question here? How does this question help pupils' existing concepts to grow? What is happening in this unit to help pupils prepare for a new concept about ...? This list of bullet points will give teachers insight into the rationale for the activities and exercises and will help them to hone their pedagogy and questioning.

**What learning will pupils have achieved at the conclusion of Question 1?**

- Pupils will have practised processing information presented visually as pictures and connecting it with concepts that they hold about everyday objects.
- Pupils will have practised talking aloud in full sentences to describe characteristics, similarities, differences and connections related to everyday objects.

**Activities for whole-class instruction**

- Pupils have practised asking what is the same and what is different about groups of objects. The learning for this question requires them to find one object that does not fit a group.
- Prepare sets of five or six concrete objects (or pictures) that are similar and add one that is different. Choose scenarios that are appropriate for your pupils. Possible ideas are:
  - 4–5 farm animals and one tractor
  - 4–5 vegetables and one fruit
  - 4–5 boats and one shark
  - 4–5 sets of shoes and one pair of socks
  - 4–5 fish and one crab
  - 4–5 identical birds flying and one perched
- Encourage the pupils to work in pairs to identify the group and recognise the one that does not belong through discussion.
- Choose a pupil to express this verbally, for example: *This is a group of (farm) animals. The one that does not belong is the tractor because it is not a (farm) animal.*

  Repeat what the pupil has said and introduce the term 'odd one out'. Say: *This is a group of (farm) animals. The odd one out is the tractor because it is not a (farm) animal.*
- Challenge pairs of pupils to use small world resources to make their own group of objects that includes an 'odd one out'. Invite pairs to identify and explain the odd one out.
- Allow pupils to work through Question 3 in the Practice Book recognising the group and identifying the object that does not belong to the group. Listen to them explaining their reasoning.

**Activities for whole-class instruction**

This is the largest section within each unit. For each question in the Practice Book, suggestions are set out for questions and activities that support pupils to form and develop concepts and deepen understanding. Suggestions are described in some detail and activities are carefully sequenced to enable coherent progression. Procedural fluency and conceptual learning are both valued and developed in tandem and in line with the Practice Book questions. Teachers are prompted to draw pupils' attention to connections and to guide them to perceive links for themselves so mathematical relationships and richly connected concepts are understood and can be applied.

The Concrete–Pictorial–Abstract (CPA) approach underpins suggestions for activities, particularly those intended to provide conceptual variation (varying the way the problem is presented without varying the structure of the problem itself). This contributes to conceptual variation by giving pupils opportunities to experience concepts in multiple representations – the concrete, pictorial and the abstract. Pupils learn well when they are able to engage with ideas in a practical, concrete way and then go on to represent those ideas as pictures or diagrams, and ultimately as symbols. It is important, however, that a CPA approach is not understood as a one-way journey from concrete to abstract and that pupils do not need to work with concrete materials in practical ways if they can cope with abstract representations – this is a fallacy. Pupils of all ages do need to work with all kinds of representations since it is 'translating' between the concrete, pictorial and abstract that will deepen understanding, by rehearsing the links between them and strengthening conceptual connections. It is these connections that provide pupils with the capacity to solve problems, even in unfamiliar contexts.

In this section, the reasons underlying certain questions and activities are explained, so teachers learn the ways in which pupils' concepts need to develop and how to improve and refine their questioning and provision.

Usually, for each question, the focus will at first be on whole-class and partner work to introduce and develop ideas and understanding relevant to the question. Once the necessary learning has been achieved and practised, pupils will complete the Practice Book question, when it will be further reinforced and developed.

### Same-day intervention

Pupils who have not been able to achieve the learning that was intended must be identified straight away so teachers can try to identify the barriers to their learning and help pupils to build their understanding in another way. (This is a principle of teaching for mastery.) In the Teacher's Guide, suggestions for teaching this group are included for each unit. Ideally, this intervention will take place on the same day as the original teaching. The intervention activity always provides a different experience from that of the main lesson – often the activity itself is different; sometimes the changes are to the approach and the explanations that enable pupils to access a similar activity.

**Same-day intervention**

- Provide worksheets to practise drawing numerals that use arrows to show the correct direction required for each stroke. Check which numerals individual pupils find difficult and provide focused support.
- Write numbers on white paper using a pink or blue highlighter pen. Give pupils a yellow highlighter and ask them to trace the numbers carefully. If they trace accurately, the colour will change from pink to orange, or from blue to green.
- Use PE small apparatus, for example, beanbags, quoits, or spot markers, for pupils to play counting games. Place the apparatus a sensible distance away. Give pairs of pupils a hoop in which to place items and then challenge them to run and collect a number of objects, for example, six beanbags. Choose a pupil to set a new challenge.

**Same-day enrichment**

- Split pupils into pairs. One pupil should make a group of everyday objects (all the same) to represent a number less than 10.
- Their partner should then use plastic counters to make a group to match that number.
- Encourage pupils to explain how they know that the groups are the same.

### Same-day enrichment

For pupils who do manage to achieve all the planned learning, additional activities are described. These are intended to enrich and extend the learning of the unit. This activity is often carried out by most of the class while others are engaged with the intervention activity.

Lessons might also have some of the following elements:

### Information point

Inserted at points where it feels important to point something out along the way.

This question allows pupils to identify links between objects according to their characteristics. Although these characteristics are not number-based, perceiving characteristics – and therefore similarities and differences – is a vital skill for mathematics. Pupils who get into good habits and are practised at noticing similarities and differences will be able to see connections more readily and be able to solve problems in future. Seeing similarities generally is also a pre-requisite for being able to say 'I have matched these two groups together because they both show 4' – that is, to match quantities that are represented in different ways.

### All say ...

Phrases and sentences to be spoken aloud by pupils in unison and repeated on multiple occasions whenever opportunities present themselves during, within and outside of the maths lesson.

*How many more are needed to make the sticks the same.* All say the sentence together.

... left-handed pupils may need additional support in forming numerals, as they cannot easily see what they are writing. They may find it easier to write an 8 in reverse. Similarly, pupils with dyspraxia will find this challenging. Ensure that such pupils are allowed to demonstrate their true cognitive abilities and are not penalised for immature motor control. These pupils should be receiving support to help with handwriting and as their handwriting skills improve, so will their ability to write clear numerals.

### Look out for ...

Common errors that pupils make and misconceptions that are often evident in a particular aspect of maths. Do not try to prevent these but recognise them where they occur and take opportunities to raise them in discussion in sensitive ways so pupils can align their conceptual understanding in more appropriate ways.

Within the guidance there are many prompts for teachers to ask pupils to explain their thinking or their answers. The language that pupils use when responding to questions in class is an important aspect of teaching with The Shanghai Maths Project. Pupils should be expected to use full sentences, including correct mathematical terms and language, to clarify the reasoning underpinning their solutions. This articulation of pupils' thinking is a valuable step in developing concepts, and opportunities should be taken wherever possible to encourage pupils to use full sentences when talking about their maths.

Ideas for resources and activities are for guidance; teachers might have better ideas and resources available. The principle guiding elements for each question should be 'What learning will pupils have achieved at the conclusion of Question X?' and the 'Information points'. If teachers can substitute their own questions and tasks and still achieve these learning objectives they should not feel concerned about diverging from the suggestions here.

## Planning

The Teacher's Guides and Practice Books for Year 3 are split into two volumes, 3A and 3B, one for each part of the year.

- Teacher's Guide 3A and Practice Book 3A cover Chapters 1–6.
- Teacher's Guide 3B and Practice Book 3B cover Chapters 7–10.

Each unit in the Practice Book will need 1–3 lessons for effective teaching and learning of the conceptual content in that unit. Teachers will judge precisely how to plan the teaching year but, as a general guide, they should aim to complete Chapters 1–4 in the autumn term, Chapters 4–8 in the spring term and Chapters 8–10 in the summer term.

The recommended teaching sequence is as set out in the Practice Books.

Statutory requirements of the National Curriculum in England 2013 (updated 2014) are fully met, and often exceeded, by the programme contained in The Shanghai Maths Project. It should be noted that some curriculum objectives are not covered in the same year group as they are in the National Curriculum Programme of Study – however, since it is end of Key Stage requirements that are statutory, schools following The Shanghai Maths Project are meeting legal curriculum requirements.

A chapter overview at the beginning of each chapter shows, in a table, how Practice Book questions and classroom activities suggested in the Teacher's Guide relate to National Curriculum statutory requirements.

### Level of detail

Within each unit, a series of whole-class activities is listed, linked to each question. Within these are questions for pupils that will:

- structure and support pupils' learning, and
- aid teachers' assessments during the lesson.

### Questions and questioning

Within the guidance for each question are sequences of questions that teachers should ask pupils. Embedded within these is the procedural variation that will help pupils to make connections across their knowledge and experience and support them to 'bridge' to the next level of complexity in the concept being learned.

In preparing for each lesson, teachers will find that, by reading the guidance thoroughly, they will learn for themselves how these sequences of questions very gradually expose more of the maths to be learned, how small those steps of progression need to be, and how carefully crafted the sequence must be. With experience, teachers will find they need to refer to the pupils' questions in the guidance less, as they learn more about how maths concepts need to be nurtured and as they become skilled at 'designing' their own series of questions.

### Is it necessary to do everything suggested in the Teacher's Guide?

Activities are described in some detail so teachers understand how to build up the level of challenge and how to vary the contexts and representations used appropriately. These two aspects of teaching mathematics are often called 'intelligent practice'. If pupils are to learn concepts so they are long-lasting and provide learners with the capacity to apply their learning fluently and flexibly in order to solve problems, it is these two aspects of maths teaching that must be achieved to a high standard. The guidance contained in this Teacher's Guide is sufficiently detailed to support teachers to do this.

Teachers who are already expert practitioners in teaching for mastery might use the Teacher's Guide in a different way from those who feel they need more support. The unit overview provides a summary of the concepts and skills learned when pupils work through the activities set out in the guidance and integrated with the Practice Book. Expert mastery teachers might, therefore, select from the activities described and supplement with others from their own resources, confident in their own 'intelligent practice'.

## Assessing

Ongoing assessment, during lessons, will need to inform judgements about which pupils need further support. Of course, prompt marking will also inform these decisions, but this should not be the only basis for daily assessments – teachers will learn a lot about what pupils understand through skilful questioning and observation during lessons.

At the end of each chapter, a chapter test will revisit the content of the units within that chapter. Attainment in the text can be mapped to particular questions and units so teachers can diagnose particular needs for individuals and groups. Analysis of results from chapter tests will also reveal questions or units that caused difficulties for a large proportion of the class, indicating that more time is needed on that question/unit when it is next taught.

## Shanghai Year 3 Learning Book

As referenced on page vii, The Shanghai Maths Project Year 3 Learning Book is a pupil textbook containing the Year 3 maths facts and full pictorial glossary to enable children to master the Year 3 maths programmes of study for England. It sits alongside the Practice Books to be used as a reference book in class or at home.

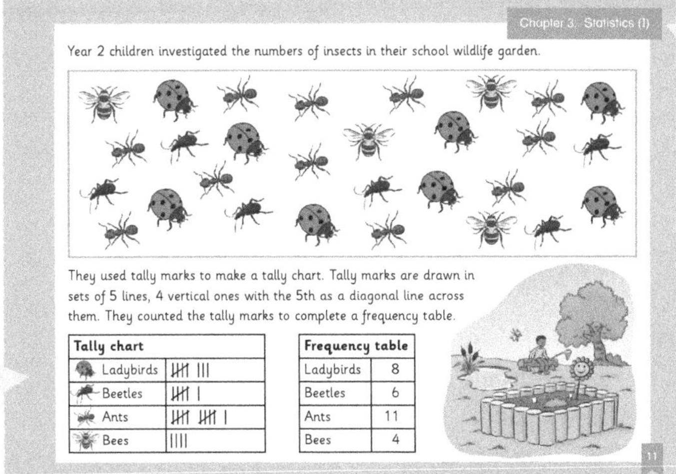

Chapter 3 Statistics (1)

Year 2 children investigated the numbers of insects in their school wildlife garden.

They used tally marks to make a tally chart. Tally marks are drawn in sets of 5 lines, 4 vertical ones with the 5th as a diagonal line across them. They counted the tally marks to complete a frequency table.

| Tally chart | |
|---|---|
| Ladybirds | 𝍸 III |
| Beetles | 𝍸 I |
| Ants | 𝍸 𝍸 I |
| Bees | IIII |

| Frequency table | |
|---|---|
| Ladybirds | 8 |
| Beetles | 6 |
| Ants | 11 |
| Bees | 4 |

11

Maths facts correspond to the chapters in the Practice Books for ease of use.

Key models and images are provided for each mathematical concept.

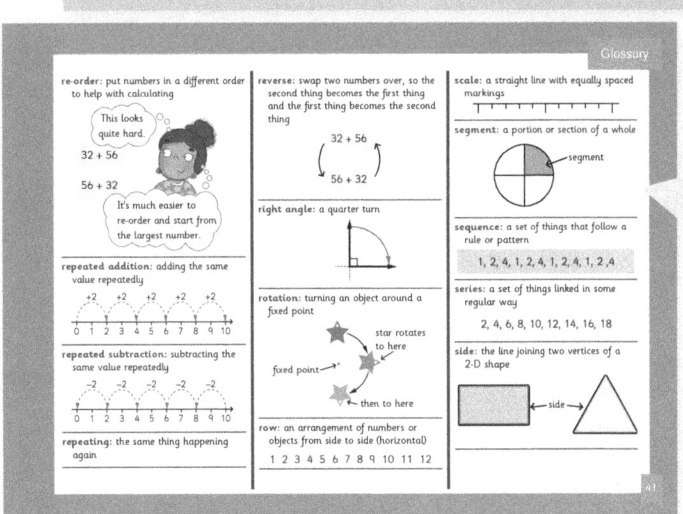

Glossary

**re-order**: put numbers in a different order to help with calculating



**repeated addition**: adding the same value repeatedly



**repeated subtraction**: subtracting the same value repeatedly



**repeating**: the same thing happening again

**reverse**: swap two numbers over, so the second thing becomes the first thing and the first thing becomes the second thing



**right angle**: a quarter turn

**rotation**: turning an object around a fixed point



**row**: an arrangement of numbers or objects from side to side (horizontal)

1 2 3 4 5 6 7 8 9 10 11 12

**scale**: a straight line with equally spaced markings

**segment**: a portion or section of a whole



**sequence**: a set of things that follow a rule or pattern

1, 2, 4, 1, 2, 4, 1, 2, 4, 1, 2, 4

**series**: a set of things linked in some regular way

2, 4, 6, 8, 10, 12, 14, 16, 18

**side**: the line joining two vertices of a 2-D shape



41

A visual glossary defines the key mathematical vocabulary children need to master.

## Homework Guides

The Shanghai Maths Project Homework Guide 3 is a photocopiable master book for the teacher. There is one book per year, containing a homework sheet for every unit, directly related to the maths being covered in the Practice Book unit. There is a 'Learning Together' activity on each page that includes an idea for practical maths the parent or guardian can do with the child.

Homework is directly related to the maths being covered in class.

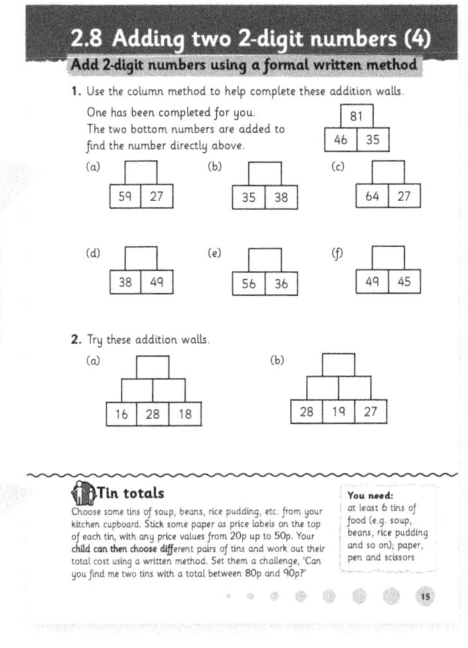

**2.8 Adding two 2-digit numbers (4)**

**Add 2-digit numbers using a formal written method**

1. Use the column method to help complete these addition walls.
   One has been completed for you.
   The two bottom numbers are added to find the number directly above.



2. Try these addition walls.



**Tin totals**

Choose some tins of soup, beans, rice pudding, etc. from your kitchen cupboard. Stick some paper as price labels on the top of each tin, with any price values from 20p up to 50p. Your child can then choose different pairs of tins and work out their total cost using a written method. Set them a challenge, 'Can you find me two tins with a total between 80p and 90p?'

**You need:** at least 6 tins of food (e.g. soup, beans, rice pudding and so on); paper, pen and scissors

15

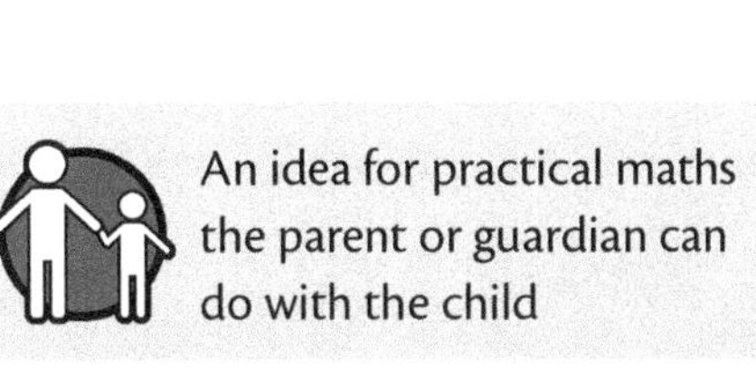

An idea for practical maths the parent or guardian can do with the child

## Collins Connect

Collins Connect is the home for all the digital teaching resources provided by The Shanghai Maths Project.

The Collins Connect pack for The Shanghai Maths Project consists of four sections: Teach, Resources, Record, Support.

### Teach

The Teach section contains all the content from the Teacher's Guides and Homework Guides, organised by chapter and unit.

- The entire book can be accessed at the top level so teachers can search and find objectives or key words easily.
- Chapters and units can be re-ordered and customised to match individual teachers' planning.
- Chapters and units can be marked as complete by the teacher.
- All the teaching resources for a chapter are grouped together and easy to locate.
- Each unit has its own page from which the contents of the Teacher's Guide, Homework Guide and any accompanying resources can be accessed.
- Teachers can record teacher judgements against National Curriculum attainment targets for individual pupils or the whole class with the record-keeping tool.
- Units from the Teacher's Guide and Homework Guide are provided in PDF and Word versions so teachers can edit and customise the contents.
- Any accompanying resources can be displayed or downloaded from the same page.

### Resources

The Resources section contains 35 interactive whiteboard tools and an image bank for front-of-class display.

- The 35 maths tools cover all topics, and can be customised and used flexibly by teachers as part of their lessons.
- The image bank contains the images from the Teacher's Guide, which can support pupils' learning. They can be enlarged and shown on the whiteboard.

### Record

The Record section is the home of the record-keeping tool for The Shanghai Maths Project. Each unit is linked to attainment targets in the National Curriculum for England, and teachers can easily make records and judgements for individual pupils, groups of pupils or whole classes using the tool from the 'Teach' section. Records and comments can also be added from the 'Record' section, and reports generated by class, by pupil, by domain or by National Curriculum attainment target.

- View and print reports in different formats for sharing with teachers, senior leaders and parents.
- Delve deeper into the records to check on the progress of individual pupils.
- Instantly check on the progress of the class in each domain.

### Support

The Support section contains the Teacher's Guide introduction in PDF and Word formats, along with CPD advice and guidance.

# Chapter 7
# Addition and subtraction with 3-digit numbers

## Chapter overview

| Area of mathematics | National Curriculum statutory requirements for Key Stage 2 | Shanghai Maths Project reference |
|---|---|---|
| Number – number and place value | Year 3 Programme of study:<br>Pupils should be taught to: | |
| | ■ recognise the place value of each digit in a three-digit number (hundreds, tens, ones) | Year 3, Units 7.1, 7.2, 7.3, 7.4, 7.5, 7.6, 7.7, 7.8, 7.9, 7.10 |
| | ■ identify, represent and estimate numbers using different representations | Year 3, Units 7.9, 7.10 |
| | ■ read and write numbers up to 1000 in numerals and in words | Year 3, Units 7.1, 7.2, 7.3, 7.4, 7.5, 7.6, 7.7, 7.8, 7.9, 7.10 |
| Number – addition and subtraction | Year 3 Programme of study:<br>Pupils should be taught to: | |
| | ■ add and subtract numbers mentally, including: | |
| | • a three-digit number and ones | Year 3, Units 7.3, 7.4, 7.5, 7.7 |
| | • a three-digit number and tens | Year 3, Units 7.1, 7.2, 7.5, 7.7 |
| | • a three-digit number and hundreds | Year 3, Units 7.1, 7.2, 7.5, 7.7 |
| | ■ add and subtract numbers with up to three digits, using formal written methods of columnar addition and subtraction | Year 3, Units 7.6, 7.8, 7.9, 7.10 |
| | ■ estimate the answer to a calculation and use inverse operations to check answers | Year 3, Units 7.9, 7.10 |
| | ■ solve problems, including missing number problems, using number facts, place value, and more complex addition and subtraction | Year 3, Units 7.1, 7.2, 7.3, 7.4, 7.5, 7.6, 7.7, 7.8, 7.9, 7.10 |
| Statistics | Year 3 Programme of study:<br>Pupils should be taught to: | |
| | ■ solve one-step and two-step questions [for example, 'How many more?' and 'How many fewer?'] using information presented in scaled bar charts and pictograms and tables | Year 3, Unit 7.10 |

# Unit 7.1 Addition and subtraction of whole hundreds and tens (1)

## Conceptual context

Pupils are already familiar with addition and subtraction of two-digit numbers. This unit introduces them to addition and subtraction of numbers with three-digits – specifically, those that are multiples of 100 and then of 10. Pupils are shown how to add/subtract multiples of 100 or 10 by considering them as a number of hundreds or a number of tens. For example, 340 + 120 is framed as 34 tens plus 12 tens. Thus, the concept of a three-digit calculation is linked directly to pupils' existing knowledge of working within numbers to 100. Pupils are expected to use mental methods to calculate answers.

## Learning pupils will have achieved at the end of the unit

- Three-digit addition and subtraction will be understood in terms of adding or subtracting a number of hundreds (Q1, Q2)
- By using known facts to derive the answers to mental addition and subtraction calculations involving three-digit numbers, pupils' mental strategies will have been practised and developed (Q2, Q4)
- Flexibility and fluency with number will have developed as pupils are encouraged to express three-digit multiples of 10 as a number of tens (Q3, Q4, Q5)
- Pupils will have recognised where and how to apply knowledge about addition and subtraction of three-digit multiples of 10 to solve word-based problems (Q6)

### Resources

mini whiteboards; digit cards; base 10 blocks; coloured counters

### Vocabulary

tens, hundreds, multiple, plus, minus, add, subtract, numeral

# Question 1

**1** Fill in the boxes.

(a) 300 + 200 means ☐ hundreds plus ☐ hundreds, which makes ☐ hundreds.

(b) 400 + 500 means ☐ hundreds plus ☐ hundreds, which makes ☐ hundreds.

(c) 900 − 300 means ☐ hundreds minus ☐ hundreds, which makes ☐ hundreds.

(d) 600 − 400 means ☐ hundreds minus ☐ hundreds, which makes ☐ hundreds.

## What learning will pupils have achieved at the conclusion of Question 1?

- Three-digit addition and subtraction will be understood in terms of adding or subtracting a number of hundreds.

## Activities for whole-class instruction

- Remind pupils of previous place value work up to 1000. Ask: *What does one hundred look like?* Discuss suggestions, then give two examples: a 100 square (labelled 1–100) and a base 10 block representing 100. Show different numbers of these blocks and encourage pupils to say how many hundreds they can see. Ask: *How would you write this number as a numeral?* Reverse the activity so pupils are shown multiples of 100 written as numerals and ask them to identify them. Establish that they can be described as ☐ hundreds.
- Write the sentence ☐ hundreds plus ☐ hundreds makes ☐ hundreds. Display an addition (for example 200 + 600) and ask pupils to read it aloud. Ask them to complete the first two boxes in the sentence:

  2 hundreds plus 6 hundreds makes ☐ hundreds.

| Hundreds | Tens | Ones |
| --- | --- | --- |
| ○ ○<br>○ ○<br>○ ○<br>○ ○ | | |

200 + 600

2 hundreds plus 6 hundreds make 8 hundreds

- Pupils should draw a place value grid on their mini whiteboards. Ask them to represent the first number (200) by drawing two circles in the hundreds column. They should then represent the second number by drawing six further circles below them.
- Ask: *How many hundreds are there altogether?* Complete the number sentence to show that this equals 8 hundreds. Ask: *How would you write this as a numeral?* (800)
- Repeat for further additions and subtractions of multiples of 100. For subtractions, draw the circles and then cross out the number that is being subtracted.
- Pupils should complete Question 1 in the Practice Book.

## Same-day intervention

- Place base 10 hundred blocks into two boxes (five hundreds in the first box and four hundreds in the second). Choose two pupils to take any number of blocks from each box. Ask: *How many hundreds do you each have?* Both pupils should place their blocks into a third box and ask: *How many hundreds are there altogether?* Write as a number sentence. Repeat the process to model further additions of multiples of 100. Also include subtraction calculations (put a number of hundreds into one box and then take some away). Encourage pupils to express their calculations as ☐ hundreds plus/minus ☐ hundreds equals ☐ hundreds, as well as using numerals.

## Same-day enrichment

- Provide students with the digits 3, 5, 2 and 4. Set them the challenge of inserting any of these digits into the statements ☐ hundreds plus ☐ hundreds and ☐ hundreds minus ☐ hundreds. Ask: *How many different answers can you make? Can you make the same answer in more than one way without changing the operation? Can you find an addition and a subtraction that give the same answer?* Encourage pupils to express their answers as ☐ hundreds as well as using numerals.

# Question 2

**2** Calculate mentally.

(a) 500 + 200 = ☐ (b) 900 − 300 = ☐

(c) 400 − 100 = ☐ (d) 200 + 400 = ☐

(e) 300 + 600 = ☐ (f) 300 + 200 = ☐

(g) 400 − 300 = ☐ (h) 500 − 100 = ☐

## What learning will pupils have achieved at the conclusion of Question 2?

- Three-digit addition and subtraction will be understood in terms of adding or subtracting a number of hundreds.
- By using known facts to derive the answers to mental addition and subtraction calculations involving three-digit numbers, pupils' mental strategies will have been practised and developed.

## Activities for whole-class instruction

- Ask pupils to write any three-digit multiple of 100 on their mini whiteboards. Choose two pupils to come to the front and reveal their numbers. Ask each to say their number as a number of hundreds. Decide whether they should be added or subtracted (if the numbers will result in a four-digit number when added, subtract them instead). Ask: *How would you write this as an addition/subtraction? Can you say this in terms of 'hundreds'? How do you know what the answer is?* Encourage pupils to explain why their answer is correct. Provide a place value grid and coloured counters for pupils to model the calculation after they have worked it out mentally.
- Repeat for further addition and subtraction of multiples of 100.
- Pupils should complete Question 2 in the Practice Book.

### Same-day intervention

- Practise rapid recall of addition and subtraction bonds within 10. This will help pupils when adding and subtracting numbers of hundreds.
- Provide pupils with addition and subtraction calculations featuring multiples of 100. Encourage pupils to express the calculation as ☐ hundreds plus/minus ☐ hundreds. Ask: *How could you use base 10 blocks to model this calculation?* Pupils should use the base 10 blocks to work out the answer initially, with the aim of moving towards using only mental methods.

## Same-day enrichment

- Draw the following grid on the board and ask pupils to copy it:

| 800 | 600 | 500 |
|---|---|---|
| 900 | 300 | 100 |
| 400 | 700 | 200 |

- Pupils should play the following game in pairs. Each pair should each have a set of multiples of 100 cards (from 100 to 900). Each pupil should take any two cards and decide to add or subtract them. If they can make one of the numbers on the grid, they may place a coloured counter on that square to claim it. If they are unable to make any of the numbers (or the number has already been claimed), play continues with the other pupil. The winner is the pupil who has claimed the most squares when the grid is full. Encourage pupils to consider whether any numbers are more difficult to make (for example, 100 is only made by subtracting two numbers that have a difference of 100).

# Question 3

**3** Fill in the boxes.

(a) 450 + 20 means ☐ tens plus ☐ tens, which makes ☐ tens.

(b) 450 − 20 means ☐ tens minus ☐ tens, which makes ☐ tens.

(c) 360 + 120 means ☐ tens plus ☐ tens, which makes ☐ tens.

(d) 360 − 120 means ☐ tens minus ☐ tens, which makes ☐ tens.

## What learning will pupils have achieved at the conclusion of Question 3?

- Flexibility and fluency with number will have been further developed as pupils are encouraged to express three-digit multiples of 10 as a number of tens.

## Activities for whole-class instruction

- Display the following calculations on the board:

  600 + 300

  640 + 20
- Ask: *What is the same/different about these calculations?* Establish that the first addition (HTO + HTO) adds multiples of 100 and the second addition (HTO + TO) adds multiples of 10.

- Remind pupils that the first calculation can be written 6 hundreds plus 3 hundreds. Ask pupils why the second calculation cannot be described in the same way. Establish that there are no hundreds in 20 and so 640 + 20 is described as: 64 tens plus 2 tens. Ask: *Can we describe 600 + 300 in terms of tens too?* Ensure that pupils understand that they can describe this as 60 tens plus 30 tens as well as hundreds. Ask pupils to consider which is easier to work out: 6 hundreds plus 3 hundreds or 60 tens plus 30 tens, and why this might be.
- Pupils should draw a place value grid on their mini whiteboards. Ask them to represent the first number (640) by drawing six circles in the hundreds column and four circles in the tens column. They should then represent the second number by drawing two further circles in the tens column.

| Hundreds | Tens | Ones |
|---|---|---|
| ○○<br>○○<br>○○ | ○○<br>○○<br><br>○○ | |

640 + 20

64 tens plus 2 tens makes 66 tens

- Ask: *How many tens are there altogether?* Complete the number sentence to show that it equals 66 tens. Ask: *How would you write this number as a numeral? What addition fact did you use to help you?*
- Repeat for further additions and subtractions of multiples of 10. For subtractions, pupils should draw the circles and then cross out the number of tens that is being subtracted.
- Pupils should complete Question 3 in the Practice Book.

## Same-day intervention

- Ensure pupils recognise the links between hundreds and tens. Use base 10 blocks to represent 100 in two ways (as 1 hundred square and as 10 tens rods). Ask: *How many tens are in one hundred? Two hundreds?* and so on. Write down each number and show pupils how they can cover the zero in the ones place and read the number they can see.
- Choose two pupils. The first should take a number of hundreds blocks and tens rods. The second should take a number of tens rods. Ask the first pupil to say their number. Ask the class to describe this as a number of tens. Do the same with the second pupil's number. Ask: *How can we write this as an addition?* Place the two sets of blocks into a box and ask the class to predict the number of tens that are in there. Ask: *How do you know this?* Write the addition as a number sentence using the structure ☐ tens plus ☐ tens makes ☐ tens. Encourage pupils to check inside the box to see whether they were correct. Repeat for subtraction calculations (where one pupil models a three-digit number using base 10 blocks and another pupil takes any number of tens from them (up to 9 tens).

## Same-day enrichment

- Split pupils into groups of three. Pupil A should invent a calculation where a three-digit multiple of 10 is added to a two-digit multiple of 10 (for example 480 + 30). They should only show their mini whiteboard to Pupil B, who should write the calculation in terms of tens (in this example, 48 tens plus 3 tens). Pupil B should only show their mini whiteboard to Pupil C, who should work out the answer and write it as a numeral. Pupil A and Pupil C should put their whiteboards next to each other to check that the answer matches the question.
- Pupils should swap roles and repeat the activity (including subtraction calculations).

# Question 4

(a) 12 + 7 = ☐ (b) 120 + 70 = ☐

(c) 45 − 8 = ☐ (d) 450 − 80 = ☐

(e) 35 + 8 = ☐ (f) 350 + 80 = ☐

(g) 91 − 5 = ☐ (h) 910 − 50 = ☐

## What learning will pupils have achieved at the conclusion of Question 4?

- Flexibility with number will have been developed as pupils are encouraged to express three-digit multiples of 10 as a number of tens.
- Mental strategies will have been used to solve three-digit addition and subtractions.

## Activities for whole-class instruction

- Display the calculation 74 + 5 and ask pupils to work out the answer mentally. Ask: *Can we use what we know about 74 + 5 to help answer 740 + 50?* Split pupils into pairs and ask them to come up with an explanation why this is possible. Share ideas as a class and establish that 740 + 50 is simply 74 tens + 5 tens, so pupils are still working out the same calculation. Compare the answers to both calculations.
- Display further TO + O and TO – O calculations and ask pupils to give another calculation that this can be used to help answer. Read each new calculation as ☐ tens plus (or minus) ☐ tens. Also display HTO + TO and HTO – TO calculations (multiples of 10) and ask pupils to give the number fact that they would use to help answer the question.
- Pupils should complete Question 4 in the Practice Book.

### Same-day intervention

- Write 42 + 9 = ☐ on the board. Ask pupils to work out the answer and then explain how they found it. Use base 10 blocks (tens rods and ones cubes) to model the addition. Ask: *What do you notice about what happens to the 11 ones?* Complete the number sentence. Write 420 + 90 = ☐. Ask: *How many tens are in 90? What about 420?* If pupils find it difficult to recognise that 420 is the same as 42 tens, encourage them to model the number out of base 10 blocks and then swap each hundred for 10 tens rods. Compare the two calculations and ensure pupils can read the second as 42 tens plus 9 tens equals 51 tens. Repeat for different additions and subtractions.

## Same-day enrichment

- Provide pupils with a set of 0–9 digit cards. They should shuffle the cards and take three at random. Challenge them to make as many TO + O or TO – O calculations as they can in two minutes (there are a maximum of 12 possibilities). Pupils should then write the corresponding HTO + TO or HTO – TO calculations by changing the numbers into multiples of 10. For example, the digits 5, 2 and 8 could yield the calculations 52 + 8 = 60, 52 – 8 = 44, 25 + 8 = 33 and so on. These could then be changed into 520 + 80 = 600, 520 – 80 = 440, 250 + 80 = 330 and so on. Repeat for different sets of digits.

# Question 5

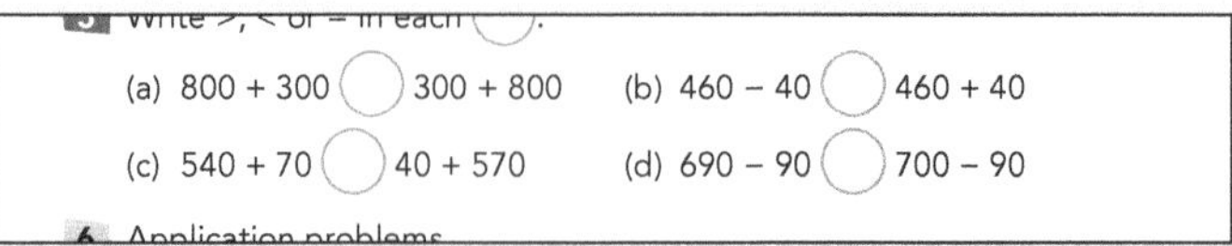
(a) 800 + 300 ◯ 300 + 800 (b) 460 – 40 ◯ 460 + 40

(c) 540 + 70 ◯ 40 + 570 (d) 690 – 90 ◯ 700 – 90

### What learning will pupils have achieved at the conclusion of Question 5?

- Flexibility and fluency with number will have been further developed as pupils are encouraged to express three-digit multiples of 10 as a number of tens.

## Activities for whole-class instruction

- Revise the symbols >, < and = by choosing pairs of pupils to write three-digit multiples of 10 on their mini whiteboards and discussing the symbol they would choose to use to compare them. For comparing equivalent numbers, use numbers expressed as three-digit numerals and as ☐ tens (for example: 89 tens = 890).
- Continue the activity, extending the information on the mini whiteboards to include HTO +/– TO calculations involving multiples of 10, for example: 350 + 60 and 620 – 30.
- Ask: *How would you say these calculations in a different way?* (35 tens plus 6 tens and 35 tens minus 6 tens.) Encourage pupils to compare both mini whiteboards and consider which value is greater. Ensure pupils perform each calculation correctly. They should then describe the relationship between the values on the whiteboards as 'more than' or 'less than', using the appropriate symbol. (By completing the activity this way around (description then symbol) it will become apparent which pupils can compare the values correctly, but have not yet learned the correct symbols.)
- Repeat for different pairs of calculations. Include some that are equivalent and some where pupils must use reasoning to explain how they can compare without actually calculating (for example, 470 + 30 is greater than 470 – 30 because they both have the same starting number, and the first calculation makes it increase and the second makes it decrease).
- Pupils should complete Question 5 in the Practice Book.

## Same-day intervention

- Place two mini whiteboards with calculations on either side of a table. Provide pupils with base 10 blocks to model each calculation. Ask pupils to describe each calculation as a number of tens, as below. They should compare both values in words and finally choose the appropriate symbol to use in a number sentence.

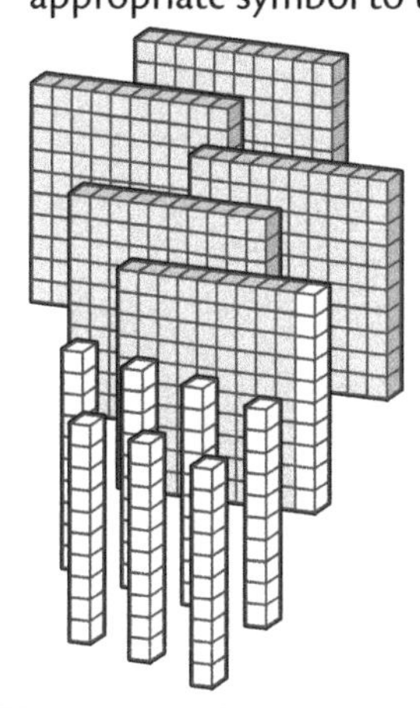

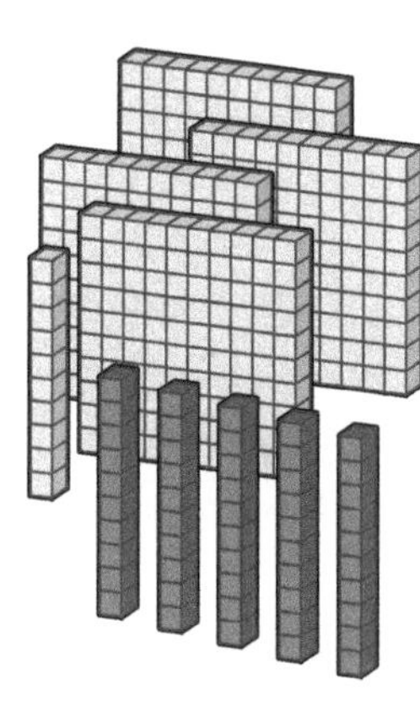

57 tens minus 8 tens = 49 tens 41 tens plus 5 tens = 46 tens

49 tens is more than 46 tens

490 > 460

## Same-day enrichment

- Ask pupils to work in pairs and give each pair a set of 0–9 digit cards. The aim of the activity is to place their cards into a given template to create a comparison of calculations that is true.
- On a mini whiteboard, pupils draw the following template (leaving space for each operation symbol and the central comparison symbol):

□□0 □0 □□0 □0

- Before beginning, pupils should decide which comparison symbol to write in the centre. This will affect where they decide to place each digit. Having decided this, the template might look like this:

□□0 □0 > □□0 □0

- Each pupil is responsible for the calculation on either side of the comparison symbol and they can each decide whether they wish to add or subtract the numbers they make. They should take turns to take a digit card and decide where to place it in the gaps to make a HTO + TO or HTO – TO calculation. The aim of the activity is for pupils to try to place their digits so that the inequality symbol makes sense. As an extension, pupils could switch the inequality symbol around and investigate whether they can make their calculations true by only swapping their digits. For example 350 + 60 > 120 – 90 can be rearranged to 530 + 60 < 910 – 20.

# Question 6

(a) A washing machine costs £230. A TV costs £400. How much cheaper is the washing machine than the TV?

£400 £230

Answer: ____________

(b) There are 530 story books and 380 science books in a library. How many story books and science books are there in total?

Answer: ____________

(c) Finn's father bought him a bike for £180. He paid the shop assistant £200. How much change should he have received?

Answer: ____________

(d) There are 340 cherry trees in an orchard, which is 270 fewer than the number of apple trees. How many apple trees are there?

Answer: ____________

## What learning will pupils have achieved at the conclusion of Question 6?

- Pupils will have recognised where and how to apply knowledge about addition and subtraction of three-digit multiples of 10 to solve word-based problems.

## Activities for whole-class instruction

- Remind pupils how to express numbers as □ tens. Write a series of three-digit multiples of 10 (including those that are also multiples of 100) and ask pupils to respond by calling out the number of tens that are being shown. For example, 700 equals 70 tens, 350 equals 35 tens and so on.
- Display the following application problem: A lorry leaves the depot and travels 270 km to deliver some goods. On the return journey it has to take a detour and ends up driving 310 km before arriving back at the depot. How many kilometres has it travelled in total?
- Ask pupils to explain which operation they would use to answer the question and why.

(i) It is important that pupils have opportunities to identify the operations required to answer word problems. By simply giving them an addition (or subtraction) problem, this takes away some of these opportunities. Try giving them two problems containing similar numbers – one an addition or subtraction problem and one a multiplication or division problem. For example:

- 480 oranges are shared equally into 60 boxes. How many oranges are in each box?
- Kieran cuts 60 cm from a piece of wood that is 480 cm long. How long is the piece he has left?

Explain that pupils only need to answer the one that is addition (or subtraction). However, to do this, they will first need to identify the operations needed before rejecting the problem that is not answered by using addition/subtraction.

- Ask: *Can you say the numbers in the problem in a different way?* (As ☐ tens.) Establish that the calculation needed is 27 tens plus 31 tens. Split pupils into pairs to discuss how they would find the answer. Share answers and ensure pupils can give the answer in the correct context (for example 580 km not 58 tens).
- Repeat for further addition and subtraction application problems.
- Pupils should complete Question 6 in the Practice Book.

## Same-day intervention

- Display the following application problem: On Saturday 370 people watched a football match. The previous week was a cup game and 520 people came to watch. How many more people watched the game the previous week?
- Ask: *What do you think you need to do to the numbers in this question to find the answer?* If it helps, alter the numbers for simpler ones less than 20 so that pupils recognise that the problem is one of subtraction. Ask: *How would you write the subtraction?* Write 520 – 370 on the board and provide base 10 blocks for pupils to model 520. Ask: *How many tens are in 520?* Pupils should swap each of their hundreds for 10 tens rods. Establish that 520 is the same as 52 tens and so 370 is the same as 37 tens. Ask: *What is 52 tens minus 37 tens?* Pupils should use mental methods to find the answer, partitioning 37 into 30 and 7 to help. Allow them to check their answer by taking away 37 tens rods from their pile of 52 and expressing the difference as a three-digit number.
- Repeat for further addition and subtraction application problems.

## Same-day enrichment

- Write 10 different numbers on the board, expressed as ☐ tens (for example 60 tens, 12 tens, 58 tens, 30 tens and so on). Challenge pupils to choose one of these numbers and write their own addition or subtraction calculation that equals their chosen number. For example, if their chosen number is 32 tens, they might write 580 – 260 (because 58 tens – 26 tens = 32 tens).
- Pupils should then write a word problem based around their calculation. For the above example this might be: 'A field is 580 m long. The farmer sells some land so that it is now 260 m shorter. How long is the field now?'
- Pupils should then share their word problems with a partner, who should solve the problem and then look for the answer as a 'tens number' on the board.

## Challenge and extension question

## Question 7

7 Which is greater, ● or ■? How much greater is it?

● + 150 = ■ – 150

Pupils are given an equation where both sides contain a variable instead of a number (● + 150 = ■ – 150). They are asked to consider whether the circle or the square is greater and how much greater it is. Pupils will need to choose a value for the circle and work out the left-hand side of the equation. They should then use this knowledge to work backwards from the right-hand side and add 150 to find the value of the square. Once deciding which is greater and working out the difference, encourage students to try different numbers and see whether the answer stays the same.

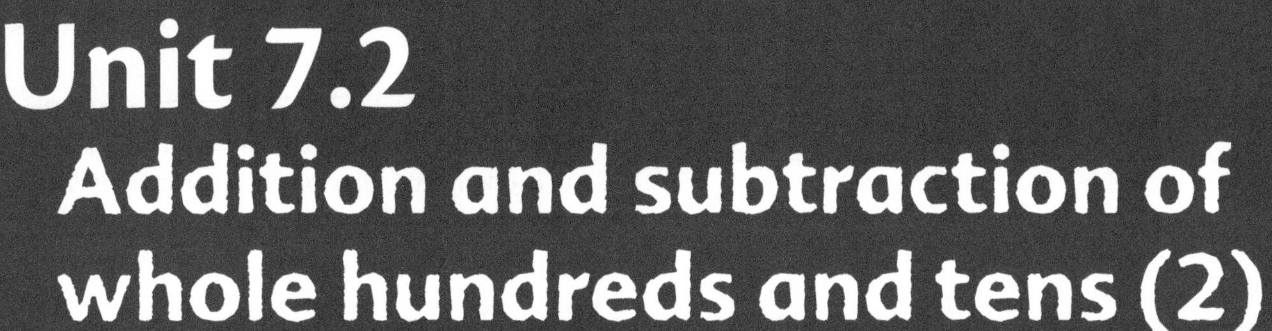

# Unit 7.2 Addition and subtraction of whole hundreds and tens (2)

## Conceptual context

In the previous unit, addition and subtraction of three-digit numbers was linked strongly to the addition and subtraction of two-digit numbers by considering 590 + 220 as being the same as 59 tens plus 22 tens. This variation is sustained and consolidated in this unit so numbers continue to be multiples of 10 and 100.

Learning is extended by combining addition and subtraction in the same problem and by working with 'application problems' in which pupils must recognise how to apply their knowledge in word problems.

In the next unit, pupils will work with three-digit numbers that are not multiples of 10.

## Learning pupils will have achieved at the end of the unit

- Mental strategies to solve three-digit addition and subtraction of multiples of 10 will have been consolidated (Q1, Q2, Q3, Q4, Q5)
- Fluency with addition and subtraction will have been extended to generate calculations from words (addend, sum / minuend, subtrahend, difference) (Q2, Q3)
- Pupils will have solved sequences of addition and subtraction calculations, including those where inverse operations are necessary (Q4)
- Pupils will have recognised where and how to apply knowledge about addition and subtraction of three-digit multiples of 10 to solve word-based problems with more than one step (Q5)

### Resources

mini whiteboards; digit cards; base 10 blocks; coloured counters; **Resource 3.7.2** Key word cards

### Vocabulary

tens, hundreds, multiple, plus, minus, add, subtract, numeral, addend, sum, minuend, subtrahend, difference

# Question 1

**1** Calculate mentally.

(a) 870 − 700 = ☐ (b) 500 + 320 = ☐
(c) 760 − 560 = ☐ (d) 900 − 190 = ☐
(e) 730 + 150 = ☐ (f) 670 + 300 = ☐
(g) 370 − 150 = ☐ (h) 640 + 90 = ☐
(i) 130 + 370 = ☐ (j) 360 − 190 = ☐
(k) 480 − 250 = ☐ (l) 1000 − 650 = ☐

## What learning will pupils have achieved at the conclusion of Question 1?

- Mental strategies to solve three-digit addition and subtraction of multiples of 10 will have been consolidated.

## Activities for whole-class instruction

- Ask pupils to explain how they would mentally add or subtract various two-digit numbers. For example, when adding the numbers 27 and 64, pupils might choose to start with the larger number, then partition 27 into 20 and 7, adding each part separately. Discuss the suggested strategies and explain that they will be going on to use these when working with three-digit numbers.
- Display the calculation 520 − 300. Ask pupils how they could use the strategies discussed to find the answer. Remind them that this can be described as 52 tens minus 30 tens. Ask pupils how this is similar to the calculations they began with. Pupils should work out 52 − 30 to help find the answer. Ask: *Is there another way to solve this?* Some pupils may notice that, as 300 is a multiple of 100, they can simply look at the hundreds digit in the first number and subtract 3 from it. Repeat for a similar three-digit addition.
- Ask: *What do you picture in your head when you imagine subtracting 300 from 520?* Do pupils visualise number lines or base 10 blocks or place value counters? Do they imagine something else? Can they describe their visual images? Encourage them to use 'mental pictures' of equipment or diagrams and procedures that are familiar.
- Ask pupils to write their own three-digit additions or subtractions where the numbers are multiples of 10. They should work out the answer and write it on their mini whiteboards. Choose a pupil to come to the front and read out their calculation as numbers of tens (for example: What is 24 tens add 17 tens?). The class should work out the answer and convert this into a written calculation (in this example, 240 + 170 = 410). The pupil at the front should reveal their mini whiteboard to check that the class answer is correct. Repeat for different calculations.
- Pupils should complete Question 1 in the Practice Book.

## Same-day intervention

- Display the calculation 490 − 180. Ask pupils to model both numbers using base 10 blocks. Ask: *How many tens are in each number?* Pupils should swap their hundreds blocks for 10 rods. Agree that the calculation can be rewritten as 49 tens minus 18 tens and ask pupils to explain what they notice about these numbers.
- Ask pupils to put the 180 to one side and concentrate on 490. Ask: *How many tens will you need to take away to subtract 180 from this number?* Encourage pupils to do this mentally, partitioning 18 into 10 and 8. They should then subtract 10 tens from 49 tens and finally subtract 8 tens. They should use their base 10 blocks to model the removal of 18 tens and then count the number of remaining tens to check their answer.
- Repeat the process to model further additions and subtractions of multiples of 10. Move towards pupils becoming less reliant on modelling using the base 10 blocks and more reliant on mental strategies. Encourage pupils to express their calculations verbally as '☐ tens plus/minus ☐ tens' as well as written using numerals.

## Same-day enrichment

- Split pupils into pairs and provide each pair with a dice (or a 0–9 spinner). They should each draw the following template:

  ☐☐0 ☐☐0

- Pupils should take turns to roll the dice or spin the spinner, deciding in which of the four spaces to write the digit that they roll. Each pupil will then end up with two three-digit multiples of 10 that they should either add or subtract. Having worked out the answer, they should swap questions for their partner to answer. If they answer correctly, they get a point.
- To increase the challenge, ask pupils to place their digits according to given objectives. For example, the winner is the pupil who can generate a calculation that yields the lowest number or whose answer is the closest to 500.

# Question 2

**2** Complete the tables.

(a)

| Addend | 280 | 210 | 330 | 140 | 240 | 390 | 190 |
|---|---|---|---|---|---|---|---|
| Addend | 230 | 160 | 150 | 360 | 410 | 220 | 810 |
| Sum | | | | | | | |

(b)

| Minuend | 160 | 240 | 430 | 650 | 710 | 480 | 610 |
|---|---|---|---|---|---|---|---|
| Subtrahend | 80 | 90 | 210 | 360 | 450 | 290 | 450 |
| Difference | | | | | | | |

## What learning will pupils have achieved at the conclusion of Question 2?

- Mental strategies to solve three-digit addition and subtraction of multiples of 10 will have been consolidated.
- Fluency with addition and subtraction will have been extended to generate calculations from words (addend, sum / minuend, subtrahend, difference).

## Activities for whole-class instruction

- Show pupils enlarged key word cards (see **Resource 3.7.2** Key word cards).

**Resource 3.7.2**

Key word cards

| minuend | subtrahend | sum |
|---|---|---|
| difference | addend | |

- Jumble them up and ask pupils to group them in the order they might find these types of numbers in an addition and a subtraction calculation. Ensure pupils revise the terms addend, minuend, subtrahend, sum and difference.
- Write the numbers 130 and 580 on the board. Ask: *If these numbers are in a subtraction question, which is the minuend, which is the subtrahend and why?* Ask pupils how they would find the difference between these numbers. Encourage them to think of the numbers as 13 tens and 58 tens. Pupils should use mental methods to subtract 13 from 58 to help find the answer. Write the numbers 250 and 680 on the board and ask pupils in which order they would place each addend if they were trying to find the sum. Ensure pupils recognise that starting with the larger number is often easier. Again, pupils should think of the numbers as 25 tens and 68 tens and use mental methods to add 68 and 25 to help find the answer. Repeat the activity for different calculations. For each calculation, ask pupils to turn to a partner and describe the mental methods they used to solve it.
- Pupils should complete Question 2 in the Practice Book.

## Same-day intervention

- Provide labels (addend, sum, minuend, subtrahend, difference) for pupils to cut out. They should use these to label the different parts of bar models showing addition and subtraction. For example:

| addend | addend |
|---|---|
| sum | |

| minuend | |
|---|---|
| subtrahend | difference |

- Give pupils the addends 420 and 140. Ask them to model these numbers using base 10 blocks, considering also the number of tens that each number consists of. For example:

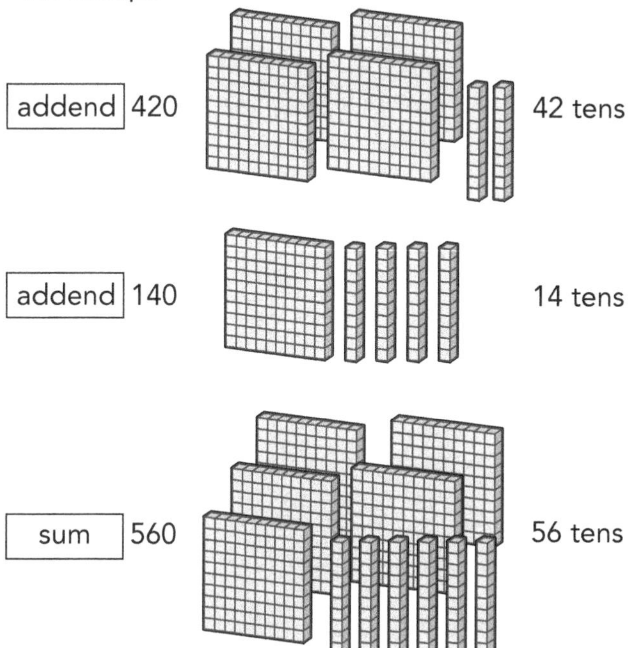

- Repeat for further addition and subtraction calculations with the aim of moving away from modelling using base 10 blocks and towards mental methods. Provide pupils with two sets of addends (for example: 350 and 140, and 230 and 430). Explain that each pair shows two addends in a question. Ask: *Are we looking for the sum or the difference? Do we need to add or subtract each pair of numbers?* Encourage pupils to add each pair using mental methods to find the answers. Repeat for two sets of minuends and subtrahends (for example: 540 and 250, and 630 and 420).

## Same-day enrichment

- Provide labels (addend, sum, minuend, subtrahend, difference) for pupils to cut out. Pupil A should write down two three-digit multiples of 10 and shuffle the cards. Pupil B should take any card and reveal it. This should show the type of calculation they are expected to do with the numbers. For example, if they turn over the card saying 'difference', they need to subtract the two numbers. If they turn over the card saying 'addend', they need to add the two numbers. They should work out the answer mentally and then match up each relevant term with the numbers in their calculation. For example:

| | |
|---|---|
| 620 | addend |
| 250 | addend |
| 870 | sum |

- Pupils should repeat the activity with different numbers and different cards.

# Question 3

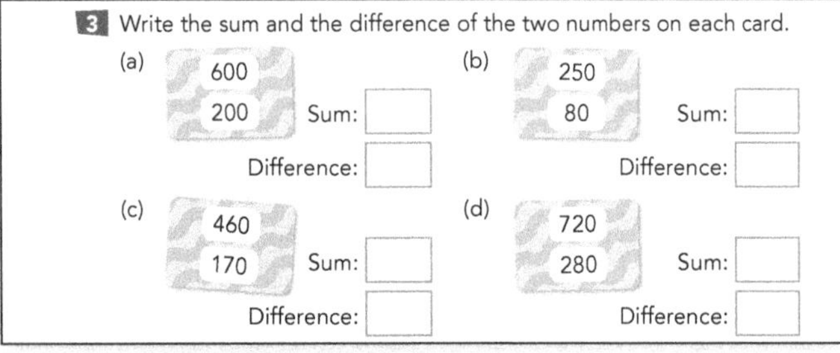

3 Write the sum and the difference of the two numbers on each card.
(a) 600 200 Sum: Difference:
(b) 250 80 Sum: Difference:
(c) 460 170 Sum: Difference:
(d) 720 280 Sum: Difference:


## What learning will pupils have achieved at the conclusion of Question 3?

- Mental strategies to solve three-digit addition and subtraction of multiples of 10 will have been consolidated.
- Fluency with addition and subtraction will have been extended to generate calculations from words (addend, sum / minuend, subtrahend, difference).

## Activities for whole-class instruction

- Display two three-digit multiples of 10, for example 150 and 660. Ask: *How would you find the difference between these numbers? How would you find the sum?* Establish that pupils need to consider the two numbers as 15 tens and 66 tens and that, for both a subtraction and addition, it is best to start with the larger number. Ask pupils whether they would expect the sum or the difference to be the larger answer and why. Give pupils time to calculate both answers mentally. Repeat for further pairs of numbers and practise using the words 'sum' and 'difference' to describe answers.
- Write the following target numbers on the board: 140, 360, 490, 470, 220, 370 and 550. Ask pupils to choose any five of these numbers and write them on their mini whiteboards. Give pupils a series of 'What is the sum of …' / 'What is the difference between …' questions, for example: What is the sum of 310 and 240? Ensure that most of these equate to one of the target numbers written on the board, although it may be interesting to include some that do not. If the answer is the same as one of the target numbers pupils have chosen, they may circle it. Keep playing until several pupils have circled all five of their chosen numbers.
- Pupils should complete Question 3 in the Practice Book.

## Same-day intervention

- Show pupils two strips of paper of different lengths. Ask pupils how they could arrange these strips to show the **sum of** the strips of paper and then the **difference between** the strips of paper. Write different three-digit multiples of 10 on each strip (the smaller number on the shorter strip and vice versa). Again, ask pupils to arrange the strips and use the corresponding modelled bar diagrams to show that two numbers can be either added or subtracted to get different results (use the terms 'sum' and 'difference').

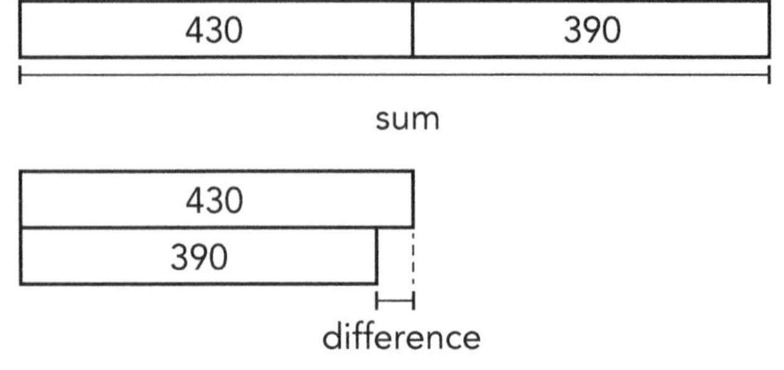

- Ask: *Which will be a larger number – the sum or the difference? Why?* Ask pupils to explain which number they would begin with when finding the sum of two numbers and why (and then the same for the difference). Pupils should then use base 10 blocks to model each calculation they can make using the same two numbers.
- Repeat for different pairs of multiples of 10.

## Same-day enrichment

- Write the following pair of numbers on the board: 130 and 150. Ask pupils to work in groups of three or four. Pupil A should use addition and subtraction to find the sum and the difference of the first pair of numbers. They should then be left with two answers that they should pass on to Pupil B to use to find the sum and difference. Pupils should aim to continue the chain round and round the group, with each pair of answers feeding into the next pupil's addition and subtraction. The chain should stop when they eventually make a sum containing four digits. As the calculation 'moves' along the chain, all pupils should check that sums and differences are being calculated correctly. Pupils could record their chain as below:
- For example, the starting numbers 130 and 150 make a chain that contains five steps:

| Numbers | Sum | Difference |
|---|---|---|
| 130 and 150 | 280 | 20 |
| 280 and 20 | 300 | 260 |
| 300 and 260 | 560 | 40 |
| 560 and 40 | 600 | 520 |
| 600 and 520 | 1120 | 80 |

- Challenge pupils to explore different pairs of starting numbers with the aim of making their chain as long as possible until they have to stop. For example, they might like to try starting with numbers that are close together like 320 and 300, or numbers that are lower like 70 and 100. Ask: *Which starting numbers have given you the longest chain?*

# Question 4

**4** Calculate and then fill in each box with your answer.

(a) 120 $\xrightarrow{+\,90}$ ☐ $\xrightarrow{+\,270}$ ☐ $\xrightarrow{+\,160}$ ☐ $\xrightarrow{+\,190}$ ☐

(b) 870 $\xrightarrow{-\,70}$ ☐ $\xrightarrow{-\,350}$ ☐ $\xrightarrow{+\,320}$ ☐ $\xrightarrow{-\,270}$ ☐

(c) 330 $\xrightarrow{+\,120}$ ☐ $\xrightarrow{-\,80}$ ☐ $\xrightarrow{+\,290}$ ☐ $\xrightarrow{-\,340}$ ☐

(d) ☐ $\xrightarrow{+\,360}$ ☐ $\xrightarrow{-\,150}$ ☐ $\xrightarrow{+\,110}$ ☐ $\xrightarrow{-\,250}$ 100

## What learning will pupils have achieved at the conclusion of Question 4?

- Mental strategies to solve three-digit addition and subtraction of multiples of 10 will have been consolidated.
- Pupils will have solved sequences of addition and subtraction calculations, including those where inverse operations are necessary.

## Activities for whole-class instruction

- Ask five pupils to sit in a row and hold a mini whiteboard. In between the chairs, write a series of operations on mini whiteboards where a two- or three-digit multiple of 10 is added or subtracted. For example:

- Ensure pupils are able to express each operation as a number of tens (for example 'plus 13 tens'). Ask the first pupil in the chain to write a three-digit multiple of 10 on their board (for example 350). Ask the class to work in pairs to calculate their way along the chain. At the same time, the pupils sitting on their chairs should work out their numbers by working their way along the chain too (the second pupil looks at the first pupil's board and adds 130 to it to get their number, then the third pupil then adds 240 to the second pupil's answer and so on along the line). They should keep the numbers on their mini whiteboards hidden from the class.
- Finally, ask the class to predict the numbers written on each of the whiteboards. Ask: *How do you know this? What strategy did you use to find the answer?* Discuss 'mental pictures' that pupils use. Repeat for different chains of calculations.

- Give pupils the opportunity to work backwards. Set up the chain of calculations as before, but this time give the fifth student a three-digit number (the answer). Ask: *How can we find out what the starting number was?* Establish that pupils need to work backwards, completing the inverse operation for each step. Provide plenty of practice for this technique and ensure pupils can use reasoning to explain how to work backwards through each step.

Look out for ... pupils who do not perform the inverse operation when working backwards. If pupils know the answer to an addition question and they need to work backwards to find the starting number, they must use subtraction. For example, to find □ + 240 = 680, they would need to start with 680 and subtract 240. Establish that pupils are aware of inverse operations and how to work backwards from an answer before continuing. A particularly useful way of showing this is through the use of bar models. For example:

| 680 | |
|---|---|
| 240 | |

240 + ______ = 680

680 – 240 = ______

- Pupils should complete Question 4 in the Practice Book.

## Same-day intervention

- Set up a series of mini whiteboards on a table-top, separated by cards showing additions and subtractions. For example:

□ $\xrightarrow{+190}$ □ $\xrightarrow{-70}$ □ $\xrightarrow{+220}$ □

- Give different pupils responsibilities for different whiteboards and ask questions about the structure of the chain of calculations, for example: What number do you need to know before you can work out the number on your whiteboard, Abdul?
- Ask the pupil in charge of the first whiteboard to write a three-digit number on their whiteboard and model it using base 10 blocks. They should then pass it to the next pupil, who should (in this example) add 190 to it, modelling their new answer using base 10 blocks and writing it on their mini whiteboard. The blocks should be passed on and so on. As pupils become more confident, take out the base 10 blocks and encourage pupils to use mental strategies alone to work out each answer in the chain.

## Same-day enrichment

- Ask pupils to work in pairs. Give each pupil five pieces of card. Ask them to lay four cards in a row. On each one they should draw an arrow to the right and write an addition or subtraction operation (with three-digit multiples of 10). For example:

$\xrightarrow{-110}$ $\xrightarrow{+530}$ $\xrightarrow{-220}$ $\xrightarrow{+190}$

- Each pupil must choose a secret three-digit start number (a multiple of 10), write it on the fifth card and turn it face down so the other pupil cannot see it. From the start number, pupils work out the answer to each step on their cards until they reach the final answer, which they should record on their mini whiteboard. Interim steps should be calculated mentally or recorded secretly.
- Pupils then swap places and, by considering only the final answer and working backwards through each step, they should find their partner's starting number. If this is too challenging, they can retrace their partner's steps, beginning with the starting number to see if they reach the same answer.

# Question 5

**5** Application problems.

(a) Meera and Caitlin took part in an 800 metre run. When Meera was 200 metres away from the finish line, Caitlin was 250 metres away. How many metres had each of them run? Who had run faster up to that point in time?

Answer: ______

(b) A school bought 250 apples and gave 90 of them to Year 3 and 110 to Year 4. How many apples were left?

Answer: ______

(c) Tom collected 150 stamps last year. He has collected 280 stamps this year, but he still has 130 stamps fewer than Yee. How many stamps has Yee collected?

Answer: ______

(d) A small cinema has 30 seats. It has 80 seats fewer than a medium-sized cinema. A large cinema has 160 seats more than the medium-sized cinema. How many seats does the large cinema have?

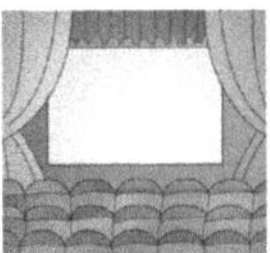

Answer: ______

## What learning will pupils have achieved at the conclusion of Question 5?

- Mental strategies to solve three-digit addition and subtraction of multiples of 10 will have been consolidated.
- Pupils will have recognised where and how to apply knowledge about addition and subtraction of three-digit multiples of 10 to solve word-based problems with more than one step.

## Activities for whole-class instruction

- Display the following application problem: Yesterday, Sanjeet read the first 250 pages of his book. Today he read another 130 pages. He now has 290 pages to go until he has finished it. How many pages are in the book altogether?
- Ask pupils to read through the problem to themselves several times. Then ask how many steps there are to the problem and what operations are needed. Agree that there are two steps – firstly, to add the pages already read (250 + 130) and secondly to add the number of unread pages to find the overall total. Ask pupils how they can use their knowledge of adding and subtracting multiples of 10 to help find the answer. Pupils should use mental methods to find the answer, sharing their strategies with the class.
- Repeat the activity for further application problems with multiple steps, including those with a mixture of operations.

By altering the information provided and the wording of an application problem, pupils can be asked to apply different concepts and work with different operations. It is important to ensure that pupils experience a wide variety of application problems to foster deep understanding of the relationship between addition and subtraction in real-world contexts.

Taking the 'reading a book' context, pupils' ability to choose an appropriate operation can be practised by varying the way the missing part of the information is presented – instead of asking about a missing sum as in the above question, simply by using the same context and the same numbers but phrasing the question differently, it becomes a subtraction question: Yesterday, Sanjeet read the first 250 pages of his book. He read 130 pages today. There are 670 pages in the book altogether. How many pages does he have left?

- Pupils should complete Question 5 in the Practice Book.

## Same-day intervention

- Display the following multi-step application problem: Charlotte has £140 in her savings account. She spends £90, but then manages to save another £220. How much money is in her account now? Ask: *What do you need to do to the numbers in this problem to solve it?* If it helps, replace the numbers with simpler numbers less than 20 so pupils recognise that the problem contains two steps – subtraction followed by addition.
- Pupils should act out the scenario using base 10 blocks. Ask: *What happens to Charlotte's money first?* Write 140 – 90 and provide base 10 blocks for pupils to model 140. Establish what the numbers are in terms of tens. Ask: *What is 14 tens minus 9 tens?* Pupils should use mental methods to find the answer, then check their answer by taking away 9 tens rods from their pile

of 14 and expressing the difference as a three-digit number. Ask: *What happens to Charlotte's money next?* Complete the same modelling activities for the second step to the problem (adding 220). Ensure pupils give the final answer in context (as a number of pounds that Charlotte has in her account).

- Repeat for further addition and subtraction application problems, particularly those that are presented in a linear way (the numbers in the above problem appear in the order they need to be worked out). Problems where the numbers are presented linearly can be less complex to solve as pupils can identify each step more clearly.

## Same-day enrichment

- In pairs, pupils should deal out four digit cards. They choose two of these digits and use them to make a two-digit number, expressing it as a number of tens.
- Challenge pupils to write a two-step calculation that equals their chosen number. To begin with, pupils may find it easier to choose a calculation that only includes one type of operation, for example: 120 + 530 + 180 = 780.
- Pupils should then write a word problem based around their calculation. For the above example this might be: 'Leah scores 120 points on Level 1 of her new computer game. She scores 530 points on Level 2 and then gets an extra 180 bonus points. How many points does she have now?'
- Pupils should share their word problems with peers to solve using mental methods. Encourage them to discuss the operations needed to find the answer and then try to display the answer as a 'number of tens' using the original digit cards.

## Challenge and extension question

# Question 6

**6** Look at the diagram. Fill in each circle with these numbers so that the sum of the four numbers in the corners of each square is 1200.

100 200 300

400 500 600

Pupils are given a rectangle constructed from six circles (3 × 2) and asked to write the multiples of 100 (from 100 to 600) in each circle such that the sum of the rectangle's four corners equals 1200. There is more than one way to do this, so encourage pupils to look for as many ways as possible. If pupils consider 1200 as 12 hundreds, this will help them with the addition of the multiples of 100.

# Unit 7.3 Adding and subtracting 3-digit numbers and ones (1)

## Conceptual context

In the previous two units pupils have been encouraged to understand three-digit numbers as a number of tens or a number of hundreds and so have been able to extend their knowledge and understanding of two-digit numbers to operate with three-digit numbers. Of course, so far, the three-digit numbers pupils have worked with have, necessarily, all had 0 in the ones column because they have been multiples of 10 and 100. In this unit, pupils' attention is focused on the digit in the ones column as they add and subtract ones to/from three-digit numbers that have any digit in the ones place.

Pupils will therefore expand their understanding of three-digit numbers. They begin the unit with deep understanding of them as a number of tens or hundreds, which brings about in them a sense of magnitude that also enables them to calculate using existing knowledge about operations; at the end of the unit pupils will have begun to connect this to other knowledge about ordering and operating with numbers that have digits in all columns/places. Pupils' knowledge is therefore likely to become robust and well-connected as it develops with further practice and challenge.

## Learning pupils will have achieved at the end of the unit

- Recall of number facts to 10 (and to 100) will have been used to help solve related calculations involving three-digit numbers (Q1)
- Mental strategies to solve HTO + O and HTO – O calculations will have been practised (Q1, Q2, Q3, Q4, Q5, Q6)
- Strategies for addition and subtraction will have been extended to include partitioning single-digit numbers to help calculate across a tens (or hundreds) boundary (Q2, Q3)
- Pupils will have developed fluency when explaining their methods (Q4)

## Resources

mini whiteboards; digit cards; base 10 blocks; place value counters and grids; ten frames; place value arrow cards; number lines; **Resource 3.7.3** Addition and subtraction cards

## Vocabulary

hundreds, tens, ones, tens boundary, hundreds boundary, plus, minus, add, subtract, numeral

# Question 1

**1** Calculate with reasoning.

(a) 23 + 2 = ☐ (b) 46 − 8 = ☐
(c) 52 − 5 = ☐ (d) 26 + 8 = ☐
(e) 323 + 2 = ☐ (f) 246 − 8 = ☐
(g) 552 − 5 = ☐ (h) 426 + 8 = ☐

## What learning will pupils have achieved at the conclusion of Question 1?

- Mental strategies to solve HTO + O and HTO − O calculations will have been practised.
- Recall of number facts to 10 (and to 100) will have been used to help solve related calculations involving three-digit numbers.

## Activities for whole-class instruction

- Remind pupils how they can use basic number facts to help answer questions. For example, display the calculations 4 + 5, 34 + 5 and 434 + 5. Ask: *What do you notice about the questions and their answers?* Encourage pupils to answer with reasoning, explaining why the answers behave in this way. Write the calculation 4 + 3 on the board and ask pupils to write two further calculations this number fact could be used to answer.
- Ask pupils to use place value arrow cards to make the number 62. Ask: *How can you use your cards to model 62 + 3? Which digit changes? Can you alter the calculation so that more digits will change?* Write the calculation 462 + 3 on the board and ask pupils to explain how 62 + 3 can be used to help find the answer. They should use reasoning to describe how only the ones digit is affected, so that any three-digit number with the same tens and ones will behave in a similar way. Call out various TO + O (or TO − O) calculations and ask pupils to model a HTO + O (or HTO − O) that the first calculation can be used to help answer. Encourage pupils to use reasoning to explain their choices.
- Pupils should complete Question 1 in the Practice Book.

## Same-day intervention

- Model the number 362 using base 10 blocks. Encourage pupils to note its make-up (3 hundreds, 6 tens, 2 ones). Cover up the three hundreds and ask pupils how they would model 62 + 7. Once they have shown this, write the completed calculation on the board. Reveal the hundreds blocks and this time model 362 + 7. Show that this has the same effect on the number as when adding to a two-digit number (in this instance, the hundreds are unchanged).

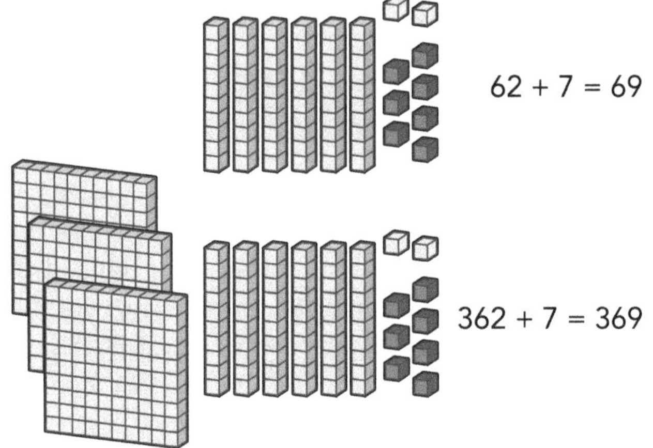


- Repeat for further calculations, including those where the tens digit changes (for example 42 − 5).

## Same-day enrichment

- Provide pairs of pupils with a place value grid and coloured counters. Without speaking, Pupil A should model a single-digit addition using counters. They should then clear the grid and model a TO + O addition, using the initial number fact as a basis. Finally, they should model a HTO + O addition. For example:

Pupil A: Pupil B:

| H | T | O | |
|---|---|---|---|
| | | | 3 + 4 = 7 |
| | | | 43 + 4 = 47 |
| | | | 243 + 4 = 247 |

- Pupil B should then write all three additions, using reasoning to explain why the calculations are linked. They get a point for each of the three additions they can recall. Pupils should swap roles and repeat for further addition and then subtraction calculations.

# Question 2

**2** Calculate mentally.

| | |
|---|---|
| (a) 326 + 8 = ☐ | (b) 113 − 5 = ☐ |
| (c) 312 + 8 = ☐ | (d) 119 − 8 = ☐ |
| (e) 223 − 4 = ☐ | (f) 233 + 8 = ☐ |
| (g) 450 − 6 = ☐ | (h) 592 + 8 = ☐ |

## What learning will pupils have achieved at the conclusion of Question 2?

- Mental strategies to solve HTO + O and HTO − O calculations will have been practised.
- Strategies for addition and subtraction will have been extended to include partitioning single-digit numbers to help calculate across a tens (or hundreds) boundary.

## Activities for whole-class instruction

- It is important that pupils are able to relate their knowledge of simple number facts to three-digit numbers. To calculate efficiently when crossing tens boundaries, pupils need to maintain high levels of fluency when counting. To develop this, begin by displaying part of a number line showing the numbers 360 to 380 (with ones marked and labelled). Start at 360 and count through to 380, then back to 360. When pupils reach a tens boundary, discuss how the digits change – why?
- Display the calculation 367 + 8. Ask: *How close is 367 to 370? Use a number line to model how to partition the* second addend (in this example, 8) into two parts: the part needed to take pupils forwards to the next tens number and the other part that needs to be added after the tens number (in this example, 3 and 5 respectively).

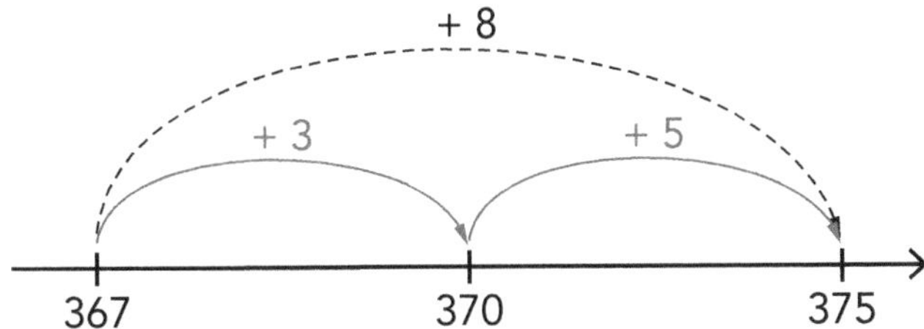


- Repeat the steps with further calculations that involve adding a single-digit to a three-digit number across the tens boundary. For each example, ask pupils to describe how the second addend can be partitioned to bridge a tens number and then recombined to aid mental calculation.
- Move on to practise the same method using subtraction, for example working out the answer to 344 – 9 by partitioning the subtrahend (in this example, 9) into two parts: the part needed to take pupils back to the previous tens number and the other part that needs to be subtracted from the tens number (in this example, 4 and 5 respectively).
- Pupils should complete Question 2 in the Practice Book.

## Same-day intervention

- Some pupils may not understand why the second addend (in an addition) or the subtrahend (in a subtraction) should be partitioned to reach a multiple of 10 and so may partition it into any two parts. Ten frames can be useful in helping pupils understand how a single-digit number can be partitioned when bridging. For example, display the calculation 425 + 9 and model 25 + 9 using ten frames. Discuss how many of the 9 counters are needed to complete the final ten frame and then how many are left to start filling another ten frame. Use the ten frames to illustrate how the partitioning of the 9 into 5 and 4 helps to make a multiple of 10 and some more. Use a number line to model both jumps. Repeat for further examples, including subtraction calculations where pupils must take away part of a number to make a multiple of 10, before taking away some more.

## Same-day enrichment

- Provide pupils with a set of digit cards. Pupil A should take the 9 and the 0 card and place them on the desk. These will form the tens digits of two three-digit numbers (in an addition and subtraction respectively) and so ensure that each calculation will cross a tens boundary. Pupil A should then shuffle the remainder of the cards and deal out four more cards. These should be placed around the 9 and the 0 to form two three-digit numbers.
  - Place tens digits 9 0
  - Deal four cards 3 9 6 8 0 5

- Pupil A should then choose a single-digit number to be added or taken away that would need to be partitioned. For example:
  - Place tens digits 9 0
  - Deal four cards 396 805
  - Choose single digit number to be added/subtracted 396 + 8 805 − 9
- Pupil B should then complete each calculation, explaining how they have partitioned the second addend or subtrahend to find the answer. Repeat for further calculations, swapping roles each time.

# Question 3

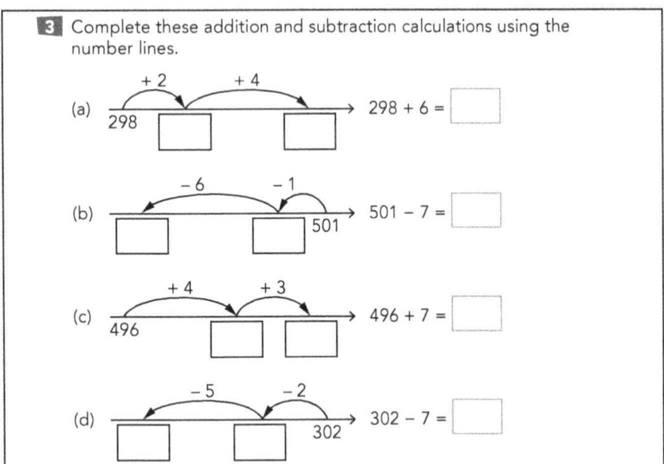


## What learning will pupils have achieved at the conclusion of Question 3?

- Mental strategies to solve HTO + O and HTO − O calculations will have been practised.
- Strategies for addition and subtraction will have been extended to include partitioning single-digit numbers to help calculate across a tens (or hundreds) boundary.

## Activities for whole-class instruction

- Display 634 + 4, 264 + 9, 125 − 8 and 736 − 6. Explain that in two calculations, only the ones digit will change. In the remaining two, the tens digit will also change. Ask pupils to identify which is which and then explain that this is because 264 + 9 and 125 − 8 cross a tens boundary. Remind pupils of the need to partition the second addend (or subtrahend).
- Display 497 + 8. Ask: *How can partitioning be used to help add 8?* Pupils should model the three-digit number using arrow cards. Ask them to predict which of the cards they will need to change. Why is this? Show pupils a number line and model the addition. Remind pupils that the tens boundary crossed is also a hundreds boundary. Ask: *What effect do you think this might have on the digits?* Challenge pupils to write HTO + O calculations that cross a hundreds boundary. Ask what these calculations have in common (the first addends should all have a 9 in the tens place). Ask: *Why is this?* Repeat for HTO − O calculations that cross a hundreds boundary (the minuends should all have a 0 in the tens place).
- Write the calculation 694 + 7 on the board. Choose three pupils to come to the front and spread themselves out in a line in order to represent the two jumps needed to model the calculation (partitioning the second addend so that it first adds to the hundreds boundary and then add the remainder). Each pupil should call out the number they are starting with and the number being added. The final pupil should call out the answer. For example:

- Try the same activity without writing the calculation for the class to see. They should work out what the original calculation was by listening to the numbers being called out. Repeat for subtractions as well as additions that cross the hundreds boundary.
- Pupils should complete Question 3 in the Practice Book.

## Same-day intervention

- Combine a number line and base 10 equipment to help pupils model addition and subtraction over a hundreds boundary. Write the calculation 295 + 8 and ask pupils to model the number using base 10 blocks. Ask them to locate the number on a number line. Ask: *How close is this number to 300?* Ensure pupils understand that adding 8 will mean crossing the hundreds boundary.
- Pupils should make the number 8 out of ones cubes. Ask: *How many ones do you need to take you from 295 to 300?* Establish that 5 ones are needed and this leaves 3. Pupils can swap 10 ones for a tens rod and then 10 tens rods for a hundred square to show that they now have 3 hundreds.
- Ask pupils to explain how they have partitioned the number 8 to help answer the question. Model this on the number line as two jumps (one from 295 to 300 and one from 300 to 303).
- Repeat for further addition and subtraction calculations that cross the hundreds boundary.

## Same-day enrichment

- Provide pairs of pupils with sets of digit cards. Pupil A should take the 9 digit and Pupil B should take the 0 digit. The remainder of the cards should be shared randomly between the two. Pupil A should use their cards to form a HTO + O calculation and Pupil B should use their cards to form a HTO – O calculation. Both pupils should try to arrange their cards to form calculations that cross the hundreds boundary (this may not always be possible). For example, Pupil A might be dealt 5, 8, 1 and 2 along with the 9 digit and so could form the addition 298 + 5.
- Both pupils should swap calculations. If their partner can answer the calculation they get a point. If they can also draw a number line to model the jumps they have made, they should get a further point. Where appropriate, encourage pupils to explain to each other how they can partition the second addend (or subtrahend) to cross the hundreds boundary.
- Repeat for further addition and subtraction calculations generated from different sets of cards.

# Question 4

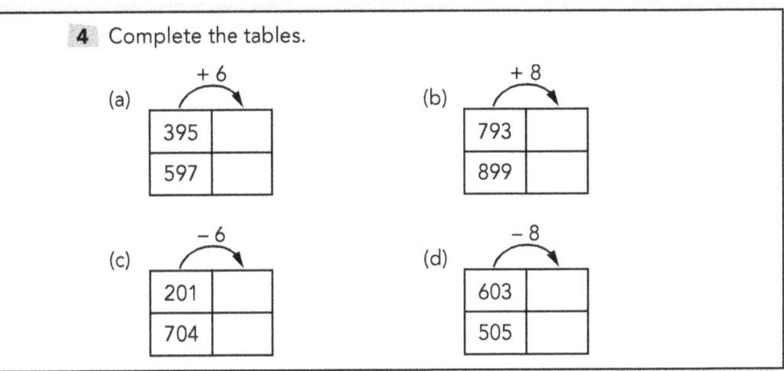

**4** Complete the tables.

(a) + 6

| 395 | |
|---|---|
| 597 | |

(b) + 8

| 793 | |
|---|---|
| 899 | |

(c) – 6

| 201 | |
|---|---|
| 704 | |

(d) – 8

| 603 | |
|---|---|
| 505 | |

## What learning will pupils have achieved at the conclusion of Question 4?

- Mental strategies to solve HTO + O and HTO – O calculations will have been practised.
- Pupils will have developed fluency when explaining their methods.

## Activities for whole-class instruction

- Display enlarged versions of **Resource 3.7.3** Addition and subtraction cards.

**Resource 3.7.3**

Addition and subtraction cards

| | | | |
|---|---|---|---|
| 452 + 4 | 874 + 5 | 354 + 9 | 407 – 9 |
| 625 – 8 | 799 + 9 | 326 – 6 | 975 + 4 |
| 915 – 5 | 371 + 6 | 287 + 4 | 355 – 8 |
| 201 – 6 | 597 + 6 | 249 – 9 | 176 + 7 |
| 534 + 6 | 827 + 3 | 206 + 9 | 518 + 4 |
| 758 + 5 | 542 + 7 | 998 – 9 | 142 – 7 |
| 667 – 3 | 303 – 4 | 231 – 8 | 192 – 3 |
| 202 – 5 | 555 – 8 | | |

© HarperCollinsPublishers 2017 283

- Ask: *How could we sort these calculations into different groups? What sorting rules could we have?* Ask pupils to sort the calculations according to the following sorting rules:
  - calculations that cross over a hundreds boundary
  - calculations that cross over a tens boundary
  - calculations that do not cross over a tens/hundreds boundary.
- Ask: *What do you notice about all the calculations that crossed a hundreds boundary?* Remind pupils that

hundreds boundaries are also tens boundaries and so these calculations should also be in the second group. Draw sorting circles on the board to demonstrate:

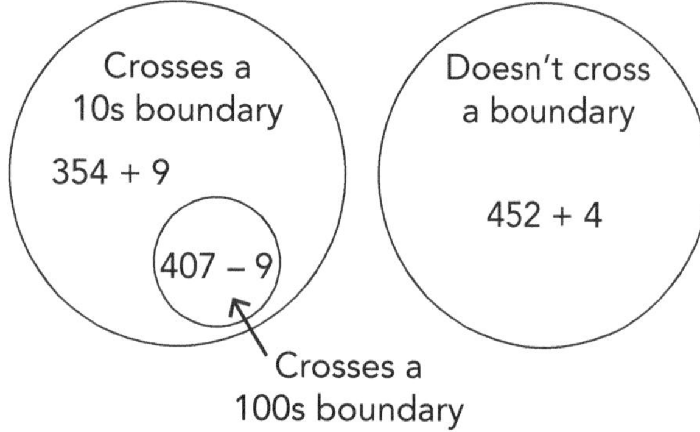


- Ask pupils whether any of their calculations needed a similar number fact to help answer them (for example 874 + 5 and 975 + 4). Use the opportunity to encourage pupils to develop their number fluency and discuss the various strategies they might use to answer these questions.
- Ask pupils to shut their eyes. Walk around the class, lightly tapping half the class on the shoulder. Explain that the 'tapped' pupils are in Group A with the rest in Group B. Only each child knows what group they are in. Ask all the pupils in Group A to write a HTO + O or HTO – O calculation on their mini whiteboard that they think is an easier calculation to answer and all the pupils in Group B to write a calculation that they think is more difficult.
- Randomly choose five pupils to come to the front and stand in a line. One at a time, they should display their mini whiteboards for the rest of the class to work out the answers. Encourage pupils to use reasoning to explain how they know that their answer is correct. Ask the class to guess whether they think the calculation was designed to be 'easier' or 'more difficult'. Why do they think this? What makes a calculation more difficult? Remind pupils that this is not about large numbers (998 – 7 is more straightforward than 102 – 7). Repeat for further groups of five questions.
- Pupils should complete Question 4 in the Practice Book.

## Same-day intervention

- Make a three-digit number out of base 10 blocks and with place value counters on a HTO grid. Count forwards and backwards along a number line in ones, adding and subtracting ones cubes and counters to help represent each new number. Discuss what happens when a tens boundary is crossed. This will help pupils visualise the quantities they are counting in and help them associate the numerals with their place value.
- Display the addition 453 + 5. Ask: *Which two digits are the most important to consider?* Ensure pupils understand that they need to know what 3 + 5 is to help answer the question. Encourage them to use the three ways of modelling the addition (the number line, base 10 blocks and place value grid). Repeat for further additions and subtractions that do not cross the tens boundary and then consider those that do, with pupils encouraged to explain what happens to the tens digit.

## Same-day enrichment

- Give pairs or small groups a set of digit cards from which four digits should be dealt. Ask each pupil to use the digits to make a secret HTO + O or HTO – O calculation. Pupil A shares their answer. The other pupils work out what the question was by using the digits to make a calculation that gives that answer. Encourage pupils to explain their working. Many will begin by using trial and error, but may begin to use other strategies. For example, if the answer is 624, the starting number must contain 6 hundreds and the ones digit should either add to make 4 (or 14) or subtract to leave 4. The group should repeat the game with each pupil's calculation and then shuffle the cards to generate a new set of calculations.

# Questions 5 and 6

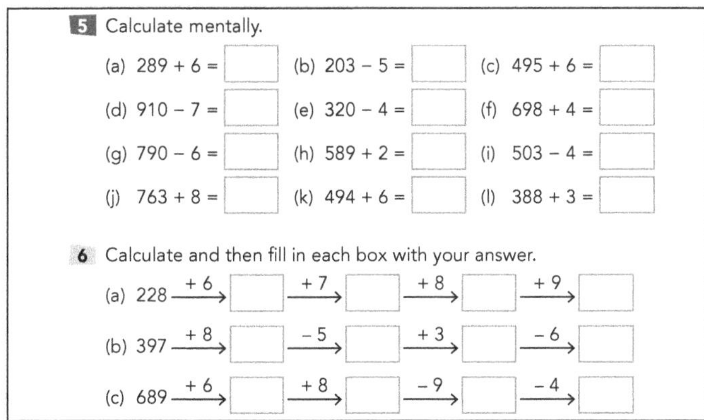

**5** Calculate mentally.

(a) 289 + 6 = ☐ (b) 203 − 5 = ☐ (c) 495 + 6 = ☐

(d) 910 − 7 = ☐ (e) 320 − 4 = ☐ (f) 698 + 4 = ☐

(g) 790 − 6 = ☐ (h) 589 + 2 = ☐ (i) 503 − 4 = ☐

(j) 763 + 8 = ☐ (k) 494 + 6 = ☐ (l) 388 + 3 = ☐

**6** Calculate and then fill in each box with your answer.

(a) 228 $\xrightarrow{+6}$ ☐ $\xrightarrow{+7}$ ☐ $\xrightarrow{+8}$ ☐ $\xrightarrow{+9}$ ☐

(b) 397 $\xrightarrow{+8}$ ☐ $\xrightarrow{-5}$ ☐ $\xrightarrow{+3}$ ☐ $\xrightarrow{-6}$ ☐

(c) 689 $\xrightarrow{+6}$ ☐ $\xrightarrow{+8}$ ☐ $\xrightarrow{-9}$ ☐ $\xrightarrow{-4}$ ☐

## What learning will pupils have achieved at the conclusion of Questions 5 and 6?

- Mental strategies to solve HTO + O and HTO − O calculations will have been practised.

## Activities for whole-class instruction

- Choose five pupils to sit in a row, holding mini whiteboards. In between each chair place a mini whiteboard showing the subtraction of a single digit.
- The first pupil should write a three-digit number on their mini whiteboard. Encourage the class to work in pairs subtracting their way along the chain. The row of pupils in the chain should simultaneously work out their numbers by working their way along from the starting number. They should not reveal their whiteboards to the class. Ask the class to predict the numbers written on each of the whiteboards, explaining the strategy that they used to find the answer. Discuss the 'mental pictures' that pupils use and encourage them to share key facts that they may have used to help.
- Repeat for different chains of calculations, moving from all subtraction and all addition to a combination of both. Also remind pupils that adding and subtracting over a tens or hundreds boundary can be trickier and encourage them to choose a starting number and series of operations that they think will ensure that the class practise this skill.
- Pupils should complete Questions 5 and 6 in the Practice Book.

## Same-day intervention

- Set up a series of mini whiteboards on a table-top, separated by cards showing addition and subtractions. For example:

☐ +4 ☐ −8 ☐ +9 ☐

- Give different pupils responsibilities for different mini whiteboards and ask questions about the structure of the chain of calculations, for example: What number do you need to know before you can work out the number on your whiteboard, Gemma?
- Ask the pupil in charge of the first whiteboard to write any three-digit number on their whiteboard and model it using base 10 blocks. They should then pass it to the next pupil, who should (in this example) add 4 to it, modelling their new answer using base 10 blocks and writing it on their mini whiteboard. The blocks should be passed on and so on. As pupils become more confident, take out the base 10 blocks and encourage pupils to use mental strategies alone to work out each answer in the chain.

## Same-day enrichment

- Remind pupils of their previous work with inverse operations, working backwards from a given answer to find the original starting number. In pairs, pupils should design a chain of four operations adding and subtracting single-digit numbers (with arrows drawn to show the direction of the chain). For example:

____ $\xrightarrow{+4}$ ____ $\xrightarrow{+3}$ ____ $\xrightarrow{-8}$ ____ $\xrightarrow{-9}$ ____

- Pupil A should secretly choose a starting three-digit number and, without Pupil B seeing, they should work their way from left to right until they end with an answer. They should then write the answer at the end of the chain. Pupil B should then use their knowledge of inverse operations to work backwards and find the starting number. They get a point for doing so correctly. Pupils repeat the activity, swapping roles each time.

## Challenge and extension question

# Question 7

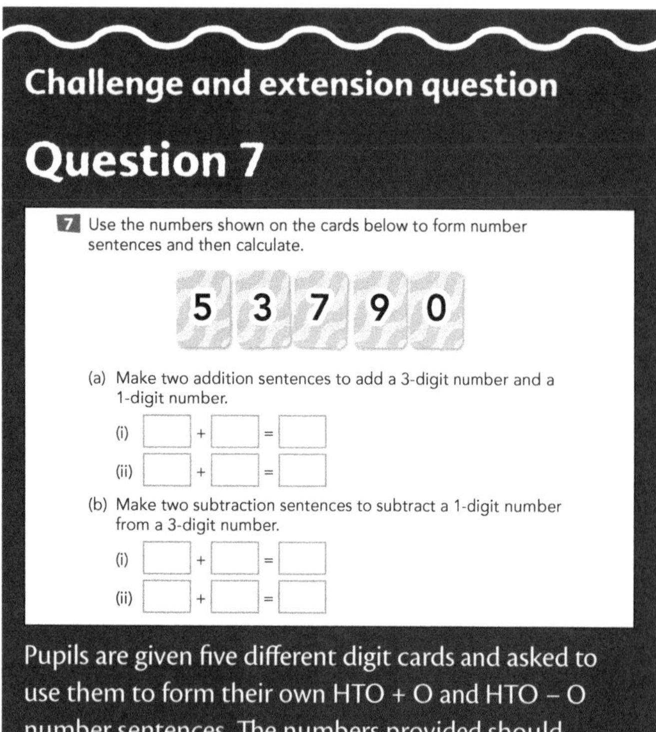
7 Use the numbers shown on the cards below to form number sentences and then calculate.

5 3 7 9 0

(a) Make two addition sentences to add a 3-digit number and a 1-digit number.

(i) ☐ + ☐ = ☐

(ii) ☐ + ☐ = ☐

(b) Make two subtraction sentences to subtract a 1-digit number from a 3-digit number.

(i) ☐ + ☐ = ☐

(ii) ☐ + ☐ = ☐

Pupils are given five different digit cards and asked to use them to form their own HTO + O and HTO – O number sentences. The numbers provided should ensure that pupils will need to add and subtract across tens and possibly hundreds boundaries. As a further extension, pupils could be challenged to give two clues for others to guess what the calculation is. These should be:

- the tens (or hundreds) boundary they calculated across
- the first part of their partitioned number.

For example: 'I added across 540. I partitioned the addend into 3 and another number.'

Using the digits provided (5, 3, 7, 9 and 0), the above description can only refer to 537 + 9 = 546.

# Unit 7.4 Adding and subtracting 3-digit numbers and ones (2)

## Conceptual context

This unit consolidates previous work on the addition or subtraction of a single-digit number to any three-digit number. Mental strategies are revised – including the partitioning of single-digit numbers to help add or subtract across a tens boundary.

Unit 7.5 introduces written methods for HTO +/– HTO calculations and this unit provides preparation for the adding and subtracting of ones in that particular context.

## Learning pupils will have achieved at the end of the unit

- Mental strategies to add and subtract single-digit numbers to and from three-digit numbers will have been consolidated (Q1)
- Fluency with number will have been extended, particularly when considering ways to find an unknown number and different ways to make the same answer (Q2, Q3)
- Reasoning will have been used to explain why addition or subtraction is most appropriate to solve visual and word-based problems (Q2, Q4)
- Pupils will have recognised where and how to apply knowledge to solve word-based problems, including those with more than one step (Q4)

### Resources

mini whiteboards; digit cards; base 10 blocks; number lines; sand timer/stopwatch; interlocking cubes; luggage tags; string; cardboard; container (e.g. a plant pot); **Resource 3.7.4** 3-digit numbers and ones

### Vocabulary

hundreds, tens, ones, tens boundary, hundreds boundary, plus, minus, add, subtract, numeral

## Question 1

**1** Calculate mentally.

(a) 325 + 8 = ☐ (b) 590 − 9 = ☐ (c) 708 + 9 = ☐

(d) 377 − 8 = ☐ (e) 278 − 6 = ☐ (f) 498 + 6 = ☐

(g) 300 − 3 = ☐ (h) 799 + 2 = ☐ (i) 702 − 4 = ☐

(j) 375 + 5 = ☐ (k) 256 + 6 = ☐ (l) 173 + 7 = ☐

### What learning will pupils have achieved at the conclusion of Question 1?

- Mental strategies to add and subtract single-digit numbers to and from three-digit numbers will have been consolidated.

### Activities for whole-class instruction

- Display the calculation 436 + ? on the board. Explain that the question mark stands for a single-digit number. Discuss with pupils what they know about the calculation and what the answer might be. For example:
  - If the missing number is 4 or more, the calculation will involve crossing a tens boundary.
  - The answer will still have 4 hundreds in it because ...?
- Reveal the missing number as 8. Ask pupils to find the solution using mental methods and consider how they got there. Discuss strategies and collect them on the board. Ask: *What picture did you use in your mind to help work out the answer?* (For example, some pupils may have partitioned 8 into 4 and 4 to add to the nearest 10 and beyond.)
- Show pupils a 3 × 3 grid containing a selection of HTO + O and HTO − O calculations. For example:

| 737 + 8 | 595 − 9 | 446 + 5 |
|---|---|---|
| 257 + 4 | 402 − 8 | 201 − 6 |
| 611 + 6 | 287 − 4 | 367 + 5 |

- Before asking for each answer, ask pupils to group the calculations according to the strategies they would choose to use to solve them. Ask: *Which questions would you use a similar strategy to answer?* (For example, 737 + 8 and 257 + 4 might both be answered by using partitioning.) Encourage pupils to suggest further additions that they could use the same mental methods to answer.
- Pupils should complete Question 1 in the Practice Book.

### Same-day intervention

- Provide pupils with opportunities to model calculations and so embed mental strategies. Provide them with blank number lines to help visualise calculations. For example, show pupils the calculation 523 + 5 and ask: *Which part of the first addend will change? Will any other digit change? How do you know?*
- Repeat for further addition and subtraction calculations, including those that cross tens boundaries. Provide several examples of these at a time so pupils can familiarise themselves with the strategies needed to partition the second addend or subtrahend each time.

### Same-day enrichment

- Split pupils into pairs and give them access to a timer (for example a one-minute sand timer or stopwatch) as well as two sets of digit cards. Ask them to shuffle the digit cards and lay them out to form a 4 × 4 grid. They time one minute and try to create and solve as many HTO + O and HTO − O calculations as possible, taking their numbers from the rows and columns in the grid they have created. For example:

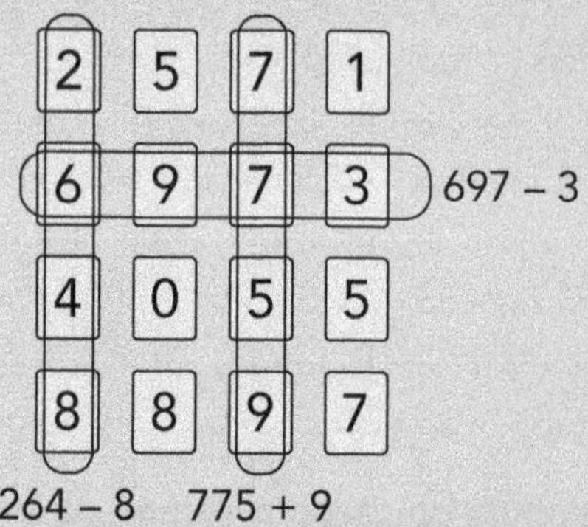


- If time allows, pupils can deal further grids of cards and attempt to beat their personal best.

# Question 2

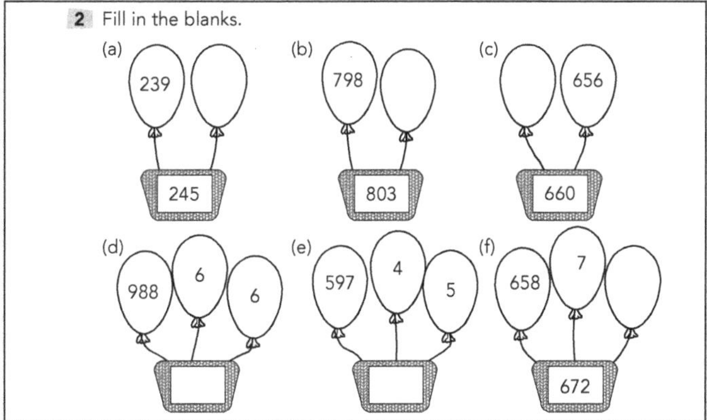


## What learning will pupils have achieved at the conclusion of Question 2?

- Fluency with number will have been extended, particularly when considering ways to find an unknown number and different ways to make the same answer.
- Reasoning will have been used to explain why addition or subtraction is most appropriate to solve visual and word-based problems.

## Activities for whole-class instruction

- Begin by showing a variety of bar diagrams representing HTO + O combinations with an unknown in different places.

A
578 | 7
?

B
? | 9
703

C
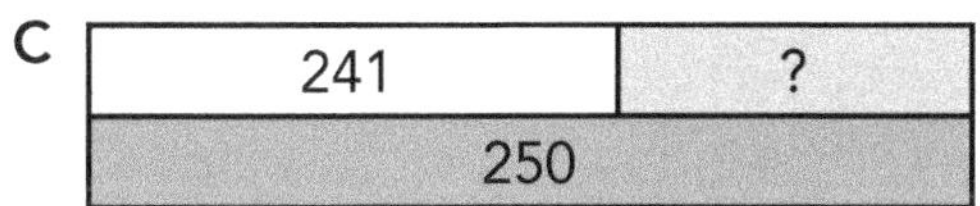


- Discuss the strategies that pupils would use to identify each missing number:

  A: The missing number is the sum; this is solved by addition (578 + 7).

  B: The missing number is an addend; this is solved by subtraction (703 – 9).

  C: The missing number is an addend; this can be solved by subtraction (250 – 241). Pupils have not practiced three-digit subtraction yet. However, because the numbers are close together, it is more efficient to count on from 241 to 250, or pupils might simply use number bonds and know that 9 must be added to 40 to reach 50.

- Practise several examples of these to allow pupils to remind themselves of each type of bar model.
- Expand each bar model (this would work best if they are drawn on pieces of paper and physically moved apart) to show that the sort of diagram depicted in Question 2 is simply a version of a bar model.

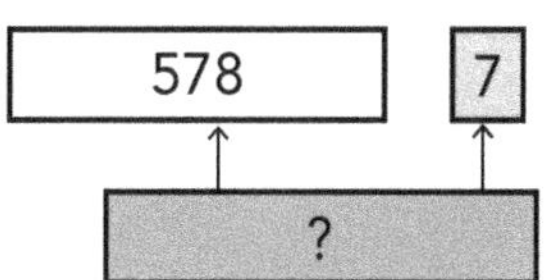


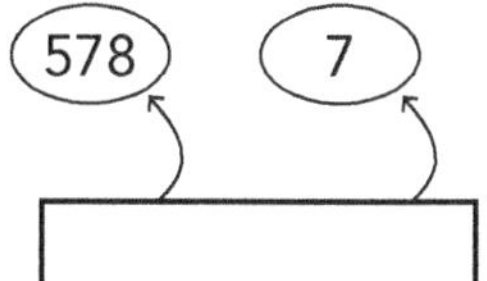


- Practise further examples of this new layout, encouraging pupils to use their knowledge of bar models to explain how they would find each missing number.
- Pupils should complete Question 2 in the Practice Book.

## Same-day intervention

- Revise bar models with pupils. Display the following bar model and cover up the different numbers in turn.

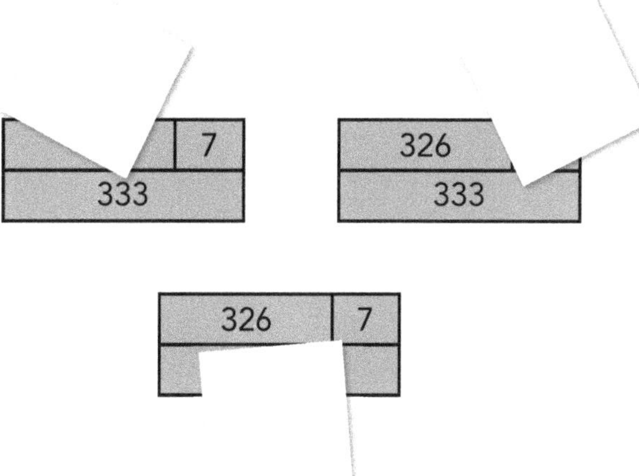


- Ask: *What if we don't know this number? How can we find it?* By using the same bar model, pupils already know the missing numbers and can therefore concentrate on understanding the operations needed to find them. Repeat for different bar models and encourage pupils to begin to explain why they should add or subtract to find the unknown value.
- If pupils need further intervention in drawing links between the three parts to each bar model, encourage them to model simple examples using interlocking cubes. Once they are able to identify whether addition or subtraction is needed, progress to giving pupils missing number problems as above.

## Same-day enrichment

- Split pupils into groups of three. Ask them to begin by drawing a blank version of the diagram used in Question 2.

- Pupil A should begin by writing any number in one of the empty spaces. They then pass the diagram to Pupil B who writes a second number in any one of the remaining spaces (leaving one number missing), then passes the diagram to the final pupil. Pupil C then completes the diagram, explaining the calculation they need to do to find the missing number. Encourage pupils to explore different missing numbers as they repeat the activity and even work with diagrams depicting the sum of two single-digit numbers and a three-digit number.

# Question 3

**3** Draw lines to match the calculations with the correct answers.

| | | | |
|---|---|---|---|
| (a) | 627 + 5 | 702 | 702 – 7 |
| (b) | 689 + 6 | 632 | 710 – 8 |
| (c) | 697 + 5 | 695 | 641 – 9 |

## What learning will pupils have achieved at the conclusion of Question 3?

- Fluency with number will have been extended, particularly when considering ways to find an unknown value and different ways to make the same answer.

## Activities for whole-class instruction

- Explore different ways of reaching 451. Write the number 451 on the board and ask: *If 451 is the answer, what was the question?* Limit pupils to suggest questions that are HTO + O or HTO – O calculations. Record as a spider diagram.

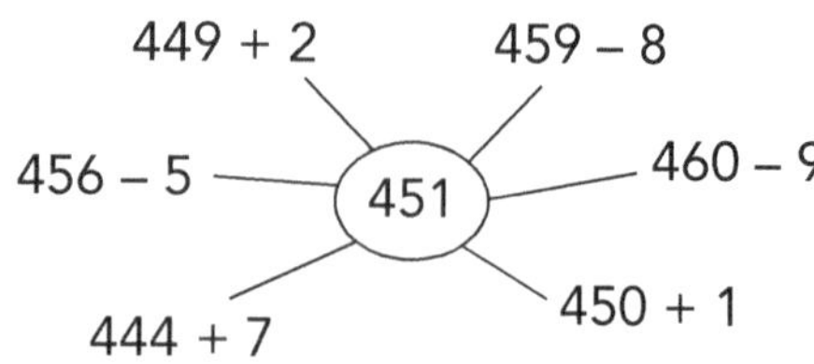


- Repeat the activity, this time as an individual challenge. Ask: *If 804 is the answer, what was the question?* Give pupils two minutes to add as many 'legs' as they can to their spider by finding calculations. Discuss the strategies they used to find possibilities.
- Split pupils into pairs. In each pair, one pupil should write a HTO + O calculation on their mini whiteboard and the other should write a HTO – O calculation so that both have the same answer (for example 783 + 7 and 795 – 5). (It does not matter if some pairs have chosen calculations with the same answer; most will be different.) Pupils should walk around the class separately, carrying their mini whiteboards. Call: *SWAP!* Pupils should swap their whiteboard with the person nearest to them. Each pupil will now have a board showing a calculation with an answer that is different from the answer they started with. Repeat. At this point, the mini whiteboards should be thoroughly mixed up around the room.
- Ask pupils to work out the answer to the sentence on the board that they now have and then find a person with a number sentence that has the same answer. Both pupils should then hold their boards in the air. Give them the example of a pupil holding a mini whiteboard showing 632 – 8. Ask: *What sort of question should they be looking for?* (An addition that equals 624.) The matching game can be played several times using the same boards as long as pupils swap their calculations each time. To add more challenge to the task, ask pupils to only write calculations that have an answer between a limited range (for example between 350 and 390). The similarities between the calculations will mean pupils will need to work out each answer carefully.
- Pupils should complete Question 3 in the Practice Book.

## Same-day intervention

- Display a number line from 350 to 380. Ask pupils to locate the number 361 on it. Challenge pupils to use the number line to show HTO + O and HTO – O calculations that have 361 as their answer. Pupils could move a counter to show the calculations. Ask: *If two numbers are added to make 361, will the starting number be lower or higher than 361?* Ask the same question of numbers that are being taken away.

- Give pairs of pupils a piece of cardboard with a three-digit target number written on it, two pieces of string tied to it and two luggage tags tied to the other end of the pieces of string. On each luggage tag, pupils should write a HTO + O and a HTO – O calculation that equals their target number, using the number line to help.

- Place all the completed chains into a container (such as a plant pot) so that the target numbers are inside and the calculations dangle outside. Choose various pupils to pick a calculation, work it out, then find its equivalent and pull the target number out of the container to see whether they were correct.

## Same-day enrichment

- Show pupils **Resource 3.7.4** 3-digit numbers and ones.

**Resource 3.7.4**

3-digit numbers and ones

| | | | | | |
|---|---|---|---|---|---|
| 750 + 3 | 756 – 5 | 760 – 8 | 746 + 6 | 752 – 1 | 750 – 5 |
| 749 – 8 | 751 + 1 | 752 – 7 | 744 + 8 | 758 – 4 | 747 + 6 |
| 760 – 6 | 743 + 9 | 759 – 7 | 758 – 6 | 768 + 9 | 760 – 9 |
| 761 – 7 | 748 + 4 | 750 + 6 | 747 + 7 | 755 – 5 | 744 + 6 |
| 756 – 5 | 755 – 3 | 752 + 6 | 758 – 7 | 752 + 9 | 741 + 9 |
| 748 + 9 | 757 – 5 | 751 – 9 | 747 – 5 | 764 + 3 | 751 – 7 |

284 © HarperCollinsPublishers 2017

- Explain that several of the calculations within the grid have the same answer of 752. (To make the challenge more difficult, do not tell pupils the number.) Explain that if they colour each of the squares containing calculations that equal 752 it will make a letter of the alphabet.
- Following the activity, challenge pupils to design their own similar puzzles by filling in a blank 6 × 6 grid of squares. Encourage pupils to consider their target number and the different ways it can be made by using HTO + O and HTO – O calculations.

# Question 4

**4** Application problems.

(a) During an environment project some Year 2 pupils collected 203 plastic containers, which was 9 fewer than the number collected by Year 3. How many containers did the Year 3 pupils collect?

Answer: ____________

(b) Dillon is 132 cm tall. He is 5 cm taller than Asha. How tall is Asha?

Answer: ____________

(c) An appliance shop had 256 TVs. They sold 8 TVs in the morning and 7 in the afternoon. How many TVs did the shop have left?

Answer: ____________

(d) Max, May and Jo were skipping. Max did 142 skips, which was 6 skips fewer than Jo. May did 8 skips fewer than Jo. How many skips did May do?

Answer: ____________

## What learning will pupils have achieved at the conclusion of Question 4?

- Pupils will have recognised where and how to apply knowledge to solve word-based problems, including those with more than one step.
- Reasoning will have been used to explain why addition or subtraction is most appropriate to solve visual and word-based problems.

## Activities for whole-class instruction

- Provide a selection of both addition and subtraction problems and encourage pupils to begin by identifying the operation needed to solve them. Explain that they are not required to work out the answer, but instead to decide **how** they would find it out. The problem could even include blanks where the numbers should be to show pupils that they are simply being asked to identify the operation needed. Practise this skill until pupils can do so confidently.

- Display the following problem: It is 1 year and 7 days until Jack is 9 years old. There are 365 days in a year. How many days altogether are there until Jack is 9?
- Choose pupils to act out the scenario and discuss whether it can be solved by adding or subtracting the numbers. Why? Are there any clues in the wording? Ask pupils to represent this information by writing the word problem as a number sentence (365 + 7 = ?).
- Split pupils into pairs to calculate the answer, using strategies that they choose. Share strategies and answers as a class and use the opportunity to highlight the more efficient strategies as good practice. Encourage pupils to use these next time.
- Repeat for different application problems. Ensure that each problem is worded differently so pupils gain experience of identifying 'clues' in different places and writing number sentences. Problems might include the following:
  - A parcel delivery van has 5 fewer parcels to deliver today than it did yesterday. Yesterday it delivered 168 parcels. How many will it deliver today?
  - There are 208 tins of tomato soup in a supermarket store room. There are 9 more tins of chicken soup than there are of tomato soup. How many tins of chicken soup are there?
- Pupils should complete Question 4 in the Practice Book.

## Same-day intervention

- Give pupils several word problems. Explain that they are not required to find the answer, but simply to identify whether it is an addition or subtraction problem. If it helps, encourage pupils to act out the scenario or choose how to model it using objects or sketches to represent the question. For example:
  1. Liam cuts a piece of string that is 9 cm longer than Izzy's. Izzy's string is 238 cm long. How long is Liam's piece? (+)
  2. A cake stall makes £167 on Monday. On Tuesday, it makes £8 less. How much does it make on Tuesday? (–)
  3. There are 204 people on the beach. 8 people decide to go home. How many people are now on the beach? (–)
  4. The school library has 589 books on its shelves. During the morning, 7 books are returned. How many books are now in the library? (+)
- Use bar models to help pupils visualise what each question is asking and to draw links between the scenario and the operation needed to solve it.
- Once pupils are becoming more confident identifying the operation needed, move on to writing it as a number sentence and solving the calculation. Support pupils with this step and provide base 10 blocks to allow them to model the calculation that is needed.
- Repeat for further one-step word problems.

## Same-day enrichment

- Provide pupils with opportunities to solve more complex versions of each problem type. Provide examples where complexity is built by adding another step to each of the four application problems. For example:

  Tom is 132 cm tall. He is 5 cm taller than Shreeya. Pippa is 8 cm shorter than Shreeya. How tall is Pippa?
- Pupils should share these problems for each other to answer as well as devising their own multi-step application problems based on HTO + O and HTO – O calculations.

## Challenge and extension question

# Question 5

**5** Look at the digit cards and answer the questions.

4 8 9 2

(a) What is the greatest number that can be made from the sum of a 3-digit number and a 1-digit number made using these digit cards? Write the number sentence.

(b) What is the smallest number that can be made from the difference of a 3-digit number and a 1-digit number made using these digit cards? Write the number sentence.

Pupils are given a limited set of digits (4, 8, 9 and 2) and challenged to form a HTO + O and HTO – O calculation so that the sum is the greatest and difference is the least, respectively. Pupils will need to draw on their knowledge of place value when deciding where to position each digit. Encourage pupils to explore different possibilities. Although there are limited options, it is interesting to note that when adding it does not matter which ones digit is used (so 984 + 2 and 982 + 4 are both possible answers). Ask pupils to explain why this is and why the same does not apply for the subtraction.

# Unit 7.5
# Addition with 3-digit numbers (1)

## Conceptual context

Over the previous units pupils have developed a sound understanding of how three-digit numbers are made up. At first they were introduced to, for example, 420 as 42 tens and they understood that since 10 tens are 100, 40 tens are 4 hundreds. So, 42 tens is also 4 hundreds and 2 tens. Once this knowledge of three-digit multiples of tens was consolidated and pupils soundly grasped that a number of tens could be represented as hundreds and tens, they started to also include some ones. Therefore, at this point in the development of their understanding, pupils possess a flexible, connected concept of three-digit numbers that incorporates knowledge of place value (column value) and the magnitude of the values represented by the numbers (quantity value).

Pupils will now review and extend their knowledge of calculation methods to operate with three-digit numbers. Pupils will be familiar with the usefulness of partitioning when adding from their work in Year 2 when adding two-digit numbers. Written strategies will include partitioning both numbers (adding the hundreds, tens and ones separately, then recombining) and partitioning only the second addend (adding its hundreds, tens and ones to the first addend, creating a running total). These extended written methods encourage pupils to think in the way they will need to do when using the column method in the next unit.

## Learning pupils will have achieved at the end of the unit

- Understanding of place value and partitioning will have been applied to a range of addition calculations (Q1, Q2, Q3, Q4)
- Written methods will have been extended to introduce the addition of three-digit numbers (Q1)
- Fluency in written calculation strategies will have developed as pupils make decisions to select their preferred strategy for a calculation (Q2, Q3, Q4)

### Resources

mini whiteboards; digit cards; base 10 blocks; place value counters and grids; place value arrow cards; **Resource 3.7.5** Decision table

### Vocabulary

hundreds, tens, ones, plus, add, sum, addend, partition

# Question 1

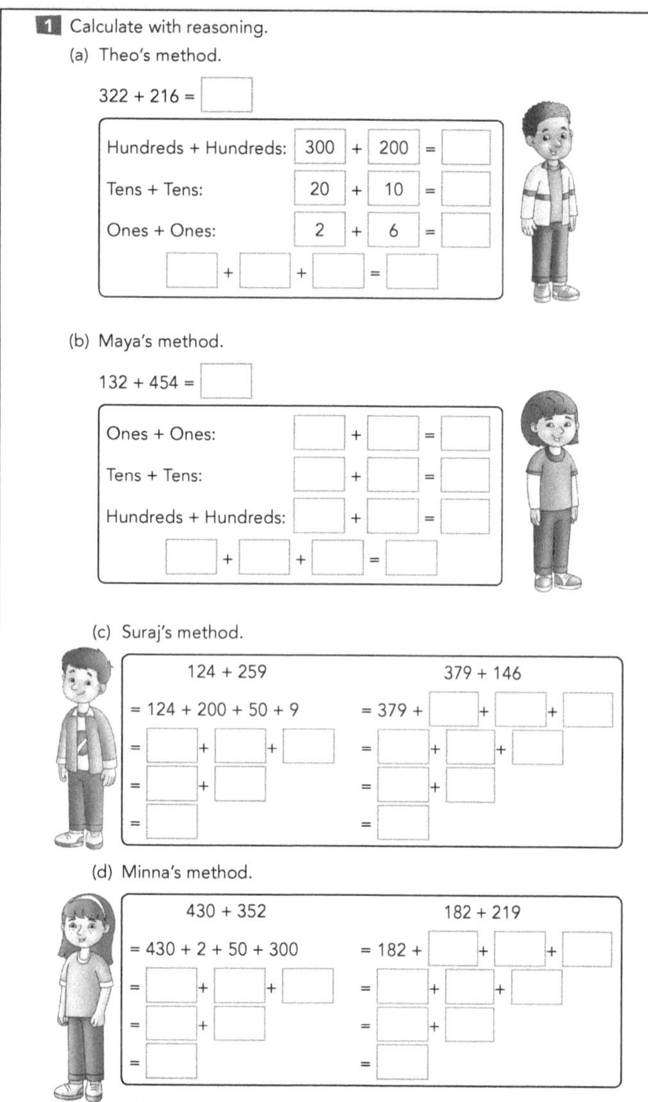

**1** Calculate with reasoning.

(a) Theo's method.

322 + 216 = ☐

Hundreds + Hundreds: 300 + 200 = ☐

Tens + Tens: 20 + 10 = ☐

Ones + Ones: 2 + 6 = ☐

☐ + ☐ + ☐ = ☐

(b) Maya's method.

132 + 454 = ☐

Ones + Ones: ☐ + ☐ = ☐

Tens + Tens: ☐ + ☐ = ☐

Hundreds + Hundreds: ☐ + ☐ = ☐

☐ + ☐ + ☐ = ☐

(c) Suraj's method.

124 + 259 = 124 + 200 + 50 + 9 = ☐ + ☐ + ☐ = ☐ + ☐ = ☐

379 + 146 = 379 + ☐ + ☐ + ☐ = ☐ + ☐ + ☐ = ☐ + ☐ = ☐

(d) Minna's method.

430 + 352 = 430 + 2 + 50 + 300 = ☐ + ☐ + ☐ = ☐ + ☐ = ☐

182 + 219 = 182 + ☐ + ☐ + ☐ = ☐ + ☐ + ☐ = ☐ + ☐ = ☐

## What learning will pupils have achieved at the conclusion of Question 1?

- Written methods will have been extended to introduce the addition of three-digit numbers.
- Understanding of place value and partitioning will have been applied to a range of addition calculations.

## Activities for whole-class instruction

- Write 44 + 35. Ask pupils for strategies to find the total. Highlight any suggestions of partitioning either or both numbers and explain that pupils will be exploring similar strategies when adding three-digit numbers together. Write a hundreds digit for both numbers so pupils recognise that the problem is very similar (for example 644 + 235). Ask: *How could you partition these numbers to help add them?* Accept suggestions, without commenting to begin with, to allow pupils to give their initial responses.
- Introduce four written methods of addition by way of two decisions pupils need to take using **Resource 3.7.5** Decision table.

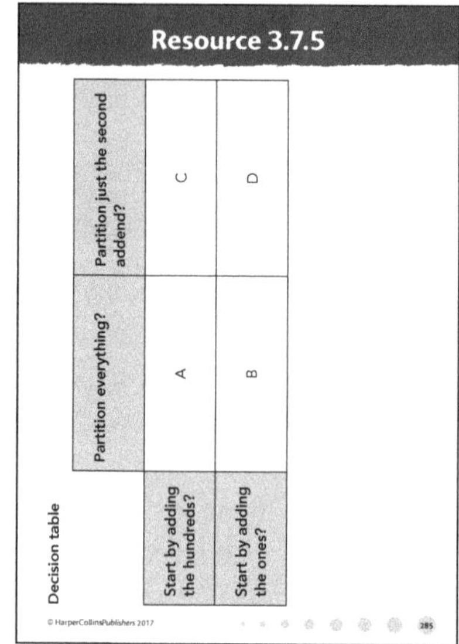

Resource 3.7.5

Decision table

| | Partition everything? | Partition just the second addend? |
|---|---|---|
| Start by adding the hundreds? | A | C |
| Start by adding the ones? | B | D |

© HarperCollinsPublishers 2017

- Explain that pupils can partition both addends or keep the first addend and just partition the second. They can also start by adding the hundreds (then the tens, then the ones) or vice versa and start by adding the ones.
- Discuss how these two decisions combine to create four different methods (the letters in the grid are for reference only, but do correspond with the parts to Question 1 and the order in which the methods should be introduced).
- Begin with the first column and model how pupils can partition both numbers to find the answer. For example, take a set of place value arrow cards and make the numbers 644 and 235. Then choose a pupil to demonstrate how to partition both numbers. Point to the first cell in Column 1 (Method A) and complete the written addition for 644 + 235 by starting with the hundreds as follows:

| | |
|---|---|
| (Partition both numbers.) | 600 + 40 + 4 + 200 + 30 + 5 |
| (Start by adding the hundreds.) | 600 + 200 = 800 |
| (Add the tens.) | 40 + 30 = 70 |
| (Add the ones.) | 4 + 5 = 9 |
| (Find the total.) | 800 + 70 + 9 = 879 |

- Ask: *Would there be any difference if you partitioned both numbers and started with the ones instead?* Model this method as Method B in the table.
- Point to the second column and remind pupils that when adding two numbers pupils don't have to start from zero;

they can simply start from the first number (often the largest) and add to it (so only the second addend needs to be partitioned). Write the addition 561 + 423 and choose a pupil to make the numbers 561 and 423 using place value arrow cards. Keep 561 together and ask pupils how 423 can be partitioned to help. Point to the first cell in Column 2 (Method C) and complete the written method as follows:

| | |
|---|---|
| (Partition the second addend.) | 561 + 400 + 20 + 3 |
| (Start by adding the hundreds.) | 961 + 20 + 3 |
| (Add the tens.) | 981 + 3 |
| (Add the ones.) | 984 |

- Ask: *What is the difference between this method and the one where you partition both numbers?* Elicit that there is one less step – pupils do not need to add at the end to find the overall total as they are adding to 561 as they go, keeping a running total. Model how to use Method D, starting by adding the ones:

| | |
|---|---|
| (Partition the second addend, ones first.) | 561 + 3 + 20 + 400 |
| (Start by adding the ones.) | 564 + 20 + 400 |
| (Add the tens.) | 584 + 400 |
| (Add the hundreds.) | 984 |

- Keep the table visible and give pupils time to practise each strategy with different additions, including those where the total of the ones or tens crosses a 10 or 100 boundary. Ask: *Which strategy are you most comfortable using?* Explain that there is no correct strategy at this stage and that they all will find the correct answer.
- Pupils should complete Question 1 in the Practice Book.

## Same-day intervention

- Provide pupils with their own set of place value arrow cards. Display the calculation 156 + 243 and ask them to make each number using their cards. Encourage them to talk about the different parts to each number as they combine the cards to form it. Ask pupils to suggest how each number could be partitioned without separating their cards. Remind them that, although numbers can be partitioned in many different ways, splitting them into their hundreds, tens and ones is a simple way to do so when adding. Pupils should separate out their cards to show this and then group the hundreds, tens and ones separately.

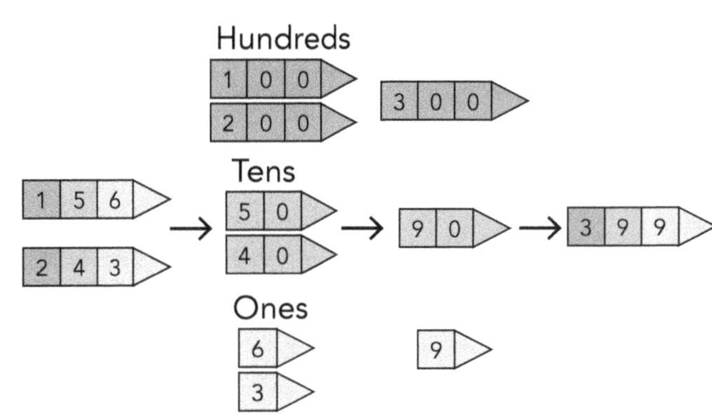


- Go through each grouping, finding the totals, then encourage pupils to recombine them to find the overall total. For each step, write the corresponding addition on the board:

  100 + 200 = 300
  50 + 40 = 90
  6 + 3 = 9
  300 + 90 + 9 = 399

- Use arrow cards to help scaffold the three remaining methods. Use a 'What if …?' structure to encourage pupils to explore each new strategy: What if we split both numbers, but we start by adding the ones first? What if we only partition one of the numbers?
- Encourage pupils to record their workings using written additions to reflect the manipulations of the arrow cards.

## Same-day enrichment

- Provide pairs of pupils with a copy of **Resource 3.7.5** Decision table, a set of digit cards and two plastic counters. They should deal out six digit cards and use them to make a three-digit addition. Both pupils then take a plastic counter and drop it from head height onto the grid. The grid cell where their counter lands shows them the strategy they need to use to answer the question. Both pupils should use their method and then compare answers to check that they have found the sum correctly. They should repeat for different sets of digit cards, practising the different strategies.

# Question 2

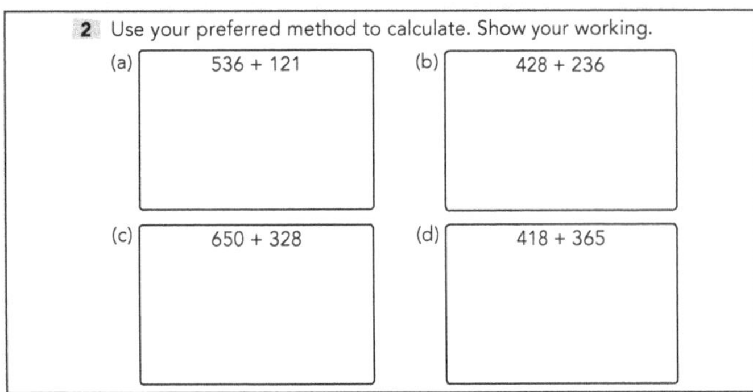

2 Use your preferred method to calculate. Show your working.
(a) 536 + 121
(b) 428 + 236
(c) 650 + 328
(d) 418 + 365


## What learning will pupils have achieved at the conclusion of Question 2?

- Fluency in written calculation strategies will have developed as pupils select their preferred strategy for a calculation.
- Understanding of place value and partitioning will have been applied to a range of addition calculations.

## Activities for whole-class instruction

- The focus of this unit is on developing efficient written calculation strategies. The use of manipulatives will be helpful in parallel with pictorial and abstract representations to support understanding to some extent. Most pupils will need little if any work with manipulatives. Do not restrict use of manipulatives if pupils need them to develop and consolidate understanding. Ultimately, the aim is to develop an efficient written strategy.
- Split pupils into four groups – A, B, C and D. Remind them of the strategy table they considered when working with Question 1 and explain that each group should use the strategy denoted by the letter used in the original table.
- Display the calculation 357 + 146. Ensure each group is aware of how to use its particular strategy to find the total. For example, pupils in Group A should partition both addends and add the ones, then the tens, then the hundreds, before adding all three totals:

  ones + ones = 7 + 6 = 13
  tens + tens = 50 + 40 = 90
  hundreds + hundreds = 300 + 100 = 400
  400 + 90 + 13 = 503
- Choose one pupil from each group to share their strategy. Swap the group letters around in the table so pupils have the opportunity to practise each of the different strategies. Finally, rub out all the letters and ask pupils to choose their preferred method. Encourage them to explain why they have chosen that particular method. Highlight any examples of reasoning where pupils mention the fact their chosen method is quicker (and therefore more efficient).

Look out for ... pupils whose approach to calculation is purely procedural and who do not look for more efficient strategies. Some pupils adopt and adhere to a 'partition both' strategy as it is a strategy that is reliable even though it can be inefficient. Encourage them to consider the previous units where they have learned how to add multiples of 100 and 10 and single digits to three-digit numbers. They therefore have the skills to be able to only partition the second addend.

- Pupils should complete Question 2 in the Practice Book.

### Same-day intervention

- Begin with the calculation 437 + 242. Provide pupils with place value arrow cards and discuss the make-up of each number as they model both addends using the cards. Encourage pupils to say each number as they make it: '4 hundreds and 3 tens and 7 makes 437. 2 hundreds and 4 tens and 2 makes 242.'
- Ask: *How can we partition these numbers to be able to add them?* Encourage pupils to partition both numbers and place the hundreds, tens and ones arrow cards together.

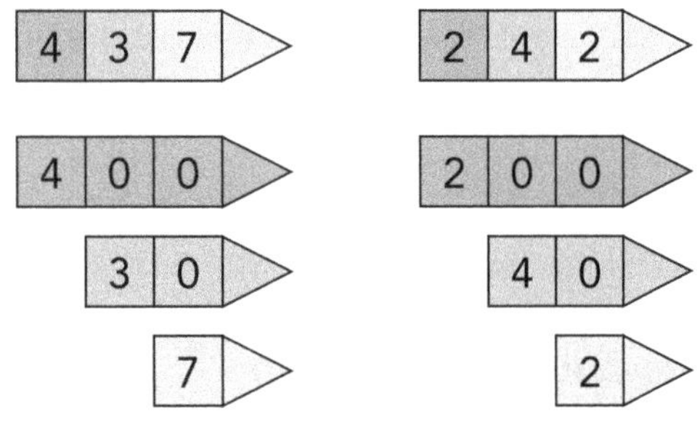


- They can then model each total (600, 70 and 9) out of arrow cards before recombining to show the total.
- Remind pupils that they do not have to partition both numbers. Repeat the activity with a new addition – this time only partitioning the second addend.
- Provide pupils with further additions to model using the arrow cards. Encourage them to use the strategy of their choice. Include additions where either the ones or tens total adds to more than 10 or 100 (for example 368 + 125).

## Same-day enrichment

- Starting with the number 558 ask pupils to suggest second addends to give a sum that is:
  - between 600 and 700
  - more than 900
  - of 789
  - of 824
  - a multiple of 10.
- After finding one solution for each statement, pupils should work in pairs, writing their own starting number and set of five statements for their partner to solve. Pupils should explain to each other the strategies they used to work out the answers.

# Question 3

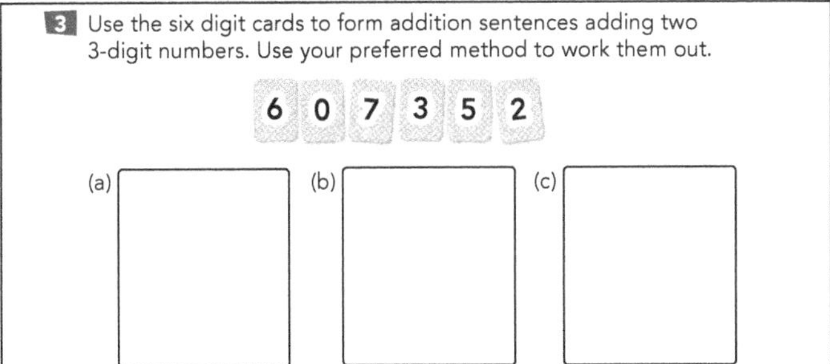

3 Use the six digit cards to form addition sentences adding two 3-digit numbers. Use your preferred method to work them out.

6 0 7 3 5 2

(a) (b) (c)

## What learning will pupils have achieved at the conclusion of Question 3?

- Fluency in written calculation strategies will have developed as pupils make decisions to select their preferred strategy for a calculation.
- Understanding of place value and partitioning will have been applied to a range of addition calculations.

## Activities for whole-class instruction

- Display the following digits on large digit cards: 5, 8, 2, 1, 4, 3. Ask pupils to come to the front and rearrange the digits to make different three-digit additions (for example 342 + 185, 528 + 431 and so on). Write each suggestion on the board.
- Choose one of the additions and give pupils the answer. Ask: *What different methods could you suggest to find this answer?* Discuss suggestions and model them.

(i) Giving pupils the answer to a question at the beginning can be an effective strategy for encouraging them to focus less on the answer and more on the strategy that is used to find it – the 'how' of a question, rather than the 'what'. This is particularly useful when considering calculations where a variety of strategies can be used (as in this case) and word-based problems.

- Choose a second addition from the set generated and give pupils time to work in pairs, choosing the strategy they prefer to find its sum. Discuss why pupils have opted for that particular strategy. Ask: *Is this a method you would use every time, or did you choose it because of the numbers in the calculation?* Repeat for further additions generated from the digit cards.
- Pupils should complete Question 3 in the Practice Book.

## Same-day intervention

- Split pupils into three groups. The first group should have base 10 blocks; the second group should have place value grids and counters; the third group should have place value arrow cards. Each pupil should record their working in written form as well as using the equipment they have been given. Show pupils the following digit cards: 4, 6, 0, 3, 2, 5. Ask pupils to suggest ways of arranging them to create a three-digit addition.
- Decide on a strategy to use (for example, partition the second addend and add the ones first), then encourage pupils to show how their equipment can be used to model the calculation. For example, if the addition is 423 + 506, then they might model this strategy as follows:

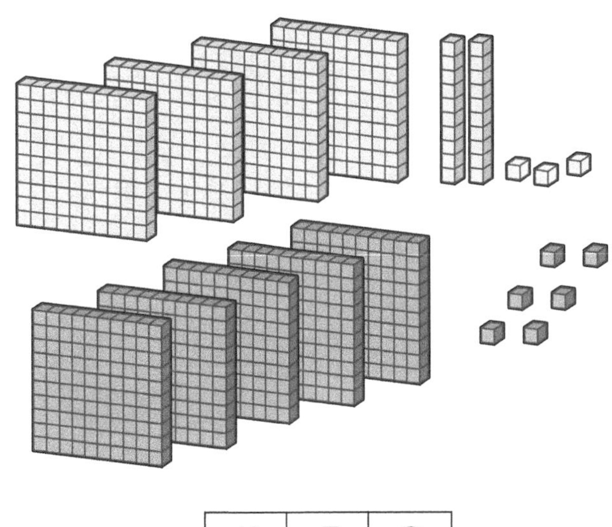

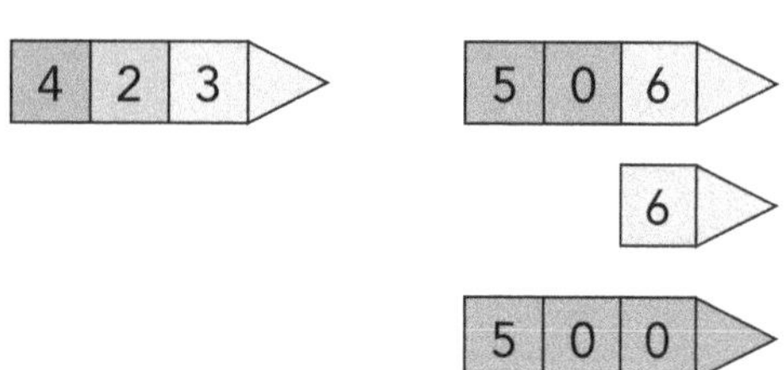


423 + 506
= 423 + 6 + 500
= 429 + 500
= 929

- Repeat for different sets of digits and strategies.

## Same-day enrichment

- Provide pairs with two sets of digit cards, which should be shuffled and dealt face down on the table-top. Each pupil should take six cards, turn them over and use their six digits to create two additions. The first addition should be designed to make the greatest sum. For example, if Pupil A picks the cards 4, 6, 2, 1, 0 and 7, they might make the addition 741 + 620.
- Pupils should use the strategy of their choice to add their numbers together and then compare their totals to see which is greater. The pupil with the larger total gets a point. They should then rearrange their digits to make an addition with the smallest possible sum. The pupil with the smaller total gets a point. Pupils should repeat the game, choosing different digits each time.

# Question 4

**4** Write a number sentence for each question.

(a) One addend is 239 and the other is 384. What is the sum?

Number sentence: ______________________

(b) What number is 168 more than 574?

Number sentence: ______________________

## What learning will pupils have achieved at the conclusion of Question 4?

- Fluency in written calculation strategies will have developed as pupils select their preferred strategy for a calculation.
- Understanding of place value and partitioning will have been applied to a range of addition calculations.

## Activities for whole-class instruction

- Practise recognition of the terms that are used to describe additions. Call out different calculations described in words, ensuring that pupils hear a variety of question types, not just addition. This will help them to concentrate on identifying additions. Ask pupils to call out 'STOP!' when they hear an addition question. Possible calculations might include:
  - What is the product of 351 and 425?
  - What is the sum of 628 and 214?
  - What is the difference between 663 and 435?
  - What is the total of 742 and 235?
  - One addend is 301. The other is 245. What is the sum?
  - The minuend is 680. The subtrahend is 278. What is the difference?
  - What are 577 and 535 altogether?
- For each addition, discuss how pupils know that they need to add the numbers together. Give them time to pause and use the written strategy of their choice to find the answer. Discuss their preferred strategies and why they prefer them.
- Pupils should complete Question 4 in the Practice Book.

## Same-day intervention

- Display the following word calculation: One addend is 450. The other is 274. What is the sum?
- Ask: *Which words give you a clue about what sort of calculation this is?* What do you think you need to do to find the answer? Remind pupils of the meanings of the words 'addend' and 'sum' and show that this is an addition calculation. Encourage pupils to write the calculation using numerals. Ask: *How might you work out the answer?* Prior to using written strategies, ensure that pupils attempt to clearly describe the method they would use. Talking about what they plan to do will help to embed the strategy. Provide place value arrow cards for pupils to model the way they partition and recombine numbers. Repeat for further word-based calculations involving terms like 'sum', 'total', and 'addend'.

## Same-day enrichment

- Provide pupils with simple word-based calculations involving unknowns. In pairs they should explain what they notice about the relationships between the numbers and use this knowledge to solve each problem.
  - If A is 136, and B is 357 more than A, what is B? What is the sum of A and B?
  - If B is 572 greater than A and A is 203, what is B? What is the total of A and B?
  - What could A and B be if A is 199 more than B? What is the sum of your two numbers?
- Pupils should then devise their own similar problems for peers to answer.

## Challenge and extension question

# Question 5

**5** Fill in the boxes.

(a) The sum of the smallest 3-digit number and the smallest 3-digit number is a ☐-digit number.

(b) The sum of the greatest 3-digit number and the greatest 3-digit number is a ☐-digit number.

(c) The sum of two 3-digit numbers can be a ☐-digit number or a ☐-digit number.

Pupils are challenged to consider the range of totals that are possible from adding two three-digit numbers. Specifically, they are asked to think about the number of digits in the total when the two smallest three-digit numbers are added (100 + 100) and when the two greatest three-digit numbers are added (999 + 999). As well as concluding that the sum of two three-digit numbers can either have three or four digits, pupils may also be able to note that each total must lie somewhere between 200 and 1998.

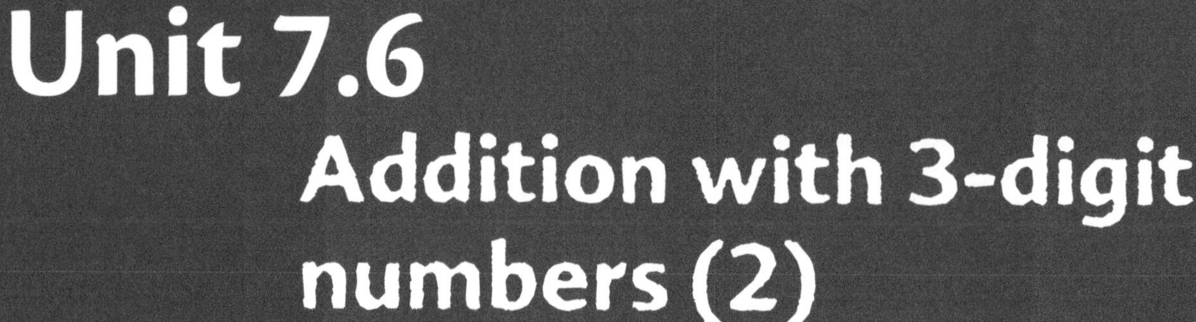

# Unit 7.6 Addition with 3-digit numbers (2)

## Conceptual context

Pupils' fluency in a range of mental and extended written methods of addition involving three-digit numbers has developed. They are already familiar with the column method of addition, having used it to add two-digit numbers, and so this unit extends this to adding numbers with three digits. The expanded written methods used in the previous unit are conceptually linked to the column method and it is important that pupils are able to see the links between them. Pupils will be encouraged to explain each step and justify their answers; retaining their focus on the mathematical processes as well as the written procedures so that their conceptual understanding about addition continues to be richly connected.

## Learning pupils will have achieved at the end of the unit

- The formal written method of addition will have been revised and extended to include three-digit numbers (Q1)
- Understanding of place value, partitioning and re-grouping numbers will have been applied to a range of three-digit addition calculations (Q1, Q2, Q3, Q4, Q5)
- Pupils will have developed their problem-solving skills (Q2, Q4, Q5)
- Reasoning will have been applied to deduce the missing digits in a column addition and to identify errors (Q2, Q4)
- Pupils' understanding and application of the addition method will have been applied to solve word-based problems (Q5)

### Resources

digit cards; base 10 blocks; mini whiteboards; **Resource 3.7.5** Decision table; **Resource 3.7.6** What's wrong here?

### Vocabulary

addition, total, column method, vertical, hundreds column, tens column, ones column, hundreds, tens, ones, addend, sum

# Question 1

**1** Use the column method to calculate.

(a) 450 + 234 =

```
  4 5 0
+ 2 3 4
```

(b) 308 + 126 =

```
  3 0 8
+ 1 2 6
```

(c) 703 + 224 =

```
  7 0 3
+ 2 2 4
```

(d) 372 + 143 =

(e) 346 + 251 =

(f) 597 + 188 =

## What learning will pupils have achieved at the conclusion of Question 1?

- The formal written method of addition will have been revised and extended to include three-digit numbers.
- Understanding of place value, partitioning and re-grouping numbers will have been applied to a range of three-digit addition calculations.

## Activities for whole-class instruction

- Display the calculation 362 + 265. Ask pupils to think back to the previous unit and to describe some of the different ways they could find the answer to an addition like this. Ensure that they can recall the written methods they used for partitioning one or both of the addends and then adding the hundreds, tens and ones separately. Display **Resource 3.7.5** Decision table and remind pupils of the four different methods they used.

**Resource 3.7.5**

Decision table

| | Partition everything? | Partition just the second addend? |
|---|---|---|
| Start by adding the hundreds? | A | C |
| Start by adding the ones? | B | D |

© HarperCollinsPublishers 2017 285

- Ask: *Is there a way to write the addition that will help you to add it?* Remind pupils of their work with column addition in Year 2 and that they can set the addition out vertically. Provide them with digit cards and ask them to arrange them so that they model where each digit should be placed. Point to different digits and ask pupils to give their value. Pupils will probably not have used column addition with three digits before, so ensure that they understand the value of the hundreds column.
- Ask: *Which of the four methods (A, B, C or D) is the column method most similar to? Why do you think this?* Pupils should note that both numbers are in effect being partitioned (ones added to ones, tens added to tens and so on) and the calculation begins with the ones, so it is most similar to Method B. Ensure that pupils understand that the column method is simply a more efficient way of writing addition (remind them of the several lines they had to complete for each addition in the previous unit).
- Go through each column and discuss with pupils how to record each total. When they add the tens, ask: *What is 6 tens plus 6 tens? How can we record this?* Remind pupils of the need to exchange the 10 tens for 1 hundred. Model this using base 10 blocks.

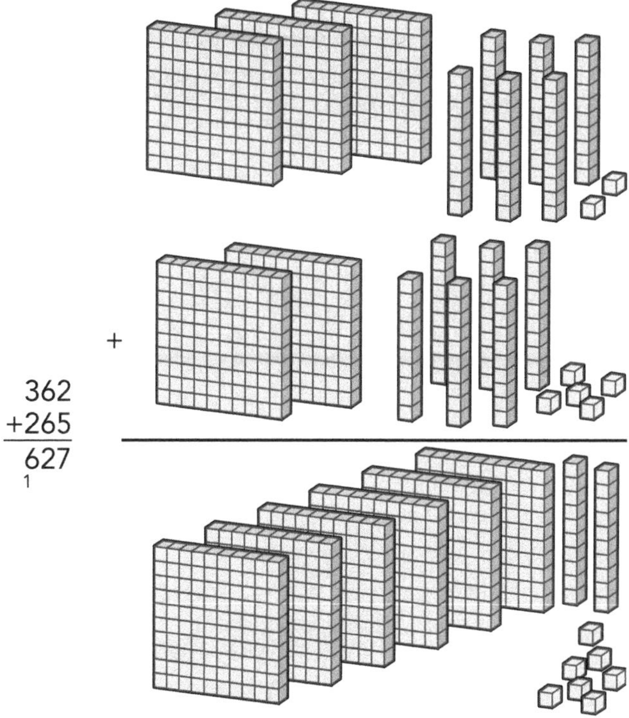


- Ask: *Which part of column addition do you think is the most important to remember? Why?* There is no 'correct' answer to this question, but it will deepen pupils' understanding if they discuss the process and the mathematics underlying it.
- Repeat for further column additions.
- Pupils should complete Question 1 in the Practice Book.

## Same-day intervention

- Draw a place value grid and ask pupils to model the number 362 using base 10 blocks. Refer to the column addition and, for each column (beginning with the ones), ask pupils to add the relevant number of base 10 blocks. Where necessary use the blocks to model how 10 ones are exchanged for 1 ten when there are more than 9 ones (and how 10 tens are exchanged for 1 hundred).

## Same-day enrichment

- Pupil pairs should write and solve three-digit addition calculations using the column method. Each pupil should devise five calculations that do not involve exchange and five that do. Pupils should consider how they know whether an addition will require exchange or not (whether a pair of digits adds to 10 or more). After writing each set of calculations, pupils should swap and solve each other's additions, before returning them to the first pupil to check that they have been solved correctly.

# Question 2

**2** Are these calculations correct? Put a ✓ for yes or a ✗ for no in the box and then make corrections.

| (a) | (b) | (c) |
|---|---|---|
| 5 8 1 | 3 7 8 | 3 5 4 |
| + 3 3 | + 1 2 6 | + 1 2 8 |
| 9 1 1 | 4 9 4 | 4 8 2 |
| ☐ | ☐ | ☐ |

Corrections:

## What learning will pupils have achieved at the conclusion of Question 2?

- Understanding of place value, partitioning and re-grouping numbers will have been applied to a range of three-digit addition calculations.
- Pupils will have developed problem-solving skills.
- Reasoning will have been applied to deduce the missing digits in a column addition and to identify errors.

## Activities for whole-class instruction

- Pupils' ability to locate errors in calculations is important not just when checking their own work for mistakes, but also to develop number sense when deciding whether an answer is reasonable and when consolidating the steps involved in a procedure.
- Explain to pupils that the roles have been reversed and that you are going to add some three-digit numbers on the board and they must 'be the teacher', watching out for any mistakes you might make. Encourage pupils to help you use the column method for addition correctly. Write several examples of three-digit additions and, as you describe your method, make a number of mistakes. The errors should include the following:
  - aligning the digits incorrectly
  - beginning with the hundreds and adding from left to right (where exchange is necessary)
  - 'forgetting' to carry a ten or hundred
  - carrying a ten or hundred, but neglecting to add it.
- Provide several opportunities for pupils to correct these types of errors. Also include one or two examples where the method is used correctly.
- Pupils should complete Question 2 in the Practice Book.

## Same-day intervention

- Pupils should be given experience of identifying errors while calculations are being worked out as well as being presented with completed calculations containing errors. Share a selection of possible mistakes when using the formal written method (see **Resource 3.7.6** What's wrong here?). Model each mistake so pupils understand what each one refers to.

**Resource 3.7.6**

What's wrong here?

Mistake 1: 411 + 233 = 14 — Just added the digits

Mistake 2: 538 + 126 = 691 (4) — Right answer, wrong way round

Mistake 3: 256 + 219 = 465 — Where's the 10 (or 100)?

Mistake 4: 337 + 482 = 711 (1) — Don't forget the 100 (or the 10)!

Mistake 5: 416 + 205 = 4365 — Right question, wrong layout

Mistake 6: 837 + 115 = 722 — Mixed-up operations!

© HarperCollinsPublishers 2017

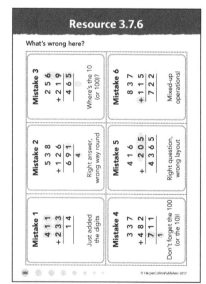

- Ask: *If there was a seventh card, what mistake do you think might be on it?* Encourage pupils to share their ideas about some of the other errors that are made when completing vertical calculations.

- Use the error cards to play a game of 'Error bingo'. Give pupils a set each and ask them to pick any four error cards from their set and place them face up on the table. Model several calculations where mistakes are made on purpose. If pupils recognise that one of the mistakes matches one of their error cards, they may turn the card over. The first player to have all four cards turned over is the winner. To make the game longer, repeat some of the mistakes and also include one or two examples where the calculation is completely correct.
- Where appropriate, encourage pupils to identify each error by writing the question out for themselves on a mini whiteboard and working through each column, comparing each step with the calculation in front of them.

## Same-day enrichment

- Ask pupils to play a game of 'Hide the mistake' in pairs, where the aim is to hide errors from their partner without them noticing. Pupils should refer to the error cards (**Resource 3.7.6** What's wrong here?) for ideas. Pupil A writes down five three-digit additions set out in columns and includes their answers. Within the five calculations, they should aim to include three incorrect answers. Encourage pupils to use ideas from **Resource 3.7.6**.
- Pupil B must look closely at the additions, but is not allowed to write anything down. They score a point for every incorrect answer they spot. If they wrongly identify an answer as incorrect, they lose a point. Encourage pupils to refer to **Resource 3.7.6** when explaining what the mistake is.
- Pupil A gets two points for every incorrect answer that is not identified by their partner and therefore remains hidden.

# Question 3

**3** Complete the table.

| Addend | 327 | 204 | 534 | 178 | 257 | 689 |
|---|---|---|---|---|---|---|
| Addend | 150 | 328 | 265 | 433 | 465 | 311 |
| Sum | | | | | | |

## What learning will pupils have achieved at the conclusion of Question 3?

- Understanding of place value, partitioning and re-grouping numbers will have been applied to a range of three-digit addition calculations.

## Activities for whole-class instruction

- Remind pupils of the words 'addend' and 'sum' – two terms that they should be familiar with. Write a vertical addition on the board and ask pupils to label each number correctly. Discuss the meaning of each term.
- Draw a table similar to the one in Question 3, partially completing each column with two three-digit addends and a missing sum. Include examples that do and that do not require a ten or hundred to be 'carried'. Ask: *How is this the same as a vertical addition? How is it different?* Ask pupils to sketch bar models to represent one of the columns and ask them to describe what they have drawn. Work through some examples of vertical additions taken from the table and then encourage pupils to find each sum by completing each calculation on their mini whiteboards.
- To add an extra layer of challenge, give pupils different clues about the answers. For example:
  - One of the missing sums has 4 ones in it. Which calculation is it?
  - Which calculation makes a sum that is an odd number?
- Encourage them to use reasoning to explain how they know their chosen calculation is correct.
- Pupils should complete Question 3 in the Practice Book.

## Same-day intervention

- Build links between written vertical addition of three-digit numbers and more concrete ways of representing it. For example, show pupils two three-digit addends in a calculation where one of the columns adds to a two-digit answer. For example:

| addend | 353 |
|---|---|
| addend | 293 |
| sum | |

- Ask three pupils to model 353 using base 10 blocks, one holding the hundreds, one the tens and the other the ones. Ask: *How many ones do we need to add to the ones we already have?* Repeat for the tens and ask: *If 5 tens plus 9 tens equals 14 tens, how can we record this answer?* Model how the second pupil should exchange 10 tens for 1 hundred and then give that to the pupil holding the hundreds. Finally, add the hundreds column and discuss the sum.
- Repeat for different additions and lead pupils towards being able to complete the calculation without modelling it.

## Same-day enrichment

- Split pupils into pairs. Pupil A should work out an addition of his/her choice using the formal written method on their mini whiteboard secretly. Pupil A should give Pupil B the numbers by giving clues about each addend (for example: the first addend is between 600 and 700, contains a 2 and a 5 and is an even number). When they have worked out the addends, Pupil B should use their knowledge of the formal written method to find the sum.
- Pupils should compare calculations to check and Pupil B gets a point if they match. They should repeat the activity for different calculations, swapping roles each time.

# Question 4

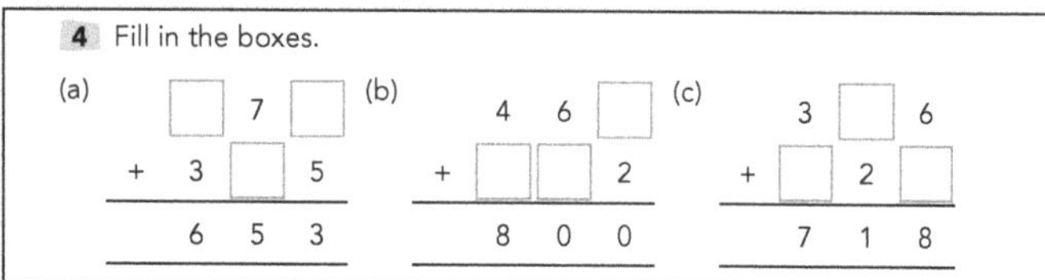


## What learning will pupils have achieved at the conclusion of Question 4?

- Understanding of place value, partitioning and re-grouping numbers will have been applied to a range of three-digit addition calculations.
- Pupils will have developed problem-solving skills.
- Reasoning will have been applied to deduce the missing digits in a column addition and to identify errors.

## Activities for whole-class instruction

- Use large digit cards to make the following vertical addition on the board: 746 + 134 = 880. However, stick the cards with their reverse showing so that none of the digits are visible. Explain to pupils that the nine cards make a vertical addition and that their aim is to identify what the calculation is without all of the cards being revealed.
- Reveal the ones digit in the answer and then ask questions based on it. For example:

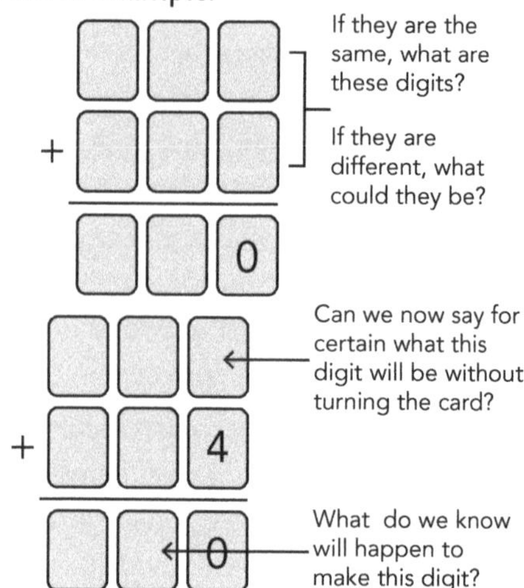

If they are the same, what are these digits?
If they are different, what could they be?
+
0
Can we now say for certain what this digit will be without turning the card?
+
4
What do we know will happen to make this digit?
0


- Repeat, digit by digit, until pupils can identify the entire addition, using reasoning to explain what the missing digits are.
- Provide further examples and encourage pupils to discuss what they need to know to work out each missing digit.
- Pupils should complete Question 4 in the Practice Book.

## Same-day intervention

- Set up a 'secret' addition calculation using nine digit cards face down, ensuring pupils have not seen the numbers on the cards.
- Place nine pieces of paper on the table in a 3 by 3 array on the left of the digit cards. Ensure pupils understand that each piece of paper represents a digit and draw a + symbol and an equals sign. Tell pupils that they need to find out what the numbers in the calculation are. They can request to see the value of any two digits in a column and work out the third.

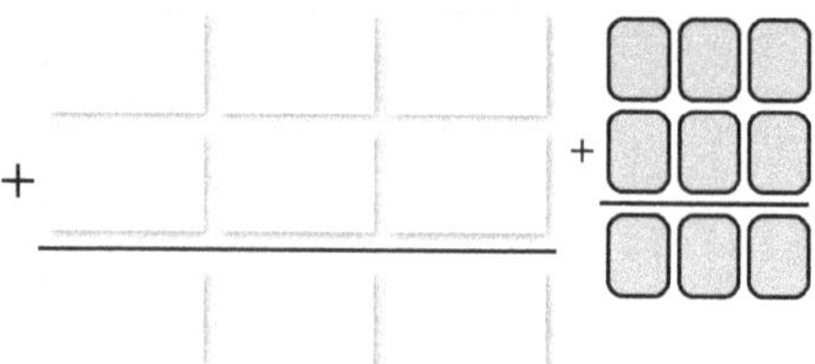

- For each digit revealed, place base 10 blocks to the value of that digit on the corresponding piece of paper. For example, they may request to see the top digit and bottom digit in the ones column:

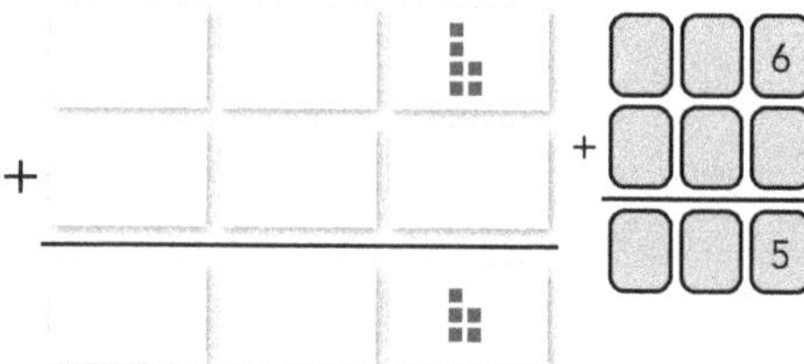

- In this example, pupils can then deduce that as 6 + ? cannot equal 5, the answer must be 15 and so the missing digit in the ones column must be 9.
- Pupils could then turn over the 9 and add the 9 blocks before going on to consider what they now know about the next column. They should realise that they already have 1 ten in the next column, carried over from adding all the ones together, and they should decide where to put that (more cards and paper may be needed). Next, pupils should choose which two cards to reveal from the tens column, and so on.
- Give pupils time to invent their own three-digit vertical additions and go through the process again.

## Same-day enrichment

- Ask pupils to work in pairs, inventing a three-digit vertical addition each and writing it secretly on a mini whiteboard. Pupil A should use digit cards to model their calculation, turning each card over so that the digit cannot be seen to begin with.
- Pupil B should turn over one card at a time until they have enough information to be able to reason what the entire addition is, based on the clues they can see. Encourage them to answer the following questions in their pairs: How many out of the nine cards did you need to turn over before you could work out the others? Why did you choose to turn over the cards that you did?
- Pupils should repeat the activity several times, swapping roles.
- Encourage them to consider the questions in the Practice Book and whether there is a pattern in the missing digits. Ask: *How many digits are revealed in each column each time? Does it matter where they are? Do you think you could work out the answer if you only had one digit revealed in a column? Why/why not?*

# Question 5

**5** Application problems.

(a) An electrician cut 312 metres from a coil of electric wire. He then cut off another 268 metres. How many metres did he cut off in total?

Ans wer: ______

(b) Ollie was reading a book. In the first week he read 162 pages. This was 135 fewer pages than in the second week. How many pages did he read in the second week?

(c) At Laptop World, a used laptop computer is priced at £138. A new laptop is priced at £162 more. What is the price of the new laptop?

£138

Answer: ______

## What learning will pupils have achieved at the conclusion of Question 5?

- Understanding of place value, partitioning and re-grouping numbers will have been applied to a range of three-digit addition calculations.
- Pupils will have developed problem-solving skills.
- Pupils' understanding and application of the addition method will have been applied to solve word-based problems.

## Activities for whole-class instruction

- Remind pupils of the bar models they can use to show a 'combine' word problem, where parts combine to find a final total (solved by addition). For example:

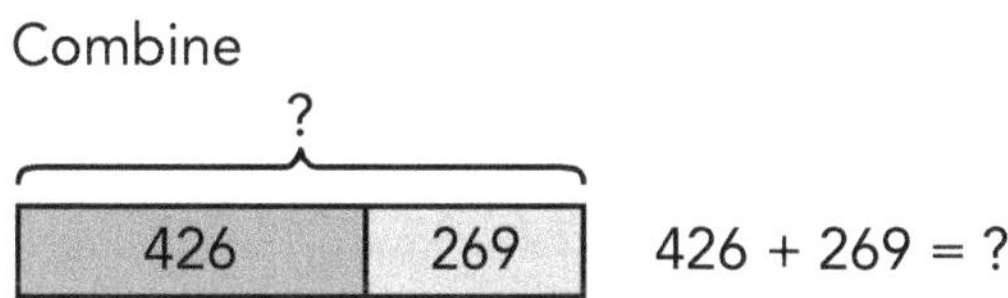


- Tell pupils that word problems often do not contain words like 'add' or 'plus' – and sometimes we might see words that we think are helpful but are actually misleading – so it is really important to understand what is happening in the problem situation to work out what calculation is needed to find the answer. In Chapter 2 pupils identified 'linked facts' to help them focus and orientate themselves around relevant information and ignore distracting information in word problems. This will be a helpful strategy now.

- Remind pupils that they know how to identify 'linked facts' when they look at information in word problems. Tell them you are going to look at some problems together and decide **how** to solve the problem, without actually working out the answer. For example:
  - A helicopter flies 389 km before stopping. It then flies another 145 km. How far does it travel in total?
  - A market stall sells £469 worth of second-hand computer games over the weekend. This is £173 less than it sold last weekend. How much did it sell last weekend?
  - Tickets are being sold for a pop concert. 752 tickets have been sold online and there have been 388 people who have bought tickets by queuing at a ticket office. How many tickets have been sold altogether?
- Display the following problem: Jermain takes £136 out of his bank account. The next day, he takes £245 out. How much money has he taken out of his account altogether?
- Choose pupils to act out the scenario and ask them whether they would use addition or subtraction to solve the problem. Why? Note that, although the question seems to be about taking money away, it is an addition calculation as the total that has been taken out is being asked for. Ask: *How can you write the problem as a number sentence?*
- Split pupils into pairs to calculate the answer. Ask: *What efficient written method could you use to add the two numbers together?* Give them time to find the answer using the vertical written method.
- Pupils should complete Question 5 in the Practice Book.

## Same-day intervention

- Pupils should be enabled to visualise what each question is asking, making connections between the scenario and the operation (in this case addition) needed to solve it. Once pupils are able to identify the operation comfortably, move on to writing it as a number sentence and then solving the calculation. Provide base 10 blocks for pupils to use as a concrete way to model the addition and encourage them to simultaneously record their addition using the vertical written method.

## Same-day enrichment

- Challenge pupils to create their own three-digit word problems. Write the following themes on the board:
  - SHOPPING
  - AT THE THEME PARK
  - LIBRARY TIME
  - ON A JOURNEY
- In pairs, pupils should write their own word problems (one for each theme): three addition questions and one subtraction. They should pass their problems to their partner to only solve the three addition problems. Firstly, they should work out which of the problems involve addition and then use the vertical written method to solve all three. Pupils should pass their working back to their partner to check.

## Challenge and extension question

# Question 6

**6** When Alisa was doing an addition sentence, by mistake she thought the digit 3 in the hundreds place was 2 and the digit 7 in the ones place was 1. The sum she got was 675. What is the correct sum?

The correct sum is: ____________.

Pupils are given a scenario where an error is described using words. Pupils are required to use the clues about the mistakes in order to work out what the wrong calculation is and, from this, work out what the correct sum should be. Using the clues they are given, they should be able to start by deducing the following:

| What Alisa thinks: | What Alisa should have written: |
|---|---|
| 2 ? 1<br>+ ? ? ?<br>6 7 5 | 3 ? 7<br>+ ? ? ?<br>7 8 1<br>(carried 1) |

Discuss the fact that in the tens column there are two mystery digits and so there are several possibilities.

# Unit 7.7 Subtraction with 3-digit numbers (1)

## Conceptual context

At this point in the development of their understanding, pupils' knowledge of place value for three-digit numbers includes both a recognition of place value (column value) and also the magnitude of the values represented by the numbers (quantity value).

In this unit, pupils will continue to extend their knowledge of calculation methods to now subtract using three-digit numbers. Written strategies will include partitioning both numbers (subtracting the hundreds, tens and ones separately) and partitioning only the subtrahend (subtracting its hundreds, tens and ones from the minuend). These expanded written methods encourage pupils to think in the ways they will need to do when using the column method in the next unit.

## Learning pupils will have achieved at the end of the unit

- Understanding of place value and partitioning will have been applied to a range of subtraction calculations (Q1, Q2, Q3, Q4)
- Written methods will have been extended to introduce the subtraction of three-digit numbers (Q1)
- Fluency in written calculation strategies will have developed as pupils make decisions to select their preferred strategy for a calculation (Q2, Q3, Q4)

### Resources

mini whiteboards; digit cards; base 10 blocks; place value grids and counters; place value arrow cards; **Resource 3.7.5** Decision table

### Vocabulary

hundreds, tens, ones, subtract, take away, minuend, subtrahend, less than, partition

# Question 1

**1** Calculate with reasoning.

(a) Theo's method.

467 – 253 = ☐

Hundreds – Hundreds: 400 – 200 = ☐
Tens – Tens: 60 – 50 = ☐
Ones – Ones: 7 – 3 = ☐
☐ – ☐ – ☐ = ☐

(b) Maya's method.

856 – 543 = ☐

Subtract hundreds first: 856 – 500 = ☐
Then subtract tens: ☐ – ☐ = ☐
Finally subtract ones: ☐ – ☐ = ☐
☐ + ☐ + ☐ = ☐

(c) Suraj's method.

356 – 185
= 356 – 100 – 80 – 5
= ☐ – ☐ – ☐
= ☐ – ☐
= ☐

637 – 249
= 637 – ☐ – ☐ – ☐
= ☐ – ☐ – ☐
= ☐ – ☐
= ☐

(d) Minna's method.

606 – 347
= 606 – 7 – 40 – 300
= ☐ – ☐ – ☐
= ☐ – ☐
= ☐

534 – 397
= 534 – ☐ – ☐ – ☐
= ☐ – ☐ – ☐
= ☐ – ☐
= ☐

## What learning will pupils have achieved at the conclusion of Question 1?

- Understanding of place value and partitioning will have been applied to a range of subtraction calculations.
- Written methods will have been extended to introduce the subtraction of three-digit numbers.

## Activities for whole-class instruction

- Write 67 – 25. Ask pupils for strategies to find the difference. Highlight any suggestions of partitioning one or both numbers and explain that they will be exploring similar strategies when subtracting three-digit numbers. Write a hundreds digit for both numbers so pupils recognise that the problem is very similar (for example 867 – 525). Ask: *How could you partition these numbers to help subtract them?*
- Remind pupils of the written methods of addition they used in Unit 7.5 by displaying **Resource 3.7.5** Decision table and discussing the two decisions they needed to make (how to partition the numbers and the order in which to add them).

**Resource 3.7.5**

Decision table

| | Partition everything? | Partition just the second addend? |
|---|---|---|
| Start by adding the hundreds? | A | C |
| Start by adding the ones? | B | D |

© HarperCollinsPublishers 2017 285

- Explain to pupils that they can use similar methods to practise subtracting numbers too. Method B will be slightly different for subtraction and so a similar grid for subtraction will not be useful in labelling each strategy. Instead, model four ways of working out the answer to 973 – 231. These should be:
  - Method A: Partition both numbers and treat the hundreds, tens and ones separately. Subtract each and then add the differences.
  - Method B: Partition the subtrahend only and describe each step in words as the hundreds, then the tens and ones are subtracted.
  - Method C: Partition the subtrahend only and write it as one number sentence starting by subtracting the hundreds, then the tens, then the ones.
  - Method D: Partition the subtrahend only and write it as one number sentence starting by subtracting the ones, then the tens, then the hundreds.
- These should look as follows:

**Method A:**

973 – 231

| | |
|---|---|
| hundreds – hundreds: | 900 – 200 = 700 |
| tens – tens: | 70 – 30 = 40 |
| ones – ones: | 3 – 1 = 2 |
| | 700 + 40 + 2 = 742 |

**Method B:**

973 – 231

Subtract hundreds first: 973 – 200 = 773

Then subtract tens: 773 – 30 = 743

Finally, subtract ones: 743 – 1 = 742

**Method C:**

973 – 231

= 973 – 200 – 30 – 1

= 773 – 30 – 1

= 743 – 1

= 742

**Method D:**

973 – 231

= 973 – 1 – 30 – 200

= 972 – 30 – 200

= 942 – 200

= 742

- Encourage pupils to examine each method through questioning. For example, ask: *Which method(s) partition both numbers? Which partition only one of the numbers? Which method(s) include a lot of writing? How many steps are involved?*
- Write the calculation 532 – 281 on the board and ask pupils why Method A would not be helpful to use in this example (the tens in the first number are less than those in the second and 30 – 80 goes below zero). Emphasise that it is useful to have a range of strategies so pupils can choose the best one to use.
- Repeat for further modelled examples and encourage pupils to take a lead in explaining how to use each method.
- Pupils should complete Question 1 in the Practice Book.

## Same-day intervention

- Provide pupils with their own set of place value arrow cards. Display the calculation 468 – 215. Pupils should make each number using their cards. Encourage them to talk about the different parts of each number as they combine the cards to form it. Without separating their cards, ask pupils how each number could be partitioned. Pupils should separate out their cards to show this and then group the hundreds together, the tens together and the ones together.

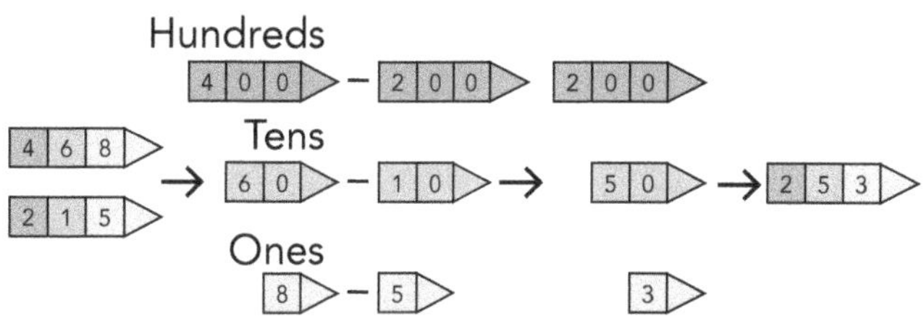


- Go through each grouping, finding the differences, and then encourage pupils to recombine them to find the overall answer. For each step, write the corresponding subtraction and the final addition on the board:

  400 – 200 = 200

  60 – 10 = 50

  8 – 5 = 3

  200 + 50 + 3 = 253
- Use arrow cards to help scaffold the three remaining methods. Use a 'What if ...?' structure to encourage pupils to explore each new strategy: What if the tens in the minuend are smaller than the tens in the subtrahend?
- Encourage pupils to consider how they will need to regroup the minuend so that there are more tens – by transferring 1 hundred (10 tens) into the tens column. Ask: *What if we only partition one of the numbers?* Encourage pupils to consider whether this makes things more efficient as they have a 'running total', rather than having to recombine their cards at the end.
- Pupils should record their workings using written subtractions to reflect the manipulations of the arrow cards.

## Same-day enrichment

- Provide pairs of pupils with a set of digit cards. They should deal out six digit cards and use them to make a three-digit subtraction. Each pupil should then choose the strategy that they would like their partner to use (based on the four strategies they have practised already). Both pupils should use their allocated method and then compare answers to check that they have found the difference correctly. They should repeat for different sets of digit cards, practising the different strategies.

# Question 2

> **2** Use your preferred method to calculate. Show your working.
> (a) 788 − 323 (b) 900 − 167
> (c) 459 − 366 (d) 558 − 263

## What learning will pupils have achieved at the conclusion of Question 2?

- Understanding of place value and partitioning will have been applied to a range of subtraction calculations.
- Fluency in written calculation strategies will have developed as pupils make decisions to select their preferred strategy for a calculation.

## Activities for whole-class instruction

- The aim of the unit is to develop efficient written calculation strategies. As such, although manipulatives will be useful when used alongside pictorial and abstract representations to support understanding, most pupils will require little, if any, work with manipulatives. If needed to develop and consolidate understanding, continue to use them, but aim to guide pupils towards an efficient written strategy.
- Split pupils into four groups – A, B, C and D. Remind pupils of the four strategies they considered when working with Question 1 and explain that each group should use the strategy denoted by the letter used for each part of the question.
- Display the calculation 657 – 316. Ensure each group knows how to use its particular strategy to find the difference. For example, pupils in Group A should partition both the minuend and the subtrahend and subtract the hundreds, then the tens, then the ones, before adding all three differences:

  hundreds – hundreds = 600 – 300 = 300
  tens – tens = 50 – 10 = 40
  ones – ones = 7 – 6 = 1
  300 + 40 + 1 = 341

- Choose one pupil from each group to share their strategy. Swap the group letters around so that pupils have the opportunity to practise each of the different strategies. Include examples where the ones and/or tens in the subtrahend are larger than those in the minuend (for example: 427 – 381). In these examples, Method A will not be possible because one of the individual subtractions will have a minuend smaller than the subtrahend. Discuss this with pupils as a limitation with Method A and encourage the group assigned to Method A to choose one of the other methods to use for those questions.
- Finally, ask pupils to choose their preferred method. Encourage pupils to explain why they have chosen that particular method. Highlight any examples of reasoning where pupils mention the fact their chosen method is quicker (and therefore more efficient).
- Pupils should complete Question 2 in the Practice Book.

## Same-day intervention

- Begin with the calculation 648 – 131. Provide pupils with place value arrow cards and discuss the make-up of each number as they model the minuend and the subtrahend using the cards. Encourage pupils to describe each number as they make it: '6 hundreds and 4 tens and 8 makes 648. 1 hundred and 3 tens and 1 makes 131.'
- Ask: *How can we partition both numbers to be able to subtract them?* Encourage pupils to partition both numbers, placing the hundreds, tens and ones arrow cards from both numbers next to each other.
- Pupils should then go through each subtraction (600 – 100, 40 – 30 and 8 – 1), modelling the answers using arrow cards and then discussing how to combine the differences to show the final answer.
- Repeat the activity with the subtraction 579 – 281. Ask: *Why can't we work out the answer by partitioning both numbers? Is there another way to find the answer?* Remind pupils that they can just partition the subtrahend if they prefer.
- Provide pupils with further subtractions to model using the arrow cards. Encourage them to use the strategy of their choice.

## Same-day enrichment

- Write the number 804 on the board. Explain that this will be the minuend in a three-digit subtraction. Ask pupils to suggest a three-digit subtrahend to give a difference that:
  - is between 300 and 400
  - is more than 700
  - equals 824
  - ends in a 7
  - is a multiple of 5.
- After finding one solution for each statement, pupils should work in pairs, writing their own starting number and set of five statements for their partner to solve. Pupils should explain to each other the strategies they used to work out the answers.

# Question 3

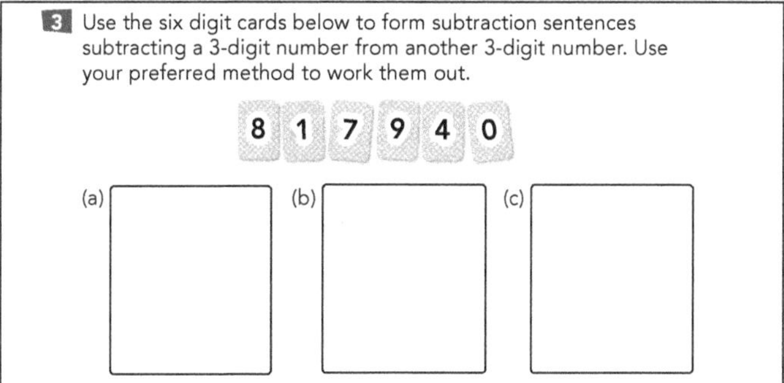
3 Use the six digit cards below to form subtraction sentences subtracting a 3-digit number from another 3-digit number. Use your preferred method to work them out.

8 1 7 9 4 0

(a) (b) (c)

## What learning will pupils have achieved at the conclusion of Question 3?

- Understanding of place value and partitioning will have been applied to a range of subtraction calculations.
- Fluency in written calculation strategies will have developed as pupils make decisions to select their preferred strategy for a calculation.

## Activities for whole-class instruction

- Place the following large digit cards at the front of the class: 3, 9, 7, 6, 8, 2. Choose different pupils to rearrange the digits to make different three-digit subtractions (for example 976 – 328, 862 – 379 and so on). Write each suggestion on the board.
- Choose one of the subtractions and give pupils the answer. Ask: *How can you get from the question to the answer?* Discuss different methods and model them.
- Choose a second subtraction from the set generated and give pupils time to work in pairs, choosing the strategy they prefer to find the difference. Discuss why pupils have opted for that particular strategy. If pupils choose to partition both numbers, encourage them to consider why this might not be the most efficient strategy of the four (and why it does not work for every subtraction). Ask: *Is this a method you would use every time, or did you choose it because of the numbers in the calculation?* Repeat for further subtractions generated from the digit cards.
- Pupils should complete Question 3 in the Practice Book.

## Same-day intervention

- Split pupils into three groups. The first group should have base 10 blocks; the second group should have place value grids and counters; the third group should have place value arrow cards. Each pupil should record their working in written form as well as using the equipment they have been given. Show pupils the following digit cards: 5, 9, 1, 4, 7, 3. Ask pupils to suggest ways of arranging them to create a three-digit subtraction.
- Decide on a strategy to use (for example, partition the subtrahend and take away the hundreds first), then encourage pupils to show how their equipment can be used to model the calculation. For example, if the subtraction is 974 – 531, they might model this strategy as follows:

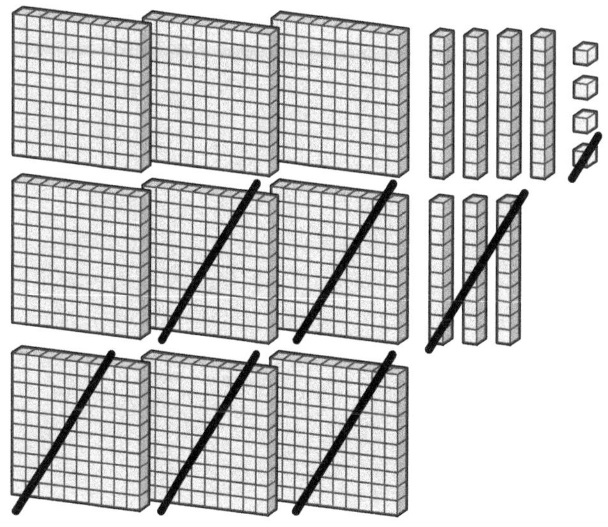

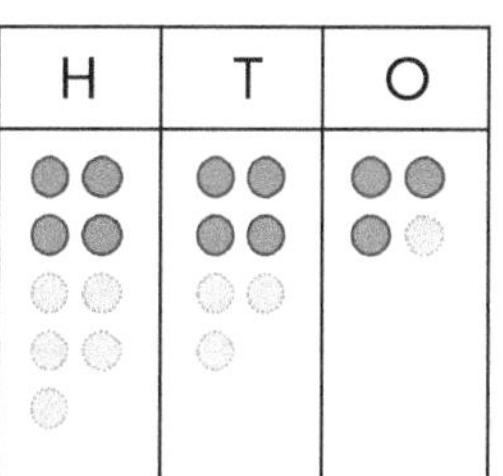

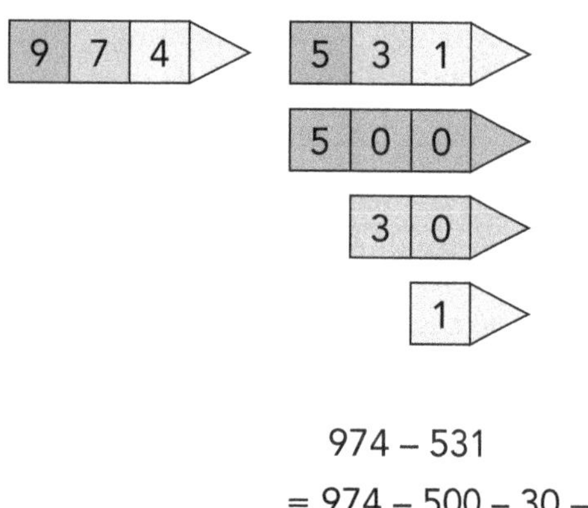


$$974 - 531$$
$$= 974 - 500 - 30 - 1$$
$$= 474 - 30 - 1$$
$$= 444 - 1$$
$$= 443$$

- Groups should compare the representations they have constructed.
- Repeat for different sets of digits and strategies.

## Same-day enrichment

- Ask pairs of pupils to shuffle two sets of digit cards and deal face down on the table-top. Each pupil takes six cards, turns them over and use their six digits to create two subtractions. The first subtraction should be designed to leave the smallest difference (i.e. two numbers that are as close together as possible). For example, if Pupil A picks the cards 7, 4, 5, 1, 8 and 9, they might choose to make the subtraction 517 – 498 (which gives a difference of 19).
- Pupils should use the strategy of their choice to subtract their numbers and then compare their differences to see which is smallest. The pupil with the smaller answer gets a point. They should then rearrange their digits to make a subtraction with the largest possible difference (i.e. one larger number and one smaller number). This time the pupil with the larger answer gets a point. Pupils should repeat the game, choosing different digits each time.

# Question 4

**4** Write a number sentence for each question.

(a) The minuend is 429 and the subtrahend is 290. What is the difference?

Answer: ______

(b) What number is 348 less than 695?

Answer: ______

## What learning will pupils have achieved at the conclusion of Question 4?

- Understanding of place value and partitioning will have been applied to a range of subtraction calculations.
- Fluency in written calculation strategies will have developed as pupils make decisions to select their preferred strategy for a calculation.

## Activities for whole-class instruction

- Discuss with pupils the vocabulary that is used to describe subtractions. Call out different calculations described in words, ensuring that pupils are provided with a variety of different question types, not just subtraction. The aim of this is to help pupils focus on the language used in subtraction questions. Ask pupils to call out 'STOP!' when they hear a subtraction question. Examples of possible calculations include:
  - What is the difference between 704 and 682?
  - What is the product of 374 and 139?
  - What is the sum of 895 and 455?
  - What is 151 less than 384?
  - One addend is 562. The other is 420. What is the sum?
  - The minuend is 680. The subtrahend is 278. What is the difference?
- For each subtraction, discuss how pupils know that they need to take the numbers away. Give sufficient time for them to then use the written strategy of their choice to find the answer. Discuss their preferred strategies and why they prefer them. Encourage pupils to sketch bar models to represent the subtraction calculations that are called out. Point out the different ways that subtraction can be modelled. For example:

| 692 | |
|---|---|
| | 274 |

$692 - 274 = ?$

- The minuend is 849. The subtrahend is 572. What is the difference?

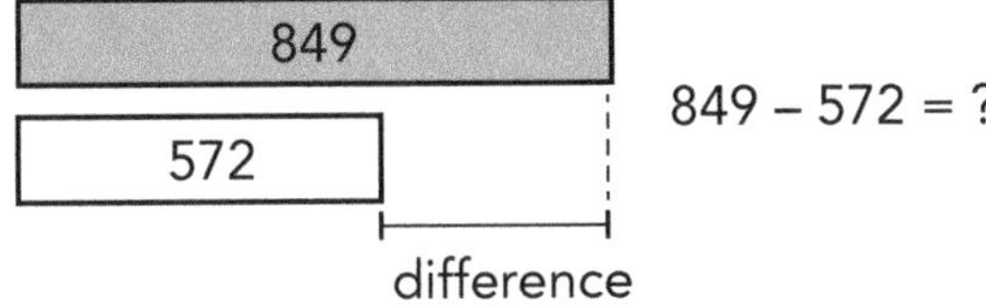


- Pupils should complete Question 4 in the Practice Book.

## Same-day intervention

- Display the following word calculation: The minuend is 533. The subtrahend is 341. What is the difference?
- Ask: *How do you know what sort of calculation this is? What do you think you need to do to find the answer?* Remind pupils of the meanings of the words 'minuend', 'subtrahend' and 'difference' and link them to subtraction. Encourage pupils to write the calculation as a number sentence. Ask: *How might you work out the answer?* Prior to using written strategies, ensure that pupils attempt to clearly describe the method they would use. Talking about what they plan to do will help to embed the strategy. Provide place value arrow cards for pupils to model the way they partition a number. Repeat for further word-based calculations involving terms like 'minuend, 'subtrahend', 'difference' and 'less than'.

## Same-day enrichment

- Provide pupils with simple word-based calculations involving unknowns. In pairs they should explain what they notice about the relationships between the numbers and use this knowledge to solve each problem.
  - If A is 832, and B is 227 less than A, what is B?
  - If A is 482 and B is 146, what is the difference between A and B?
  - What could A and B be if the difference between them is 543?
- For each problem, pupils should sketch the relevant bar model to show how the subtraction can be represented.
- Pupils should then devise their own similar problems for peers to answer. As well as providing the word-based calculation, they could give their partner a bar model labelled with the letters A and B to provide a visual clue to the relationship between A and B, as set out in their problem.

## Challenge and extension question

# Question 5

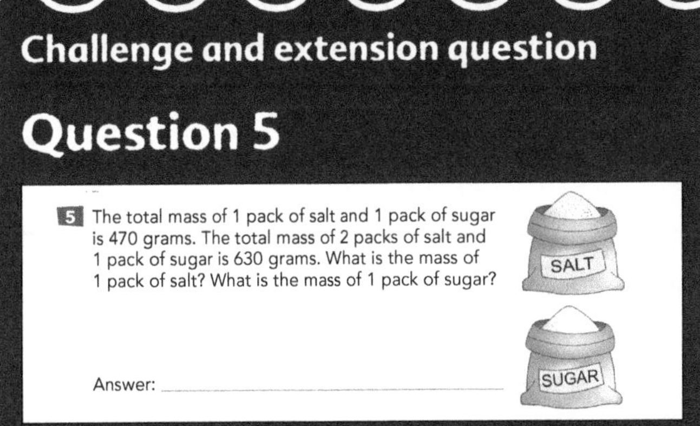
**5** The total mass of 1 pack of salt and 1 pack of sugar is 470 grams. The total mass of 2 packs of salt and 1 pack of sugar is 630 grams. What is the mass of 1 pack of salt? What is the mass of 1 pack of sugar?

Answer: ____________



Pupils are given information about the total mass of one pack of salt and one pack of sugar (470 g). They are then given information about the total mass of two packs of salt and one pack of sugar (630 g). Pupils should recognise that they can find the mass of a pack of salt by subtracting the first mass from the second. Once they have worked out the mass of a pack of salt, they can use this information (again in a subtraction) to find the mass of a pack of sugar. Pupils should be encouraged to use their preferred written strategy to solve each subtraction.

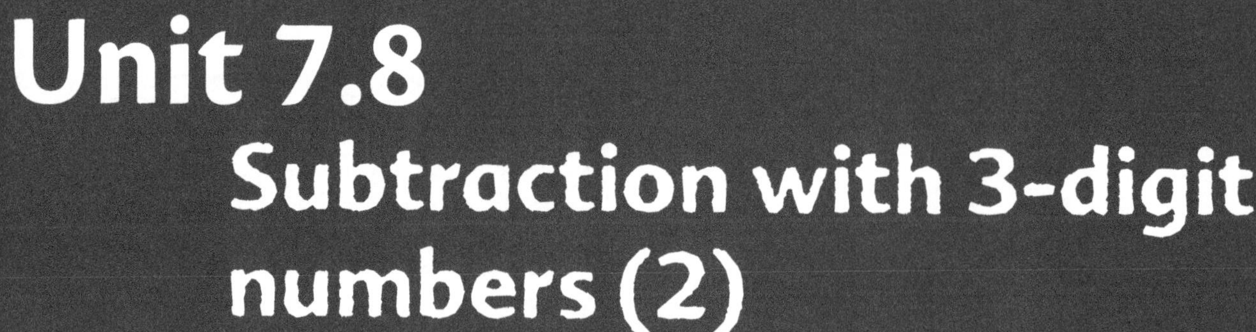

# Unit 7.8 Subtraction with 3-digit numbers (2)

## Conceptual context

Pupils have developed a range of mental and extended written methods of three-digit subtraction, and will now learn how to use the column method with three-digit numbers, having previously learned how to use it with two-digit numbers. The expanded written methods used in the previous unit are intrinsically linked to the column method and it is important that pupils are able to see the links between the procedures. Pupils will be encouraged to explain each step and justify their answers; retaining their focus on the mathematical processes as well as the written procedures so that their conceptual understanding about subtraction continues to be richly connected.

## Learning pupils will have achieved at the end of the unit

- The formal written method for subtraction will have been extended to include three-digit numbers (Q1)
- Understanding of place value and regrouping numbers will have been applied to a range of three-digit subtractions (Q1, Q2, Q3, Q4, Q5)
- Pupils will have further developed problem-solving skills (Q2, Q4, Q5)
- Reasoning will have been used to deduce the missing digits in column subtraction and to identify errors (Q2, Q4)
- Pupils' understanding and application of column subtraction will have been applied to solve word problems (Q5)

### Resources

digit cards; base 10 blocks; mini whiteboards

### Vocabulary

subtraction, take away, difference, column method, vertical, hundreds column, tens column, ones column, hundreds, tens, ones, minuend, subtrahend

# Question 1

**1** Use the column method to calculate.

(a) 187 − 31 =

```
  1 8 7
-   3 1
-------
```

(b) 129 − 88 =

```
  1 2 9
-   8 8
-------
```

(c) 151 − 75 =

```
  1 5 1
-   7 5
-------
```

(d) 433 − 265 =

```
  4 3 3
- 2 6 5
-------
```

(e) 800 − 468 =

```
  8 0 0
- 4 6 8
-------
```

(f) 105 − 76 =

```
  1 0 5
-   7 6
-------
```

## What learning will pupils have achieved at the conclusion of Question 1?

- The formal written method for subtraction will have been extended to include three-digit numbers.
- Understanding of place value and regrouping numbers will have been applied to a range of three-digit subtractions.

## Activities for whole-class instruction

- Write 549 − 381. Ask pupils to describe the four written methods they used in the previous unit. Check that they are able to recall how to partition either the minuend and subtrahend or just the subtrahend and then subtract the hundreds, tens and ones separately.
- Remind pupils of their previous work using column addition and ask them how they could write this subtraction using a similar method. Ask: *How will the layout of the subtraction change? What do you need to remember?* Use digit cards to model the layout of the vertical subtraction. Revise each digit's place value by asking questions based on its position in the number.
- Discuss the meaning of the word 'efficient' in relation to strategies used in maths. Ask: *Why do you think that column subtraction is a more efficient method than any of the written methods you used in the last unit?*
- Use base 10 blocks to model the minuend. Begin by asking: *Should I start on the left with the hundreds or on the right with the ones? Why?* Can pupils explain that it is more efficient to start on the right because when starting on the left it is often necessary to retrace steps when regrouping becomes necessary?
- Ask: *What do we need to do if the lower digit is larger than the upper digit in a column?* Remind pupils that although this does happen when we look at individual columns, the subtraction can still be worked out as the minuend as a whole is larger than the subtrahend as a whole.
- Go through the subtraction, column by column, modelling each action using the blocks as below:

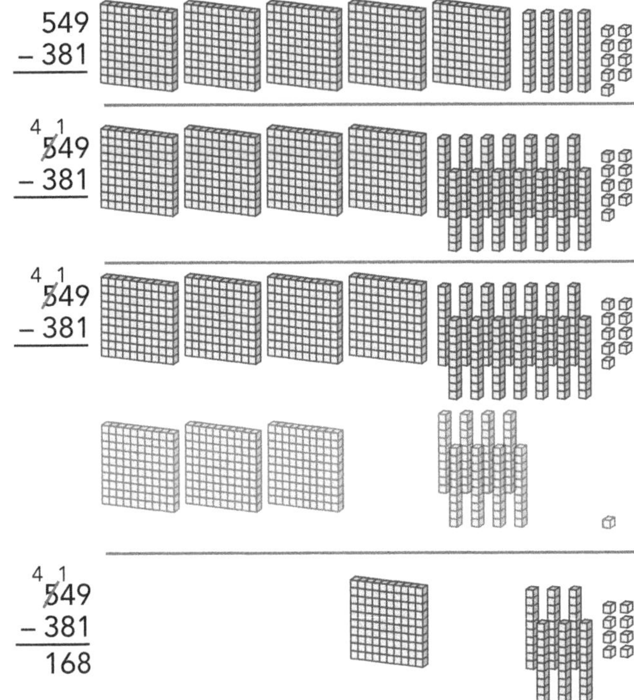


- Ask: *Which part of column subtraction do you think is the most important to remember? Why?* Use this question as an opportunity for extended discussion.
- Repeat for further subtractions.
- Pupils should complete Question 1 in the Practice Book.

## Same-day intervention

- Write 459 − 145 as a vertical calculation. Provide pupils with place value grids and ask them to model the minuend using base 10 blocks. Ask: *How can 145 be partitioned to help us take it away? Which part of the number should we subtract first in a column subtraction? Are you happy that you will be able to subtract each column without re-grouping the minuend?*
- Refer to the column subtraction and, for each column (starting with the ones), ask pupils to subtract the relevant number represented by base 10 blocks (5, then 40, then 100).
- Repeat for different subtractions and begin to include those where pupils will need to regroup the minuend (for example 532 − 319). Encourage pupils to identify the need to regroup prior to starting the subtraction. After regrouping, discuss how the regrouped number (in this case 'five hundred and twenty-twelve') has the same value as the initial minuend. (Using base 10 blocks means that the total number of blocks is visible.)

## Same-day enrichment

- Ask pupils to work in pairs. Each should devise five subtractions that do not need regrouping to solve and five that do. These should be jumbled up. Pupils share their ten calculations with their partner who should be encouraged to consider how to work out whether a calculation needs regrouping. Each pupil should then solve their partner's calculations, before returning them so that the writer can check that they have been solved correctly.

# Question 2

**2** Are these calculations correct? Put a ✓ for yes or a ✗ for no in the box and then make corrections.

(a)
```
  6 4 3
- 3 0 7
  3 6 4
```
(b)
```
  4 1 3
- 3 3 1
  1 4 2
```
(c)
```
  1 0 5
-   3 9
    7 6
```

Corrections:

## What learning will pupils have achieved at the conclusion of Question 2?

- Understanding of place value and regrouping numbers will have been applied to a range of three-digit subtractions.
- Pupils will have developed problem-solving skills.
- Reasoning will have been used to deduce the missing digits in column subtraction and to identify errors.

## Activities for whole-class instruction

- Write: 706 – 482. Give pupils time to consider the calculation. Model the calculation vertically as follows (making deliberate mistakes). First, subtract from left to right (beginning with the hundreds). Then, when you reach the tens column, 'subtract upwards' from bottom to top (8 – 0 = 8).

```
  7 0 6        7 0 6
– 4 8 2      – 4 8 2
               3 8 8
```

- Notice the pupils who correctly spot that the question has been answered incorrectly, then ask them to explain to the class and to demonstrate how to work out each step of the calculation correctly. Tell pupils that the mistake of 'subtracting upwards' is a common error.

Remind them that they are subtracting 'four hundred and eighty two' from 'seven hundred and six'.

(i) It is good practice to refer to three-digit numbers by their 'word names' and not as a series of digits – that is 'four hundred and eighty two' and not 'four, eight, two' – at all times when talking about numbers. The latter encourages a focus on each digit, rather than on the whole number, and it is this narrow focus on digits that leads pupils to 'subtract upwards', looking only for a small number to subtract from a larger one.

- Repeat for further calculations. As well as 'subtracting up', also make the mistake of:
  - confusing the operation for addition
  - aligning the digits wrongly
  - regrouping incorrectly in different ways.
- For each example, ask pupils to identify and correct the mistakes.
- Write: 723 – 482. Ask pupils to close their eyes. Walk around the class and tap one pupil on their shoulder. Explain that everyone in the class should work out the subtraction making a deliberate mistake unless they have felt a tap on their shoulder, in which case they should work out the answer correctly (this will just be one pupil). No one should show their answers to anyone else.
- Choose three pupils to come to the front – the pupil who was tapped and two others (whose answers contain deliberate mistakes). Ask the rest of the class to identify the correct calculation and the mistakes that the other two pupils have made. Repeat the activity for different subtractions.
- Pupils should complete Question 2 in the Practice Book.

## Same-day intervention

- Display the following numbers: 248, 538, 942, 103, 449 and 757. Choose any two numbers from the set and use them to form a column subtraction. Complete the subtraction twice, ensuring that one calculation is correct and the other contains a deliberate error. Include common errors such as:
  - reading the operation symbol incorrectly (adding instead of subtracting)
  - neglecting to regroup the minuend or doing so incorrectly
  - subtracting upwards to avoid having to use regrouping
  - aligning the digits incorrectly in either the question or the answer.

- Ask pupils to close their eyes (to encourage individual decision-making) and ask them to raise either their right or left hand depending on which calculation they think is correct. Note pupils who may need additional support.
- Ask: *What do you think the mistake is? How can we avoid making mistakes like this?* Encourage pupils to create their own pairs of subtractions, sharing them with the rest of the group to spot which is correct and what the error is.

## Same-day enrichment

- Explain to pupils that they will not only be identifying errors, but also providing advice to those who find vertical subtraction tricky. Write a variety of three-digit subtractions on the board, including those that do and do not need regrouping to answer. Give each pupil a strip of cardboard divided into three equal sections.
- In the first of the three sections, pupils should choose any one of the calculations and answer it using vertical subtraction, but making a deliberate mistake. They then should swap their pieces of card so that each pupil has a different calculation in front of them. Pupils should then complete the second section of the piece of card by writing a description of the error that has been made.
- Finally, pupils should swap their pieces of card once more and in the third section they should model the correct way of answering the question on the card, writing a sentence of advice about how to avoid making the same mistake again. Pupils should return the strips to their original owner to check and see whether the error analysis and final calculation are correct.
- Use these as revision strips (showing an incorrect calculation, a description of the error and advice about how to avoid making the same mistake) to support any pupils who are finding vertical subtraction more difficult to master.

# Question 3

**3** Complete the table.

| Minuend | 737 | 562 | 656 | 770 | 312 | 707 |
|---|---|---|---|---|---|---|
| Subtrahend | 133 | 266 | 475 | 634 | 134 | 668 |
| Difference | | | | | | |

## What learning will pupils have achieved at the conclusion of Question 3?

- Understanding of place value and re-grouping numbers will have been applied to a range of three-digit subtractions.

## Activities for whole-class instruction

- Write the words 'quotient', 'factor', 'minuend', 'divisor', 'difference', 'addend', 'product' and 'subtrahend' on the board. Remind pupils that these are all ways of describing the different numbers that appear in number sentences. Ask: *Which words are used to describe parts of subtractions? What do the three words refer to?*
- Draw a table similar to the one shown in Question 3, completing each column with both a minuend and a subtrahend, leaving the difference empty. Ask: *How has the table been drawn to help you with vertical subtraction? How would you sketch this subtraction using a bar model?* Encourage pupils to describe their sketches in terms of a difference between two bars. For example:

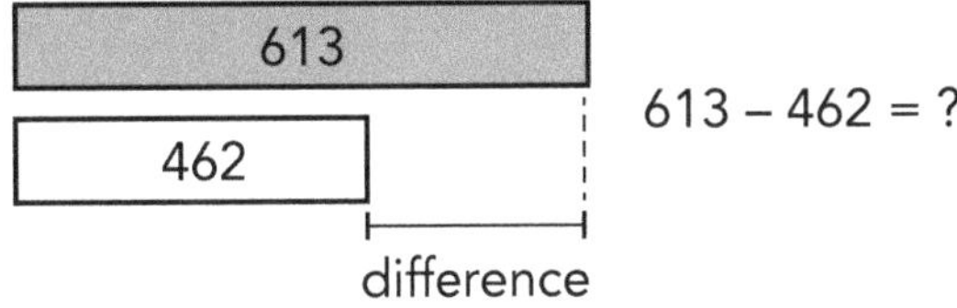


- Ask them to point out the subtrahend and the minuend on their bar model. Emphasise that the difference between them is known as just that – the 'difference'. Go through some examples of vertical subtractions taken from the table and then encourage pupils to find each difference by completing similar subtractions on their mini whiteboards.
- Provoke further thought by giving pupils clues about some of the answers. For example:
  - Two of the numbers have a difference of less than 100. Which are they?
  - Which calculation has an answer that has 8 ones?

  Encourage pupils to use reasoning to explain how they know that their chosen calculation is correct, particularly if they can do so before actually working out the answer.
- Pupils should complete Question 3 in the Practice Book.

## Same-day intervention

- Make connections between the vertical subtraction of three-digit numbers using written methods and more concrete ways to represent the same calculations. For example, show pupils the following information:

  MINUEND: 864

  SUBTRAHEND: 351

  DIFFERENCE:
- Choose three pupils to model 864 using base 10 blocks. Ask: *How many ones/tens/hundreds do we need to subtract from those we already have?* Model the subtraction as each is taken away, leaving the answer. Show how each step can be written as a vertical subtraction.
- Repeat for different subtractions, including those where pupils will need to regroup the minuend in order to be able to subtract that particular column. Lead pupils towards being able to complete the calculation without modelling it.

## Same-day enrichment

- Split pupils into pairs. Ask pupils to write the words 'MINUEND', 'SUBTRAHEND' and 'DIFFERENCE' vertically on their mini whiteboards. Pupil A should take six cards from a set of digit cards and use these to make two three-digit numbers, placing each next to the word 'MINUEND' and 'SUBTRAHEND' to form the basis of a three-digit subtraction. Pupil A should work out the difference between their numbers and make a note of it. They should then pass their mini whiteboard to Pupil B to calculate the difference for themselves.
- Pupils should compare calculations to check; Pupil B gets a point if they match. They should repeat the activity for different calculations, swapping roles each time.
- To add an extra layer of challenge, pupils could provide their partner with a completed set of 'MINUEND', 'SUBTRAHEND' and 'DIFFERENCE', but with one digit card missing from each of the hundreds, tens and ones columns. Pupils should use their knowledge of vertical methods to identify the missing digits.

# Question 4

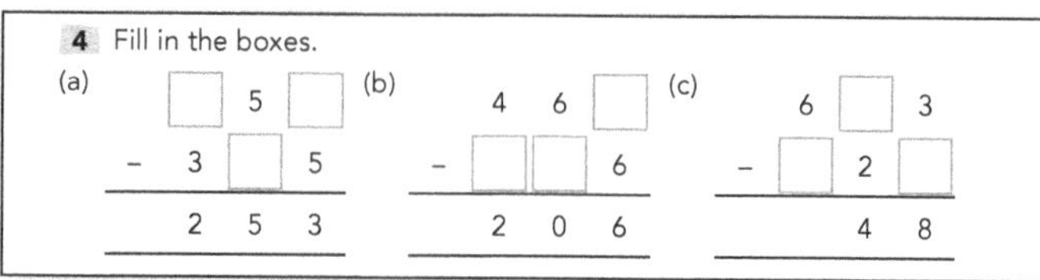


## What learning will pupils have achieved at the conclusion of Question 4?

- Understanding of place value and regrouping numbers will have been applied to a range of three-digit subtractions.
- Pupils will have developed problem-solving skills.
- Reasoning will have been used to deduce the missing digits in column subtraction and to identify errors.

## Activities for whole-class instruction

- Use large digit cards to show 841 – 257 = 584 on the board as a vertical subtraction. However, turn all nine cards so that their reverse is showing (hiding the digits). Explain that the cards represent a vertical subtraction and remind pupils of a similar 'mystery digit' activity they completed when working with vertical addition (see Unit 7.6). Ask: *How many digits do you think you need to know in each column in order to work out what the calculation is?* Ask pupils to choose which two digits to reveal in the ones column and then ask questions based on their choices. For example:

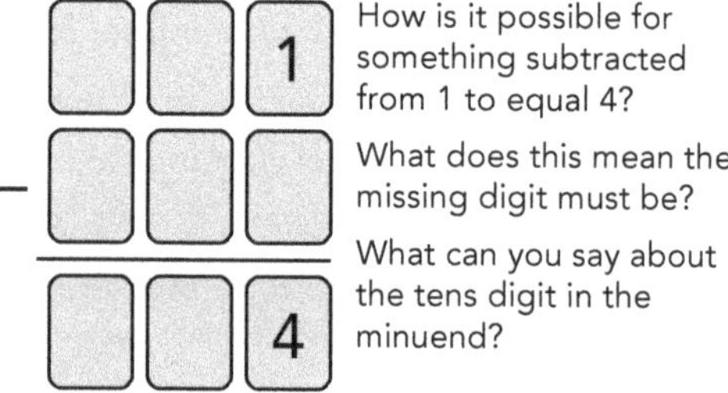

1
−
4
How is it possible for something subtracted from 1 to equal 4?
What does this mean the missing digit must be?
What can you say about the tens digit in the minuend?


- Repeat the same activity for any two digits in the tens column.

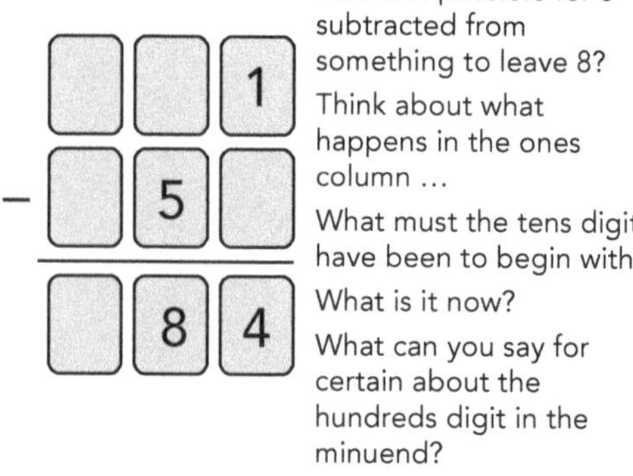

1
− 5
8 4
How is it possible for 5 subtracted from something to leave 8?
Think about what happens in the ones column …
What must the tens digit have been to begin with?
What is it now?
What can you say for certain about the hundreds digit in the minuend?

- Finally, repeat this for the hundreds digits, by which time pupils should be able to identify the entire subtraction.
- Give pupils further examples, varying the positions of the missing digits. Encourage them to use reasoning to explain what they think each missing digit is and why. Ask: *Which column should you work out first? Why?*
- Pupils should complete Question 4 in the Practice Book.

## Same-day intervention

- Use base 10 blocks to model similar problems to the ones in Question 4. For example, show pupils the following vertical subtraction with three missing digits:

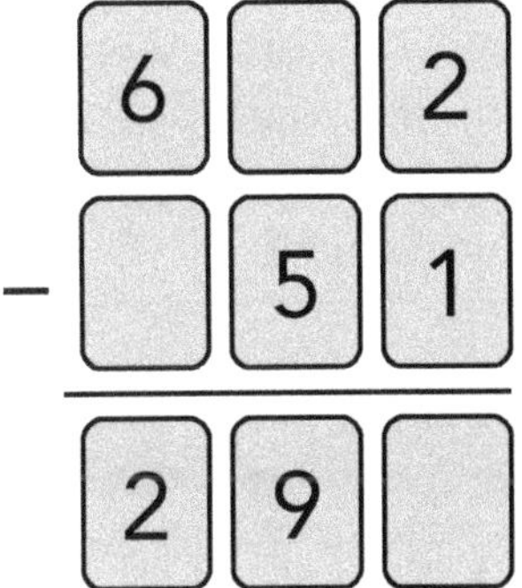


- Use base 10 blocks and targeted questioning to go through each column and help pupils to work out what the missing digits are. For example:
  - Make 2 ones out of base 10 blocks and ask: *How many ones will you have if you subtract 1 one?*
  - Take 5 tens from an imaginary pile of tens rods. Explain that there are 9 tens left and ask: *How many must there have been to begin with? How can there be a two-digit number in the tens place? What do we know must happen to the hundreds digit?*
  - Focus on the hundred blocks and ask: *There were 6 hundreds at the start but the minuend has been regrouped. How many hundreds blocks are there now? So how many hundreds must be in the subtrahend if the difference has 2 hundreds?*
- Repeat for further subtractions, using the base 10 blocks to help pupils reason about each missing digit.

## Same-day enrichment

- Ask pupils to work in pairs. One pupil should devise their own three-digit vertical subtraction and record it on a mini whiteboard without their partner seeing, and then use digit cards to model their calculation, turning each card upside-down so that the digit is face down on the table.
- Partners reveal one digit at a time until they have enough information to be able to deduce what the entire calculation is based on the information they have revealed. Encourage pupils to consider the following questions: How many cards did you need to see before you could work out what the subtraction was? Is there a rule about which cards to turn over?
- Repeat the activity, with pupils swapping roles each time. Encourage pupils to devise a rule about the cards that should be turned over (for example: two cards in every column need to be revealed, but these can be any two cards).

# Question 5

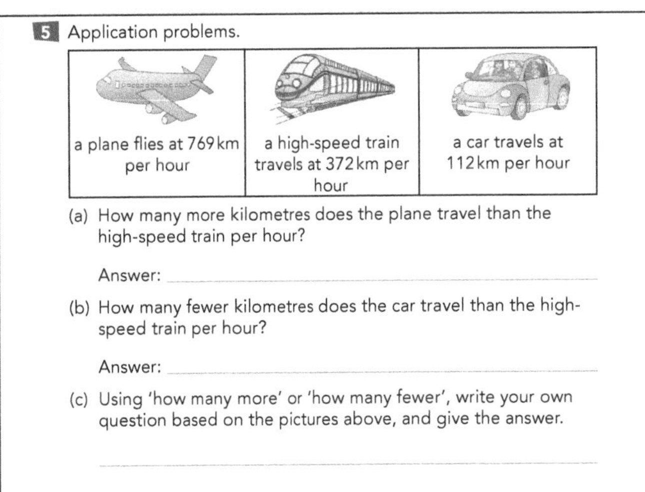

5 Application problems.
a plane flies at 769 km per hour
a high-speed train travels at 372 km per hour
a car travels at 112 km per hour
(a) How many more kilometres does the plane travel than the high-speed train per hour?
Answer:
(b) How many fewer kilometres does the car travel than the high-speed train per hour?
Answer:
(c) Using 'how many more' or 'how many fewer', write your own question based on the pictures above, and give the answer.


## What learning will pupils have achieved at the conclusion of Question 5?

- Understanding of place value and regrouping numbers will have been applied to a range of three-digit subtractions.
- Pupils will have developed problem-solving skills.
- Pupils' understanding and application of column subtraction will have been applied to solve word problems.

## Activities for whole-class instruction

- Recap the different bar models that pupils can use to show 'change' and 'compare' type word problems, both of which are solved by subtraction.

| 613 | |
|---|---|
| | 151 |

613 – 151 = ?

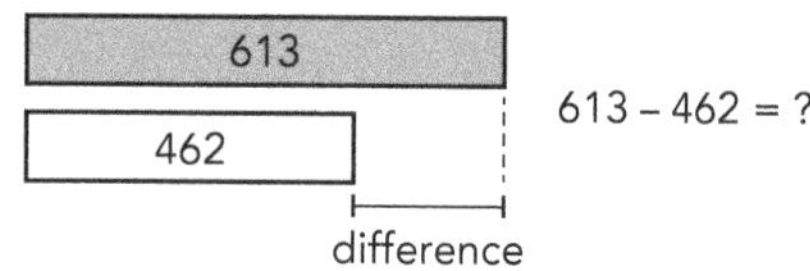


- Remind pupils that subtraction word problems often do not contain words like 'subtract', 'minus' or 'take away', so it is important that they understand the situation being described in order to work out that subtraction is needed. Remind them that they know how to identify 'linked facts' when they look at information in word problems.
- Read out a series of word problems, including both three-digit addition and three-digit subtraction. Encourage pupils to stand up if they think a scenario needs subtraction to solve it. Ask: *How do you know that you need to take the numbers away in order to solve the problem? What clues are in the question?* As with the similar addition activity (see Unit 7.6), remove the numbers from the problems so pupils can focus completely on the **how** of the question, rather than the **what**.
- Display the following problem: The High Street is 374 m long. Coppice Lane is 145 m long. How much longer in metres is the High Street than Coppice Lane?
- Ask pupils to model the scenario using whatever equipment or sketches they choose. Ask: *Would you use addition or subtraction to solve this problem? Why?* Point out that, although the problem uses the word 'longer' (which might seem to point to addition), it is a compare problem and the difference between the two measurements is found through subtraction. Ask: *How would you write the problem as a number sentence?*
- Encourage pupils to work in pairs. Ask them to name all the different methods they could use to solve the problem. Ask: *Which is the most efficient? Why?* Pupils should use the vertical method to find the answer.
- Work through the following word problems involving three-digit addition and subtraction together. Identify 'linked facts' and draw bar models to represent the situation each time, before using the column method to calculate the answer:
  - On Monday, 769 people visited the town library. On Tuesday, 903 people visited. How many more people visited the library on Tuesday than Monday?
  - Year 3 are reading a class book together. They have already read 175 pages and their teacher says, 'We've got another 298 pages to go.' How many pages are in the book?
  - Deepa has 353 megabytes of memory left on her laptop. She wants to download an eBook that is 148 megabytes. How much memory will she have left?
- Pupils should complete Question 5 in the Practice Book.

## Same-day intervention

- Pupils should be enabled to visualise what each question is asking, making connections between the scenario and the operation (in this case subtraction) needed to solve it. Encourage them to sketch or act out the scenario and then represent it using a bar model. Ask: *What operation do you need to do to find the answer? How do you know?* Once pupils are able to identify the operation comfortably, move onto writing it as a number sentence and then solving the calculation. Provide base 10 blocks for pupils to use as a concrete way to model the subtraction (by removing blocks from the minuend) and encourage them to simultaneously record their subtraction using the vertical written method.

## Same-day enrichment

- Challenge pupils to create their own three-digit word problems. Write the following themes on the board:
  - THE CINEMA
  - IN THE CHOCOLATE FACTORY
  - NEWS OF THE DAY
  - AT THE ZOO
- In pairs, pupils write their own subtraction word problems (one for each theme). They should pass their problems to their partner to solve. First, they should check that each of the problems requires subtraction and then use the column method of subtraction to solve them. Pupils then pass their working back to their partner to check.
- To extend pupils further, they could be challenged to consider how to use vertical addition to check that the answer is correct (i.e. by working backwards – adding the difference to the subtrahend and checking that it equals the minuend).

## Challenge and extension question

# Question 6

**6** Complete the sentences.

```
    5 ( ) 2
  - 4  3  9
  ---------

  ---------
```

(a) If the difference is a 3-digit number, the smallest possible number in the ◯ is ☐.

(b) If the difference is a 2-digit number, the greatest possible number in the ◯ is ☐.

Pupils are provided with a vertical subtraction question with one missing digit (and no answer). They should be able to reason (from their work in Question 4) that they have slightly less information than they need to be able to fill in the missing digits as there are two missing digits in the tens column. This means that there are several possible answers. The question asks pupils to find the smallest possible number where the difference is a three-digit answer and the greatest possible answer where the difference is a two-digit answer. Although both tasks can be solved through trial and error, pupils should be encouraged to try and use reasoning to suggest why a particular digit is/is not suitable.

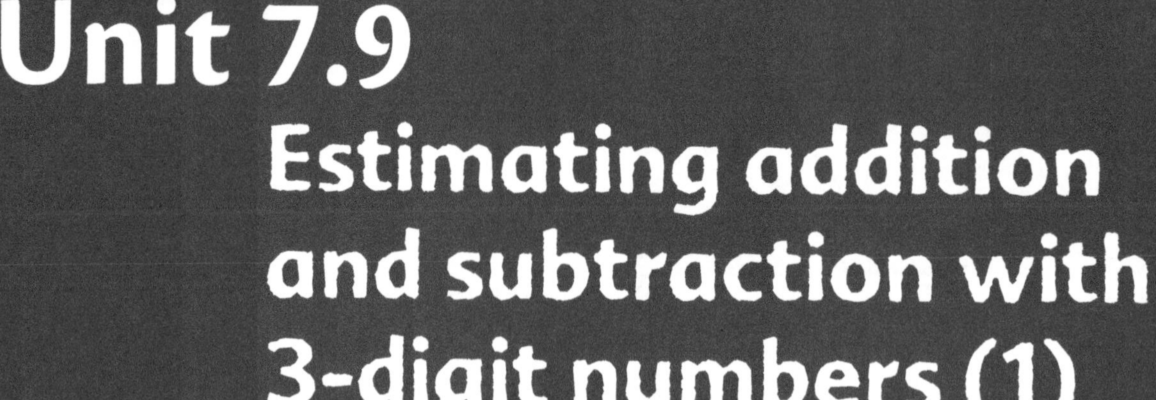

# Unit 7.9 Estimating addition and subtraction with 3-digit numbers (1)

## Conceptual context

Pupils have now extended their formal written addition and subtraction skills; they also need to be able to look at a three-digit calculation and have an idea of what a reasonable answer would be. The concept of estimation is not simply about the ability to suggest an answer more quickly than actually working it out (important though this is) – it is also about applying a sense of number. In this unit, pupils will be encouraged to develop number fluency so that they begin to regard estimation as a way of predicting an approximate answer. The skills of vertical addition and subtraction are used here as a method for checking, with the focus of the unit being on rounding to the nearest 10 or 100 in order to estimate.

## Learning pupils will have achieved at the end of the unit

- Pupils will have revised mental strategies to add and subtract three-digit multiples of 10 (Q1)
- Pupils will have learned how to round numbers to the nearest 10 and 100 (Q2)
- Estimation based on rounding numbers will have been introduced and practised (Q3, Q4)
- Pupils will have used vertical written methods to check the accuracy of estimates (Q3, Q4)
- Problem-solving skills will have been developed to include estimation (Q5)

### Resources

digit cards; base 10 blocks; mini whiteboards; number lines

### Vocabulary

multiple of 10, multiple of 100, tens number, hundreds number, estimate/estimation, approximate, round up, round down, calculate

# Question 1

**1** Calculate mentally.

(a) 320 + 80 = ☐ (b) 310 − 90 = ☐

(c) 580 + 100 = ☐ (d) 102 − 29 = ☐

(e) 720 − 60 = ☐ (f) 490 + 60 = ☐

(g) 670 − 600 = ☐ (h) 390 + 200 = ☐

## What learning will pupils have achieved at the conclusion of Question 1?

- Pupils will have revised mental strategies to add and subtract three-digit multiples of 10.

## Activities for whole-class instruction

- Explain to pupils the context of the unit – that they will be using tens numbers and hundreds numbers to help estimate answers. Ensure that they understand the meaning of the word 'estimate'.

  (i) A useful definition of estimation is the idea of a 'thoughtful guess'. This is the sort of estimation used when, for example, suggesting the number of people in a crowd. It is a guess, but there is some sort of reasoning behind it. In the following units, however, estimation is used in a more specific way than this. Three-digit numbers are rounded to the nearest 10 or 100 and then added or subtracted in order to approximate an answer. Therefore, estimation here involves the concept of a rough (rounded) calculation rather than an educated guess.

- Display: 439 + 157 and 380 + 260. Ask: *Which calculation would you find easier to answer? Why?* Choose pupils to describe how they would find both answers. Write the statement: Adding two three-digit multiples of 10 involves the same skills as adding two two-digit numbers. Ask: *Is this true? Why do you think this?* Recap the fact that multiples of 10 show a number of tens and so 380 + 260 can be answered by considering 38 tens plus 26 tens.
- Ask pupils to write a HTO + HTO or HTO − HTO calculation involving multiples of 10 on their mini whiteboards. One by one, pupils should reveal their calculation and the rest of the class should respond immediately with the two-digit calculation they would use to help. For example 570 + 160 and 57 + 16.
- One pupil should write a calculation involving multiples of 10 on the board and choose another pupil to come to the front and describe how they found the answer. Then they should write their own 'multiples of 10' calculation underneath and so on. Ensure there is a balance between addition and subtraction and that pupils consider each calculation as a number of tens. If pupils choose to use other methods (for example partitioning), praise them for doing so and discuss these methods as a class – it is important that pupils know they do not have to rely on one specific strategy.
- Pupils should complete Question 1 in the Practice Book.

## Same-day intervention

- Show pupils a 100 square. Ask: *How do you add 10/20/30 using a 100 square?* Ask similar questions for addition and subtraction of ones.
- Display the calculation 520 − 360. Ask: *How can we say each of these numbers as a number of tens?* (52 tens minus 36 tens) *What number fact can we use to help?* Choose a pupil to demonstrate how to start on 52 on the 100 square, then count back 3 tens and 6 ones to find the answer to 52 − 36. Ask: *How does the answer to this question help us answer 520 − 360?* (Because the answer, 16, tells us the answer is 16 tens, which is 160.)
- Repeat for different addition and subtraction of multiples of 10 and 100 as revision. When pupils are able to move away from using the 100 square to scaffold their learning, encourage them to do so.

## Same-day enrichment

- Provide pairs with a set of digit cards. Each player takes one card at a time, placing it into the gaps in the following grid:

- They should choose where to place each digit as they pick it, then use these multiples of 10 to form an addition or subtraction calculation, which they should find the answer for. Encourage pupils to set their own challenges – for example, to make a subtraction that yields the highest number or an addition whose answer is closest to 400. For every round, the winner gets a point.

# Question 2

**2** Complete the table. One has been done for you.

| | 232 | 527 | 659 | 707 | 348 | 499 |
|---|---|---|---|---|---|---|
| The nearest tens number | 230 | | | | | |
| The nearest hundreds number | 200 | | | | | |

## What learning will pupils have achieved at the conclusion of Question 2?

- Pupils will have learned how to round numbers to the nearest 10 and 100.

## Activities for whole-class instruction

- Provide pupils with a number line with 100 divisions, with each ten clearly marked with a longer line. Explain that 300 is at one end of the number line and 400 is at the other. Ask: *Why do number lines often show some notches longer than others?* Explain that the numbers that end in a zero (multiples of 10 or 'tens numbers') or two zeros (multiples of 100 or 'hundreds numbers') are like markers between which the other numbers fit. They act as signposts or benchmarks to help us place each number where it belongs. Point to various notches and ensure that pupils are able to say what number they represent.
- Write the number 384 on the board. Ask: *Which two hundreds numbers is this number between? Which hundreds number is it nearest to?* Establish that 384 lies between 300 and 400 and is nearer to 400.

*384 rounded to the nearest 100 is 400.*

- Ask: *Which two tens numbers is this number between? Which tens number is it nearest to?* Establish that 384 lies between 380 and 390 and is nearer to 380.

*384 rounded to the nearest 10 is 380.*

- Ask: *If someone didn't know how to find the two tens numbers or hundreds numbers either side of a number, how would you help them?* Discuss strategies pupils use. Repeat for further three-digit numbers between 300 and 400.

Look out for ... pupils who are unsure what to do with the mid-point between two round numbers. This is any number that ends in 5 when rounding to 10 (for example 245, 385) or any number that ends in 50 when rounding to 100 (for example 850, 350). They are always rounded upwards. The best way for pupils to learn this is with thorough practice. Provide plenty of examples of these mid-point numbers for pupils to practise.

- Pupils should work in pairs and draw a blank number line on their mini whiteboards. Think of a three-digit number (for example 456) and say: *I have thought of a number. When I round it to the nearest 100, it is 500. Show on your number line the lowest and highest numbers that my number might be.* Pupils might label their number line to show 450 on the left and 549 on the right.

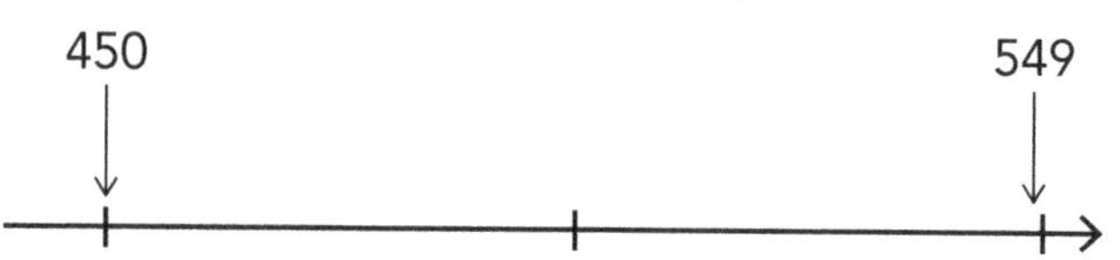


- Agree that this includes all of the numbers that, when rounded to the nearest 100, would be 500.
- Continue by saying: *I'm still thinking of the same number I started with. When it is rounded to the nearest 10, it is 460. Show on the number line that you have drawn the lowest and highest numbers that my number might be.* Pupils should add labels to their number line to show a section within the previous section that includes the numbers from 455 to 464.

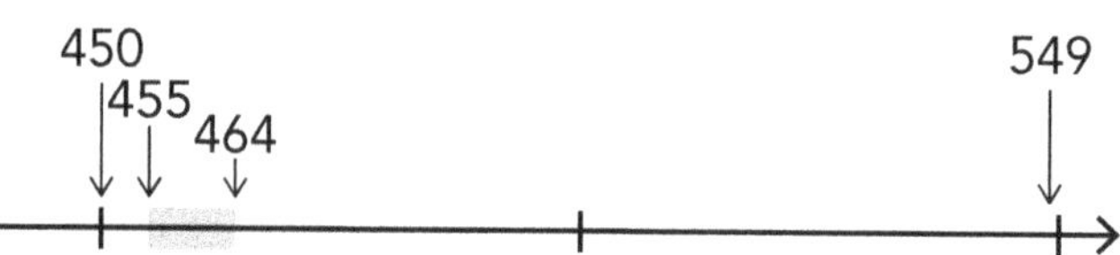


- Repeat with a different three-digit number. Can pupils list all possible outcomes?
- Pupils should complete Question 2 in the Practice Book.

## Same-day intervention

- Provide pupils with a number line with 100 divisions representing 300 to 400, labelled with tens and hundreds numbers. Ask: *Where is the number 342 on the line?* Pupils should draw an arrow to label its position. Ask: *Which tens numbers is 342 between? How do you know? Is there a way to know without using the number line to help?* Ask pupils to say which of the two tens numbers the number is nearest to. They should be able to see this visually, but encourage them to count the notches either side too. Ask the same question as before: *Is there a way to know without using the number line to help? Which hundreds number is it nearest to?*
- Repeat for other numbers that belong on the number line. Include the number 350 as well as various examples that end in the digit 5 in order to practise rounding up a mid-point number.
- If time allows, provide pupils with their own blank number lines in pairs and encourage them to ask each other similar rounding questions based on different hundreds.

## Same-day enrichment

- Display large digit cards showing the digits 2, 5 and 9 on the board, but reversed so that the digits are hidden from view. Explain to pupils that the three digits can be used to form numbers that can be rounded to 300, 500, 600, 900 and 1000 when rounded to the nearest 100. Challenge them to work out what the hidden digits are and what all the different numbers are (259 and 295 are rounded to 300, 529 is rounded to 500, 592 is rounded to 600, 925 is rounded to 900, and 952 is rounded to 1000). Encourage pupils to devise their own similar challenges for a partner to solve. Ask: *Is it possible to use three digits to make numbers that can be rounded to six different hundreds numbers?*

# Questions 3 and 4

**3** Estimate to the nearest 10 first and then calculate.

(a) 212 + 168 Estimate: Calculate:
(b) 438 + 321 Estimate: Calculate:
(c) 192 + 306 Estimate: Calculate:
(d) 626 + 322 Estimate: Calculate:
(e) 674 – 418 Estimate: Calculate:
(f) 813 – 479 Estimate: Calculate:

**4** Estimate to the nearest 100 first and then calculate.

(a) 388 + 217 Estimate: Calculate:
(b) 657 + 129 Estimate: Calculate:
(c) 290 + 426 Estimate: Calculate:
(d) 587 + 349 Estimate: Calculate:
(e) 477 – 286 Estimate: Calculate:
(f) 529 – 380 Estimate: Calculate:

## What learning will pupils have achieved at the conclusion of Questions 3 and 4?

- Estimation based on rounding numbers will have been introduced and practised.
- Pupils will have used vertical written methods to check the accuracy of estimates.

## Activities for whole-class instruction

- Ask pupils to consider when they might need to have a rough idea to what the answer to an addition or subtraction might be without actually working it out.

  (i) The skill of estimation is one that pupils will already have experience of in everyday life. As well as being useful as a way of mentally approximating an answer quickly, it is also useful for getting a rough idea of what the answer to a calculation could be (so pupils know what an answer 'should look like'). This test for reasonableness is important to emphasise.
- Write the following calculations: 478 + 213 = 581 and 675 – 164 = 517. Without giving pupils time to work out the correct answers, ask: *How can we tell whether these answers seem reasonable?* Introduce the concept of using

rounding to help estimate an answer. Explain that to 'estimate' means to give an approximate answer based on information pupils already know and that it is quicker to estimate than to calculate the actual answer.

- Highlight the two numbers in the first calculation and ask pupils what each number is, rounded to the nearest 10. Ask: *What is the total?* Show that this process of estimation involves the combining of two skills pupils have practised in the unit already, namely rounding a number to the nearest 10 and adding the resulting multiples of 10 together. Say: *480 plus 210 equals 690, so we would estimate that the answer to the calculation should be somewhere near to 690. The answer 581 is not reasonable.*
- Repeat the activity for the second calculation. This time, say: *680 minus 160 equals 520, so we would estimate that the answer to the calculation should be somewhere near to 520. The answer 517 is reasonable.*
- Ask: *What if we rounded each number to the nearest 100? Is the answer still reasonable?* Go through each number in the calculations and ask pupils what the two hundreds numbers either side of the number are. For example, 478 comes between 400 and 500. Choose pupils to come to the front and stick a hundreds place value arrow card on top of each number to show what it is rounded to. Pupils should then complete each calculation. Ask: *How is estimating to the nearest 100 the same as estimating to the nearest 10? How is it different? Would you expect this to be closer to the actual answer than if you estimated to the nearest 10? Why/why not?*
- Encourage pupils to calculate the answers using column methods. Compare the actual answer with both estimates. Ask: *Which was most effective – rounding to the nearest 10 or rounding to the nearest 100? How reasonable were the answers when you rounded to the nearest 100, compared to when you rounded to the nearest 10?*
- Repeat the activity for further three-digit addition and subtraction calculations. Include some that feature numbers in the mid-point (those that end with 50 or 5) so pupils can practise rounding up.
- Pupils should complete Questions 3 and 4 in the Practice Book.

## Same-day intervention

- Write the following steps on the board to make the process of estimation clear to pupils:

  STEP 1: ROUND the numbers to the nearest 10 or 100.

  STEP 2: ADD or SUBTRACT the multiples of 10 or 100 that you have made. This is the estimate.

  STEP 3: ADD or SUBTRACT the original numbers using vertical methods. This is the actual answer.
- Go through a series of examples, taking pupils through each step. Ask: *Which step do you find easiest/most difficult? Why?* Ensure that pupils understand that none of the steps are new to them and that they have practised these skills already. Note any difficulties pupils have with specific parts of the process and give support where necessary.

## Same-day enrichment

- Pupils can play 'Prove it!' in pairs. Pupil A deals six cards from a pack of digit cards. They arrange their cards to form an addition and then a subtraction of their choice, writing down both and including an answer. One should be a reasonable attempt at the answer, the other should be a completely unreasonable attempt (they should use estimation to work out what is reasonable in order to know what is unreasonable). Neither should be the correct answer.
- For example, the cards 5, 2, 3, 9, 0 and 4 could be arranged to make the following:

  904 – 235 = 584 593 + 204 = 805
- Pupil A should show both calculations to their partner. Pupil B should then act as teacher and prove to Pupil A which of the two calculations is a reasonable answer and why, using estimation to the nearest 10 or 100 to help.

  904 – 235 = 584 593 + 204 = 805

  900 – 200 = 600 (unreasonable)

  600 + 200 = 800 (reasonable)
- Pupils should complete the activity several times, swapping roles and dealing a new set of digits each time.

# Question 5

**5** Application problems.

(a) A school organises 228 Year 3 and 198 Year 4 pupils to go swimming at a local pool. There cannot be more than 450 children in the swimming pool at the same time. Estimate whether all these children can swim at the same time.

Answer: ____________

(b) There are 287 apple trees and 343 pear trees in an orchard. Estimate the total number of apple trees and pear trees, and the difference between the two types of tree.

Number of apple and pear trees: ____________

Difference: ____________

(c) Erin's mum went to a furniture shop with £200. She wanted to buy two rugs for £79 and a set of kitchen chairs for £114.

(i) Estimate whether Erin's mum had enough money for the rugs and chairs she wanted to buy.

Answer: ____________

(ii) If she had enough money, how much change should she get? If she did not have enough, how much was she short?

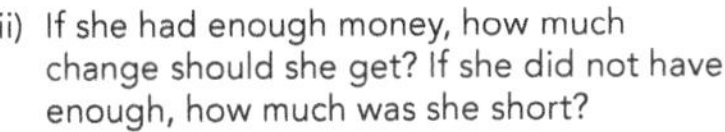

Answer: ____________

## What learning will pupils have achieved at the conclusion of Question 5?

- Problem-solving skills will have been developed to include estimation.

## Activities for whole-class instruction

- Give pupils a series of everyday contexts – for example at the shops, preparing a meal, travelling on a journey or going to a football match. Ask them to consider when it might be useful to be able to estimate a total or a difference quickly, without knowing the exact amount. These might include:
  - looking at the price of two items in a shop and knowing roughly whether you have enough to pay for them
  - estimating how much of a journey there is still to go by rounding up the total distance and taking away an estimate of how far you have travelled already.
- Display the following problem for pupils to consider: Jake is trying to save £358 to buy a new laptop. So far he has saved £189. Roughly how much does he still need to save?
- Ask: *Is this an addition or subtraction question? How do you know? Do you think this question is best solved by rounding to the nearest 100 or the nearest 10? Why?* Establish that rounding to the nearest 10 will give a closer estimate and it is more helpful in this case. Pupils should round each number to the nearest 10 and use these numbers to estimate how much money Jake still needs to save.

(i) Where a question asks for an estimate, the temptation for many pupils is to work out the actual answer because they don't believe that teachers want anything except a 'correct' answer. However, limiting themselves to what the question asks is a good habit to get into. It could be argued that it is more challenging to approximate than to calculate and it certainly shows a pupil's knowledge, understanding and number sense more deeply.

- Repeat for further application problems. Each time, encourage pupils to decide the operation needed to solve it and to replace the numbers in the problem for rounded equivalents before estimating.
- Pupils should complete Question 5 in the Practice Book.

## Same-day intervention

- Give pupils the following word problem: A rugby match is being watched by 478 home fans and 354 away fans. You are the stadium announcer and have to tell the crowd roughly how many fans have attended. How would you estimate the total number?
- Ask pupils to model both numbers using base 10 blocks. Ask: *Is this an addition or subtraction problem? How do you know that you don't have to work out the actual answer?* Go through each number and encourage pupils to round them to the nearest 10. They should do this physically, by removing/adding ones cubes and exchanging for tens rods so that they are left with the numbers 480 and 350. They should use their knowledge of adding multiples of 10 to find the approximate answer.
- Repeat for further application problems, modelling both the original number and the rounded numbers using base 10 blocks.

## Same-day enrichment

- Pupil pairs should read and respond to their own written two-step problems based on estimation. Give all pupils the sample problem:

  Kim is going on holiday driving through Europe. Her dad says that they drove 146 miles yesterday and have already driven 127 miles today. She knows that the whole journey to their campsite should be around 430 miles. About how many more miles do they have left to travel?
- All pupils should write a similar problem for their partner to solve, using bar models to help select the correct operations and using estimation to check reasonableness of their answers.
- Can pupils write a second two-step problem?

## Challenge and extension question

# Question 6

6 A number consists of three digits: **6**, **4** and **2**.

(a) If you add the number to 350, the result is between 600 and 700. This number is ☐.

(b) If you subtract 350 from the number, the result is between 100 and 200. This number is ☐.

Pupils are given three digits from which to make two numbers and use given clues to work out what those numbers might be. Pupils should use reasoning to explain each digit's positioning. For example, the result of their number plus 350 equals a number between 600 and 700. This means they can deduce that the hundreds digit must be 2 (because 4 hundred and 6 hundred would give a hundreds digit greater than 6). To make a total greater than 600, the tens digit needs to be greater than 5, so the answer must be 264. Encourage pupils to test their answer by calculating the addition to check that the result is between 600 and 700. Similar reasoning should be encouraged when deducing the second number, which gives an answer between 100 and 200 when 350 is subtracted from it.

# Unit 7.10 Estimating addition and subtraction with 3-digit numbers (2)

## Conceptual context

Pupils have now been introduced to the estimation of three-digit additions and subtractions and this unit seeks to consolidate their knowledge and understanding of this concept. Pupils are again given the opportunity to practise mental addition and subtraction of multiples of 10 to develop fluency for estimating. Pupils' reasoning will also be 'exercised' as they solve problems based on a series of related calculations.

## Learning pupils will have achieved at the end of the unit

- Mental strategies to solve three-digit addition and subtraction of multiples of 10 will have been revisited (Q1)
- Pupils' ability to round three-digit numbers to the nearest 10 and 100 will have been consolidated (Q2, Q4)
- Rounding will have been used to estimate answers to three-digit calculations to the nearest 10 and/or 100 (Q2, Q4)
- Pupils will have learned that using 'round numbers' provides an efficient starting point from which to derive a series of solutions to related calculations (Q3)
- Pupils will have continued to develop their ability to interpret data from tables and use it in related calculations (Q5)
- Estimation will have been used in real-life contexts (Q5)

### Resources

digit cards; base 10 blocks; mini whiteboards

### Vocabulary

multiple, estimate/estimation, approximate, round up, round down, calculate, the nearest 10, the nearest 100

# Question 1

**1** Calculate mentally.

| | |
|---|---|
| (a) 450 + 160 = ☐ | (b) 660 − 450 = ☐ |
| (c) 370 + 270 = ☐ | (d) 610 − 270 = ☐ |
| (e) 480 − 330 = ☐ | (f) 530 + 160 = ☐ |
| (g) 360 + 550 = ☐ | (h) 1000 − 430 = ☐ |

## What learning will pupils have achieved at the conclusion of Question 1?

- Mental strategies to solve three-digit addition and subtraction of multiples of 10 will have been revisited.

## Activities for whole-class instruction

- Begin by revising the addition and subtraction of two-digit numbers. Draw a 3 by 3 grid on the board and populate it with any nine digits. Ask pupils to write on mini whiteboards a two-digit addition or subtraction based on making a journey through four squares of the grid. For example:

| | | |
|---|---|---|
| 7 | 8 | 1 |
| 5 | 2 | 9 |
| 3 | 0 | 4 |

| | | |
|---|---|---|
| 7 | 8 | 1 |
| 5 | 2 | 9 |
| 3 | 0 | 4 |

75 – 29

- Choose different pupils to stand up and call out their calculations as a quick-fire questioning activity, sometimes asking pupils to explain their answers. Emphasise the strategies of partitioning the second number or using known facts to help.
- Write the calculation 580 − 370 = ☐ on the board. Ask: *What is the link between this calculation and the grid activity that you have just done?* Remind pupils that 580 − 370 can be considered as '58 tens minus 37 tens' and so knowing how to work out the answer to 58 − 37 is helpful. Say: *Write down an addition/subtraction where we could use this strategy.* Do pupils write calculations involving three-digit multiples of 100 and/or 10? Choose some pupils who have not shared their original quick-fire calculations and ask them to change their two-digit numbers into multiples of 10 and show their new calculations with the class. Ask: *What do you think their original calculation was? How do you know?*
- Choose pupils to come to the front and take part in a 'Say what you're thinking' activity. Give them addition and subtraction calculations involving multiples of 10. Encourage the pupil answering to talk through their thoughts as they work out the answer as a commentary on the mental strategies they are using. Model this beforehand so pupils know what to do.
- Pupils should complete Question 1 in the Practice Book.

## Same-day intervention

- Display the calculation 670 + 240. Ask pupils to model both numbers using base 10 blocks. Ask: *How many tens are in each number?* Encourage pupils to consider each hundreds square as a block of 10 tens. Establish that the calculation can be rewritten as 67 tens plus 24 tens.
- Ask pupils to move the 240 to one side and concentrate on the first addend (670). Ask: *How many tens do we need to add?* Encourage pupils to do so mentally and then model the addition using the base 10 blocks, for example starting with 67 and adding 20 then 4.
- Pupils should use their base 10 blocks as a way of checking their answer is correct.
- Repeat for further additions and subtractions involving multiples of 10. Encourage pupils to stop using the base 10 blocks if they are able and to explain the mental strategies they are using instead, expressing their calculations verbally as 'X tens plus/minus Y tens' as well as using written numerals.

## Same-day enrichment

- Ask pupils to play the following game in small groups. Display the numbers: 460, 850, 250, 370 and 670. Pupils can use any of these numbers to create four additions, using the mental strategies they have already practised to find each total and write them on paper or mini whiteboards. For example:

  460 + 370 = 830    850 + 250 = 1100
  250 + 460 = 710    670 + 370 = 1040

- Pupils take turns to read out one of their addition sentences. If someone else has the same sentence they shout 'Match' and all pupils with that sentence cross it out on their list. Pupils miss their turn if all their sentences have already been crossed out. The winner is the last pupil to have a sentenced unmatched.
- Encourage the groups to repeat the game, this time using a new set of multiples of 10 and practising subtracting them to find the difference.

# Question 2

**2** Estimate first and then calculate.

(a) 431 + 278

To the nearest 10:

To the nearest 100:

Calculate:

(b) 516 + 483

To the nearest 10:

To the nearest 100:

Calculate:

(c) 878 − 356

To the nearest 10:

To the nearest 100:

Calculate:

(d) 623 − 399

To the nearest 10:

To the nearest 100:

Calculate:

## What learning will pupils have achieved at the conclusion of Question 2?

- Pupils' ability to round three-digit numbers to the nearest 10 and 100 will have been consolidated.
- Rounding will have been used to estimate answers to three-digit calculations to the nearest 10 and/or 100.

## Activities for whole-class instruction

- Ask: *Why is estimation an important skill?* Remind pupils of the usefulness of having a rough idea about the answer to a question. Ensure that they understand that this is a way of self-checking their work and making changes if they think they may have made a mistake.
- Bring six pupils to the front and give each one a large digit card. Ask them to arrange the cards to make a three-digit addition. Give a seventh pupil an = card. Ask the class: *How can we work out roughly what the answer will be?* Revise the need to round the numbers to either the nearest 10 or 100 and then add them together. Ask pupils to round each number to the nearest 10 to begin with. What is the calculation? Do the same for the nearest 100.
- For example, if the digit cards are 2, 5, 7, 4, 1 and 9, pupils might generate the addition 427 + 159, which could then be estimated as follows:

  427 + 159

  To the nearest ten: 430 + 160 = 590

  To the nearest hundred: 400 + 200 = 600

- Ask pupils what they notice about both answers. Ask: *Do totals of two multiples of 10 always end in a zero? Is it possible for them to have two zeros? Do they always make three-digit totals?* They should then calculate the actual answer using vertical addition.

$$\begin{array}{r} 4\ 2\ 7 \\ +\ 1\ 5\ 9 \\ \hline 5\ 8\ 6 \\ \hline {\scriptstyle 1}\ \ \end{array}$$

- Provide further opportunities for pupils to estimate twice, then calculate using both addition and subtraction.
- Pupils should complete Question 2 in the Practice Book.

## Same-day intervention

- Write the following numbers on the board: 200, 210, 220, 230, 240, 250, 260, 270, 280, 290, 300. Ask pupils to choose any five of these numbers and write them on their mini whiteboards. Call out different three-digit numbers between 200 and 300 and ask pupils to practise rounding them to the nearest 10. If they round to one of their five chosen numbers they may circle it. The first player to circle all five numbers is the winner.
- Use some of the numbers that have been called out to form addition and subtraction calculations. Use the same rounding skills to model how each calculation can be estimated. Once pupils have grown in confidence, extend the activity to include any three-digit numbers.

## Same-day enrichment

- Write the following statement on the board: I think that rounding to the nearest 100 gives an estimate nearer to the actual answer than rounding to the nearest 10.
- Ask pupils whether they think this statement is true or not and challenge them to explore whether one method gives a closer estimate than the other. Pupils should take six cards from a pack of digit cards and use them to make a three-digit addition or subtraction. They should estimate the total to the nearest 10, then the nearest 100, and finally calculate the actual answer, recording which of their estimates is closest. Encourage pupils to do this for ten additions and subtractions altogether to test which of the two estimates is closer.
- Pupils should share their results and may be able to use reasoning to suggest why one particular method of estimation gives a closer result than the other.

# Question 3

**3** Calculate with reasoning. Start with the easiest calculation. Think carefully about which one to start with.

| | | | |
|---|---|---|---|
| (a) | 97 + 238 = ☐ | (e) | 456 + 98 = ☐ |
| (b) | 98 + 238 = ☐ | (f) | 456 + 99 = ☐ |
| (c) | 99 + 238 = ☐ | (g) | 456 + 100 = ☐ |
| (d) | 100 + 238 = ☐ | (h) | 456 + 101 = ☐ |
| (i) | 200 − 130 = ☐ | (m) | 550 − 97 = ☐ |
| (j) | 199 − 130 = ☐ | (n) | 550 − 98 = ☐ |
| (k) | 198 − 230 = ☐ | (o) | 550 − 99 = ☐ |
| (l) | 197 − 230 = ☐ | (p) | 550 − 100 = ☐ |

## What learning will pupils have achieved at the conclusion of Question 3?

- Pupils will have learned that using 'round numbers' provides an efficient starting point from which to derive a series of solutions to related calculations.

## Activities for whole-class instruction

- Write the following series of calculations on the board:

| | |
|---|---|
| 467 + 98 | 500 − 160 |
| 467 + 99 | 499 − 160 |
| 467 + 100 | 498 − 160 |
| 467 + 101 | 497 − 160 |

- Give pupils two minutes to discuss in pairs the similarities and differences between both sets of calculations. What do they notice? Gather their ideas.
- Ask: *Which of the calculations in each set do you think is the easiest to work out? Why is this?* Circle the calculation in each set that shows a multiple of 100. Discuss what pupils notice about the sequence of calculations and how the 'easiest' calculation fits into this sequence. Ask: *How can you use the 'easiest' calculation to find the answers to the others, without using the vertical written method?* Explain that pupils can look at the way the numbers change around the 'easiest calculation' and adjust the answer accordingly.
- Again split pupils into pairs and ask them to answer each set of calculations by only actually working out the 'easiest calculation' and using reasoning to explain what the others will be. Share answers as a class. Encourage pupils to use number sense to explain patterns. For example: 'I worked out 500 − 160 first, which is 340. The next calculation starts with a number that is one less than 500, so the answer won't be as big. It will be one less, which is 339. Each minuend is one less each time, so this will affect the answers in the same way. They are 340, 339, 338 and 337.'
- Show pupils the calculation 849 − 300. Ask them to work out the answer. Then, quickly reveal further calculations (either above or below the displayed subtraction), for example 849 − 299, 849 − 298 and so on. Pupils should respond with the answer immediately, without working out the answer. Practise this quick response activity with different calculations.
- Extend pupils' number sense when working with estimation by asking: *How could you use what you have practised here to help estimate the answer to a calculation?* For example, if pupils are presented with a calculation where one of the numbers is near to a multiple of 100 (603 + 332), they could work out the answer to 600 + 332 and then adjust. Give pupils several examples to try for themselves to build fluency.
- Pupils should complete Question 3 in the Practice Book.

### Same-day intervention

- Use bar models to emphasise the reasoning needed to use known facts to find related facts. For example, display two strips of differently-coloured paper. Write the numbers 489 and 300 on them respectively. Place the strips together so that they are combined. Ask: *What is the total? Why is it fairly easy to work out?* Sketch the related bar model. Take the 300 strip and cut a small amount off the end. Change the number to 299 and ask: *How will this affect the total?* Show how the third bar is now one less.

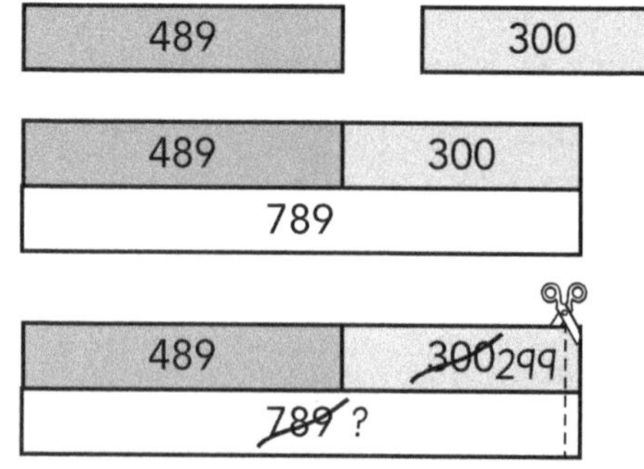


- Repeat for further sequences of addition and subtraction calculations, always starting with the 'easier' calculation and extrapolating in both directions. If a sequence needs to be continued by adding 1, ensure that the initial strip of paper is folded back slightly. Open out more of it as it increases by 1.

## Same-day enrichment

- Ask pairs of pupils to draw two 3 by 3 grids. The first should contain three-digit numbers that are near to a multiple of 100. The second can contain any three-digit numbers. For example:

| 295 | 403 | 602 |
|---|---|---|
| 797 | 598 | 304 |
| 106 | 203 | 896 |

| 258 | 839 | 214 |
|---|---|---|
| 375 | 466 | 162 |
| 525 | 271 | 843 |

- Pupil A drops two counters from a small height so that one lands on each grid, choosing a random number from each. They then combine the two to form either an addition or subtraction calculation. Pupil B should then round the number from Grid 1 to the nearest 100, say what the answer is and then use this to help give the answer to Pupil A's calculation.
- Pupils should repeat the activity for different numbers, alternating the operation needed.

# Question 4

**4** (a) Estimate and then write the letters of the number sentences.

A. 213 + 176 B. 323 + 268 C. 334 + 178 D. 352 + 278

E. 138 + 363 F. 233 + 171 G. 268 + 326 H. 382 + 156

(i) Estimating to the nearest 100, the number sentence(s) with a result of:

400 is/are ____, with result of 500 is/are ____, and with a result of 600 is/are ____.

(ii) Estimating to the nearest 10, the number sentence(s) with a result of:

400 is/are ____, with a result of 500 is/are ____, and with a result of 600 is/are ____.

(b) Now calculate.

(i) 213 + 176 = ☐ (ii) 323 + 268 = ☐

(iii) 334 + 178 = ☐ (iv) 352 + 278 = ☐

(v) 138 + 363 = ☐ (vi) 233 + 171 = ☐

(vii) 268 + 326 = ☐ (viii) 382 + 156 = ☐

## What learning will pupils have achieved at the conclusion of Question 4?

- The ability to round three-digit numbers to the nearest 10 and 100 will have been consolidated.
- Rounding will have been used to estimate the answers to three-digit calculations to the nearest 10 and/or 100.

## Activities for whole-class instruction

- Write the calculations 536 + 266 and 544 + 274 on the board. Ask pupils to use estimation to find both totals to the nearest 10 and then to the nearest 100. Ask: *What do you notice?* Explain that the actual answers are different, but that each addend rounds to the same number in every case so the estimations are the same.

| | Estimated to nearest ten | Estimated to nearest hundred | Actual |
|---|---|---|---|
| 536 + 266 | 540 + 270 = 810 | 500+ 300 = 800 | 802 |
| 544 + 274 | 540 + 270 = 810 | 500+ 300 = 800 | 818 |

- Use this as a way of showing that different calculations can give the same estimated answer.
- Display the following calculations:

  145 + 352 276 + 316 402 + 104

  168 + 326 214 + 279
- Split the class into three groups. Group A should estimate each answer to the nearest 10, Group B should estimate each answer to the nearest 100, and Group C should use the vertical written method to find the actual answers.
- Share results as a class. Ask: *Which calculations give the same answer when you estimate to the nearest 100?* Give pupils time to work in pairs and identify those with the same answer. Do the same for estimating to the nearest 10.
- Repeat for further three-digit estimations.
- Pupils should complete Question 4 in the Practice Book.

## Same-day intervention

- Display the following calculations on cards or mini whiteboards:

  478 + 119 245 + 254 361 + 237

  138 + 455 367 + 125
- Ask: *Do you think these calculations will have the same or different answers? How do you know?* Encourage pupils to go through each number and round it to the nearest 100, forming a new, estimated addition. They should then use their knowledge of addition of multiples of 100 to find the estimated totals. Ask: *Which answers are the same when rounded to the nearest 100?* Pupils should group the cards accordingly.
- Repeat the activity estimating to the nearest 10. Pupils should again go through each number, rounding it before working out each calculation. Provide base 10 blocks for pupils who find these useful when adding multiples of 10.
- If time allows, repeat for further sets of calculations.

## Same-day enrichment

- Ask pupils to work in small groups. Write the target numbers 200, 300 and 400 on the board and ask each pupil to think of an addition (include subtraction as well if pupils are confident) involving multiples of 10 that equals one of these numbers. They should then write an 'unrounded' three-digit calculation that, when rounded to the nearest 10, equals their 'multiple of 10' calculation.

  For example:

| Target number: | Multiple of 10 calculation: | 'Unrounded' calculation: |
|---|---|---|
| 300 | 130 + 170 | 127 + 166 |
| 200 | 640 – 440 | 644 – 438 |

- Pupils should write several of these 'unrounded' calculations on cards and shuffle them, spreading them out on the table. They should then take turns to try and spot pairs of calculations that have the same answer when rounded to the nearest 10. Do any have the same answer when rounded to the nearest 100 too? Pupils should find each pair of actual answers using the vertical written method.

# Question 5

**5** Use the information in the table to estimate the answers.

| Name of building in London | Broadgate Tower | One Churchill Place | Canary Wharf Tower | The Shard |
|---|---|---|---|---|
| Height (metres) | 178 | 156 | 244 | 310 |

(a) About how many metres higher is The Shard than Broadgate Tower?

Answer: ______

(b) About how many metres shorter is One Churchill Place than Canary Wharf Tower?

Answer: ______

(c) Write two more estimation questions of your own and work out the answers.

______

______

## What learning will pupils have achieved at the conclusion of Question 5?

- Pupils will have continued to develop their ability to interpret data from tables and use it in related calculations.
- Estimation will have been used in a real-life context.

## Activities for whole-class instruction

- Display the following information as a table:

| Name of UK river | Avon | Bann | Clyde | Severn | Thames | Trent | Wye |
|---|---|---|---|---|---|---|---|
| Length in km | 154 | 159 | 176 | 354 | 346 | 297 | 215 |

- Ask pupils a series of questions based on rounding the river lengths directly from the table. Use different wording, for example:
  - About how many kilometres long is the Clyde?
  - Which river is approximately 300 kilometres long?
- Encourage pupils to consider the data carefully and think about whether it is more helpful to round to the nearest 100 or the nearest 10.
- Display a similar question comparing any two of the river lengths. For example:
  - About how many kilometres longer is the Thames than the Avon?
- Ask: *What do you need to calculate here? How do you know?* Split pupils into two groups. Ask Group A to decide on an estimate for the difference between the two river lengths and Group B to calculate the difference using the vertical method. Compare both answers.
- Ask pupils to suggest comparison questions of their own. These do not have to be limited to subtraction (for example: About how many kilometres is the total length of the Trent added to the Clyde?).
- Continue the activity, using pupils' questions and swapping the roles of each group so they practise both estimating and calculating using the data.
- Pupils should complete Question 5 in the Practice Book.

## Same-day intervention

- Use several packs of digit cards to deal three digits to each pupil in the group. Ask them to arrange their digits to make any three-digit number. Ask: *How can we display these numbers so that we can see whose is whose and compare them easily?* Establish that putting each number next to each other on the table is a good way to compare each number, as is writing them in a table.

- Go through each number, asking pupils to round them to the nearest 10. Draw an extra row to the table and record pupil answers so that the numbers are already rounded. For example:

| **Name** | Aisha | Ben | Charlotte | Daniel |
|---|---|---|---|---|
| **Number** | 278 | 564 | 912 | 385 |
| **Rounded to nearest 10** | 280 | 560 | 910 | 390 |

- Discuss how pupils can use the rounded numbers to help estimate what the actual answers to questions might be. For example, ask them about how much the difference in score is between Ben and Aisha. Ask: *What do the words 'about how much' mean? How would you give an estimate?* Encourage pupils to use their rounded numbers to give an approximate answer (in this case 56 tens – 28 tens = 28 tens, so the difference is about 280).
- Repeat for similar questions using data from the table. Pupils could model each calculation using tens rods if it helps them visualise the calculation in terms of tens.

## Same-day enrichment

- Show pupils the following grid, which is populated with the heights of some UK mountains.

| | | |
|---|---|---|
| Slieve Donard 850 m | Goat Fell 874 m | Snaefell 621 m |
| Scafell Pike 912 m | Cadair Idris 608 m | Helvellyn 712 m |
| Ben Hope 772 m | Skiddaw 709 m | Sgurr Alasdair 992 m |

- Encourage pupils to devise their own two-part questions based on the information in the grid. Part 1 should be based on estimating either the difference or the total of two heights. Give pupils the following sentence starters to help:
  - About how much is the difference between ... and ...?
  - About how much is the total height of ... and ...?
- Part 2 should be about calculating the actual answer. Again, give pupils a possible sentence starter:
  - What is their actual difference/total?
- Pupils should write their questions onto cards (with the answers on the back) and then share these with others in the group. They should use rounding to help solve the estimated answer and then vertical addition or subtraction to help find the actual answer.

## Challenge and extension question

## Question 6

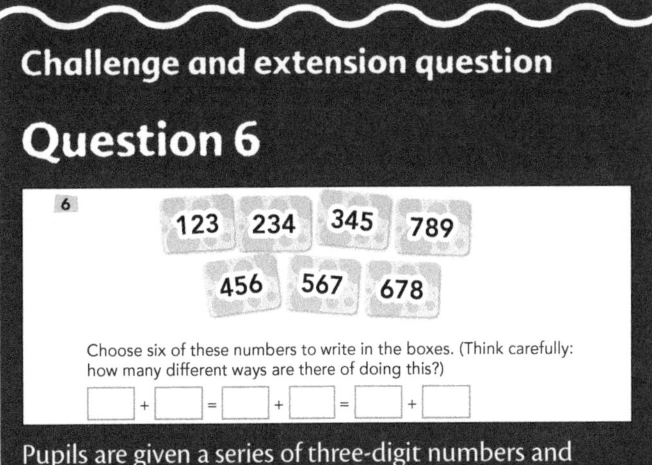

6
123
234
345
789
456
567
678
Choose six of these numbers to write in the boxes. (Think carefully: how many different ways are there of doing this?)
+ = + = +


Pupils are given a series of three-digit numbers and challenged to find combinations of pairs that are equal. They may choose to use trial and error as a strategy to begin with, but should be encouraged to consider the nature of the numbers they have been given. These are not randomly chosen numbers, but they each have a difference of 111 (123, 234, 345 and so on). Pupils should use reasoning to think about how to pair the numbers to make the same totals (for example, choosing to start with the largest number and the smallest number, then find the total of the next largest number and the next smallest number and so on).

## Chapter 7 Test (Practice Book 3B, pages 33–37)

| Test Question number | Relevant Unit | Relevant questions within unit |
|---|---|---|
| 1 | 7.1 | 2, 4 |
| | 7.2 | 1 |
| | 7.3 | 2, 5 |
| | 7.4 | 1 |
| | 7.9 | 1 |
| | 7.10 | 1 |
| 2 | 7.6 | 1 |
| | 7.8 | 1 |
| 3 | 7.9 | 3 |
| | 7.10 | 2 |
| 4 | 7.6 | 4 |
| | 7.8 | 4 |
| 5 | 7.5 | 4 |
| | 7.7 | 4 |
| 6, 7, 8, 9, 10 | 7.6 | 5 |
| | 7.8 | 5 |

# Chapter 8
# Simple fractions and their addition and subtraction

## Chapter overview

| Area of mathematics | National Curriculum statutory requirements for Key Stage 2 | Shanghai Maths Project reference |
|---|---|---|
| Number – fractions | Year 3 Programme of study<br>Pupils should be taught to: | |
| | ■ count up and down in tenths; recognise that tenths arise from dividing an object into 10 equal parts and in dividing one-digit numbers or quantities by 10 | Year 3, Unit 8.1 |
| | ■ recognise, find and write fractions of a discrete set of objects: unit fractions and non-unit fractions with small denominators | Year 3, Units 8.1, 8.2, 8.3 |
| | ■ recognise and use fractions as numbers: unit fractions and non-unit fractions with small denominators | Year 3, Units 8.1, 8.4 |
| | ■ recognise and show, using diagrams, equivalent fractions with small denominators | Year 3, Units 8.2, 8.3 |
| | ■ add and subtract fractions with the same denominator within one whole (e.g. $\frac{5}{7} + \frac{1}{7} = \frac{6}{7}$) | Year 3, Unit 8.4 |
| | ■ compare and order unit fractions, and fractions with the same denominators | Year 3, Units 8.1, 8.2, 8.3 |
| | ■ solve problems that involve all of the above | Year 3, Units 8.1, 8.2, 8.3, 8.4 |

# Unit 8.1 Unit fractions and tenths

## Conceptual context

In Book 2, pupils explored the concept of unit fractions and used their understanding of this to identify unit fractions of objects and quantities. This first unit on fractions in Book 3 will deepen this understanding and will lead to a focus on tenths of objects and quantities. Pupils will already appreciate the importance of splitting objects or items into equal parts or groups when dealing with fractions; now they will understand that tenths arise from dividing an object or quantity into 10 equal parts. This will lay the foundations for later work on decimals in Book 4.

Pupils will draw on their multiplication and division facts when finding tenths of quantities involving non-unit fractions. This will continue to be supported by the array representation to help pupils make connections between fractions, multiplication and division.

In Book 2, pupils were introduced to the idea that fractions are also numbers in their own right. This concept will be further developed as pupils explore tenths on a number line.

## Learning pupils will have achieved at the end of the unit

- Understanding of the role of the numerator and denominator will have been developed when exploring and comparing unit fractions (Q1, Q2)
- Pupils will understand that tenths arise from dividing an object into ten equal parts (Q1, Q3, Q4)
- Understanding of unit fractions will have been used to find and write fractions of a discrete set of objects (Q2)
- Pupils will know that tenths arise from dividing quantities by 10 (Q2)
- Pupils will understand that fractions are themselves numbers (Q3)
- Counting forwards and backwards in tenths will have been developed (Q3)
- Pupils will have solved problems involving dividing an object into 10 equal parts (Q4)

### Resources

strips of paper; mini whiteboards; two different colours of interlocking cubes; images of shapes which show unit and non-unit fractions (see Question 1); fraction cards labelled with unit fractions $\frac{1}{2}$ to $\frac{1}{10}$; chocolate bar in a 4 by 5 array formation; 12 sweets; double-sided counters; 10-sided spinners labelled with $\frac{1}{10}$, $\frac{2}{10}$, $\frac{3}{10}$, $\frac{4}{10}$, $\frac{5}{10}$, $\frac{6}{10}$, $\frac{7}{10}$, $\frac{8}{10}$, $\frac{9}{10}$, $\frac{10}{10}$; blank dice labelled with 10, 20, 30, 40, 50, 100; dotted paper in which dots line up to make squares; 10 cm strips of card; chalks; circles divided into 10 equal parts; scissors; counting stick; **Resource 3.8.1** Shape fractions

### Vocabulary

unit fraction, non-unit fraction, tenths, denominator, numerator

# Question 1

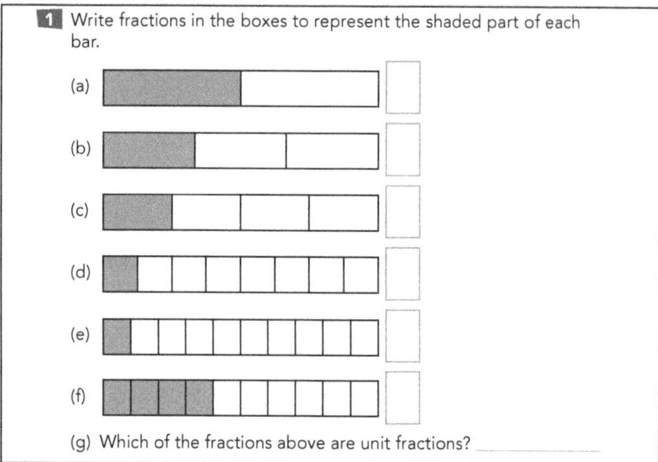

**1** Write fractions in the boxes to represent the shaded part of each bar.

(a)

(b)

(c)

(d)

(e)

(f)

(g) Which of the fractions above are unit fractions? ________

## What learning will pupils have achieved at the conclusion of Question 1?

- Understanding of the role of the numerator and denominator will have been developed when exploring and comparing unit fractions.
- Pupils will understand that tenths arise from dividing an object into 10 equal parts.

## Activities for whole-class instruction

- Provide pupils with a strip of paper, one per pair. Ask them to fold the paper so that it is divided into any number of equal parts.
- Once the strips of paper have been folded into equal parts, ask pupils to open them out.
- Ask: *Who has divided their paper into halves? Who has divided their paper into quarters? What other fractions have people divided their paper into?*
- Share alternative responses and establish what fraction each strip of paper has been divided into. Ask pupils to shade one of the parts on their strip of paper.
- Create a class display by ordering the strips of paper, starting with the one divided into the fewest equal parts, for example:

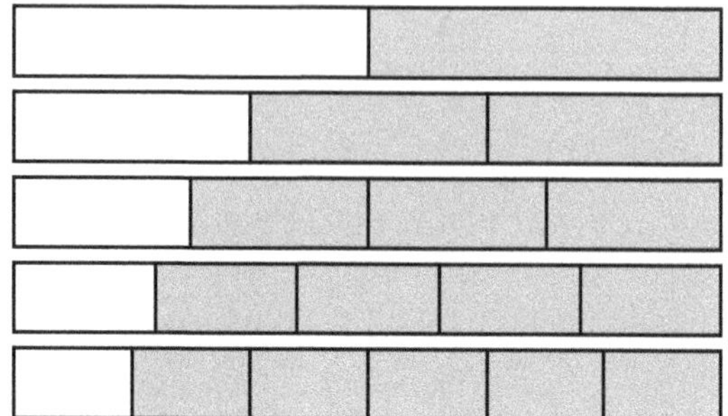

- Ask: *What can we label the shaded part on each strip?* Ask pupils to record responses on their mini whiteboards. Identify and discuss any incorrect responses. Record the symbolic notation on the display next to each strip of paper.

... pupils who represent the fraction as a ratio, for example, $\frac{1}{4}$ is written as $\frac{1}{3}$ because they compare the shaded part with the unshaded part(s), rather than counting all of the parts.

- Explain that these are all called 'unit fractions' because *one* part of the whole has been selected. Focus pupils' attention on the symbolic representations.
- Ask: *How do we know one part has been selected in each of these fractions?* Establish that the top number in the fraction is 1 each time. Remind pupils that the top number in a fraction is called the 'numerator'. When exploring parts of a whole, the numerator identifies the number of parts the fraction refers to.

All say ... *In a unit fraction, the numerator is always 1.*

- Present the unit fractions $\frac{1}{2}, \frac{1}{3}, \frac{1}{4}, \frac{1}{5}, \frac{1}{6}, \frac{1}{7}, \frac{1}{8}, \frac{1}{9}, \frac{1}{10}$ on the board. Provide pupils with copies of **Resource 3.8.1** Shape fractions.

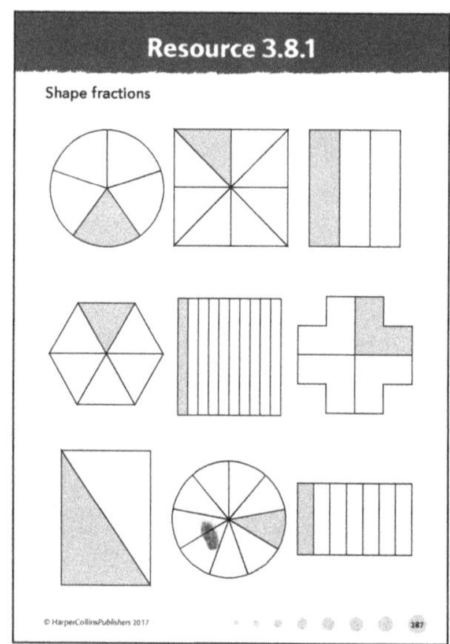

**Resource 3.8.1**

Shape fractions

© HarperCollinsPublishers 2017

- Working individually or in pairs, pupils should label the fractions represented on **Resource 3.8.1**.
- Display the following fractions on the board: $\frac{1}{5}, \frac{1}{10}, \frac{3}{10}, \frac{1}{8}$.
- Ask pupils to talk to their partner and identify which fraction could be the odd one out and why.
- Can they see that $\frac{3}{10}$ is the only one with a numerator which is greater than one?
- Tell pupils that this is called a 'non-unit fraction'.

*In a non-unit fraction, the numerator is always greater than 1.*

- Introduce a stack of 10 interlocking cubes of the same colour; this will be the whole.
- Ask: *What fractions could we be dealing with if this is the whole?* Pupils might identify that halves or fifths could be represented. Acknowledge that these are correct, but then establish that for the time being, you would like to focus on the whole being split into tenths.
- Ask pupils if they can see that each cube is $\frac{1}{10}$ because there are 10 of them in the whole and they are all the same. Remind pupils that the denominator tells us how many equal parts the whole has been divided into. Identify that, because the whole is divided into 10 equal parts, the denominator will be 10.

*The denominator tells us how many equal parts the whole has been divided into.*

- Swap one of the cubes for a different colour (for example, red) and reconstruct the tower, for example:

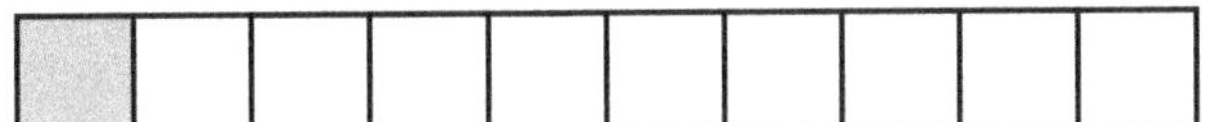

- Ask: *What fraction is red?* Establish that one tenth is red. Record this symbolically for pupils to see. Construct a second stack of 10 interlocking yellow cubes. Ask: *How many cubes will I need to change if I would like to represent $\frac{2}{10}$ of the stack as red?* Establish that two will need to be changed. Record $\frac{2}{10}$.
- Ask pupils to create their own stacks of 10 interlocking cubes to represent $\frac{3}{10}$, $\frac{4}{10}$, $\frac{5}{10}$, and so on.
- Ask: *What is the same and what is different about each stack? What is the same and what is different about each fraction when recorded symbolically?* Identify that the denominator remains the same, but the numerator changes each time.
- Pupils should complete Question 1 in the Practice Book.

## Same-day intervention

- Provide pupils with a selection of cards that show unit and non-unit fractions of shapes.
- Ask pupils to sort them into two groups: those which represent a unit fraction and those which represent a non-unit fraction.
- Ask: *Can you record the value of the unit fraction using fraction notation? What will the numerator be? What will the denominator be? How do you know?*

## Same-day enrichment

- Provide pairs of pupils with a set of nine cards which have $\frac{1}{2}, \frac{1}{3}, \frac{1}{4}, \frac{1}{5}, \frac{1}{6}, \frac{1}{7}, \frac{1}{8}, \frac{1}{9}, \frac{1}{10}$ written on them, one fraction per card.
- Ask pupils to randomly select two cards. Ask: *Which fraction is the largest? Which fraction is the smallest? Which unit fractions belong between these two?* Pupils should describe why one fits between two others. Pupils should take turns to identify unit fractions which will be between the two fractions.
- Repeat with different unit fraction cards.

# Question 2

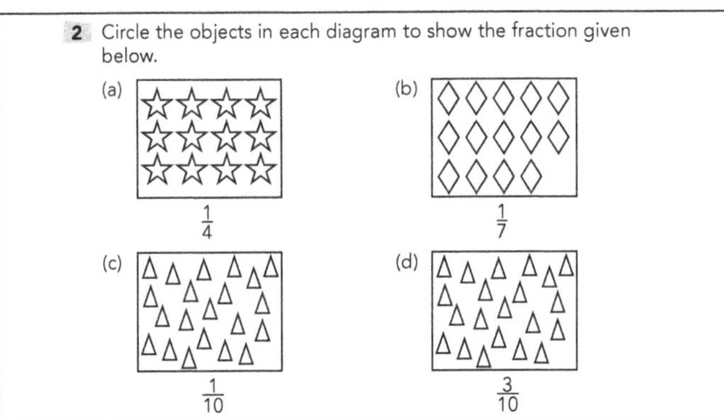

2 Circle the objects in each diagram to show the fraction given below.
(a)
1/4
(b)
1/7
(c)
1/10
(d)
3/10


## What learning will pupils have achieved at the conclusion of Question 2?

- Understanding of the role of the numerator and denominator will have been developed when exploring and comparing unit fractions.
- Understanding of unit fractions will have been used to find and write fractions of a discrete set of objects.
- Pupils will understand that tenths arise when dividing quantities by 10.

## Activities for whole-class instruction

- Show pupils a bar of chocolate in a 4 by 5 array formation, for example:

- Ask: *If I was going to eat $\frac{1}{4}$ of the chocolate bar, how many pieces would I eat?* Take responses. Ask: *What can you see 4 of? There are 4 rows.* Dynamically demonstrate that 1 row is $\frac{1}{4}$ of the whole bar. There are 5 pieces of chocolate in 1 row.
- Reconstruct the bar so it represents a 4 by 5 array formation. Ask: *If I was going to eat $\frac{1}{5}$ of the chocolate bar, how many pieces would I eat?* Take responses. Ask: *What can you see five of? There are five columns.* Demonstrate that one column represents $\frac{1}{5}$ of the whole bar. There are four pieces of chocolate in one column.
- Ask: *What mathematical image does the chocolate bar remind you of?* Ensure pupils notice that the chocolate bar shows an array formation.
- Pupils work in pairs. Ask Pupil A to draw an array formation on a mini whiteboard to represent a chocolate bar of any dimensions. Pupil B identifies what fraction of the whole bar 1 row would be. Pupil A identifies what fraction of the whole bar 1 column would be. Swap roles and repeat with a different array representation.
- Show pupils a pile of 12 sweets. Tell pupils that we need to find $\frac{1}{5}$ of the pile of sweets. Remind pupils that the whole will need to be divided into 6 equal groups when we are dealing with sixths. Give pupils time to talk to their partner to identify how we can find out how many sweets represent $\frac{1}{5}$ of 12.
- Ask: *How could we arrange the 12 sweets so we can easily identify the value of $\frac{1}{5}$?* Ask a pupil to demonstrate how they would arrange the sweets to help establish the value of $\frac{1}{5}$. Hint that it should be something that can be split into 6 equal groups easily. If they do not arrange the sweets in a 2 by 6 or 6 by 2 formation, demonstrate this representation to pupils, for example:

- Identify that $\frac{1}{5}$ of 12 is 2, by pointing to two sweets.
- Ask: *What if I had 15 sweets and was allowed to eat $\frac{1}{5}$ of them? How would I arrange them to find the value of $\frac{1}{5}$?* Give pupils time to explore. Identify that a 3 by 5 array formation helps to see that $\frac{1}{5}$ of 15 is 3. Repeat with different numbers if necessary.
- Place ten chairs at the front of the classroom and invite ten pupils to sit on the chairs. Ask one pupil to stand up. Ask: *What fraction of the whole group are standing?* Establish that one out of ten are standing, so $\frac{1}{10}$ of the whole are standing. Ask a second pupil to stand up. Ask: *What fraction are standing now?* Repeat with three pupils standing.
- Record on the board:

  $\frac{1}{10}$ of 10 = 1

  $\frac{2}{10}$ of 10 = 2

  $\frac{3}{10}$ of 10 = 3
- Ask: *What do you notice about the pattern?* Ask pupils to continue the pattern.
- Pupils should complete Question 2 in the Practice Book.

## Same-day intervention

- Provide pupils with ten double-sided counters. Ask them to arrange them in a line with the yellow side facing up. Ask: *This line of counters is my whole – how many equal parts can we see? Which number in a fraction shows how many equal parts the whole has been divided into?*
- Turn one counter over. Ask: *What fraction is now red?* Establish that $\frac{1}{10}$ is red. Turn a second counter over. Ask: *What fraction is now red?* Repeat the process for further counters until they have all been turned over.

## Same-day enrichment

- Provided dotted paper in which dots line up to make squares. Pupils work in pairs. Pupil A spins a 10-sided spinner labelled with $\frac{1}{10}, \frac{2}{10}, \frac{3}{10}, \frac{4}{10}, \frac{5}{10}, \frac{6}{10}, \frac{7}{10}, \frac{8}{10}, \frac{9}{10}, \frac{10}{10}$. Pupil B rolls a dice with 10, 20, 30, 40, 50, 100 written on it. They work together to find the fraction of the amount rolled, using the dotted paper to show 10 by 10 grids for support. Each time, pupils write the fraction sentence. For example:

  $\frac{4}{10}$ of 30 = 12

  $\frac{7}{10}$ of 50 = 35
- How many fraction sentences can each pair list in three minutes?

# Question 3

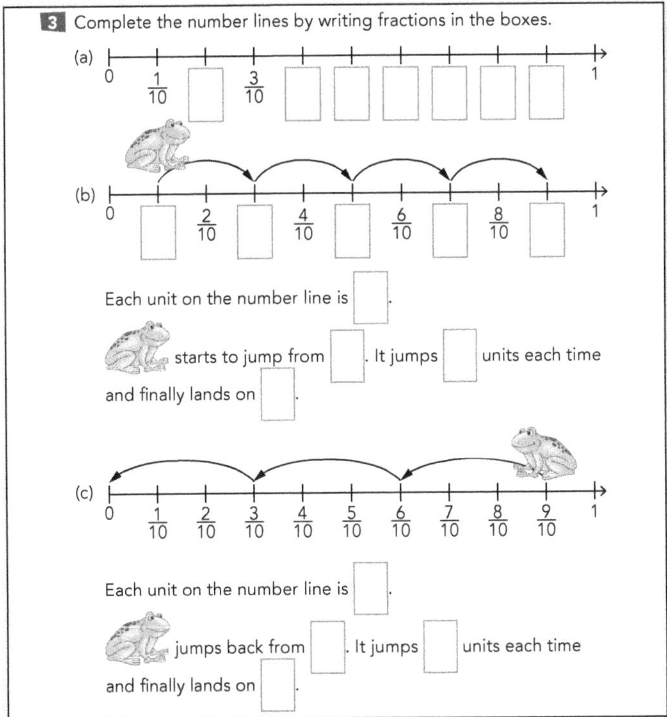
3 Complete the number lines by writing fractions in the boxes.

(a) 0, $\frac{1}{10}$, ☐, $\frac{3}{10}$, ☐, ☐, ☐, ☐, ☐, ☐, 1

(b) 0, ☐, $\frac{2}{10}$, ☐, $\frac{4}{10}$, ☐, $\frac{6}{10}$, ☐, $\frac{8}{10}$, ☐, 1

Each unit on the number line is ☐.

starts to jump from ☐. It jumps ☐ units each time and finally lands on ☐.

(c) 0, $\frac{1}{10}$, $\frac{2}{10}$, $\frac{3}{10}$, $\frac{4}{10}$, $\frac{5}{10}$, $\frac{6}{10}$, $\frac{7}{10}$, $\frac{8}{10}$, $\frac{9}{10}$, 1

Each unit on the number line is ☐.

jumps back from ☐. It jumps ☐ units each time and finally lands on ☐.

## What learning will pupils have achieved at the conclusion of Question 3?

- Pupils will understand that fractions are themselves numbers.
- Pupils will know that tenths arise from dividing an object into 10 equal parts.
- Counting forwards and backwards in tenths will have been developed.

## Activities for whole-class instruction

- Provide each pupil with a 10 cm strip of card. Tell pupils that this is $\frac{1}{10}$ of a metre.
- Ask: *What can you find in the classroom that is $\frac{1}{10}$ of a metre?* Give pupils time to explore and feedback. Ask: *What can you find in the classroom that is $\frac{2}{10}$ of a metre?* Take feedback. Give pupils time to explore other fractions of a metre if appropriate.
- Use ten 10 cm strips of card and line them up along a counting stick. Establish that ten 10ths of a metre is equal to one metre. Explain that you have been exploring fractions of a whole, but that fractions are also numbers and that they can be shown as places on a number line.
- Using the counting stick, place 0 at one end and 1 at the other.

0 1

- Ask: *If this represents a number line from 0 to 1, what is the value of the first division along the line?* Establish that it is $\frac{1}{10}$. Ask a child to place a number card with $\frac{1}{10}$ in this position on the counting stick.
- Ask: *How do we know?* Encourage pupils to notice that there are 10 'jumps' along the counting stick so each point will represent 1 tenth.
- Ask: *What is the value of the second division along the number line?* Take responses. Ask a child to place a number card with $\frac{2}{10}$ in this position on the counting stick. Ask: *Where would $\frac{4}{10}$ go?* Give pupils time to discuss and share responses. Position $\frac{4}{10}$ on the correct position on the number line. Position $\frac{8}{10}$ incorrectly on the counting stick. Ask: *Are you happy with the position of this?* Encourage pupils to identify that it is incorrectly placed and point out where it should be. Ask individual pupils to place the remaining tenths along the counting stick.
- Using the counting stick labelled in tenths, ask the whole class to count forwards in tenths from 0 to 1. Repeat the process, but count backwards this time. Remove a few fraction cards and repeat the process. Remove further fraction cards and repeat the process again. Remove all the cards apart from 0 and 1 and repeat the process one more time.
- Reconstruct the counting stick with the tenths labels. Ask: *If I started at zero and counted on two tenths, where would I land?* Ask pupils to record responses on mini whiteboards. Point (dynamically for effect) one jump of a tenth and then a second jump of a tenth and identify that we land on $\frac{2}{10}$.
- Ask: *Where would we land if we jumped on two more tenths?* Ask pupils to record responses on mini whiteboards. Indicate one jump of a tenth and then a second jump of a tenth and identify that we land on $\frac{4}{10}$. Repeat as appropriate.
- Say: *Now we will explore counting backwards on our tenths number line.* Ask: *If I started at $\frac{9}{10}$ and counted back two tenths, where would I land?* Ask pupils to record responses on mini whiteboards. Point dynamically for effect one jump back of a tenth and then a second jump back of a tenth and identify that we land on $\frac{7}{10}$.
- Ask: *Where would we land if we jumped back two more tenths?* Ask pupils to record responses on mini whiteboards. Indicate one jump back of a tenth and then a second jump back of a tenth and identify that we land on $\frac{5}{10}$. Repeat as appropriate.
- Take pupils to the playground. Provide pairs of pupils with chalk and ask them to construct a number line from 0 to 1 and label it in tenths. Pupils then take it in turns to

'instruct' their partner which fraction to stand on and how many jumps to move up or down the number line. Partners check their jumps for accuracy. Swap roles. If this isn't possible, pupils can construct a large number line in pairs using one sheet of paper per tenth, and complete the activity inside the classroom.

- Pupils should complete Question 3 in the Practice Book.

## Same-day intervention

- Present pupils with the following sequence: $\frac{4}{10}$, $\frac{5}{10}$, $\frac{6}{10}$, $\frac{7}{10}$, $\frac{9}{10}$. Ask: *What is the mistake? Can you explain why? What is the correct sequence?*
- Present a second sequence: 1, $\frac{8}{10}$, $\frac{6}{10}$, $\frac{4}{10}$, $\frac{3}{10}$. Ask: *What is the mistake? Can you explain why? What is the correct sequence?* Repeat with different sequences as appropriate.

## Same-day enrichment

- Say: *Visualise a number line divided into tenths. If I made two equal-size jumps and landed on $\frac{9}{10}$, what size could the jumps have been? Where could I have started?* Ask pupils to find all the possibilities.

# Question 4

**4** Mum divided a cake into 10 equal pieces for 4 children to share. Express the amount of cake each child was given in tenths.

(a) Joe took 1 piece. The amount is ☐ of the cake.

(b) Jenna took 3 pieces. The amount is ☐ of the cake.

(c) Meera took 2 pieces. The amount is ☐ of the cake.

(d) Theo took 4 pieces. The amount is ☐ of the cake.

(e) Write your fractions from (a) to (d) in order, from the least to the greatest.

☐ ☐ ☐ ☐

## What learning will pupils have achieved at the conclusion of Question 4?

- Pupils will understand that tenths arise from dividing an object into 10 equal parts.
- Pupils will have solved problems involving dividing an object into 10 equal parts.

## Activities for whole-class instruction

- Explain that pupils are going to explore sharing a pizza. A pizza has already been sliced into 10 equal pieces.

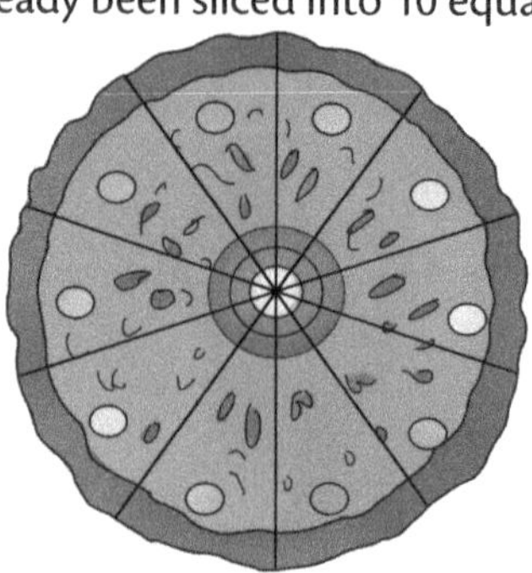

- Ask: *What fraction of the whole pizza is each slice worth?* Identify that each slice is worth $\frac{1}{10}$. Ask: *What fraction of the whole pizza is two slices worth?* Identify that two slices are worth $\frac{2}{10}$.
- Provide pairs of pupils with paper circles divided into 10 equal parts. Ask them to explore how the slices could be shared between three people. Agree that it will not be possible to divide 10 slices into 3 equal parts – each person will not get the same number of tenths (without cutting one of the slices).
- Encourage pupils to cut the circles into segments to support their problem solving if necessary. Ask: *Can you find five different ways to share out the pizza so that everyone gets at least one slice?*
- Ask: *If one person had four slices, what fraction of the whole pizza did they eat? What about if they had five slices? What fraction of the whole did they eat?*
- Pupils should complete Question 4 in the Practice Book.

## Same-day intervention

- Pupils consider sharing 10 slices of pizza between four people.
- Introduce the following table to pupils:

| Person 1 | | Person 2 | | Person 3 | | Person 4 | |
|---|---|---|---|---|---|---|---|
| Slices | Tenths | Slices | Tenths | Slices | Tenths | Slices | Tenths |
| 1 | $\frac{1}{10}$ | 1 | $\frac{1}{10}$ | 1 | $\frac{1}{10}$ | 7 | $\frac{7}{10}$ |
| 1 | $\frac{1}{10}$ | 1 | $\frac{1}{10}$ | 2 | $\frac{2}{10}$ | | |
| 1 | $\frac{1}{10}$ | | | 2 | $\frac{2}{10}$ | 3 | $\frac{3}{10}$ |
| 1 | $\frac{1}{10}$ | 5 | $\frac{5}{10}$ | | | 2 | $\frac{2}{10}$ |
| | | | | | | | |

- Ask pupils to fill in the gaps in the table, explaining their reasoning. The first row is already completed. Use the words 'slices' and tenths' interchangeably. Use the circular image divided into tenths to support explanations. Ask pupils to now add their own row to the table. Ask: *How else could the pizza be shared between four people?*

## Challenge and extension question

## Question 5

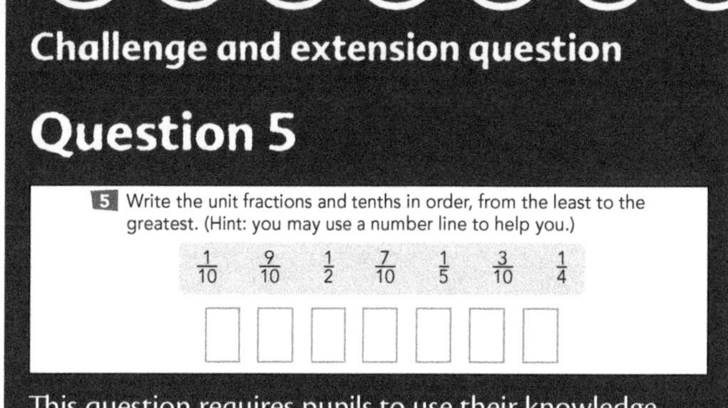
5 Write the unit fractions and tenths in order, from the least to the greatest. (Hint: you may use a number line to help you.)

$\frac{1}{10}$ $\frac{9}{10}$ $\frac{1}{2}$ $\frac{7}{10}$ $\frac{1}{5}$ $\frac{3}{10}$ $\frac{1}{4}$

This question requires pupils to use their knowledge and understanding of unit fractions and tenths to order fractions from least to greatest.

## Same-day enrichment

- Pupils consider sharing 10 slices of pizza between four people. Say: *Person 1 gets twice as much as person 2. Person 3 gets twice as much as person 1. Person 4 eats the rest. What fraction of the whole pizza does each person get? Show this as a bar model.*
- Pupils should complete the table. The first row is already completed.

| Person 1 | | Person 2 | | Person 3 | | Person 4 | |
|---|---|---|---|---|---|---|---|
| Slices | Tenths | Slices | Tenths | Slices | Tenths | Slices | Tenths |
| 1 | $\frac{1}{10}$ | 1 | $\frac{1}{10}$ | 1 | $\frac{1}{10}$ | 7 | $\frac{7}{10}$ |
| 1 | $\frac{1}{10}$ | 1 | $\frac{1}{10}$ | 2 | $\frac{2}{10}$ | | |
| 1 | $\frac{1}{10}$ | | | 2 | $\frac{2}{10}$ | 3 | $\frac{3}{10}$ |
| 1 | $\frac{1}{10}$ | 5 | $\frac{5}{10}$ | | | 2 | $\frac{2}{10}$ |
| | | | | | | | |

- Pupils should show Rows 2, 3 and 4 as three different bar models.

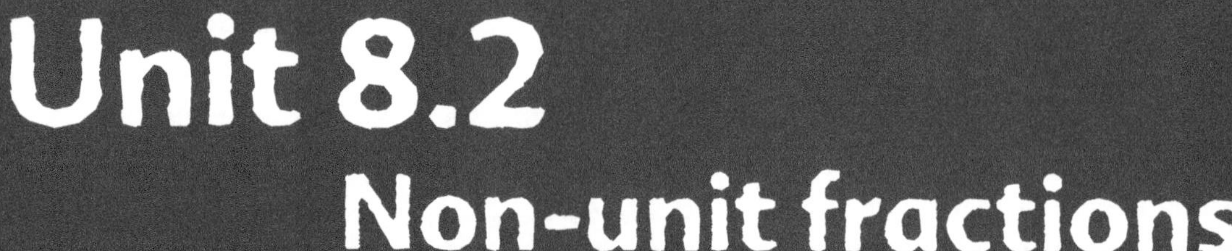

# Unit 8.2 Non-unit fractions

## Conceptual context

In this unit, pupils will become increasingly aware of the role of the numerator as they are introduced to non-unit fractions, and will use this knowledge to help them identify and represent fractions of a whole and fractions of quantities.

When finding fractions of shapes, pupils' attention will be drawn to noticing equivalent parts; this is a precursor to the work they will do on equivalent fractions in the next unit.

Pupils will continue to use arrays to support their work on fractions; this will enable them to see how their knowledge of multiplication facts can support them when calculating fractions of quantities.

Pupils' awareness of fractions as numbers will continue to be broadened as they order fractions with the same denominator; this will be further developed in the next unit.

## Learning pupils will have achieved at the end of the unit

- Pupils will understand how to find fractions of a discrete set of objects for both unit fractions and non-unit fractions (Q1, Q4)
- Pupils will understand the difference between unit and non-unit fractions (Q1)
- Understanding of non-unit fractions of shapes will have been developed (Q2, Q3)
- Pupils will have used diagrams to interpret and show equivalent fractions with small denominators (Q2, Q3)
- Pupils will understand how to order fractions with the same denominator (Q5)

### Resources

picture of an ice-cream sundae (see Question 1); counters in four different colours; mini whiteboards; scissors; copies of fraction images (see Question 2); paper circles; copies of fraction images (see Question 3); paper equilateral triangles; paper regular hexagons; 1-litre bottle of juice; plastic jugs which measure 1 litre; plastic cups; large sugar paper; 0–12 number cards; $\frac{0}{5}$–$\frac{5}{5}$ fraction cards; 2 by 3 paper rectangles; washing line; **Resource 3.8.2a** Animal arrays; **Resource 3.8.2b** Shaded shapes 1; **Resource 3.8.2c** Shaded shapes 2; **Resource 3.8.2d** Odd shape out; **Resource 3.8.2e** Sorting images; **Resource 3.8.2f** Ordering images

### Vocabulary

unit fractions, non-unit fractions, numerator, denominator

# Question 1

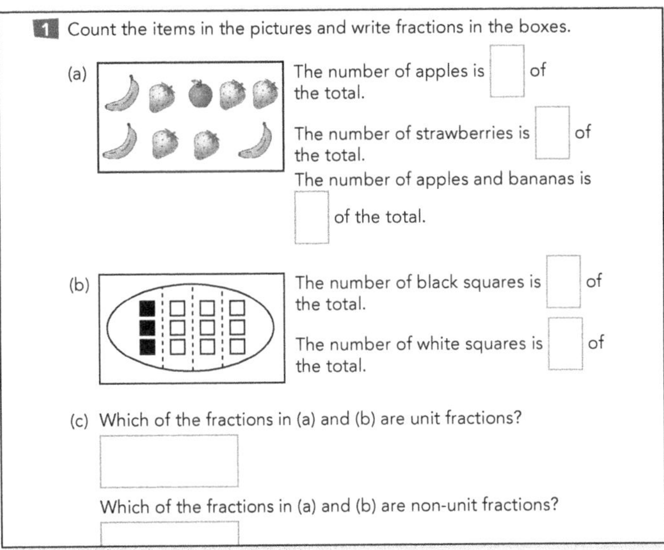

**1** Count the items in the pictures and write fractions in the boxes.

(a) The number of apples is ☐ of the total.

The number of strawberries is ☐ of the total.

The number of apples and bananas is ☐ of the total.

(b) The number of black squares is ☐ of the total.

The number of white squares is ☐ of the total.

(c) Which of the fractions in (a) and (b) are unit fractions?

☐

Which of the fractions in (a) and (b) are non-unit fractions?

☐

## What learning will pupils have achieved at the conclusion of Question 1?

- Pupils will understand how to find fractions of a discrete set of objects for both unit fractions and non-unit fractions.
- Pupils will understand the difference between unit and non-unit fractions.

## Activities for whole-class instruction

- Ask: *Who has eaten an ice-cream sundae before? What is an ice-cream sundae?* Establish that ice-cream sundaes often have a combination of ice-cream flavours. Share a visual representation of an ice-cream sundae, for example:

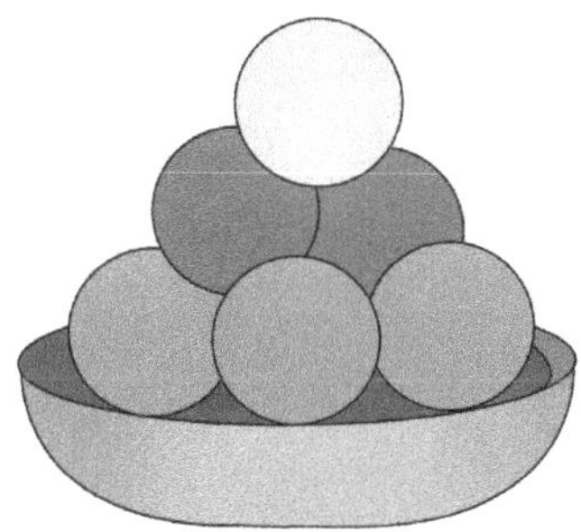

- Establish that this ice-cream sundae has six scoops of ice-cream and that three scoops are strawberry, two scoops are chocolate and one scoop is vanilla. Ask: *What fraction of the total amount of ice-cream is vanilla?* Identify that there are six scoops and that one of those scoops is vanilla, therefore, vanilla is $\frac{1}{6}$ of the total amount of ice-cream.
- Ask: *What fraction of the total amount of ice-cream is chocolate?* Identify that there are six scoops and that two of those scoops are chocolate, therefore, chocolate is $\frac{2}{6}$ of the total amount of ice-cream. Ask: *What fraction of the total amount of ice-cream is strawberry?* Identify that there are six scoops and that three of those scoops are strawberry, therefore, strawberry is $\frac{3}{6}$ of the total amount of ice-cream.
- Ask: *How could we rearrange the scoops into an array formation to help us identify what fraction of the whole each flavour is?* Share the following images with the class.

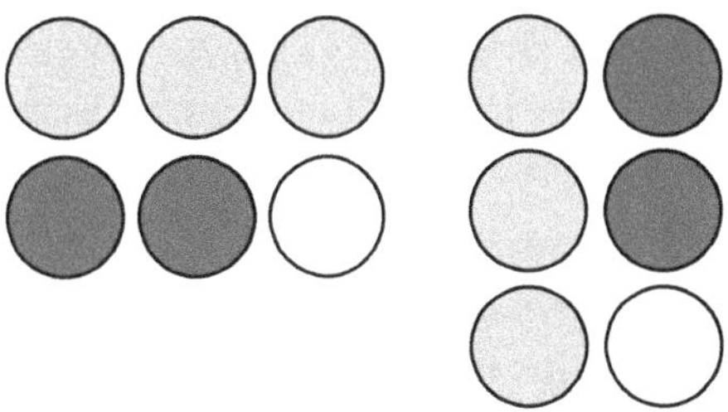

- Using the above images, ask pupils to convince you why $\frac{3}{6}$ of the sundae is strawberry. Take responses. Ask: *Can anyone see another fraction which will identify how much of the sundae is made up of strawberry flavour ice-cream?* Identify that 1 out of 2 rows are strawberry, therefore $\frac{1}{2}$ of the whole is strawberry. Ask: *Can we see the half on the second image? Explain to a partner where it is.* Ask: *How could we rearrange the coloured circles to make it easier to identify that $\frac{2}{6}$ are chocolate?*

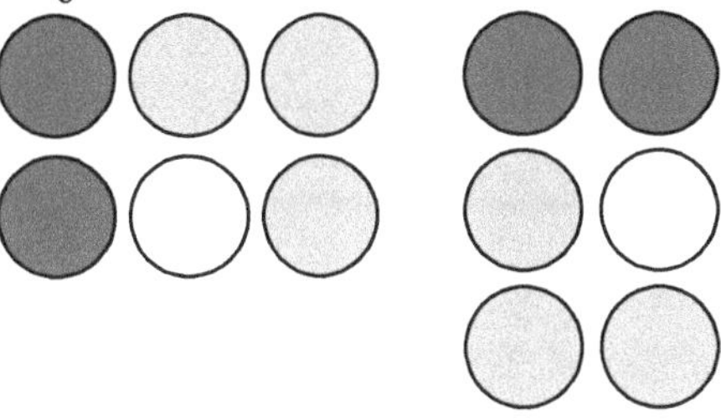

- Using the first image above, ask pupils to consider another fraction that will identify how much of the sundae is made up of chocolate ice-cream. Establish that 1 out of 3 columns are chocolate, therefore $\frac{1}{3}$ is chocolate. Ask: *Can we see the $\frac{1}{3}$ in the second image? Explain to a partner where it is.*
- Ask pupils to work in pairs to design their own ice-cream sundae. Ask pupils to think about how many scoops of ice-cream it will have, what flavours it will include and what it will be called. Once pupils have designed their ice-cream sundae, ask them to record what fraction of the total amount of ice-cream each flavour represents. Ask pupils to share their design with another pair and talk through the fractional amounts. Ask: *Does the other pair agree with the fractional amounts? If not, why not? Have they included $\frac{1}{5}$s, $\frac{1}{3}$s and halves?* (If so, they are demonstrating mastery.)

... pupils who record the numerator and the denominator the wrong way round.

- Present pupils with an image of a group of counters, similar to the one below.

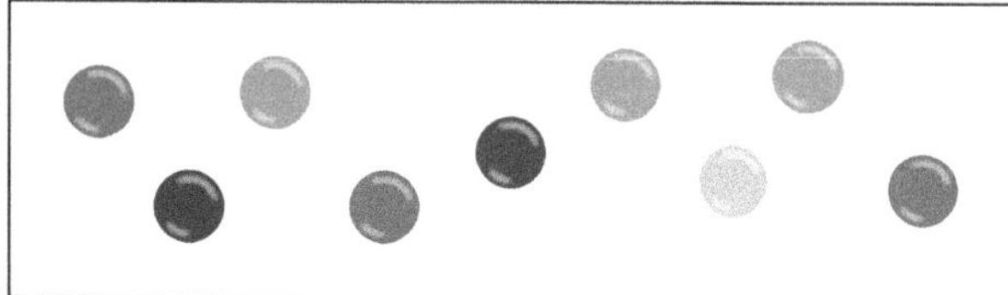

Ensure that your image shows a selection of four different-coloured counters arranged randomly, for example three red, three green, two blue and one yellow.

- On mini whiteboards ask pupils to record the total number of counters which are: red, yellow, green and blue. Ask pupils to record how many counters there are altogether. Ask: *What fraction of the total number of counters is red or yellow?* Identify that 4 out of 9 counters are red or yellow, therefore, 4/9 of the total number of counters are red or yellow. Ask: *What fraction of the total number of counters are green or blue?* Identify that five out of nine counters are green or blue, therefore, 5/9 of the total number of counters are green or blue. Ask pupils to work with a partner to take turns asking and answering further fractional questions involving two colours relating to the nine counters. Share findings with the whole class. Ask: *Can anyone ask a question which explores what fraction of the total three colours are?* Share responses.
- Using the image of the counters above, identify which colours are represented by a unit fraction and which are represented by a non-unit fraction. Take responses, drawing out the fact that unit fractions identify one part of the whole and that this is symbolically represented by a fraction which has a numerator of 1.
- Put two headings on the board: 'Unit fractions' and 'Non-unit fractions'. Ask individual pupils to come to the board and write a fraction in the correct position under either of the headings. Ask the class: *Do you agree? Why/why not?* Ask different pupils to add further fractions under the two headings. Ask the class to check the positions are correct. Add further fractions and position one 'incorrectly'. Encourage pupils to identify this error and justify why it is in the wrong position. Correct the position of the fraction so it is under the right heading.
- Ask pupils to work in pairs to agree responses to the following questions:
  - What are unit fractions?
  - What are non-unit fractions?

Share responses and establish that a unit fraction is a fraction where one 'unit' or part of the whole has been selected. This is represented by a fraction which has a numerator of 1. Non-unit fractions are fractions where more than one 'unit' or part of the whole has been selected. This is represented by a fraction that has a numerator greater than 1.

- Provide pairs of pupils with counters of four different colours. Ask Pupil A to take a small handful of counters. Pupil B then identifies what fraction of the handful are red. Pupil A finds what fraction of the whole a second colour is. Check that pupils understand how to find what the denominator should be in their fraction. Pupils take it in turns to identify what fraction of the whole each colour is, ensuring their partner agrees each time. Repeat with another pile of counters as necessary.

Look out for ... pupils who record the fraction as a ratio because they compare one colour with the other three colours rather than comparing one colour with the total number of counters.

- Pupils should complete Question 1 in the Practice Book.

## Same-day intervention

- Provide pupils with a copy of **Resource 3.8.2a** Animal arrays.

Resource 3.8.2a

Animal arrays

- Ask pupils to cut up the sheet so they have 20 cards with pictures of animals. Working with a partner, ask pupils to arrange the 20 cards in arrays which will help them to identify what fraction of the 20 cards is represented by each animal. Ask: *What fraction of the total number of cards are fish? What about dogs? Which animal is shown on half of all the cards? What about rabbits?* Organise the cards into different arrays to support recognition of the different fractions.

## Same-day enrichment

- Ask pupils to write down their first name. Ask: *What fraction of your first name is made up of vowels? What fraction of your first name is made up of consonants?* Check responses. Ask: *Can you think of a name which is made up of $\frac{2}{5}$ vowels? What about one that is made up of $\frac{1}{2}$ consonants? What fractions of vowels and consonants are the names of children in the class/group?*

# Question 2

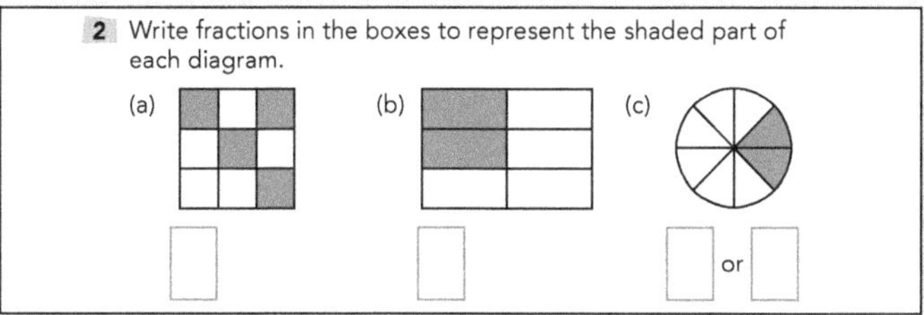
**2** Write fractions in the boxes to represent the shaded part of each diagram.

(a) (b) (c)

or

## What learning will pupils have achieved at the conclusion of Question 2?

- Understanding of non-unit fractions of shapes will have been developed.
- Pupils will use diagrams to interpret and show equivalent fractions with small denominators.

## Activities for whole-class instruction

- Provide pupils with a copy of **Resource 3.8.2b** Shaded shapes 1.

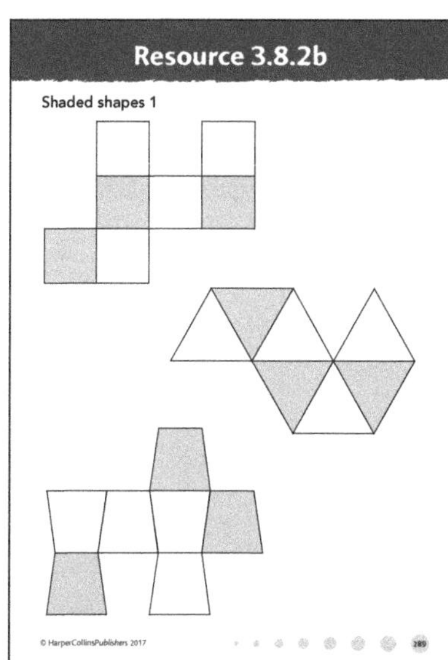


- Ask: *What is the same and what is different about the three images?* Give pupils time to talk with their partner to establish what is the same and what is different. Take responses. Identify that each image is made up of seven identical shapes and that three of the shapes are shaded. Identify that the shapes and configuration are different in each of the images. Establish that even though these three images look quite different, they all represent $\frac{3}{7}$ because the whole has been divided into seven equal parts, and three of these parts have been identified. On mini whiteboards, ask pupils to sketch a further image of a shape which represents $\frac{3}{7}$. Compare pupils' different responses.

... pupils who do not draw a shape split into seven equal parts.

- Give pupils **Resource 3.8.2c** Shaded shapes 2.

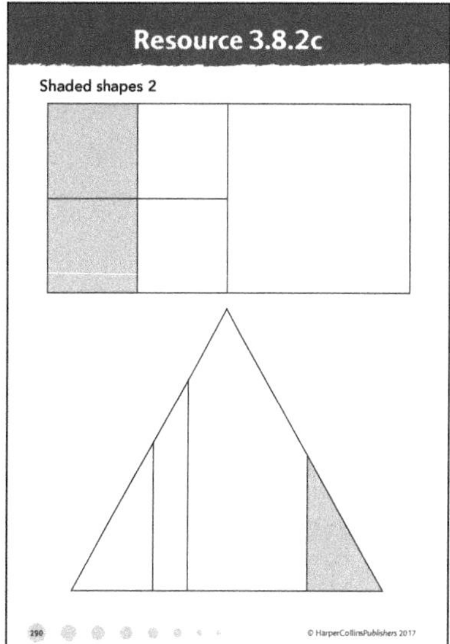


- Focus on the first image:

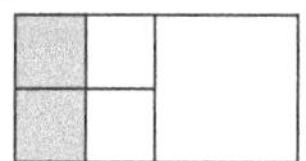

- Explain that some people may think that $\frac{2}{5}$ of this shape is shaded. Ask: *Can you explain why this mistake may occur? How would you help someone to understand what fraction of the whole is actually shaded?* Pupils should draw on, fold or cut the first image on **Resource 3.8.2c** to support their explanations.
- Ask them to work in pairs to rehearse their responses before sharing with the rest of the class. Ask: *Who thinks $\frac{2}{8}$ are shaded? Why? Who thinks $\frac{1}{4}$ is shaded? Are they both correct? How do you know?* Annotate the diagram to help pupils to see that both responses represent the same value.
- Ask pupils to look at the second image on **Resource 3.8.2c**:

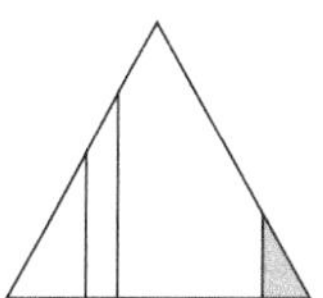

- Ask: *Is $\frac{1}{4}$ of this shape shaded?* Pupils should fold, cut or draw on the second image on **Resource 3.8.2c** to support their explorations.
- Ask pupils to work in pairs to rehearse their responses before sharing with the rest of the class. Agree that the shaded part does not represent $\frac{1}{4}$ because the one part cannot be replicated four times in the whole shape to exactly fill the space.

When identifying a fraction of a shape that has been split into different-sized parts, pupils need to understand that counting those parts does not always help them to know the denominator of the fraction. In some cases, it will be possible to show that the one part they have can be replicated through the whole shape to exactly fill the space, but in other cases, multiples of the part do not fill the space exactly so that part is not a fraction of the whole.

- Pupils should complete Question 2 in the Practice Book.

## Same-day intervention

- Provide pupils with a sheet of A4 paper. Ask them to work in pairs and ask Pupil A to fold the paper in half and label each part. Ask Pupil B to fold the paper into quarters and label each part. Ask them to cut their paper into either halves or quarters respectively. Explain that you would like them to swap a part or parts of their whole with their partner so that the whole remains the same but that the parts will no longer all be the same size. Each pupil should end up with $\frac{1}{4}$, $\frac{1}{4}$ and $\frac{1}{2}$. Ask pupils to hold up $\frac{1}{4}$. Then ask: *What about $\frac{2}{4}$? What would $\frac{3}{4}$ look like?*
- Now ask pupils to take a third sheet of A4 paper, fold and then cut it into eighths. They label each part. Ask: *What part of your rectangle could you swap for eighths that will cover exactly the same space?* Explore different responses.

## Same-day enrichment

- Introduce the following image.

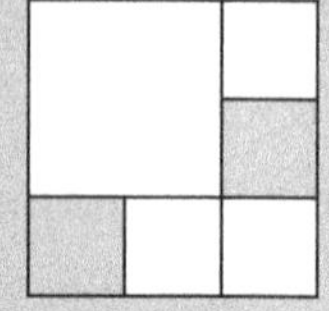

- Ask: *What fraction of the whole is shaded? How can you convince me? What fraction of the shape is not shaded?*

# Question 3

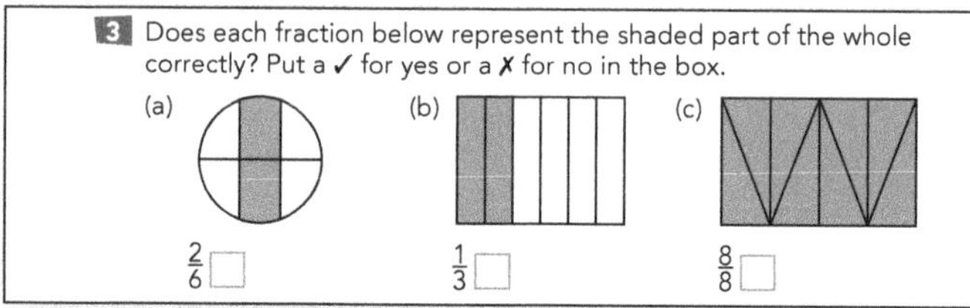

3 Does each fraction below represent the shaded part of the whole correctly? Put a ✓ for yes or a ✗ for no in the box.
(a)
(b)
(c)
2/6
1/3
8/8


## What learning will pupils have achieved at the conclusion of Question 3?

- Understanding of non-unit fractions of shapes will have been developed.
- Pupils can use diagrams to interpret and show equivalent fractions with small denominators.

## Activities for whole-class instruction

- Show pupils the following image.

- Explain that a fictional pupil thinks that $\frac{1}{3}$ of this triangle has been shaded. Ask: *Do you agree?* Give pupils time to discuss their responses. Take some feedback. Establish that the three parts are not the same size, therefore this cannot represent $\frac{1}{3}$.

Look out for ... pupils who think that just because the large triangle is split into three parts, and one of the parts are shaded, this is $\frac{1}{3}$. They do not appreciate that each part needs to be the same size.

- Give pupils **Resource 3.8.2d** Odd shape out

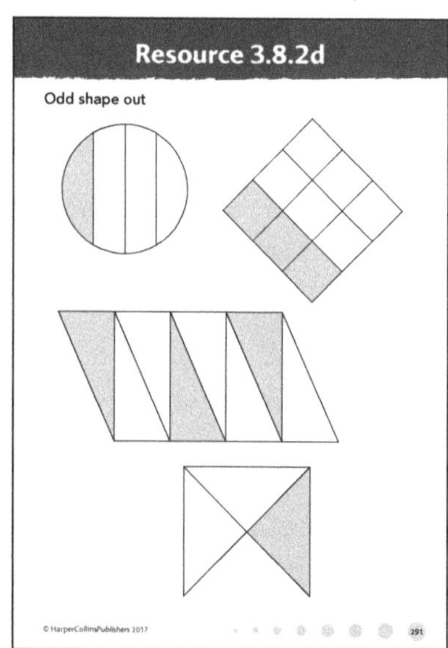

- Ask: *Which one could be the odd one out and why?* Give pupils time to work in pairs to discuss responses. Encourage pupils to notice the similarities and differences between the four shaded shapes. Take responses focusing on pupils' justifications. Ensure pupils notice that one of the above images does not represent a fractional amount because it is not split into equal parts or parts which can be made equal. Identify that it is the circle.
- Provide pupils with paper circles. Ask: *Show me what $\frac{1}{4}$ of a circle looks like.* Give pupils time to represent $\frac{1}{4}$ of a circle through folding and shading. Ask: *What is the same and what is different between your circle and the circle drawn on the board?* Identify that both are divided into four parts, but the circle on the board is not in equal parts.
- Explain that two of the images on **Resource 3.8.2d** represent $\frac{1}{3}$ of the shape being shaded. Ask: *Which two of the images on your sheet represent $\frac{1}{3}$?* Allow some discussion, then demonstrate cutting the second and fourth shape into three equal parts to prove that these images represent $\frac{1}{3}$.
- Pupils should complete Question 3 in the Practice Book.

## Same-day intervention

- Provide pupils with copies of **Resource 3.8.2e** Sorting images.

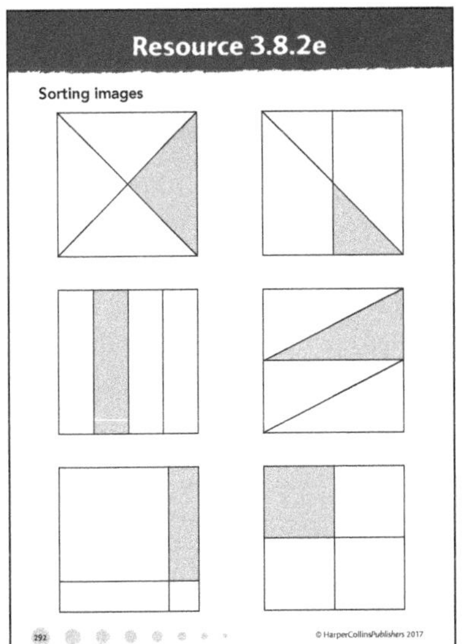


- Ask pupils to sort the images into 'those that represent $\frac{1}{4}$' and 'those that do not represent $\frac{1}{4}$'. Add a further representation to each group.

## Same-day enrichment

- Provide pupils with a paper copy of an equilateral triangle. Ask them to find $\frac{1}{4}$ of the triangle. Can they convince a partner that they have identified $\frac{1}{4}$ correctly by cutting or folding? Does the partner agree? Repeat with a regular hexagon. Ask: *Which one was easier? Why?*

# Question 4

**4** Fill in the boxes.

(a) A strip of ribbon, with a length of 1 metre, is cut into 7 equal pieces. Each strip is [ ] metres long. 4 pieces are [ ] metres long.

(b) (i) $\frac{2}{15}$ of 15 ▲ is [ ] ▲. (ii) $\frac{1}{5}$ of 15 ▲ is [ ] ▲.

(iii) $\frac{2}{5}$ of 15 ▲ is [ ] ▲. (iv) $\frac{3}{5}$ of 15 ▲ is [ ] ▲.

## What learning will pupils have achieved at the conclusion of Question 4?

- Pupils will have understood how to find fractions of a discrete set of objects for both unit fractions and non-unit fractions.

## Activities for whole-class instruction

- Tell pupils that there is a 1-litre bottle of juice which is going to be shared equally between six people. Share the juice equally between six cups. Ask: *What fraction of the whole bottle of juice is in one cup? What about two cups? Three cups?* Now ask: *What fraction of a litre is in one cup? What about two cups? Three cups?*
- Establish that $\frac{1}{6}$ of a litre is in one cup, $\frac{2}{6}$ of a litre are in two cups. Focus pupils' attention on the fact that the fractions are the same, but that first you were referring to the whole as a bottle of juice, then you were referring to the whole as 1 litre of juice. Establish that the fractions are the same because they both relate to the same whole.
- Ask pupils to work in groups of four. Provide each group with a 1-litre jug of water and a stack of cups (a different number for each group). Ask each group to share the water equally between the number of cups they have been given. On a large sheet of paper, ask each group to record what fraction of a litre will be in one cup, two cups, three cups, and so on. Pupils then present findings to the rest of the class. Ask: *Can we make any generalisations about the fractions of the whole?* Establish that the denominator was determined by the number of cups the liquid was shared between.

*The denominator tells how many parts the whole has been divided into.*

- Provide pupils with 12 counters of the same colour. Ask: *How many different ways can 12 counters be divided equally?* Give pupils time to explore before taking responses. Use arrays to illustrate that the counters can be divide into 12 groups of 1, 6 groups of 2, 4 groups of 3, 3 groups of 4, 2 groups of 6 and 1 group of 12, for example:

- Ask: *What multiplication facts can you see within these arrays?* Record the multiplication facts and corresponding division facts on the board to help remind pupils of the connections between multiplication and division. Ask: *How does our knowledge of multiplication and division facts to 12 help us to find fractions of 12?* Ensure pupils see the connection between division and finding fractions through their use of arrays.
- Ask: *If you know $\frac{1}{12}$ of 12 is 12, how do you work out $\frac{2}{12}$?* Give pupils time to discuss this before taking responses. Ask: *What about $\frac{3}{12}$?*
- Provide pupils with 0–12 number cards to enable them to show their responses. Ensure pupils use arrays to support them when answering the following questions:
  - What is $\frac{4}{12}$ of 12? What is $\frac{5}{12}$ of 12? What is $\frac{6}{12}$ of 12?
  - What is $\frac{1}{5}$ of 12? What is $\frac{2}{6}$ of 12? What is $\frac{3}{6}$ of 12?
  - What is $\frac{1}{4}$ of 12? What is $\frac{2}{4}$ of 12? What is $\frac{3}{4}$ of 12?
  - What is $\frac{1}{3}$ of 12? What is $\frac{2}{3}$ of 12?
  - What is $\frac{1}{2}$ of 12?
- Use arrays to identify correct answers and inform explanations.
- Pupils should complete Question 4 in the Practice Book.

## Same-day intervention

- Provide pupils with a stack of 20 interlocking cubes of the same colour. Ask pupils to break the stack into two equal groups.
- Ask: *What is $\frac{1}{2}$ of 20?* Ensure that pupils understand that, because we have two equal groups of 10, 10 is $\frac{1}{2}$ of 20. Ask pupils to reconstruct the stack of 20 interlocking cubes and then break the stack into four equal groups.
- Ask: *What is $\frac{1}{4}$ of 20?* Ensure that pupils understand that, because there are four equal groups of five, $\frac{1}{4}$ of 20 is five. Say: *Show me $\frac{2}{4}$ of 20.* Check that pupils hold up two stacks of five cubes. Ask: *Can you see that this is the same as $\frac{1}{2}$?* Lead pupils to noticing that there are 10 cubes in $\frac{2}{4}$, therefore $\frac{2}{4}$ is the same as $\frac{1}{2}$.
- Ask: *How many cubes are there in $\frac{3}{4}$?* Ask pupils to reconstruct the stack of 20 interlocking cubes and explore breaking it into five equal groups. Ask: *How many cubes are there in $\frac{1}{5}$? What about $\frac{2}{5}$? What about $\frac{3}{5}$?* Ensure pupils use the cubes to support their thinking.

## Same-day enrichment

- Say to pupils: *This shows $\frac{2}{5}$ of a bag of sweets.*

  *How many sweets are in the whole bag?*

# Question 5

**5** Write the numbers in order, from the least to the greatest.

(a) $\frac{1}{7}$ $\frac{5}{7}$ $\frac{6}{7}$ $\frac{4}{7}$ $\frac{2}{7}$ ☐ ☐ ☐ ☐ ☐

(b) $\frac{4}{9}$ $\frac{2}{9}$ $\frac{8}{9}$ $\frac{7}{9}$ 1 ☐ ☐ ☐ ☐ ☐

## What learning will pupils have achieved at the conclusion of Question 5?

- Pupils will understand how to order fractions with the same denominator.

## Activities for whole-class instruction

- Provide pupils with a copy of **Resource 3.8.2f** Ordering images

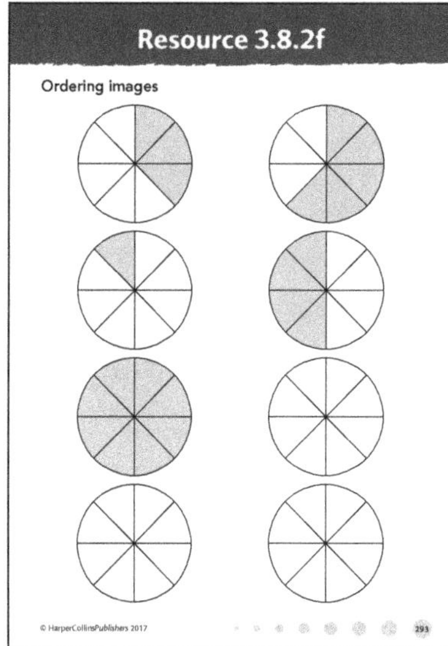


- Ask pupils to order the images, from those with the smallest part shaded to those with the largest part shaded. Ask individual pupils to label the fractional part represented by each image. Ask: *Could we add an image to represent eighths which would go between $\frac{1}{8}$ and $\frac{3}{8}$?* Establish that $\frac{2}{8}$ could be added to go between $\frac{1}{8}$ and $\frac{3}{8}$. Provide additional paper circles divided into eighths and ask a pupil to create a representation for $\frac{2}{8}$.
- Ask: *Can you think of any further representations for eighths which could also be added to this sequence?* Provide further paper circles divided into eighths. Ask pupils to create visual representations and position these correctly within the sequence.
- Provide pairs of pupils with fraction cards, $\frac{0}{5}$ to $\frac{5}{5}$, jumbled up. Ask them to sequence the fraction cards in order, starting with the least. Now ask them to sequence the fraction cards in order, starting with the greatest. Ask: *What do you notice?* Ensure pupils are aware that they reversed the order.
- Provide pupils with a set of blank digit cards. Ask them to work in pairs to write down five different fractions which have the same denominator. Ask pupils to order these, starting with the smallest. Now provide each pupil with a further blank digit card. Allow pupils to walk round the room, examining the fraction sequences created by other pairs. Ask them to select someone else's sequence and write a fraction on their blank card which could be added to the sequence.
- Pupils should complete Question 5 in the Practice Book.

## Same-day intervention

- Provide pupils with 2 by 3 paper rectangles, for example:

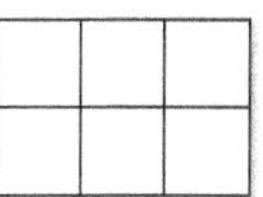

Ask one pupil to shade $\frac{1}{5}$, another to shade $\frac{2}{6}$, another to shade $\frac{3}{6}$. Repeat for $\frac{4}{6}$, $\frac{5}{6}$ and $\frac{6}{6}$. Once each fraction representation has been shaded, pupils should work together to order the rectangles along the washing line from the smallest fraction to the largest. Provide sticky labels. Ask pupils to label each fraction, using symbolic notation.

## Same-day enrichment

- Provide pupils with a fraction sequence with an error, for example,
$\frac{0}{12}, \frac{3}{12}, \frac{4}{12}, \frac{7}{12}, \frac{6}{12}, \frac{8}{12}, \frac{11}{12}, \frac{12}{12}$.
- Ask: *What is wrong with this sequence? Can you correct it?* Repeat, as appropriate.

## Challenge and extension question

# Question 6

6 Calculate and fill in the boxes. (Hint: you may draw diagrams to help you find the answers.)

(a) $\frac{2}{18}$ of 36 ▲ is ☐ ▲. (b) $\frac{2}{12}$ of 36 ▲ is ☐ ▲.

(c) $\frac{2}{9}$ of 36 ▲ is ☐ ▲. (d) $\frac{2}{6}$ of 36 ▲ is ☐ ▲.

(e) $\frac{2}{4}$ of 36 ▲ is ☐ ▲. (f) $\frac{2}{3}$ of 36 ▲ is ☐ ▲.

This question requires pupils to calculate non-unit fractions of quantities.

# Unit 8.3 Equivalent fractions

## Conceptual context

In this unit, pupils will build on their knowledge of the equivalence between halves and quarters, and will extend this to other fractions. They will draw on their understanding of the role of the numerator and denominator to compare unit fractions and fractions with the same denominator.

A variety of representations will be used to support pupils' conceptual understanding of equivalent fractions, including arrays, which are particularly helpful for communicating the relationships between multiplication, division and fractions.

Pupils' understanding of equivalent fractions will be required when they begin to compare fractions and solve calculations involving the addition and subtraction of fractions with different denominators in Book 4.

## Learning pupils will have achieved at the end of the unit

Pupils will understand that the whole is made up of the sum of all the parts and how this is represented symbolically (Q1, Q3)

Knowledge of arrays will be extended to support pupils' understanding of equivalent fractions (Q2)

Pupils will compare fractions with the same denominator and unit fractions with different denominators (Q3)

Pupils will recognise equivalent fractions with small denominators (Q4)

### Resources

strips of paper; scissors; squared paper; A4 paper; double-sided counters; mini whiteboards; 2 strips of the same-length ribbon; fraction cards labelled $\frac{1}{2}, \frac{1}{3}, \frac{1}{4}, \frac{1}{5}, \frac{1}{6}, \frac{1}{7}, \frac{1}{8}, \frac{1}{9}, \frac{1}{10}$; piece of card with > on one side and = on the other; blank cards; **Resource 3.8.3a** Matching fractions; **Resource 3.8.3b** Equivalent fractions; **Resource 3.8.3c** Fraction pairs

### Vocabulary

denominator, numerator, is equivalent to, unit fraction

# Question 1

**1** Look at the diagram and then fill in the boxes.

(a) [ | | | ]

(i) The rectangle is divided into 4 equal parts. What fraction of the rectangle does each part represent? [ ]

(ii) What fraction of the rectangle does 4 parts represent? [ ]

(iii) What whole number is this equal to? [ ]

(b) What is 6 one-sixths as a fraction? [ ]
This is equal to 1.

## What learning will pupils have achieved at the conclusion of Question 1?

- Pupils will understand that the whole is made up of the sum of all the parts and how this is represented symbolically.

## Activities for whole-class instruction

- Provide pupils with a strip of paper, one per pair. Ask them to fold the paper so that it is divided into any number of equal parts, and then open it out. Ask: *Who has divided the whole into two equal parts? Who has divided the whole into four equal parts? Who has divided the whole into a different number of equal parts?* Ask pupils to tell their partner what fraction of the whole each part represents on their strip of paper.

*The denominator tells us how many equal parts the whole has been divided into.*

- Show pupils a strip of paper that has been divided into seven equal parts, for example:

- Ask: *How many equal parts has the whole been divided into?* Agree that it is seven. Ask: *What fraction of the whole is each part?* Establish each part is $\frac{1}{7}$ because the whole has been split into seven equal parts and one part has been selected. Label each part $\frac{1}{7}$. Ask pupils to label each part on their strip of paper to show what fraction of the whole each part represents.
- Shade two parts of the whole, for example:

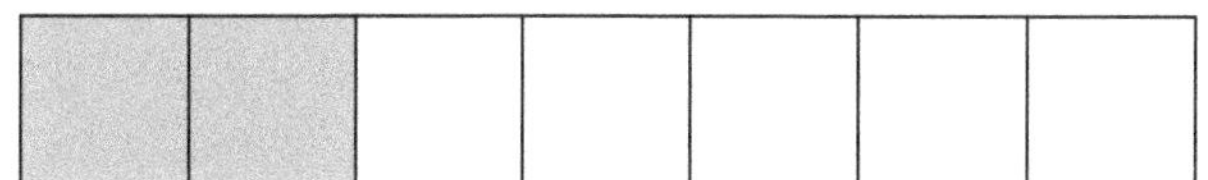

*The numerator tells us how many equal parts of the whole have been selected.*

- Ask pupils to shade two parts of the whole on their strip of paper. Say: *Can you tell your partner how many parts of the whole have been shaded? Can you tell your partner what fraction of the whole has been shaded?* If a pair have shaded $\frac{2}{2}$, draw pupils' attention to this example. Alternatively, make your own strip that has been folded in two and has both parts shaded, for example:

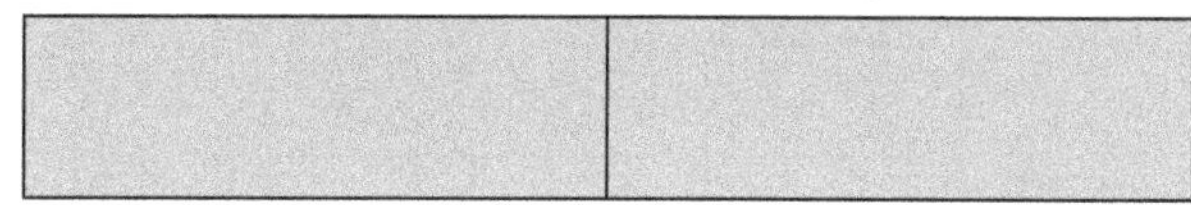

- Ask: *What fraction of the whole has been shaded?* Establish that two parts of the whole have been shaded and that this is two halves because the whole has been split into two equal parts. Record this symbolically: $\frac{2}{2}$.
- Ask pupils to shade all the parts on their strip of paper. Ask: *What fraction of the whole is shaded?* Say the fraction aloud. Pupils record the symbolic notation on their whiteboards, for example: $\frac{4}{4}$ (four quarters, not four fourths), $\frac{8}{8}$, $\frac{5}{5}$.
- Ask: *What do you notice about this group of fractions?* Encourage children to articulate that the numerator and the denominator both have the same value in all of the fractions. Ask: *Can anyone explain why the numerator and the denominator have the same value?* Agree that all of the parts of the whole have been selected, therefore the numerator and the denominator are the same.
- Explain that when all parts of the whole are selected, this is equivalent to one whole, or we can say it is equivalent to one. Record this symbolically on the board next to each fraction, for example: $\frac{4}{4} = 1$, $\frac{8}{8} = 1$, $\frac{5}{5} = 1$.

*When all parts of the whole have been selected, this is equivalent to one.*

- Pupils should complete Question 1 in the Practice Book.

## Same-day intervention

- Provide pairs of pupils with a copy of **Resource 3.8.3a** Matching fractions.

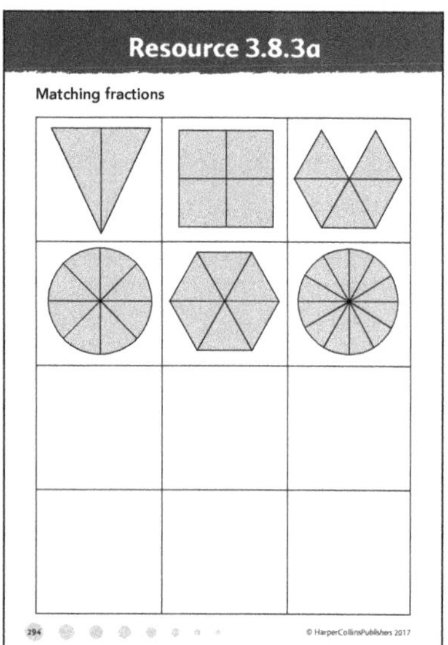


- On the blank cards, ask pupils to record a fraction which represents each of the shaded shapes, one fraction per card. Cut the cards up and turn them face down on the table. Play 'Equivalent pairs'.

## Same-day enrichment

- Say to pupils: *Sophie says '$\frac{8}{8}$ of a shape has been shaded'.* Ask: *What could the shape look like?* Provide pupils with squared paper and ask them to explore possible solutions.

# Question 2

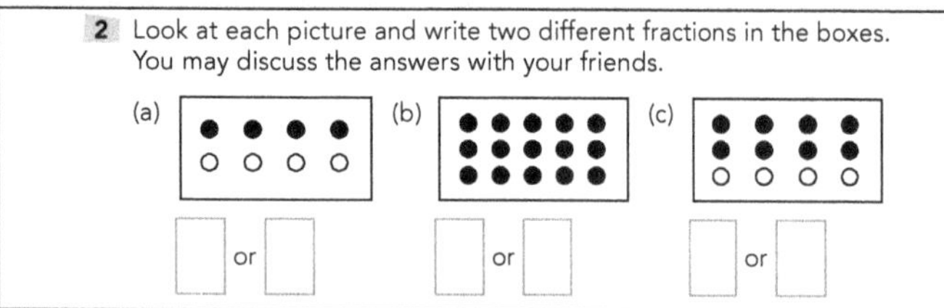

2 Look at each picture and write two different fractions in the boxes.
You may discuss the answers with your friends.
(a)
(b)
(c)
or
or
or


## What learning will pupils have achieved at the conclusion of Question 2?

- Knowledge of arrays will have been extended to support pupils' understanding of equivalent fractions.

## Activities for whole-class instruction

- Provide pupils with an A4 sheet of paper, one per pair. Ask them to fold it into two equal parts. Ask: *What fraction of the whole is each part?* Establish that they are halves. Ask the pupils to label one half $\frac{1}{2}$.
- Now ask them to fold the same piece of paper into four equal parts. Ask: *What fraction of the whole is each part now?* Agree that each of the four parts shown by the folded lines is $\frac{1}{4}$. Ask pupils to label $\frac{1}{4}$ and $\frac{1}{4}$ in the unlabelled parts, for example:

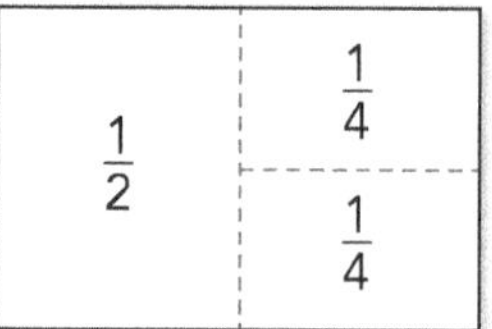


Write the following statement on the board: $\frac{1}{2} = \frac{?}{4}$. Ask: *What is the missing number?* Agree that $\frac{1}{2} = \frac{2}{4}$ because $\frac{1}{4}$ and $\frac{1}{4}$ cover the same amount of space as $\frac{1}{2}$. Prove this by cutting or folding.

- Provide pupils with a second sheet of paper. Ask them to fold it into four equal parts. Ask them to label two of the quarters $\frac{1}{4}$ and $\frac{1}{4}$. Now ask them to fold the same piece of paper into eight equal parts. Ask: *What fraction of the whole is each part now?* Establish that each of the eight parts is one-eighth of the whole. Ask pupils to label $\frac{1}{8}, \frac{1}{8}, \frac{1}{8}$ and $\frac{1}{8}$ in the unlabelled parts, for example:

| $\frac{1}{4}$ | $\frac{1}{8}$ | $\frac{1}{8}$ |
|---|---|---|
| $\frac{1}{4}$ | $\frac{1}{8}$ | $\frac{1}{8}$ |

- Write the following statement on the board: $\frac{1}{4} = \frac{?}{8}$. Ask: *What is the missing number?* Take responses from the class and agree that $\frac{1}{4} = \frac{2}{8}$ because $\frac{1}{8}$ and $\frac{1}{8}$ cover the same area as $\frac{1}{4}$. Prove this by cutting or folding.
- Write $\frac{2}{4} = \frac{?}{8}$ on the board. Ask: *What is the missing number?* Take responses and agree that $\frac{2}{4} = \frac{4}{8}$ because $\frac{2}{4}$ covers the same area as $\frac{4}{8}$. Prove this by folding or cutting.
- Using double-sided counters, arrange six counters in a 2 by 3 array and tell pupils that this is the whole. Draw a box around the whole array.
- Turn one counter over.

- Ask: *What fraction of the whole group is red?* Establish that the red counter represents $\frac{1}{6}$ because the whole is a group

of six counters, so one counter is what you get when the group is divided into six equal parts – one counter is one-sixth of the whole. Draw a circle round the one red counter.

- Turn two counters over.

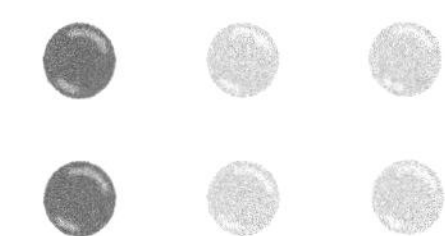

- Ask: *What fraction of the whole is red?* Establish that the red counters represent $\frac{2}{6}$ of the whole because the whole is a group of six counters. One counter is what you get when the group is divided into six equal parts and two of them are red, so two red counters is $\frac{2}{6}$.
- Say: *We can see that the whole is set out in three columns.* Draw a circle round the two red counters. Ask: *So what fraction is each column of the whole?* Agree $\frac{1}{3}$. Ask pupils if they can see that $\frac{2}{6}$ is the same as $\frac{1}{3}$. Record $\frac{2}{6} = \frac{1}{3}$ on the board.

*When two fractions represent the same amount, they are equivalent.*

- Using the same 6 counters show the following array in a box.

- Say: *We can think of this array as 2 rows of 3. There are 2 rows of 3 in the array. What fraction of the whole is each row?* Establish that $\frac{3}{6}$ and $\frac{1}{2}$ represent the same quantity, therefore, they are equivalent. Record $\frac{3}{6} = \frac{1}{2}$ on the board.

Pupils have already used arrays to support their work on multiplication and division. This knowledge will support their work on fractions, and through counters in arrays, pupils will see the relationships between multiplication, division and fractions.

- Provide pairs of pupils with 12 double-sided counters and ask them to arrange them in a 2 by 6 array formation with the yellow side facing up, for example:

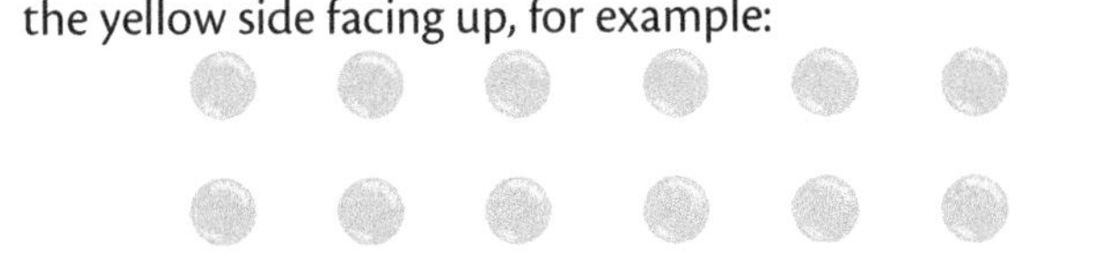

- Turn two counters over. Say: *We can see that the whole is set out in six columns.* Draw a circle round the two red counters. Ask: *So what fraction is each column of the whole?* Agree $\frac{1}{5}$. Ask pupils if they can see that $\frac{2}{12}$ is the same as $\frac{1}{5}$. Record $\frac{2}{12} = \frac{1}{5}$ on the board.
- Turn four counters over. Say: *This is $\frac{4}{12}$ of the whole. What is this equivalent to?* Record $\frac{4}{12} = \frac{2}{6}$. Ask pupils to repeat with $\frac{6}{12}$, $\frac{8}{12}$, $\frac{10}{12}$ and $\frac{12}{12}$.
- Ask pupils to arrange the counters in a 3 by 4 formation. Turn three counters over and draw a circle round the three red counters. Ask: *What fraction is each column of the whole? We can see the whole is set out in four columns.* Agree $\frac{1}{4}$. Ask pupils if they can see that $\frac{3}{12}$ is the same as $\frac{1}{4}$. Record $\frac{3}{12} = \frac{1}{4}$ on the board.

Look out for ... pupils who think $\frac{2}{10}$ is double the size of $\frac{1}{5}$ because both the numerator and denominator are doubled.

- Pupils should complete Question 2 in the Practice Book.

## Same-day intervention

- Provide pupils with four double-sided counters. Establish that this is the whole and that you would like $\frac{1}{4}$ of the counters to be red. Ensure counters are laid out in a line, for example:
- Provide pupils with 10 double-sided counters. Establish that this is the whole and that you would like $\frac{1}{5}$ of the counters to be red. Ensure counters are laid out in 2 × 5 array, for example:

- Ask: *Can this be expressed as an equivalent fraction?* Agree that this is equivalent to $\frac{2}{10}$ if one counter represents one part of the whole. Ask pupils to record $\frac{1}{5} = \frac{2}{10}$.
- Provide pupils with 12 double-sided counters. Establish that this is the whole and that you would like $\frac{1}{4}$ of the counters to be red. Ensure counters are laid out in a 3 by 4 array, for example:

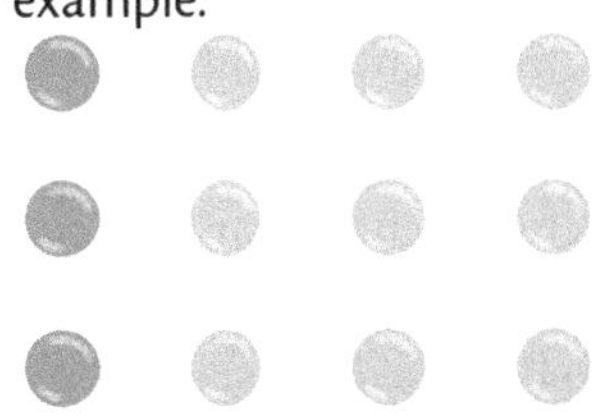

- Ask: *Can this be expressed as an equivalent fraction?* Agree that this is equivalent to $\frac{3}{12}$ if one counter represents one part of the whole. Ask pupils to record $\frac{1}{4} = \frac{2}{8} = \frac{3}{12}$.
- Repeat with 16 counters and 20 counters, if appropriate.

## Same-day enrichment

- Provide pupils with a copy of **Resource 3.8.3b** Equivalent fractions.

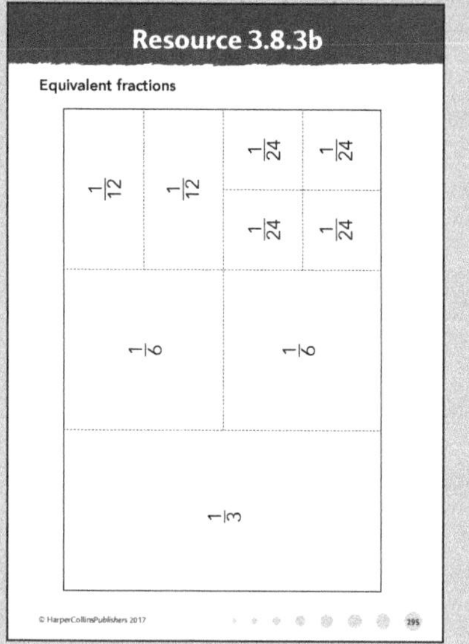
Resource 3.8.3b

Equivalent fractions

| $\frac{1}{12}$ | $\frac{1}{12}$ | $\frac{1}{24}$ | $\frac{1}{24}$ |
|---|---|---|---|
| | | $\frac{1}{24}$ | $\frac{1}{24}$ |
| $\frac{1}{6}$ | | $\frac{1}{6}$ | |
| $\frac{1}{3}$ | | | |

© HarperCollinsPublishers 2017 295

- Ask pupils how many pairs of equivalent fractions they can identify.

# Question 3

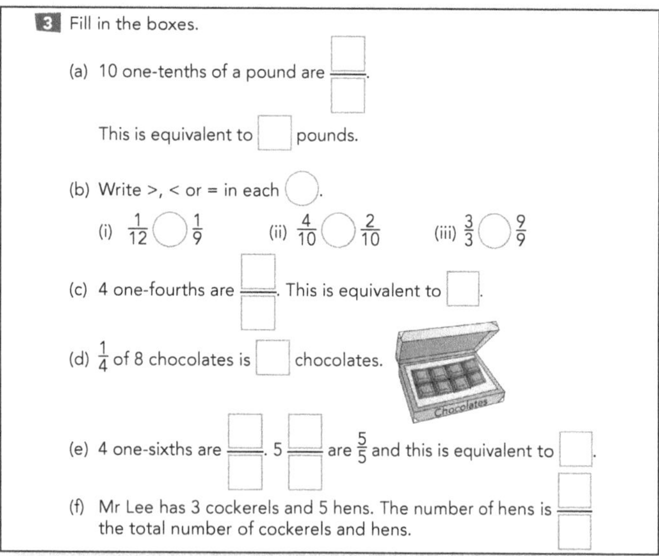
**3** Fill in the boxes.

(a) 10 one-tenths of a pound are $\frac{\square}{\square}$.

This is equivalent to ☐ pounds.

(b) Write >, < or = in each ◯.

(i) $\frac{1}{12}$ ◯ $\frac{1}{9}$ (ii) $\frac{4}{10}$ ◯ $\frac{2}{10}$ (iii) $\frac{3}{3}$ ◯ $\frac{9}{9}$

(c) 4 one-fourths are $\frac{\square}{\square}$. This is equivalent to ☐.

(d) $\frac{1}{4}$ of 8 chocolates is ☐ chocolates.



(e) 4 one-sixths are $\frac{\square}{\square}$. 5 $\frac{\square}{\square}$ are $\frac{5}{5}$ and this is equivalent to ☐.

(f) Mr Lee has 3 cockerels and 5 hens. The number of hens is $\frac{\square}{\square}$ the total number of cockerels and hens.

## What learning will pupils have achieved at the conclusion of Question 3?

- Pupils will know that where the numerator and denominator are equal, this is equivalent to a whole and be able to explain why.
- Pupils will compare fractions with the same denominator and unit fractions with different denominators.

## Activities for whole-class instruction

- Introduce the class to an image of a fraction wall, for example:

| 1 | | | | | |
|---|---|---|---|---|---|
| $\frac{1}{2}$ | | | | | |
| $\frac{1}{3}$ | | | | | |
| $\frac{1}{4}$ | | | | | |
| $\frac{1}{5}$ | | | | | |
| $\frac{1}{6}$ | | | | | |

- Provide pupils with mini whiteboards. Using the image of the fraction wall, ask pupils to record a fraction which is equivalent to one. Now ask them to record a different fraction which is equivalent to one. Agree $\frac{2}{2}, \frac{3}{3}, \frac{4}{4}, \frac{5}{5}$ and $\frac{6}{6}$ are all equivalent to one.
- Using the image of the fraction wall, ask pupils to record a fraction which is equivalent to $\frac{1}{2}$. Now record a different fraction which is equivalent to $\frac{1}{2}$. Establish both $\frac{2}{4}$ and $\frac{3}{6}$ are equivalent to $\frac{1}{2}$ by shading, cutting or overlaying.
- Ask: *Can anyone identify a fraction which is close to $\frac{1}{2}$?* Identify that $\frac{2}{5}$ is quite close to a half on the above fraction wall. Ask: *Can anyone identify two other fractions which are close to each other?*
- Shade $\frac{1}{2}, \frac{1}{3}, \frac{1}{4}, \frac{1}{5}$ and $\frac{1}{6}$. Ask: *What do you notice about the size of the fraction as the denominator gets bigger?* Establish that the larger the denominator, the smaller each part will be. Illustrate this dynamically by cutting a ribbon into four equal parts and a second strip of ribbon of the same length into eight equal parts. Compare the size of the strips from both ribbons. Identify that the greater the number of parts the whole is split into, the smaller each part will be.
- Ask pupils to complete the sentences:
  - The greater the number of parts the whole is divided into, the __________ each part will be.
  - When the denominator gets bigger, the size of the fraction gets __________.

*The greater the number of parts the whole is divided into, the smaller each part will be. When the denominator gets bigger, the size of the fraction gets smaller.*

... pupils who think $\frac{1}{6}$ is larger than $\frac{1}{3}$ because 6 is larger than 3.

- Present the following statement to pupils: $\frac{1}{?} > \frac{1}{?}$. Ask pupils to come up with suggestions to make this inequality statement correct. Record a range of responses on the board. Ask: *What do you notice about the size of the denominator on each size of the inequality?* Lead pupils to notice that the smaller fraction has a larger denominator. Ask: *Has anyone written a fraction smaller than $\frac{1}{15}$? How do you know? Who has written the smallest fraction? How do you know?*

*The greater the number of parts the whole is divided into, the smaller each part will be. When the denominator gets bigger, the size of the fraction gets smaller.*

- Present the following statement to pupils: $\frac{?}{6} < \frac{?}{6}$. Ask pupils to come up with suggestions to make this inequality statement correct. Record a range of responses on the board. Ask: *What do you notice about the size of the numerator on each size of the inequality?* Lead pupils to notice that the smaller fraction has a smaller numerator. Look back at the fraction wall to establish why this is the case. Identify that when comparing two fractions with the same denominator, the numerator identifies how many parts have been selected in each fraction.

*When comparing fractions with the same denominator, a smaller numerator means the fraction is smaller.*

- Focus children's attention on the sixths row on the fraction wall and shade two-sixths, for example:

| $\frac{1}{6}$ | $\frac{1}{6}$ | $\frac{1}{6}$ | $\frac{1}{6}$ | $\frac{1}{6}$ | $\frac{1}{6}$ |
|---|---|---|---|---|---|

- Ask: *What fraction of the whole is yellow?* Give pupils time to agree their responses with a partner. Agree $\frac{2}{6}$ are yellow. Ask: *What fraction of the whole is green?* Give pupils time to agree their responses with a partner. Agree $\frac{4}{6}$ are green.
- Ask pupils to imagine this bar represents a context. For example, yellow represents the number of girls and green represents the number of boys in a team. Ask: *What fraction of the team are girls? What fraction are boys?* Share and agree responses. Ask pupils to come up with their own context for this visual representation.
- Pupils should complete Question 3 in the Practice Book.

## Same-day intervention

- Provide pairs of pupils with a set of fraction cards labelled $\frac{1}{2}, \frac{1}{3}, \frac{1}{4}, \frac{1}{5}, \frac{1}{6}, \frac{1}{7}, \frac{1}{8}, \frac{1}{9}, \frac{1}{10}$ and a piece of card with > on one side and = on the other. Arrange all the fraction cards face down on the table. Pupils take it in turns to turn over two fraction cards and use the equality card to make a correct mathematical statement. They see if their partner agrees and then swap roles. Provide pupils with a fraction wall to support their thinking, if required.

## Same-day enrichment

- Ask: *Can you think of a fraction which is less than a quarter? Now come up with an example that you think no one else will come up with. Explain how you know the fraction is less than a quarter. Draw an image to prove it.*

# Question 4

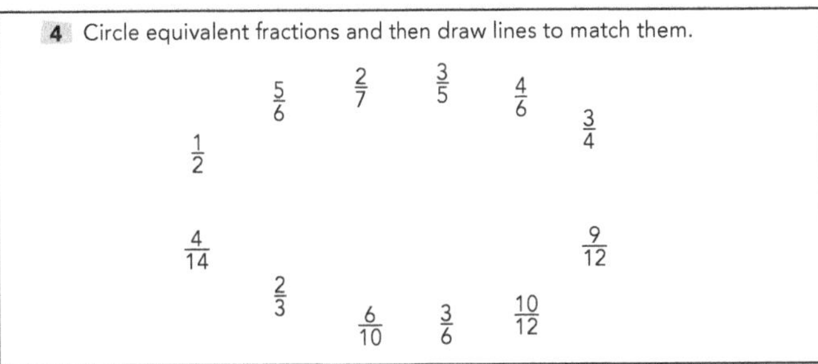


## What learning will pupils have achieved at the conclusion of Question 4?

- Pupils will have recognised equivalent fractions with small denominators.

## Activities for whole-class instruction

- Share an image of $\frac{1}{2}$ a pizza, $\frac{2}{4}$ of a pizza and $\frac{4}{8}$ of a pizza, for example:

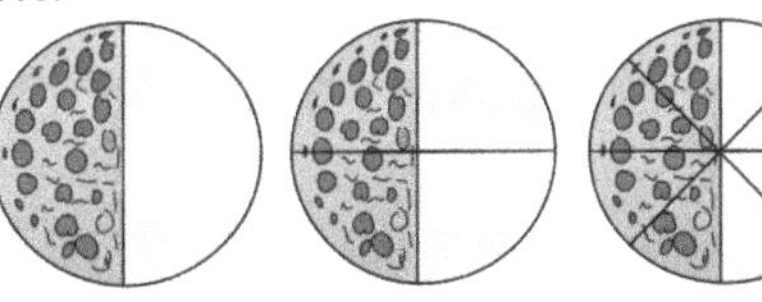

- Ask: *What is the same about these three images? What is different?* Give pupils time to discuss responses. Establish that all three images represent the same amount of pizza, but that they are cut into different-sized pieces and that there are a different number of pieces in each image. Ask: *Do we agree that the amount of pizza in all 3 images is equal?* Add an equals symbol between each of the pictures and identify that these three images are considered to be equivalent.
- Ask: *What fraction of a whole pizza does each image represent?* Give pupils time to discuss responses. Record $\frac{1}{2} = \frac{2}{4} = \frac{4}{8}$ on the board. Ask: *What do you notice about the numerator and the denominator in each fraction?* Identify that the numerator is half of the denominator / the denominator is double the numerator in each fraction. Ask for other fractions where the numerator is half the size of the denominator. List them on the board, for example $\frac{5}{10}, \frac{10}{20}$.

- Re-focus pupils' attention on $\frac{1}{2} = \frac{2}{4}$. Ask: *What do you notice about the relationship between the numerators? What do you notice about the relationships between the denominators?* Agree that the numerator in $\frac{2}{4}$ is double the numerator in $\frac{1}{2}$ and that the denominator in $\frac{2}{4}$ is double the denominator in $\frac{1}{2}$. Record this on the board, for example:

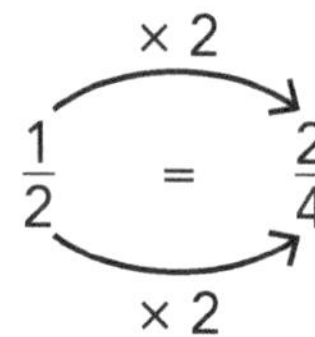


- Record $\frac{1}{2} = \frac{4}{8}$ on the board. Ask: *What is the relationship between the numerators? What is the relationship between the denominators?* Establish that the numerator in $\frac{4}{8}$ is four times the numerator in a $\frac{1}{2}$ and the denominator in $\frac{4}{8}$ is four times the denominator in a $\frac{1}{2}$. Ask pupils to work in pairs, exploring other fractions which are equivalent to $\frac{1}{2}$. Ask: *What is the numerator and the denominator being multiplied by each time?*
- Provide pairs of pupils with a copy of **Resource 3.8.3c** Fraction pairs.

**Resource 3.8.3c**

Fraction pairs

| | | | |
|---|---|---|---|
| $\frac{1}{2}$ | $\frac{6}{10}$ | $\frac{3}{4}$ | $\frac{3}{15}$ |
| $\frac{2}{3}$ | $\frac{1}{4}$ | $\frac{1}{3}$ | $\frac{1}{7}$ |
| $\frac{3}{9}$ | $\frac{8}{16}$ | $\frac{8}{8}$ | $\frac{3}{5}$ |
| $\frac{2}{14}$ | $\frac{4}{6}$ | $\frac{4}{10}$ | 1 |
| $\frac{1}{5}$ | $\frac{6}{8}$ | $\frac{3}{12}$ | $\frac{2}{5}$ |

296 © HarperCollinsPublishers 2017

- Ask them to cut up and match the fractions on the cards. Ask pupils to justify why they have paired the fractions together.

... pupils who cannot reason about equivalences even if their answer is correct.

- Pupils should complete Question 4 in the Practice Book.

## Same-day intervention

- Provide pairs with 12 blank cards and fraction walls. Ask pupils to record $\frac{1}{2}, \frac{1}{3}, \frac{1}{4}, \frac{2}{3}, \frac{2}{5}, \frac{3}{4}$ on six of the cards. Then ask pupils to write fractions which are equivalent to the fractions on the remaining six cards. Once the cards have been created, give pupils time to turn the cards face down and play 'Matching pairs'.

## Same-day enrichment

- Ask pupils to consider whether the following statements are true or false:
  - Equivalent fractions have the same value.
  - Equivalent fractions take up the same amount of space.
  - Equivalent fractions can have the same numerator.
  - Equivalent fractions can have the same denominator.
  - Equivalent fractions occupy the same position on a number line.
- Ask pupils to jusfiy each answer.

## Challenge and extension question

# Questions 5 and 6

**5** Write a fraction to represent the shaded part in each diagram.

(a) (b)

**6** Think carefully about how to answer these.

(a) If 48 bottles of water are divided into 8 equal parts, each part has ☐ bottles of water. If they are divided into 6 equal parts, each part has ☐ bottles of water.

(b) If Lily takes away $\frac{3}{8}$ of the water and Ellis takes away $\frac{2}{6}$, then __________ takes more.

(c) If Holly wants to take $\frac{1}{5}$, is it possible? Explain why/why not.

(d) What fraction of water can Holly take? Explain why.

Pupils will be required to use their understanding of equivalent fractions to identify fractions of shapes and solve problems involving fractions of quantities.

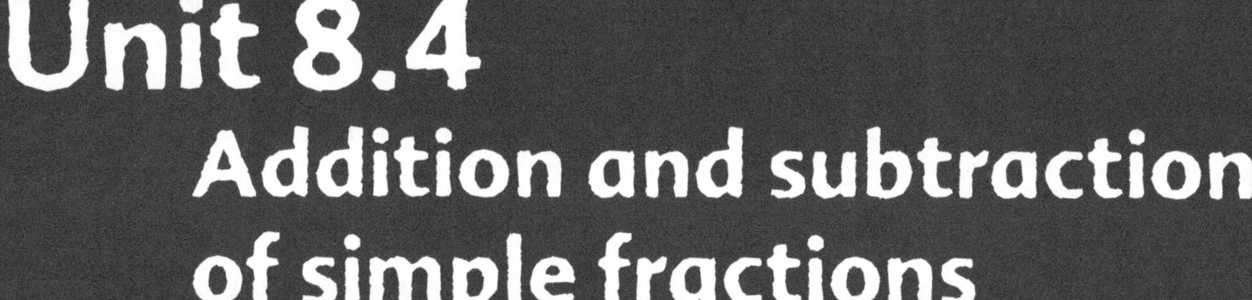

# Unit 8.4 Addition and subtraction of simple fractions

## Conceptual context

This unit will broaden pupils' understanding of the inverse relationship between addition and subtraction which was introduced in Year 1, and has since been continually developed. They will use this knowledge to identify knowns and unknowns in addition and subtraction calculations. Pupils may also draw on their knowledge of number bonds to support their calculations with fractions.

When solving addition and subtraction calculations involving fractions, pupils will apply their understanding of equivalent fractions which was developed in the previous unit.

A range of concrete and visual representations will be used to extend pupils' understanding of the addition and subtraction of fractions. These will include a variety of shapes, bar models and number lines. They will enable pupils to develop a range of visual images which will help them to solve more complex addition and subtraction fraction calculations in Book 4.

## Learning pupils will have achieved at the end of the unit

- Pupils will understand how to add fractions with the same denominator within one whole using pictorial representations to support their thinking (Q1)
- Understanding of adding and subtracting fractions with the same denominator within one whole will have been developed (Q2, Q3, Q4)
- Pupils will use their understanding of adding and subtracting fractions with the same denominator to solve contextualised problems (Q5)

### Resources

**Resource 3.8.4a** Sliced eighths; **Resource 3.8.4b** Pie sixths; **Resource 3.8.4c** Parallelograms; **Resource 3.8.4d** Total fractions; **Resource 3.8.4e** Fraction towers; **Resource 3.8.4f** Comparing twelfths; scissors; mini whiteboards; strips of paper divided into equal parts; colouring pens / pencils; interlocking cubes; counting stick; dice labelled $\frac{1}{12}$, $\frac{2}{12}$, $\frac{3}{12}$, $\frac{4}{12}$, $\frac{5}{12}$, $\frac{6}{12}$; cards labelled $\frac{0}{12}$, $\frac{1}{12}$, $\frac{2}{12}$, $\frac{3}{12}$, $\frac{4}{12}$, $\frac{5}{12}$, $\frac{6}{12}$, $\frac{7}{12}$, $\frac{8}{12}$, $\frac{9}{12}$, $\frac{10}{12}$, $\frac{11}{12}$, $\frac{12}{12}$; sweets; counters

### Vocabulary

numerator, denominator, equivalent, inverse

# Question 1

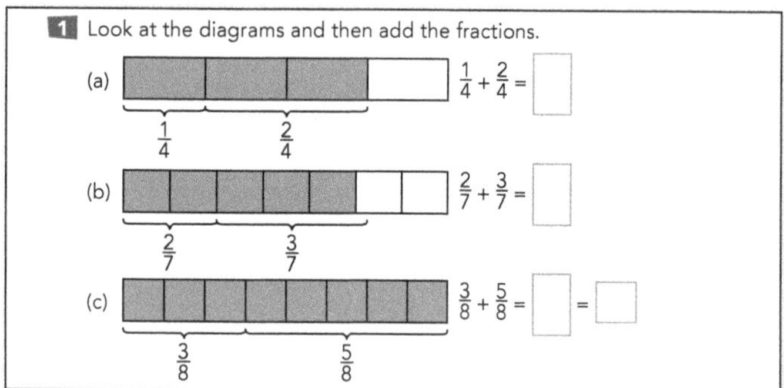

1 Look at the diagrams and then add the fractions.
(a) $\frac{1}{4}+\frac{2}{4}=$
$\frac{1}{4}$ $\frac{2}{4}$
(b) $\frac{2}{7}+\frac{3}{7}=$
$\frac{2}{7}$ $\frac{3}{7}$
(c) $\frac{3}{8}+\frac{5}{8}=$ =
$\frac{3}{8}$ $\frac{5}{8}$


## What learning will pupils have achieved at the conclusion of Question 1?

- Pupils will understand how to add fractions with the same denominator within one whole using pictorial representations to support their thinking.

## Activities for whole-class instruction

- Show pupils an image of a strawberry tart divided into eight equal parts (see **Resource 3.8.4a** Sliced eighths).

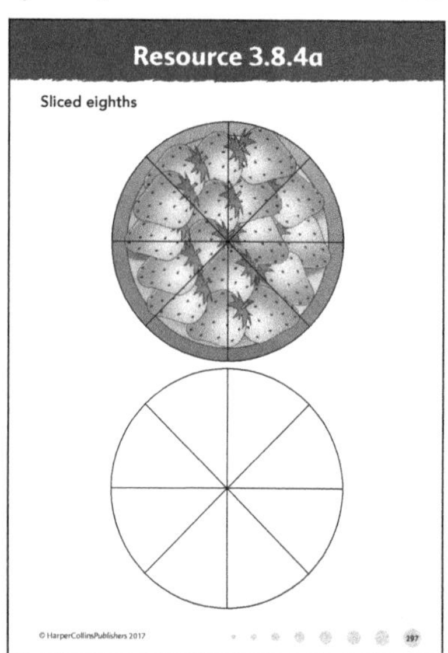


- Ask: *What fraction of the whole does each part represent?* Agree that each part represents one-eighth because the whole has been divided into eight equal parts.
- Ask: *How do we write one-eighth with numbers or symbols?* Revisit the role of the numerator and denominator if necessary. Cut the image into eighths. Ask various pupils to label each part $\frac{1}{8}$. Hold up two parts of the whole, one in each hand. Ask: *What fraction of the whole is this?* Agree that it is $\frac{2}{8}$.
- Record the number sentence on the board $\frac{1}{8}+\frac{1}{8}=\frac{2}{8}$. Ask: *What do you notice about this calculation?* Discuss that the parts you are considering are the slices and that one slice add one slice is two slices. Say: *Each slice in this case is an eighth, so when you add two together there are two-eighths.*
- Stick the two parts onto a circle the same size as the strawberry tart which has also been divided into eight equal parts (see **Resource 3.8.4a** Sliced eighths).
- Stick a third slice of strawberry tart onto the diagram. Ask: *What fraction of the whole does this represent now?* Agree this is $\frac{3}{8}$ because 3 out of the 8 parts have been stuck on. Ask pupils to record an addition number sentence on mini whiteboards which shows that three-eighths are being added together. Repeat with $\frac{4}{8}, \frac{5}{8}, \frac{6}{8}, \frac{7}{8}$ identifying equivalences as appropriate.
- Show the representation with all eighth slices added. Ask: *What fraction of the whole does this represent?* Identify that this is $\frac{8}{8}$ and that it is equivalent to one whole so we can say it is equivalent to one.

*When all parts of the whole have been selected, this is equivalent to one.*

- Show pupils a strip of paper divided into nine equal parts, for example:

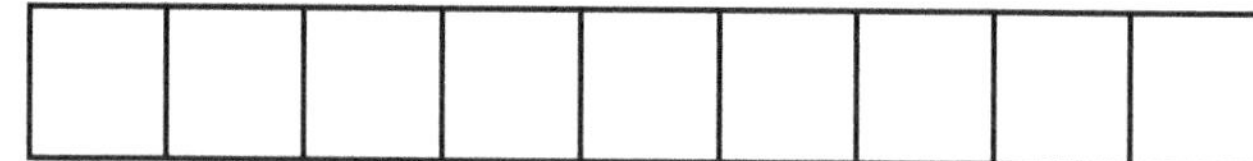

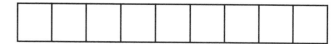

- Ask: *What fraction of the whole does each part represent?* Establish that each part represents one-ninth because the whole has been divided into nine equal parts. Select pupils to label each part of the fraction strip with $\frac{1}{9}$.
- Select a different pupil to shade any number of parts on the strip of paper. Ask: *What fraction of the whole has been shaded?* Confirm the correct response by counting in ninths the number of shaded parts.
- Using a different-coloured pen, ask a second pupil to shade any number of parts on the strip of paper that are yet to be shaded. Ask: *What fraction of the whole has the second pupil shaded?* Confirm the correct response by counting in ninths the number of shaded parts.
- Ask: *What fraction of the whole has been shaded altogether?* Confirm the correct response by counting in ninths the number of shaded parts altogether. Ask: *What addition number sentence will represent this image?* Record the answer on the board, agreeing the correct values for the numerators and denominators, for example:

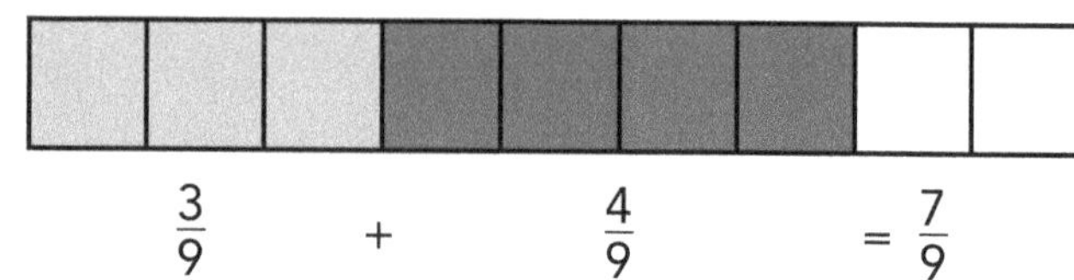

- Provide pairs of pupils with a strip of paper divided into nine equal parts. Repeat the activity in pairs, with each pupil selecting a number of parts to be shaded. Pupils work together to calculate the total number of shaded parts and record the corresponding number sentence. Repeat as appropriate.

Avoid representing the fractions to be added on separate diagrams at this stage, as it may lead to pupils misinterpreting the visual representation and identifying the incorrect denominator, for example:

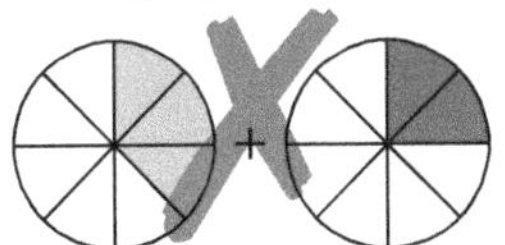

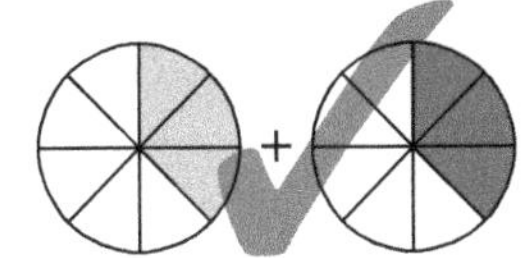

- Pupils should complete Question 1 in the Practice Book.

## Same-day intervention

- Provide pupils with a strip of paper divided into seven equal parts and a selection of cards labelled $\frac{1}{7}, \frac{2}{7}, \frac{3}{7}, \frac{4}{7}$. Ask a pupil to select one of these cards. Shade the number of parts on the strip of paper. Ask a second pupil to select another fraction card and shade this number of parts on the strip of paper in a different colour.
- Ask: *How many parts have been shaded?* Agree the answer. Ask: *What fraction of the whole has been shaded?* All count in sevenths to identify what fraction of the whole has been shaded. Repeat as appropriate.

## Same-day enrichment

- Provide pupils with strips of paper divided into seven equal parts. Ask pupils to investigate number sentences which make this statement correct: $\square + \square = \frac{6}{7}$.
- Ask pupils:
  - *How many different possibilities can you find?*
  - *What about this number sentence:* $\square + \square + \square = \frac{6}{7}$?

# Question 2

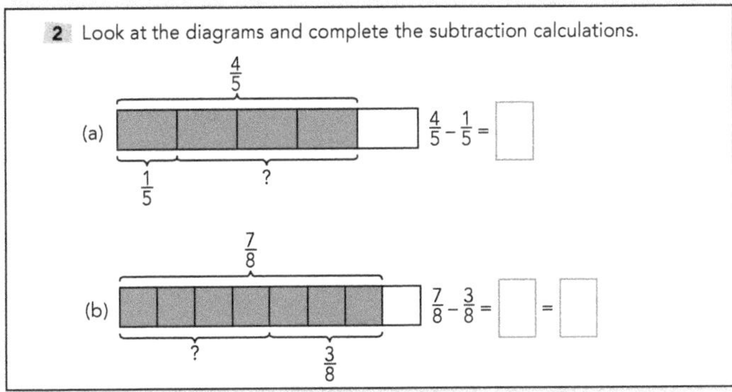


## What learning will pupils have achieved at the conclusion of Question 2?

- Pupils will understand how to subtract fractions with the same denominator, for numbers less than one, using pictorial representations to support their thinking.

## Activities for whole-class instruction

- Show pupils a strip of paper divided into nine equal parts, for example:

- Revise what fraction is represented by each part, and label each part $\frac{1}{9}$. Ask: *If I start with one whole and take away* $\frac{1}{9}$, *what fraction of the whole will remain?* Fold $\frac{1}{9}$ behind the rest of the bar. Together, count the remaining sections: one-ninth, two-ninths, three-ninths, and so on, up to eight-ninths. Record the number sentence on the board $1 - \frac{1}{9} = \frac{8}{9}$. It is important to frequently unfold the strip of paper to reveal all nine parts.
- Ask: *If I start with one whole and take away* $\frac{2}{9}$, *what fraction of the whole will I be left with?* Fold $\frac{2}{9}$ behind the rest of the bar so pupils can see the remaining sections. Ask the whole class to count in ninths the remaining sections. Record the number sentence on the board $1 - \frac{2}{9} = \frac{7}{9}$.
- Provide pairs of pupils with strips of paper divided into nine equal parts. Ask one pupil to fold over a certain number of part(s) and show their partner the remaining part(s). The other pupil records the corresponding number sentence. Ensure both pupils agree that the number sentence is correct. Swap roles and repeat as necessary.

- Provide pupils with an image of $\frac{5}{6}$ of a pie (see **Resource 3.8.4b** Pie sixths), for example:

- Ask: *What fraction of the whole pie is this?* Give pupils time to discuss their responses. Establish that this is $\frac{5}{6}$ of the whole pie because the pie was divided into six equal parts and five parts remain.
- Ask: *How much pie will remain if another $\frac{1}{5}$ is taken away?* Give pupils time to discuss. Physically remove or cover $\frac{1}{5}$ so pupils can see that $\frac{4}{6}$ remain. Record the number sentence $\frac{5}{6} - \frac{1}{5} = \frac{4}{6}$. Ask: *How much pie will remain if I have $\frac{5}{6}$ to begin with and $\frac{3}{6}$ are eaten?* Provide pupils with copies of **Resource 3.8.4b** Pie sixths to support their thinking. Repeat with other sixths.

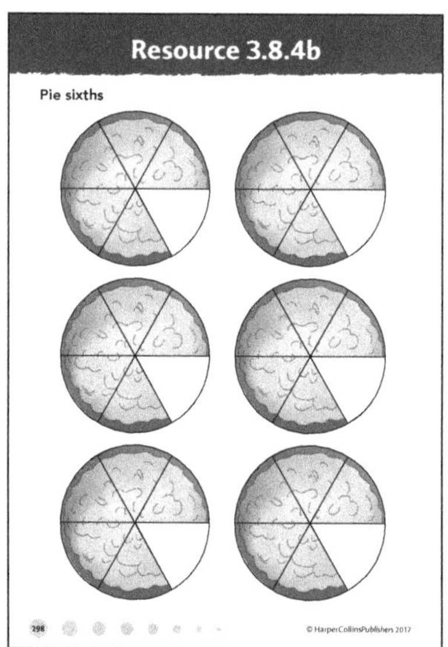


- Provide pupils with an image similar to the one below.

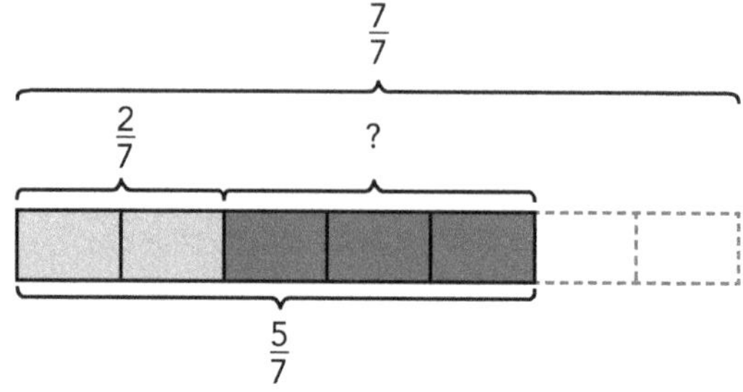


- Ask: *Why are the fractions labelled sevenths and not fifths?* Share responses, acknowledging that the whole has been split into seven equal parts, but that only five parts remain. Introduce that this image represents the calculation $\frac{5}{7} - \frac{2}{7} = \frac{3}{7}$. Ask pupils to consider how they would explain why the image represents this calculation.
- Circulate and identify a pupil who is counting up from $\frac{2}{7}$ to $\frac{5}{7}$. Also identify a pupil who has solved this by counting down from $\frac{5}{7}$ to $\frac{2}{7}$. Ask pupils to feed back the two different strategies. Ask: *Did anyone solve it in a different way?* Take responses.
- Record the following calculations on the board:

$\frac{2}{7} + \frac{3}{7} = \frac{5}{7}$

$\frac{3}{7} + \frac{2}{7} = \frac{5}{7}$

$\frac{5}{7} - \frac{2}{7} = \frac{3}{7}$

$\frac{5}{7} - \frac{3}{7} = \frac{2}{7}$

- Explain that this image shows the relationship between $\frac{2}{7}$, $\frac{3}{7}$ and $\frac{5}{7}$ and demonstrates the inverse relationship between addition and subtraction.
- Ask pupils to draw a bar model to represent $\frac{5}{7} - \frac{4}{7}$. Work with partners to identify what fraction of the whole remains. Ask: *Can you identify any other addition or subtraction calculations relating to $\frac{5}{7} - \frac{4}{7} = \frac{1}{7}$ using your knowledge of inverse relationships?*
- Pupils should complete Question 2 in the Practice Book.

## Same-day intervention

- Provide pairs of pupils with a strip of paper divided into seven equal parts, with each part being a 2 cm by 2 cm square (each square the same size as one interlocking cube), for example:

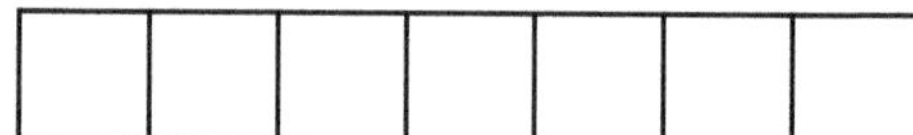

- Explain that this is the whole. Provide red and yellow interlocking cubes and ask pupils to position six yellow cubes onto the strip of paper, for example:

- Ask: *What fraction of the whole has been covered?* Establish that 6/7 have been covered because the whole has been split into seven equal parts and six parts have been covered. Swap one of the yellow interlocking cubes for a red one, for example:

- Ask: *What fraction of the whole is covered by cubes now?* Establish that $\frac{6}{7}$ are still covered by cubes. Ask: *What fraction of the whole is covered by yellow cubes?* Count the yellow cubes in sevenths and agree that $\frac{5}{7}$ are yellow. Ask: *What fraction of the whole is covered by red cubes?* Agree the answer $\frac{1}{7}$. Introduce that this image can represent two addition and two subtraction number sentences. Ask: *What are they?* Record the number sentences together.
- Swap a second yellow interlocking cube for a red one, for example:

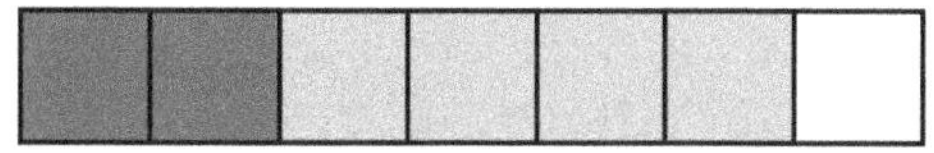

- Ask pupils to work in pairs to explore addition and subtraction number sentences for this image. Repeat for 3 red cubes, 4 red cubes, 5 red cubes, and 6 red cubes. Ensure pupils record the appropriate number sentences for the image represented.

## Same-day enrichment

- Say to pupils: *After a party, $\frac{1}{8}$ of a Hawaiian pizza was left, $\frac{2}{8}$ of a margarita was left and $\frac{5}{8}$ of a pepperoni pizza was left. How much pizza was left altogether? Emma ate $\frac{3}{8}$ of the leftover pizza, how much was left now?*
- Ask children to write their own questions like this for a partner to solve.

# Question 3

**3** Add the fractions.

(a) $\frac{1}{2}+\frac{1}{2}=$ ☐ (b) $\frac{2}{7}+\frac{4}{7}=$ ☐ (c) $\frac{1}{4}+\frac{3}{4}=$ ☐

(d) $\frac{1}{3}+\frac{1}{3}=$ ☐ (e) $\frac{5}{9}+\frac{2}{9}=$ ☐ (f) $\frac{3}{5}+\frac{2}{5}=$ ☐

## What learning will pupils have achieved at the conclusion of Question 3?

- Understanding of adding fractions with the same denominator within one whole will have been developed.

## Activities for whole-class instruction

- Introduce a counting stick labelled in tenths, for example:

$\frac{0}{10}$ $\frac{1}{10}$ $\frac{2}{10}$ $\frac{3}{10}$ $\frac{4}{10}$ $\frac{5}{10}$ $\frac{6}{10}$ $\frac{7}{10}$ $\frac{8}{10}$ $\frac{9}{10}$ $\frac{10}{10}$

- Ask the whole class to count in tenths from zero to one, using the counting stick for support. Progress to counting round the class with individual pupils continuing the count. Revisit counting in jumps of $\frac{2}{10}$ from zero and then from $\frac{1}{10}$, using the counting stick for support.
- Ask: *If I start at $\frac{2}{10}$ and count on five jumps of one-tenth, where will I land?* Give pupils time to discuss. Use the counting stick to illustrate 5 jumps of $\frac{1}{10}$ counting on from $\frac{2}{10}$. With the whole class, count together '$\frac{3}{10}$, $\frac{4}{10}$, $\frac{5}{10}$, $\frac{6}{10}$, $\frac{7}{10}$'. Agree the answer is $\frac{7}{10}$.
- Record the number sentence $\frac{2}{10}+\frac{1}{10}+\frac{1}{10}+\frac{1}{10}+\frac{1}{10}+\frac{1}{10}=\frac{7}{10}$. Ask: *Do we agree that this number sentence represents the calculation we have just done?* Ask: *Who can think of a more efficient way of recording this calculation?* Identify that this calculation can also be recorded as $\frac{2}{10}+\frac{5}{10}=\frac{7}{10}$ because five jumps of $\frac{1}{10}$ is equal to $\frac{5}{10}$.
- Ask: *Who can think of two other fractions which, when they are added together, are equal to $\frac{7}{10}$?* Give pupils time to identify the possible answers. Ask individual pupils to record different addition number sentences on the board. Identify all possibilities. Circle $\frac{1}{10}+\frac{6}{10}=\frac{7}{10}$ and $\frac{6}{10}+\frac{1}{10}=\frac{7}{10}$ in the same colour.
- Ask: *What do you notice about these two calculations?* Draw pupils' attention to the commutative nature of these calculations. Ask: *Who can spot another 'pair of calculations' where the numbers being added have swapped positions?* Circle other pairs in different colours.
- Introduce an image of a parallelogram divided into 12 equal triangles such as the ones on **Resource 3.8.4c** Parallelograms.

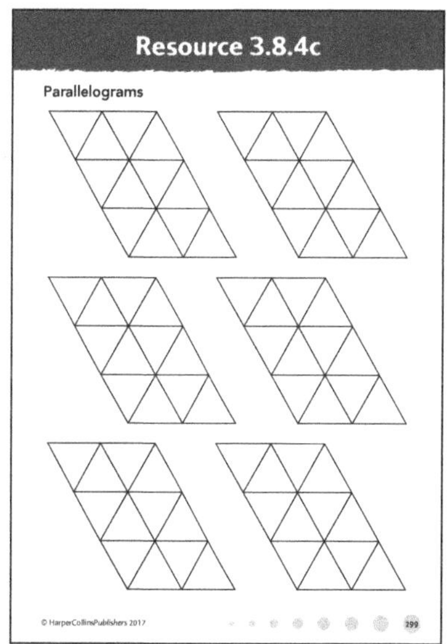


- Write the calculation on the board $\frac{7}{12}+\frac{5}{12}=$ ? Ask one pupil to shade $\frac{7}{12}$ of the image in one colour. Ask a second pupil to shade $\frac{5}{12}$ in a different colour. Ask: *What is the answer to the calculation?* Establish that $\frac{7}{12}+\frac{5}{12}=1\frac{2}{12}$. This is equal to one.

- Provide pairs of pupils with copies of **Resource 3.8.4c** Parallelograms, a dice labelled $\frac{1}{12}$, $\frac{2}{12}$, $\frac{3}{12}$, $\frac{4}{12}$, $\frac{5}{12}$, $\frac{6}{12}$ and two different-coloured pencils. Pupil A rolls the dice and shades the fraction of the whole that has been rolled on the first parallelogram. Pupil B rolls the dice and shades the fraction they have rolled using any unshaded triangles on the same parallelogram. Pupils agree and record the addition number sentence represented on the diagram.
- Pupil A rolls the dice again and shades the fraction rolled. Pupils agree and record the addition number sentence now represented on the diagram. They continue to take turns in this way. The winner is the person who rolls a fraction which enables them to shade the final part(s) of the parallelogram. Repeat as appropriate using the other images on **Resource 3.8.4c**.

Look out for ... pupils who add the numerators and the denominators together, for example, $\frac{2}{12} + \frac{3}{12} = \frac{5}{12}$. If pupils do this, then you will need to remind them that each part represents $\frac{1}{12}$, therefore, the denominator does not change. Encourage children to count on in twelfths from the first number to reinforce this.

- Pupils should complete Question 3 in the Practice Book.

## Same-day intervention

- Provide pupils with a copy of **Resource 3.8.4d** Total fractions.

**Resource 3.8.4d**

Total fractions

| | |
|---|---|
| $\frac{1}{11}$ | $\frac{3}{11}$ |
| $\frac{5}{11}$ | $\frac{6}{11}$ |
| $\frac{4}{11}$ | $\frac{8}{11}$ |
| $\frac{7}{11}$ | $\frac{2}{11}$ |
| | |

300 © HarperCollinsPublishers 2017

- Ask pupils to pair up the fractions to total $\frac{9}{11}$. Draw an image of a fraction bar for support, if required. Record each calculation as a number sentence.
- Ask: *Can you now pair up the fractions to total* $\frac{10}{11}$? *Which fractions do not have a pair? What fraction do they need to be paired with?* Ask pupils to record these fractions on the two blank cards. Record each calculation as a number sentence.

## Same-day enrichment

- Provide pupils with a copy of **Resource 3.8.4e** Fraction towers.

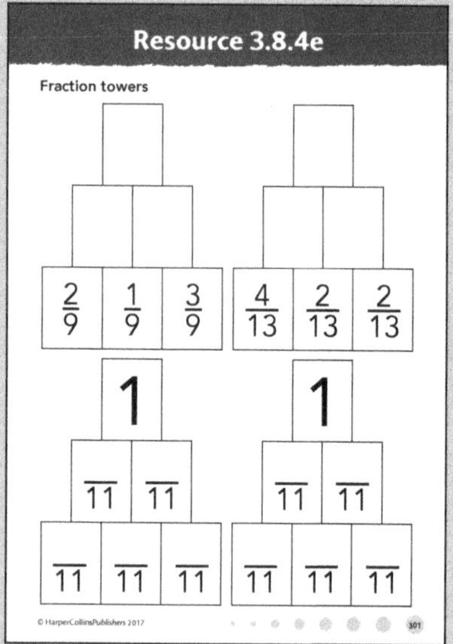
**Resource 3.8.4e**

Fraction towers

$\frac{2}{9}$ $\frac{1}{9}$ $\frac{3}{9}$  $\frac{4}{13}$ $\frac{2}{13}$ $\frac{2}{13}$

1  1

11 11  11 11

11 11 11  11 11 11

© HarperCollinsPublishers 2017  301

- Pupils find the total to the two adjoining squares and record the answer in the square above.
- Ask pupils to create their own addition pyramid for elevenths which has one whole in the top square.

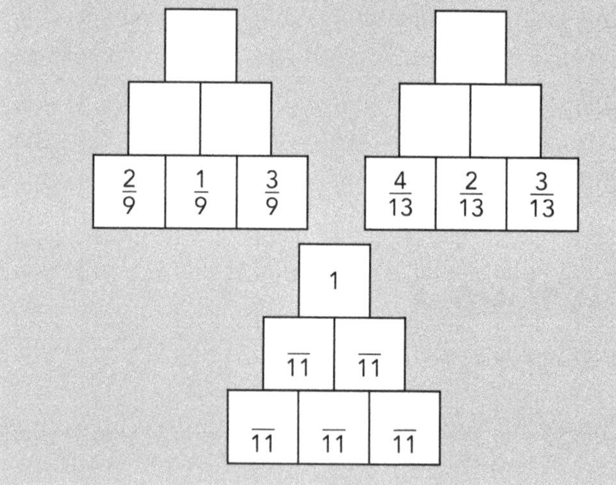


## Question 4

**4** Subtract the fractions.

(a) $\frac{5}{8} - \frac{3}{8} = \square$  (b) $1 - \frac{1}{2} = \square$  (c) $\frac{4}{9} - \frac{4}{9} = \square$

(d) $\frac{6}{7} - \frac{1}{7} = \square$  (e) $\frac{3}{4} - \frac{1}{4} = \square$  (f) $\frac{4}{5} - 0 = \square$

### What learning will pupils have achieved at the conclusion of Question 4?

- Understanding of subtracting fractions with the same denominator within one whole will have been developed.

## Activities for whole-class instruction

- Introduce a counting stick labelled in tenths, for example:

$\frac{0}{10}$ $\frac{1}{10}$ $\frac{2}{10}$ $\frac{3}{10}$ $\frac{4}{10}$ $\frac{5}{10}$ $\frac{6}{10}$ $\frac{7}{10}$ $\frac{8}{10}$ $\frac{9}{10}$ $\frac{10}{10}$

- Ask the whole class to count back in tenths from one to zero using the counting stick for support. Progress to counting round the class with individual pupils continuing the count. Revisit counting back in jumps of $\frac{2}{10}$ from one and then from $\frac{9}{10}$, using the counting stick for support.
- Divide the class into four groups. Allocate each group a different 'counting rule': forwards $\frac{1}{10}$, forwards $\frac{2}{10}$, back $\frac{1}{10}$, back $\frac{2}{10}$. Introduce the starting number, for example, $\frac{5}{10}$ and select one of the four groups to continue the count using their 'counting rule'. Then select different groups to continue the count from the number reached using their 'counting rule'. Swap rules if appropriate.
- Ask: *If I start at $\frac{9}{10}$ and count back five jumps of one-tenth, where do I land?* Give pupils time to discuss. Use the counting stick to illustrate five jumps of $\frac{1}{10}$, counting back from $\frac{9}{10}$. Ask the whole class to count together: $\frac{8}{10}$, $\frac{7}{10}$, $\frac{6}{10}$, $\frac{5}{10}$, $\frac{4}{10}$. Agree the answer is $\frac{4}{10}$. Record the number sentence $\frac{9}{10} - \frac{1}{10} - \frac{1}{10} - \frac{1}{10} - \frac{1}{10} - \frac{1}{10} = \frac{4}{10}$.
- Ask: *Do we agree that this number sentence represents the calculation we have just done?* Ask: *Who can think of a more efficient way of recording this calculation?* Agree that this calculation can also be recorded as $\frac{9}{10} - \frac{5}{10} = \frac{4}{10}$ because five jumps of $\frac{1}{10}$ is equal to $\frac{5}{10}$.
- Introduce an image of a shape divided into 12 equal squares, such as the one on **Resource 3.8.4f**, Comparing twelfths.

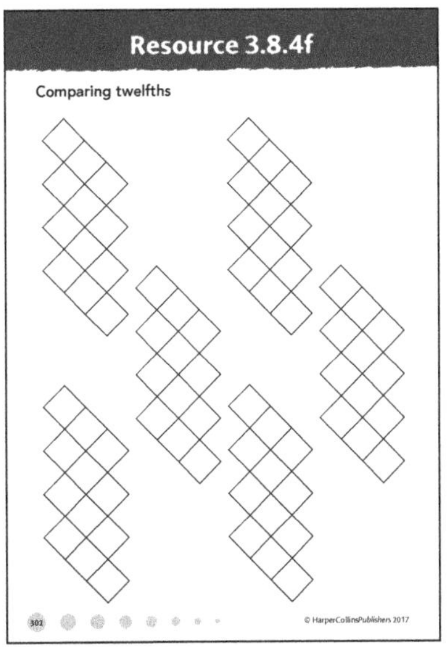


- Write the calculation on the board $\frac{7}{12} - \frac{5}{12} = ?$ Ask one pupil to shade $\frac{7}{12}$ of the image and say: *This represents how much of the whole we have.* Ask a second pupil to put a cross through five of the shaded squares and say: *This represents how much is being subtracted.* Ask: *How much is left after $\frac{5}{12}$ is subtracted from $\frac{7}{12}$?* Establish that there are two shaded squares without a cross and this represents $\frac{2}{12}$. Agree $\frac{7}{12} - \frac{5}{12} = \frac{2}{12}$. Repeat with other subtraction calculations as appropriate.
- Provide pairs of pupils with copies of **Resource 3.8.4f** and cards labelled $\frac{0}{12}$, $\frac{1}{12}$, $\frac{2}{12}$, $\frac{3}{12}$, $\frac{4}{12}$, $\frac{5}{12}$, $\frac{6}{12}$, $\frac{7}{12}$, $\frac{8}{12}$, $\frac{9}{12}$, $\frac{10}{12}$, $\frac{11}{12}$, $\frac{12}{12}$. Ask pupils to select two fraction cards. They identify the largest fraction and shade this number of squares. They identify the smaller fraction and put a cross through the number of shaded squares. This represents the amount being subtracted. They then record the calculation as a subtraction number sentence. Repeat as appropriate, using the other images on **Resource 3.8.4f**.
- Pupils should complete Question 4 in the Practice Book.

## Same-day intervention

- Introduce this image to pupils and say that it represents fifths because it has been divided into five equal parts.

- Record the incomplete number sentence $\frac{?}{5} - \frac{?}{5} = \frac{?}{5}$. Ask: *What are the missing numbers and why?* Give pupils time to explore responses before taking feedback. Agree this is $\frac{4}{5} - \frac{2}{5} = \frac{2}{5}$. Ask pupils to draw a similar image which represents $\frac{4}{5} - \frac{3}{5} = \frac{1}{5}$. Repeat with other fractions as appropriate.

## Same-day enrichment

- Ask pupils: *The answer is $\frac{1}{2}$, what could the subtraction calculation be? How many possibilities can you find? The answer is $\frac{2}{9}$, what could the subtraction calculation be? Find 10 possible calculations. The answer is $\frac{3}{12}$, what could the subtraction calculation be? Find 10 possible calculations.*

# Question 5

**5** Anna was reading a book. The book had 24 pages in total. She read 3 pages on the first day, 4 pages on the second day and 5 pages on the third day.

(a) Write the fraction of the book Anna read on each day.

First day: ☐

Second day: ☐

Third day: ☐

(b) What fraction of the book did Anna read on the first two days? ☐

(c) What fraction of the book had Anna read after three days? ☐

(d) What fraction of the book had Anna not read? ☐

How many pages had she not read? ☐

## What learning will pupils have achieved at the conclusion of Question 5?

- Pupils will have used their understanding of adding and subtracting fractions with the same denominator to solve contextualised problems.

## Activities for whole-class instruction

- Show pupils a bag of sweets. Ask a pupil to count the sweets and establish that there are 20 sweets in the bag. Ask: *What fraction of the whole bag is one sweet?* Pupils record responses on mini whiteboards. Agree it is $\frac{1}{20}$. Ask: *What fraction of the whole bag is three sweets?* Pupils record responses on mini whiteboards. Agree it is $\frac{3}{20}$. Repeat with other fractions as appropriate.
- Tell pupils that on Monday you will give away two sweets, on Tuesday you will give away three sweets and on Wednesday you will give away five sweets. Ask pupils to record what fraction of the whole bag of sweets will be given away on each day. Share responses and use sweets to illustrate the fractions of the whole as appropriate. Ask: *What fraction of the whole will I have given away after the three days?* Share responses and use sweets to illustrate the fractions of the whole as appropriate.
- Ask: *What fraction of the whole will be left for me to eat after the three days?* Share responses and use sweets to illustrate the fractions of the whole as appropriate.

**Look out for** ... pupils who find fractions of the remaining amount rather than fractions of the whole. These pupils would benefit from addition practice in the intervention activity.

## Same-day intervention

- Say to pupils: *You have 25 sweets. Pupil A is given four sweets. Pupils B is given five sweets, and Pupil C is given six sweets.* Ask pupils to model this scenario using counters. Discuss what fraction of the whole is given to each using the counters to support thinking. Ask addition/subtraction questions involving this scenario. Ask pupils to solve this, using the counters to support.

## Same-day enrichment

- Say to pupils: *You have 25 sweets. Write your own scenario and fraction questions involving giving a different number of sweets away to some of your friends.*

## Challenge and extension question

# Question 5

**6** Maya's grandma bought 12 pears to share. She gave Maya and her brother Theo 3 pears each. She then kept 1 pear to herself and gave the rest to the children's mum.

(a) Complete the sentence by writing the correct fractions in the boxes.

Grandma got ☐ of all the pears; Maya got ☐ of all the pears;

Theo got ☐ of all the pears; and Mum got ☐ of all the pears.

(b) What fraction of all the pears did Maya and Theo get in total? Write the number statement and calculate the answer.

Number statement: ____________

(c) What fraction of all the pears did Maya, Theo and Mum get altogether?

Number statement: ____________

(d) Who got the most pears? Who got the least? What is the difference? Write the number statement and find the difference.

Answer: ________ got the most; ________ got the least.

The difference is: ____________ = ______ of the total number of pears.

Express the difference as a whole number. It is ☐ pears.

This question requires pupils to use their understanding of adding and subtracting fractions with the same denominator to solve a contextualised problem.

## Chapter 8 test (Practice Book 3B, pages 52–55)

| Test question number | Relevant unit | Relevant questions within unit |
|---|---|---|
| 1 | 8.1 | 4 |
| | 8.2 | 4 |
| | 8.3 | 1, 3 |
| 2 | 8.3 | 3 |
| 3 | 8.3 | 4 |
| 4 | 8.2 | 5 |
| 5 | 8.4 | 1, 3 |
| 6 | 8.2 | 1 |
| | 8.4 | 5 |
| 7 | 8.4 | 5 |
| 8 | No specific unit | |

# Chapter 9 Multiplying and dividing by a 1-digit number

## Chapter overview

| Area of mathematics | National Curriculum statutory requirements for Key Stage 2 | Shanghai Maths Project reference |
|---|---|---|
| Number – multiplication and division | Year 3 Programme of study<br>Pupils should be taught to: | |
| | ■ recognise the place value of each digit in a three-digit number (hundreds, tens, ones) | Year 3, Unit 9.7 |
| | ■ recall and use multiplication and division facts for the 3, 4 and 8 multiplication tables | Year 3, Units 9.1, 9.2, 9.3, 9.4, 9.5, 9.6, 9.7, 9.8, 9.9, 9.10, 9.11, 9.12, 9.14, 9.15, 9.17, 9.19, 9.20 |
| | ■ write and calculate mathematical statements for multiplication and division using the multiplication tables that they know, including for two-digit numbers times one-digit numbers, using mental calculations and progressing to formal written methods | Year 3, Units 9.1, 9.2, 9.3, 9.4, 9.5, 9.6, 9.10, 9.11, 9.12, 9.14, 9.15, 9.16, 9.17, 9.18, 9.19, 9.20 |
| | ■ solve problems, including missing number problems, involving multiplication and division, including positive integer scaling problems and correspondence problems in which n objects are connected to m objects. | Year 3, Units 9.11, 9.12, 9.14, 9.15, 9.16, 9.17, 9.18, 9.19, 9.20 |

| | | |
|---|---|---|
| Number – multiplication and division | Year 4 Programme of study<br>Pupils should be taught to: | |
| | ■ recall multiplication and division facts for multiplication tables up to 12 × 12 | Year 3, Units 9.1, 9.2, 9.3, 9.4, 9.5, 9.6, 9.7, 9.8, 9.9, 9.10, 9.11, 9.12, 9.13, 9.14, 9.15, 9.16, 9.17, 9.19, 9.20 |
| | ■ use place value, known and derived facts to multiply and divide mentally, including: multiplying by 0 and 1; dividing by 1; multiplying together three numbers | Year 3, Units 9.1, 9.2, 9.3, 9.4, 9.9, 9.10, 9.11, 9.12, 9.13, 9.14, 9.15, 9.16, 9.17, 9.18, 9.19, 9.20 |
| | ■ recognise and use factor pairs and commutativity in mental calculations | Year 3, Units 9.1, 9.2, 9.3, 9.9 |
| | ■ multiply two-digit and three-digit numbers by a one-digit number using formal written layout | Year 3, Units 9.5, 9.6, 9.7, 9.8, 9.9 |
| | ■ solve problems involving multiplying and adding, including using the distributive law to multiply two-digit numbers by one digit, integer scaling problems and harder correspondence problems, such as n objects are connected to m objects. | Year 3, Units 9.4, 9.5, 9.6, 9.7 |
| Number – multiplication and division | Year 5 Programme of study<br>Pupils should be taught to: | |
| | ■ divide numbers up to four digits by a one-digit number using the formal written method of short division and interpret remainders appropriately for the context. | Year 3, Units 9.12, 9.13, 9.14, 9.15, 9.16, 9.17, 9.18, 9.19, 9.20 |

# Unit 9.1 Multiplying by whole tens and hundreds (1)

## Conceptual context

Pupils have previously learned all of their multiplication tables and have explored relationships between them.

In this unit, pupils will extend what they know about multiplying by one-digit numbers and link it with their understanding about place value to be able to multiply by a number of tens. They must begin with sound understanding of 'tens numbers' and 'hundreds numbers' and a number of tens and a number of hundreds so that multiplying, for example 40 by 3 is simply a matter of multiplying 4 tens by 3.

Success with this conceptual variation relies on pupils' fluency with multiplication and division by 10 and 100.

## Learning pupils will have achieved at the end of the unit

- Pupils will understand that multiplying by multiples of 10 and 100 is simply an extension of single-digit multiplication since 3 × 40 is the same as 3 × 4 tens rods (12 tens rods) and 6 × 700 is the same as 6 lots of 7 hundreds blocks (42 hundreds blocks) (Q1, Q2, Q5)
- Pupils will relate repeated addition of tens numbers or hundreds numbers to multiplying tens and hundreds (Q2, Q6)
- Pupils will understand the significance of zeros at the end of two- and three-digit numbers where they appear (Q2, Q3, Q4)
- Pupils will be able to mentally multiply a one-digit number by tens numbers and hundreds numbers using their knowledge of multiplication facts and place value (Q3, Q4, Q5, Q6)
- Pupils will be able to use multiplication facts to quickly compare the products of different numbers of tens or hundreds, for example 7 × 30 must be larger than 6 × 20 because both calculations are one-digit numbers multiplied by tens numbers, but 7 × 3 = 21 and this product is larger than 12 (Q3, Q4)
- The effect of place value will have been explored as pupils begin to recognise the effect it has on the size of the numbers, for example 8 × 40 and 8 × 400 (Q3, Q4)
- The inverse relationship of multiplication and division will have been further developed to help find missing numbers (Q5, Q6)
- Pupils will have practised applying their knowledge of multiplying a one-digit number by tens and hundreds to a range of problems with and without a context (Q6, Q7)

### Resources

base 10 blocks; cubes; counters; dice; 0–9 digit cards; place value counters; **Resource 3.9.1a** Find the largest product; **Resource 3.9.1b** Multiplying ones, tens and hundreds; **Resource 3.9.1c** Array multiplication

### Vocabulary

tens, hundreds, multiply, multiplication, product, times, factor, place value, zero, sum of

# Question 1

**1** Calculate with reasoning.

(a) $4 \times 7 =$ ☐ (b) $5 \times 3 =$ ☐ (c) $6 \times 9 =$ ☐

(d) $4 \times 70 =$ ☐ (e) $50 \times 3 =$ ☐ (f) $60 \times 9 =$ ☐

(g) $4 \times 700 =$ ☐ (h) $500 \times 3 =$ ☐ (i) $6 \times 90 =$ ☐

## What learning will pupils have achieved at the conclusion of Question 1?

- Pupils will understand that multiplying by multiples of 10 and 100 is simply an extension of single-digit multiplication since 3 × 40 is the same as 3 × 4 tens rods (12 tens rods) and 6 × 700 is the same as 6 lots of 7 hundreds blocks (42 hundreds blocks).

## Activities for whole-class instruction

- Ask pupils to work in groups of 3–4. Give each group some base 10 blocks. Ask: *How would you show three groups of one, with base 10 blocks and as a number sentence?*
- Pupils should set out three separate cubes and record: 3 × 1 = 3.

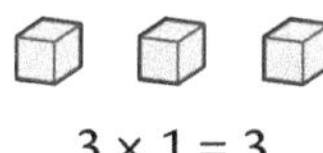

3 × 1 = 3

- Ask: *How would you show three groups of ten, with base 10 blocks and as a number sentence?*
- Pupils should set out three tens rods and record: 3 × 10 = 30.

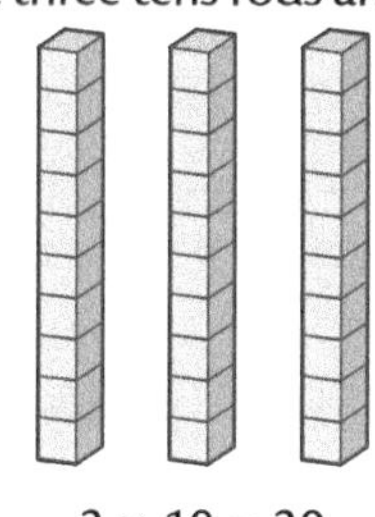

3 × 10 = 30

- Ask: *How would you show three groups of one hundred, with base 10 blocks and as a number sentence?*
- Pupils should set out three one hundred blocks and record: 3 × 100 = 300.

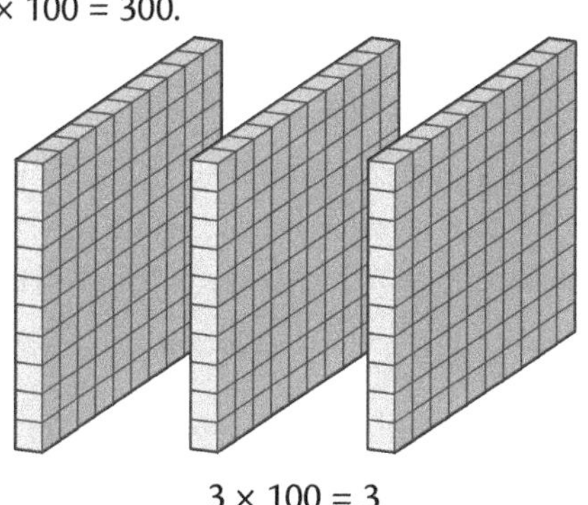

3 × 100 = 3

- Show the following table.

| 5 × 4 | 6 × 8 | 9 × 5 |
|---|---|---|
| 5 × 40 | 6 × 80 | 9 × 50 |
| 5 × 400 | 6 × 800 | 9 × 500 |

- Ask: *What patterns can you see?* Can pupils see that:
  - the product is ten times bigger when the multiplier is ten times bigger? Can they explain why, using base 10 blocks or arrays/squared paper?
  - there is one zero on the product after multiplying by a tens number?
  - the product is 100 times bigger when the multiplier is 100 bigger? Can they explain why, using base 10 blocks or arrays/squared paper?
  - there are two zeros on the product after multiplying by a hundreds number?
- Pupils should complete Question 1 in the Practice Book.

## Same-day intervention

- Give pupils **Resource 3.9.1a** Find the largest product.

**Resource 3.9.1a**

Find the largest product

1. 4 × 6 = ☐ 2. 3 × 5 = ☐
3. 8 × 2 = ☐ 4. 6 × 3 = ☐
5. 7 × 4 = ☐ 6. 9 × 6 = ☐
7. 5 × 6 = ☐ 8. 4 × 7 = ☐

| 1000 | 100 | 10 | 1 |
|---|---|---|---|
| | | | |

© HarperCollinsPublishers 2017 103

- Ask pupils to play a game in pairs and take it in turns to go first. They each select a different calculation from their sheet to give the largest product or a product larger than their partner's choice. They represent the product using digit cards or counters on a place value grid and then make it ten times larger. They represent it by moving the digits and using zero as a place holder.
- Pupils record the number of tens and then write a multiplication sentence that gives the new product. For the first multiplication fact (4 × 6), they record this as 24 tens and sentences as 40 × 6 = 240 or 4 × 60 = 240, and so on.

- They then see who has made the largest product. They can score a point for the largest product.
- The game continues, but when a calculation has been used it must be crossed out and cannot be used again.

## Same-day enrichment

- Ask pupils to explain why 60 × 9 has the same product as 6 × 90. Look for pupils who can talk about the commutativity of multiplication and have used this quickly to work out that the product for both can be found as 54 tens.
- Ask pupils to write number stories for 60 × 9 and 6 × 90. For example:

  *A school has two classes of 30 in each year group. There are nine year groups in the school. How many pupils attend the school?*
- Pupils may find thinking of a context for the numbers tricky. Ask them to think about when we see or use tens numbers. Give them clues by using their immediate experiences such as school or home.

# Question 2

**2** Fill in the boxes.

(a) (i) 60 + 60 + 60 + 60 = ☐

☐ × ☐ = ☐

(ii) 200 + 200 + 200 + 200 + 200 = ☐

☐ × ☐ = ☐

(b) When calculating 6 × 30 mentally, you can think of it as

6 multiplied by ☐ tens, which is ☐ tens.

So the answer to 6 × 30 is ☐.

(c) There are ☐ zeros at the end of the product of 700 × 9.

## What learning will pupils have achieved at the conclusion of Question 2?

- Pupils will understand that multiplying by multiples of 10 and 100 is simply an extension of single-digit multiplication, since 3 × 40 is the same as 3 × 4 tens rods (12 tens rods) and 6 × 700 is the same as 6 lots of 7 hundreds blocks (42 hundreds blocks).
- Pupils will relate repeated addition of tens numbers or hundreds numbers to multiplying by a tens number or hundreds number.
- Pupils will understand the significance of zeros at the end of two- and three-digit numbers where they appear.

## Activities for whole-class instruction

- Give groups of 2–3 pupils a set of one, ten and hundred place value counters.
- Ask them to arrange their counters in these three sets:

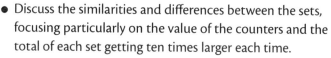

1 1 1 1   10 10 10 10   

- Discuss the similarities and differences between the sets, focusing particularly on the value of the counters and the total of each set getting ten times larger each time.

  **Look out for** ...pupils who may find it beneficial to use base 10 blocks, as these show the relative size of the numbers and pupils will be able to see how a 'one' relates each time.
- Using **Resource 3.9.1b** Multiplying ones, tens and hundreds, label each set on the top row as shown.

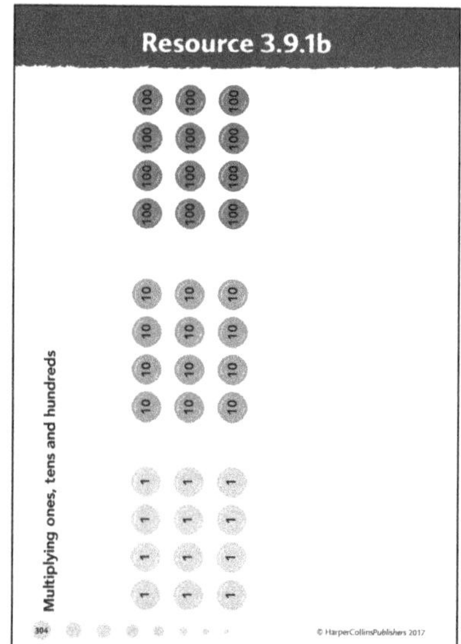


- Discuss how to label each set of counters on **Resource 3.9.1b**. Model the top row as follows:

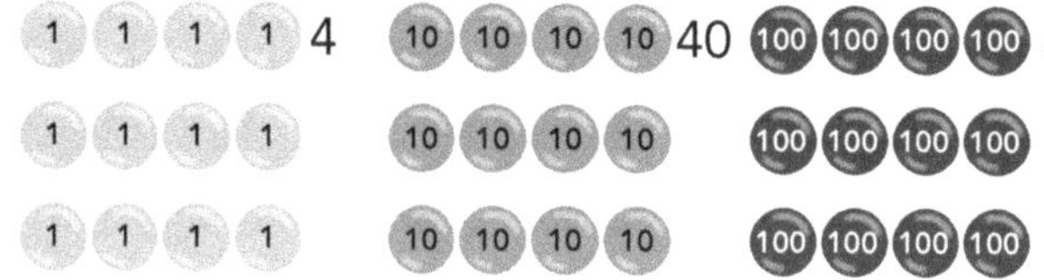


- Pupils should label other rows in the same way.
- Ask: *What is the value of the whole set of 'ones' counters now? Is there a quick way to calculate?*
- Record this as 4 + 4 + 4 = 12 and as 3 × 4 = 12.
- Now ask pupils to record addition and multiplication sentences for the 'tens' counters. Relate repeated addition of four tens to repeated addition of four ones.

  40 + 40 + 40 = 120, 3 × 40 = 120 and 30 × 4 = 120

*Three multiplied by 40 is the same as three multiplied by four tens or 12 tens.*

- Discuss the 'hundreds' counters in the same way and record, relating repeated addition of four hundreds to repeated addition of four ones and 3 × 400 to 3 × 4:

  400 + 400 + 400 = 1200, 3 × 400 = 1200 and 3 × 40 = 1200

*Three multiplied by 400 is the same as three multiplied by four hundreds or 12 hundreds.*

- Establish that the total value of the 'tens' counters is ten times larger than the 'ones' and the total of the 'hundreds' counters is one hundred times larger than the 'ones'.
- Say that you have noticed something – there is one zero at the end of the product of 3 × 4 for the calculation 3 × 40, but there are two zeros at the end of the product 3 × 4 in the calculation 3 × 400. Can pupils explain why?
- Now look down the columns to check that the totals are the same each time. Ask pupils to add another two rows of counters to each set and quickly find the new products. Ask: *How will each of the number sentences change?*
- Record matching addition and multiplication sentences.

*Five multiplied by 40 is the same as five multiplied by four tens or 20 tens.*

- Agree that 5 × 400 can be seen as 20 hundreds.
- Suggest that the following addition sentences match the counters in the columns:

  5 + 5 + 5 + 5

  50 + 50 + 50 + 50

  500 + 500 + 500 + 500

- Ask pupils to write the matching multiplication sentences.
- Work together to confirm that the products are the same as for the rows.

*Five multiplied by four tens is equal to four multiplied by five tens. There are 20 tens.*

- Look together at the number of zeros at the end of the product 5 × 4 for 5 × 40 and 5 × 400.
- Pupils should complete Question 2 in the Practice Book.

## Same-day intervention

- Give groups of pupils a dice and base 10 blocks. Introduce the activity.
- Tell pupils that they should roll the dice to find the number of blocks in each group, for example, roll a three and make a group of three ones, three tens and three hundreds.
- Blocks should be placed in rows as before.
- Tell pupils to think carefully about the value of each set of blocks each time.
- Say that they should continue to add blocks one row at a time, as in the whole-class session, and record and answer the matching addition and multiplication sentences. How many different products can they find?

## Same-day enrichment

- Give pupils a copy of the multiplication table for nine up to 9 × 9.
- While you are introducing the activity to the intervention group, they should discuss how it could be changed to become the multiplication table for 90 or the multiplication table for 900 and test some of their ideas, for example, multiply the one-digit number by nine tens rather than nine ones.
- Ask pupils to select a fact up to 9 × 9, for example 3 × 9 = 27, and write the multiplication sentences needed to find the product that is ten times larger (for example 3 × 90 = 270) and one hundred times larger.
- Look at the commutativity of multiplication, for example 3 × 90 = 270 or 27 tens and 90 × 3 = 270 or 27 tens.
- Ask: *What helpful tips would you give to someone else about multiplying tens by a one-digit number?*

  *How can we adapt our tips to help someone multiply hundreds by a one-digit number?*

# Question 3 and Question 4

**3** Write >, < or = in each ◯.

(a) 9 × 50 ◯ 90 × 5 (b) 40 × 2 ◯ 3 × 20

(c) 8 × 200 ◯ 500 × 6 (d) 300 × 3 ◯ 5 × 200

(e) 7 × 90 ◯ 6 × 600 (f) 600 × 4 ◯ 4 × 600

**4** Draw lines to match each calculation to the correct answer.

| | |
|---|---|
| (a) 5 × 70 | 3500 |
| (b) 500 × 7 | 35 |
| (c) 5 × 7000 | 350 |
| (d) 5 × 7 | 35 000 |

## What learning will pupils have achieved at the conclusion of Questions 3 and 4?

- Pupils will understand the significance of zeros at the end of two- and three-digit numbers where they appear.
- Pupils will have used multiplication facts to quickly compare the products of different numbers of tens or hundreds, for example 7 × 30 must be larger than 6 × 20 because both calculations are one-digit by tens, but 7 × 3 = 21 and this product is larger than 12.
- The effect of place value is explored as pupils begin to recognise the effect it has on the size of the numbers, for example 8 × 40 and 8 × 400.
- Pupils can mentally multiply a one-digit number by tens numbers and hundreds numbers, using their knowledge of multiplication facts and place value.

## Activities for whole-class instruction

- Show some of the helpful tips for multiplying a tens number by a single-digit number developed by pupils in the previous enrichment activity.
- Using the example 4 × 60 (four multiplied by six tens equals 24 tens), test the tips. Do pupils agree that they are helpful?
- Ask: *What do you notice about the number of zeros at the end of the product 240?* (one zero) *Why do you think this is?* Agree that the product of 4 × 60 is ten times larger than the product of 4 × 6 because 60 is ten times 6.
- Ask: *How many zeros are at the end of the product of 4 times 600? Why?*
- Use place value counters to show this array:

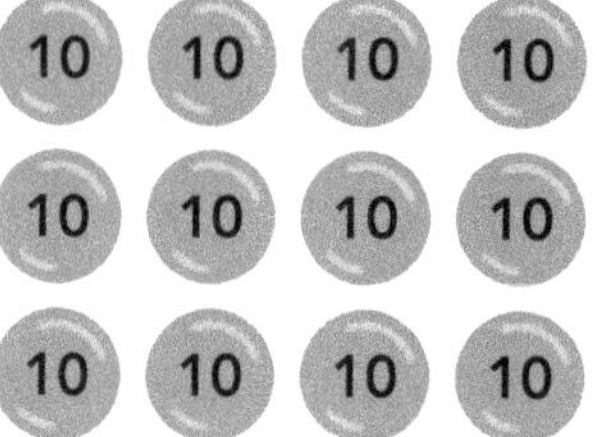

- Ask: *How much is the array worth altogether?* (120) Agree that it shows three multiplied by four tens or 3 × 40.
- Say: *Looking at the columns, we can also see four multiplied by three tens or 4 × 30.*
- See if pupils can explain that they know that 3 × 40 and 4 × 30 give the same product because they each have 12 tens.
- Rearrange the 12 counters as shown:

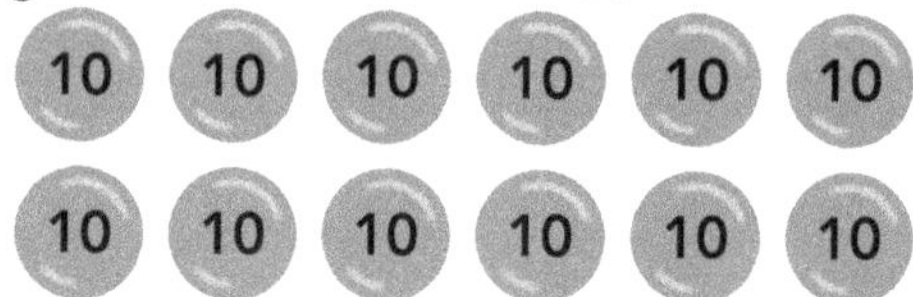

- Ask: *What is represented this time?*
- See if pupils can explain that the product of 2 × 60 and 6 × 20 must be equal to 3 × 40 and 4 × 30 because the number of tens in the product is the same.
- Record equalities such as:

  3 × 40 = 30 × 4

  3 × 40 = 2 × 60

  30 × 4 = 20 × 6, discussing the number of tens in the product each time.
- Adding another column of two counters, write the following sentence: 3 × 40 = 2 × 70. Ask: *Is it true? What sign should be used instead?*
- Record the inequality as 3 × 40 < 2 × 70.
- Continue by using the 100 place value counters to explore 3 × 400 and 2 × 600 to show the product is the same. Then explore an inequality by taking away a column of two counters. Record this as 3 × 40 > 2 × 50.
- Pupils should complete Question 3 and Question 4 in the Practice Book.

## Same-day intervention

- Give pupils **Resource 3.9.1c** Array multiplication.

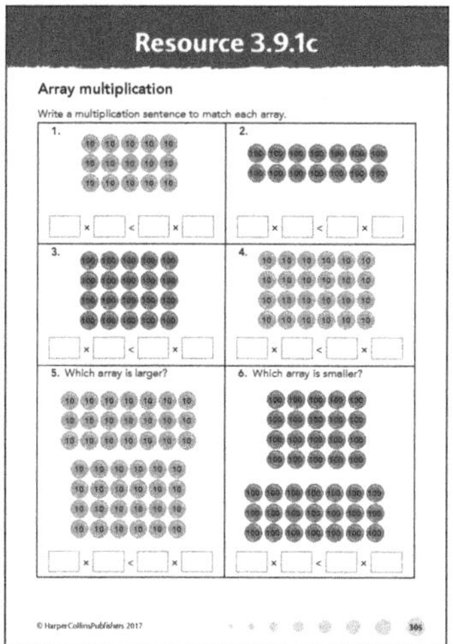
Resource 3.9.1c

Array multiplication

Write a multiplication sentence to match each array.

5. Which array is larger?

6. Which array is smaller?

- Ask pupils to write the multiplication sentences to match the arrays.

## Same-day enrichment

- Ask pupils to choose one of these numbers to be represented with tens (red) place value counters.

240　　180　　300

- Pupils make an array and write two multiplication sentences, for example: 3 × 80 = 8 × 30. The array should be rearranged and an equivalent calculation recorded, for example 3 × 80 = 6 × 40.
- Pupils should add or subtract a column or row of counters, recording the sentence using the symbols < or >.
- Ask pupils to use their knowledge of place value to write each of the sentences using hundreds.
- Repeat with the other numbers from the list.

# Question 5

**5** Fill in the boxes.

(a) □ × 3 = 1200　　(b) 700 × □ = 1400

(c) 2000 = □ × 400　　(d) 3200 = 800 × □

## What learning will pupils have achieved at the conclusion of Question 5?

- Pupils will understand that multiplying by multiples of 10 and 100 is simply an extension of single-digit multiplication since 3 × 40 is the same as 3 × 4 tens rods (12 tens rods) and 6 × 700 is the same as 6 lots of 7 hundreds blocks (42 hundreds blocks).
- Pupils can mentally multiply a one-digit number by tens numbers and hundreds numbers using their knowledge of multiplication facts and place value.
- The inverse relationship of multiplication and division is further developed to help find missing numbers.

## Activities for whole-class instruction

- Pupils use place value counters to make the following arrangement.

10 10 10 10 10 10

10 10 10 10 10 10

10 10 10 10 10 10

- Ask: *How many groups of six tens are there? What are the counters worth altogether?* (18 tens or 180)
- Agree that the array shows three rows of six tens. Record this as three multiplied by six tens, 18 tens and 3 × 60 = 180. Ask: *How we can describe the array using the columns?* Explain that you will re-arrange the 18 counters to make rows of two tens. Record this as: □ multiplied by 2 tens or □ tens is 180 and □ × 20 = 180. Pupils arrange 18 counters to show rows of two tens.
- Say: *There are nine rows of two tens so the array shows 9 × 20.* Complete the number sentence to show 9 × 20 = 180.
- Look together at the columns. Write the sentences: 2 × □ = 180 and 180 = 2 × □ on the board. Ask: *What is the missing number each time?*
- Ask pupils to use the hundreds counters to make an arrangement to help find the missing number in the sentences: 7 × □ = 2800 and 2800 = 7 × □.
- Take feedback and together agree that seven rows of four hundreds or 28 hundreds is 2800 or 7 × 400 = 2800.

  Complete the missing numbers in the number sentences. Using the columns this time, ask pupils to find the missing values in: □ × 4 = 2800 and 2800 = 4 × □.
- Pupils should complete Question 5 in the Practice Book.

## Same-day intervention

- Pupils use place value counters to represent each of the multiplication sentences in the Practice Book.
- For each array, they record two multiplication sentences – one looking at the rows and the other at the columns.

## Same-day enrichment

- Give pupils the following problem to explore.

  The products of three sets of multiplication sentences are 320, 360 and 2400.

  How many different multiplication sentences can you find to make each product?

| Product is 320 | Product is 360 | Product is 2400 |
|---|---|---|
| | | |

# Question 6 and Question 7

**6** Write a number sentence for each question.

(a) What is the sum of 40 nines?

Number sentence: ______

(b) What is 3 times 600?

Number sentence: ______

(c) A number is divided by 400 and both its quotient and the remainder are 8. What is the number?

Number sentence: ______

**7** A pack of salt weighs 500 grams. How many kilograms do 8 packs of salt weigh? (Note: 1 kilogram = 1000 grams)

SALT
500g

Answer: ______

## What learning will pupils have achieved at the conclusion of Questions 6 and 7?

- Pupils will relate repeated addition of tens numbers or hundreds numbers to multiplying tens and hundreds.
- Pupils will be able to mentally multiply a one-digit number by tens numbers and hundreds numbers using their knowledge of multiplication facts and place value.
- The inverse relationship of multiplication and division will have been further developed to help find missing numbers.
- Pupils will have practised applying their knowledge of multiplying a one-digit number by tens and hundreds to a range of problems with and without a context.

## Activities for whole-class instruction

- Rehearse the multiplication tables for 4 and 8, remembering to include division facts. Relate facts to multiples of four tens and eight tens, looking also at the relationship between the tables, for example, three multiplied by eight tens is double three multiplied by four tens.
- Introduce some contexts for the multiplications, for example:

  *There are 300 marbles in a jar. How many marbles are in four jars? And in eight?*

  *A box weighs 600 g. What is the mass of four of these boxes?*
- Develop the activity further to consider multiples of four hundreds and eight hundreds.
- Write one of the facts from the starter activity on the board, for example, 8 × 40 = 320. Ask: *What is the total of 40 eights? How can we work this out?*
- Pupils discuss the problem and suggest ideas. It could be described as 8 + 8 + 8 + 8 + ... and so on.
- See if pupils can explain that 40 eights is the same as 40 × 8 or 4 tens multiplied by 8. Agree that the total or the sum of 40 eights is 320.

*The sum of 40 eights is 320.*

- Ask: *What is the sum of 400 eights? How can you use what you know about 40 eights?* Agree that this is 3200 which is ten times larger than 40 eights and a hundred times larger than four eights.
- Ask: *Why will '8 times 400' give the same product, 3200?*
- Introduce this problem:

  *I am thinking of a number from the starting activity. When it is divided by 80, the quotient is 3.*
- Pupils discuss the problem. Do they recognise that the number is a product rather than a factor? Together, draw out the division sentence ☐ ÷ 80 = 3. Ask: *What multiplication sentence matches my division sentence? How will this help us?* Agree that 3 × 80 = ☐ will be useful, as it will help to identify the dividend, 240. Practise a few more examples, encouraging pupils to find the matching division and multiplication sentences.
- Pupils should complete Question 6 and Question 7 in the Practice Book.

## Same-day intervention

- Give pupils a range of multiplication or division problems in a context, for example:
- *A bus holds 50 people. How many people can seven buses hold?*
- *Amy has a 2500 cm length of string. She cuts it into five equal parts. How long is each piece?*
- Work through the problems together, using place value counters or base 10 blocks to support application of place value as required.

## Same-day enrichment

- Give pupils the number 3600, explaining that this is the answer to a question.
- Pupils then create different questions (with or without a context) with the answer 3600.

  For example: *What is the sum of 600 sixes?*
- *A number is divided by 900. Its quotient is four. What is the number?*
- *A small ship holds 600 people. How many people do six of these ships hold?*
- Encourage them to use a range of different language as explored in the lessons.

## Challenge and extension question

# Question 8

**8** One plastic box contains 50 pens. 8 plastic boxes can fit into one large case. The price of each pen is £3. How much will two large cases of pens cost?

Answer: ______

This question requires pupils to recognise multiplying by tens in a context. They should draw out the multiplication 8 × 50 or 50 × 8 to first find the number of pens in one large case.

However, the problem is in two parts, as they are asked to find the price of the pens when one pen is £3.

They should recognise that the next calculation requires them to multiply 3 by 400 which is the number of pens in one large case.

# Unit 9.2 Multiplying by whole tens and hundreds (2)

## Conceptual context

Pupils have extended what they know about multiplying by one-digit numbers and, using their understanding of place value, have been introduced to multiplying by a number of tens or hundreds.

In this unit, pupils will further develop their understanding of a number of tens and a number of hundreds so that when multiplying, for example, 6 × 800 as 6 multiplied by 8 hundreds, they identify the product of 6 × 8 as 48 and recognise that the 6 × 800 is equal to 48 hundreds. This concept will be extended to include even larger numbers.

Pupils will apply their understanding to solve a range of routine and non-routine problems.

## Learning pupils will have achieved at the end of the unit

- Conceptual understanding of multiplying a one-digit number by tens and hundreds will have been further developed through the use of manipulatives and other representations (Q1, Q2)
- Pupils' concept of place value will have been deepened as they explore the effect multiplication has on the size of numbers (Q1, Q2, Q3, Q4)
- Multiplication of tens or hundreds numbers by 10 or 100 will have been practised so that pupils perceive patterns for themselves and understand why a number ending with zeros is always a multiple of 10 or 100 respectively (Q2, Q3, Q4)
- Pupils will be able to mentally multiply a one-digit number by tens and hundreds, using their knowledge of multiplication facts and place value (Q3, Q4, Q5, Q6)
- Pupils will relate repeated addition of tens numbers or hundreds numbers to multiplying by a tens number or hundreds number (Q5)
- The inverse relationship of multiplication and division will have been further developed to help find missing numbers (Q5)
- Pupils will have practised applying their knowledge of multiplying a one-digit number by tens and hundreds to a range of problems with and without a context (Q5, Q6)

### Resources

base 10 apparatus; dice; 0–9 digit cards; place value counters; balancing scales; **Resource 3.9.2a** Base 10, ones and tens; **Resource 3.9.2b** Array; **Resource 3.9.2c** Comparing arrays; **Resource 3.9.2d** Balancing multiplications; **Resource 3.9.2e** Changing arrays; **Resource 3.9.2f** Multiplication problems; **Resource 3.9.2g** Problem arrays; **Resource 3.9.2h** Writing problems

### Vocabulary

tens, hundreds, multiply, multiplication, product, times, factor, place value, zero, sum of

# Question 1 and Question 2

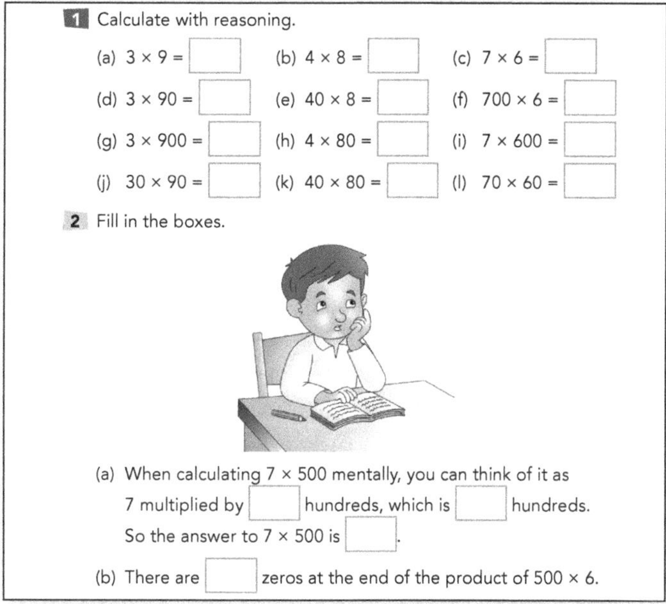

**1** Calculate with reasoning.

(a) $3 \times 9 =$ ☐ (b) $4 \times 8 =$ ☐ (c) $7 \times 6 =$ ☐

(d) $3 \times 90 =$ ☐ (e) $40 \times 8 =$ ☐ (f) $700 \times 6 =$ ☐

(g) $3 \times 900 =$ ☐ (h) $4 \times 80 =$ ☐ (i) $7 \times 600 =$ ☐

(j) $30 \times 90 =$ ☐ (k) $40 \times 80 =$ ☐ (l) $70 \times 60 =$ ☐

**2** Fill in the boxes.

(a) When calculating $7 \times 500$ mentally, you can think of it as 7 multiplied by ☐ hundreds, which is ☐ hundreds. So the answer to $7 \times 500$ is ☐.

(b) There are ☐ zeros at the end of the product of $500 \times 6$.

## What learning will pupils have achieved at the conclusion of Question 1 and Question 2?

- Conceptual understanding of multiplying a one-digit number by tens and hundreds will have been further developed through the use of manipulatives and other representations.
- Multiplication of tens or hundreds numbers by 10 or 100 will have been practised so that pupils perceive patterns for themselves and understand why a number ending with zeros is always a multiple of 10 or 100 respectively.
- Pupils' concept of place value will have been deepened as they explore the effect multiplication has on the size of numbers.

## Activities for whole-class instruction

- Show pupils **Resource 3.9.2a** Base 10, ones and tens.

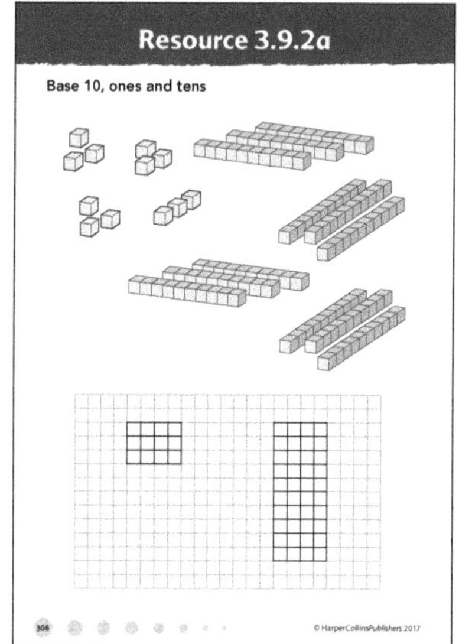


- Ask pupils to discuss the similarities and differences between the images of the base 10 blocks – one shows groups of ones and the other shows groups of tens.
- Ask: *What are the images of squares showing?* See if pupils can tell you that:
  - the squares represent the cubes above, as arrays
  - the number of tens blocks in each group is the same as the number of ones cubes in each group, but each is worth ten times more
  - there are three groups of four ones (12 ones) and three groups of four tens (12 tens).

*3 × 40 is ten times larger than 3 × 4.*

- Record these multiplication sentences on the board, lining up the digits carefully to show place value:

  $3 \times 4 = 12$ (3 multiplied by 4 ones)

  $4 \times 3 = 12$ (4 ones multiplied by 3)

  $3 \times 40 = 120$ (3 multiplied by 4 tens)

  $40 \times 3 = 120$ (4 tens multiplied by 3)

- Ask pupils to reason about the product of the array on **Resource 3.9.2b** Array. Ask: *What do you notice this time? What does it represent?*

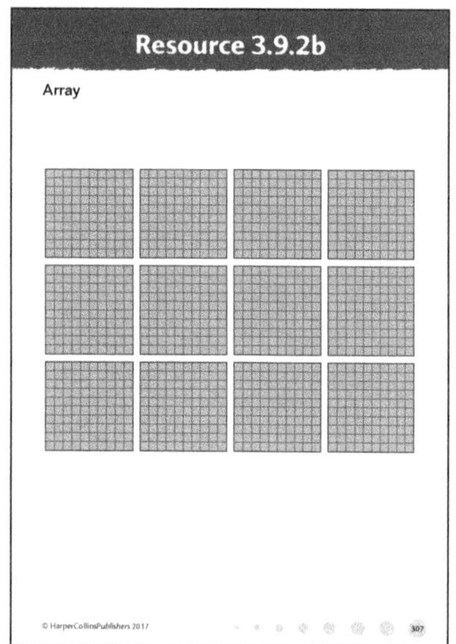


- The array shows 3 × 400 or 3 multiplied by 4 hundreds or 12 hundreds, so the product is 1200.
- Ask: *How many times larger is 3 × 400 than 3 × 4?*
- Agree that the product of three multiplied by four hundreds (or 12 hundreds) is a hundred times larger than the product of three multiplied by four ones (or 12 ones).
- Record 3 × 400 = 1200 (three multiplied by four hundreds) and 400 × 3 = 1200 (four hundreds multiplied by three) on the board beneath the two rows recorded previously.
- Look together at the:
  - diagonal patterns in the place value of digits as the factor and products gets ten times larger
  - number of zeros at the end of the products to show 'tens' and 'hundreds'.
- Give groups enough base 10 blocks to represent the image from **Resource 3.9.2b** Array.
- Agree that the array shows 3 × 400, as there are three rows of four hundreds.

*Three multiplied by four hundreds, or 12 hundreds.*

- Look closely at each 100 block. Place ten ten rods on top of one one hundred block to show that it is made up of ten tens.
- Now push the 100 blocks together to show 30 rows of 40.

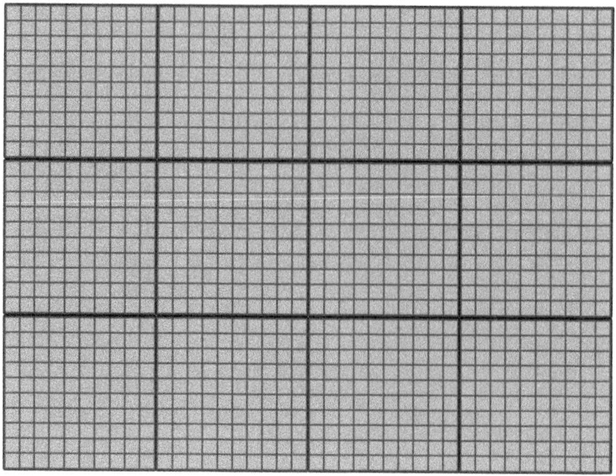

- Ask: *How do you know the total number of rows without counting?* Agree that there are 30 rows because there are three groups of 10 rows. There are 40 squares in each row because there are four tens.
- Establish that this is a 30 × 40 array, but it still has the same value as 3 × 400.
- Say: *We can check this as:*

  10 rows of 40 (10 × 4 tens) is 400

  20 rows of 40 (20 × 4 tens) is 800 relating 20 rows to double ten rows

  30 rows of 40 (30 × 4 tens) is 1200
- Record 3 × 400 = 1200 and 30 × 40 = 1200.
- Pupils should now make a 3 × 40 array.

- Ask: *How would you change this 3 × 40 array into a 30 × 40 array?* Agree that each tens rod would need to be changed for a hundred block. Establish that this means that 30 × 40 (1200) is ten times more than 12 tens (120).
- Make a 30 × 40 array with 100 blocks and compare with the 3 × 40 array so that pupils appreciate the magnitude of multiplying the two tens numbers. Re-count the number of rows in the larger array to confirm there are 30 rows of 40 which is 10 times more than 3 rows of 40.
- Remove three 100 blocks so the array shows 30 × 30. Ask pupils how they can use what they know about 3 × 300 to find the product of 30 × 30.
- Pupils should complete Question 1 and Question 2 in the Practice Book.

## Same-day intervention

- Ask pupils to roll two 1–6 dice and to practise making and recording multiplication sentences with the numbers rolled. For example, if they roll a 5 and a 6, they can make 5 × 6 and 6 × 5.

- Ask pupils to make an array using 'ones' cubes or place value counters to check their first product.
- Look together at the rows and columns, focusing on the commutativity of multiplication.
- Pupils should swap each of their ones for tens and write the new multiplications and product. They can then swap the tens for hundreds. How does the multiplication and product change this time?
- Pupils choose another of their recorded multiplication sentences and explore making the product ten and a hundred times larger in the same way.

## Same-day enrichment

- Introduce this activity while the intervention group are making multiplication sentences using dice.
- Give pupils one copy of the first array on **Resource 3.9.2c** Comparing arrays, showing 4 × 60 and up to eight copies of the second array showing 10 × 60.

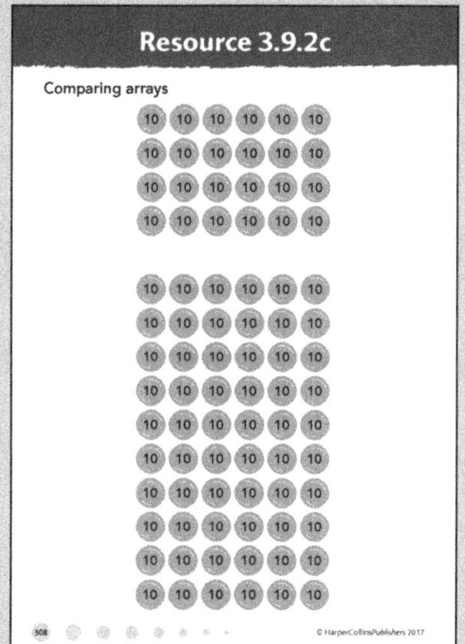


- Ask pupils to compare the size of the arrays for 4 × 60 and 10 × 60, agreeing that the larger array shows 60 tens which is six rows of six tens more than the smaller array.
- Tell pupils to explore making different arrays to find larger products that are the result of multiplying tens by tens. Suggest that they first try to represent 20 × 60 by putting two arrays together. Agree that this is the same as double 10 × 60.
- They should continue adding arrays, comparing the values each time and recording number sentences.

# Question 3 and Question 4

**3** Write >, < or = in each ◯.

(a) 6 × 50 ◯ 60 × 5 (b) 400 × 5 ◯ 40 × 50

(c) 7 × 700 ◯ 900 × 5 (d) 60 × 30 ◯ 300 × 6

(e) 7 × 800 ◯ 50 × 10 (f) 900 × 2 ◯ 3 × 600

**4** Draw lines to match each calculation with the correct answer.

| | |
|---|---|
| (a) 5 × 80 | 4000 |
| (b) 500 × 8 | 40 |
| (c) 50 × 800 | 400 |
| (d) 5 × 8 | 40 000 |

## What learning will pupils have achieved at the conclusion of Question 3 and Question 4?

- Multiplication of tens or hundreds numbers by 10 or 100 will have been practised so that pupils perceive patterns for themselves and understand why a number ending with zero is always a multiple of 10 or 100 respectively.
- Pupils will be able to mentally multiply a one-digit number by tens and hundreds, using their knowledge of multiplication facts and place value.
- Pupils' concept of place value will have been deepened as they explore the effect multiplication has on the size of numbers.

## Activities for whole-class instruction

- Write the following calculations on the board:

  7 × 30 = ☐ 6 × 40 = ☐ 8 × 300 = ☐
  400 × 5 = ☐ 6 × 400 = ☐ 80 × 30 = ☐

- Suggest that some of these will also result in the same product. Pupils should complete the multiplication sentences and find those with the same solutions.
- Ask: *Which solutions are multiples of 100 and which are multiples of 10? How do you know?*
- Now show pupils the following number sentence. Ask: *Is it true? Why?*

  4 × 600 = 400 × 5

- Establish that the product of 4 × 600 is greater than the product of 400 × 5.

- You could sketch the following balancing scales to represent this:

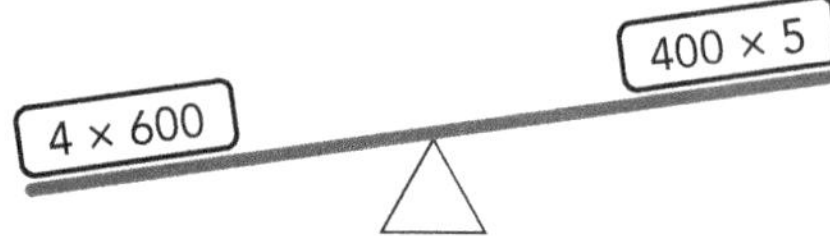


- Ask pupils to explain which symbol we need to used instead of the equals sign to make the sentence correct. Record this as 4 × 600 > 400 × 5.
- Return to the incorrect sentence 4 × 600 = 400 × 5. Ask: *Can we change the numbers in the sentences and keep the equals sign so that the sentence is correct?*
- Record possible solutions as 4 × 500 = 400 × 5, 40 × 50 = 400 × 5, 4 × 600 = 8 × 300, and so on.
- Ask pupils to sketch their own balancing scales to show one of these equalities, for example:

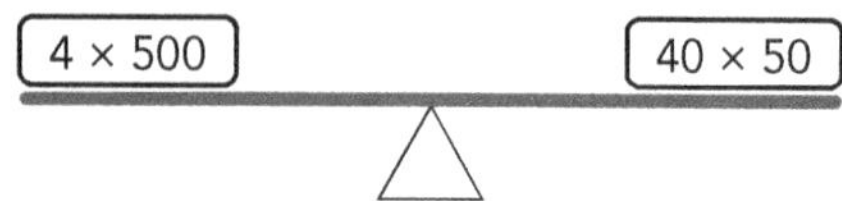


- Look together at the multiplication sentences:

  4 × 5 = ☐

  4 × 50 = ☐

  4 × 500 = ☐

  40 × 50 = ☐
- Discuss the similarities and differences, agreeing that they all use 4 × 5 to find the product 20, but then place value is applied to find 20 tens, 20 hundreds or 20 multiplied by ten tens.
- Write 40 × 500 on the board. Ask: *What do you think you will need to do this time? Can you use the product 20 and place value to help you?*
- Agree this as 20 multiplied by 100 tens. Use the place value chart to first multiply 20 by 100 and by 10 again. Can pupils explain that this is the same as multiplying 20 by a thousand?

  (i) Although 40 × 500 results in a much larger product than pupils are familiar with, this task looks principally at how numbers of tens and hundreds can be easily multiplied using, in this case, the product of 4 × 5 and applying knowledge of place value.
- Pupils should complete Question 3 and Question 4 in the Practice Book.

## Same-day intervention

- Using base 10 apparatus, place three 100 blocks into one pan on a set of balancing scales. Ask pupils to put an equal value of base 10 in the other pan using only tens sticks.
- Ask pupils to work together to predict how many tens they need to use before doing it practically.
- Pupils should balance the scales using 30 tens. Can they explain why 3 × 100 = 30 × 10?
- Take the three hundreds from the scales and place them on the table. Arrange the tens sticks on top so that pupils can clearly see that they have the same total value.

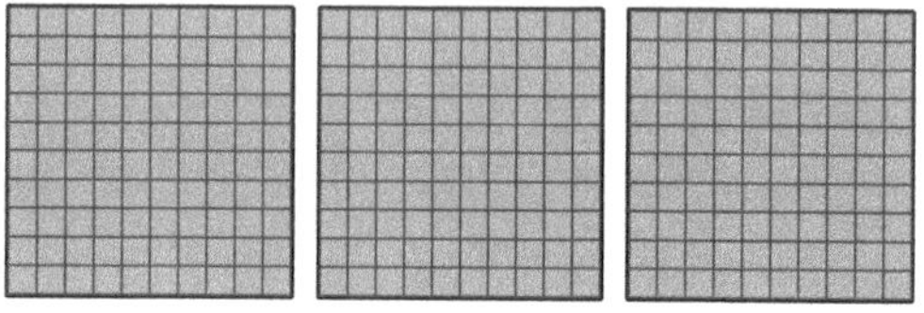

- Say that you will put four hundreds blocks in one scale pan. Ask: *What will happen when 30 tens are placed in the other pan?* Agree that 4 × 100 is more than 30 × 10. Record this as 4 × 100 > 30 × 10.
- Pupils should explore other numbers of hundreds and tens, for example 5 × 100 and 40 × 10, deciding whether they are equivalent in value or not.

## Same-day enrichment

- Give pupils **Resource 3.9.2d** Balancing multiplications.

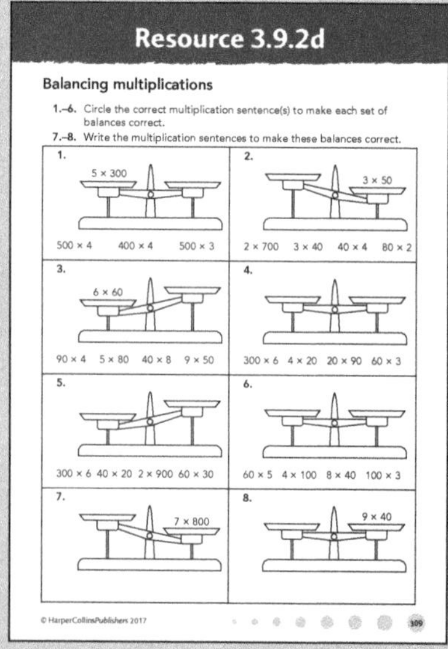

Resource 3.9.2d

**Balancing multiplications**

1.–6. Circle the correct multiplication sentence(s) to make each set of balances correct.

7.–8. Write the multiplication sentences to make these balances correct.

1. 5 × 300

   500 × 4 400 × 4 500 × 3

2. 3 × 50

   2 × 700 3 × 40 40 × 4 80 × 2

3. 6 × 60

   90 × 4 5 × 80 40 × 8 9 × 50

4. 300 × 6 4 × 20 20 × 90 60 × 3

5. 300 × 6 40 × 20 2 × 900 60 × 30

6. 60 × 5 4 × 100 8 × 40 100 × 3

7. 7 × 800

8. 9 × 40

© HarperCollinsPublishers 2017 109

- They should compare the products of multiplication sentences shown on balancing scales and complete missing information to make each example true.
- Pupils can make up their own balancing scale problems for others to solve.

## Question 5

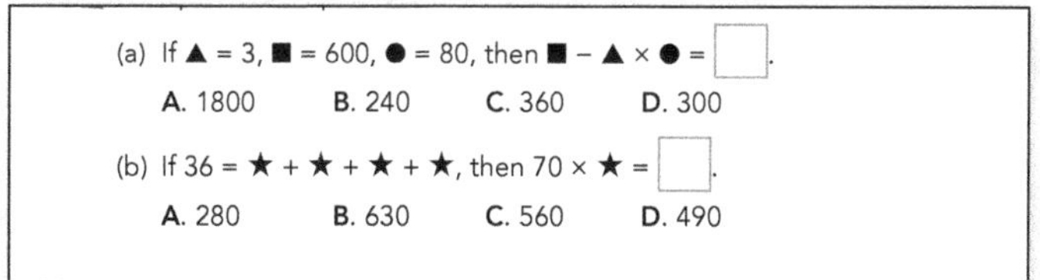

(a) If ▲ = 3, ■ = 600, ● = 80, then ■ − ▲ × ● = ☐.

A. 1800  B. 240  C. 360  D. 300

(b) If 36 = ★ + ★ + ★ + ★, then 70 × ★ = ☐.

A. 280  B. 630  C. 560  D. 490

### What learning will pupils have achieved at the conclusion of Question 5?

- Pupils will relate repeated addition of tens or hundreds numbers to multiplying by a tens or hundreds number.
- Pupils will be able to mentally multiply a one-digit number by tens and hundreds using their knowledge of multiplication facts and place value.
- The inverse relationship of multiplication and division will have been further developed to help find missing numbers.
- Pupils will have practised applying their knowledge of multiplying a one-digit number by tens and hundreds to a range of problems with and without a context.

### Activities for whole-class instruction

- Show the number sentence: 28 = 7 + 7 + 7 + 7. Ask: *How do we know that this is correct? Can we write it using the multiplication symbol?*
- Now replace one of the sevens as shown: 28 = 7 + 7 + 7 + ☐. Ask: *How do we know that the missing value must still be seven?*
- Finally show the number sentence: ☐ + ☐ + ☐ + ☐ + ☐ + ☐ + ☐ = 42. Ask: *Can each of the missing numbers be 7 this time? What can you do to check?*
- Establish that the missing numbers cannot be 7 as 7 × 7 is 49. Say: *We can easily find the value of each missing number by using the inverse 42 ÷ 7 as 42 is grouped into seven numbers. Each missing number is 6.*

- Show image 1 on **Resource 3.9.2e** Changing arrays.

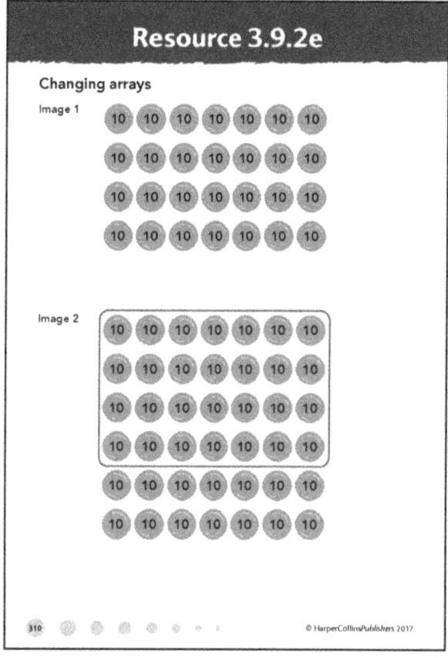


- Ask pupils to quick find the total value of the array. Establish that for the rows they can use 4 × 70 and for the columns 7 × 40. Agree that the product (280) is the same as they both have 28 tens.
- Now show image 2. Ask pupils to discuss what has changed and what has stayed the same.
- Ask pupils if they can explain that the value of each row is still 70 but there are now two more rows.
- Establish that the value of each column is now 60 and the total value can be found as 6 × 70 or 7 × 60, which is 42 tens or 420.
- Focus on the original array that is outlined in image 2. Suggest that we can describe the new array in different ways. Write the following on the board for pupils to discuss:

  6 × 70  4 × 70 + 140  280 + 2 × 70  280 + 7 × 20
- Explore each of the number sentences in turn, establishing that the three to the right use the value of the original array and then show the rows (or columns) that have been added.
- Ensure that pupils are clear that for 280 + 2 × 70 and 280 + 7 × 20, the multiplication that represents the second array must be completed first before it is added to 280 otherwise the total will not match the array.

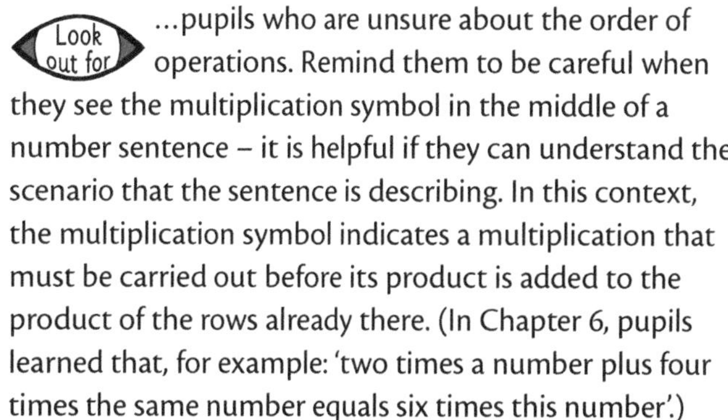


...pupils who are unsure about the order of operations. Remind them to be careful when they see the multiplication symbol in the middle of a number sentence – it is helpful if they can understand the scenario that the sentence is describing. In this context, the multiplication symbol indicates a multiplication that must be carried out before its product is added to the product of the rows already there. (In Chapter 6, pupils learned that, for example: 'two times a number plus four times the same number equals six times this number'.)

- Crossing through each line of the original 4 × 70 array, explain that you are taking away the four rows and leaving only the 2 × 70 array.
- Ask: *What number sentence can we use to explain what I have done? Is there more than one possibility?*
- Pupils work together and make suggestions. Take feedback and discuss ideas, checking that each is correct.
- These should include:

  420 – 280 = 140, 6 × 70 – 280 = 140, 420 – 4 × 70 = 140, 420 – 7 × 60 = 140, 420 – 280 = 2 × 70
- Practise the concept again by starting, this time, with a 4 × 700 array and adding two rows of 700.
- Ask pupils to explain what is the same and what is different this time.
- Pupils should complete Question 5 in the Practice Book.

## Same-day intervention

- Use place value counters or base 10 apparatus to represent the first problem in Question 5. Work together to make the array that is represented by ▲ × ●, that is 3 × 80.
- Ask pupils to quickly find the product describing this as 24 tens or 240.
- Now return to the problem ■ – ▲ × ● = □. Agree that we now know that ▲ × ● = 240 and that the square is worth 600.
- Write the sentence as 600 – 240 = □. Revisit subtraction to confirm that the missing number is 360. Pupils can use the inverse of addition to check this.
- Give pupils a similar problem, encouraging them to find the product of the multiplication first, for example: ■ + ▲ × ● = □ where the ■ = 320, ▲ = 5 and the ● = 80.

## Same-day enrichment

- Give pupils two dice and a set of tens and hundreds place value counters. They roll the dice to find their first array to make with tens or hundreds counters, for example if they roll a 6 and a 4, they make a 6 × 40 or 4 × 60 array with tens counters.
- They write a multiplication sentence to describe their array, for example 6 × 40 = 240. They roll one dice again to find the number of rows of counters to add or subtract, for example, if they roll a 2, they add two rows.
- Pupils then describe their new array in different ways, including using addition.
- Ask pupils to see if they can use their arrays to make up some problems as in Question 5a for others to solve.

  For example: If ▲ = 6, ● = 40 and ■ = 80, then ▲ × ● + ■ = □.
- Pupils repeat the activity, alternating between using tens counters and hundreds counters.

# Question 6

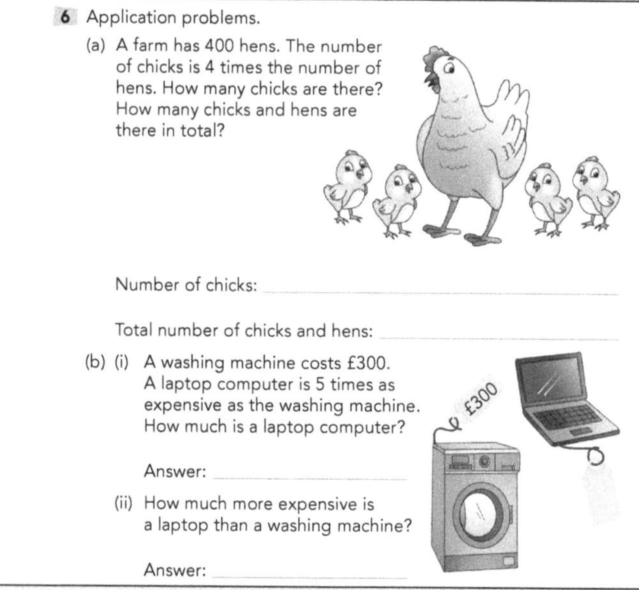
6 Application problems.

(a) A farm has 400 hens. The number of chicks is 4 times the number of hens. How many chicks are there? How many chicks and hens are there in total?

Number of chicks: ____________

Total number of chicks and hens: ____________

(b) (i) A washing machine costs £300. A laptop computer is 5 times as expensive as the washing machine. How much is a laptop computer?

Answer: ____________

(ii) How much more expensive is a laptop than a washing machine?

Answer: ____________



## What learning will pupils have achieved at the conclusion of Question 6?

- Pupils will be able to mentally multiply a one-digit number by tens and hundreds using their knowledge of multiplication facts and place value.
- Pupils will have practised applying their knowledge of multiplying a one-digit number by tens and hundreds to a range of problems with and without a context.

## Activities for whole-class instruction

- Using **Resource 3.9.2f** Multiplication problems, show pupils the three different word problems and three number sentences (two of the number sentences match the third problem).

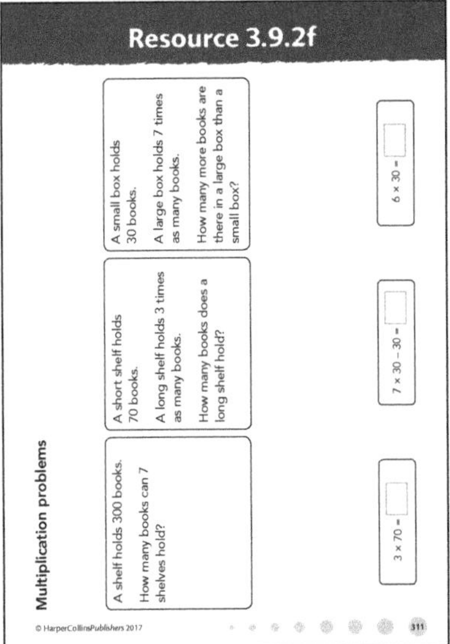

Resource 3.9.2f

Multiplication problems

A shelf holds 300 books. How many books can 7 shelves hold?

A short shelf holds 70 books. A long shelf holds 3 times as many books. How many books does a long shelf hold?

A small box holds 30 books. A large box holds 7 times as many books. How many more books are there in a large box than a small box?

3 × 70 = □

7 × 30 − 30 = □

6 × 30 = □

© HarperCollinsPublishers 2017 311

- Ask: *Which word problem matches each of the number sentences? How do you know?* Look together at the language used to describe multiplication here.
- Ask pupils to quickly find the answer to the three calculations. Discuss the strategies they use.
- Discuss why two of the number sentences match the last problem and why 6 × 30 is the same as 7 × 30 – 30.
- Together, construct a number sentence that could be used to match the first word problem. Ask pupils if they can change the numbers in the first problem but keep the product as 2400 books, for example, 6 × 400, 80 × 30.
- Invite pupils to make up three more problems to match the following calculations. They can use a context of their choice.

  90 × 6 = □ 5 × 800 = □ 6 × 90 + 90 = □
- Ask pupils to represent and explain each of their calculations concretely or pictorially.
- Pupils should complete Question 6 in the Practice Book.

## Same-day intervention

- Give pupils **Resource 3.9.2g** Problem arrays.

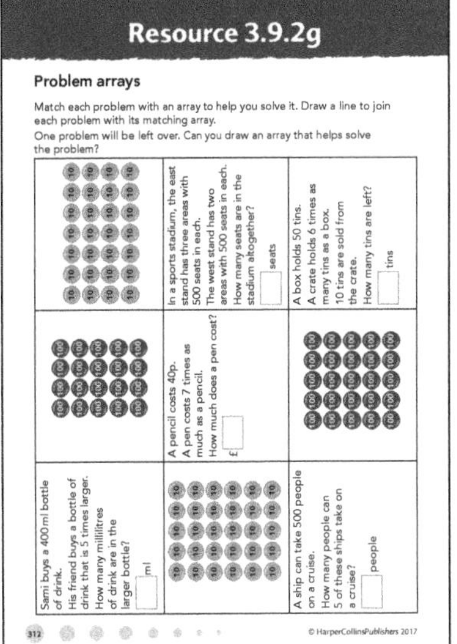

Resource 3.9.2g

Problem arrays

Match each problem with an array to help you solve it. Draw a line to join each problem with its matching array.
One problem will be left over. Can you draw an array that helps solve the problem?

In a sports stadium, the east stand has three areas with 500 seats in each. The west stand has two areas with 500 seats in each. How many seats are in the stadium altogether? □ seats

A box holds 50 tins. A crate holds 6 times as many tins as a box. 10 tins are sold from the crate. How many tins are left? □ tins

A pencil costs 40p. A pen costs 7 times as much as a pencil. How much does a pen cost? £□

Sami buys a 400 ml bottle of drink. His friend buys a bottle of drink that is 5 times larger. How many millilitres of drink are in the larger bottle? □ ml

A ship can take 500 people on a cruise. How many people can 5 of these ships take on a cruise? □ people

312 © HarperCollinsPublishers 2017

- Ask pupils to match each of the problems with an array. They then write the number sentence and answer the question.
- One problem is left over because the array is missing. Ask pupils to show it pictorially or concretely and explain why it matches the problem.

## Same-day enrichment

- Give pupils **Resource 3.9.2h** Writing problems, showing six different arrays.

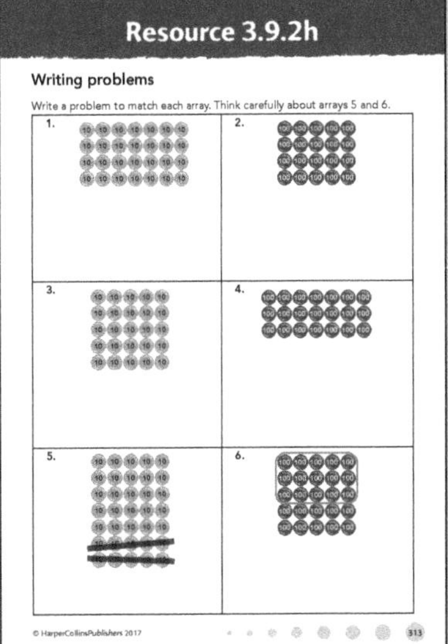

Resource 3.9.2h

Writing problems

Write a problem to match each array. Think carefully about arrays 5 and 6.

1. 2. 3. 4. 5. 6.

© HarperCollinsPublishers 2017 313

- Ask pupils to write a word problem to match each array. They then swap their word problem with a friend who should then match the problems to the correct array.

- For examples 5 and 6, pupils will need to include a subtraction and an addition in the problem.
  For example: *A box holds 50 tins.*
  *A crate holds six times as many tins as a box.*
  *Ten tins are sold from the crate.*
  *How many tins are left?*

## Challenge and extension question

# Question 7

**7** Fill in the boxes.

2000 × 8 = 200 × ☐ = ☐ × 800 = ☐ × 4 = 1000 × ☐ = 100 × ☐ = ☐ × 40 = 500 × ☐

In this question, pupils need to think flexibly about the different ways that the same product can be achieved.

The key to the problem is finding the product of 2000 × 8 and then recognising that each of the following sentences are equivalent to this.

Pupils may find it useful to use a place value grid to check the effect of multiplying by tens and hundreds.

# Unit 9.3
# Writing number sentences

## Conceptual context

Pupils have developed their understanding of multiplying a number of tens or hundreds, for example 7 × 50, by identifying the product of 7 × 5 as 35 and recognising that 7 × 50 is equal to 35 tens.

In this unit, pupils apply this understanding and draw on other multiplication facts to solve a range of routine problems in context. The focus of this work is to identify the number sentence needed each time from the information that has been given.

## Learning pupils will have achieved at the end of the unit

- Pupils will have applied their knowledge in order to identify the processes and the numbers involved when problems are presented in context (Q1, Q2)
- Understanding of multiplication will have been deepened further as pupils create their own word problems (Q2)
- Pupils will have applied their understanding of mentally multiplying a one-digit number by tens and hundreds, using their knowledge of multiplication facts and place value (Q1, Q2)
- Pupils will have practised using multiplication facts, including multiplying by tens in a range of problems in context (Q1, Q2)

### Resources

Number rods; **Resource 3.9.3a** Write word problems; **Resource 3.9.3b** Multiplication sentences; **Resource 3.9.3c** Multiplication word problems

### Vocabulary

tens, multiply, multiplication, product, times, factor, sum of

# Question 1

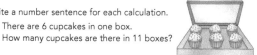

**1** Write a number sentence for each calculation.

(a) There are 6 cupcakes in one box.
How many cupcakes are there in 11 boxes?

Number sentence: ______________________

(b) Evie and 3 friends are going on a trip. Everyone needs to pay £30 for the trip. How much do they pay in total?

Number sentence: ______________________

(c) There are 4 packets of nuts in one box. Each pack costs £12. How much will 3 packs of nuts cost?

Number sentence: ______________________

## What learning will pupils have achieved at the conclusion of Question 1?

- Pupils will have applied their knowledge in order to identify the processes and the numbers involved when problems are presented in context.
- Pupils will have applied their understanding of mentally multiplying a one-digit number by tens and hundreds using their knowledge of multiplication facts and place value.
- Pupils will have practised multiplication facts, including multiplying by tens in a range of problems in context.

## Activities for whole-class instruction

- Allocate groups of pupils to the 4, 8 or 12 times tables. They should quickly complete a double-sided number line to show their multiplication table up to 12 times, as shown.

0 4 8 12 16 20 24 28 32 36 40 44 48

0 1 2 3 4 5 6 7 8 9 10 11 12

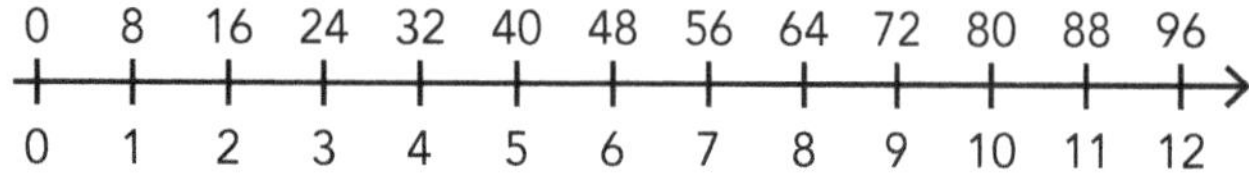


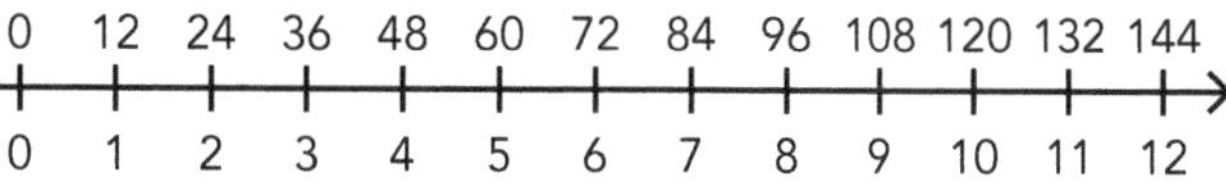


- Draw out related facts from each table, for example 3 × 4, 3 × 8 and 3 × 12, looking at the relationships between the factors and the products.
- Ask pupils to explain why the product of 3 × 8 is double 3 × 4, and why the product of 3 × 12 is three times more than 3 × 4 or is the sum of the product of 3 × 4 and 3 × 8.

*Three multiplied by eight is double three multiplied by four.*

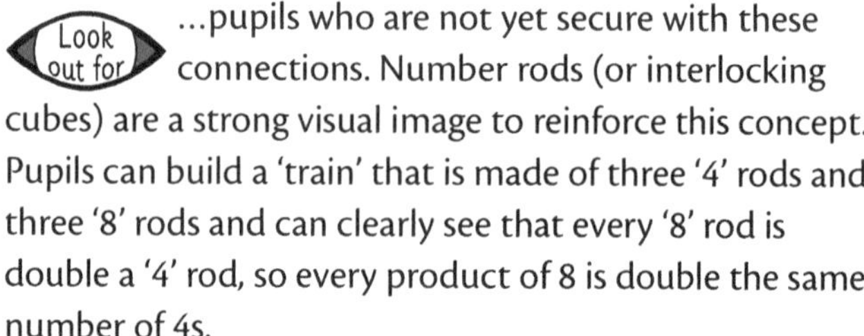


...pupils who are not yet secure with these connections. Number rods (or interlocking cubes) are a strong visual image to reinforce this concept. Pupils can build a 'train' that is made of three '4' rods and three '8' rods and can clearly see that every '8' rod is double a '4' rod, so every product of 8 is double the same number of 4s.

- Discuss facts that have the same product, for example, 6 × 4, 3 × 8 and 2 × 12, focusing on the fact that there are two fours in eight, so double the number of fours are needed to give the same product as 3 × 8.
- Show pupils the following problems:

  *A chair has four legs.*

  *How many legs do nine of these chairs have?*
- Ask: *Who has the fact on their number line that matches this problem? How do you know?*
- Ask pupils to write the number sentence for the problem: 9 × 4 = 36 or 4 × 9 = 36.
- Now change the question slightly to: *How many legs do 12 of these chairs have?*
- Ask pupils to explain who has the fact that matches the problem on their number line. Look together at the commutativity of multiplication to agree that both 12 × 4 and 4 × 12 match, so the fact can be found on two of the number lines. Record the number sentences together.
- Introduce three more problems. Ask pupils to write the matching number sentences:

> A spider has eight legs.
>
> Amy finds three spiders in the garden and another two spiders in the shed.
>
> How many spider legs does she see?

> A pack of stickers costs 40p.
>
> How much will 12 packs cost?

> A cake costs 40p.
>
> There are six cakes in a box.
>
> How much will two boxes cost?

- Explore each question in turn, discussing those that have two steps, for example three spiders and two spiders is five spiders, so 5 × 8 legs were seen.
- Ask pupils to explain why the multiplication fact 12 × 40 can be used for the sticker problem and the cake problem.
- Establish that there are 12 cakes in two boxes, and each costs 40p.
- Finally reveal a final problem:

  *A cake costs 40p.*

  *There are six cakes in a box.*

  *How many cakes will be in two boxes?*
- Suggest that the same number sentence 12 × 40 can be used for this problem because the information is the same. Ask pupils to discuss this. Ask pupils to explain why you are wrong and the number sentence this time is 2 × 6. Explain that some problems may include redundant information, that is, information that is not important or needed to answer the question.
- Pupils should complete Question 1 in the Practice Book.

## Same-day intervention

- Look together at the three problems in Question 1. Ask: *Which problems could you solve using the double-sided number lines that we made earlier?*
- Agree that the second problem, 4 × 30, uses the fact 4 × 3 or 3 × 4 to find 12 tens and the third problem uses the fact 3 × 12 = 36. Discuss why the number of packets of nuts in one box is irrelevant here and is redundant information.
- Present the following problem: *There are four packets of nuts in one box. Each box costs £12. How many packets are in three boxes of nuts?*
- Ask: *What information is important this time? Will the number sentence still be 3 × 12?* Agree that the cost of a box is redundant information and the number sentence needed is 3 × 4 = 12.
- Finally look at the first problem. It used different multiplication facts. Can pupils quickly make up a double-sided number line to help them? Will they choose × 6 or × 11?
- Look together at the commutativity of multiplication to agree that the answer to the problem can be found in both tables as 11 × 6 and 6 × 11.

## Same-day enrichment

- Give pupils **Resource 3.9.3a** Write word problems.

**Resource 3.9.3a (1 of 2)**

**Write word problems**

Use facts from the number lines to help make up the following types of question.

| 0 | 4 | 8 | 12 | 16 | 20 | 24 | 28 | 32 | 36 | 40 | 44 | 48 |
|---|---|---|---|---|---|---|---|---|---|---|---|---|
| 0 | 1 | 2 | 3 | 4 | 5 | 6 | 7 | 8 | 9 | 10 | 11 | 12 |

| 0 | 8 | 16 | 24 | 32 | 40 | 48 | 56 | 64 | 72 | 80 | 88 | 96 |
|---|---|---|---|---|---|---|---|---|---|---|---|---|
| 0 | 1 | 2 | 3 | 4 | 5 | 6 | 7 | 8 | 9 | 10 | 11 | 12 |

| 0 | 12 | 24 | 36 | 48 | 60 | 72 | 84 | 96 | 108 | 120 | 132 | 144 |
|---|---|---|---|---|---|---|---|---|---|---|---|---|
| 0 | 1 | 2 | 3 | 4 | 5 | 6 | 7 | 8 | 9 | 10 | 11 | 12 |

1. Write a word problem to match the fact: 6 × 12 = 72.

2. Write a different word problem to match a fact from the eights number line.

3. Write a different word problem to match a fact from the fours number line.

314 © HarperCollinsPublishers 2017

**Resource 3.9.3a (2 of 2)**

4. Write a problem with two steps. Make the first step multiplication and the second step subtraction.

5. Complete this maths story with numbers of your choice:
   Amy buys 7 packets of 4 stickers on the way to school.
   On the way home, she buys another ☐ packets of 4 stickers.
   She calculates that altogether she has ☐ × 4 = ☐ stickers.

6. Write a word problem for the fact: 9 × 4 = 36. Include some information in the problem that is not needed to solve it.

© HarperCollinsPublishers 2017 315

- Pupils create word problems to match different facts from their double-sided number lines. Ask pupils to try to include two steps in their problems.
- Challenge pupils to make up a problem that combines the multiplication facts for four with the facts for eight so that the solver will need to use multiplication facts for 12.
- Ask pupils if they can make up a problem that includes redundant information. They should write a number sentence and answer for each problem and test them out on their friends.

# Question 2

**2** Look at the pictures. Draw a line to match each question to the correct number sentence.

| BAKED BEANS | | Rice 10kg |
|---|---|---|
| 12 cans per box<br>£70 per box | 12 bottles per box<br>£45 per box | 10 kilograms per sack<br>£50 per sack |

(a) How much do 2 boxes of baked beans cost? 4 × 10

(b) How much do 2 boxes of milk cost? 2 × 12

(c) How many bottles of milk are there in 2 boxes? 2 × 70

(d) What is the weight of 4 sacks of rice? 2 × 45

## What learning will pupils have achieved at the conclusion of Question 2?

- Pupils will have applied their knowledge in order to identify the processes and the numbers involved when problems are presented in context.

- Understanding of multiplication will have been deepened further as pupils create their own word problems.
- Pupils will have practised multiplication facts, including multiplying by tens in a range of problems in context.

## Activities for whole-class instruction

- Show pupils image 1 on **Resource 3.9.3b** Multiplication sentences.

- Ask: *What different multiplication sentences can you make from the picture?* Pupils should work together to come up with a range of number sentences, explaining which part of the picture they represent. This could include the following:

  4 × 4 = 16 people rowing boats or cost of hiring a boat for four people

  4 × 16 = 64 cost of hiring the four boats

  3 × 35 = 105 cost of three balloons

  9 × 35 = 315 cost of nine balloons

  5 × 4 = 20 people altogether (4 groups of 4 in river and 1 group of 4 on the river bank)

  6 × 2 = 12 cones

  4 × 70 = 280 cost of four boxes of popcorn

  12 × 50 = 600 cost of 12 cones

  6 × 80 = 480 cost of 6 cups of tea

  4 × 50 = 200 if one boat of 4 had an ice-cream cone each, and so on.

- Explore each of the number sentences and scenarios in turn. Ask pupils to write or say a word problem to match each scenario discussed. Ask them to see if they can include more than one step or some redundant information.
- Discuss ideas together and agree a set of word problems.
- Show image 2 from **Resource 3.9.3b** that captures parts of the original picture but now with changes.
- Ask pupils to amend the original number sentences and problems to match the new information.
- Share some of the ideas together and agree new problems and number sentences.
- Pupils should complete Question 2 in the Practice Book.

## Same-day intervention

- Pupils work together to create their own multiplication picture. They can use the same theme as before or change it to one of their own, for example in the sea, at the supermarket, on a tropical island.
- They could use sticky-notes, or similar, to write different word problems to match their picture, making sure they record the number sentence and the answer on the back of each note.

## Same-day enrichment

- Give pupils **Resource 3.9.3c** Multiplication word problems.

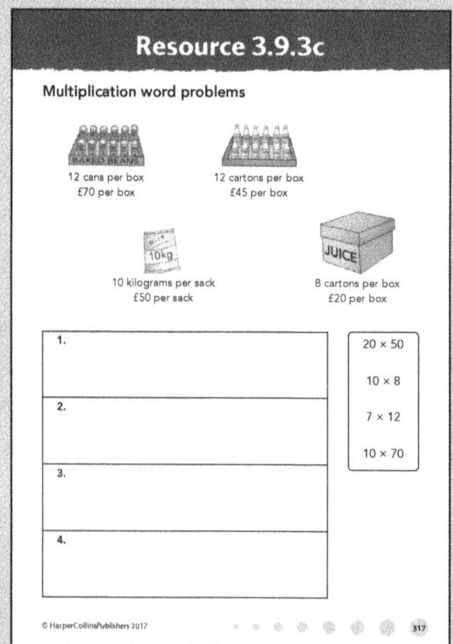


- The pictures shown are the same as those used in the Practice Book, along with another image showing a box of juice cartons.
- Ask pupils to write new word problems for the given multiplication sentences so that others can draw lines to match the problems with the number sentences.

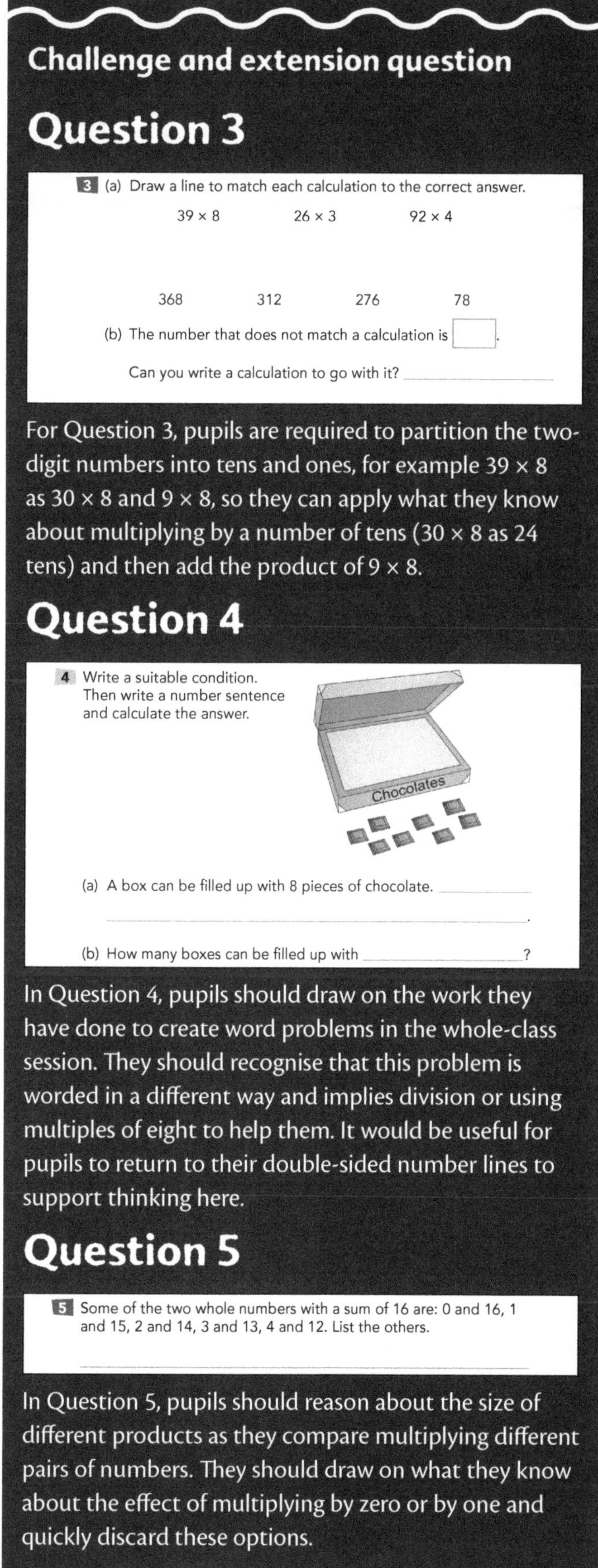

## Challenge and extension question

## Question 3

3 (a) Draw a line to match each calculation to the correct answer.

39 × 8    26 × 3    92 × 4

368    312    276    78

(b) The number that does not match a calculation is ☐.

Can you write a calculation to go with it? ____________

For Question 3, pupils are required to partition the two-digit numbers into tens and ones, for example 39 × 8 as 30 × 8 and 9 × 8, so they can apply what they know about multiplying by a number of tens (30 × 8 as 24 tens) and then add the product of 9 × 8.

## Question 4

4 Write a suitable condition. Then write a number sentence and calculate the answer.



(a) A box can be filled up with 8 pieces of chocolate. ____________

____________.

(b) How many boxes can be filled up with ____________?

In Question 4, pupils should draw on the work they have done to create word problems in the whole-class session. They should recognise that this problem is worded in a different way and implies division or using multiples of eight to help them. It would be useful for pupils to return to their double-sided number lines to support thinking here.

## Question 5

5 Some of the two whole numbers with a sum of 16 are: 0 and 16, 1 and 15, 2 and 14, 3 and 13, 4 and 12. List the others.

____________

In Question 5, pupils should reason about the size of different products as they compare multiplying different pairs of numbers. They should draw on what they know about the effect of multiplying by zero or by one and quickly discard these options.

# Unit 9.4
# Multiplying a 2-digit number by a 1-digit number (1)

## Conceptual context

In previous units in this chapter, pupils have applied their knowledge of single-digit multiplication facts to multiply by a number of tens or hundreds. They know that (and understand why) they can use multiplication facts to find products of factors that are ten or a hundred times bigger than those within the tables that they know.

They have also learned that arrays can be partitioned to represent part products. Pupils' understanding of part products will now be developed so that they begin to perceive opportunities to partition two-digit numbers in order to create two-part products that can be added together. In this way they will, over the coming units, naturally understand the process of multiplying a two-digit number by a one-digit number as adding together part products found when the number to be multiplied is partitioned.

## Learning pupils will have achieved at the end of the unit

- Pupils will recognise and explain why it is easier to partition a two-digit number to be multiplied into tens and ones (Q1, Q2)
- Pupils will have shown their ability to mentally multiply a one-digit number by tens as part of the whole calculation (Q1, Q2, Q3)
- Pupils will be able to write number sentences to match representations, identifying the operation and the numbers involved (Q1, Q2, Q3)
- Pupils will be able to compare multiplication sentences and reason about which will give the larger product (Q3)
- Pupils will have practised using multiplication facts and multiplying a one-digit number by tens in a range of problems in context (Q3)

### Resources

base 10 blocks; place value counters; dice; **Resource 3.9.4a** Strawberry array; **Resource 3.9.4b** Partitioning arrays with strawberries; **Resource 3.9.4c** Place value arrays; **Resource 3.9.4d** 2-digit × 1-digit multiplication; **Resource 3.9.4e** Word problem arrays

### Vocabulary

tens, multiply, multiplication, product, partition

# Question 1

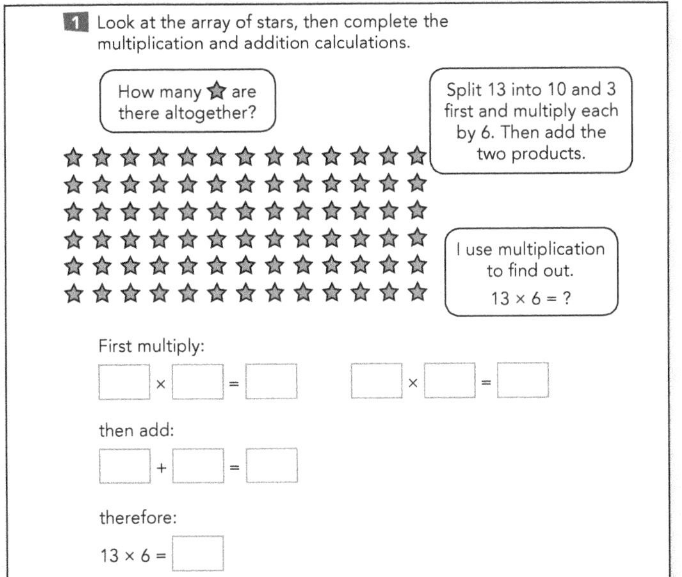

1 Look at the array of stars, then complete the multiplication and addition calculations.
How many ☆ are there altogether?
Split 13 into 10 and 3 first and multiply each by 6. Then add the two products.
I use multiplication to find out. 13 × 6 = ?
First multiply:
then add:
therefore:
13 × 6 =


## What learning will pupils have achieved at the conclusion of Question 1?

- Pupils will recognise and explain why it is easier to partition a two-digit number to be multiplied into tens and ones.
- Pupils will have shown their ability to mentally multiply a one-digit number by tens as part of the whole calculation.
- Pupils will be able to write number sentences to match representations, identifying the operation and the numbers involved.

## Activities for whole-class instruction

- Begin by practising 10 × multiplication facts to include examples using commutativity, such as 7 × 10 and 10 × 7.
- Pupils should use base 10 blocks to represent the product each time as a number of tens rods or sticks.
- Draw an array of squares for 3 × 10. Agree this represents three tens rods or sticks:

- Agree that the product is 30 as 3 × 10 = 30 and 10 × 3 = 30.
- Ask: *How will you need to change the representation to show 12 × 3 or 3 × 12?* Discuss ideas, ensuring that pupils add two extra cubes in each row to show 12 in each row.
- Draw two more squares in each row, using a different colour.

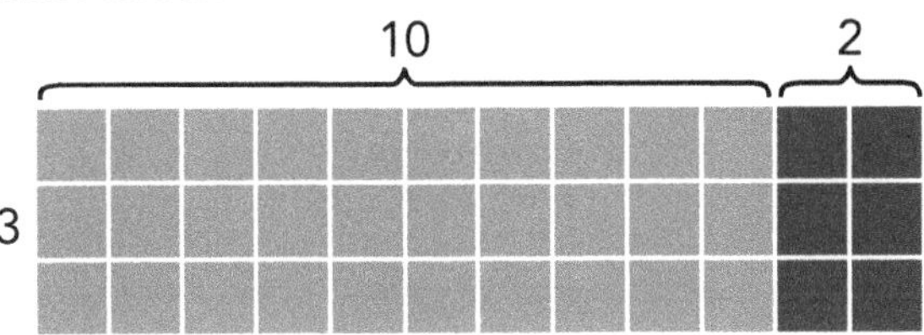


- Tell pupils that they can quickly find the product of 12 × 3 by partitioning 12 into 10 + 2 and looking at the tens part first and then the ones part. Ask: *Why is it useful to partition 12 into 10 + 2 rather than 9 + 3?*
- Pupils should be able to explain that multiplying by 10 is an easy calculation.

(i) Recognising that multiplying by 10 or 100 is an easy calculation is an important development point so pupils can make informed decisions about the most efficient strategy to use.

- Ask pupils to explain the value of the tens part (10 × 3 = 30) and the value of the ones part (2 × 3 = 6). Explain that to find the value of 12 × 3, we can simply add the products of 10 × 3 and 2 × 3.
- Record this as:

  10 × 3 = 30 2 × 3 = 6

  30 + 6 = 36

  12 × 3 = 36
- Ask pupils to change their array to show 13 × 4. Ask: *What do you need to do?* Discuss how 13 is partitioned this time into 10 and 3.
- Ask pupils to complete the calculation by first looking at the tens and the ones separately, and then adding the products. Ask pupils to record the number sentences to show what they have done.
- Look together at using the inverse division to check answers.
- Practise a few more examples using the same method, for example 13 × 5 and 14 × 4.

- Finally, show the image on **Resource 3.9.4a** Strawberry array.

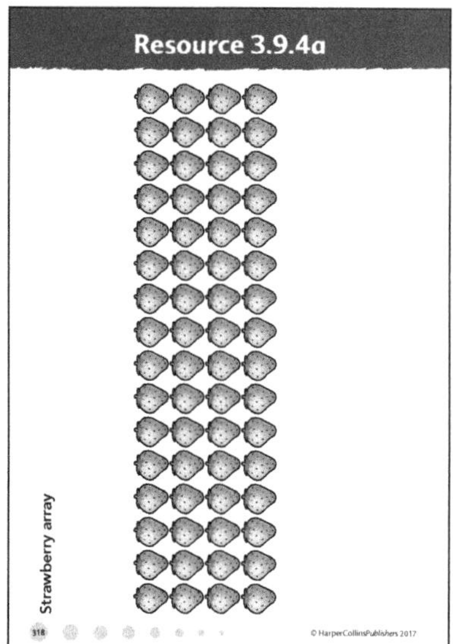


- Ask: *What multiplication sentence can we write to describe this array?*
- Discuss how to find the product of 16 × 4 by partitioning the array into tens and ones as before.
- Draw a line on the array to show how it has been partitioned.
- Record the calculation as:

  10 × 4 = 40 6 × 4 = 24

  40 + 24 = 64

  16 × 4 = 64
- Pupils should complete Question 1 in the Practice Book.

## Same-day intervention

- In groups, give pupils the following multiplications to represent using base 10 blocks or place value counters.

  13 × 5 12 × 6 14 × 4 15 × 7
- They compare the size of each array and together discuss which will give the largest and smallest product and why.
- Pupils record the multiplication sentences needed to find the product of their array, using partitioning, then calculate. Ask pupils if their predictions were correct.
- Ask pupils to now make an array to show a calculation with a product that is smaller than the arrays shown.

## Same-day enrichment

- Give pupils the problem on **Resource 3.9.4b** Partitioning arrays with strawberries, to explore.

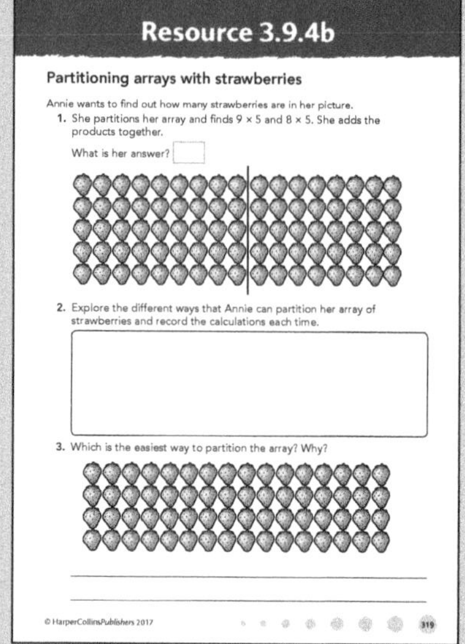
Resource 3.9.4b

Partitioning arrays with strawberries

Annie wants to find out how many strawberries are in her picture.

1. She partitions her array and finds 9 × 5 and 8 × 5. She adds the products together.

   What is her answer?

2. Explore the different ways that Annie can partition her array of strawberries and record the calculations each time.

3. Which is the easiest way to partition the array? Why?

© HarperCollinsPublishers 2017 319

- The problem involves partitioning arrays in different ways to reinforce the fact that using tens is easier. Pupils should record their ideas in their books.

# Question 2

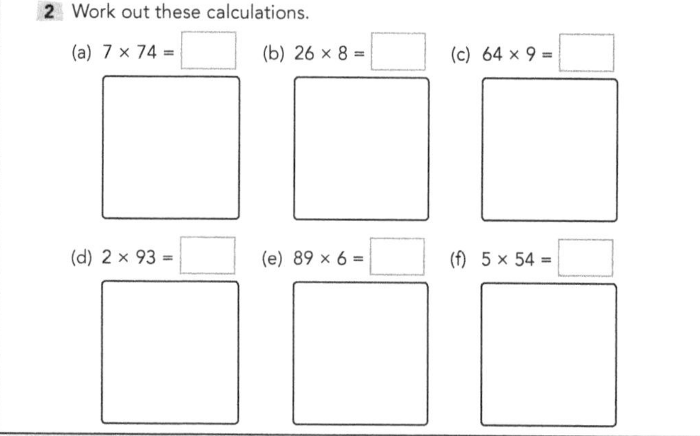
2 Work out these calculations.

(a) 7 × 74 = (b) 26 × 8 = (c) 64 × 9 =

(d) 2 × 93 = (e) 89 × 6 = (f) 5 × 54 =

## What learning will pupils have achieved at the conclusion of Question 2?

- Pupils will recognise and explain why it is easier to partition a two-digit number to be multiplied into tens and ones.
- Pupils will have shown their ability to mentally multiply a one-digit number by tens as part of the whole calculation.
- Pupils will be able to write number sentences to match representations, identifying the operation and the numbers involved.

## Activities for whole-class instruction

- Show pupils the following sets of calculations. Ask them to reason about the products each time, using what they know about multiplication facts and multiplying by a number of tens.

| | | | |
|---|---|---|---|
| $4 \times 3 =$ | $7 \times 5 =$ | $9 \times 8 =$ | $6 \times 3 =$ |
| $40 \times 3 =$ | $7 \times 50 =$ | $9 \times 80 =$ | $60 \times 3 =$ |

- Go through the answers together, focusing on the products of, for example $40 \times 3$ as $4 \times 3$ tens or 12 tens so $40 \times 3$ is ten times larger than $4 \times 3$.
- Look at the two facts $40 \times 3$ and $6 \times 3$. Agree that both numbers are multiplied by three.
- Show image 1 on **Resource 3.9.4c** Place value arrays.

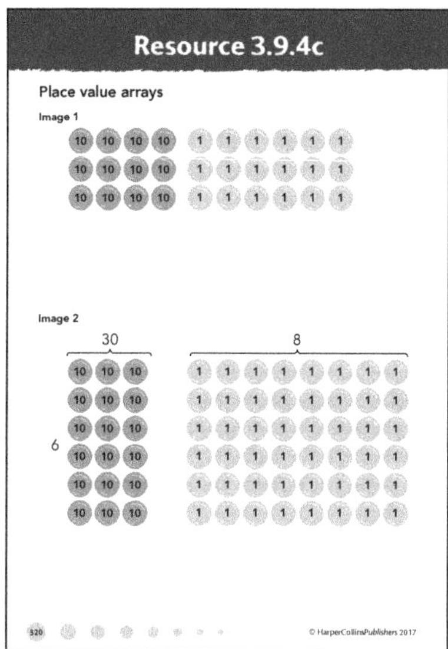


- Agree that the arrays of place value counters represent $40 \times 3$ and $6 \times 3$.
- Ask: *What do we know about the product of 46 × 3? Where can you see 46 in the representation?*
- Pupils should discuss their ideas. Take feedback and establish that $46 \times 3$ must be the total of the products of $40 \times 3$ and $6 \times 3$. Again, partitioning has been used to show the number of tens and the number of ones.
- Record the calculation as:

$46 \times 3 =$

$40 \times 3 = 120$

$6 \times 3 = 18$

$120 + 18 = 138$

All say ... *46 × 3 is the same as 40 × 3 add 6 × 3.*

Look at the calculation $38 \times 6$. Ask pupils to describe the array that would represent $38 \times 6$.

- Show image 2 from **Resource 3.9.4c** to confirm ideas.
- Ask: *What is 38 × 6? Will the product be the same for 6 × 38?*
- Record the calculation, using partitioning as before.
- Pupils should complete Question 2 in the Practice Book.

### Same-day intervention

- Look together at some of the calculations from Question 2. Ask: *Which calculation gave the largest product? Which gave the smallest? Which part of the number helps you to decide?*
- Compare $7 \times 74$ with a new calculation, $6 \times 89$. Ask: *Which do you think will give the larger product? Why?*
- Look together at $7 \times 70$ and $6 \times 80$, ensuring that pupils recognise this as 49 tens and 48 tens. Agree that $7 \times 70$ gives a larger product, but it is important to check the ones part of the calculation too.
- Compare $7 \times 4$ and $6 \times 9$ and ask: *What are the products? Which is larger?*
- Establish that $7 \times 74$ is the same as $70 \times 7$ add $7 \times 4$ and is the total of $490 + 28$ (518), and that $6 \times 89$ is the same as $6 \times 80$ add $6 \times 9$ and is the total of $480 + 54$ (534). So, $7 \times 74$ is actually less than $6 \times 89$.
- Select other calculations to compare in the same way.

## Same-day enrichment

- Give pupils **Resource 3.9.4d** 2-digit × 1-digit multiplication.

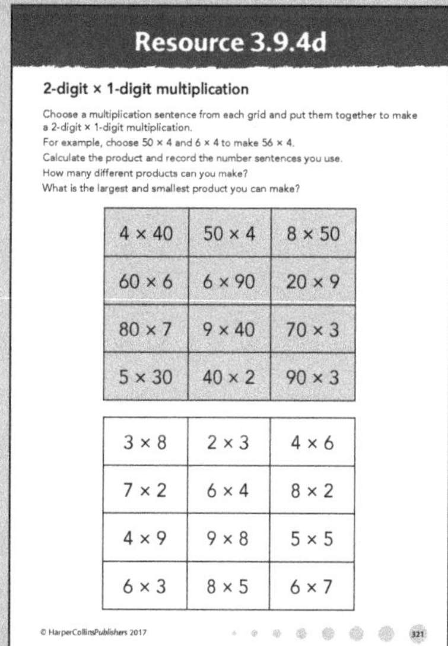

Resource 3.9.4d

2-digit × 1-digit multiplication

Choose a multiplication sentence from each grid and put them together to make a 2-digit × 1-digit multiplication.

For example, choose 50 × 4 and 6 × 4 to make 56 × 4.

Calculate the product and record the number sentences you use.

How many different products can you make?

What is the largest and smallest product you can make?

| | | |
|---|---|---|
| 4 × 40 | 50 × 4 | 8 × 50 |
| 60 × 6 | 6 × 90 | 20 × 9 |
| 80 × 7 | 9 × 40 | 70 × 3 |
| 5 × 30 | 40 × 2 | 90 × 3 |

| | | |
|---|---|---|
| 3 × 8 | 2 × 3 | 4 × 6 |
| 7 × 2 | 6 × 4 | 8 × 2 |
| 4 × 9 | 9 × 8 | 5 × 5 |
| 6 × 3 | 8 × 5 | 6 × 7 |

© HarperCollinsPublishers 2017 321

- They should select two multiplications to combine to make two-digit × one-digit multiplications.
- Pupils are asked to find as many different products as they can, including the largest and smallest possible product.

# Question 3

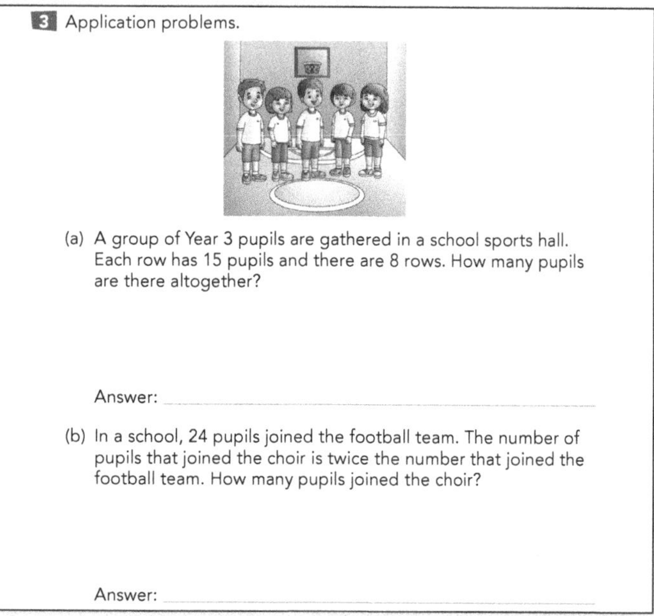

**3** Application problems.

(a) A group of Year 3 pupils are gathered in a school sports hall. Each row has 15 pupils and there are 8 rows. How many pupils are there altogether?

Answer: ______

(b) In a school, 24 pupils joined the football team. The number of pupils that joined the choir is twice the number that joined the football team. How many pupils joined the choir?

Answer: ______

## What learning will pupils have achieved at the conclusion of Question 3?

- Pupils will have shown their ability to mentally multiply a one-digit number by tens as part of the whole calculation.
- Pupils will be able to write number sentences to match representations, identifying the operation and the numbers involved.
- Pupils will be able to compare multiplication sentences and reason about which will give the larger product.
- Pupils will have practised using multiplication facts and multiplying a one-digit number by tens in a range of problems in context.

## Activities for whole-class instruction

- Show pupils the following two problems and three different arrays, using **Resource 3.9.4e** Word problem arrays.

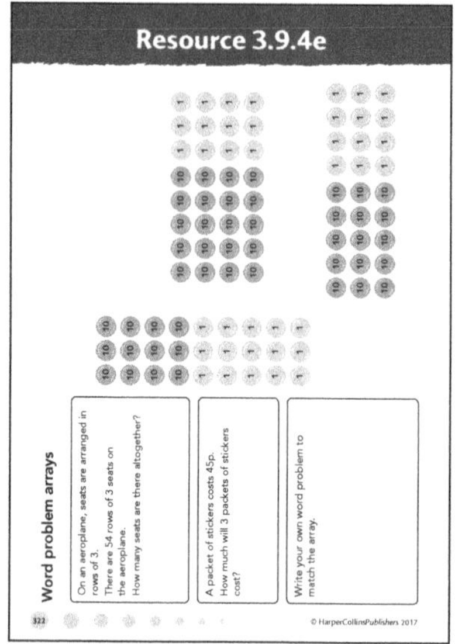

Resource 3.9.4e

Word problem arrays

On an aeroplane, seats are arranged in rows of 3. There are 54 rows of 3 seats on the aeroplane. How many seats are there altogether?

A packet of stickers costs 45p. How much will 3 packets of stickers cost?

Write your own word problem to match the array.

- Read through the problems together and decide what each one is asking. Establish that each requires us to multiply.
- Ask: *What is the same and what is different about the problems?* Pupils should notice that some of the digits are the same but are in a different order within the calculations needed to solve the problems.
- Look together at the three arrays. Ask pupils to explain which array matches each problem. Ask them to decide which calculation will give the largest product. Ask: *How does the array help you to decide? What part of the array is it important to look at when making this decision?*
- Agree that it is useful to look at the tens part first, but we must check the ones as well.
- Ask pupils to work out the answer to each problem and record the number sentences each time.
- Ask pupils to make up their own problem to match the array. Make up a question for the third box to go with the unmatched array and together complete the calculation.
- Pupils should complete Question 3 in the Practice Book.

## Same-day intervention

- Give pupils the following problem with missing numbers and introduce the activity.

  *One jar holds ☐ marbles.*

  *How many marbles will ☐ of these jars hold?*
- Pupils roll a dice three times to make a two-digit and a one-digit number to write into the problem.
- They solve the problem using their numbers.
- Ask them to rearrange the three digits to make another one-digit and two-digit number to find a larger answer.
- They repeat the activity to find the largest and smallest answer to the problem.

## Same-day enrichment

- Give pupils the following problem to discuss and solve while you are introducing the activity to the intervention group.

  *A red jar holds 34 marbles. A green jar holds 46 marbles.*

  *There are 7 full jars of each colour.*

  *How many more marbles in total are in the green jars than in the red jars?* ☐
- Look together at the solution to the problem and discuss how this problem differs from the ones solved in the whole-class session. Agree that there is more than one step to this problem.
- Remove all the numbers for the problem and give pupils the following criteria.
  - The number of marbles in each jar is a two-digit number.
  - The difference between the number of marbles in a green jar and a red jar is also a two-digit number.
  - The number of jars each time is always a one-digit number.
- Ask pupils to work together with their own numbers to find different solutions with between 30 and 50 more marbles in total in the green jars than red jars.

## Challenge and extension question

## Question 4

**4** Write < or > in each ◯.

(a) $14 \times 7$ ◯ $17 \times 4$　　(b) $27 \times 3$ ◯ $23 \times 7$

(c) $19 \times 5$ ◯ $15 \times 9$　　(d) $45 \times 2$ ◯ $42 \times 5$

What did you notice?

In this question, pupils should be encouraged to look carefully at the numbers involved before calculating.

Ask them to make estimates about which product may be larger by quickly looking first at the number of tens, for example one, comparing 7 tens ($10 \times 7$) and 4 tens ($10 \times 4$). Look for pupils who may think that $14 \times 7$ and $17 \times 4$ will give the same product as all the digits are the same.

Pupils can use place value counters or sketch their own arrays to assist calculations.

# Unit 9.5 Multiplying a 2-digit number by a 1-digit number (2)

## Conceptual context

Pupils have begun to focus on part products to multiply two-digit numbers, built on their ability to multiply easily by ten. In the previous unit, the concept of partitioning a two-digit number into tens and ones and multiplying each of those by the multiplier to find part products before combining those to find the complete product, was introduced and pupils explored a number of examples.

In this unit, they will explore ways of recording those part products, including column methods. The first method emphasises partitioning and records part products separately; this method is used as a transition to the more compact method, where multiplying by ones and tens is recorded in the same answer space and any 'movement' across columns becomes part of the process. Pupils continue to use mental methods to check their working and, at times, this may still be the most appropriate method for the numbers involved.

## Learning pupils will have achieved at the end of the unit

- Conceptual understanding of multiplying a two-digit number by a one-digit number has been developed using manipulatives. Pupils represent multiplication as arrays and understand how the partitioned product relates to the process of multiplication in a written method (Q1, Q2, Q3, Q4)
- Pupils will be able to compare multiplication sentences and reason about which will give the larger product (Q1, Q2)
- Pupils will have shown their ability to mentally multiply a one-digit number by tens as part of the whole calculation (Q1, Q2, Q3)
- Knowledge of partitioning into tens and ones will have been applied to mental and written methods of multiplication (Q1, Q2, Q3)
- Pupils will have been introduced to the compact method for short multiplication (Q1, Q2, Q3, Q4)
- Pupils will have practised applying their knowledge of multiplication facts and multiplying a one-digit number to check answers to calculations (Q4)

## Resources

base 10 blocks; place value counters; **Resource 3.9.5a** 3-digit calculations; **Resource 3.9.5b** Twice the price; **Resource 3.9.5c** Missing numbers

## Vocabulary

ones, tens, multiply, multiplication, product, partition

# Question 1

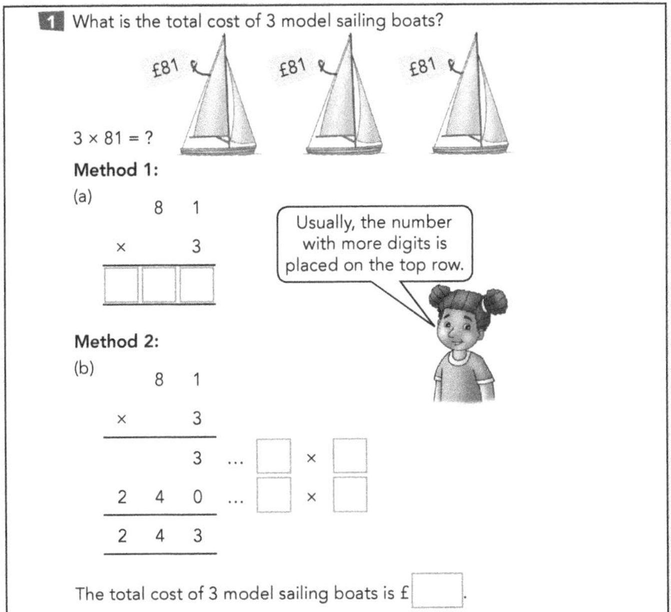

1 What is the total cost of 3 model sailing boats?

£81 £81 £81

3 × 81 = ?

**Method 1:**

(a)

$$\begin{array}{r} 8\ 1 \\ \times\quad 3 \\ \hline \square\square\square \end{array}$$

Usually, the number with more digits is placed on the top row.

**Method 2:**

(b)

$$\begin{array}{rl} 8\ 1 & \\ \times\quad 3 & \\ \hline 3 & \dots \square \times \square \\ 2\ 4\ 0 & \dots \square \times \square \\ \hline 2\ 4\ 3 & \end{array}$$

The total cost of 3 model sailing boats is £$\square$.

## What learning will pupils have achieved at the conclusion of Question 1?

- Conceptual understanding of multiplying a two-digit number by a one-digit number will have been developed using manipulatives. Pupils represent multiplication as arrays and understand how the partitioned product relates to the process of multiplication in a written method.
- Pupils will be able to compare multiplication sentences and reason about which will give the larger product.
- Pupils will have shown their ability to mentally multiply a one-digit number by tens as part of the whole calculation.
- Knowledge of partitioning into tens and ones will have been applied to mental and written methods of multiplication.
- Pupils will have been introduced to the compact method for short multiplication.

## Activities for whole-class instruction

- Give pupils the following set of multiplication calculations to compare:

  80 × 4    4 × 82    6 × 50    51 × 6    70 × 5

- Ask: *Which do you think will give the largest product and the smallest product? Why?* Agree that 35 tens for 70 × 5 is larger than 30 tens for 51 × 6, and so on.
- Ask pupils to complete each calculation, using partitioning where needed. Look for pupils who recognise that for 4 × 82 and 51 × 6, we already know the answer to the tens part of the calculation because we have worked out 80 × 4 and 6 × 50.
- Discuss the answers and compare these against the predicted largest and smallest products.
- Explain that you are going to show two different methods to calculate 4 × 82. These are written methods rather than mental methods, but knowledge of multiplication facts and place value will still be needed.
- Show pupils the following example, explaining that the number with more digits is usually placed at the top.

$$\begin{array}{r} 8\ 2 \\ \times\quad 4 \\ \hline 8 \\ 3\ 2\ 0 \\ \hline 3\ 2\ 8 \end{array}$$

- Say: *These numbers are a record of a calculation. What do you think the calculation was? Why do you think that? What are the numbers showing?*
- Ask: *Where can you see 4 × 80* (4 × 8 tens) *and 4 × 2?* Agree that 82 has still been partitioned into 80 and 2 and that the products of the two multiplications have been added at the end.
- Annotate the calculation to show this as:

$$\begin{array}{rl} 8\ 2 & \\ \times\quad 4 & \\ \hline 8 & (4 \times 2) \\ 3\ 2\ 0 & (4 \times 80) \\ \hline 3\ 2\ 8 & \end{array}$$

- Ask pupils to use the method to try 61 × 5. Ask them to explain each part of the method to show how 61 has been partitioned.

  Look out for ...pupils who would still benefit from setting out the calculation as an array using place value counters and then using what they know about the number of ones and tens to complete the written calculation.

- Take feedback to check that everyone understands how the method works.

  i This expanded method helps pupils relate a written method to what they have done previously. It also provides a useful building block so that pupils can clearly see how combining steps in the short method of multiplication results in the same product.

- Work through further examples:
  - 43 × 3 = $\square$
  - 22 × 4 = $\square$

- 51 × 6 = □

- Say that you will now show another written method for 51 × 6.
- Ask pupils to discuss what is different this time.

```
   5 1
×    6
 3 0 6
```

- They should notice that the answer is the same but there is only one line of working.
- Talk through the steps that are needed to complete the method, paying particular attention to 6 × 5 as 6 × 5 tens as the product is larger than 9 tens. Say: *We know that 6 × 5 tens is 30 tens which is the same as 300, so the digit '3' is placed in the hundreds column to show 300 or 30 tens.*
- Pupils should now try this second method for 82 × 4.
- Share the following problem and ask what the answer will be. Ask: *Do we need to calculate? Why not?*

  *The cost of one ticket for a train journey is £51.*

  *How much will it cost for six people to go on this train journey?*
- Agree that the calculation is still 51 × 6, but is simply in pounds (£).
- Pupils should complete Question 1 in the Practice Book.

## Same-day intervention

- Show pupils the cost of three different items, for example a banana 43p, a lemon 32p and an orange 55p.
- Ask: *Will it cost more to buy three bananas or four lemons?*
- Pupils should now use the first method shown in the whole-class session that uses partitioning, to find the prices of three bananas and of four lemons. Look together at the second method, discussing similarities and differences.
- Ask: *Will it cost more to buy two oranges than three lemons?* Pupils find the costs using a written method of their choice.

## Same-day enrichment

- Give pupils **Resource 3.9.5a** 3-digit calculations.

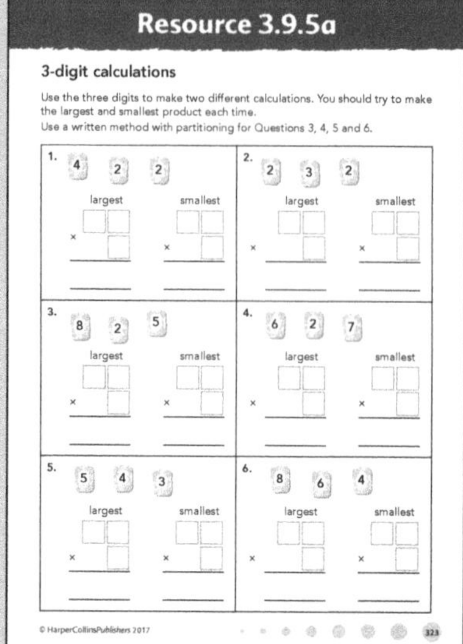

**Resource 3.9.5a**

3-digit calculations

Use the three digits to make two different calculations. You should try to make the largest and smallest product each time.
Use a written method with partitioning for Questions 3, 4, 5 and 6.

1. 4 2 2 — largest / smallest
2. 2 3 2 — largest / smallest
3. 8 2 5 — largest / smallest
4. 6 2 7 — largest / smallest
5. 5 4 3 — largest / smallest
6. 8 6 4 — largest / smallest

© HarperCollinsPublishers 2017 323

- Pupils should use the digits to find the largest and smallest product each time, using a written method of multiplication.

# Question 2

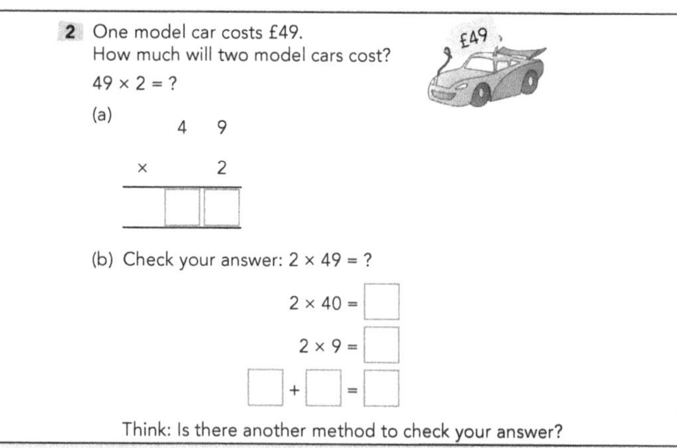

**2** One model car costs £49.
How much will two model cars cost?
49 × 2 = ?

(a)
```
  4 9
×   2
  □ □
```

(b) Check your answer: 2 × 49 = ?

2 × 40 = □
2 × 9 = □
□ + □ = □

Think: Is there another method to check your answer?



## What learning will pupils have achieved at the conclusion of Question 2?

- Conceptual understanding of multiplying a two-digit number by a one-digit number will have been developed using manipulatives. Pupils represent multiplication as arrays and understand how the partitioned product relates to the process of multiplication in a written method.
- Pupils will be able to compare multiplication sentences and reason about which will give the larger product.

- Pupils will have shown their ability to mentally multiply a one-digit number by tens as part of the whole calculation.
- Knowledge of partitioning into tens and ones will have been applied to mental and written methods of multiplication.
- Pupils will have been introduced to the compact method for short multiplication.

## Activities for whole-class instruction

- With pupils, practise mentally doubling some two-digit numbers using partitioning to first double the tens and then the ones. For example: 45, 36, 54, 67, 24.
- Ask pupils to predict which numbers, when doubled, will result in a three-digit number. Ask: *What can you use to help make a decision?* Agree that numbers that are 50 or more will result in a three-digit number, as we know that double 50 is 100.
- Use base 10 blocks to model doubling the numbers with carry-overs, for example, double 36, showing first three sticks of ten and six ones. Say: *Double three tens to give six tens and then double six ones to give 12 ones.* Agree that six tens add 12 ones is 72, so double 36 is 72.
- Remind pupils of the written methods of multiplication that they used in the previous session. Ask: *How can we use the methods to show some of the calculations we have just been using?*
- Begin with using the partitioning method for double 36 as follows, agreeing together that doubling is the same as multiplying by two.
- Show the base 10 blocks alongside each step of the calculation, for example, 2 × 6 ones and 2 × 3 tens:

$$\begin{array}{r} 3\,6 \\ \times\quad 2 \\ \hline 1\,2 \\ 6\,0 \\ \hline 7\,2 \end{array}$$

- Now ask pupils to look carefully at the second method. Ask: *What is different this time?*

$$\begin{array}{r} 3\,6 \\ \times\quad 2 \\ \hline 7\,2 \\ \hline {\scriptstyle 1}\phantom{2} \end{array}$$

- Ask: *Where can you see the product of 2 × 6? And the product of 2 × 3 tens?* Establish that the one ten in the product 12 has been written in the tens column, under the bottom line, ready to be added to the product of 2 × 3 tens.

*When the product of the ones is ten or more, the tens must be written in the tens column, under the bottom line, ready to be added to the product of the tens.*

- Ask pupils to use both methods to show the product of 67 × 2. Give pupils time to work on both methods, using base 10 blocks as necessary to represent parts of the calculation.
- Say that we can check that the answer is correct using the mental method that we have been practising in previous sessions:

67 × 2

2 × 60 = 120

2 × 7 = 14

120 + 14 = 134

- Pupils should complete Question 2 in the Practice Book.

### Same-day intervention

- Give pupils **Resource 3.9.5b** Twice the price.

**Resource 3.9.5b**

**Twice the price**

How much does it cost to buy two of each of these items?
Use a written column method to calculate the cost and a mental method to check your answers.

| | |
|---|---|
| 1. 46p | 2. 38p |
| 3. £27 | 4. 49p |
| 5. £54 | 6. £63 |

324

© HarperCollinsPublishers 2017

- Ask pupils to find the cost of buying two of each item, using a column method.
- They should also use a mental method to check each calculation.

## Same-day enrichment

- Ask pupils to imagine a shop where everything costs from £36 to £69. Challenge them to find out whether the following statement is true or false.

  *The cost of buying three items at one price is always more than the cost of buying two items at a different price.*
- Explore an example. If the two prices are £36 and £52: three items at £36 and two items at £52, the three items cost more. However, if the £52 items were £55 then these would cost more.
- Pupils should test many examples, making estimates before checking with the column method for each example they try.
- Ask if pupils are able to make any generalisations about the prices. For example: When you buy three identical items that are less than £45 and two items that are more than £67, then two items always cost more.

# Question 3 and Question 4

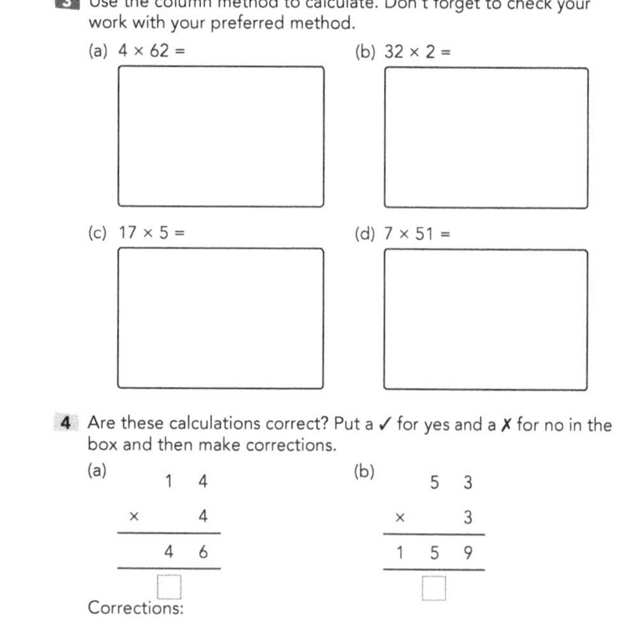

3 Use the column method to calculate. Don't forget to check your work with your preferred method.

(a) 4 × 62 = (b) 32 × 2 =

(c) 17 × 5 = (d) 7 × 51 =

4 Are these calculations correct? Put a ✓ for yes and a ✗ for no in the box and then make corrections.

(a)
$$\begin{array}{r} 1\ 4 \\ \times\ \ \ 4 \\ \hline 4\ 6 \end{array}$$

(b)
$$\begin{array}{r} 5\ 3 \\ \times\ \ \ 3 \\ \hline 1\ 5\ 9 \end{array}$$

Corrections:

## What learning will pupils have achieved at the conclusion of Question 3 and Question 4?

- Conceptual understanding of multiplying a two-digit number by a one-digit number will have been developed using manipulatives. Pupils represent multiplication as arrays and understand how the partitioned product relates to the process of multiplication in a written method.
- Pupils will have shown their ability to mentally multiply a one-digit number by tens as part of the whole calculation.
- Knowledge of partitioning into tens and ones will have been applied to mental and written methods of multiplication.
- Pupils will have been introduced to the compact method for short multiplication.
- Pupils will have practised applying their knowledge of multiplication facts and multiplying a one-digit number to check answers to calculations.

## Activities for whole-class instruction

- Begin by practising some multiplication facts and recording each product in tens and ones, for example 7 × 8 = 56 and then also record the product as 56 = 50 + 6 and '5 tens and 6 ones'.
- You could also give pupils the product in tens and ones, for example 4 tens and 8 ones, and pupils suggest possible multiplication facts that will give the product.
- Show some calculations that you have completed. Ask pupils to explain whether your working is accurate and correct any mistakes you have made. They could prove their decisions using base 10 blocks. Again look carefully at the tens part of each calculation that results in a product that is greater than nine tens and, therefore, uses the hundreds column.

$$\begin{array}{r} 5\ 8 \\ \times\ \ \ 2 \\ \hline 1\ 0\ 6 \end{array} \qquad \begin{array}{r} 4\ 7 \\ \times\ \ \ 2 \\ \hline 9\ 4 \end{array} \qquad \begin{array}{r} 9\ 6 \\ \times\ \ \ 2 \\ \hline 1\ 9\ 4 \end{array}$$

- Take feedback and model any corrections to be made. Look at describing each product in tens and ones (and hundreds), for example 2 × 8 = 16 which is one ten and six ones, and using this to reinforce the process of carrying tens and hundreds to the appropriate columns.

*When the product of the ones is ten or more, the tens must be written in the tens column, under the bottom line, ready to be added to the product of the tens.*

- Show another set of calculations. Pupils should notice that some of the factors are the same as in the previous examples.

$$\begin{array}{r} 58 \\ \times\ 3 \\ \hline \\ \hline \end{array} \qquad \begin{array}{r} 47 \\ \times\ 4 \\ \hline \\ \hline \end{array} \qquad \begin{array}{r} 96 \\ \times\ 5 \\ \hline \\ \hline \end{array}$$

- Look together at the first example. Ask: *What is 3 × 8? How can we describe this in tens and ones?*

*24 is two tens and four ones.*

- Use base 10 blocks or place value counters to model this as follows:

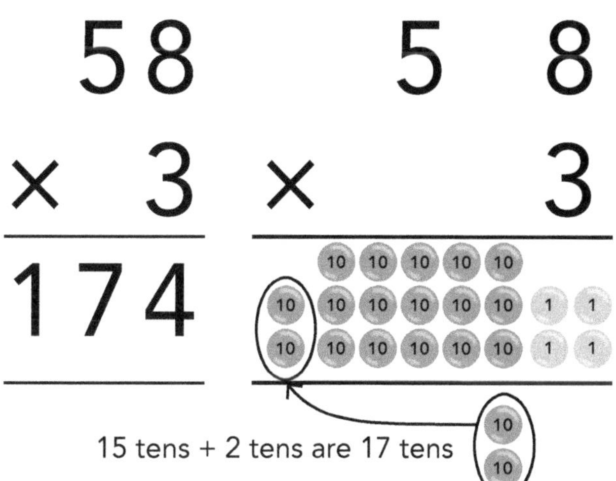


- Agree that four ones should be placed in the ones column in the answer space and the two tens must be written in the tens column, under the bottom line, ready to be added to the product of the tens.
- Say: *Look at the next column. This is 3 × 5 tens or 15 tens, but we have two more tens to add. We now have 17 tens.*
- Complete the answer space to show that 58 × 3 = 174.
- Ask pupils to check the answer using a mental method.

  Record examples:

  58 × 3 =

  50 × 3 = 150

  8 × 3 = 24

  150 + 24 = 174

- Ask pupils to practise the method using 47 × 4 and 96 × 5. They should practise using the language of 'ones' and 'tens' as they multiply. They should remember to check their answers using a mental method.
- Pupils should complete Question 3 and Question 4 in the Practice Book

## Same-day intervention

- Look together at the calculations in Question 3 in the Practice Book.
- Ask pupils to represent each calculation using place value counters and explain the method using the language of 'ones' and 'tens'.

## Same-day enrichment

- Give pupils **Resource 3.9.5c** Missing numbers.

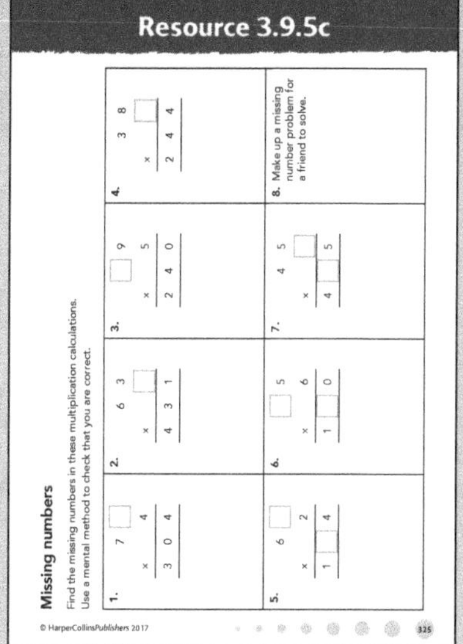
Resource 3.9.5c

Missing numbers

Find the missing numbers in these multiplication calculations. Use a mental method to check that you are correct.

8. Make up a missing number problem for a friend to solve.

© HarperCollinsPublishers 2017

- A number is missing from each of the multiplications on the top row of the sheet.
- Pupils should use what they know about their multiplication facts and the written method of multiplication to help find the missing number. On the bottom row, two numbers are missing each time. Note that in some cases there is more than one possible solution.

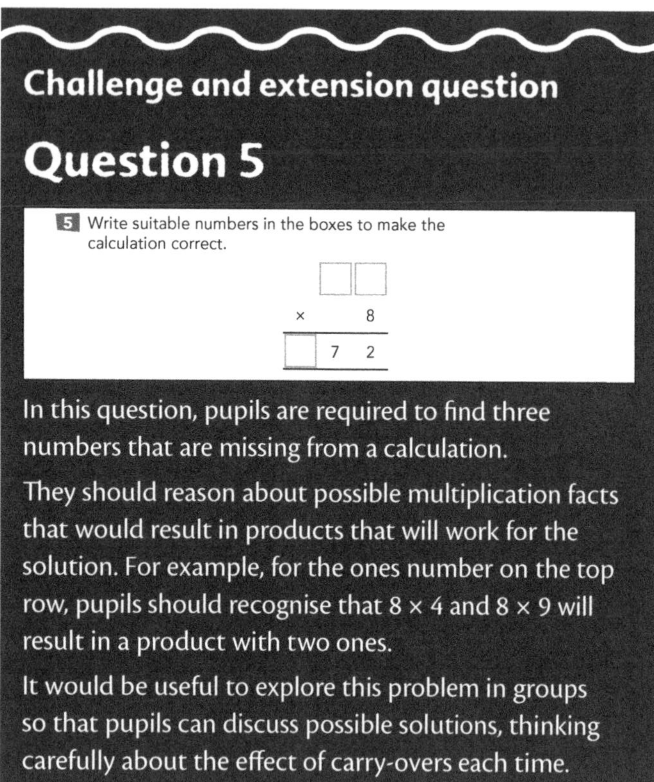

## Challenge and extension question

# Question 5

**5** Write suitable numbers in the boxes to make the calculation correct.

$$\begin{array}{r} \square\square \\ \times \quad 8 \\ \hline \square\,7\,2 \end{array}$$

In this question, pupils are required to find three numbers that are missing from a calculation.

They should reason about possible multiplication facts that would result in products that will work for the solution. For example, for the ones number on the top row, pupils should recognise that 8 × 4 and 8 × 9 will result in a product with two ones.

It would be useful to explore this problem in groups so that pupils can discuss possible solutions, thinking carefully about the effect of carry-overs each time.

# Unit 9.6
# Multiplying a 2-digit number by a 1-digit number (3)

## Conceptual context

Pupils will continue to multiply two-digit numbers by one-digit numbers, using methods learned in the previous units, both mental and written, before extending to three-digit × one-digit numbers in the next unit (9.7). Pupils are encouraged to estimate, then check using the column method.

Pupils' conceptual understanding about numbers and multiplication becomes increasingly connected through work in this unit, completing a short series of units in which they have learned to bring together what they know about multiplying by ten, recording calculations using place value, the structure of arrays and ways to partition them and increase or decrease them.

## Learning pupils will have achieved at the end of the unit

- Combining multiplication and addition in mental calculation will have been explored further, including the effect of multiplying by one and zero (Q1)
- Commutativity will have been explored further, as pupils make decisions about which facts to use when multiplying (Q1)
- Conceptual understanding will have been strengthened by representing multiplication as arrays and understanding of how the partitioned product relates to the process of multiplication in a written method (Q1, Q2)
- Pupils will have compared multiplication sentences and reasoned about which will give the larger product (Q1, Q2, Q3)
- Pupils will have become more proficient with the compact written method for multiplication (Q1, Q2, Q3, Q4, Q5, Q6)
- Using knowledge of multiplying tens numbers, pupils will have made informed estimates about the size of a product and will be able to explain which two multiples of ten it will lie between (Q3, Q4, Q5, Q6)
- Fluency with multiplication facts, including multiplying by ten, will have been developed further as pupils solve problems with or without a context (Q3, Q6)

## Resources

base 10 blocks; place value counters; squared paper; 0–9 dice or 0–9 spinners; **Resource 3.9.6a** Multiplication methods; **Resource 3.9.6b** Product range; **Resource 3.9.6c** Sorting calculations; **Resource 3.9.6d** Shop multiplication problems

## Vocabulary

ones, tens, multiply, multiplication, product, partition, estimate

# Question 1 and Question 2

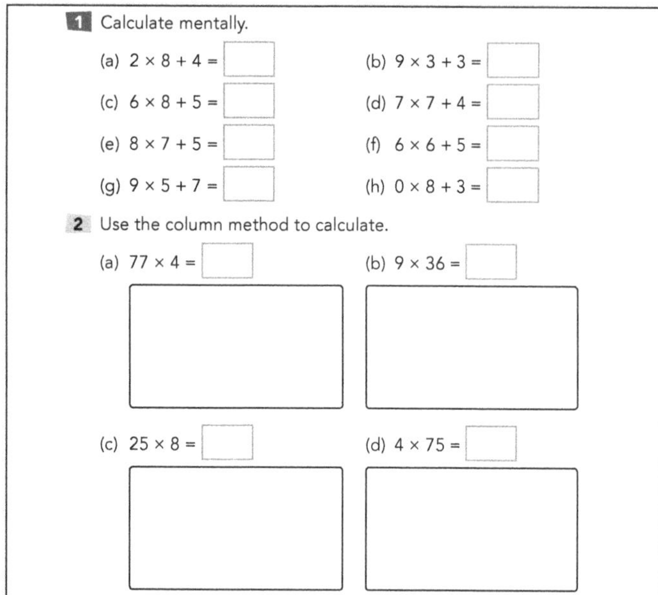

1 Calculate mentally.

(a) $2 \times 8 + 4 =$ ☐ (b) $9 \times 3 + 3 =$ ☐

(c) $6 \times 8 + 5 =$ ☐ (d) $7 \times 7 + 4 =$ ☐

(e) $8 \times 7 + 5 =$ ☐ (f) $6 \times 6 + 5 =$ ☐

(g) $9 \times 5 + 7 =$ ☐ (h) $0 \times 8 + 3 =$ ☐

2 Use the column method to calculate.

(a) $77 \times 4 =$ ☐ (b) $9 \times 36 =$ ☐

(c) $25 \times 8 =$ ☐ (d) $4 \times 75 =$ ☐

## What learning will pupils have achieved at the conclusion of Question 1 and Question 2?

- Combining multiplication and addition in mental calculation will have been explored further, including the effect of multiplying by one and zero.
- Commutativity will have been explored further as pupils make decisions about which facts to use when multiplying.
- Conceptual understanding will have been strengthened by representing multiplication as arrays and understanding of how the partitioned product relates to the process of multiplication in a written method.
- Pupils will be able to compare multiplication sentences and reason about which will give the larger product.
- Pupils will have become more proficient with the compact method for short multiplication.

## Activities for whole-class instruction

- Begin by playing a game, using three spinners or dice with the numbers 0–9 to generate three numbers. Split the class into two teams – one team is 'lowest number' and the other is 'highest number'.
- Show pupils the following number sentence:

  ☐ × ☐ + ☐ = ☐

- Generate the first three numbers, for example, 5, 3 and 8. Pupils should reason about where to put each digit to result in the 'highest number' or 'lowest number', according to the team they are in.
- Take feedback, discussing which part of the calculation will have the largest effect on the answer, that is, the multiplication part as long as the digits are not 1 or 0. Remind pupils about commutativity.
- Now show the number sentence:

  ☐ × ☐ – ☐ = ☐ and repeat with three new numbers.

- Repeat with 3 new numbers, giving pupils the choice of which sentence to use.
- Remind pupils about the written methods of multiplication that were used in the previous session. Revisit the two methods to reinforce the procedures, using an array and place value counters to represent the parts of the calculation as shown on **Resource 3.9.6a** Multiplication methods.

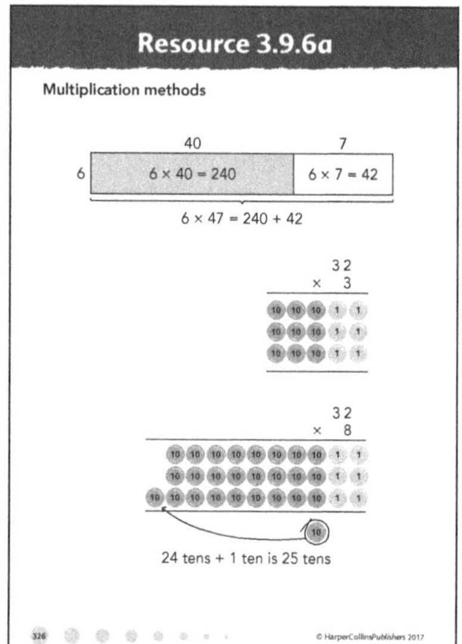

Resource 3.9.6a

Multiplication methods

| | 40 | 7 |
|---|---|---|
| 6 | $6 \times 40 = 240$ | $6 \times 7 = 42$ |

$6 \times 47 = 240 + 42$

$32 \times 3$

$32 \times 8$

24 tens + 1 ten is 25 tens

326 © HarperCollinsPublishers 2017

- Look together at the three examples below that do and do not require tens to be carried across to the tens column, reinforcing place value at all times.

*When the product of the ones is ten or more, the tens must be written in the tens column, under the bottom line, ready to be added to the product of the tens.*

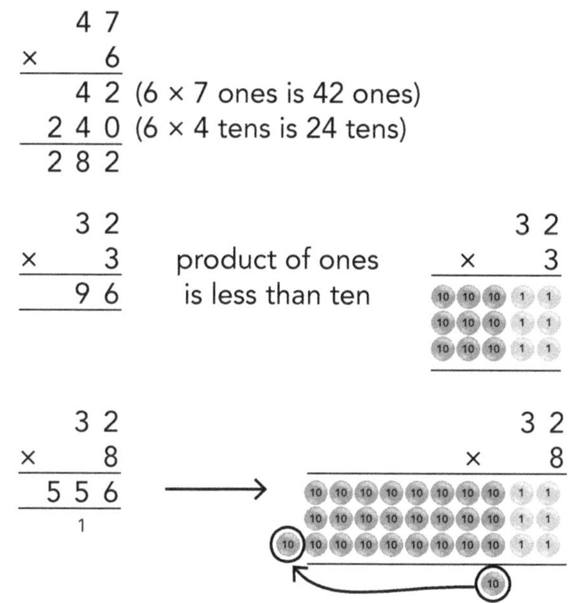


**Look out for** ...pupils who carry across the wrong part of a product, for example for the product 16, they write the six ones rather than the one ten in the tens column. Place value counters or base 10 blocks are useful here – ask pupils to build the product and then discuss which part is a ten and which is made up of ones, reinforcing that only 'ones' can be placed in the 'ones' position.

- Pupils should complete Question 1 and Question 2 in the Practice Book.

## Same-day intervention

- Give pupils the three spinners or dice as used in the whole-class session.
- Show the calculation this time as follows:

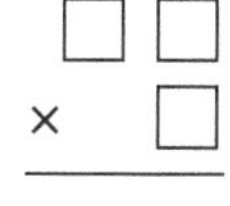

- Ask pupils to reason about and find the largest and smallest product.
- They should think carefully about the position of the digits, using what they learned from the whole-session to help them make decisions.

## Same-day enrichment

- Give pupils the following problem to think about as you are introducing the intervention task.

  *Ahmed uses two odd digits and one even digit to complete his calculation.*

  *The product is a three-digit odd number that is also a multiple of five.*

  *Ahmed adds 5 to his product. The answer is now a multiple of 50.*

  *What three digits could he have used in his calculation?*

- Pupils should reason about the position of the digits in order to result in an odd product.

  (Possible answers are 29 × 5, 49 × 5, 69 × 5, 89 × 5.)

# Question 3

**3** First estimate, and then calculate using the column method.

(a) 49 × 7 = ☐
I estimate the product is between ☐ and ☐.
Calculate:

(b) 75 × 6 = ☐
I estimate the product is between ☐ and ☐.
Calculate:

(c) 88 × 8 = ☐
I estimate the product is between ☐ and ☐.
Calculate:

**4** Are these calculations correct? Put a ✓ for yes and a ✗ for no in the box and then make corrections.

(a) (b) (c)

## What learning will pupils have achieved at the conclusion of Question 3?

- Pupils will have compared multiplication sentences and reason about which will give the larger product.
- Pupils will have become more proficient with the compact method for short multiplication.
- Using knowledge of multiplying tens numbers, pupils will be able to make informed estimates about the size of a product and will be able to explain which two multiples of ten it will lie between.

- Fluency with multiplication facts, including multiplying by ten, will have been developed further as pupils solve problems with or without a context.

## Activities for whole-class instruction

- Tell pupils that you want to buy presents for three of your friends. The presents are all the same. Explain that you only have £100 to spend in total.
- Draw three sets of similar presents with prices as shown:

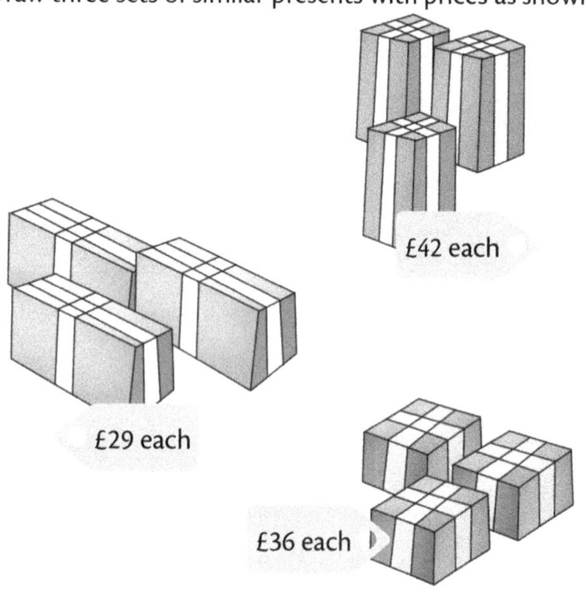


- Ask: *Using estimation, do you think any of these sets of presents might be the ones I bought? Why?*
- See if pupils can tell you that:
  - it could be the first set because 29 is just under 30 and 3 × 30 is 90 which is less than 100
  - it cannot be the second set because 42 is close to 40 and 3 × 40 is 120 which is more then 100
  - it might be the second set because 36 is between 30 and 40 so the total price will be between £90 and £120, so an accurate calculation is needed for this one to be sure about the product.
- Ask pupils to check, using a written method for multiplication to find the actual cost of buying each set of presents. Ask: *Do you recognise that when 3 × £6 is added to 3 × £30 for the third set of presents, the total now exceeds £100?*
- Agree that only the first set of presents costing £29 each can be purchased with a £100 budget.
- Tell pupils they are going to make some more estimates, deciding which two numbers a product will lie between. Show the following calculations:

  65 × 4   72 × 8   52 × 7

- Say that the product for the first calculation must be greater than 240 but less than 280.
- Ask: *How do I know this? What have I done here?*
- Establish that you have multiplied the tens number on each side of 65 and multiplied that by 4 because it will be more than 60 × 4 and less than 70 × 4.
- Model using arrays to show that the product of 65 × 4 is larger than 60 × 4, but less than 70 × 4.

| | 60 | | | 65 | | | 70 |
|---|---|---|---|---|---|---|---|
| 4 | 240 | $<$ | 4 | ? | $<$ | 4 | 280 |

Previously, pupils have used squares or dots to show each 'one' represented in an array, so this representation will need some discussion. Pupils will not be able to represent 60 with squares so they might need some practise with drawing the rectangle and labelling the sides and the product, rather than actually seeing every 'one' individually.

- Ask pupils to reason about the other calculations 72 × 8 and 52 × 7 in the same way. They should sketch arrays like those above to show the tens numbers that each product lies between.
- Take feedback, looking at each calculation in turn.

All say...  *The product of 72 × 8 is greater than 70 × 8 but less than 80 × 8.*

- Ask pupils: *What can you say about the product of 52 × 7?*
- Pupils should complete Question 3 in the Practice Book

### Same-day intervention

- Look together at the calculations in Question 3 and the tens numbers that the products lie between, for example the product of 49 × 7 is between 280 and 350 because 40 × 7 = 280 and 50 × 7 = 350.
- Ask: *How can we use what we know to find another calculation with a product that is also between 280 and 350?*
- Agree that other calculations between 40 × 7 and 50 × 7, for example 43 × 7 would also be possible.
- Ask pupils to calculate 43 × 7 using the written method.
- Look at 75 × 6 and 88 × 8 in the same way, agreeing that calculations such as 72 × 6 and 83 × 8 would also result in products within the same ranges.

## Same-day enrichment

- Give pupils **Resource 3.9.6b** Product range.

**Resource 3.9.6b**

**Product range**

Replace each triangle with one of these digits once only in order to make the calculations correct.

3 5 6 7 8 9

Remember to estimate first and then write the answer each time.

1. 48 × △ = □ The product is between 320 and 400.
2. △ × 63 = □ The product is between 180 and 210.
3. □ = 29 × △ The product is between 160 and 240.
4. 75 × △ = □ The product is between 350 and 400.
5. □ = △ × 65 The product is between 420 and 490.
6. △ × 84 = □ The product is between 480 and 540.

© HarperCollinsPublishers 2017 327

- Pupils are required to reason about calculations that will result in products within a specified range.
- They will need to think about which of the given digits can be used as the value of the empty triangle to suit the criteria each time. They should then complete the calculations.

# Question 4 and Question 5

**4** Are these calculations correct? Put a ✓ for yes and a ✗ for no in the box and then make corrections.

(a)
$$\begin{array}{r} 9\ 9 \\ \times\ \ \ 9 \\ \hline 8\ 8\ 1 \\ \hline \end{array}$$
□

(b)
$$\begin{array}{r} 2\ 6 \\ \times\ \ \ 8 \\ \hline 1\ 9\ 6 \\ \hline \end{array}$$
□

(c)
$$\begin{array}{r} 6\ 8 \\ \times\ \ \ 5 \\ \hline 3\ 0\ 0 \\ \hline \end{array}$$
□

Corrections:

**5** Draw a line to match each calculation with the correct answer.

25 × 7 = 56 × 4 = 9 × 42 = 5 × 63 =

315 378 224 175

## What learning will pupils have achieved at the conclusion of Question 4 and Question 5?

- Pupils have become more proficient with the compact method for short multiplication.
- Using knowledge of multiplying tens numbers, pupils make informed estimates about the size of a product and can explain which two multiples of ten it will lie between.

## Activities for whole-class instruction

- Show pupils the following number line. (Leave space to extend the line to 550 later.)

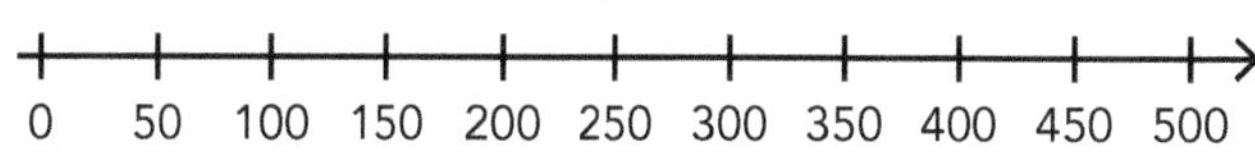


- Challenge pupils by saying: *Write down two different multiplication sentences with products between 0 and 50, where one of the factors is a two-digit number.*
- In groups, ask pupils to focus on different sections of the number line (for example, 50 to 100, 100 to 150, and so on) to explore products that sit within these intervals. Ask pupils if they can use estimates to make decisions about possible two-digit by one-digit numbers.
- Collect examples from different groups and ask others to check these are possible using estimating. Record a calculation in each interval of the number line.
- Extend the number line to 550. Write these calculations on the board:

7 × 45 = □

63 × 8 = □

52 × 9 = □

76 × 7 = □

8 × 93 = □

- Ask: *Which of these calculations will definitely not have products that lie between 500 and 550? Which ones are possible? Can we use estimating to check?*
- Pupils should discard 7 × 45, 52 × 9 and 8 × 93 and explain why.
- Work through the column method on the board to find the actual products of 63 × 8 and 76 × 7, making deliberate mistakes.

$$\begin{array}{r} 6\ 3 \\ \times\ \ \ 8 \\ \hline 5\ 0\ 2 \\ \hline {\scriptstyle 2}\ \ \ \end{array} \qquad \begin{array}{r} 7\ 6 \\ \times\ \ \ 7 \\ \hline 5\ 2\ 2 \\ \hline {\scriptstyle 4}\ \ \ \end{array}$$

- Ask pupils to check your working. They should explain and correct any mistakes that you have made.
- Pupils should complete Question 4 and Question 5 in the Practice Book.

## Same-day intervention

- Give pupils a set of calculations to sort using **Resource 3.9.6c** Sorting calculations.

**Resource 3.9.6c**

Sorting calculations

| The product is between 100 and 150. | The product is between 150 and 200. |
|---|---|
| The product is between 200 and 250. | The product is between 250 and 300. |
| The product is between 300 and 350. | The product is between 350 and 400. |
| The product is between 400 and 450. | The product is between 450 and 500. |

| | | | | | | |
|---|---|---|---|---|---|---|
| 45 × 6 | 93 × 5 | 3 × 62 | 3 × 64 | 19 × 8 | 78 × 4 | 8 × 61 |
| 6 × 75 | 34 × 3 | 55 × 6 | 47 × 4 | 57 × 3 | 9 × 55 | 72 × 3 |
| 9 × 47 | 2 × 99 | 7 × 71 | 48 × 6 | 73 × 4 | 83 × 2 | 32 × 9 |

328 © HarperCollinsPublishers 2017

- Pupils can play this as a game in pairs. They take it in turns to pick a calculation from the file and estimate which section the product will go in. They place the calculation in this section on the sheet.
- The other player calculates the actual answer using a written method. If the estimate is correct, the 'estimator' scores a point, but if it is incorrect, the 'calculator' scores a point.
- The calculation should be recorded on the sheet in the correct section.
- The winner is the first player to reach five points.

## Same-day enrichment

- Give pupils a set of calculations to reason about. Ensure that some are correct and others are not.
- For the incorrect calculations, some should be able to be discarded through estimation and others only through calculation, for example, 47 × 6 = 262 could be correct as a result of an estimation, but through calculation, pupils would prove that the actual product is 282, whereas 53 × 5 = 425 would be discarded after an estimation.
- Pupils should sort the calculations into 'possible products' and 'impossible products' groups initially, and then use a written method to check the actual products for all calculations in the 'possible product' group.
- Ask pupils to use other knowledge to discard any 'possible products' without calculating, for example, noticing that:
  - the product is a multiple of five, but neither factor is a multiple of five
  - the product is even but both factors are odd
  - the number ends in a '2' but the ones digits when multiplied end with a different ones digit, and so on.

# Question 6

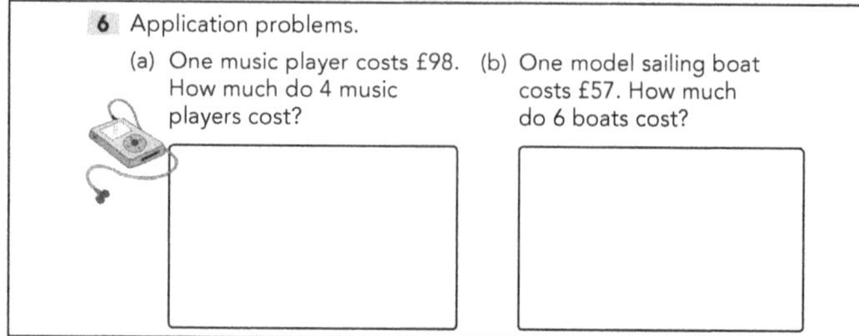
**6** Application problems.

(a) One music player costs £98. How much do 4 music players cost?

(b) One model sailing boat costs £57. How much do 6 boats cost?

## What learning will pupils have achieved at the conclusion of Question 6?

- Pupils will have become more proficient with the compact method for short multiplication.
- Using knowledge of multiplying tens numbers, pupils will have made informed estimates about the size of a product and will be able to explain which two multiples of ten it will lie between.
- Fluency with multiplication facts, including multiplying by ten, will have been developed further as pupils solve problems with or without a context.

## Activities for whole-class instruction

- Begin by practising multiplying one-digit numbers by a number of tens. Focus on some of the multiplication facts that pupils find more difficult, for example the multiplication table of seven.
- You could use the seven times table and work together to find the 70 times table, building these up using tens blocks or place value counters if needed.

  1 × 7 = 7: because 1 × 7 ones = 7 ones, then 1 × 70 = 70 because 1 × 7 tens = 7 tens

  2 × 7 = 14: because 2 × 7 ones = 14 ones, then 2 × 70 = 140 because 2 × 7 tens = 14 tens

  and so on.

- Show pupils the following three items that are sold in a local shop.

Say that the shopkeeper wants to calculate how much money has been taken for these items at the end of the day. The shop has sold eight computer games, seven skateboards and five scooters.

- Ask pupils to estimate the amount taken for each item. Ask: *Was more money taken for scooters or skateboards? How do you know?*
- Next, pupils should calculate the actual amount taken and compare these to the estimates. Refer to multiplying by seven tens from the initial activity when calculating the cost of seven skateboards.
- Write the following problem on the board:
  *One scooter costs £75. How much do 6 scooters cost?*
- Do pupils recognise that the calculation 6 × 75 or 75 × 6 is needed to solve this problem? Can they explain that this is £75 more than the cost of five scooters?
- Ask pupils to write a similar problem about the skateboards. Ask: *What calculation would someone need to use to solve it?*
- Pupils should complete Question 6 in the Practice Book.
- Following the activity, look together at the first problem involving the calculation 4 × 98 and explore the mental method of rounding and adjusting. Pupils should recognise that 98 is close to 100 and can calculate 4 × 100 as the first step and then adjust by subtracting 4 × 2.

## Same-day intervention

- Look together at a set of word problems.
  *The cost of one skateboard is £49. What is the cost of seven skateboards?*
  *I have £100. Do I have enough money to buy two skateboards?*
- Discuss the calculation that is needed each time and why each problem implies multiplication. Pupils should make an estimate first before calculating.
- Ask pupils if they recognise that multiplying by two is the same as doubling.
- Use place counters to reinforce the process of the written method as necessary.

## Same-day enrichment

- Give pupils **Resource 3.9.6d** Shop multiplication problems.

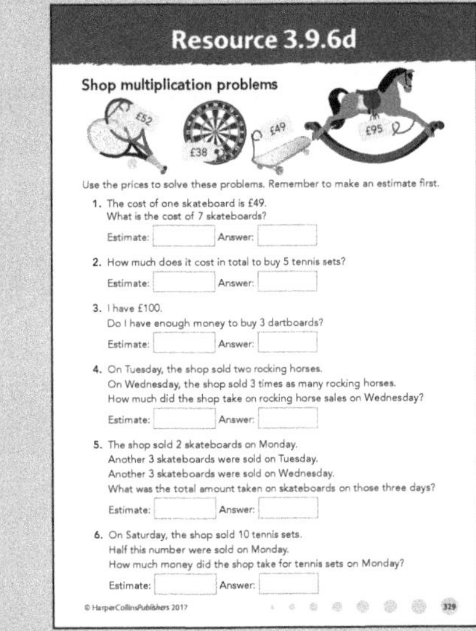

**Resource 3.9.6d**

**Shop multiplication problems**



Use the prices to solve these problems. Remember to make an estimate first.

1. The cost of one skateboard is £49.
   What is the cost of 7 skateboards?
   Estimate: ☐ Answer: ☐
2. How much does it cost in total to buy 5 tennis sets?
   Estimate: ☐ Answer: ☐
3. I have £100.
   Do I have enough money to buy 3 dartboards?
   Estimate: ☐ Answer: ☐
4. On Tuesday, the shop sold two rocking horses.
   On Wednesday, the shop sold 3 times as many rocking horses.
   How much did the shop take on rocking horse sales on Wednesday?
   Estimate: ☐ Answer: ☐
5. The shop sold 2 skateboards on Monday.
   Another 3 skateboards were sold on Tuesday.
   Another 3 skateboards were sold on Wednesday.
   What was the total amount taken on skateboards on those three days?
   Estimate: ☐ Answer: ☐
6. On Saturday, the shop sold 10 tennis sets.
   Half this number were sold on Monday.
   How much money did the shop take for tennis sets on Monday?
   Estimate: ☐ Answer: ☐

© HarperCollinsPublishers 2017 329

- They should make an estimate before solving each problem about items and sales at the shop.

## Challenge and extension question

# Question 7

**7** Write suitable numbers in the boxes to make the calculation correct.

```
    1 □ □
  ×     8
  -------
  □ 5 □ 0
```

In this missing number question, the calculation is extended to a three-digit number multiplied by a one-digit number. Pupils are required to find four possible digits that would work in the given calculation, set out using the written method.

They should recognise that the digit in the hundreds position is one, so that to result in a four-digit product, the tens and ones part of the three-digit number must result in a product that is larger than 200.

Pupils should reason about the ones position and consider possible multiples of eight that result in a product ending with a zero, for example 8 × 5 or 8 × 10, but recognise that 8 × 10 cannot be used as 10 is not a one-digit number.

They should use what they know about carry-overs to make decisions about the value of the tens and hundreds digits in the three-digit number and try out possible solutions.

# Unit 9.7

# Multiplying a 3-digit number by a 1-digit number (1)

## Conceptual context

In previous units in this chapter, pupils have learned that arrays can be partitioned to represent part products. Pupils' understanding of part products has been developed and applied to the partitioning of two digit-numbers in order to create two-part products that can be added together. This concept has been further embedded and has been used as a building block (conceptual variation) to help pupils make sense of the steps taken as part of a written procedure.

In this unit, the concepts developed so far are varied procedurally so that pupils are able to extend what they understand to be able to multiply three-digit numbers using and developing the same knowledge.

## Learning pupils will have achieved at the end of the unit

- Pupils will be able to compare multiplication sentences and reason about which will give the larger product using understanding about place value to help make decisions (Q1, Q6)
- Using knowledge of place value, pupils will have partitioned three-digit numbers into hundreds, tens and ones (Q2)
- Pupils will be able to recognise and explain why it is useful to partition a three-digit number into hundreds, tens and ones if the number needs to be multiplied (Q3, Q4)
- Pupils will have shown their ability to mentally multiply a one-digit number by tens and hundreds as part of the whole calculation (Q3, Q4, Q5)
- Conceptual understanding of multiplying a three-digit number by a one-digit number will have been developed using manipulatives and other representations (Q3, Q4, Q5, Q6)
- Pupils' understanding of how to carry out a written procedure for multiplying a two-digit number by a one-digit number will have been extended to multiplying a three-digit number (Q4, Q5, Q6)
- Through application of multiplying hundreds numbers, pupils will have made informed estimates about the size of a product and can predict which two multiples of a hundred it will lie between (Q5, Q6)

### Resources

base 10 blocks; place value counters; place value arrow cards; 0–9 dice or 0–9 spinners; **Resource 3.9.7a** Connect 3; **Resource 3.9.7b** Money multiplication; **Resource 3.9.7c** Finding whole numbers; **Resource 3.9.7d** Partitioning arrays; **Resource 3.9.7e** Finding values; **Resource 3.9.7f** Multiplication: written methods; **Resource 3.9.7g** Largest and smallest products

### Vocabulary

ones, tens, hundreds, multiply, multiplication, product, partition, estimate

# Question 1

**1** Calculate mentally.

(a) 3 × 800 = ☐ (d) 20 × 8 = ☐
(b) 3 × 80 = ☐ (e) 200 × 8 = ☐
(c) 3 × 8 = ☐ (f) 2 × 8 = ☐

(g) 900 × 7 = ☐ (j) 60 × 6 = ☐
(h) 90 × 7 = ☐ (k) 700 × 4 = ☐
(i) 9 × 7 = ☐ (l) 3 × 9 = ☐

## What learning will pupils have achieved at the conclusion of Question 1?

- Pupils will be able to compare multiplication sentences and reason about which will give the larger product, using understanding about place value to help make decisions.

## Activities for whole-class instruction

- Show pupils the grid of numbers on **Resource 3.9.7a** Connect 3.

**Resource 3.9.7a**

Connect 3

| 12 | 3600 | 56 | 240 | 420 |
|---|---|---|---|---|
| 4200 | 54 | 2800 | 540 | 1200 |
| 560 | 42 | 120 | 280 | 360 |
| 24 | 5600 | 36 | 2400 | 28 |

330 © HarperCollinsPublishers 2017

- Ask pupils to find trios of numbers that are connected in some way. They should be prepared to explain or prove the connection either verbally, numerically or pictorially.
- Focus on trios of numbers, such as 42, 420 and 4200, referring to these as 42 ones, 42 tens and 42 hundreds.
- Say that you want to record multiplication sentences that will result in these products:

☐ × ☐ = 42 ☐ × ☐ = 420 ☐ × ☐ = 4200

- Ask: *Tell me all the different ways you can make these number sentences true.*
- Give pupils time to come up with a set of solutions. Do they use commutativity to help find further examples? See if pupils recognise that 6 × 700 and 60 × 70 both result in the product 4200.
- Look at each sentence in turn and reinforce that multiplying by a number of tens or hundreds is simply an extension of a one-digit multiplication, that is, 6 × 7 = 42 and 6 × 70 is ten times larger because 42 tens is ten times larger than 42 ones.
- Explore 12, 120 and 1200 in the same way, describing these as 12 ones, 12 tens and 12 hundreds. Ask pupils to use base 10 blocks or place value counters to represent these products using groups or arrays.
- Compare representations, agreeing, for example that 6 × 2 = 3 × 4 and 20 × 6 = 30 × 4, and so on.

*The product of 12 tens is ten times larger than the product of 12 ones.*

*The product of 12 hundreds is a hundred times larger than the product of 12 ones.*

- Explain that one set of three numbers is incomplete as only two can be found on the grid (54 and 540).
- Ask: *What is the third member of this group? How do you know?*
- Pupils should complete Question 1 in the Practice Book.

## Same-day intervention

- Look together at a set of related facts, for example 4 × 7 = 28, 4 × 70 = 280 and 4 × 700 = 2800. Pupils should represent each of the sentences using base 10 blocks or place value counters, explaining the similarities and differences each time.
- See if pupils can explain that the product of 4 × 70 (28 tens) is ten times larger than the product of 4 × 7 (28 ones).
- Look at commutativity by rearranging the representations to show 7 × 4, 7 × 40 and 7 × 400. Ask pupils to explain why the product is the same.

## Same-day enrichment

- Give pupils **Resource 3.9.7b** Money multiplication.

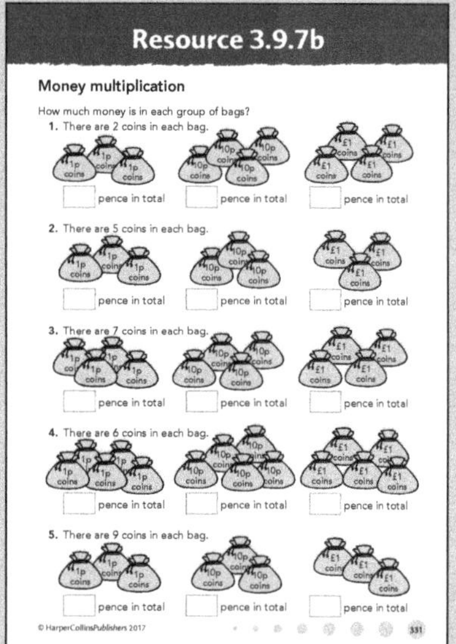

Resource 3.9.7b

Money multiplication

How much money is in each group of bags?

1. There are 2 coins in each bag.

[ ] pence in total [ ] pence in total [ ] pence in total

2. There are 5 coins in each bag.

[ ] pence in total [ ] pence in total [ ] pence in total

3. There are 7 coins in each bag.

[ ] pence in total [ ] pence in total [ ] pence in total

4. There are 6 coins in each bag.

[ ] pence in total [ ] pence in total [ ] pence in total

5. There are 9 coins in each bag.

[ ] pence in total [ ] pence in total [ ] pence in total

© HarperCollinsPublishers 2017 331

- The problem shows bags of 1p, 10p and £1 coins (100p). Pupils use the information to find the value, in pence, of each group of bags. They can also make their own money bag problems for others to solve.

# Question 2

**2** Split the numbers into hundreds, tens and ones. One has been done for you.

(a) 316 = 300 + 10 + 6

(b) 427 = [ ] + [ ] + [ ]

(c) 987 = [ ] + [ ] + [ ]

(d) 634 = [ ] + [ ] + [ ]

## What learning will pupils have achieved at the conclusion of Question 2?

- Using knowledge of place value, pupils will have partitioned three-digit numbers into hundreds, tens and ones.

## Activities for whole-class instruction

- Show pupils the following numbers made using place value arrow cards.

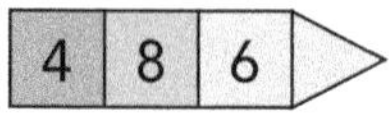


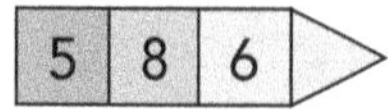


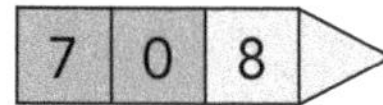

- Tell pupils that you have been building some three-digit numbers by combining different numbers of hundreds, tens and ones. Start by looking at 486.
- Ask: *How many hundreds, tens and ones were used to build 486? Which place value arrow cards did I use to build it?*
- Tell pupils to build the number using place value arrow cards. Record this as: 400 + 80 + 6 = 486 and 486 = 400 + 80 + 6

*486 can be split into 4 hundreds, 8 tens and 6 ones.*

- Now show pupils the numbers 586, 708 and 640. Ask them to use the place value arrow cards to build each of these numbers and then partition (split) the number to show the value of each digit. They should record the partitioned number each time and tell their partner the value of each part.
- Focus particularly on 708, as this has no tens (708 = 700 + 8) and 640 as this has no ones (640 = 600 + 40).
- Pupils should complete Question 2 in the Practice Book.

## Same-day intervention

- Give pupils **Resource 3.9.7c** Finding whole numbers to complete. Pupils count the hundreds, tens and ones and then find the value of the whole number.

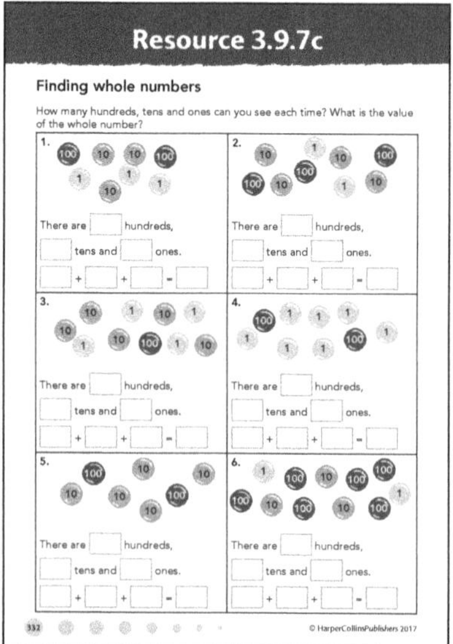

Resource 3.9.7c

Finding whole numbers

How many hundreds, tens and ones can you see each time? What is the value of the whole number?

1. There are [ ] hundreds, [ ] tens and [ ] ones. [ ] + [ ] + [ ] = [ ]

2. There are [ ] hundreds, [ ] tens and [ ] ones. [ ] + [ ] + [ ] = [ ]

3. There are [ ] hundreds, [ ] tens and [ ] ones. [ ] + [ ] + [ ] = [ ]

4. There are [ ] hundreds, [ ] tens and [ ] ones. [ ] + [ ] + [ ] = [ ]

5. There are [ ] hundreds, [ ] tens and [ ] ones. [ ] + [ ] + [ ] = [ ]

6. There are [ ] hundreds, [ ] tens and [ ] ones. [ ] + [ ] + [ ] = [ ]

332 © HarperCollinsPublishers 2017

## Same-day enrichment

- Using 12 place value counters (100s, 10s and 1s), ask pupils to show each of the following:
  - the largest three-digit number
  - the smallest three-digit number
  - an odd number that is less than 500
  - a multiple of 5 that is between 400 and 600.

- Pupils should record their ideas by showing the counters set out in place value columns each time and write it as: ☐00 + ☐0 + ☐ = ☐.

# Question 3 and Question 4

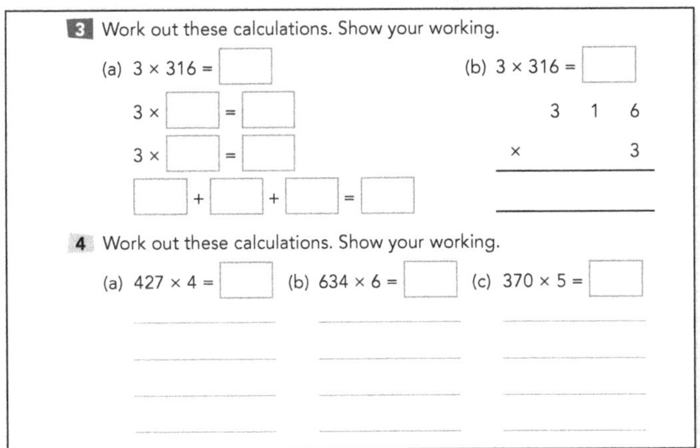

**3** Work out these calculations. Show your working.

(a) 3 × 316 = ☐

3 × ☐ = ☐

3 × ☐ = ☐

☐ + ☐ + ☐ = ☐

(b) 3 × 316 = ☐

  3 1 6
× 3

**4** Work out these calculations. Show your working.

(a) 427 × 4 = ☐ (b) 634 × 6 = ☐ (c) 370 × 5 = ☐

## What learning will pupils have achieved at the conclusion of Question 3 and Question 4?

- Pupils will be able to recognise and explain why it is useful to partition a three-digit number into hundreds, tens and ones if the number needs to be multiplied.
- Pupils will have shown their ability to mentally multiply a one-digit number by tens and hundreds as part of the whole calculation.
- Conceptual understanding of multiplying a three-digit number by a one-digit number will have been developed using manipulatives and other representations.
- Pupils' understanding of how to carry out a written procedure for multiplying a two-digit number by a one-digit number will have been extended to multiplying a three-digit number.

## Activities for whole-class instruction

- Discuss the mental strategies that pupils used to multiply two-digit numbers by a one-digit number. Agree that the method used partitioning to find 'part products' by multiplying the tens and then the ones parts of the calculation, and then adding the part products together.
- Show this again with the example 7 × 25, using arrays as shown in image 1 on **Resource 3.9.7d** Partitioning arrays.

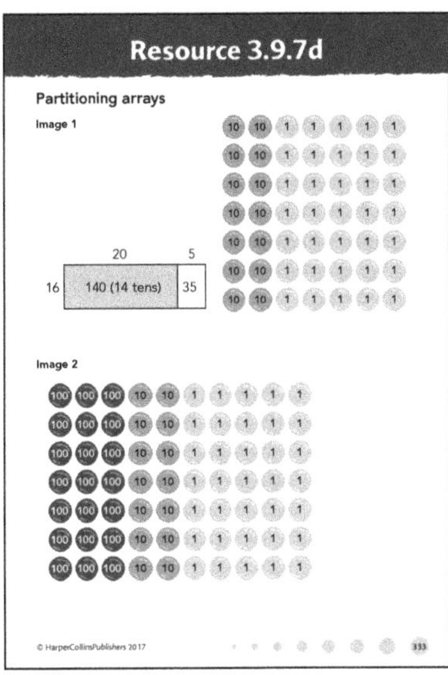


Agree that 7 × 25 = 175 as it is the sum of 7 × 20 and 7 × 5.

- Show image 2 on **Resource 3.9.7d**.
- Ask pupils to discuss the differences and similarities between this array and the one for 7 × 25. Agree that there are the same number of ones and the same number of tens, but the new array also shows 7 × 300 (7 × 3 hundreds).
- Agree that the whole array represents 7 × 325, but the calculation has been broken down into smaller parts using partitioning, for example 325 as 300 + 20 + 5.
- Record this as:

  7 × 325 =

  7 × 300 = 2100

  7 × 20 = 140

  7 × 5 = 35
- Work through the parts of the calculation together, drawing on pupils' understanding of multiplying a number of tens or a number of hundreds. Agree that 7 × 325 = 2100 + 140 + 35 = 2275.
- Finally, show an expanded method of written multiplication (as used in previous units) that keeps the part products visible. Ask pupils to compare the different parts of the calculation and the array, agreeing that these are the same.

```
     3 2 5
×        7
     3 5 (7 × 5 ones)
   1 4 0 (7 × 2 tens)
 2 1 0 0 (7 × 3 hundreds)
 2 2 7 5
```

- Practise another example together, for example 4 × 253, first describing the array and then working through the two methods shown above.

- Pupils should complete Question 3 and Question 4 in the Practice Book.

## Same-day intervention

- Show pupils the calculation 4 × 536. Ask: *What is 536 partitioned into hundreds, tens and ones?* Agree that 536 = 500 + 30 + 6.
- Tell one group to take place value counters to show five hundreds, another to show three tens, and the third to show six ones.

  Record 4 × 536 using partitioning as:

  4 × 500 =

  4 × 30 =

  4 × 6 =

- Ask: *What do you need to do to show 4 × 5 hundreds, 4 × 3 tens and 4 × 6 ones?* Pupils should add additional rows to their arrays to show four rows and say the total value, for example 4 × 3 tens is 12 tens or 120.
- Record the products next to the correct part of the partitioned calculation above.
- Agree that the product of 4 × 536 is the sum of the part products, 2000 + 120 + 24.
- Ask pupils to push their arrays together to now show 4 × 536.

## Same-day enrichment

- Give pupils **Resource 3.9.7e** Finding values. They use the information given about the partitioned multiplications to find the missing values.

**Resource 3.9.7e**

**Finding values**

Find the missing values to make these multiplications correct.

1. ☐ × 652 =
   ☐ × 600 = 4200
   ☐ × 50 = 350
   ☐ × 2 = ☐
   4200 + 350 + ☐ = ☐

2. 4 × ☐ =
   4 × ☐ = 1200
   4 × ☐ = 320
   4 × 6 = 24
   1200 + 320 + 24 = ☐

3. 491 × ☐ =
   400 × ☐ = 3600
   90 × ☐ = ☐
   1 × ☐ = 9
   3600 + ☐ + 9 = ☐

4. ☐ × 7 =
   ☐ × 7 = 5600
   ☐ × 7 = 350
   ☐ × 7 = 63
   5600 + 350 + 63 = ☐

5. ☐ × ☐ =
   ☐ × 200 = 1000
   ☐ × ☐ = 400
   ☐ × 6 = ☐
   1000 + 400 + ☐ = ☐

6. 316 × ☐ =
   300 × ☐ = 2400
   10 × ☐ = ☐
   6 × ☐ = 48
   2400 + ☐ + 48 = ☐

334 © HarperCollinsPublishers 2017

# Question 5

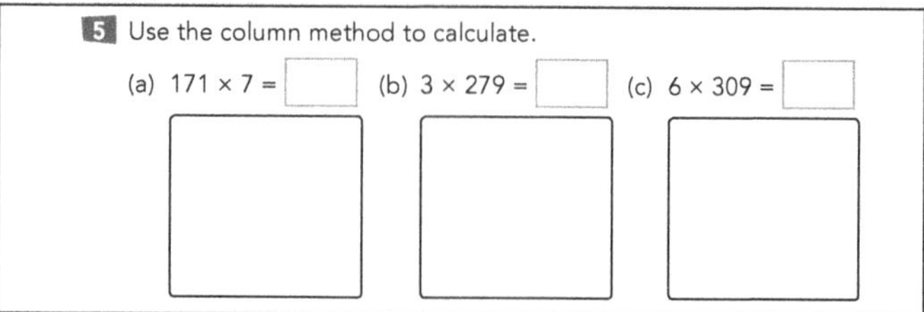
5 Use the column method to calculate.

(a) 171 × 7 = ☐ (b) 3 × 279 = ☐ (c) 6 × 309 = ☐

## What learning will pupils have achieved at the conclusion of Question 5?

- Pupils will have shown their ability to mentally multiply a one-digit number by tens and hundreds as part of the whole calculation.
- Conceptual understanding of multiplying a three-digit number by a one-digit number will have been developed using manipulatives and other representations.
- Pupils' understanding of how to carry out a written procedure for multiplying a two-digit number by a one-digit number will have been extended to multiplying a three-digit number.
- Through application of multiplying hundreds numbers, pupils will have made informed estimates about the size of a product and can predict which two multiples of a hundred it will lie between.

## Activities for whole-class instruction

- Ask pupils to partition the numbers 367 and 428 to show the value of the hundreds, tens and ones part of each. Say: *I would like to make each number three times larger. How should I do this?*
- First discuss a possible estimate for each calculation. Ask: *What estimate can I make for 3 × 367? How do I know that the product will be between 900 and 1200?*
- Agree that 3 × 367 is greater than 3 × 300 (9 hundreds) but smaller than 3 × 400 (12 hundreds).
- Revisit the methods used in the previous session with partitioning to find part products and then add these parts together, for example:

$$3 \times 367 =$$
$$3 \times 300 = 900$$
$$3 \times 60 = 180$$
$$3 \times 7 = 21$$
$$900 + 180 + 21 = 1101$$

$$\begin{array}{r} 3\ 6\ 7 \\ \times \quad\ \ 3 \\ \hline 2\ 1 \\ 1\ 8\ 0 \\ 9\ 0\ 0 \\ \hline 1\ 1\ 0\ 1 \\ \hline {}_{1}\quad\ \ \end{array}$$

- Ask pupils to use both methods to calculate 3 × 428, remembering to make an estimate first.
- Tell pupils that you are going to explain a short method of multiplication for multiplying a three-dgit number by a one-digit number. Reassure pupils that it is the same method as for multiplying a two-digit number by a one-digit number, but with an extra column.
- Look together at the methods for 3 × 67 and 3 × 367, using **Resource 3.9.7f** Multiplication: written methods.

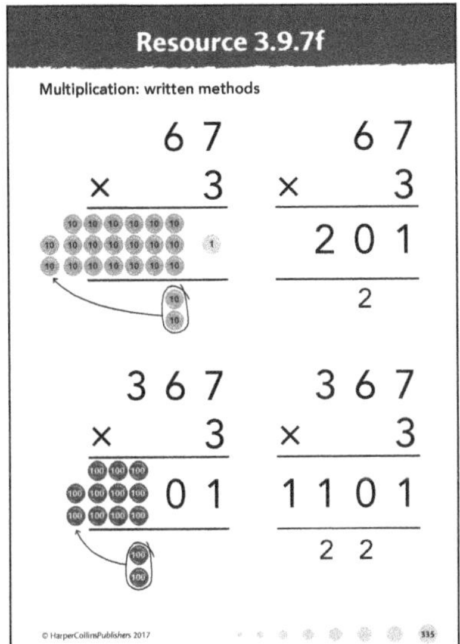


- Discuss any similarities and differences. Focus particularly on exchanging 20 tens for two hundreds that must be written in the hundreds column in the second example.
- Pupils should use place value counters to work through each stage of the calculation 3 × 367 to reinforce the process of grouping tens into hundreds where appropriate and writing them in the tens column.
- Now work together through the calculation 3 × 428, using place value counters.
- Pupils should complete Question 5 in the Practice Book.

## Same-day intervention

- Work together with pupils to look at the similarities and differences between the expanded method and the short method of multiplication for the following calculations.

  3 × 215 4 × 324 5 × 224

- Ensure that pupils recognise that values are the same even though they are set out differently.
- Use place value counters or base 10 blocks to model each stage of the calculations alongside each other so the similarities are explicit.
- For example:

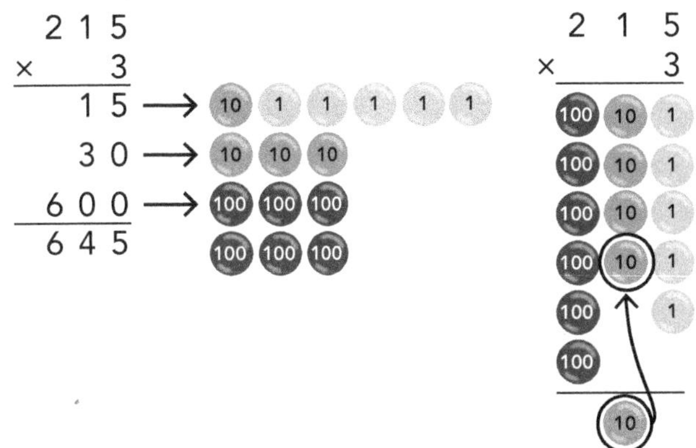


## Same-day enrichment

- Give pupils **Resource 3.9.7g** Largest and smallest products.

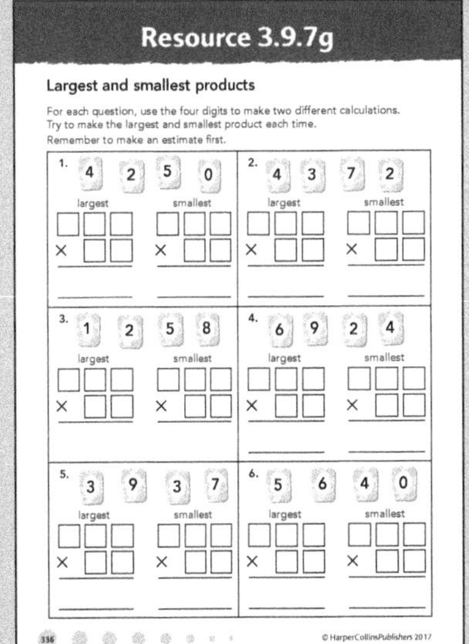


- Pupils should use the digits to find the largest and smallest product each time, using the written method of multiplication. They are reminded to make an estimate first so they have an idea of the size of the product and can spot any errors that have been made when calculating.

# Question 6

**6** Are these calculations correct? Put ✓ for yes and ✗ for no in the box and then make corrections.

(a)
```
    2 3 5
×       4
---------
    9 4 0
```
☐

(b)
```
    1 0 7
×       5
---------
    8 3 5
```
☐

(c)
```
    6 7 2
×       8
---------
  5 3 7 6
```
☐

Corrections:

## What learning will pupils have achieved at the conclusion of Question 6?

- Conceptual understanding of multiplying a three-digit number by a one-digit number will have been developed using manipulatives and other representations.
- Pupils' understanding of how to carry out a written procedure for multiplying a two-digit number by a one-digit number will have been extended to multiplying a three-digit number.
- Through application of multiplying hundreds numbers, pupils will have made informed estimates about the size of a product and can predict which two multiples of a hundred it will lie between.

## Activities for whole-class instruction

- Begin by practising a few multiplications by partitioning into hundreds, tens and ones to find part products or a written method.

  368 × 4   586 × 3   172 × 9   243 × 8   779 × 2
- Ask pupils to predict which is likely to give the largest product before calculating. Ask them to compare the number of hundreds to help them.
- Show the working that you have done for 5 × 685 and 4 × 737. Say that you had made an estimate first and decided that the product for 5 × 685 must be between 3000 and 3500 and the product of 4 × 737 must be between 2800 and 3200. Do pupils agree with the estimates?
- Write the following on the board (including deliberate errors):

```
    6 8 5          7 3 7
×       4      ×       4
---------      ---------
  2 9 2 2        2 8 4 8
    3 0            1 2
```

- Pupils should check through the calculations in pairs, explaining and correcting any errors.
- Ask pupils to represent each calculation using place value counters.
- Pupils should complete Question 6 in the Practice Book.

## Same-day intervention

- Give pupils the following calculations to check.

  4 × 235 = 930   6 × 208 = 1248

  426 × 5 = 2120   318 × 4 = 1172
- They should record an estimate for each and then check, using place value counters and recording with a written column method.

## Same-day enrichment

- Give pupils a set of calculations. Ensure that some are correct and others are not. For the incorrect calculations, some should be able to be discarded through estimation and others only through calculation: for example, estimation would predict that 358 × 6 = 2128 might be correct, however, calculation will show that the actual product is 2148; whereas 524 × 7 = 5668 would be correctly discarded after estimating.
- Pupils should sort the calculations into 'possible products' and 'impossible products' groups initially, and then use a written method to check the actual products for all calculations in the 'possible product' group.

## Challenge and extension question

# Question 7

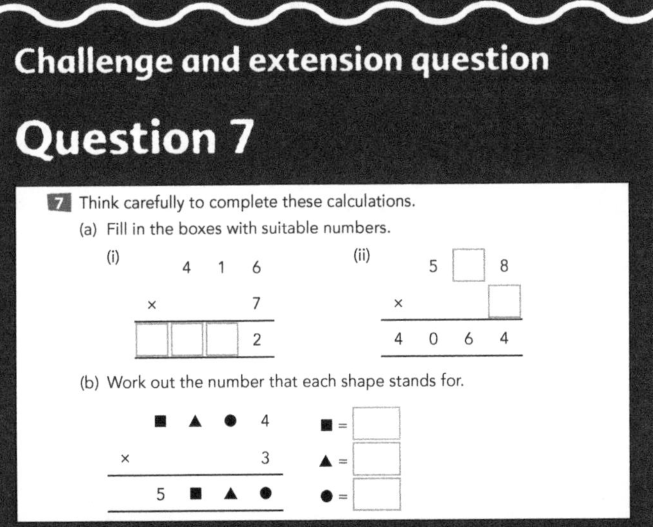
7 Think carefully to complete these calculations.

(a) Fill in the boxes with suitable numbers.

(i) 416 × 7 = □□□2

(ii) 5□8 × □ = 4064

(b) Work out the number that each shape stands for.

■▲●4 × 3 = 5■▲●

■ = □

▲ = □

● = □

For the first question, pupils are required to replace the missing numbers with values that are suitable for the size of the calculation and product. They should think about the information they already know, for example for the first example, 7 × 6 is 42 so there must be a carry-over of four tens. For the second example, the multiplication 3 × 8 and 8 × 8 would result in the digit 4 in the ones position of the answer space. However, an initial estimate would help pupils to recognise the magnitude of the product and that the multiplier must be a larger digit, that is, 8.

The second problem is quite similar and pupils should not be put off by the different shapes. However, they should notice that the three shapes appear in the calculation and in the answer space – both in the same order.

By quickly finding the value of the circle as the ones part of the product 12, pupils should work through the problem systematically filling in the values that they find along the way.

# Unit 9.8 Multiplying a 3-digit number by a 1-digit number (2)

## Conceptual context

In the previous unit, pupils used partitioning to represent part products. They applied this understanding to help make sense of an expanded and compact method for multiplying a three-digit number by a one-digit number.

In this unit, pupils will explore the size of a product resulting from multiplying a three-digit number by a one-digit number and will recognise that this will always be a three-digit or four-digit number. They reason about the number of tens or hundreds in the product and use this to determine the number of zeros.

## Learning pupils will have achieved at the end of the unit

- Multiplication of tens or hundreds numbers by 10 or 100 will have been practised so that pupils perceive patterns for themselves and understand why a number ending with one or two zeros is always a multiple of 10 or 100 respectively (Q1, Q2, Q3, Q4)
- Pupils will be able to predict the likely magnitude of a product using reasoning (Q2, Q3, Q4, Q5)
- Understanding of equivalences between multiples of ten and multiples of 100 will have become secure (Q2)
- Pupils will have become more proficient with the compact written method for multiplying a three-digit number by a one-digit number (Q2, Q3, Q4, Q5)
- Fluency with multiplication facts, including multiplying by tens and hundreds, will have been further developed as pupils solve problems in a context (Q5)

### Resources

Number rods; base 10 blocks; place value counters; 0–9 dice or 0–9 spinners; **Resource 3.9.8a** Total values; **Resource 3.9.8b** Money totals; **Resource 3.9.8c** Matching calculations; **Resource 3.9.8d** Multiplication grid

### Vocabulary

ones, tens, hundreds, multiply, multiplication, product, partition, estimate

# Question 1

**1** Calculate mentally.

| | | | |
|---|---|---|---|
| (a) | 5 × 5 = ☐ | (d) | 2 × 5 = ☐ |
| (b) | 50 × 5 = ☐ | (e) | 20 × 5 = ☐ |
| (c) | 500 × 5 = ☐ | (f) | 200 × 5 = ☐ |
| (g) | 3 × 7 = ☐ | (j) | 9 × 4 = ☐ |
| (h) | 30 × 7 = ☐ | (k) | 90 × 4 = ☐ |
| (i) | 300 × 7 = ☐ | (l) | 900 × 4 = ☐ |

## What learning will pupils have achieved at the conclusion of Question 1?

- Multiplication of tens or hundreds numbers by 10 or 100 will have been practised so that pupils perceive patterns for themselves and understand why a number ending with one or two zeros is always a multiple of 10 or 100 respectively.

## Activities for whole-class instruction

- Show pupils image 1 from **Resource 3.9.8a** Total values.

**Resource 3.9.8a**

Total values

Image 1

Image 2

- Discuss the differences between the coins on the bags, but agree that there are three of each bag.
- Tell pupils there are four coins in each bag.
- Ask pupils to discuss the total value (in pence) of each set of bags. Refer to each coin in the £1 bag being the same as 100p.
- See if pupils recognise that they can use what they know about multiplying a number of tens or hundreds to help them.
- Record the number sentences as follows, describing them as 3 × 4 ones (12 ones), 3 × 4 tens (12 tens), 3 × 4 hundreds (12 hundreds):

  3 × 4p = 12p 3 × 40p = 120p 3 × 400p = 1200p
- Say: *There are now six coins in each bag – what are the total values now?*
- Take feedback and record these as 3 × 6p = 18p, 3 × 60p = 180p and 3 × 600p = 1800p, again describing them as 3 × 6 ones (18 ones), 3 × 6 tens (18 tens) and 3 × 6 hundreds (18 hundreds).
- Look at the number of zeros at the end of the product '18' in each number sentence, asking pupils to explain why this is the case.
- Now show image 2 from **Resource 3.9.8a**. Ask pupils to explain what is different this time.
- Say: *There are three coins in each bag – do I need to calculate the total amount in each set of bags again or can I use what I already know?*
- Agree that there are now 6 × 3p = 18p, 6 × 30p = 180p and 6 × 300p = 1800p. There are still 18 ones, 18 tens and 18 hundreds. Say: *We have used the product of 6 × 3 this time rather than 3 × 6, but the result is the same because multiplication is commutative.*
- Finally, tell pupils that there are seven coins in each bag. Ask pupils to quickly find the total value for each set of bags, encouraging them to describe each calculation as: 6 × 7 ones (42 ones), 6 × 7 tens (42 tens) and 6 × 7 hundreds (42 hundreds).
- Pupils should complete Question 1 in the Practice Book

## Same-day intervention

- Pupils use a 0–9 dice or spinner to generate two digits. They then use the digits to replace the missing numbers in the sentences below. For example, if they roll a 6 and a 4, they use 6 as the number of coins each time and 4 as the number of bags.

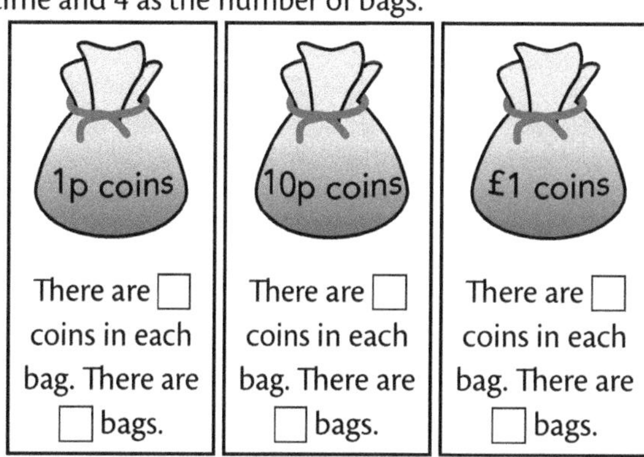

1p coins
There are ☐ coins in each bag. There are ☐ bags.
10p coins
There are ☐ coins in each bag. There are ☐ bags.
£1 coins
There are ☐ coins in each bag. There are ☐ bags.

- They should record the calculations they use each time to find the total numbers in pence.
- Ask pupils to now swap the digits in each calculation, for example, 4 coins and 6 bags. Ask pupils to explain why the total number remains the same. For the example here, there are still 24 ones, 24 tens and 24 hundreds.
- Pupils continue by generating another two digits.

## Same-day enrichment

- Ask pupils to complete **Resource 3.9.8b** Money totals.

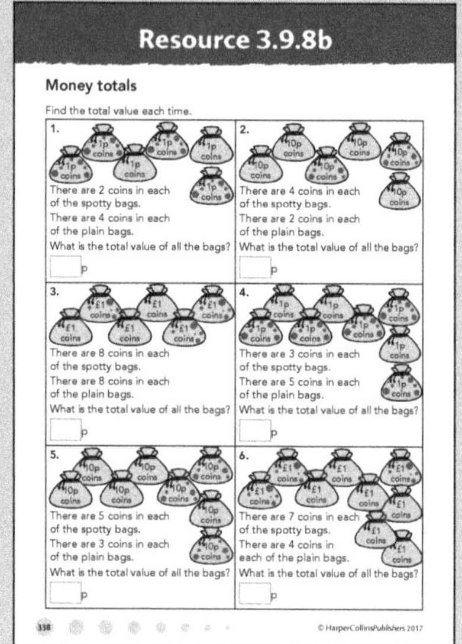

**Resource 3.9.8b**

**Money totals**

Find the total value each time.

1. There are 2 coins in each of the spotty bags. There are 4 coins in each of the plain bags. What is the total value of all the bags? ☐ p

2. There are 4 coins in each of the spotty bags. There are 2 coins in each of the plain bags. What is the total value of all the bags? ☐ p

3. There are 8 coins in each of the spotty bags. There are 8 coins in each of the plain bags. What is the total value of all the bags? ☐ p

4. There are 3 coins in each of the spotty bags. There are 5 coins in each of the plain bags. What is the total value of all the bags? ☐ p

5. There are 5 coins in each of the spotty bags. There are 3 coins in each of the plain bags. What is the total value of all the bags? ☐ p

6. There are 7 coins in each of the spotty bags. There are 4 coins in each of the plain bags. What is the total value of all the bags? ☐ p

338 © HarperCollinsPublishers 2017

# Question 2

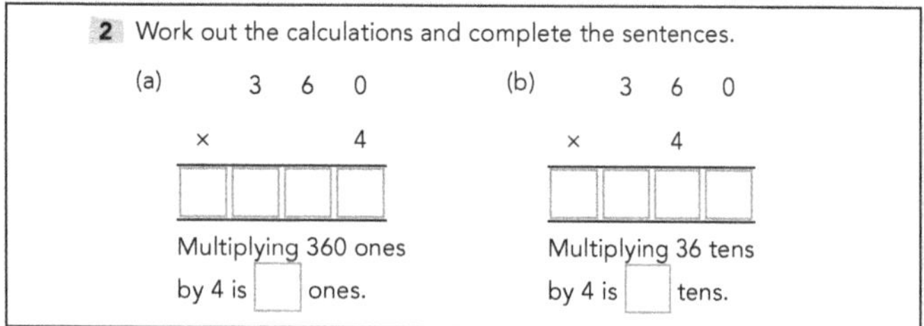

**2** Work out the calculations and complete the sentences.

(a) 360 × 4 = ☐☐☐☐

Multiplying 360 ones by 4 is ☐ ones.

(b) 360 × 4 = ☐☐☐☐

Multiplying 36 tens by 4 is ☐ tens.

## What learning will pupils have achieved at the conclusion of Question 2?

- Multiplication of tens or hundreds numbers by 10 or 100 will have been practised, so that pupils perceive patterns for themselves and understand why a number ending with one or two zeros is always a multiple of 10 or 100 respectively.
- Pupils will be able to predict the likely magnitude of a product using reasoning.
- Understanding of equivalences between multiples of ten and multiples of 100 will have become secure.
- Pupils will have shown their ability to mentally multiply a one-digit number by tens and hundreds as part of the whole calculation.
- Pupils will have become more proficient with the compact written method for multiplying a three-digit number by a one-digit number.

## Activities for whole-class instruction

- Show pupils the set of statements below involving a number of ones, tens and hundreds to reason about.
- Ask: *Is each statement correct? How do you know?*

  4 × 70 = 4 × 7 tens

  4 × 7 hundreds = 700 × 4

  20 ones = 2 tens

  280 ones = 28 tens

  450 ones = 54 tens

- Discuss each statement in turn, returning to the use of place value counters or base 10 blocks to show, for example that 4 × 70 = 4 × 7 tens because they both result in 28 tens.

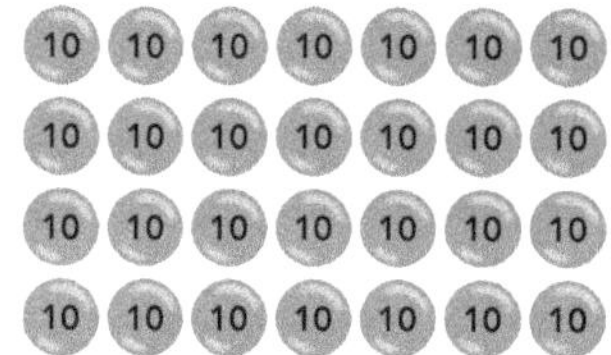


- Look at 20 ones = 2 tens in more detail, agreeing that 10 'ones' cubes is equal to one 'tens' rod. There are ten times as many cubes as rods, but the total value is the same. This means that 20 'ones' cubes are the same as 2 'tens' rods.
- Extend this thinking to consider 280 ones = 28 tens. You could also ask pupils to reason about 280 lots of 1p coins and 28 lots of 10p coins, establishing that both have the same value.
- Ask: *If I arrange 280 one pence coins into 28 equal rows, how many one pence coins will be in each row?* Look together at the result of multiplying 28 × 10, using a place value grid to show the position of the digits as the number is multiplied.
- Discuss 540 ones = 54 tens, establishing that 54 tens is larger because this is the same as 54 × 10 and we know this is 540. Model this on a place value grid to show that as the number 54 becomes ten times larger, the digits all move one place to the left to show the value as 540 (or 54 tens).

- Correct the statement to show 450 ones = 45 tens, agreeing this is correct because 45 × 10 = 450.
- Show pupils the following calculations. What do they notice about them?

$$\begin{array}{r} 2\,4\,0 \\ \times \quad\; 3 \\ \hline \\ \hline \end{array} \qquad 3 \times 24 \text{ tens} = \_\_\_\_ \text{ tens}$$

- Explain that the first calculation shows multiplying 240 ones by 3, whereas the second shows multiplying 24 tens by 3. Agree that 24 tens is equal to 240 ones.
- Work together to complete the first calculation using the column method.
- For the tens column, say: *3 times 4 tens (or 40) is 12 tens (or 120)*, writing the 10 tens (1 hundred) under the hundreds column to be added to the hundreds product and putting two tens in the tens part of the answer space to show 20.
- Describe the product of the first calculation as 720 ones.
- Ask: *How can we describe 720 ones as a number of tens?* Agree that 720 ones is the same as 72 tens, so the product of 3 × 24 tens is 72 tens.
- Pupils should complete Question 2 in the Practice Book.

## Same-day intervention

- Give pupils **Resource 3.9.8c** Matching calculations.

**Resource 3.9.8c**

Matching calculations

| | | | |
|---|---|---|---|
| 230 ones × 5 | 300 ones × 8 | 5 × 25 tens | 420 ones × 3 |
| 42 tens × 6 | 7 × 18 tens | 23 tens × 5 | 18 tens × 2 |
| 4 × 21 tens | 42 tens × 3 | 30 tens × 8 | 420 ones × 6 |
| 180 ones × 2 | 5 × 250 ones | 180 ones × 7 | 4 × 210 ones |

© HarperCollinsPublishers 2017 339

- Pupils should record the matching calculations and find the product using a written method.

For example: 230 ones × 5 = 23 tens × 5

$$\begin{array}{r} 2\,3\,0 \\ \times \quad\; 5 \\ \hline 1\,1\,5\,0 \\ \hline 1\;\;\; \end{array}$$

## Same-day enrichment

- Give pupils the following statements. They should check to see if each statement is correct using a written method of multiplication, recording their calculations and amending any errors they find by changing the symbol =, < or >, as necessary.

250 ones × 5 > 6 × 24 tens

36 tens × 7 < 360 ones × 8

180 ones × 6 = 8 × 16 tens

650 ones × 3 = 65 tens × 3

42 tens × 9 > 490 ones × 8

# Question 3

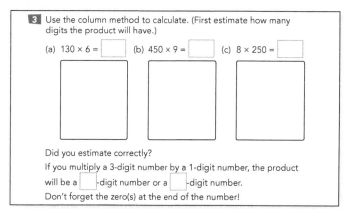

**3** Use the column method to calculate. (First estimate how many digits the product will have.)

(a) 130 × 6 = ☐ (b) 450 × 9 = ☐ (c) 8 × 250 = ☐

Did you estimate correctly?

If you multiply a 3-digit number by a 1-digit number, the product will be a ☐-digit number or a ☐-digit number.

Don't forget the zero(s) at the end of the number!

## What learning will pupils have achieved at the conclusion of Question 3?

- Multiplication of tens or hundreds numbers by 10 or 100 will have been practised so that pupils perceive patterns for themselves and understand why a number ending with one or two zeros is always a multiple of 10 or 100 respectively.
- Pupils will be able to predict the likely magnitude of a product using reasoning.
- Pupils will have shown their ability to mentally multiply a one-digit number by tens and hundreds as part of the whole calculation.
- Pupils will have become more proficient with the compact written method for multiplying a three-digit number by a one-digit number.

## Activities for whole-class instruction

- Give groups of pupils nine of the '100' place value counters. Explain that they can use no more than nine of these counters each time to represent different multiplications.
- Pupils can represent the multiplications showing arrays or simply as grouping.
- Ask: *Which of these multiplications can you represent using no more than nine of the counters? Show me.*

  300 × 3   5 × 200   3 × 400   600 × 1   500 × 3   2 × 300
- Encourage pupils to think about, for example, 300 as three hundreds, and so on, to help make decisions about how to represent each multiplication. They should use the counters and make a note of those that can be made and those that cannot.
- Share findings as a group, agreeing that 5 × 200, 3 × 400 and 500 × 3 cannot be represented as they all need more than nine counters, for example, 5 × 200 is the same as 5 × 2 hundreds or 10 hundreds. Look at the number of zeros at the end of the products to show hundreds.
- Compare each of the products, focusing on the number of digits in each – the products that could be made using the counters all have three digits while the others have four digits.
- Suggest that if the related multiplication fact using single digits gives a product that is 9 or less, for example, 3 × 3 = 9, then the number of hundreds 3 × 3 hundreds will be nine or less than nine hundreds and will be a three-digit number.
- Now show the calculation 3 × 350. Ask: *It still shows 3 × 3 hundreds, but will the product still be a three-digit number?*
- Pupils should discuss the problem, making an estimate to decide which numbers the product will sit between and then calculating using a written method.
- Agree that this is actually a four-digit number, the extra 3 × 50 added to 3 × 300 made the product 150 larger than 900.
- Finally, show the calculation 4 × 526. Ask pupils to explain how they know that the product will definitely be a four-digit number.

*Multiplying a three-digit number by a one-digit number will give a product with three or four digits.*

- Pupils should complete Question 3 in the Practice Book.

## Same-day intervention

- Give each pair of pupils a set of three-digit by one-digit multiplications on separate cards – some with products that are less than 1000 and others with larger products.
- They should take it in turns to pick a card and make an estimate first. They then decide if the product will be a three-digit or four-digit number and explain why. Their partner calculates, using a written method or place value counters, to check.
- Players score a point for a correct estimate.

## Same-day enrichment

- Give pupils the following problem to explore:

  What numbers should go in the spaces to make this statement true?

  □□□ × □ < 1000

  Which two numbers give the product closest to 1000?

  Which two numbers give the product closest to 0?

# Question 4 and Question 5

**4** (a) There are ☐ zeros at the end of the product 4 × 5 × 5.

(b) There are ☐ zeros at the end of the product 125 × 8 × 10.

**5** Application problems.

(a) Zainab finished reading a book in 9 days. She read 120 pages a day. How many pages are there in the book?

Answer: ______

(b) There are 205 cows on a farm. There are 4 times as many sheep as there are cows. How many sheep are there?

Answer: ______

## What learning will pupils have achieved at the conclusion of Question 4 and Question 5?

- Multiplication of tens or hundreds numbers by 10 or 100 will have been practised so that pupils perceive patterns for themselves and understand why a number ending with one or two zeros is always a multiple of 10 or 100 respectively.
- Pupils will be able to predict the likely magnitude of a product using reasoning.

 

- Pupils will have shown their ability to mentally multiply a one-digit number by tens and hundreds as part of the whole calculation.
- Pupils will have become more proficient with the compact written method for multiplying a three-digit number by a one-digit number.
- Fluency with multiplication facts, including multiplying by tens and hundreds, will have been further developed as pupils solve problems in a context.

## Activities for whole-class instruction

- Show pupils the grid of calculations on **Resource 3.9.8d** Multiplication grid.

**Resource 3.9.8d**

Multiplication grid

| | | | |
|---|---|---|---|
| 302 × 4 | 2 × 2 × 10 | 3 × 10 × 7 | 6 × 300 |
| 460 × 5 | 40 × 30 | 125 × 4 | 2 × 4 × 30 |
| 40 × 7 | 247 × 3 | 200 × 5 | 5 × 5 × 10 |

140 © HarperCollinsPublishers 2017

- Ask pupils to reason about the calculations using estimates as required to help them to find:
  - products with three digits
  - products with four digits
  - products ending with one zero
  - products ending with two zeros.
- Discuss each set of calculations in turn, sharing pupils' reasoning about the decisions they made and why it is helpful to estimate. Focus on calculations such as 5 × 5 × 10 and 2 × 4 × 30, showing that these can be seen as 25 × 10 and 8 × 30 respectively.
- Finally, write the calculation 125 × 4 × 10. Ask pupils to discuss what they will need to do to find the product and discuss how the number of zeros at the end of the number will change as a result.
- Explain that you are now going to share a word problem that uses the calculation 460 × 5 from the grid.

  *A cinema has 460 tickets to sell for the showing of one film.*

  *The cinema is full for the showing of 5 films.*

  *How many tickets were sold altogether?*
- Ask pupils to use what they know about 125 × 4 × 10 to help them estimate the answer to this problem. Show a second problem as:

  *A smaller cinema has 238 tickets to sell for the showing of one film.*

  *A much larger cinema can sell four times as many tickets for the showing of one film.*

  *How many tickets can the larger cinema sell?*
- Look together at the language used in each of the problems, particularly focusing on 'times as many'.
- Pupils should make an estimate to decide whether the product will have three or four digits and then complete the calculation. Ask: *What is the largest number that the 238 could be changed to for the answer to the question to have three digits? How do you know?* Pupils should explain that for the answer to be three digits, it must be less than $\frac{1}{4}$ of 1000, so they must start by finding $\frac{1}{4}$ of 1000 and then consider the greatest number below that (224).
- Pupils should complete Question 4 and Question 5 in the Practice Book.

### Same-day intervention

- Look together at some three-digit by one-digit multiplications that will result in products that are larger or smaller than 1000. Encourage pupils to make estimates and use what they know about place value to help make decisions.
- Take a problem one at a time and together, suggest some contexts, for example the ticket sales at the cinema. Ask pupils to turn the contexts into a word problem.

### Same-day enrichment

- Give pupils a set of calculations, for example:

  260 × 7   453 × 4   741 × 5   380 × 6
- Pupils should make up their own word problems to match each calculation and provide answers for each.
- They should first make an estimate before calculating. Encourage them to use a range of language to imply multiplication, including 'times as many.'

## Challenge and extension question

# Question 6

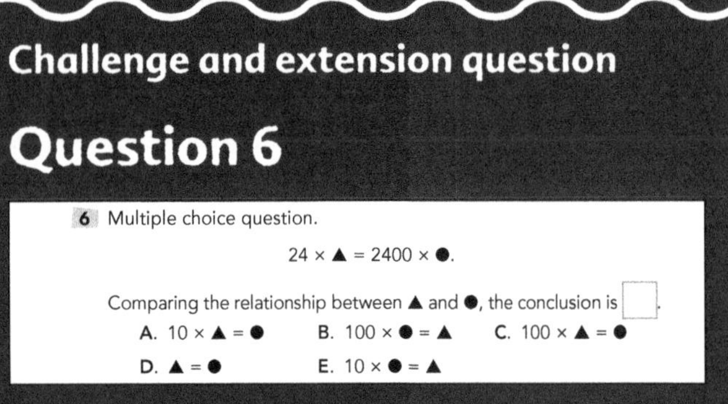
6 Multiple choice question.

24 × ▲ = 2400 × ●.

Comparing the relationship between ▲ and ●, the conclusion is ☐.

A. 10 × ▲ = ●  B. 100 × ● = ▲  C. 100 × ▲ = ●

D. ▲ = ●  E. 10 × ● = ▲

For Question 6, pupils are required to reason about the relationship between two unknown values. They should apply knowledge of place value to recognise that 2400 is the same as 24 hundreds, so 2400 is one hundred times larger than 24. This means that the value of the triangle must be one hundred times larger than the circle to make the products equal.

# Question 7

7 Look at the table. First, work out the product of the numbers in rows A and B. Then compare how the product has changed in relation to one of the other numbers multiplied. What did you find?

| A | 400 | 400 | 800 | 800 |
|---|---|---|---|---|
| B | 3 | 6 | 3 | 6 |
| A × B | | | | |

My findings: ______________________________

Question 7 is set out in a table. Pupils will need to make sense of the layout and decide what needs to be done to find the missing values. They should then reason about the products, using what they know from the whole-class session for Question 1 to spot that 400 × 6 is double 400 × 3, and that 800 × 3 is double 400 × 3, and so on.

# Unit 9.9
# Practice and exercise

## Conceptual context

In this chapter, pupils have developed a range of mental and written methods to multiply a two- or three-digit number by a one-digit number. They have further developed their understanding of place value to describe and relate calculations such as 4 × 6, 4 × 60 and 4 × 600 to a number of ones, tens and hundreds using known multiplication facts to help them. Robust conceptual knowledge has been developed as pupils use multiple representations to demonstrate the effect of multiplication.

In this unit, pupils will further consolidate their understanding of multiplication and the language used to describe it. They reason about the size of a product using estimation as a valuable tool to help make decisions.

## Learning pupils will have achieved at the end of the unit

- Pupils will have demonstrated their ability to flexibly apply mental and written methods depending on the numbers involved (Q1, Q2, Q3, Q6, Q7)
- Through reasoning about the size of a product, pupils will have shown their depth of understanding of multiplication and place value (Q3, Q4)
- Pupils will understand the significance of zeros at the end of two-, three- and four-digit numbers where they appear (Q4)
- The language of multiplication will have been consolidated so pupils associate phrases, such as, 'times as many as', 'times the number of', 'the product of', with the operation (Q5, Q6, Q7)
- Fluency with multiplication facts, including multiplying by tens and hundreds, will have been secured as pupils compare calculations and solve problems in context (Q3, Q6, Q7)

### Resources

weighing scales; base 10 blocks; place value counters; place value arrow cards; **Resource 3.9.9a** Mental and written methods; **Resource 3.9.9b** Balancing multiplications; **Resource 3.9.9c** Making number sentences

### Vocabulary

ones, tens, hundreds, multiply, multiplication, product, partition, estimate, as many, times, double

# Question 1 and Question 2

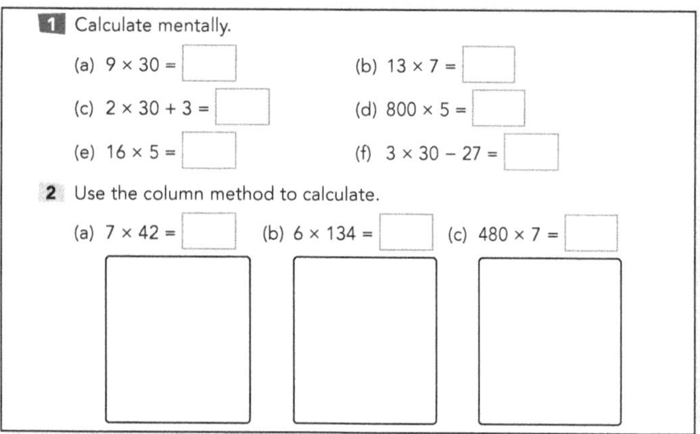

**1** Calculate mentally.

(a) 9 × 30 = ☐ (b) 13 × 7 = ☐

(c) 2 × 30 + 3 = ☐ (d) 800 × 5 = ☐

(e) 16 × 5 = ☐ (f) 3 × 30 – 27 = ☐

**2** Use the column method to calculate.

(a) 7 × 42 = ☐ (b) 6 × 134 = ☐ (c) 480 × 7 = ☐

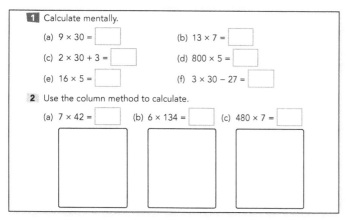

## What learning will pupils have achieved at the conclusion of Question 1 and Question 2?

- Pupils will have demonstrated their ability to flexibly apply mental and written methods depending on the numbers involved.

## Activities for whole-class instruction

- Show pupils the following set of calculations.

  300 × 6   14 × 6   4 × 60   382 × 3

  7 × 17   269 × 6   5 × 60
- Ask: *Which will you solve mentally? When will you use a column method?*
- Take feedback, discussing and modelling different methods, including partitioning a two-digit number into tens and ones and mentally adding part products for 14 × 6 and 7 × 17.
- Agree that 382 × 3 and 269 × 6 are best solved using a written method. Pupils should solve each calculation using the written method.

  (Some pupils will still benefit from representing each step of the calculation using place value counters.)
- Return to the calculations 4 × 60 and 5 × 60, adding an extra step to each calculation as:

  4 × 60 + 20 and 5 × 60 – 40.
- Tell pupils to use place value counters to represent each of the number sentences using arrays, remembering to complete the multiplication part first and then adding or subtracting as required.
- Ask: *What do you notice about the answers each time? Can you explain why this is the case?*
- Agree that the final answers are the same because the first adds some to 4 lots of 60 and the second subtracts some from 5 groups of 60.
- Give pupils the number sentence 4 × 70 + 30. Agree that this sentence shows a number added to 4 lots of 70. Challenge pupils to find the same final answer by subtracting a number from 5 groups of 70.
- Pupils should complete Question 1 and Question 2 in the Practice Book.

## Same-day intervention

- Discuss any calculations from Question 1 and Question 2 that pupils found difficult, revisiting methods of finding part products and multiplying numbers of tens and hundreds as required.
- Encourage pupils to use place value counters or base 10 blocks to model as necessary.

## Same-day enrichment

- Give pupils **Resource 3.9.9a** Mental and written methods.

**Resource 3.9.9a**

Mental and written methods

| 47 × 2 | 30 × 40 | 3 × 68 | 367 × 6 |
|---|---|---|---|
| 2 × 900 | 5 × 600 | 800 × 8 | 72 × 5 |
| 592 × 4 | 6 × 90 | 28 × 4 | 9 × 600 |
| 80 × 40 | 508 × 7 | 60 × 7 | 400 × 8 |

© HarperCollinsPublishers 2017

- Pupils work in pairs to sort the calculations into two groups – one group that they will solve mentally and the others they would solve using a written method.
- They take turns to select a calculation from each group, choosing a method to use and comparing the time taken to complete them.

## Question 3 and Question 4

**3** Write >, < or = in each ◯.

(a) 604 × 0 ◯ 236 (b) 36 × 6 ◯ 214

(c) 37 + 3 ◯ 37 × 3 (d) 28 × 8 ◯ 88 × 2

(e) 123 × 4 ◯ 124 × 3 (f) 240 × 5 ◯ 1200

**4** Complete the sentences.

(a) There are ☐ zeros at the end of the product 2500 × 8.

(b) The product of a 1-digit number and a 3-digit number is a ☐-digit number or a ☐-digit number.

(c) The product of 49 × 5 is a ☐-digit number. The product is between ☐ and ☐.

### What learning will pupils have achieved at the conclusion of Question 3 and Question 4?

- Pupils will have demonstrated their ability to flexibly apply mental and written methods depending on the numbers involved.
- Through reasoning about the size of a product, pupils will have shown their depth of understanding of multiplication and place value.
- Pupils will understand the significance of zeros at the end of two-, three- and four-digit numbers where they appear.
- Fluency with multiplication facts, including multiplying by tens and hundreds, will have been secured as pupils compare calculations and solve problems in context.

### Activities for whole-class instruction

- Draw the image below on the board. Ask: *Is this representation correct? Do both sides, 7 × 49 and 9 × 47, have the same value?*

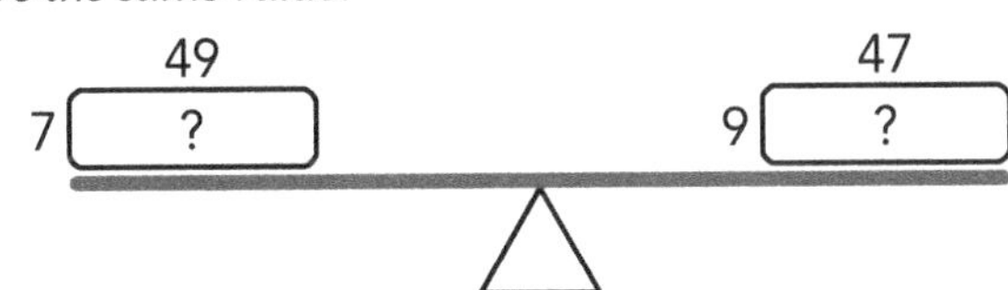


Pupils should discuss the problem and explain their thinking, using estimates to help them. Using the estimates, determine that each product will be a three-digit number.

Look out for ... pupils who mistake 7 × 49 and 9 × 47 as showing commutativity because the digits 7 and 9 are swapped in the calculations. Show that 7 × 49 and 49 × 7 are not commutative, by checking both products.

- Use a mental method to find part products or a written method to model the calculations. Confirm that the product of 7 × 49 is less than 9 × 47, so the representation is incorrect. (You could also look at a rounding and adjusting method here as 47 and 49 are both close to 50.)
- Record this as 7 × 49 < 9 × 47, focusing on the fact that there are two more groups of 47 than there are of 49.

*The product of 7 times 49 is less than the product of 9 times 47.*

- Draw this image on the board:

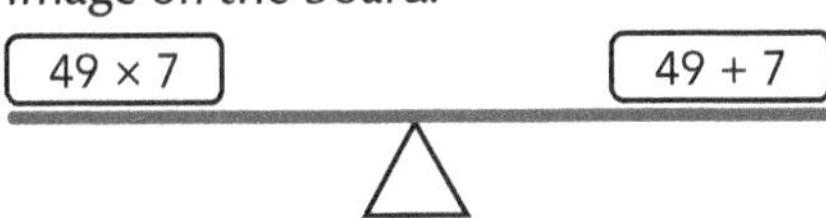


- Ask: *What is the same and what is different about each side of the balance this time? Is the representation correct?*
- Ensure that pupils recognise that 343 is the product of 49 × 7 as 7 × 49 was found previously. Agree that the representation is not correct, as 49 + 3 gives a much smaller answer than 49 × 7 so the left side of the balance should be lower because 49 × 7 > 49 + 7.
- Draw this image on the board:

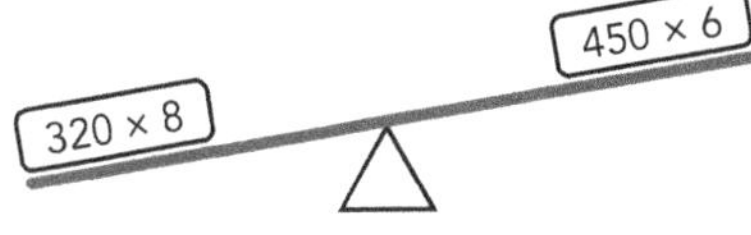


- Ask: *How many tens are there in the numbers 320 and 450? Can you use this to predict the number of zeros that will be at the end of the products 32 × 8 and 45 × 6?*
- Pupils should complete the calculations using a method of their choice. Confirm that 320 × 8 = 2560 or 256 tens, whereas 450 × 6 = 2700 or 270 tens or 27 hundreds. It has two zeros to show hundreds.
- Say: *Both these products are four-digit numbers, so multiplying a three 3-digit number by a one-digit number will give a three-digit or a four-digit product.*
- Pupils should complete Question 3 and Question 4 in the Practice Book.

### Same-day intervention

- Pupils use a pan balance and base 10 blocks to check the following statements:

| | |
|---|---|
| 3 × 40 = 4 × 30 | 124 × 2 < 62 × 4 |
| 26 + 4 = 26 × 4 | 324 × 1 > 2 × 162 |

- For example, pupils put three groups of four tens in one pan and four groups of 30 tens in the other to check to see if they balance. Pupils should correct any statements by changing the symbols.

## Same-day enrichment

- Ask pupils to complete **Resource 3.9.9b** Balancing multiplications.

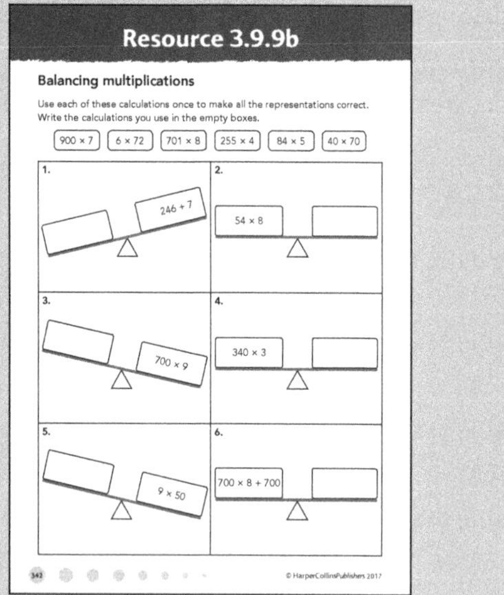

**Resource 3.9.9b**

**Balancing multiplications**

Use each of these calculations once to make all the representations correct. Write the calculations you use in the empty boxes.

900 × 7 | 6 × 72 | 701 × 8 | 255 × 4 | 84 × 5 | 40 × 70

1. 246 + 7
2. 54 × 8
3. 700 × 9
4. 340 × 3
5. 9 × 50
6. 700 × 8 + 700

342

© HarperCollinsPublishers 2017

- Ask pupils to then make up a representation of their own for a friend to check.

# Question 5

**5** Write a number sentence for each question.

(a) What is the product of 650 multiplied by 7?

Number sentence: ______

(b) What is the sum of 4 lots of seven hundred and twenty-threes?

Number sentence: ______

(c) What is 5 times 106?

Number sentence: ______

(d) Find the product of 38 and 8.

Number sentence: ______

## What learning will pupils have achieved at the conclusion of Question 5?

- The language of multiplication will have been consolidated so pupils can associate phrases, such as 'times as many as', 'times the number of', 'the product of', with the operation.

## Activities for whole-class instruction

- Rehearse the multiplication tables for 3 and 6, remembering to include division facts. Relate facts to multiples of three hundreds and six hundreds, looking also at the relationship between the tables, for example 7 multiplied by 6 hundreds is double 7 multiplied by 3 hundreds.
- Introduce some contexts for the multiplications, for example:

  *There are 500 pencils in a box. How many pencils in 3 boxes? And in 6?*

  *A bag of potatoes weighs 700 g. What is the mass of 6 of these bags?*
- Write one of the facts from the starter activity on the board, for example 5 × 300 = 320. Ask: *What is the total of five three hundreds? How can we work this out?*
- Ask pupils to discuss the problem and suggest ideas. It could be described as 300 + 300 + 300 + 300 + 300. Can pupils explain that five three hundreds is the same as 5 × 300 or five multiplied by three hundreds?

  Agree that the total or the sum of three hundred added 5 times is 1500.

*Five three hundreds is 1500.*

- Ask: *What is the sum of three hundred and sixty added five times? How could you use what you know about 5 × 60 to help you?*

  Agree that this is the same as 360 + 360 + 360 + 360 + 360 or 5 × 360.

*Five 360s is 1800.*

- Discuss other language that could be used to describe multiplication, for example 'times', 'product', 'times as many', 'multiplied by'.
- Ask pupils to use the language to describe the calculation 5 × 360 in other ways.
- Check they know they can say 'the product of 360 multiplied by 5' and 'the product of 360 and 5' to describe 5 × 360. They might also mention 'groups of', 'lots of'.
- Pupils should complete Question 5 in the Practice Book.

## Same-day intervention

- Give pupils the following language prompts and the calculation 43 × 5:

| the product of | multiplied by | times |
| --- | --- | --- |

- Work together to record different ways to describe 43 × 5, using each of the language prompts in turn. Reinforce any language as necessary, giving your own examples or discussing other questions that pupils have solved previously.
- Then ask pupils to choose a language prompt of their own to describe 4 × 350.

## Same-day enrichment

- Give pupils the calculations 6 × 235, 35 × 6 and 62 × 5. They should use a range of 'multiplication' language to create different questions to match these calculations. For example: What is the product of 235 and 6? What is the product of 6 times thirty-five? What is 5 times as many as 62?
- Pupils can swap questions, explaining why each matches the calculations given.

# Question 6 and Question 7

6 Finn's weight is 39 kilograms. His father's weight is twice the weight of Finn's. What is his father's weight?

Answer: ______

7 Ella was reading a book. She read 18 pages per day for 9 days and still had 42 pages left. How many pages were there in the book?

Answer: ______

## What learning will pupils have achieved at the conclusion of Question 6 and Question 7?

- Pupils will have demonstrated their ability to flexibly apply mental and written methods depending on the numbers involved.
- The language of multiplication will have been consolidated so pupils can associate phrases, such as 'times as many as', 'times the number of', 'the product of', with the operation.
- Fluency with multiplication facts, including multiplying by tens and hundreds, will have been secured as pupils compare calculations and solve problems in context.

## Activities for whole-class instruction

- Give pairs of pupils a set of place value arrow cards. Ask them to quickly build the number that is twice as many as 26.
- Now ask them to build the number that is double 260. Pupils may decide to partition the numbers to find part products. Ask pupils to compare the products and say what they notice.
- Look at the language 'twice as many' and 'double'. Agree that both are the same as 'multiplying by two'. Record the number sentences as 26 × 2, 2 × 26, 260 × 2 and 2 × 260. Say:

  *There are 26 ducks on a pond.*

  *There are twice as many frogs as ducks.*

  *How many frogs are there?*
- Pupils should recognise that they already know the answer to this.
- Ask pupils to adapt the problem to use the word 'double'.
- Ask pupils to use place value arrow cards to build the number 37. Ask if they can partition the number and use this to explain the part products for 37 × 6. They should build the product.
- Say: *There are 6 equal rows of chairs in the school hall.*

  *There are 37 chairs in each row.*

  *When all the people come into the hall there are not enough chairs and 25 people have to stand.*

  *How many people are in the hall?*
- Ask: *What is different about this problem?* Agree that it involves addition and multiplication as we need to find the number of chairs available to seat people and then add the number of people standing.
- Suggest that the calculation is 6 × 25 + 37. Can pupils explain why you are mistaken? Establish that the calculation is 6 × 37 + 25, and that the multiplication part must be completed first.
- Pupils should calculate using a method of their choice, remembering to add the 25 extra people.
- Pupils should complete Question 6 and Question 7 in the Practice Book.

## Same-day intervention

- Ask pupils to practise building three-digit numbers and finding twice as many.

  For example: 237, 154, 378, 209, 543

  They use partitioning to find part products.
- Ask pupils to work together to create maths stories to match the doubling they have been doing.

  For example: *The car wash cleaned 237 cars on Friday. Twice as many were cleaned on Saturday. How many were cleaned on Saturday?*

## Same-day enrichment

- Give pupils **Resource 3.9.9c** Making number sentences.

**Resource 3.9.9c**

Making number sentences

| | | | | |
|---|---|---|---|---|
| 45 × 3 | 67 × 6 | 600 × 7 | add 99 | subtract 12 |
| 35 × 4 | 5 × 240 | 939 × 1 | add 200 | subtract 1 |
| 428 × 7 | 8 × 700 | 9 × 68 | subtract 50 | add 7 |
| 66 × 7 | 40 × 30 | 566 × 2 | add 23 | subtract 40 |

© HarperCollinsPublishers 2017

- Pupils take it in turns to pick a multiplication card and a shaded card to create a number sentence, for example they take the card 45 × 3 and the card 'subtract 12'.
- They then write the number sentence, for example 45 × 3 – 12, and give it to their partner to solve.
- In the meantime, the first player makes up a problem to match the number sentence. They share their answer and problem, checking that both are correct.

## Challenge and extension question

## Question 8

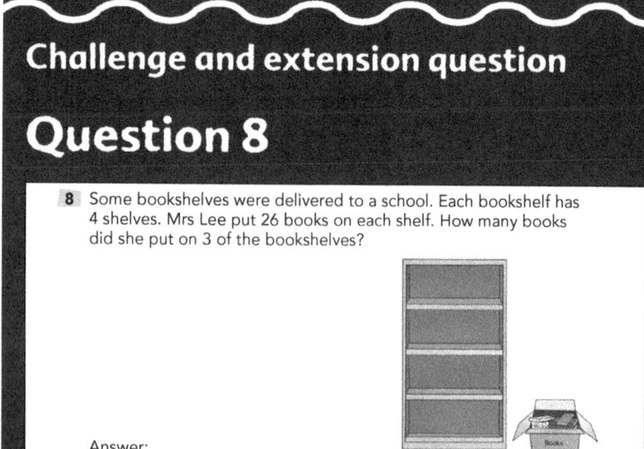
8 Some bookshelves were delivered to a school. Each bookshelf has 4 shelves. Mrs Lee put 26 books on each shelf. How many books did she put on 3 of the bookshelves?

Answer: ______

For Question 8, pupils continue to apply multiplication strategies to word problems. It is important that pupils read the problem carefully rather than calculating what they think the problem will ask.

## Question 9

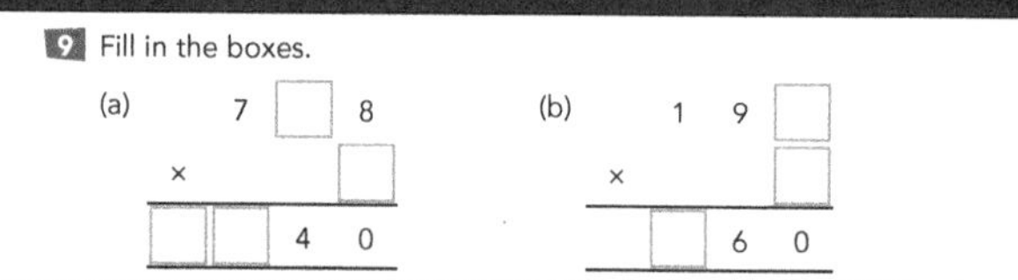
9 Fill in the boxes.

(a) 7 □ 8 × □ = □ □ 4 0

(b) 1 9 □ × □ = □ 6 0

For Question 9, look out for pupils who immediately spot that both calculations involve multiplying a three-digit number by a one-digit number, but that the first product is a four-digit number and the second is a three-digit number. This is particularly important in the second example, as pupils should recognise that the number to be multiplied is about 200, so the largest possible number to multiply by to give a product that is less than 1000 is the number 5.

# Unit 9.10 Dividing whole tens and whole hundreds

## Conceptual context

In this chapter, pupils have multiplied a number of tens and hundreds, recognising that they can use known multiplication facts and understanding about place value to quickly determine new products.

In this unit, pupils will deepen their understanding about the relationship between multiplication and division, using manipulatives and other representations to demonstrate this. Pupils will make a connection between dividing a number of tens or hundreds to dividing a number of ones. They will begin to explain why the dividend and quotient in a division involving, say, tens is ten times larger than dividing the same number of ones by the same divisor.

## Learning pupils will have achieved at the end of the unit

- Pupils should be able to understand that dividing a number of tens or hundreds is simply an extension of the related division fact using 'ones', for example 18 tens divided by six is three tens and 18 hundreds divided by six is three hundreds (Q1, Q2)
- Pupils will have demonstrated their ability to find related multiplication and division facts, applying understanding about place value to reason about product or dividends that are multiples of ten or a hundred (Q2, Q3)
- Understanding of the inverse relationship of multiplication and division will have been deepened as pupils explore a range of representations both practically and pictorially (Q2, Q3, Q4, Q5)
- The language of multiplication will have been developed to include, 'divided by', 'equal groups', 'how many times' (Q4, Q5)
- Fluency with division facts, including dividing by a number of tens, will have been developed as pupils solve problems with and without a context (Q4, Q5)

### Resources

base 10 blocks; place value counters; 0–9 dice or spinner; squared paper; interlocking cubes; **Resource 3.9.10a** Relating divisions; **Resource 3.9.10b** Multiplication and division arrays; **Resource 3.9.10c** Array division; **Resource 3.9.10d** Division problem arrays

### Vocabulary

ones, tens, hundreds, division, dividend, divisor, quotient, equal groups, multiply, multiplication, product

# Question 1

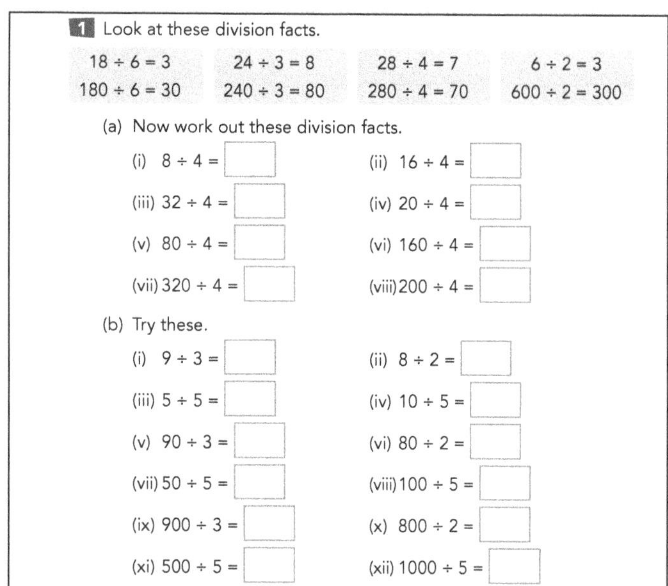

**1** Look at these division facts.

| 18 ÷ 6 = 3 | 24 ÷ 3 = 8 | 28 ÷ 4 = 7 | 6 ÷ 2 = 3 |
|---|---|---|---|
| 180 ÷ 6 = 30 | 240 ÷ 3 = 80 | 280 ÷ 4 = 70 | 600 ÷ 2 = 300 |

(a) Now work out these division facts.

(i) 8 ÷ 4 = ☐ (ii) 16 ÷ 4 = ☐
(iii) 32 ÷ 4 = ☐ (iv) 20 ÷ 4 = ☐
(v) 80 ÷ 4 = ☐ (vi) 160 ÷ 4 = ☐
(vii) 320 ÷ 4 = ☐ (viii) 200 ÷ 4 = ☐

(b) Try these.

(i) 9 ÷ 3 = ☐ (ii) 8 ÷ 2 = ☐
(iii) 5 ÷ 5 = ☐ (iv) 10 ÷ 5 = ☐
(v) 90 ÷ 3 = ☐ (vi) 80 ÷ 2 = ☐
(vii) 50 ÷ 5 = ☐ (viii) 100 ÷ 5 = ☐
(ix) 900 ÷ 3 = ☐ (x) 800 ÷ 2 = ☐
(xi) 500 ÷ 5 = ☐ (xii) 1000 ÷ 5 = ☐

## What learning will pupils have achieved at the conclusion of Question 1?

- Pupils should be able to understand that dividing a number of tens or hundreds is simply an extension of the related division fact using 'ones', for example 18 tens divided by six is three tens and 18 hundreds divided by six is three hundreds.

## Activities for whole-class instruction

- Ask pupils to work in groups of 3–4 and give each group some base 10 blocks. Ask: *How would you use the blocks to show four ones divided by four? How would you record this as a number sentence?*
- Pupils should set out four 'ones' cubes and separate them into four equal groups of one.

  Record it as: 4 ÷ 4 = 1.

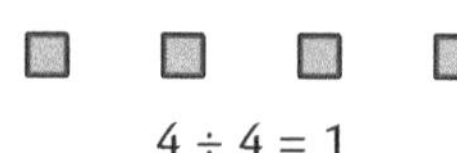

4 ÷ 4 = 1

*Four ones divided by four is one one.*

- Ask: *How would you use the blocks to show four tens divided by four?* How would you record this as a number sentence?
- Pupils should set out four tens and separate them into four equal groups of ten. Record it as: 40 ÷ 4 = 10.

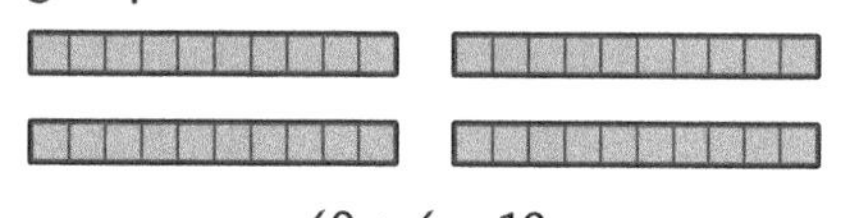

40 ÷ 4 = 10

*Four tens divided by four is one ten.*

- Ask: *How would you use the blocks to show four hundreds divided by four? How would you record this as a number sentence?*
- Pupils should set out four hundreds and separate them into four equal groups of one hundred. Record it as: 400 ÷ 4 = 100.

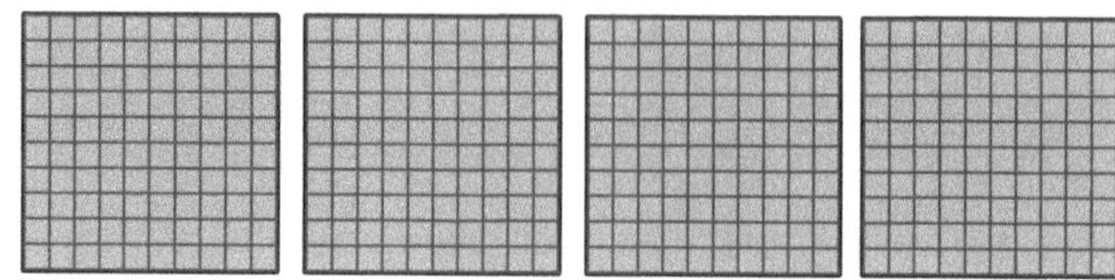

400 ÷ 4 = 100

Four hundreds divided by four is one hundred.

- Ask: *What patterns can you see?*

  Find out if pupils can see that:

  - the quotient is ten times larger when the dividend is the times larger. Ask pupils to explain why, using base 10 blocks or arrays/squared paper
  - there is one zero on the quotient after dividing a number of tens by the same number of ones
  - the quotient is 100 times larger when the dividend is 100 times larger. Ask pupils to explain why, using base 10 blocks or arrays/squared paper
  - there are two zeros on the quotient after dividing a number of hundreds by the same number of ones.
- Look together at the following sets of division sentences. Ask pupils to use base 10 blocks to represent each set of divisions, explaining any patterns they see. Ask pupils to use a given fact to reason about any missing quotients.

| 8 ÷ 2 = 4 | 15 ÷ 5 = 3 | 10 ÷ 2 = 5 |
|---|---|---|
| 80 ÷ 2 = 40 | 150 ÷ 5 = | 100 ÷ 2 = |
| 800 ÷ 2 = 400 | 1500 ÷ 5 = | 1000 ÷ 2 = |

(i) Pupils should understand that dividing a number of tens or hundreds is simply an extension of the related division fact using 'ones', for example 18 tens divided by six is three tens and 18 hundreds divided by six is three hundreds.

- Pupils should complete Question 1 in the Practice Book.

## Same-day intervention

- Give pupils 12 base 10 'ones' cubes or ones place value counters. Ask them to divide the ones into two equal groups and record the division sentence.
- Tell pupils to now swap the ones in each group for tens.
- Ask: *What is the value of each equal group now? How many times larger is this than the same number of ones?*
- Agree this as six tens which is ten times larger than six ones.
- Ask pupils to write the division sentence and explain why the dividend and quotient are ten times larger.
- Now tell pupils to swap the tens in each group for hundreds.
- Ask: *What is the value of each equal group now? How many times larger is this than the same number of ones?*
- Agree this as six hundreds which is a hundred times larger than six ones.
- Ask pupils to write the division sentence and explain why the dividend and quotient are a hundred times larger than the division using ones.
- Explore other ways of arranging 12 ones into equal groups, representing related divisions using tens and hundreds.

## Same-day enrichment

- Give pupils copies of **Resource 3.9.10a** Relating divisions.

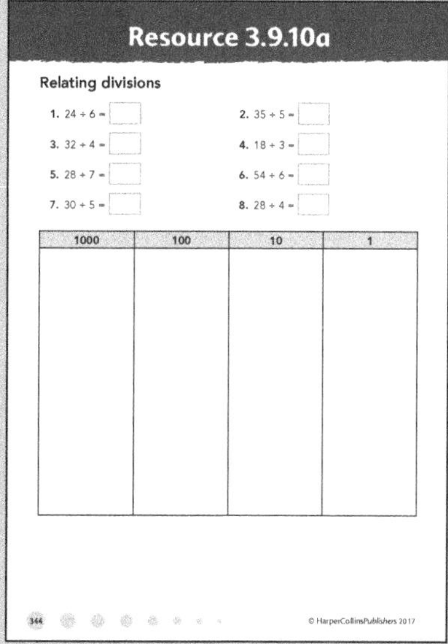
Resource 3.9.10a

Relating divisions

1. 24 ÷ 6 = ☐ 2. 35 ÷ 5 = ☐
3. 32 ÷ 4 = ☐ 4. 18 ÷ 3 = ☐
5. 28 ÷ 7 = ☐ 6. 54 ÷ 6 = ☐
7. 30 ÷ 5 = ☐ 8. 28 ÷ 4 = ☐

| 1000 | 100 | 10 | 1 |
|---|---|---|---|
| | | | |

- Pupils play a game in pairs, taking it in turns to go first. They each select a different calculation and find the quotient. They represent the quotient using digit cards or counters on the place value grid and then make it ten times larger. They represent this by moving the digits and using zero as a placeholder.
- Their partner should then write a division sentence using the same divisor, but resulting in the new quotient.
- Ask pupils to explain why the dividend is ten times larger this time. Pupils might find it useful to model their calculations using place value counters.
- They repeat the game, making the quotient one hundred times larger.

# Question 2

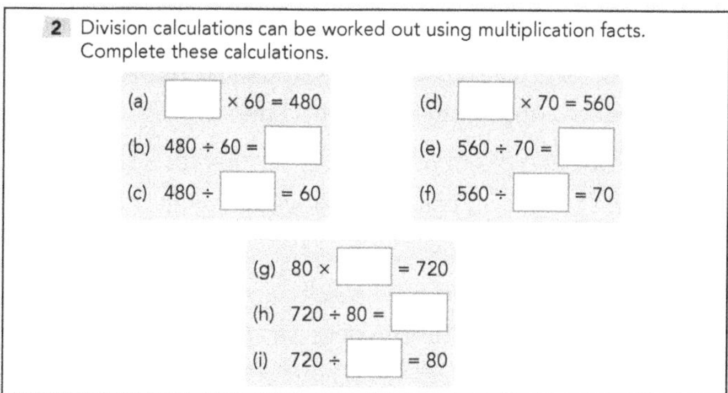
**2** Division calculations can be worked out using multiplication facts. Complete these calculations.

(a) ☐ × 60 = 480 (d) ☐ × 70 = 560
(b) 480 ÷ 60 = ☐ (e) 560 ÷ 70 = ☐
(c) 480 ÷ ☐ = 60 (f) 560 ÷ ☐ = 70

(g) 80 × ☐ = 720
(h) 720 ÷ 80 = ☐
(i) 720 ÷ ☐ = 80

## What learning will pupils have achieved at the conclusion of Question 2?

- Pupils should be able to understand that dividing a number of tens or hundreds is simply an extension of the related division fact using 'ones', for example 18 tens divided by six is three tens and 18 hundreds divided by six is three hundreds.
- Pupils will have demonstrated their ability to find related multiplication and division facts, applying understanding about place value to reason about product or dividends that are multiples of ten or a hundred.
- Understanding of the inverse relationship of multiplication and division will have been deepened as pupils explore a range of representations both practically and pictorially.

## Activities for whole-class instruction

- Show pupils the following array, using place value counters:
- Ask: *Can you write two multiplication and division facts to match the array?*
- Take feedback, establishing the product of each multiplication as 15 and the dividend of each division as 15. Look together at the commutativity of multiplication.

  Record the related facts as:

  $3 \times 5 = 15$

  $5 \times 3 = 15$

  $15 \div 5 = 3$

  $15 \div 3 = 5$
- Tell pupils to make an array with the same number of rows and columns, but with 'tens' counters.
- Ask: *What two multiplication and division facts can you write this time? Can you use what you already know to help you?*
- Take feedback, recording the following facts next to those recorded previously for the ones array.

  $3 \times 50 = 150$

  $5 \times 30 = 150$

  $150 \div 5 = 30$

  $150 \div 3 = 50$
- Ask pupils to explain why the products and the dividends are ten times larger this time. Do they recognise that dividing 15 tens by three results in a quotient that is ten times larger than dividing 15 ones by three?
- Ask: *Can we use what we know to find the quotient when 150 is divided by 30?* Agree that $150 \div 30 = 5$ because $5 \times 3$ tens is 15 tens or 150.
- Ask pupils to make a further array with the same number of rows and columns, but with hundreds counters.

  Ask: *What are the missing values in this set of related facts? How do you know?*

  $3 \times \square = 1500$

  $5 \times 300 = \square$

  $\square \div 5 = 300$

  $1500 \div \square = 500$
- Look together at the division sentences.

*15 hundreds divided by three is a hundred times larger than 15 ones divided by three.*

- Ask pupils to compare the divisions $15 \div 5 = 3$ and $1500 \div 5 = 300$ using the language of ones and hundreds. Discuss the quotient when 1500 is divided by 500. Agree that $1500 \div 500 = 3$ because $3 \times 5$ hundreds is 15 hundreds or 1500.
- Pupils should complete Question 2 in the Practice Book.

### Same-day intervention

- Give pupils **Resource 3.9.10b** Multiplication and division arrays.

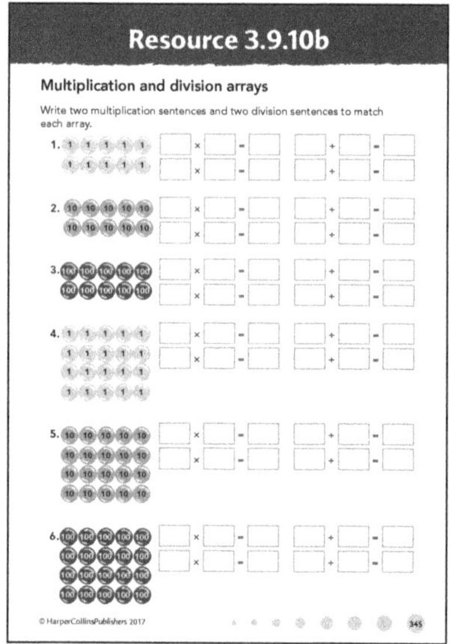

Resource 3.9.10b

Multiplication and division arrays

Write two multiplication sentences and two division sentences to match each array.

© HarperCollinsPublishers 2017

345

- Pupils should write two multiplication and division facts to match each array. Ask them to explain why the same arrangement of tens counters results in a product and a dividend that is ten times larger than the same arrangement using ones counters. Do they recognise how this affects the quotient?

### Same-day enrichment

- Give pupils the following problem to explore:

  *The dividends and products for three sets of related facts are 320, 3600 and 240.*

  *How many different sets of related facts can you find for each?*

| 320 | 3600 | 240 |
|---|---|---|

# Question 3

**3** Work out these calculations using your preferred method.

(a) 400 ÷ 50 = ☐ (b) 210 ÷ 7 = ☐

(c) 540 ÷ 90 = ☐ (d) 40 ÷ 2 = ☐

(e) 400 ÷ 8 = ☐ (f) 210 ÷ 30 = ☐

(g) 540 ÷ 6 = ☐ (h) 40 ÷ 20 = ☐

(i) 120 ÷ 30 = ☐ (j) 250 ÷ 50 = ☐

(k) 150 ÷ 30 = ☐ (l) 810 ÷ 90 = ☐

(m) 360 ÷ 60 = ☐ (n) 630 ÷ 90 = ☐

(o) 490 ÷ 70 = ☐ (p) 450 ÷ 90 = ☐

## What learning will pupils have achieved at the conclusion of Question 3?

- Pupils will have demonstrated their ability to find related multiplication and division facts, applying understanding about place value to reason about product or dividends that are multiples of ten or a hundred.
- Understanding of the inverse relationship of multiplication and division will have been deepened as pupils explore a range of representations both practically and pictorially.

## Activities for whole-class instruction

- Give pupils a set of place value counters. Say that an array is made up of three equal rows and the product is 180. They should work with a partner, using place value counters, to represent this.
- Ask: *How many counters are in the array altogether if the product is 180?*

This is a key point – pupils should recognise that 18 tens counters are needed and they simply need to consider factor pairs that give a product of 18 where one factor is three. The most efficient strategy is to divide 18 by three using tables facts – this will show how many counters should be in each row.

- Establish that the array is made up of three rows of 60 or six tens. Ask: *What is the quotient when 180 is divided by three? How many times larger is this quotient than for 18 divided by three?*

*18 tens divided by three is ten times larger than 18 ones divided by three.*

- Explain that division sentences can be found using multiplication sentences to help us. Ask: *How can we use what we know about 6 × 30 = 180 to find 180 ÷ 6?*
- Ask pupils to write two multiplication and two division sentences to match the array. Can pupils explain that 180 ÷ 6 = 30 using the facts to help them?
- Now show pupils the two arrays on **Resource 3.9.10c** Array division.

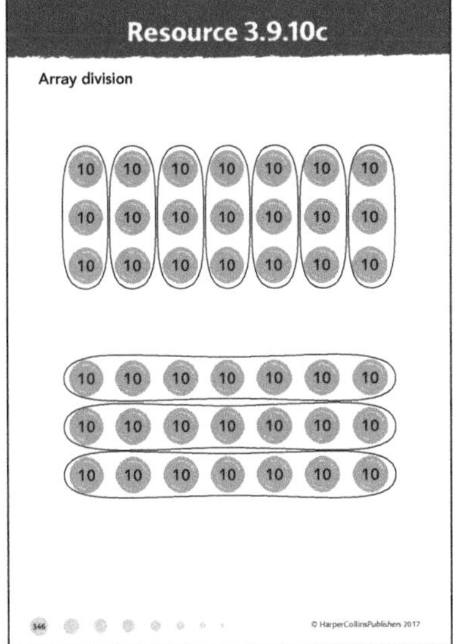


- Explain that this time, the first array shows 180 divided into equal groups of three tens or 30. Ask: *What does the second array show?*
- Establish that the second array shows 18 tens divided into equal groups of six tens or 60. Can pupils write the division sentences to match each array?
- Record these as 180 ÷ 30 = 6 and 180 ÷ 60 = 3.
- Finally, ask pupils to use place value counters to make an array with a product of 1800 that is arranged in two equal rows. Ask them to use the array to find the missing values in the number sentences below.

2 × 900 = ☐

200 × 9 = ☐

1800 ÷ 9 = ☐

1800 ÷ 20 = ☐

- Pupils should complete Question 3 in the Practice Book.

### Same-day intervention

- Pupils should represent the divisions in the first column of Question 3 using place value counters.
- Ask pupils how many different related facts they can write to show multiplication and division.
- Encourage them to think about rows and columns, determining the size of the group each time.

## Same-day enrichment

- Ask pupils to use a 0–9 dice or a spinner to generate two numbers, for example they roll a 5 and a 7. They then use tens place value counters or squared paper to make or sketch an array using the generated numbers, for example 5 rows of 7. How many related multiplication and division facts can they write to match their array?
- Pupils then roll the dice again to make another array. They could swap their division and multiplication facts with a partner. Can they use the facts to recreate an appropriate array?

# Question 4

4 Write a number sentence for each question.

(a) The dividend is 270 and the divisor is 3. What is the quotient?

Number sentence: ______

(b) How many times 50 is 350?

Number sentence: ______

(c) Divide 640 into 8 equal parts. How much is each part?

Number sentence: ______

## What learning will pupils have achieved at the conclusion of Question 4?

- The language of multiplication will have been developed to include, 'divided by', 'equal groups', 'how many times'.
- Fluency with division facts, including dividing by a number of tens, will have been developed as pupils solve problems with and without a context.

## Activities for whole-class instruction

- Ask pupils to reason about the quotients for each of these sets of divisions.

| 28 ÷ 7 = | 36 ÷ 4 = | 30 ÷ 6 = |
|---|---|---|
| 280 ÷ 7 = | 360 ÷ 4 = | 300 ÷ 6 = |
| 2800 ÷ 7 = | 360 ÷ 40 = | 300 ÷ 60 = |

Tell pupils, in pairs, to choose one set and represent each division as an array, either using place value counters or by sketching an array on squared paper. Ask pupils to explain to another pair how to find the quotient for each division, using the array.

- Show pupils another array representing the multiplication 3 × 70. Ask pupils to reason about the answers to the following questions about the array. You may wish to assign a different question to each group of pupils.
  - The dividend is 210 and the divisor is 3. What is the quotient?
  - The dividend is 210 and the divisor is 70. What is the quotient?
  - How many times 3 is 210?
  - How many times 70 is 210?
  - Divide 210 into 3 parts equally. How much is each part?
- Discuss each question in turn, using the array to make sense of the answers.
- Clarify any language as necessary and record the number sentences using division.
- Finally, ask pupils to return to the array they made earlier. Pupils ask their partner their own questions about the array using the examples above as a model.
- Pupils should complete Question 4 in the Practice Book.

## Same-day intervention

- Give pupils 20 tens counters to make an array of their choice. Ask them to look at the number of rows to help find the missing values in the following question:

  *The dividend is* □ *and the divisor is* □. *The quotient is* □.
- Using the different arrays, agree that the divided is the same each time (200 or 20 tens). Look together at the different number of equal rows used to represent a divisor. Ask: *What is the quotient each time?*
- Selecting one of the arrays, ask pupils to explain how many times □ goes into 200, for example how many times 40 goes into 200.
- Ask pupils to look at the other arrays, using the language 'how many times' to ask questions about them.

## Same-day enrichment

- Give pupils the following problem to solve.

  *Asha answered three problems about division.*

  *The answer to the first problem is 480.*

  *The answer to the next problem is 6.*

  *The answer to the last problem is 80.*

  *What three problems could Asha have answered?*
- Encourage pupils to use a range of language as used in the whole-class session. Can they write more than one problem for each of the answers?
- Pupils then swap problems with a partner. Their partner tries to work out which answer is used each time.

# Question 5

**5** Application problems.

(a) A primary school receives a donation of 720 books. The books are shared equally with 9 classes. How many books does each class receive?

Answer: ______

(b) The price of a large screen television is £1500. It is three times the price of a small screen television. How much does a small screen television cost?

Answer: ______

(c) In a hotel kitchen, 240 litres of cooking oil has been used from a large bottle. The amount of oil left in the bottle is 4 times the amount that has been used. How many litres of oil were in the bottle to start with?

Answer: ______

## What learning will pupils have achieved at the conclusion of Question 5?

- The language of multiplication will have been developed to include 'divided by', 'equal groups', 'how many times'.
- Fluency with division facts, including dividing by a number of tens, will have been developed as pupils solve problems with and without a context.

## Activities for whole-class instruction

- Give each group of 3–4 pupils a tray of cubes to represent division problems. Ask pupils to make a group of seven cubes. Tell pupils that each cube represents ten cars. Ask: *How many cars does your group of cubes represent?* (70)

  Say that:

  *In a multi-storey car park, there are spaces for 70 cars on each level.*

  *There are spaces for 420 cars altogether.*

  *There are 6 levels in the car park.*
- Ask pupils to represent the division story using their cubes. Ask them to explain how they know that their representation matches the story. Some pupils will benefit from using place value counters to represent the problem.
- Write the following number sentences and ask pupils to discuss how each one relates to the car park story:

  $\square \div 6 = \square$ $\quad\quad$ $\square \div 70 = \square$

  Say that:

  *Another car park also has spaces for 420 cars.*

  *There are 7 levels in the car park that each have an equal number of spaces.*

  *How many car parking spaces are on each level?*
- Discuss the problem together, agreeing on the division sentence needed and the quotient that represents the number of spaces on each level. Relate the division $420 \div 7 = 60$ (or 42 tens divided by 7) to 42 ones divided by 7.
- Show pupils the following representation using cubes.

- Remind pupils that each cube represents 10 cars. Ask: *How many cars does this representation show? How do you know?*
- Record this using multiplication and addition as: $6 \times 70 + 30$. Discuss how the car park stories can be adjusted to match the new array.

  For example:

  *In a multi-storey car park, there are 6 levels with spaces for 70 cars on each.*

  *There is also space for a further 30 cars on the top level.*

  *There are spaces for 450 cars altogether.*

- Finally, share this problem:

  *There are spaces for 60 cars on the first level of the car park.*

  *The remaining levels in the car park have a total of 5 times as many spaces as the first level.*

  *How many spaces are in the car park in total?*
- Say that the problem can be solved using multiplication and addition.
- Use cubes to separately represent the number of cars on the first floor and the other levels.

level 1 remaining levels

- Ask pupils to find the missing values for the number sentence ☐ × ☐ + ☐ needed to answer the problem.
- Agree the total number of cars is the sum of the two arrays of cubes, where each cube represents ten cars.
- Pupils should complete Question 5 in the Practice Book.

## Same-day intervention

- Revisit the problems in Question 5 of the Practice Book, working together to represent problems using place value counters or base 10 blocks. Discuss how the arrays relate to each problem, establishing the answers each time and recording the division sentences used.
- Ask pupils to adapt the first problem so it matches the division sentence 630 ÷ 7 = 90.

## Same-day enrichment

- Give pupils **Resource 3.9.10d** Division problem arrays, showing four different representations using arrays.

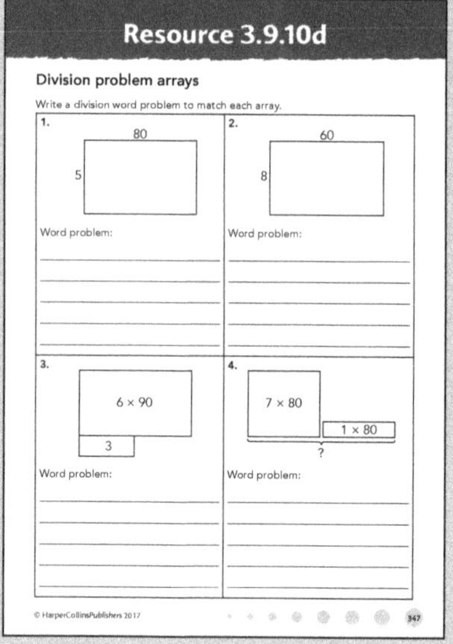

**Resource 3.9.10d**

**Division problem arrays**

Write a division word problem to match each array.

1. 80, 5

Word problem:

2. 60, 8

Word problem:

3. 6 × 90, 3

Word problem:

4. 7 × 80, 1 × 80, ?

Word problem:

© HarperCollinsPublishers 2017 347

- Ask pupils to write a division word problem to match each of the representations. Can they write another word problem that uses the same numbers but does not match the representation?
- They then swap word problems with a partner, who should reason about and explain why a problem does or does not match each representation.

## Challenge and extension question

# Question 6

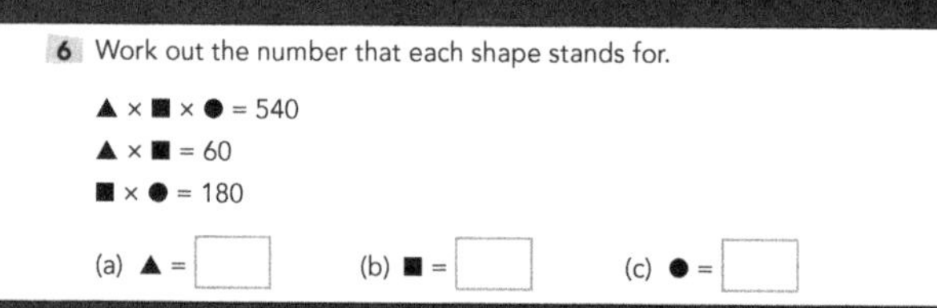

6 Work out the number that each shape stands for.

▲ × ■ × ● = 540

▲ × ■ = 60

■ × ● = 180

(a) ▲ = ☐ (b) ■ = ☐ (c) ● = ☐

For this problem, pupils should use what they know about multiplication and related division facts to help find possible factors involving numbers of tens each time. All the number sentences are shown as multiplications, so pupils should apply knowledge of the inverse to divide the given dividend or reason about factors with products that match the dividends. They will also need to consider factors that are common to more than one product, for example for 180, pairs of factors would include 2 × 90, 20 × 9, 30 × 6 and 3 × 60.

# Unit 9.11

# Dividing a 2-digit number by a 1-digit number (1)

## Conceptual context

In Book 2, pupils began to understand division and how it relates to multiplication. Pupils' knowledge of multiplication is now growing through their learning this year and links with division will be developed in line with that. This unit, and those that follow, move pupils towards an efficient and accurate procedure to use flexibly with understanding when dividing a two-digit number by a single digit.

Different ways of considering division (for example, as sharing or as repeated subtraction to make equal groups) are used through the unit, and care should be taken to not favour one particular method, but to ensure that pupils experience different ways of thinking about dividing. Connections between division and multiplication are also made through the unit and these should be discussed and explored.

Ensure that the correct vocabulary (dividend, divisor, quotient, remainder) is used throughout.

## Learning pupils will have achieved at the end of the unit

- Pupils will be able to use formal and informal strategies as appropriate to divide a two-digit number by a one-digit number and express the quotient with a remainder (Q1, Q2, Q3, Q4, Q5)
- Pupils will be able to work flexibly, using known division facts to calculate unknown divisions (Q3, Q4)
- Pupils will understand different images for division, accurately interpreting word problems that are structurally different to each other (Q5, Q6)

### Resources

place value counters; counters; number plates; tens rods; mini whiteboards and pens; **Resource 3.9.11a** Sweet share ; **Resource 3.9.11b** Division questions

### Vocabulary

multiple, divide, division, dividend, divisor, quotient, remainder

# Question 1

**1** Calculate mentally.

(a) 9 ÷ 2 = ☐    (b) 25 ÷ 4 = ☐

(c) 27 ÷ 5 = ☐    (d) 38 ÷ 6 = ☐

(e) 19 ÷ 3 = ☐    (f) 36 ÷ 5 = ☐

(g) 39 ÷ 4 = ☐    (h) 47 ÷ 5 = ☐

## What learning will pupils have achieved at the conclusion of Question 1?

- Pupils will be able to use informal strategies to divide a two-digit number by a one-digit number and express the quotient with a remainder.

## Activities for whole-class instruction

- Have printouts of multiplication tables available to pupils. Together, practise multiplication tables for six and seven. Ask questions in the format: *How many sixes in 36? How many sevens in 28? How many sevens in 63?* Encourage pupils to try to respond without looking at the tables printouts, but to refer to them if they are stuck.
- Pupils should work in pairs to chant tables together, and then ask each other questions, using the tables printouts for support where necessary.
- Review remainders as 'leftovers' and notation, for example 11 ÷ 2 = 5 r1.
- Pupils should complete Question 1 in the Practice Book, without referring to the tables printouts.

## Same-day intervention

- Use place value counters to create a two-digit number (say, 63). Use this as the dividend and ask pupils to share the dividend equally between a given number of boxes. Ensure that the divisor is such that the quotient is a whole number, for example ask pupils to share 63 equally between three. In this example, the place value counters will not need to be decomposed since 63 = 3 × 20 + 3 × 1. Ensure that pupils record their sharing using correct notation (63 ÷ 3 = 21).

*63 divided by three is the same as 21.*

- A progression in questions might be:
  - 63 ÷ 3 (no decomposition necessary, no remainder)
  - 37÷ 3 (no decomposition necessary, remainder)
  - 47÷ 3 (decomposition needed, remainder)
- Ensure that pupils have mastered each stage of this progression.

## Same-day enrichment

- Focus on the 7 ×, 8 × and 9 × tables. Ask pupils to answer the list of division questions on **Resource 3.9.11a** Division questions, with and without remainders.

**Resource 3.9.11a**

Division questions

| | | |
|---|---|---|
| 1. 42 ÷ 9 = ☐ | 19. 37 ÷ 8 = ☐ | 37. 28 ÷ 8 = ☐ |
| 2. 48 ÷ 9 = ☐ | 20. 43 ÷ 7 = ☐ | 38. 23 ÷ 9 = ☐ |
| 3. 62 ÷ 7 = ☐ | 21. 24 ÷ 8 = ☐ | 39. 50 ÷ 8 = ☐ |
| 4. 69 ÷ 8 = ☐ | 22. 24 ÷ 9 = ☐ | 40. 53 ÷ 7 = ☐ |
| 5. 63 ÷ 7 = ☐ | 23. 65 ÷ 9 = ☐ | 41. 13 ÷ 7 = ☐ |
| 6. 53 ÷ 9 = ☐ | 24. 16 ÷ 9 = ☐ | 42. 51 ÷ 8 = ☐ |
| 7. 63 ÷ 9 = ☐ | 25. 46 ÷ 8 = ☐ | 43. 50 ÷ 7 = ☐ |
| 8. 43 ÷ 9 = ☐ | 26. 66 ÷ 9 = ☐ | 44. 60 ÷ 8 = ☐ |
| 9. 41 ÷ 9 = ☐ | 27. 23 ÷ 7 = ☐ | 45. 43 ÷ 8 = ☐ |
| 10. 45 ÷ 8 = ☐ | 28. 49 ÷ 9 = ☐ | 46. 52 ÷ 8 = ☐ |
| 11. 44 ÷ 7 = ☐ | 29. 42 ÷ 8 = ☐ | 47. 33 ÷ 7 = ☐ |
| 12. 60 ÷ 9 = ☐ | 30. 65 ÷ 7 = ☐ | 48. 59 ÷ 7 = ☐ |
| 13. 26 ÷ 9 = ☐ | 31. 36 ÷ 9 = ☐ | 49. 56 ÷ 7 = ☐ |
| 14. 73 ÷ 7 = ☐ | 32. 26 ÷ 8 = ☐ | 50. 36 ÷ 7 = ☐ |
| 15. 33 ÷ 8 = ☐ | 33. 33 ÷ 9 = ☐ | 51. 32 ÷ 7 = ☐ |
| 16. 46 ÷ 9 = ☐ | 34. 53 ÷ 8 = ☐ | 52. 32 ÷ 8 = ☐ |
| 17. 46 ÷ 7= ☐ | 35. 23 ÷ 8 = ☐ | |
| 18. 42 ÷ 9 = ☐ | 36. 57 ÷ 7 = ☐ | |

348

© HarperCollinsPublishers 2017

# Question 2

**2** What is the greatest number you can write in each box?

(a) 6 × ☐ < 32    (b) ☐ × 9 < 60

(c) ☐ × 8 < 53    (d) 8 × ☐ < 50

(e) 7 × ☐ < 62    (f) ☐ × 9 < 78

## What learning will pupils have achieved at the conclusion of Question 2?

- Pupils will have used their knowledge of multiplication to find the greatest multiple less than a given number.

## Activities for whole-class instruction

- This question helps pupils practise a skill necessary for column division calculations that they first encountered in Chapter 2, that of identifying the greatest multiple that is less than a given number.

- Show a 100 square. Point to 42 and ask pupils: *If I were counting up in fives, but had to stop before I reached this point, what would be the last number I would say?*
- Record answers on the board.
- Show pupils this array:

- Count in fives, pointing to each column in turn. This makes the conceptual link between the columns of the array and skip-counting.
- Repeat this, counting up in fours, but stopping before the same number, or counting up in fives again, but staying beneath a different value, if necessary.
- Using the last example, write on the board: $5 \times 8 < 42$.
- Discuss how all the following are also correct:

  $5 \times 1 < 42$

  $5 \times 2 < 42$

  $5 \times 3 < 42$

  $5 \times 4 < 42$

  $5 \times 5 < 42$

  $5 \times 6 < 42$

  $5 \times 7 < 42$
- Finally, ask pupils to decide what the largest whole number is that can be used to complete the inequality:

  $5 \times \square < 42$
- Pupils should complete Question 2 in the Practice Book.

## Same-day intervention

- Use number plates or tens rods and explain to pupils that, using only the threes plate/rod, you want to get as close to 20 as possible. Ask them initially to predict how many threes plates/rods they will need, then count up with them to see how close their estimate was. As you count up, also mark the jumps on a number line.
- Work with pupils and draw their attention to the efficiencies of using known facts to minimise the effort needed. Use the number line to record these known facts. It might be, for example that pupils know that $5 \times 3 = 15$, and so you can make this in one jump, then consider how many more jumps are possible before reaching 20.
- Work with some more questions and encourage pupils to use the number line to calculate, then to use the tiles or rods to check their calculation.

## Same-day enrichment

- Give pupils 25 counters and ask them to make an array using all of the counters so that they have:
  - 1 left over
  - 3 left over
  - 4 left over
  - 5 left over.
- Ask pupils to find as many different ways as possible, and ask them to consider the best way to record their arrays using mathematical notation.

# Question 3

**3** Five children share 73 sweets equally between them. How many sweets does each child have?

$73 \div 5 = ?$

(a) **Minna's solution:**

$5 \times 10 = \square$

$50 \div 5 = \square$

$73 - 50 = \square$

$23 \div 5 = \square$ r $\square$

$10 + 4 = \square$

$73 \div 5 = \square$ r $\square$

(b) **Asif's solution:**

$50 \div 5 = \square$

$23 \div 5 = \square$ r $\square$

$73 \div 5 = \square$ r $\square$

## What learning will pupils have achieved at the conclusion of Question 3?

- Pupils will be able to understand the steps necessary to record when dividing a two-digit number by a one-digit number.

## Activities for whole-class instruction

- Show pupils this list of calculations and ask: *What is the same about these?*
  - $82 \div 6 = \square$
  - $67 \div 4 = \square$
  - $59 \div 3 = \square$
  - $75 \div 5 = \square$
- Have pupils noticed that the dividend is at least ten times the divisor?

- Show pupils this array. Say: *When Jay works out 82 ÷ 6 = □ this is what he thinks about.*

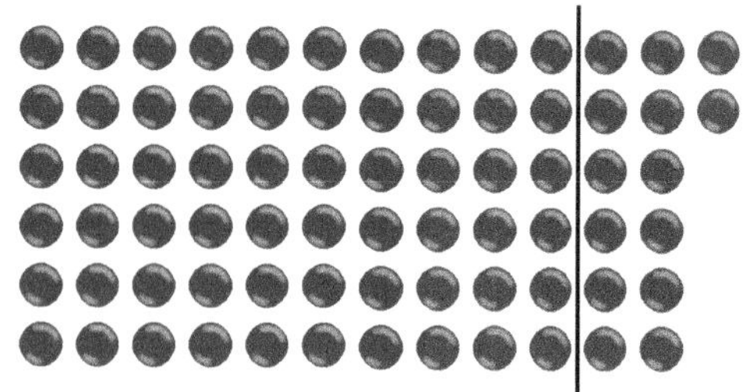

- Explain that this array shows 82 counters. Ask pupils to describe how it has been partitioned.
- Say: *Jay works out the answer to the problem 82 ÷ 6 = □ by doing this:*

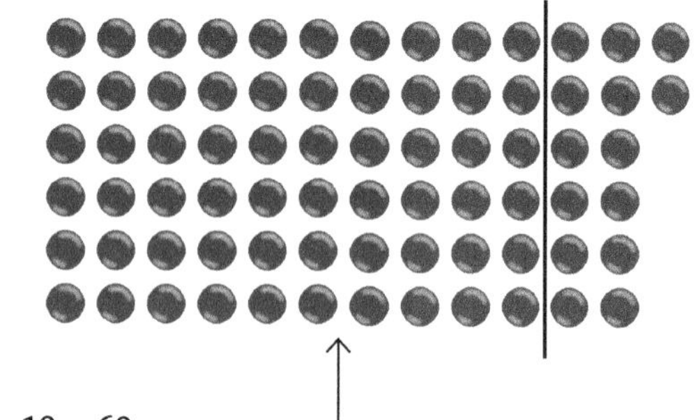

  - 6 × 10 = 60
  - 60 ÷ 6 = 10
  - 82 − 60 = 22
  - 22 ÷ 6 = 3 r 4
  - 10 + 3 = 13
  - 82 ÷ 3 = 13 r 4
- Repeat for 48 ÷ 4 = □.
- Pupils should complete Question 3 in the Practice Book.

## Same-day intervention

- Use counters and enact the steps needed to make the calculation 68 ÷ 5. Tell pupils that the 68 counters must be divided equally into 5 columns. Ask: *Do we need to share them out one at a time? What else could we do?*
- Guide pupils to see that they could put multiple counters into each column each time. They could put 2, 5, 10 each time. Pupils should physically put ten counters into the first column, then ten into the second, then ten into the third, and so on.
- Ask: *How can we record what we've done?*

68 ÷ 5 = □:

6 × 10 = 60 →

60 ÷ 6 = 10

- Agree that next, the 60 must be subtracted from the starting number (the dividend) to see whether there are any more 6s.

So:

68 − 60 = 8 →

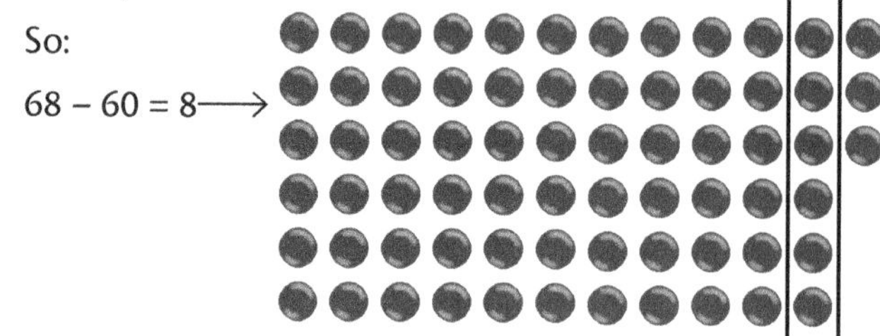

There is one more 6 and 3 more ones left over.

8 ÷ 6 = 1 r 3

All the sixes must be added together:

10 + 1 = 11. So,

68 ÷ 6 = 11 r 3

- Work through 39 ÷ 3 together in the same way.
- Leave pupils with the place value counters and ask them to use the same structure to complete the calculation 92 ÷ 4.

## Same-day enrichment

- Ask pupils to complete **Resource 3.9.11b** Sweet share.

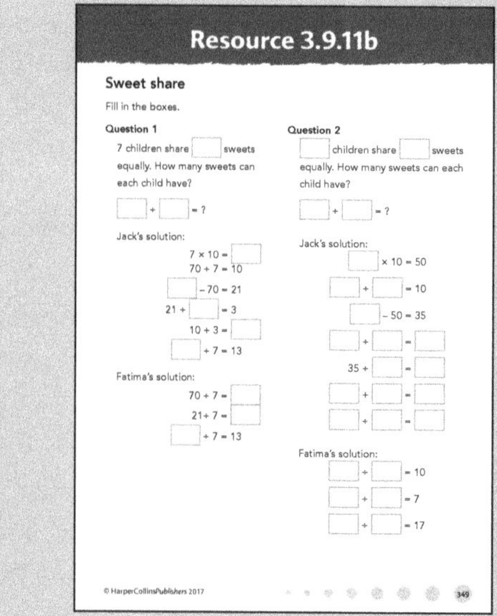

Resource 3.9.11b

Sweet share

Fill in the boxes.

Question 1

7 children share □ sweets equally. How many sweets can each child have?

□ + □ = ?

Jack's solution:

7 × 10 = □

70 + 7 = 10

□ − 70 = 21

21 + □ = 3

10 + 3 = □

□ + 7 = 13

Fatima's solution:

70 + 7 = □

21 + 7 = □

□ + 7 = 13

Question 2

□ children share □ sweets equally. How many sweets can each child have?

□ + □ = ?

Jack's solution:

□ × 10 = 50

□ + □ = 10

□ − 50 = 35

□ + □ = □

35 + □ = □

□ + □ = □

□ + □ = □

Fatima's solution:

□ ÷ □ = 10

□ ÷ □ = 7

□ ÷ □ = 17

© HarperCollinsPublishers 2017

349

- Ask pupils to select which method they prefer – Jack's or Fatima's – and prepare an explanation for why they prefer it, using the vocabulary of division.

## Question 4

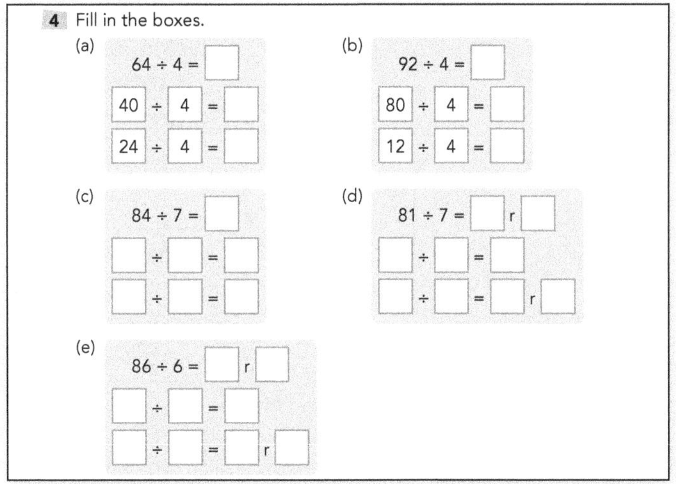

4 Fill in the boxes.

(a) 64 ÷ 4 = ☐
40 ÷ 4 = ☐
24 ÷ 4 = ☐

(b) 92 ÷ 4 = ☐
80 ÷ 4 = ☐
12 ÷ 4 = ☐

(c) 84 ÷ 7 = ☐
☐ ÷ ☐ = ☐
☐ ÷ ☐ = ☐

(d) 81 ÷ 7 = ☐ r ☐
☐ ÷ ☐ = ☐
☐ ÷ ☐ = ☐ r ☐

(e) 86 ÷ 6 = ☐ r ☐
☐ ÷ ☐ = ☐
☐ ÷ ☐ = ☐ r ☐

### What learning will pupils have achieved at the conclusion of Question 4?

- Pupils will be able to combine known division facts to calculate the results of other division calculations.

### Activities for whole-class instruction

- Write the following on the board:

  40 ÷ 4 = 10

  12 ÷ 4 = 3
- Ask pupils to work in pairs on mini whiteboards and to explain how they would use these calculations to work out 52 ÷ 4.
- Link back to the whole-class task in Question 3, and represent the results using an array like this:

Or:

- Explain to pupils that it is often useful to partition a dividend to first work with 10 × the divisor, and then work with the rest.
- Give pupils a second example (such as 91 ÷ 7) and ask them to consider how they would partition it and how that will help them to find an answer. Pupils should represent the calculation using an array, perhaps using manipulatives for support.
- Pupils should complete Question 4 in the Practice Book.

### Same-day intervention

- Using counters, work with pupils to solve two or three simple division questions. For example, ask pupils to work on the first set of calculations from Question 4, 64 ÷ 4, 40 ÷ 4 and 24 ÷ 4, but ensure that you have all three calculations represented by counters at the same time. You should do this by counting up in fours, until you reach the dividend, or by starting with the dividend and sharing into four groups. Alternatively, use a different set of three calculations such as 28 ÷ 2, 2 ÷ 2 and 8 ÷ 2.
- Ask: *What do you notice about the three different calculations in front of you?* Point out that combining the counters for 40 ÷ 4 and 24 ÷ 4 will give the same as the counters for 64 ÷ 4. If you have counted up in fours, this means showing them that the ten piles from 40 ÷ 4 and the six piles from 24 ÷ 4 can be combined to make 16 piles, which is the same as the number of piles created in 64 ÷ 4.
- If you are representing the division by sharing the counters into four groups, you will need to show that the four piles of ten counters created from 40 ÷ 4, and the four piles of six counters created from 24 ÷ 4 can be put together to make four piles of 16 counters, which is the same as the number of counters in the piles created by 64 ÷ 4.
- Wonder out loud if this will always happen and ask pupils to choose another set of numbers to try. Ensure that pupils notice that the way the calculation is being split to first work with 10 × the divisor and to adjust the calculation from there. Recording the methods and the steps on a number line may support pupils in seeing this strategy.

## Same-day enrichment

- Using 24 as a dividend, a chain can be constructed: 24 , 4 , 3 , 2 = 1. Ask pupils to try to find another dividend where dividing by three consecutive numbers gives a result that is a whole number with no remainder.
- Look for pupils who are able to use multiplication to find the solution (in the example 2 × 3 × 4 = 24, so a second solution with a two-digit result would be found using 3 × 4 × 5 = 60 giving the division 60 , 5 , 4 , 3 = 1. Alternatively, pupils may work with multiples of 24 and use the same consecutive digits as in the example. One possible solution using this strategy is 48 , 4 , 3 , 2 = 2.

# Question 5

**5** Write a number sentence for each question.

(a) When 95 is divided by 7, what are the quotient and remainder?

Number sentence: ____________

(b) A number times 5 is 75. What is the number?

Number sentence: ____________

(c) What number divided by 5 is 125?

Number sentence: ____________

## What learning will pupils have achieved at the conclusion of Question 5?

- Pupils will understand different images for division, accurately interpreting word problems that are structurally different to each other.

## Activities for whole-class instruction

- Draw the following spider diagram on the board and ask pupils what calculation should go in the middle.

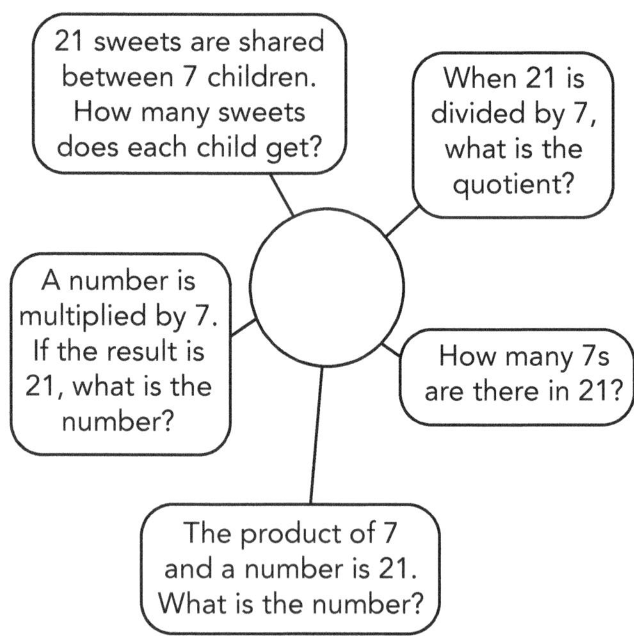


- Discuss with pupils which 'story' they feel most and least comfortable with as a way of thinking about the calculation 21 ÷ 7 = 3. This information may offer an insight into their current understanding of division and dividing which can be used to inform future lessons.
- Leave the spider diagram on the board and ask pupils to decide on a division that they know the answer to, and to create their own spider diagram for it. They should use all of the worded questions that you have given them, but also add in any extra that they can think of. Again, their own words may offer insight that can be used for future planning, or to inform same-day intervention.
- Leave the spider diagram on the board while pupils complete Question 5 in the Practice Book.

Look out for ... pupils who reverse the dividend and the divisor. It is important that pupils understand that division calculations are not necessarily said 'in order'. For example, the calculation 21÷ 3 can be read as '21 divided by three' in which case the word and the number sentence follow the same order, but can also be read as 'How many threes are there in 21?' where the order in which the digits are said is reversed. Pupils need to understand that division, unlike multiplication, is not commutative (the order in which a division calculation is carried out cannot be reversed without affecting the outcome, for example 2 × 8 = 8 × 2 but 8 ÷ 2 ≠ 2 ÷ 8).

## Same-day intervention

- Give a calculation, for example 12 ÷ 3 and ask pupils to read it to you. (Ensure that they have the dividend and the divisor the right way round: some pupils may mistakenly read this as 'three divided by twelve').
- Write down pupils' words as they read it to you (for example '12 divided by three') and then challenge them to read it again, but this time they're not allowed to use the word 'divided'. They could say '12 shared between three', or 'How many threes in 12'. The focus of the task is to develop correct use of language. Include the terms 'quotient' and 'remainder' in some examples.
- Write down two calculations, 12 ÷ 3 = ☐ and 12 × 3 = ☐.
- Now, express these in different ways – for example, 'What is 12 lots of three?', 'How many threes are in 12?' or 'What is 12 multiplied by 3?'. As you ask each question, pupils should point to the relevant calculation.

## Same-day enrichment

- Give pupils the frame:
  - How many ☐s are there in ☐☐?
  - What is ☐☐ shared between ☐?
- Tell pupils that, using any three digits from 1, 2, 3 and 4, they have to find as many ways to fill in the blanks as possible, and then find an answer to each question that they write.

# Question 6

**6** Application problems.

(a) The weight of a calf is 6 kg. The weight of a cow is 90 kg. How many times the weight of the calf is that of the cow?

Answer: ______

(b) A toy factory plans to make 96 toys in 4 days. If it makes 25 toys each day, can the target be met?

Answer: ______

## What learning will pupils have achieved at the conclusion of Question 6?

- Pupils will have built their understanding of division, applying it in a given context.

## Activities for whole-class instruction

- Use the spider diagram from the previous question (or sketch one out if you decided not to use that task to introduce Question 5) and ask pupils to give a 'story' that the calculation could describe. You might like to offer your own as a starting point, such as:

  *Matilda is 21 years old. She is seven times as old as her nephew. How old is her nephew?*

  Or:

  *There are seven cakes in each packet. Rivka needs 21 cakes. How many packets of cakes should she buy? How many will she have left over?*
- Gather pupils' stories and discuss how they know that division is to be used to find a solution.
- Ask pupils to write a new story for the same calculation. Pupils are beginning to think flexibly about different ways to consider division as an operation. They are learning what division is, as well as how to carry it out.
- Pupils should complete Question 6 in the Practice Book.

## Same-day intervention

- Help pupils to enact some situations in which they work on two images for division.
- Bundle some straws or cubes into sets of five and work out how many of these are needed if 15 straws/cubes are required. Ask pupils to describe what they are doing and record the ways they describe this. Ensure phrases such as 'how many blocks of five straws/cubes make 15' are recorded.
- Then unbundle the 15 counters/straws and share them into five equal piles. Again, ask pupils to describe what they are doing and record this in their own words. Make sure that an understanding of 'sharing' is recorded.
- Draw particular attention to areas of possible confusion, for example the question 'What is three lots of 12?' and the question 'How many lots of three are there in 12?' are both different questions and require different operations, but look very similar.
- Now ask pupils to tell a story using their earlier task as a model. You might need to offer an example, such as 'Benedict has 15 toys and he puts the same number of toys into each of five boxes. How many toys does he put in each box'.

- Use pupils' stories to assess their understanding. You might also like to tell them a similar story and ask them whether it is describing division or multiplication.
- For example, tell these stories:
  - *There are three pencils cases, and each pencil case has got seven pencils inside. James tips all of the pencils out in a pile on the table. How many pens are in the pile?*
  - *Sam puts the pencils back into the pencil cases, and also puts some rubbers into the pencil cases. He has 28 rubbers and puts the same number into each pencil case. How many rubbers go into each pencil case? How many are left over?*
- Ask pupils to identify which of them is a multiplication story and which is a division story.

## Same-day enrichment

- Give pupils the calculations:
  - How many sevens are there in 99?
  - What is 99 shared equally between seven?
- (If pupils have completed the enrichment task for Question 5, you might like to use some of their solutions for this task.)
- Now ask pupils to create some 'stories' that involve these numbers and the way they relate to each other. Pupils should create stories for both multiplication and division.
- Ask pupils which of their calculation descriptions fit with which of their stories, for example for the story 'Sarah has 99 balloons to put into bunches of seven. How many bunches can she make and how many are left over?', this might be best represented by a description of 99 ÷ 7 that involves counting up in threes, while the story 'Sarah has 99 balloons and wants to arrange them into seven bunches. How many balloons will be in each bunch and how many will she have left over?' might be best represented by a description that involves sharing.

## Challenge and extension question

# Question 7

**7** Choose from these signs: +, −, ×, ÷ or ( ) to make these equations true. One has been done for you.

(a) 4 + 4 − 4 − 4 = 0 (b) 4 4 4 4 = 3

(c) 4 4 4 4 = 1 (d) 4 4 4 4 = 5

(e) 4 4 4 4 = 2 (f) 4 4 4 4 = 8

This question challenges pupils to combine four operations to make a given total. Look for misconceptions around 4 ÷ 4, which may be a strategy used by pupils to create a '1' but which some may also believe gives them '0'.

This question also offers a useful opportunity for pupils to work with many different correct answers. You might like to discuss with pupils whether they prefer one correct solution to another and to explore why that might be.

# Unit 9.12
# Dividing a 2-digit number by a 1-digit number (2)

## Conceptual context

This unit introduces the column method as an efficient strategy for calculating a quotient.

The use of place value counters should be explicitly linked with the notation for the formal written method, or 'column method': this must be a focus of teaching for this unit. To make this connection, the 'sharing' image for division is used with the column method, using the vinculum ( $\overline{)\phantom{000}}$ ), decomposing place value counters where needed. It is important pupils use the notation as a *recording* of the process; this will involve sharing the place value counters, exchanging tens for ones when there are leftovers. As pupils become more familiar with the way in which they are recording the process, their focus will shift and they will 'compress' the process and the 'recording' will become conceptually intertwined with the 'method'. In this way, what pupils learn as a way of recording a process becomes, effortlessly and unbeknown to them, a written algorithm for division that serves them as a reliable and extendable tool for calculation for the future.

Although pupils will be encouraged to think about sharing when they begin to work with the written column method for division, the unit starts by looking at arrays and focusing on discerning the number of equal groups that can be 'seen' in arrays. The intention is that pupils develop a flexible conceptual understanding about division is as well as knowing how to divide, and it is important that different kinds of dividing (sharing between or making equal groups) are explored. This might be done by asking the same question using different vocabulary (for example, when working on the question 24¸6 you might read it as 'How many sixes are there in 24?'; 'What is 24 divided by six?'; 'What is 24 shared between six?'; or 'How many times does six go into 24?'

## Learning pupils will have achieved at the end of the unit

- Pupils will have extended their knowledge about dividing to use informal strategies to divide a two-digit number by a one-digit number and express the quotient with a remainder (Q1)
- Pupils will have extended their range of representations for division and learned to record the process of division using the vinculum symbol ( $\overline{)\phantom{000}}$ ) (Q2)
- Pupils will be able to set out and solve a division calculation using a formal written method (Q2, Q3, Q5)
- Pupils will be able to interpret a division calculation written using both symbols for division (÷ and $\overline{)\phantom{000}}$ ) or as a word problem (Q3, Q4)
- Pupils will be able to apply understanding of division structures to solve word problems (Q5)

## Resources

place value counters or blocks; counters; number plates; tens rods; mini whiteboards and pens; interlocking cubes; **Resource 3.9.12a** Matching divisions 1; **Resource 3.9.12b** Matching divisions 2; **Resource 3.9.12c** Division tables; **Resource 3.9.12d** Matching divisions 3

## Vocabulary

multiple, divide, division, dividend, divisor, quotient, remainder

# Question 1

**1** Calculate mentally.

(a) $20 \div 6 =$ ☐ (b) $31 \div 5 =$ ☐ (c) $63 \div 8 =$ ☐

(d) $43 \div 7 =$ ☐ (e) $75 \div 9 =$ ☐ (f) $62 \div 7 =$ ☐

(g) $48 \div 9 =$ ☐ (h) $39 \div 4 =$ ☐

## What learning will pupils have achieved at the conclusion of Question 1?

- Pupils will be able to use informal strategies to divide a two-digit number by a one-digit number and express the quotient with a remainder.

## Activities for whole-class instruction

- Show pupils this array:

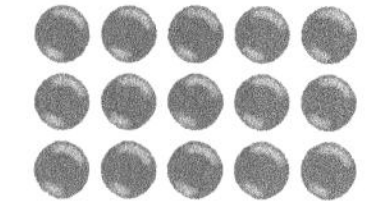

- Give the class time to familiarise themselves with the array, and to work out how many items there are in it. Can pupils see $3 \times 5$ and $5 \times 3$?
- Tell the story: *There are 15 bananas in a fruit bowl. Each night a monkey comes and takes three bananas.* Ask pupils how many nights it is before there are no bananas left in the fruit bowl.
- Give them time to discuss how to reach the answer with a partner, using a mini whiteboard to capture their methods if they need to.
- Now ask a few pairs to share their answers and the routes they took to reach them. Now ask pupils to discuss the question: *How many times can three be subtracted from 15?* Again, give them time to work on this in pairs and then select some pairs to share their answer. Ask: *How can you use the array to help?*
- Can pupils see that the two tasks are different ways of asking the same question? Ask them to write a number sentence to describe the situations. Do pupils understand that both situations can be described as $15 \div 3 = 5$?
- Ask pairs to write a word problem that can be answered using the number sentence $15 \div 5 = 3$. The intention of the tasks is to encourage pupils to see the repeated subtraction that is implicit in a division calculation in preparation for the move to column division.
- Pupils should complete Question 1 in the Practice Book.

## Same-day intervention

- Using number plates or tens rods, give pupils a supply of threes plates or rods. Ask pupils to make 21 and, when they have done so, ask them to note how many plates or rods they have used, and to record this as a number sentence. It is likely that they will use multiplication $7 \times 3 = 21$.
- Now tell pupils that, using only threes, they should make 36. Ask them first to work out how many rods or plates they will need (and give them time to work this out so that it is not just a guess). Check together by counting up in threes to 36, and then counting back in threes from 36 to zero.

*36 divided by three equals 12 means that three can be taken from 36 twelve times, or that 12 can be taken from 36 three times.*

- Ask them to now make a similar pair of statements about the calculation $56 \div 7 = 8$.
- Repeat with different numbers if necessary.

## Same-day enrichment

- Give pupils the digits 3, 4 and 5 on sticky notes, and sketch out this frame on a mini whiteboard: ☐☐ ÷ ☐.
- Ask pupils to create and solve as many division questions as they can by placing the notes into the frame.
- Challenge them to create a question with no remainder and to create the largest or the smallest answer.

# Question 2

**2** Use the column method to calculate. One has been done for you.

(a) $3\overline{)45}$ = 15: 45 − 3(0) = 15; 15 − 15 = 0

(b) $2\overline{)78}$ (c) $5\overline{)65}$

(d) $2\overline{)46}$ (e) $3\overline{)93}$ (f) $4\overline{)48}$

## What learning will pupils have achieved at the conclusion of Question 2?

- Pupils will be able to set out a division calculation using a formal written method.
- Pupils will have extended their range of representations for division and learned to record the process of division using the vinculum symbol ( $\overline{)\quad}$ ).

## Activities for whole-class instruction

- Use place value counters to represent 51 on a whiteboard.

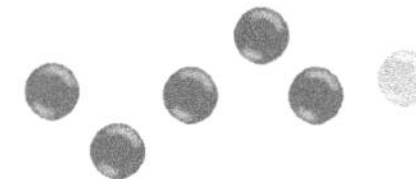

- Write: 51 ÷ 3 = □. Ask pupils to calculate an answer. Gather answers and suggestions for methods.

  Show pupils that the counters should firstly be set out as tens and ones, with a special symbol called a 'vinculum' drawn around them and the 51 drawn under the counters on the paper:

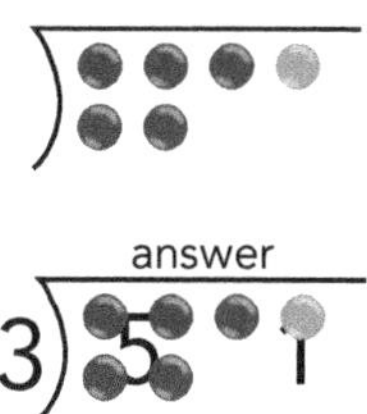


- Write 3 and 'answer' as shown. Ask: *What does this three represent?* Agree that the question was 51 ÷ 3, so 51 must be divided into three equal parts. Tell pupils you will make three columns of counters – they will be the three equal parts.
- Invite a pupil to share the tens counters between the three columns equally.

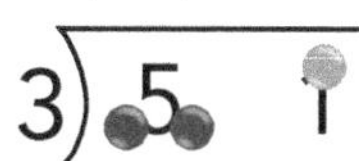


- At this point, the tens have been shared out as much as they can be. No more tens can be put into columns, the number of tens has been divided and only one ten can go into each part – each part will have one ten.
- Tell pupils that this must be recorded before you do any more. Ask: *Where should we record how many tens are in each group, each column?* Show pupils that 1 must be written above the tens counters.

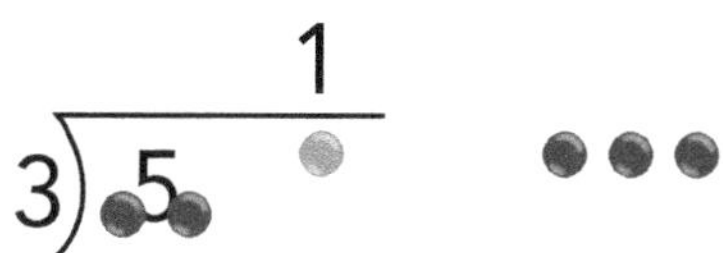


- Ask: *What do we need to do to the other counters to be able to share them out, to divide them between the columns?* Pupils should suggest exchanging the two tens counters for 20 ones.

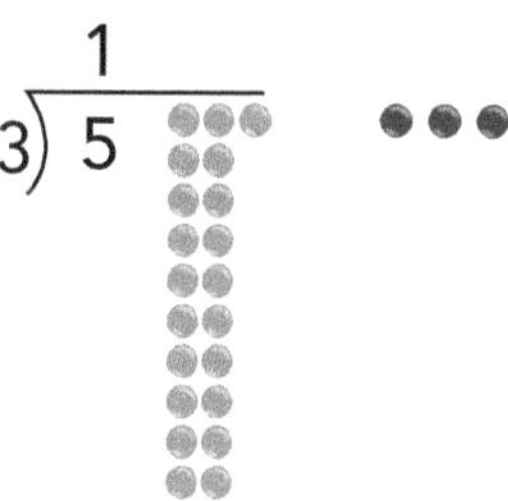


- From here, pupils should easily see that the ones can be divided among the columns equally

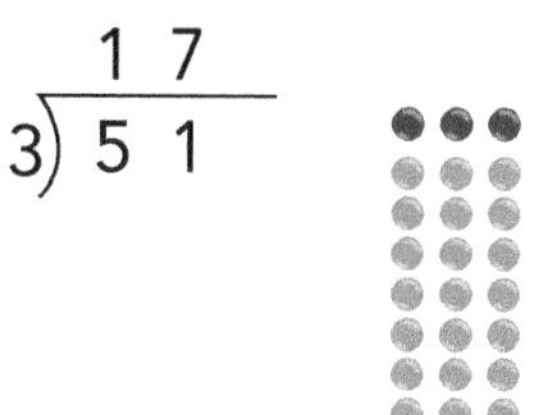


- After the ones are divided between the three columns, the number of ones in each column can be counted and recorded as above.
- Work through three more examples with pupils: 57 ÷ 3 = □ (for which pupils can almost follow exactly the same procedure, but with a small change at the end) followed by 57 ÷ 4 = □ (which leaves a remainder).
- Where there is a remainder, explain to pupils that the number left over is simply recorded as a remainder by writing r, for example, r1 as for the 57 ÷ 4 = □ example.

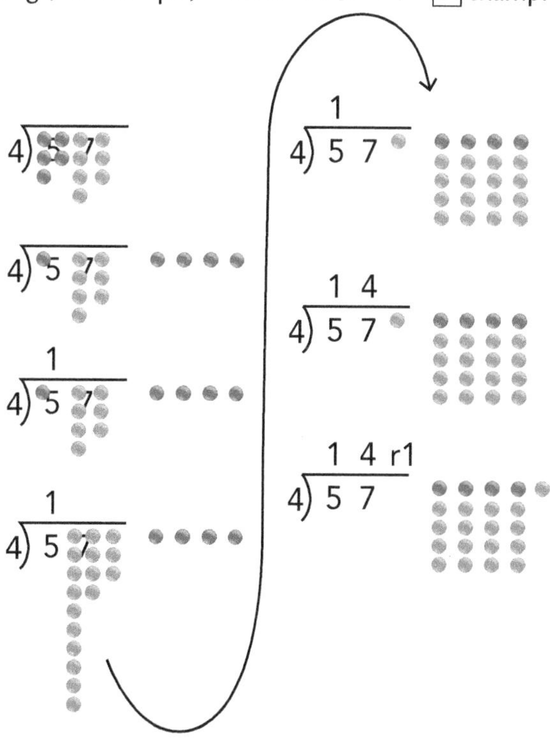


- Finally, use the calculation 68 ÷ 6 = □.

- Now ask pupils to put the place value counters away and revisit one of the calculations from earlier with which they are comfortable. Use 57 ÷ 3. Ask pupils to work in pairs to imagine and discuss how the counters would be used to solve this problem. Ask them what the steps would look like as they progress through the problem. If appropriate, allow pupils to use the counters, but only after they have tried to solve the calculation without.
- Show pupils this image of the calculation as carried out by manipulating the place value counters.

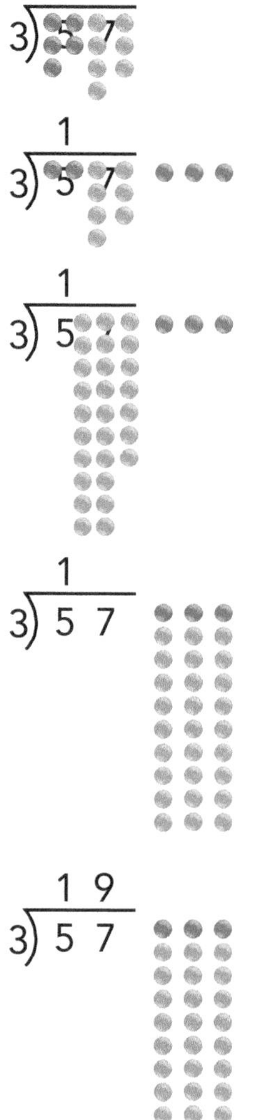


ⓘ By using place value counters 'concretely' in a physical column division layout, and by linking that with the numbers revealed beneath and the formation of equal groups alongside, pupils have had opportunities to build vital links between concepts. These connections are crucial for making sense of the written method for division, in which multiples of the divisor are subtracted from the dividend. Pupils often become overly focused on the mechanics of the procedures, relying on memorising steps and inevitably forgetting something. By understanding basic principles about the process itself – that the written method simply needs to keep track of the multiplications that have been carried out, their products and quotients, so that the quotient is built up in a sensible way – pupils can be successful with division. So far, they have learned that the process is to divide the dividend into equal groups and that visualising this as the movement of place value counters helps them make sense of this. Next, they will learn how to record each step using numbers, relying on knowledge of multiplication facts and fluency with column subtraction.

- Work through 57 ÷ 3 = ☐ together as follows:

3)57

- Sharing the tens equally uses three of the tens, which is 30. There is one ten in each column. Say: *We must write 30 under the 57 to show that 30 have been used. We must also show how many are left – how many of the dividend we started with are still to be divided, so that is 57 subtracted by the 30 we have used so far – 27.*

```
  1
3)57
  30
  --
  27
```

- Say: *We already know there are not enough tens to put another ten in every column, so what should we do?* Pupils should suggest exchanging the two tens for 20 ones.
- Say: *Breaking the two tens and combining with the ones means that there are now 27 ones to share.*

```
  19
3)57
  30
  --
  27
  27
  --
   0
```

- Say: *Sharing the 27 ones equally between the three uses all 27. We can show that as a subtraction that leaves zero. Each column has nine ones so 9 is written in the ones column of the quotient* (the answer).

*When 57 is divided by three, the quotient is 19.*

- Work through 87 ÷ 4 = ☐ together in the same way.
- Pupils should complete Question 2 in the Practice Book.

## Same-day intervention

- Use this frame and work with pupils, one row at a time, to complete the blanks represented by the movement of the place value counters.

2)3 6

2)3 6
  _ _
  ―――

2)3 6
  _ _
  ―――
  _

2)3 6
  _ _
  ―――
  _ _

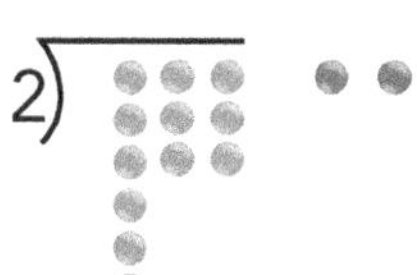

  _ _
2)3 6
  _ _
  ―――
  _ _
  _ _
  ―――
    _

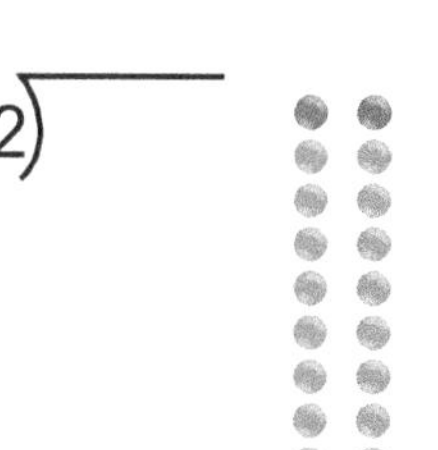

## Same-day enrichment

- Give pupils completed calculations, with either the divisor or the dividend missing, and challenge pupils to identify what the missing digits must be. For example:

```
   2 6          1 7
_) 5 3       5) _ _
   4 0          5 0
   ---          ---
   1 3          3 9
   1 2          3 5
   ---          ---
     1            4
```

- When pupils have found the missing values, they should write a complete number sentence for each of the above.
- Ask pupils to talk to a partner about their strategies.

# Question 3

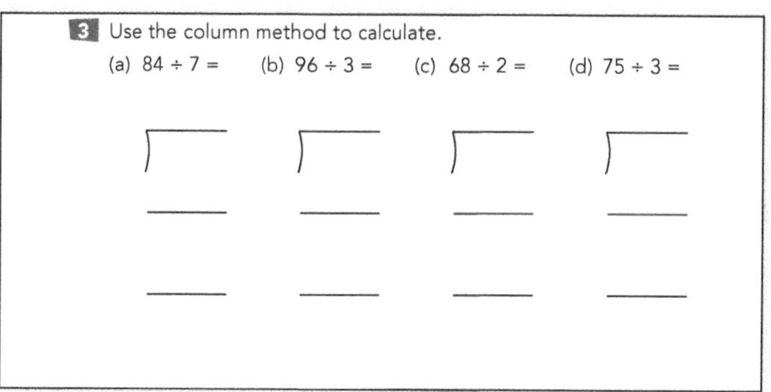

3 Use the column method to calculate.

(a) 84 ÷ 7 = (b) 96 ÷ 3 = (c) 68 ÷ 2 = (d) 75 ÷ 3 =

### What learning will pupils have achieved at the conclusion of Question 3?

- Pupils will be able to set out and solve a division calculation using a formal written method.
- Pupils will be able to interpret a division calculation written using both symbols for division (÷ and ) ̅ ) or as a word problem.

## Activities for whole-class instruction

- The intention of this task is to focus on the notation, not on the strategies for division that have been covered in the previous question.
- Write two sets of calculations on the board like this:

| | |
|---|---|
| 7)3 6 | 45 ÷ 7 |
| 4)3 2 | 42 ÷ 3 |
| 3)2 4 | 36 ÷ 7 |
| 7)4 5 | 24 ÷ 3 |

- Ask pupils which of the calculations don't have a partner, and to write the missing partner.
- Ensure that pupils also pay attention to the way that the calculation is said, drawing attention to the different positions of the dividend and divisor in the different representations.
- Pupils should complete Question 3 in the Practice Book.

## Same-day intervention

- Use **Resource 3.9.12a** Matching divisions 1, and work with pupils to match the two different ways of writing the division calculations.

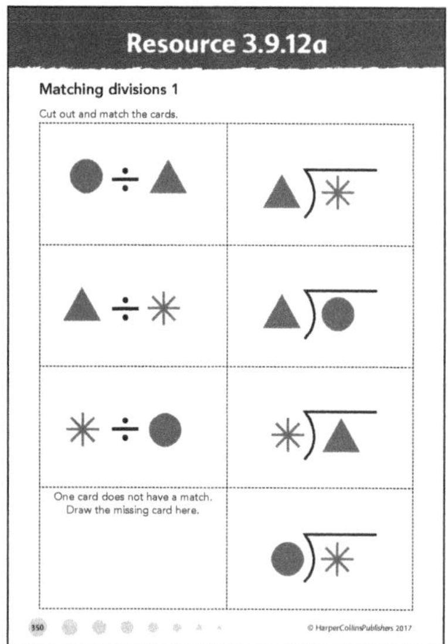


## Same-day enrichment

- Write this calculation on the board and ask pupils: *What might be in the empty boxes? Make up a word problem that uses these numbers.*

$$\square\overline{)\square\square}^{\,7} = 3\square \div 5$$

# Question 4

**4** Write a number sentence for each question.

(a) What is 39 divided 3?

Number sentence: ____________________

(b) What is 78 divided by 6?

Number sentence: ____________________

## What learning will pupils have achieved at the conclusion of Question 4?

Pupils will be able to 'read' a division calculation presented in words or symbols.

## Activities for whole-class instruction

- Pupils use mini whiteboards to write the following in two different ways (using the ÷ and the column method).
  - What is thirty-seven divided by four?
  - How many sixes are in 47?
  - How many times larger is 99 than nine?
- Discuss their ideas.
- Pupils should complete Question 4 in the Practice Book.

## Same-day intervention

- Give pupils **Resource 3.9.12b** Matching divisions 2, and work with them to match calculations with their descriptions.

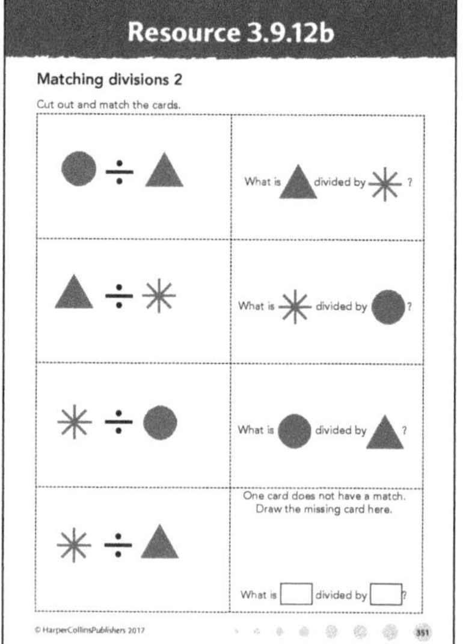


- If pupils also worked on the intervention task for Question 3, then they might notice that this task builds onto it, adding a description to the two calculations that they have already matched.

## Same-day enrichment

- Ask pupils to complete **Resource 3.9.12c** Division tables.

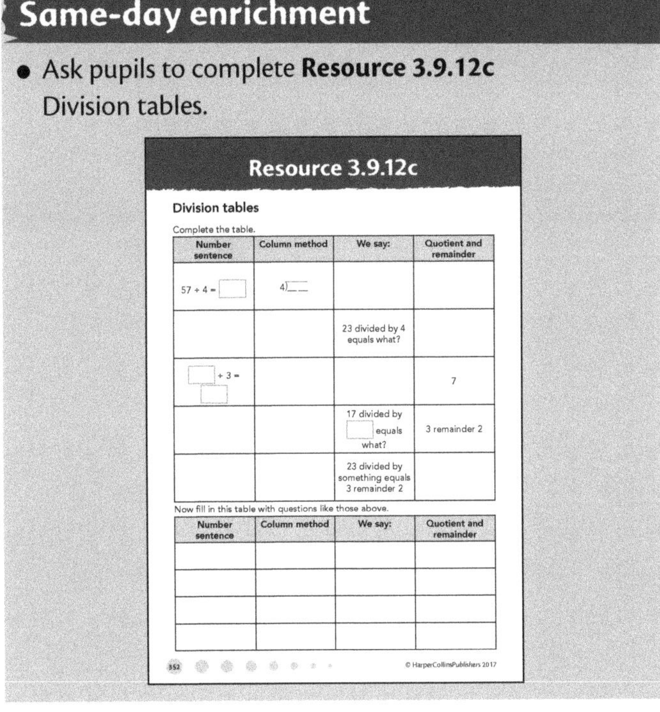

Resource 3.9.12c

Division tables

Complete the table.

| Number sentence | Column method | We say: | Quotient and remainder |
|---|---|---|---|
| 57 ÷ 4 = ☐ | 4)‾‾ | | |
| | | 23 divided by 4 equals what? | |
| ☐ ÷ 3 = ☐ | | | 7 |
| | | 17 divided by ☐ equals what? | 3 remainder 2 |
| | | 23 divided by something equals 3 remainder 2 | |

Now fill in this table with questions like those above.

| Number sentence | Column method | We say: | Quotient and remainder |
|---|---|---|---|
| | | | |
| | | | |
| | | | |
| | | | |

352 © HarperCollinsPublishers 2017

# Question 5

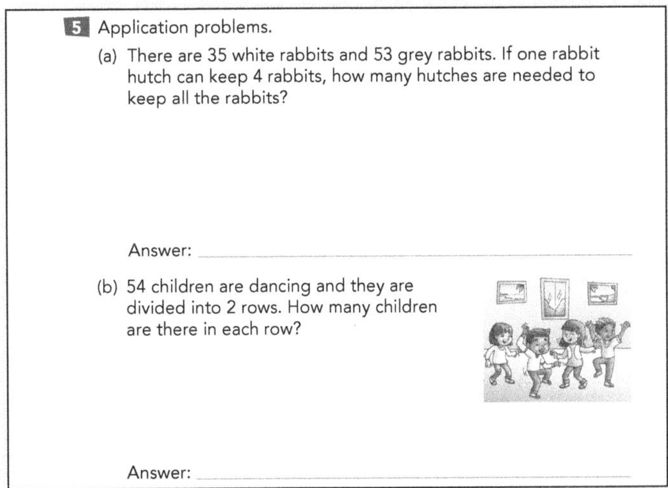

5 Application problems.

(a) There are 35 white rabbits and 53 grey rabbits. If one rabbit hutch can keep 4 rabbits, how many hutches are needed to keep all the rabbits?

Answer: ______________________

(b) 54 children are dancing and they are divided into 2 rows. How many children are there in each row?

Answer: ______________________

## What learning will pupils have achieved at the conclusion of Question 5?

- Pupils will have applied understanding of division structures to solve word problems.
- Pupils will be able to set out and solve a division calculation using a formal written method.

## Activities for whole-class instruction

- Use two equal piles of approximately 35 interlocking cubes. Select three pupils and say that you are going to share the cubes between them.
- Ask the class to predict how many cubes each pupil will get, and whether there will be any cubes left over. Gather their responses and methods and then 'check' them by sharing the cubes one at a time between the three pupils.
- Now use the other, equal pile of cubes and explain that you want to create towers that are three cubes high. Ask pupils to calculate how many towers you will be able to build, and whether there will be any cubes left over. Gather their responses and methods and again, 'check' them by modelling and building one tower at a time until it is not possible to build another.
- Explain to pupils that both of the situations you have just represented are different ways to think about division, and carry out the division on the board using the column method.
- Ask pupils to look at the numbers given in the result and explain that (for 35 ÷ 3) in the first situation the 11 represents the total number of blocks each person has and the 2 is the number of blocks left over, while in the second situation the 11 represents the total number of towers, and the 2 is again the number of blocks left over.
- Pupils should complete Question 5 in the Practice Book.

## Same-day intervention

- Ask pupils to use **Resource 3.9.12d** Matching divisions 3, to match the four calculations to the four word problems.

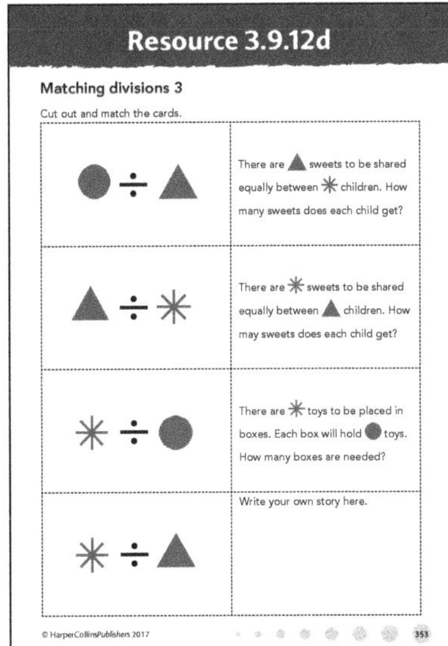

Resource 3.9.12d

Matching divisions 3

Cut out and match the cards.

| | |
|---|---|
| ● ÷ ▲ | There are ▲ sweets to be shared equally between ✳ children. How many sweets does each child get? |
| ▲ ÷ ✳ | There are ✳ sweets to be shared equally between ▲ children. How may sweets does each child get? |
| ✳ ÷ ● | There are ✳ toys to be placed in boxes. Each box will hold ● toys. How many boxes are needed? |
| ✳ ÷ ▲ | Write your own story here. |

© HarperCollinsPublishers 2017 353

- The intention is to draw pupils' attention to a calculation without the pressure of having to calculate an answer, allowing more of a focus on the structure of the question.
- Although independent of them, these word problems add to the intervention tasks used with Questions 4 and 5, so you might like to have copies of these ready should pupils need this extra support.

## Same-day enrichment

- Tell pupils that, in a farmyard, there are 24 chickens, 12 sheep, four horses and two cows. There are also seven fields that the animals can go to and 14 water troughs.
- Ask pupils to write as many division word questions as they can that might be asked about this situation.

## Challenge and extension question

# Question 6

6 Using the numbers 4, 11, 2 and 3, complete the following division calculation.

☐ ÷ ☐ = ☐ r ☐

Question 6 gives pupils a chance to explore division and to think about the relative values of the numbers in each position. Pupils will demonstrate good reasoning if they show that they understand that the 11 must be the dividend.

# Question 7

7 Lily's mother gave Lily 8 chocolates and gave the rest of the chocolates to Iram. The number of chocolates that Lily got was exactly half of the number Iram was given.

How many chocolates did Iram have?

Answer: ____________________

Question 7 adds a level of complexity to the division problem. You might like to offer pupils counters and suggest that they use these to represent the sweets, if they find the problem hard to access.

# Unit 9.13
# Dividing a 2-digit number by a 1-digit number (3)

## Conceptual context

This unit extends pupils' learning about the column method for division, introducing the column method for dividends where the first digit has a lower value than the divisor. Of course, this requires pupils to know multiplication facts, and to understand how they relate to dividing.

The unit continues to build an understanding of what division is, alongside developing fluency in dividing, using both formal and informal methods. It is important to keep this dual focus in mind, using different phrases to describe the calculation, and modelling the divisions using manipulatives, where appropriate.

## Learning pupils will have achieved at the end of the unit

- Pupils will have applied their knowledge of multiplication to find the greatest multiple less than a given number, connecting multiplication and division (Q1)
- Pupils will have made connections between the different notation used to represent division (Q2, Q3, Q4)
- Pupils will be able to calculate a quotient when the first digit of the dividend is greater than the divisor (Q2, Q3, Q4)
- Pupils will be able to calculate a quotient when the first digit of the dividend is less than the divisor (Q3, Q4)

### Resources

place value counters; counters; tens rods; base 10 blocks; mini whiteboards and pens; 100 square; multiplication square

### Vocabulary

divide, division, dividend, divisor, quotient, remainder

# Question 1

**1** What is the greatest number you can write in each box?

(a) ☐ × 7 < 45 (b) ☐ × 4 < 26 (c) 68 > 9 × ☐

(d) 3 × ☐ < 28 (e) 6 × ☐ < 35 (f) 47 > ☐ × 8

## What learning will pupils have achieved at the conclusion of Question 1?

- Pupils will have applied their knowledge of multiplication to find the greatest multiple less than a given number, connecting multiplication and division.

## Activities for whole-class instruction

- Show a 100 square on your board and point to a number, for example 23. Ask:

  *If I were counting up in twos, but had to stop before I reached this point, what would be the last number I'd say?*

  *How did you know it was 22?*

  *How many twos are in 23?*

  *How do you know it is 11?*
- Show pupils tens rods or base 10 blocks to represent 23. Ask them to use these to prove their answers. For example:

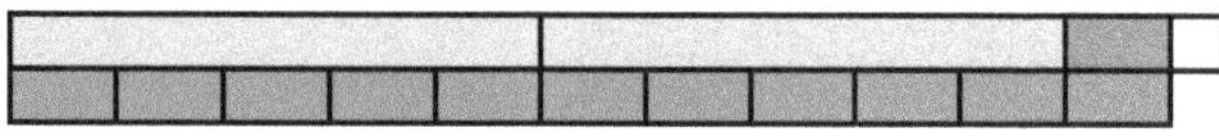

- Write 2 × 11 = 22 on the board.
- Ask: *Is there a larger number than 11 that I could use, but still keep the result less than 23? How do you know?*
- Finally, write 2 × ☐ < 23 on the board and ask pupils what the missing number might be. Ask pupils if they can see that there is more than one answer. Ask: *What is the greatest possible answer?*
- Pupils should complete Question 1 in the Practice Book.

## Same-day intervention

- Use cube sticks or tens rods and explain to pupils that, using only the five stick/rod, you want to get as close to 27 as possible.
- Ask them initially to predict how many sticks/rods they will need, then count up with them to see how close their estimate was. As you count up, also mark the jumps on a number line.
- Work with pupils and draw their attention to the efficiencies of using known facts to minimise the effort needed. Use the number line to record these known facts.

It might be, for example, that pupils know that 5 × 2 = 10, and so you can make this in one jump, then consider how many more jumps are possible before reaching 20.

- Work with some more questions and encourage pupils to use the number line to calculate, then to use the sticks or rods to check their calculation.

## Same-day enrichment

- Tell pupils that they are to use cube sticks or tens rods to make 43, but they are only allowed to use two types of stick or rod. For example, if they use threes and fours, then 43 can be made using ten fours and one three, or using 13 threes and one four.
- Ask them to choose two types of stick and to see whether they can always make 43 using just these sticks. If appropriate, they should record their answers mathematically as number sentences (so, in the examples given, these would be 10 × 4 + 3 = 43 and 13 × 3 + 4 = 43).

# Question 2

**2** Work out these division calculations. Think carefully about where to write each quotient.

(a) 6 ) 3 0 (b) 2 ) 1 9 (c) 9 ) 3 8 (d) 3 ) 2 0

(e) 6 ) 3 2 (f) 4 ) 2 1 (g) 8 ) 2 8 (h) 7 ) 4 0

## What learning will pupils have achieved at the conclusion of Question 2?

- Pupils will have understood the notation used to represent division when using the column method.
- Pupils will have used the structure of the column method to record solutions where the first digit of the dividend is less than the divisor.

## Activities for whole-class instruction

- Using place value counters, model sharing 29 ones into three equal groups. Record this using the vinculum ( $\overline{)\phantom{00}}$ ), drawing pupils' attention to the way that the quotient is recorded in the ones column.
- Now set up the counters to show 29, using two tens and nine ones, reminding pupils that the 29 is to be split into three equal groups, and is equivalent to the calculation that has just been carried out.
- Model sharing the tens out, but show that there are not enough to put one in each group. Explain that, in this instance, all of the tens need to be exchanged for ones, making 29 counters to share between the three groups.
- Now use tens and ones to make 39, and model the calculation 39 ÷ 4, showing again that there are not enough tens to share one into each group. Ask pupils to work together on mini whiteboards (or, where appropriate, using place value counters) to calculate the quotient. Point out that they might be able to use known multiplication facts to help them find the solution and that they probably do not actually need to group the counters.
- Gather their solutions and methods, ensuring that pupils are aware of efficient strategies using known facts to work out the quotient.
- Pupils should find quotients for:

| | | |
|---|---|---|
| $5\overline{)30}$ | $2\overline{)18}$ | $3\overline{)54}$ |
| $2\overline{)44}$ | $3\overline{)48}$ | $7\overline{)77}$ |
| $3\overline{)27}$ | $7\overline{)63}$ | $5\overline{)35}$ |

- Ask pupils to group the calculations into those that have two-digit quotients and those that have one-digit quotients. Ask: *What is the same among the calculations in each group?*
- Ask pupils if they can see that, where the divisor is bigger than the first digit of the dividend, the answer (the quotient) has only one digit. Ask if they can explain why.
- Pupils should complete Question 2 in the Practice Book.

## Same-day intervention

- Use a multiplication square to work with pupils on division calculations in which the first digit of the dividend is less than the divisor.
- Use these calculations:

$5\overline{)40}$ $4\overline{)39}$ $6\overline{)30}$

$5\overline{)42}$ $4\overline{)38}$ $6\overline{)31}$

$5\overline{)47}$ $4\overline{)37}$ $6\overline{)37}$

- Ensure that pupils can interpret this notation correctly as a division, with the correct dividend and divisor.
- Work with pupils to use the multiplication square to solve these divisions and interpret the remainders in each calculation.

## Same-day enrichment

- Ask pupils to work out 20 ÷ 7, 20 ÷ 8 and 20 ÷ 9, and to record their results using the column method.
- Ask them to comment on and to explain any patterns that they notice in the remainders of their answers.
- Follow this up by asking if they can find another number that gives the same patterns in its remainders when it is divided by 7, 8 and 9.

## Question 3

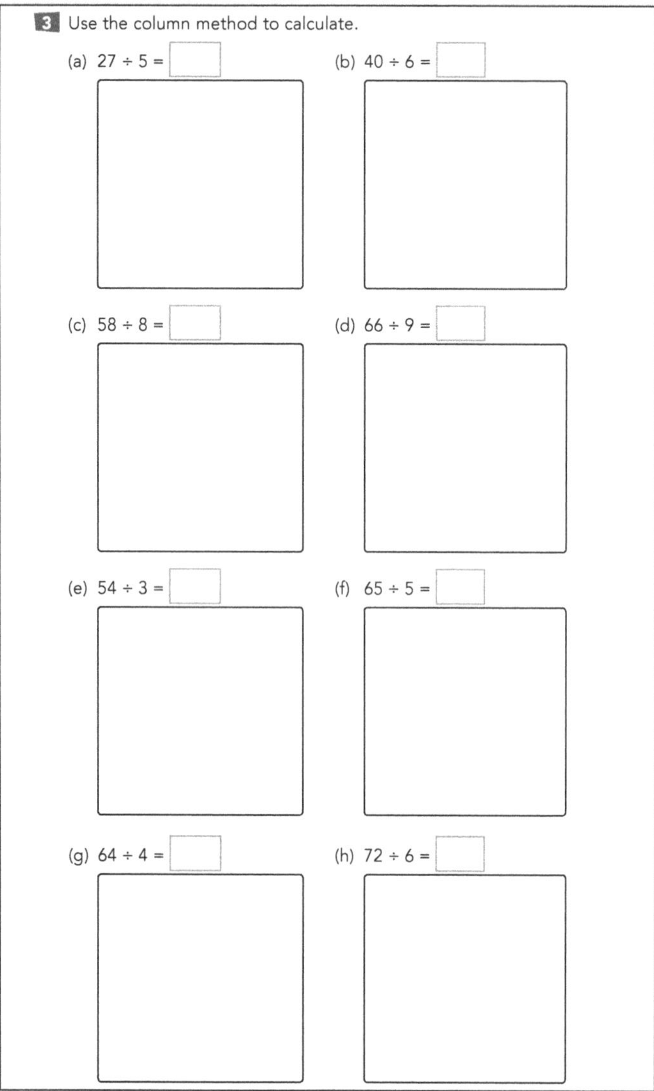

3 Use the column method to calculate.

(a) 27 ÷ 5 = ☐ (b) 40 ÷ 6 = ☐

(c) 58 ÷ 8 = ☐ (d) 66 ÷ 9 = ☐

(e) 54 ÷ 3 = ☐ (f) 65 ÷ 5 = ☐

(g) 64 ÷ 4 = ☐ (h) 72 ÷ 6 = ☐

- Pupils should complete Question 3 in the Practice Book.

### Same-day intervention

- For this activity, pupils might need to use place value counters. Ensure that they are able to make the connections between the obelus notation and the vinculum notation. The counters represent the dividend, and the numbers underneath the counters, so they are revealed as the counters are redistributed.
- Calculations for pupils to work on are:

  90 ÷ 6

  95 ÷ 6

  96 ÷ 8

  90 ÷ 8
- As before, ensure that pupils understand that they can count up, or use known multiplication facts to make their arranging of the counters, or calculation of the quotient, more efficient.

### Same-day enrichment

- Using the digits 4, 6 and 8, ask pupils to see how many different ways they can find to complete ☐☐ ÷ ☐.
- Ask pupils how they can be sure that they have all possible arrangements.
- Ask: *Which arrangement of digits gives the greatest quotient? Which gives the lowest?* Ask pupils to justify why this particular arrangement gives the lowest.

### What learning will pupils have achieved at the conclusion of Question 3?

- Pupils will be able to calculate a quotient when the first digit of the dividend is greater or less than the divisor.

### Activities for whole-class instruction

- Write a calculation using the ÷ symbol (the obelus), for example, 33 ÷ 5. Explain to pupils that this can be rewritten using the column method and write the calculation this way.
- The intention of this task is to connect the obelus notation with the column method, which uses the vinculum symbol ( $\overline{)\quad}$ ), and to give pupils an opportunity to practise the column method.
- Place value counters can be provided, but pupils should be encouraged to use the formal written method without counters, where possible.

## Question 4

4 Application problems.

(a) 27 pupils took part in a school art competition. They were divided into 3 groups. How many pupils were there in each group?

Answer: __________

(b) 88 balls are put into 5 baskets in equal numbers. How many balls are put into each basket? How many balls are left over?

Answer: __________

(c) Each coat needs 5 buttons. How many coats can 78 buttons be sewn on to? How many buttons are left over?

Answer: __________

## What learning will pupils have achieved at the conclusion of Question 4?

- Pupils will have interpreted worded questions and will represent them as division calculations.

## Activities for whole-class instruction

- Write 36 ÷ 4 = 9 on the board.
- Now tell a 'story' that the calculation might represent.
- For example:

  *Each car on a rollercoaster will hold four people.*

  *There are 36 people in the queue.*

  *The rollercoaster is full when all the people in the queue have got on.*

  *There are 9 cars on the rollercoaster.*
- Ask pupils to work together on mini whiteboards to write their own story for the same calculation and share some of these stories. Look for pupils' stories that suggest different representations for division (the rollercoaster example might be thought of as 'How many fours are there in 36?' while the story: *Sarah has 36 sweets to give out to four friends. If she gives each person the same number of sweets, how many sweets will each of them get?* offers a different, sharing image for division) so that pupils are able to see the variety of ways to think about the same calculation.
- If your original example does not include a remainder, you might now adjust the question so that a remainder is added. For example, rewriting the calculation as 39 ÷ 4 = 9 remainder 3 might change the story to: *Each car on a rollercoaster will hold four people. There are 39 people in the queue. When all the people in the queue have got on, one car has one space in it. There are 9 full cars and one with 3 people in it.*
- Pupils should adapt their stories to include a remainder. Discuss examples.
- Pupils should complete Question 4 in the Practice Book.

### Same-day intervention

- Use blocks or counters to carry out a process that can be represented by a division calculation. For example, use twelve blocks and split them into three equal piles. Work with pupils to represent this as a number sentence, writing 12 ÷ 4 = 3 and drawing attention to where each of the numbers (the 12, the 4 and the 3) can be seen in the piles of counters.
- Now give pupils a number sentence such as 24 ÷ 6 = 4 and ask them to represent the number sentence using the counters.
- If appropriate, give pupils a calculation with a division and again ask them to represent this calculation using the counters. Again, work with pupils to explicitly identify where each of the numbers in the calculation (now including the remainder) can be seen in the piles of counters.
- 'Act out' some of the stories that the other pupils have created, writing the related number sentence.

### Same-day enrichment

- Give pupils the number sentence 154 ÷ 9 = 17 remainder 1. (Although this is a larger dividend than pupils have been used to, this should not impact on the level of challenge as they are not calculating. This is a task about interpreting remainders in a division.)
- Ask pupils to use this calculation to answer (without calculating):

  155 ÷ 9

  156 ÷ 9

  164 ÷ 9

## Challenge and extension question

## Question 5

**5** A teacher bought some special pencils as prizes for 6 winners of a mental maths competition. She gave each winner 1 pencil, and then continued to give them a pencil each until she no longer had enough pencils to give each winner. The number of pencils left over is the same as the number of pencils each winner has in total.

How many pencils did the teacher buy? Give as many answers as you can find.

If pupils find Question 5 difficult to access, encourage them to represent it as a number sentence, using blanks where necessary, or to use counters to represent the erasers. The key to the problem is for pupils to identify that the structure of the solutions is 'one more than one lot of six, two more than two lots of six…' and so on, and to use this structure to calculate the numerical solutions and identify that the solutions are multiples of 7.

# Unit 9.14

# Dividing a 2-digit number by a 1-digit number (4)

## Conceptual context

This unit continues to build pupils' understanding of division by providing further opportunities to practise dividing two-digit numbers by one-digit numbers.

Pupils will also explore the effect of multiplying the dividend or the divisor by a given value, and by making connections with multiplication. This is, initially, through seeing how the quotient halves when the divisor doubles, but also through the use of place value where pupils will find that the quotient becomes ten times larger if the dividend becomes ten times larger. Generalisations about these relationships will become understood, so that pupils are more able to calculate flexibly and fluently. It is important to focus on the connections between (for example) $600 \div 3$, $6 \div 3$, $3 \times 2$ and $300 \times 2$, and make explicit the ways in which knowledge of one leads to knowledge of the others.

## Learning pupils will have achieved at the end of the unit

- Pupils will have practised using multiplication facts when dividing a two-digit number by a one-digit number, (Q1, Q2, Q4, Q5)
- Pupils will have explored why doubling the value of the divisor halves the value of the quotient, enabling flexible thinking (Q2)
- Pupils will have understood the importance of the use of a zero for place value when using the column method for division (Q3)
- Pupils will have built on their understanding of division with two-digit numbers to work with simple multiples of ten (Q4, Q5, Q6)
- Pupils will have used known facts to work out multiplication and division calculations (Q1, Q2, Q5)
- Pupils will be able to identify the necessary number sentence and calculate the solution from a problem written in words (Q6)
- Pupils will have solved word problems requiring division, including identifying the correct operation (Q7)

### Resources

place value counters; counters; number plates; tens rods; mini whiteboards and pens; multiplication square

### Vocabulary

divide, division, dividend, divisor, quotient, remainder

# Question 1

**1** Calculate mentally.

(a) $30 \div 3 =$ ☐ (b) $40 \div 2 =$ ☐

(c) $80 \div 4 =$ ☐ (d) $500 \div 5 =$ ☐

(e) $39 \div 3 =$ ☐ (f) $48 \div 2 =$ ☐

(g) $84 \div 4 =$ ☐ (h) $6000 \div 3 =$ ☐

## What learning will pupils have achieved at the conclusion of Question 1?

- Pupils will have practised using multiplication facts when dividing a two-digit number by a one-digit number.

## Activities for whole-class instruction

- Display two calculations, for example $65 \div 5$ and $75 \div 5$, and ask pupils, without calculating, to predict which will give the larger quotient. Give them time to discuss, to reason and explain their answer.
- Ask: *How much larger is 75 ÷ 5 than 65 ÷ 5? How can you tell without calculating the result of each division?*
- Ask pupils if they can explain why an increase of two fives in the dividend will result in an increase of just two in the quotient.
- Show pupils this array to support pupils in 'seeing' the structure of the calculation.

- Pupils should complete Question 1 in the Practice Book.

## Same-day intervention

- Write a division, such as $30 \div 6 = 5$, and use an array to represent the division, enacting the division with pupils.

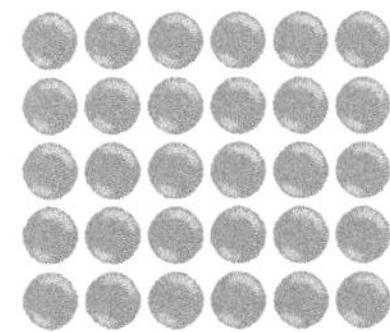

- Ensure that pupils understand the connection between the number sentence and the array, and have identified where each of the numbers in the calculation can be seen in the array.
- Now add another column to the array, and adjust the number sentence to show this, so that your number sentence now reads $36 \div 6 = 6$. Draw pupils' attention to the similarities and differences in each representation.
- Now add another column and invite pupils to adjust the number sentence accordingly.
- Ask: *What will the quotient be if another three columns are added to the array?* Can pupils tell you that the two arrays of the same height can be combined to make a third array?
- Ask: *What would happen to the quotient if the array (the dividend) increased by 6? By 12? By 18? By 24? What is the pattern?*
- Ask: *How much would the dividend need to be increased by for the quotient to increase by another five?*
- Ask pupils to use the array to explain why increasing the dividend by a multiple of the divisor will increase the quotient.

## Same-day enrichment

- Show pupils the calculation ☐ $\div 3 +$ ☐ $\div 3 = 10$ and ask them to find as many numbers as they can that fill the boxes to complete the calculation correctly.
- Ask pupils what the pairs of numbers all have in common and ask them to explain why this is always the case.

## Question 2

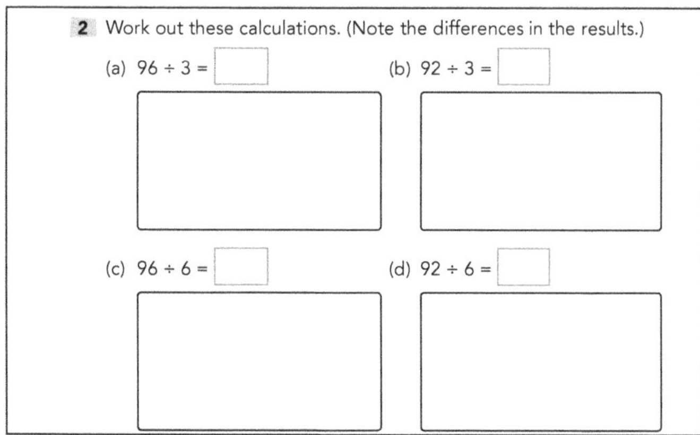

2 Work out these calculations. (Note the differences in the results.)

(a) 96 ÷ 3 = □ (b) 92 ÷ 3 = □

(c) 96 ÷ 6 = □ (d) 92 ÷ 6 = □

### What learning will pupils have achieved at the conclusion of Question 2?

- Pupils will further develop an image for dividing a two-digit number by a one-digit number.
- Pupils will understand why doubling the value of the divisor halves the value of the quotient.

### Activities for whole-class instruction

- Use place value counters to model dividing a two-digit number by a one-digit number. For example, use the calculation 72 ÷ 3. Use the place value counters to make 72 and share this into three equal piles, recording your calculation as a number sentence after you have shared out the tens (giving the number sentence 60 ÷ 3 = 2) and then again after you shared out the ones (giving the number sentence 12 ÷ 3 = 4). Then combine these two sentences to make 72 ÷ 3 = 24.
- Repeat with:

  105 ÷ 5 = □

  112 ÷ 7 = □
- Pupils should complete Question 2 in the Practice Book.
- The following task gives pupils the opportunity to explore the connections that they noticed while working on Question 2.
- Show the class an array to represent a division, for example, 24 ÷ 3 = 8.

- Ensure that pupils have connected each of the numbers in the calculation with the counters in the array. Can pupils identify the dividend, divisor and quotient in the array?
- Now move the counters so that the height of the array is doubled.

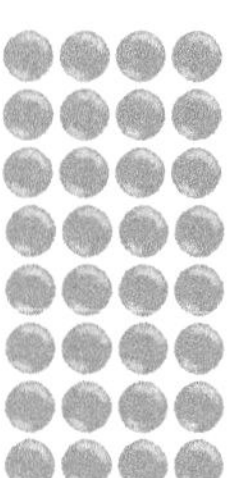

- As you move the counters, make sure that pupils notice that the number of counters is not changing, and that half of the counters are moving. Draw their attention to the way that the height has doubled, but the width has halved, and again make the connection with the numbers in the number sentences 24 ÷ 3 = 8 and 24 ÷ 6 = 4.
- Give pupils the calculation 54 ÷ 3 = 18 and ask them to discuss in pairs how they would use this to work out 54 ÷ 6.
- Gather ideas. Can pupils explain that, for a constant dividend, doubling the divisor will halve the quotient?
- Repeat for other arrays, repositioning counters to change from:

  6 × 2 to 3 × 4

  10 × 2 to 5 × 4

  8 × 6 to 4 × 12

### Same-day intervention

- Use the counters again to show a second image for division. Arrange the 24 counters into three groups, each of eight counters, and write the number sentence 24 ÷ 3 = 8.
- Now halve each group to create six groups, each containing four counters, and write the number sentence 24 ÷ 6 = 4. Check that the connections between the counters and the numbers are clear to pupils.
- Discuss with pupils how halving the dividend will double the quotient, and doubling the dividend will halve the quotient, using counters to model.

### Same-day enrichment

- Give pupils a number sentence such as 36 ÷ 3 = 12 and ask them what happens to the quotient if:
  - the dividend is doubled, but the divisor stays the same
  - the divisor is doubled, but the dividend stays the same
  - both the divisor and the dividend are doubled?
- Ask: *Why does this happen?*

# Question 3

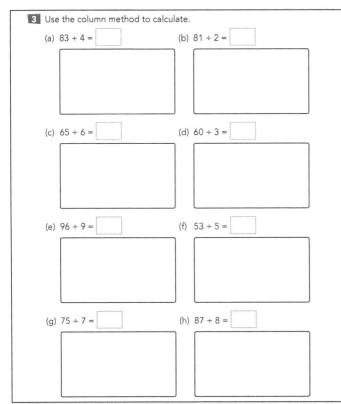

**3** Use the column method to calculate.

(a) 83 ÷ 4 = ☐ (b) 81 ÷ 2 = ☐

(c) 65 ÷ 6 = ☐ (d) 60 ÷ 3 = ☐

(e) 96 ÷ 9 = ☐ (f) 53 ÷ 5 = ☐

(g) 75 ÷ 7 = ☐ (h) 87 ÷ 8 = ☐

## What learning will pupils have achieved at the conclusion of Question 3?

- Pupils will have applied their knowledge about the use of zero as a placeholder in the context of division.

## Activities for whole-class instruction

- Show pupils the written calculation 62 ÷ 3 and ask them to show how it would look if the question were written ready to use the column method.

  **Look out for** ... the possible misconception that, using the obelus (÷), the dividend is written first, followed by the divisor, while when written using a vinculum ( ) ), the divisor comes first.

- Show a second division, 91 ÷ 3, and ask pupils to write this on mini whiteboards, using the column method, but not to solve it yet. Check that pupils have represented it correctly.
- Now show pupils the following solution to the first calculation, written using a column method. Tell them that the calculation is not correct. Ask them to work in pairs to identify where the mistake has been made and to find the correct answer.

```
  2  r2
3)6 2
  6 0
    2
```

- Do pupils notice that the zero is missing in the ones column?
- Review the method needed to find the quotient, reminding pupils how the place value counters would be shared. Stress the importance of inserting a zero as a place holder.
- Ask pupils to use the column method to solve 91 ÷ 3, imagining the movement of the place value counters if possible, but offering place value counters for pupils to use if appropriate.
- Pupils should complete Question 3 in the Practice Book.

## Same-day intervention

- Use place value counters to model the calculation 83 ÷ 4 = ☐ and record each step using the column method.
- Start by making 83 using the place value counters, and then describe the calculation as sharing this into four equal groups.

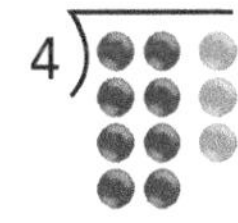

```
4)8 3
```

- Divide the counters into four groups and record that all eight of the tens, worth 80, have been used.
- Record that there are two tens in each pile.

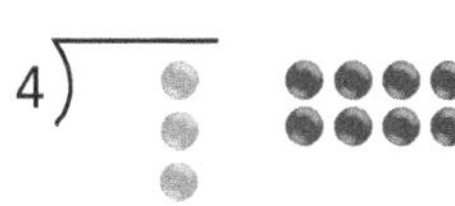

```
  2
4)8 3
  8 0
    3
```

- Now show pupils that there are three ones to share out, and demonstrate that it is not possible to share these equally between the four groups so these are all left over. Zero must be written in the ones column in the quotient and there is a remainder of 3.

```
  2 0
4)8 3
  8 0
    3
```

- Now ask pupils to carry out the division 62 ÷ 3, using place value counters and to record each step as they do. Support them with this as appropriate.

  **Look out for** ... pupils who may not yet understand the importance of writing '0' in the ones position to show that none of the ones have been shared, as you come to divide the three ones in 83 ÷ 4. It is this mistake that the question is aiming to expose and address.

## Same-day enrichment

- Ask pupils to find as many solutions as they can that will complete the first frame below, then the second and then the third:

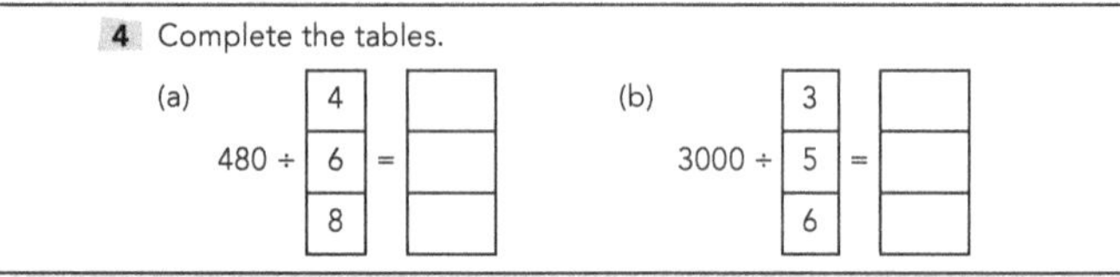

- Ask: *What do you notice about the solutions? What do you notice about the number of possible solutions? Can you explain why there are fewer solutions to each frame?*

# Question 4

**4** Complete the tables.

(a) 480 ÷ [4 / 6 / 8] = [ / / ]

(b) 3000 ÷ [3 / 5 / 6] = [ / / ]

## What learning will pupils have achieved at the conclusion of Question 4?

- Pupils will have built on their understanding of division with two-digit numbers to work with simple multiples of ten.

## Activities for whole-class instruction

- Use place value counters to make 96 and model the calculations 96 ÷ 4 = ☐ and 96 ÷ 6 = ☐ using the counters, recording your steps using the column method. Leave your working on the board and make 960 using place value counters and model 960 ÷ 4 and 960 ÷ 6, recording your steps using the column method beside the earlier calculations. (Adding a third column is, of course, a straightforward extension of the process, but you should be aware that pupils are doing this for the first time.)
- Ask pupils to discuss, in pairs, the similarities and differences, and to explain why they have happened.
- Now give pupils the number sentence 96 ÷ 8 = 12 and ask them to use it to calculate 960 ÷ 8 = ☐ and 9600 ÷ 8 = ☐.
- Gather responses and discuss pupils' methods. Ensure that pupils notice from these examples that making the dividend ten times larger, with the same divisor, will also make the quotient ten times larger.
- Pupils should complete Question 4 in the Practice Book.

## Same-day intervention

- Use the place value counters to make 12 and 120. Also, make 12 and 120 with base 10 blocks.
- Split each pile of counters and each set of blocks into two. Record the process and result as the number sentences 12 ÷ 2 = 6 and 120 ÷ 2 = 60.
- Repeat this, by splitting 12 and 120 into three, four and six piles.
- For each set of calculations, draw pupils' attention to the similarities between the 12 and the 120, and the corresponding quotients.

## Same-day enrichment

- Give pupils the frame: ☐☐0 ÷ 6 = ☐ and ask them to fill in the blanks in as many ways as they can so that the calculation does not give a remainder.
- Now give pupils the statement 'Any number that ends in a zero can be divided by five without a remainder', asking them whether they think it is true or false, and to explain why.
- You might like to follow up with 'Any number that ends in a zero cannot be divided by seven without a remainder' and again, ask them whether they think it is true or false, and to explain why.

# Question 5

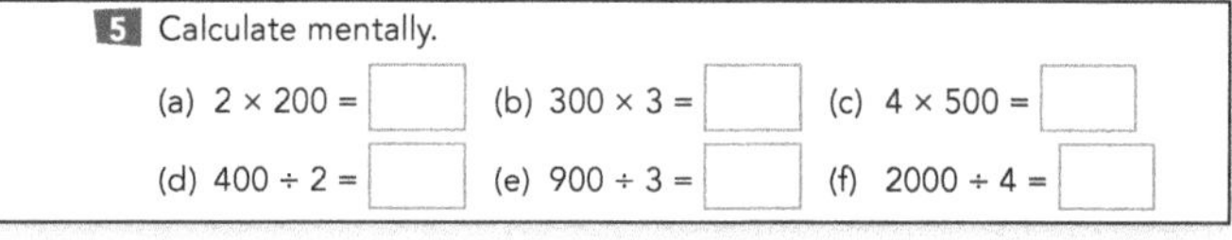

**5** Calculate mentally.

(a) 2 × 200 = ☐ (b) 300 × 3 = ☐ (c) 4 × 500 = ☐

(d) 400 ÷ 2 = ☐ (e) 900 ÷ 3 = ☐ (f) 2000 ÷ 4 = ☐

## What learning will pupils have achieved at the conclusion of Question 5?

- Pupils will have used known facts to work out multiplication and division calculations, and identify the relationship between multiplication and division.

## Activities for whole-class instruction

- Show an array with the four different calculations that it might represent, such as:

2 × 3 = 6
3 × 2 = 6
6 ÷ 3 = 2
6 ÷ 2 = 3

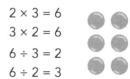

- Now show a second set of calculations:

  $20 \times 3 =$

  $30 \times 2 =$

  $60 \div 3 =$

  $60 \div 2 =$

- Ask pupils: *What should I do to the array to make it represent these number sentences?* Do pupils suggest swapping the white counters for red ones – that is, ones for tens?
- To support pupils in generalising, show two sets of number sentences using more complex numbers, such as:

  $14 \times 9 = 126$

  $9 \times 14 = 126$

  $126 \div 9 = 14$

  $126 \div 14 = 9$

- Ask pupils to complete the second set:

  $140 \times 9 =$

  $90 \times 14 =$

  $1260 \div 9 =$

  $1260 \div 14 =$

- Ask: *If I made arrays with counters to represent these two sets of number sentences, what would be the difference between the arrays?*
- Finally, give one calculation, such as $37 \times 8 = 296$, and ask pupils to write as many multiplication and division facts based on this calculation as they can.
- Gather the results in and share their strategies. Explain that, if they know one multiplication or division fact, they can use this to work out many more.
- Pupils should complete Question 5 in the Practice Book.

## Same-day intervention

- Give pupils place value counters. Ask them to make the number 800 and to split it into four equal piles. Work with them to record this as the number sentence $800 \div 4 = 200$.
- Now ask them to make 80 and to split this into four equal piles, and to record this as a number sentence.
- Finally, ask pupils to make eight and to split this into four equal piles, again recording this as a number sentence.
- Draw pupils' attention to the relationship between the three calculations and ask them to predict what might happen if 8000 were shared into four equal piles. Model this with the counters and record the number sentence.

- Give pupils this set of calculations:

  $6000 \div 2 =$

  $600 \div 2 =$

  $60 \div 2 =$

  $6 \div 2 =$

- Pupils should predict the answers and check, using place value counters.

## Same-day enrichment

- Give pupils these frames for pairs of calculations, and ask them to find as many ways as possible to fill in the boxes.
- The boxes can be filled with any of the digits from 1 to 9.

  5 × □00 = □□00

  □□00 ÷ 5 = □00

  4 × □00 = □00

  □00 ÷ 4 = □00

  49 × □00 = □00

  □00 ÷ 9 = □00

# Question 6

**6** Write a number sentence for each question.

(a) What is 82 divided by 2?

Number sentence: ____________

(b) What is 900 divided by 3?

Number sentence: ____________

(c) 640 is divided equally into 2 parts. How much is each part?

Number sentence: ____________

(d) How many 4s are there in 320?

Number sentence: ____________

## What learning will pupils have achieved at the conclusion of Question 6?

- Pupils will be able to identify the necessary number sentence and calculate the solution from a problem written in words.

## Activities for whole-class instruction

- Show the class two number sentences, 6 ÷ 3 = 2 and 6 × 3 = 18 and describe questions that would use these numbers. For example, some questions might be:
  - How many threes are there in six?
  - What number is three times larger than six?
  - How many times does three go into six? (Note that both this and the previous questions use 'times' which may be a trigger for multiplication.)
  - If six is split into three equal pieces, how large will each piece be?
  - What are three lots of six?
- Pupils should discuss and decide which calculation they would use to answer each of these questions.
- Pupils should complete Question 6 in the Practice Book.

### Same-day intervention

- Give pupils a calculation, such as 36 ÷ 3, and explain that the calculation can be said in several different ways. Explain that some ways to say the calculation are: *thirty-six divided by three, thirty-six split (or shared) equally between three*, or *How many threes are there in thirty-six?*
- Record these three different ways (and any other that you or pupils offer) with the calculation, and then give a second calculation, such as 35 ÷ 7, and ask pupils to tell you as many different ways of expressing this calculation as possible.

## Same-day enrichment

- Tell pupils that your nephew, Tom, told you that:

When we multiply, we can put the two numbers in any order, so 6 multiplied by 14 is the same as 14 multiplied by 6. That must mean that 20 divided by 5 is the same as 5 divided by 20.


- Ask: *Is Tom correct? Prove it.*

# Question 7

> **7** A patch of grass the size of a classroom can produce enough oxygen daily for 3 people. How many of the patches of grass are needed to produce enough oxygen daily for 210 people?
>
> Number sentence: ____________

### What learning will pupils have achieved at the conclusion of Question 7?

- Pupils will have identified the calculation required to solve a word problem.

## Activities for whole-class instruction

- Show pupils a 3 by 4 array and describe the mathematical relationships that it might be used to represent (3 × 4 = 12, 4 × 3 = 12, 12 ÷ 4 = 3 and 12 ÷ 3 = 4).
- Now describe a 'story' that the calculation might be used to represent.

  For example:
  - *Raj has three dogs who like getting very muddy, so he decides to buy them all some dog welly boots. How many dog welly boots does he need?*
  - *Raj has 12 dog biscuits that he shares between his three dogs. How many biscuits does each dog get?*
- Ask pupils to imagine an array with 120 dots and ask them how high and wide it might be. Gather their responses and record and describe the number sentences that they represent.
- Finally, ask them again to describe a 'story' that their 120 array and number sentence would fit.
- Pupils should complete Question 7 in the Practice Book.

### Same-day intervention

- Ask pupils to draw an alien with:
  - three eyes
  - five legs
  - two arms.
- Use all pupils' aliens to construct some multiplication facts. For example, if you are working with three pupils, find the total number of legs and represent that as a number sentence: 5 × 3 = 15.
- Tell pupils that some aliens have got together for a party, and that there are 65 legs in the room. Ask pupils: *How many aliens are at the party?*
- Work with pupils to represent this as a number sentence (have number plates, tens rods or cubes available to represent this problem).

- Tell them that some of the aliens had to leave, and there were 24 eyes in the room. Ask them to write a number sentence that could be used to find out how many aliens are still at the party and work with them, drawing connections between any different number sentences that they have written (for example, some may have written 3 × ☐ = 24 while others have written 24 ÷ 3 = ☐. If there is not more than one number sentence offered, prompt pupils to write a second number sentence, or offer one yourself).

## Same-day enrichment

- Give pupils a number sentence involving large numbers such as 370 × 40 = 14 800.
- Pupils should write three related number sentences and then a 'story' that matches each number sentence.

## Challenge and extension question

# Question 8

**8** A monkey is playing a game with 12 little monkeys to help them learn maths.

The rules are as follows.

(1) All the 12 little monkeys line up.

(2) The little monkeys in the 1st, 3rd, 5th, 7th, 9th and 11th places are given 1 banana each and then asked to leave. The other monkeys remain in the line.

(3) The little monkeys in the 1st, 3rd and 5th places in the new line are given 2 bananas each and then asked to leave. The other monkeys, again, remain in the line.

(4) The little monkeys in the 1st and 3rd places in the line are given 3 bananas each and then asked to leave the line.

(5) Finally, the remaining little monkey is given the top prize, which is 5 bananas.

If a monkey can choose any place in the line at the beginning, what place do you think it should choose in order to receive the top prize?

Answer: ______________________

This question challenges pupils to work on and model a complex problem, and to work systematically and logically. Ensure that they read through the problem carefully and ask pupils to think about the best way to tackle the problem before starting it. Provide counters or other objects that pupils could use to represent the monkeys in the problem.

Challenge pupils to see if it is always the same monkey that gets the most bananas. Extend the problem by asking pupils to predict what would happen if there were 10 monkeys or 14 monkeys instead of 12, then ask them to test their predictions.

# Unit 9.15

# Dividing a 2-digit number by a 1-digit number (5)

## Conceptual context

In this unit, pupils will revisit formal and informal methods of division, building their familiarity and fluency with the methods and deepening understanding of the mathematical process.

As with previous units, ensure that connections are made between any manipulatives being used and the written calculation strategies that they are modelling.

## Learning pupils will have achieved at the end of the unit

- Pupils will have revisited strategies for multiplying by and division of tens numbers and hundreds numbers (Q1)
- Pupils will have revisited the column method for division, developing familiarity and fluency (Q2)
- Pupils will be able to carry out division calculations to solve word problems, including where a calculation needs to be carried out to find the dividend (Q3)

### Resources

place value counters; base 10 blocks; counters; tens rods; mini whiteboards and pens

### Vocabulary

divide, division, dividend, divisor, quotient, remainder

# Question 1

**1** Calculate mentally.

(a) $30 \times 2 =$ ☐  (b) $120 \times 3 =$ ☐

(c) $9000 \div 3 =$ ☐  (d) $2000 \times 4 =$ ☐

(e) $46 \div 2 =$ ☐  (f) $300 \times 5 =$ ☐

(g) $60 \div 9 =$ ☐  (h) $1000 \times 7 =$ ☐

(i) $21 \times 3 =$ ☐  (j) $840 \div 4 =$ ☐

(k) $240 \div 6 =$ ☐  (l) $2000 \div 5 =$ ☐

## What learning will pupils have achieved at the conclusion of Question 1?

- Pupils will have revisited strategies for multiplying by and division of tens numbers and hundreds numbers.

## Activities for whole-class instruction

- Read out questions in pairs, for example say: *five times two* and then follow this with *50 times two*, or *six divided by three* and then *60 divided by three* and ask pupils to answer on their mini whiteboards. Ensure that the starting calculation in each pair is one that is accessible to pupils, as the key idea in this task is multiplying by and division of tens numbers and hundreds numbers.
- After one or two pairs of questions, ensure that all pupils are making the connection between the questions in each pair, and either ask a pupil to explain their strategy or give your own explanation. Use base 10 blocks to model the calculation to remind pupils of the conceptual connection, for example modelling $6 \div 3$ by placing six 'ones' into three piles, and then modelling $60 \div 3$ by repeating this with six 'tens'.
- Pupils should complete Question 1 in the Practice Book.

### Same-day intervention

- Give pupils pairs of calculation as in the whole-class task, but so that pupils can focus only on multiplying by and division of tens numbers and hundreds numbers, provide the answer to the first calculation.
- For example:

  $3 \times 5 = 15$ so $30 \times 5 = 150$

  $2 \times 7 = 14$ so $20 \times 7 =$ ☐

  $3 \times 7 = 21$ so $3 \times 70 =$ ☐

  $6 \div 3 = 2$ so $60 \div 3 =$ ☐

  $5 \div 5 = 1$ so $50 \div 5 =$ ☐

**Look out for** ... pupils who talk simply about 'adding a 0 to the end' without any explanation about digits moving to the column to the left and needing a zero to be a placeholder. Simply 'adding a 0' should be discouraged; it is a misconception which can cause problems when pupils meet decimals (since the 'add a 0' rule does not work with a pair such as $3 \times 1.5 = 4.5$ and $30 \times 1.5 = 45$).

## Same-day enrichment

- Challenge pupils to write five pairs of questions, following the same pattern as in the whole-class activities section (so questions are structured as, for example, '7 times 3' followed by '7 times 30') but to make the pairs such that they will be difficult for a partner to answer. They might do this by going from '7 times 3' to '70 times 30', or even from '6 times 20' to '60 times 2'. The key is for pupils to explore the impact of multiplying or dividing one part of the calculation by 10, not both. Ask pupils to decide which of them has created the most difficult set of questions, or who has written the most interesting set of questions and what makes the questions difficult or interesting.

# Question 2

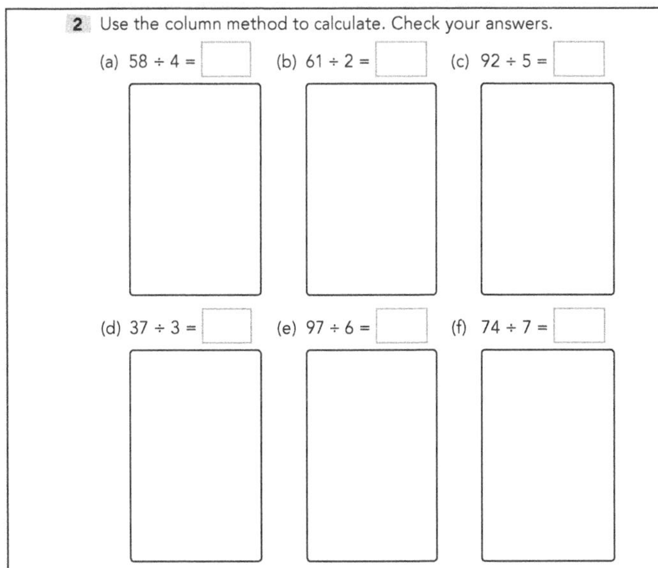

**2** Use the column method to calculate. Check your answers.

(a) $58 \div 4 =$ ☐  (b) $61 \div 2 =$ ☐  (c) $92 \div 5 =$ ☐

(d) $37 \div 3 =$ ☐  (e) $97 \div 6 =$ ☐  (f) $74 \div 7 =$ ☐

## What learning will pupils have achieved at the conclusion of Question 2?

- Pupils will have revisited the column method for division, developing familiarity and fluency.

## Activities for whole-class instruction

- Provide place value counters and show pupils a set of calculations carried out using the column method for division, but in which mistakes have been made.
- Ask pupils to work in pairs to spot which are correct and to correct any mistakes. Encourage pupils to use place value counters to set out calculations, as in previous lessons, although some pupils might be confident to carry out calculations without them. If so, check that they are not making mistakes. Pupils should not work without place value counters unless they can consistently achieve correct answers without difficulty.

```
   1 2        2 2        1 2        2 0
5)6 8      3)6 8      5)6 2      3)6 2
  5 8        6 0        5 0        6 0
  1 0        0 8        1 2          2
  1 0          6        1 0
    0          2          2
```

- Pupils should complete Question 2 in the Practice Book.

### Same-day intervention

- Use place value counters to represent and model the column method, as in the whole-class task in Unit 9.12 Question 2.
- Model a calculation such as 58 ÷ 4 by making 58 using the manipulative, and by sharing it into four equal pieces, starting by sharing the 50 and recording this in the column method. Then decompose the remaining ten into ten ones and sharing them with the eight other 'ones' into the four piles too. Make sure that you make the connection between the manipulative and the notation.

### Same-day enrichment

- Provide place value counters for pupils to use. Give pupils this calculation and ask them to work in pairs to find the missing digits.

```
   _ _
5) _ _
   8 0
   1 6
   1 6
     0
```

# Question 3

**3** Application problems.

(a) There are 96 sheep and 3 horses on a farm. How many times more sheep are there than horses?

Answer: ____________

(b) A book has 63 pages. Mo is reading 7 pages a day. In how many days' time will he finish the book?

Answer: ____________

(c) Maya helps her brother to ice some cupcakes. She ices 8 cupcakes every minute. How many minutes does it take her to ice 96 cupcakes?

Answer: ____________

(d) 39 girls and 45 boys from Year 3 went to work in an orchard. They were divided into groups of 4. How many groups were they divided into?

Answer: ____________

(e) Joe put 45 sweets into 15 sweet jars. He put 5 sweets in each jar. Did he have enough sweet jars? If your answer is yes, how many sweet jars were left over?

Answer: ____________

### What learning will pupils have achieved at the conclusion of Question 3?

- Pupils will be able to solve word problems involving division, including where the dividend needs to be found.

## Activities for whole-class instruction

- Show pupils a table with word problems, a description of the appropriate calculation, and the number sentence needed to solve the question.

For example, in the first instance, show:

| Problem | Description of method | Number sentence |
|---|---|---|
| *Sam has three times as many apples as Cassidy. Sam has 15 apples. How many apples does Cassidy have?* | Divide 15 by 3 | 15 ÷ 3 = 5 |

- Use a bar model to represent the problem.

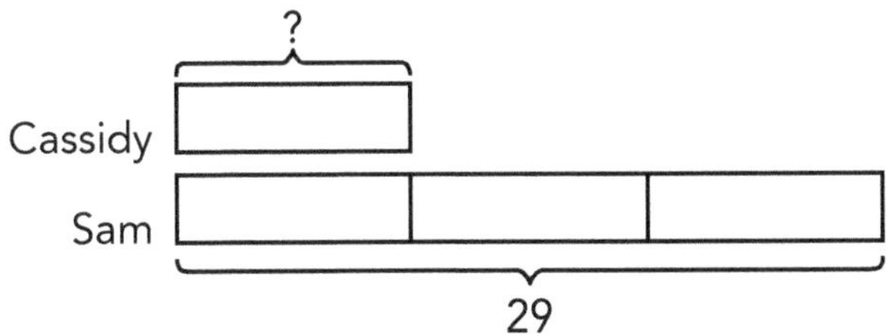


- Make the connection between the text and the image explicit to pupils, and demonstrate how the bar model can help structure thinking when solving a problem.
- Now show pupils some more word problems.

| Problem | Description of method | Number sentence |
|---|---|---|
| *Sam has 3 times as many apples as Cassidy. Sam has 15 apples. How many apples does Cassidy have?* | Divide 15 by 3 | 15 ÷ 3 = 5 |
| *Grace puts 3 apples into a bag and Emily puts two more apples in. Adam says, 'I've got 3 times as many apples as are in that bag!' How many apples does Adam have?* | | |
| *Max has 3 more apples than Matilda. Max has 7 apples. How many does Matilda have?* | | |
| *Sarah has 10 apples and Richard has 5 apples. James doesn't have any apples. They decide to share the apples between them so that each of them has the same. How many apples does each person get?* | | |

- Ask pupils to work in pairs to decide which of these problems is a division problem and draw a bar model to represent the problem. Ask them to describe how they would tackle the problem and write their solution using a number sentence (or number sentences).
- Gather the responses and draw out from pupils what prompts they used to identify the division question. Explore with them whether the question was difficult (was it more difficult than the example that you offered?), and why.
- Draw attention to the way that work had to be done to calculate the dividend (adding 5 apples and 10 apples) and the divisor (identifying that there were three people), and so neither the dividend or the divisor are 'named' in the question. Explain that this happens in one of the questions they are about to work on.
- If appropriate, ask pupils to work on the other questions in the table and to complete the descriptions and number sentences for them (see the Same-day enrichment task), but key to this task is identifying the division and which numbers to use as the divisor and the dividend.
- Pupils should complete Question 3 in the Practice Book.

## Same-day intervention

- Give pupils a calculation (or use one of the calculations from an earlier question which pupils have already solved successfully) and tell a story to represent the calculation (for example, the calculation 37 ÷ 3 might represent the story '37 apples are to be placed into bags of 3. There will be 13 bags and 1 apple will be left over'.
- Now ask pupils to tell you a story for the same calculation.
- Challenge and prompt as necessary, then tell them another story for the calculation.
- Take turns in telling the stories for the calculation, working with pupils to identify the common features of the stories and building their flexibility in thinking about division.

## Same-day enrichment

- Ask pupils to identify and describe the other calculations in the table.
- Now ask them to write a word question which might fit these number sentences:
  3 + 7 + 2 = 12
  12 ÷ 3 = 4
- Finally, ask pupils to write their own word question. The question must include division, but the division needs to be as 'hidden' as possible, and with other calculations needed to work out both the divisor and the dividend.

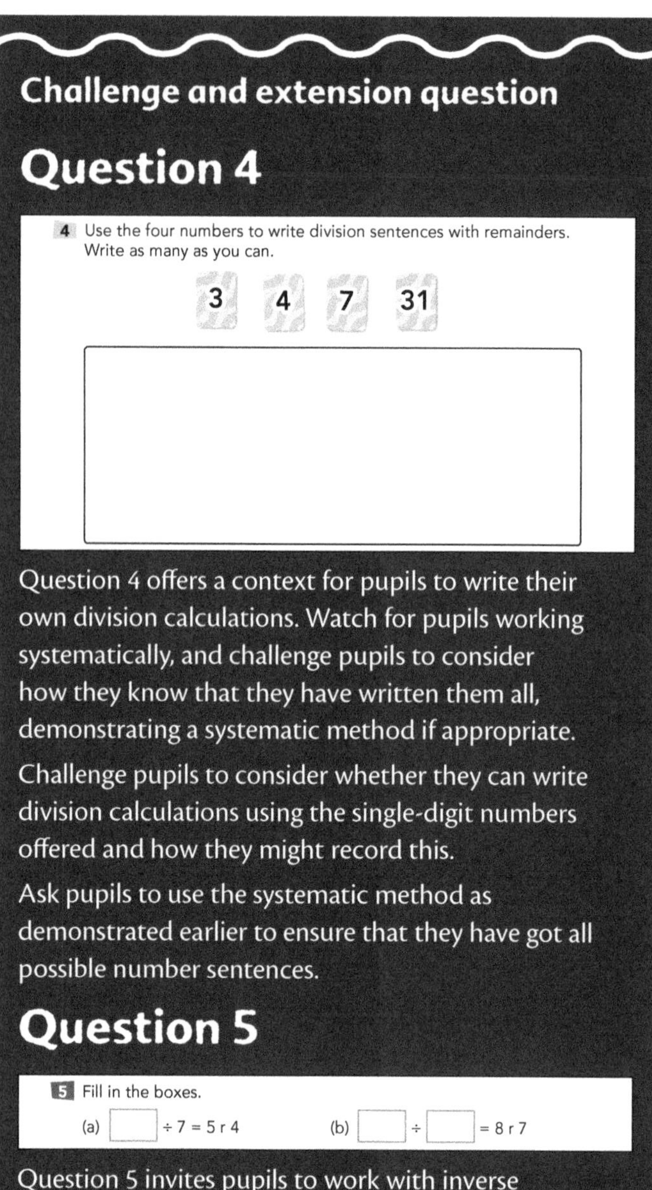

## Challenge and extension question

## Question 4

4 Use the four numbers to write division sentences with remainders. Write as many as you can.

3 4 7 31

Question 4 offers a context for pupils to write their own division calculations. Watch for pupils working systematically, and challenge pupils to consider how they know that they have written them all, demonstrating a systematic method if appropriate.

Challenge pupils to consider whether they can write division calculations using the single-digit numbers offered and how they might record this.

Ask pupils to use the systematic method as demonstrated earlier to ensure that they have got all possible number sentences.

## Question 5

5 Fill in the boxes.

(a) □ ÷ 7 = 5 r 4 (b) □ ÷ □ = 8 r 7

Question 5 invites pupils to work with inverse calculations. Offer pupils resources such as tens rods or counters to support them in unpicking the problem. Remind them of the way that division is linked with multiplication and use an array to make this link apparent (so, for the first question, the array would be 5 by 7 and there will be 4 counters 'left over').

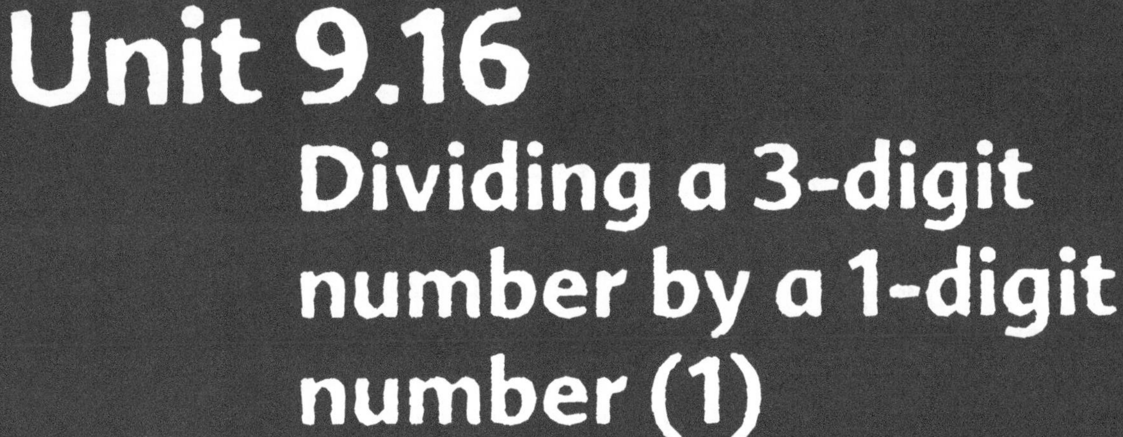

# Unit 9.16 Dividing a 3-digit number by a 1-digit number (1)

## Conceptual context

This chapter introduces the column method for dividing a three-digit number by a one-digit number.

While this uses exactly the same concept as previous chapters, the additional digit adds a layer of complexity for pupils that can lead to confusion. It is important that pupils understand that the column method is both a way of recording the mathematics that is taking place (partitioning the dividend into multiples of the divisor) and a method to support that mathematics. The explicit linking of base 10 manipulatives and the notation used on the column method is key to this and should be reinforced through the chapter.

You might like to offer some pupils place value counters to use to support them through this chapter, although it is important that these are put away as soon as they stop being necessary for pupils to access the procedure, so that abstraction and fluency can be developed.

## Learning pupils will have achieved at the end of the unit

- Pupils will be more fluent at calculating quotients, using flexible understanding of place value (Q1, Q2)
- Pupils will expand the dividend before adding the part quotients to divide a three-digit number (Q3)
- Pupils will divide a three-digit number by a single-digit using the column method (Q4)
- Pupils will use the information given in a word problem to identify the dividend and divisor before calculating the quotient (Q5)

### Resources

place value counters; counters; number plates; tens rods; mini whiteboards; money; sticky notes; **Resource 3.9.16a** Division stories; **Resource 3.9.16b** Division odd one out

### Vocabulary

multiple, divide, division, dividend, divisor, quotient, remainder

# Question 1

**1** Calculate mentally.

(a) 160 ÷ 8 = ☐ (b) 300 ÷ 6 = ☐

(c) 200 ÷ 5 = ☐ (d) 1600 ÷ 8 = ☐

(e) 3000 ÷ 6 = ☐ (f) 2000 ÷ 5 = ☐

(g) 220 ÷ 2 = ☐ (h) 840 ÷ 4 = ☐

## What learning will pupils have achieved at the conclusion of Question 1?

- Pupils will be more fluent at calculating quotients, using flexible understanding of place value.

## Activities for whole-class instruction

- Use play money (or 20 sticky notes with £10 written on each) to represent £200 in £10 units. Tell pupils that you are going to share the 20 notes between four of them (ignore the value of the notes for the time being) and ask how many notes each will get. Give time for pupils to discuss then gather in answers.
- Carry out the division, grouping the notes into four equal piles, and count in ones as you do so. Write on the board: 20 ÷ 4 = 5.
- Now explain that each note is worth £10. Remind pupils that the original 20 notes were worth £200 and ask pupils how much each pile is worth. Allow time for discussion then gather the answers.
- Write on the board, alongside the previous calculation: 200 ÷ 4 = 50. Ask pupils to discuss and explain the similarities between the two calculations, and gather responses. Ensure that pupils notice the way that place value can be used to calculate the quotient.
- Now tell them that you are going to share the £200 between five people. Ask them to work it out mentally, then tell their partner what calculation they did, and finally to write down the calculation they used on a mini whiteboard.
- Gather their responses and draw attention to any variety in the methods being used. The purpose is to encourage pupils to see the calculation flexibly, to have a range of strategies that they can use efficiently, but to ensure that they understand the way that place value can be used to inform their strategies.
- Carry out another example using £100 notes in place of the £10 notes.
- Pupils should complete Question 1 in the Practice Book.

## Same-day intervention

- Use place value counters. Give pupils six 1000 counters, six 100 counters, six 10 counters and six 1 counters.
- Ask them to use the counters to show 6000 ÷ 3, 600 ÷ 3, 60 ÷ 3 and 6 ÷ 3, and to record the calculation and the answer on mini whiteboards.
- Discuss with pupils the similarities and differences between the four calculations, then give them a second set of calculations to do that follow a similar structure, giving them only the tens place value counters.
- For example, you might give them twelve 10 counters and ask them to calculate and record 12 000 ÷ 4, 1200 ÷ 4, 120 ÷ 4 and 12 ÷ 4.
- Observe as pupils work on these questions and ensure that they understand the way that place value can be used to simplify the calculations.

## Same-day enrichment

- Give pupils a set of calculations, such as:
  - 36 000 ÷ 3 = 12 000
  - 3600 ÷ 3 = 1200
  - 360 ÷ 3 = 120
  - 36 ÷ 3 = 12
- Tell them that you have two more sets just like this, but some of the numbers have been blocked out.
  - Ask them to find the missing digits.
  - ☐☐000 ÷ ☐ = ☐000
  - 1☐☐☐ ÷ ☐ = ☐☐☐
  - ☐2☐ ÷ ☐ = ☐☐
  - ☐ ÷ 3 = ☐

  - ☐000 ÷ ☐ = ☐000
  - 5☐☐☐ ÷ ☐ = 8☐☐
  - ☐6☐ ÷ ☐ = ☐☐
  - ☐☐ ÷ ☐ = ☐

# Question 2

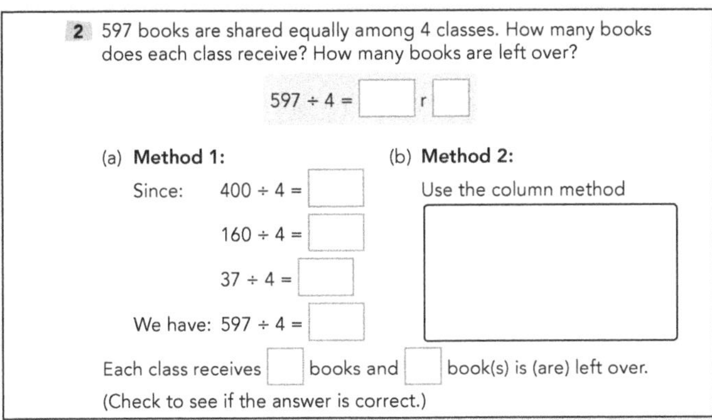

**2** 597 books are shared equally among 4 classes. How many books does each class receive? How many books are left over?

597 ÷ 4 = ☐ r ☐

(a) **Method 1:**

Since: 400 ÷ 4 = ☐

160 ÷ 4 = ☐

37 ÷ 4 = ☐

We have: 597 ÷ 4 = ☐

(b) **Method 2:**

Use the column method

Each class receives ☐ books and ☐ book(s) is (are) left over.

(Check to see if the answer is correct.)

## What learning will pupils have achieved at the conclusion of Question 2?

- Pupils use place value to divide a three-digit number by a one-digit number.

## Activities for whole-class instruction

- Show a 34 × 8 array.

- Ask: *How could we partition this array to make it easy to work out how many spots there are?* Agree that there are many ways. Agree that we usually use tens and ones when we calculate but other ways will give us the same total.
- Write 58 ÷ 4 = ☐. Pupils should use the column method to work out the answer, with one pair of pupils working on the board at the front of the room so that you can use their work as an example to explore ideas. Remind pupils that you are mainly interested in their methods as they have already found the answer in an earlier unit.
- Remind pupils that the calculation 58 ÷ 4 = 14 remainder 2 means that there are 14 fours in 58, and there are two 'left over'.
- Together as a class devise a story that the number sentence 48 ÷ 4 = 14 remainder 2 might represent.
- Ask: *What if, instead of there being 58 objects being shared between four, there were 458 being shared between four? How would that change what you need to do?* Give pupils time to discuss and share ideas.
- Make 458 with place value counters and divide them into four equal groups, talking through each step and recording it as you go along using the column method.

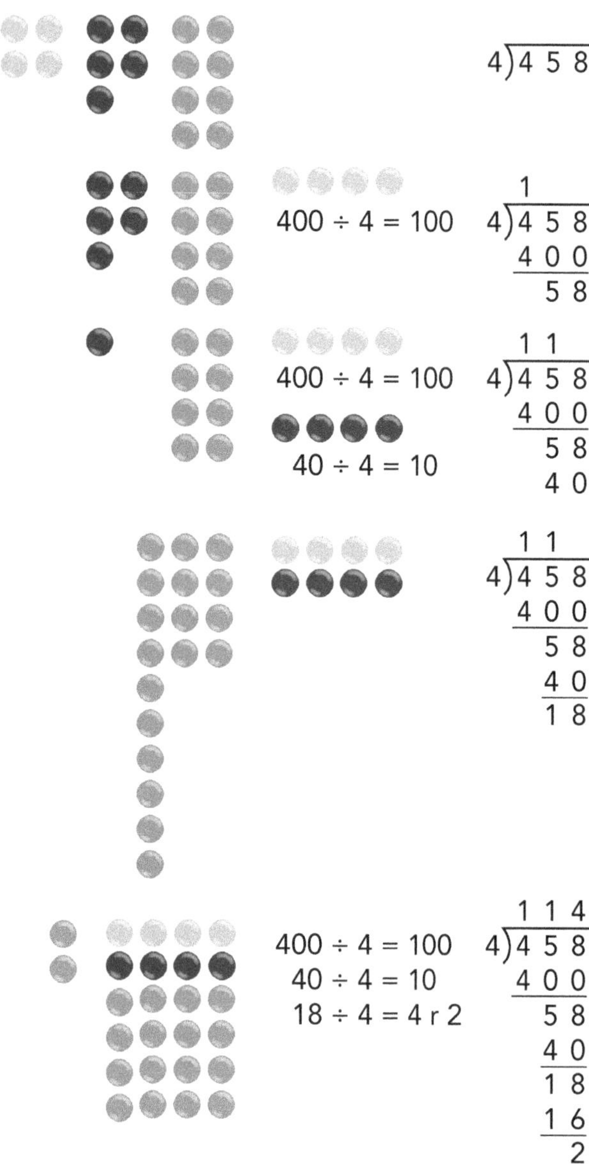


- Write 858 ÷ 4 = □ on the board and provide a sharing story to go with it, echoing the context of Question 2, saying: *858 books are given to four classes equally. How many books does each class get? How many books are left over?*
- Ask pupils to use the column method as exemplified on the board to calculate the quotient for this calculation.
- Give pupils time to work together on mini whiteboards and use the information these offer to support and explain as necessary. Supply pupils with place value counters as necessary to support them in making sense of the calculation and the notation.
- Ask pupils to look at Question 2 in the Practice Book. Draw their attention to Method 1 as an example of partitioning the dividend in a different way. Ask: *Do you think this is easier or harder than the column method? Why?*
- Pupils should complete Question 2 in the Practice Book.

## Same-day intervention

- Use place value counters to work with pupils to build up calculations. Start by sharing 8 hundreds into two equal groups. Then share 4 tens equally into the two groups. Then share 8 ones equally into the two groups. Work with pupils to find the total value of each group, and record the calculations that you have just carried out.
- Write 800 ÷ 2 = 400, 40 ÷ 2 = 20 and 8 ÷ 2 = 4.
- Now discuss with pupils the total value of the number that has been shared equally into the two groups and record this as a calculation: 848 ÷ 2 = 424.
- Gather the counters together and repeat the sharing, this time using the column method to record the movements as you make them, and making the connection between the sharing and grouping and the notation being used.
- Ensure pupils understand that the notation is a way of capturing the movement of the place value counters.

## Same-day enrichment

- Pupils should complete **Resource 3.9.16a** Division stories.

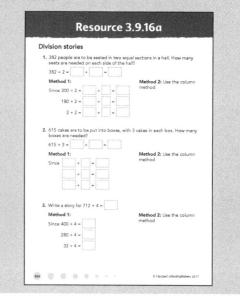

**Resource 3.9.16a**

**Division stories**

1. 382 people are to be seated in two equal sections in a hall. How many seats are needed on each side of the hall?

   382 ÷ 2 = □ + □ = □

   **Method 1:**
   Since 200 ÷ 2 = □ + □ = □
   180 ÷ 2 = □ + □ = □
   2 ÷ 2 = □ + □ = □

   **Method 2:** Use the column method

2. 615 cakes are to be put into boxes, with 3 cakes in each box. How many boxes are needed?

   615 ÷ 3 = □ + □ = □

   **Method 1:**
   Since □ + □ = □
   □ + □ = □
   □ + □ = □

   **Method 2:** Use the column method

3. Write a story for 712 ÷ 4 = □

   **Method 1:**
   Since 400 ÷ 4 = □
   280 ÷ 4 = □
   32 ÷ 4 = □

   **Method 2:** Use the column method

354 © HarperCollinsPublishers 2017

# Question 3

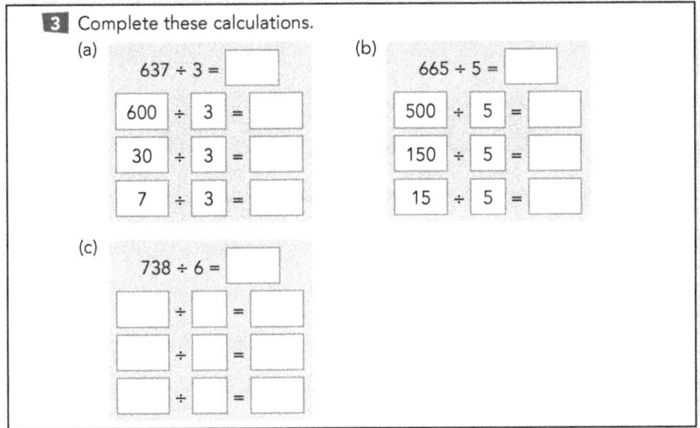
3 Complete these calculations.

(a) 637 ÷ 3 = ☐

600 ÷ 3 = ☐

30 ÷ 3 = ☐

7 ÷ 3 = ☐

(b) 665 ÷ 5 = ☐

500 ÷ 5 = ☐

150 ÷ 5 = ☐

15 ÷ 5 = ☐

(c) 738 ÷ 6 = ☐

☐ ÷ ☐ = ☐

☐ ÷ ☐ = ☐

☐ ÷ ☐ = ☐

## What learning will pupils have achieved at the conclusion of Question 3?

- Pupils will expand the dividend before adding the part quotients to divide a three-digit number.

## Activities for whole-class instruction

- Use place value counters and make a three-digit number, say 846. Explain that you're going to create three piles of equal value using all the counters. Show pupils each stage of the division, starting with the 8 hundreds, and dealing out the counters one at a time.
- Model the calculation using the counters and record the results in a grid as in Question 3, writing the result of each stage of the calculation as you go along.

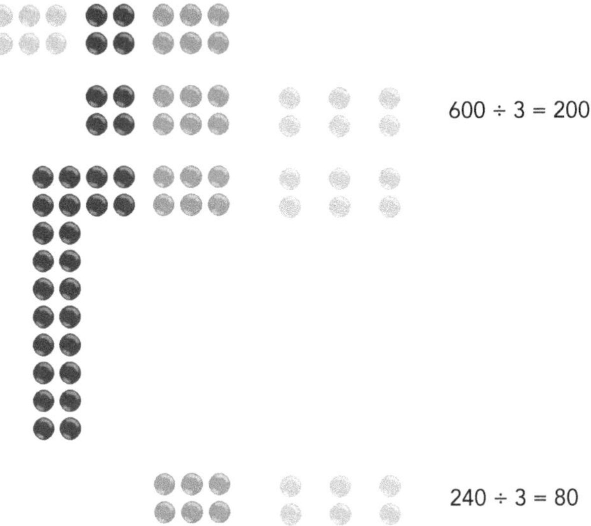


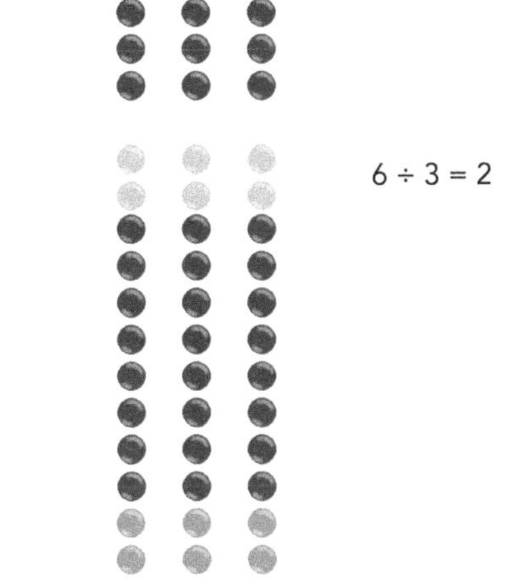


| 846 ÷ 3 = |
|---|
| 600 ÷ 3 = 200 |
| 240 ÷ 3 = 80 |
| 6 ÷ 3 = 2 |

Ensure that you start with the second row, working downwards, returning to the top row at the end.

- Discuss with pupils how the work you've done with the counters and the frame allow you to calculate the result for 846 ÷ 3, and explain that you can combine the three part quotients to find the quotient of the whole dividend.
- Demonstrate this also by showing that all the place value counters together still have the value of 846.

- Now ask pupils to imagine using place value counters to work on 746 ÷ 3 = ☐

| 746 ÷ 3 = |
|---|
| 600 ÷ 3 = |
| 140 ÷ 3 = |
| 6 ÷ 3 = |

- Ask pupils, working in pairs, to describe what would be happening to the place value counters at each stage of the frame, but not to use the counters unless absolutely necessary.
- Gather in pupils' descriptions of their calculation and use these to discuss any misconceptions or challenges.
- Pupils should complete Question 3 in the Practice Book.

## Same-day intervention

- Give pupils the place value counters and ask them to make 456.
- Ask them to divide 456 into two equal piles and to use this to complete:

400 ÷ 2 =
40 ÷ 2 =
16 ÷ 2 =

- Ask them to divide 456 into three equal piles and use the piles to complete :

300 ÷ 3 =
150 ÷ 3 =
6 ÷ 3 =

- Ask them to divide 456 into four equal piles and use the piles to complete:

400 ÷ 4 =
40 ÷ 4 =
16 ÷ 4 =

- If appropriate you might like to ask them to sketch what one pile looks like for each question in order to record the result.
- Now ask pupils to use the information to calculate 456 ÷ 2, 456 ÷ 3 and 456 ÷ 4, and ensure that they understand that this is done by combining the partitions that they have created.

## Same-day enrichment

- Ask pupils to complete **Resource 3.9.16b** Division odd one out.

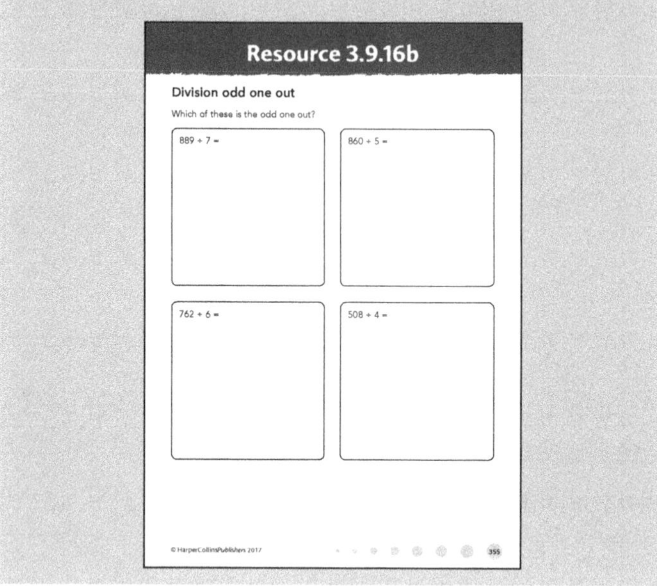

Resource 3.9.16b

Division odd one out

Which of these is the odd one out?

889 ÷ 7 =

860 ÷ 5 =

762 ÷ 6 =

508 ÷ 4 =

© HarperCollinsPublishers 2017

355

# Question 4

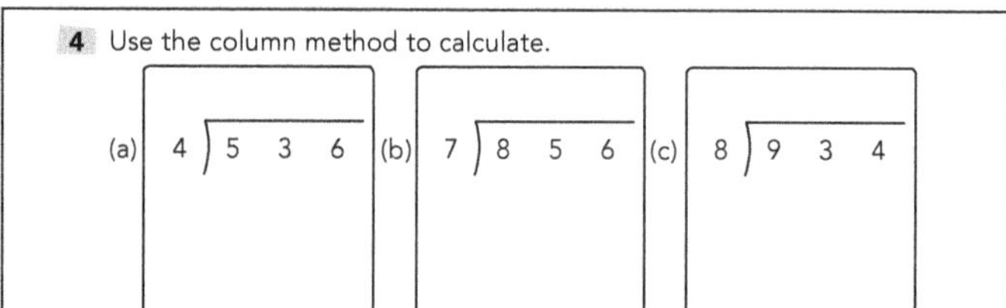

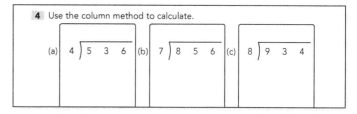

4 Use the column method to calculate.

(a) 4 ) 5 3 6 (b) 7 ) 8 5 6 (c) 8 ) 9 3 4

## What learning will pupils have achieved at the conclusion of Question 4?

- Pupils will divide a three-digit number by a single-digit using the column method.

## Activities for whole-class instruction

- Write on the board:

```
   ☐ ☐ ☐
5)6  3  5
  5  0  0
  1  3  5
  1  0  0
     3  5
     3  5
        0
```

- Ask pupils to discuss what digits might go in the boxes.
- Gather pupils' responses and use them to decide whether to set pupils onto Question 4, or whether to continue with the explanation.

- Use place value counters to make 635 and carry out the division, sharing the 635 into five piles of equal value, and drawing connections between the counters, their value and the way that this is recorded in the column method.

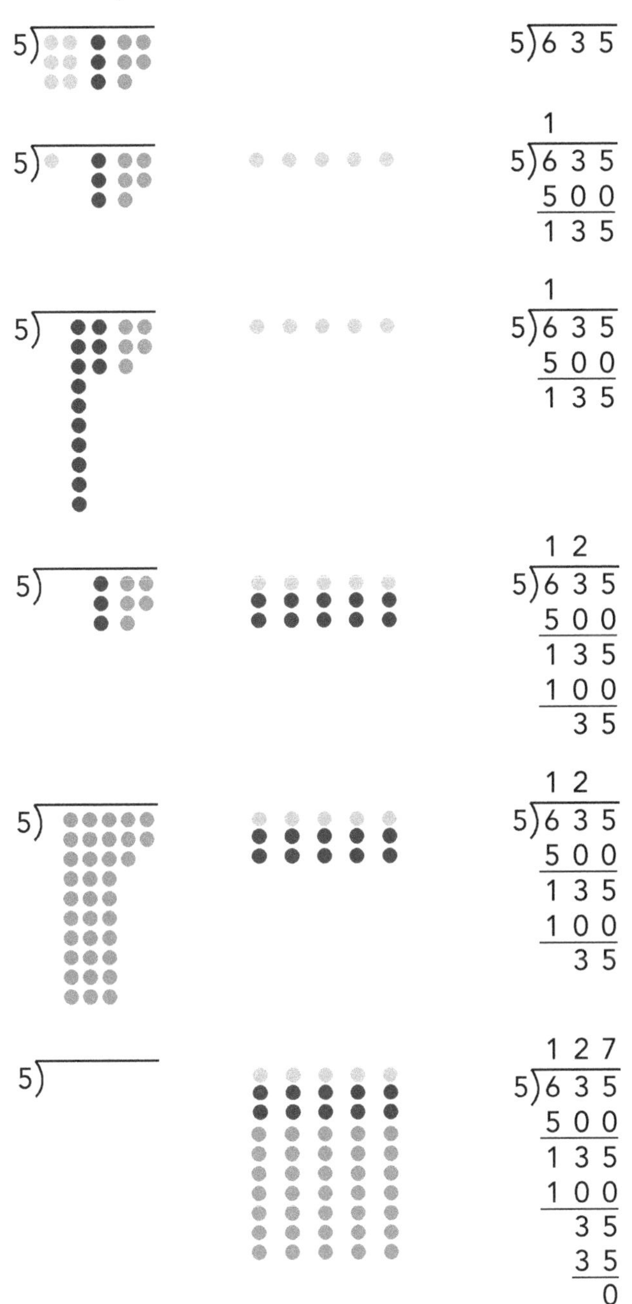


- Now use this explanation to explain the meaning of the digits in the boxes, and to work with pupils to complete the boxes.
- Before starting pupils on Question 4, you might like to model a second calculation on the board. Maintaining the 5 as a divisor, but adjusting the dividend slightly, may offer more of an insight into the structure for pupils so you might like to work with 735 ÷ 5, or 645 ÷ 5.
- Pupils should complete Question 4 in the Practice Book.

## Same-day intervention

- Use place value counters to work with pupils. Ask pupils to make 405 using the place value counters, and to share 405 into three equal groups. As they do this, record the steps that they take using the column method on the board.
- Now ask pupils to make 705 using place value counters and again to share them into three equal groups. This time ask one pupil to take your place, recording the steps made using column notation.
- Repeat this as necessary. A sequence of calculations to work on is:
  - 708, 6
  - 714, 6
  - 756, 6

## Same-day enrichment

- Ask pupils to calculate 575 ÷ 5 = ☐, 675 ÷ 5 = ☐, 775 ÷ 5 = ☐, 875 ÷ 5 = ☐ and 975 ÷ 5 = ☐, and to explain and justify the pattern in their results.

# Question 5

**5** Application problems.

(a) A group of pupils picked 266 apples from the apple trees in the school's garden. 62 apples were saved for visitors. The rest were shared equally among the 6 classes in Year 1. How many apples did each class get?

Answer: ______

(b) A school bought 4 boxes of books. Each box contains 100 books. How many books did the school buy in total? If the books are given to 5 year groups (from Year 1 to Year 5) equally, how many books will each year group receive?

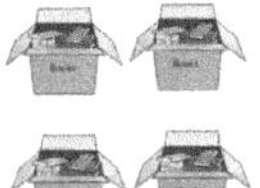

Answer: ______

## What learning will pupils have achieved at the conclusion of Question 5?

- Pupils will use the information given in a word problem to identify the dividend and divisor before calculating the quotient.

## Activities for whole-class instruction

- Act out a story about five children who all have some sweets. Bring five pupils to the front. Give them bags labelled 50, 80, 100, 120, 235.
- Explain that five children have some sweets. One of them has 80 sweets, one has 100 sweets, one has 120 sweets, one has 235 sweets and the last one has 50 sweets.
- Tell pupils that the children want to share the sweets equally between themselves. Ask them to work out how they should do this.
- Give pupils time to explore and discuss, using mini whiteboards to capture their thinking and work on their method. Then gather in their ideas.
- Draw attention to the work that was necessary to calculate the dividend before being able to calculate the quotient, and explain that this is the focus of Question 5.
- If appropriate for your class, you might also ask pupils to discuss what mistakes they think pupils might have made when working out the answer (or what mistakes *they* made) and share these with the class.
- Pupils should complete Question 5 in the Practice Book.

### Same-day intervention

- Use a frame or set of questions to work with pupils to identify what they know and what they need to know to solve the problem.
- Model this using the following question: Two teachers are sorting out their pens. Between them they have three boxes of pens. One box has 18 pens in it, one has 56 pens and the last contains 150 pens. The teachers tip the pens into a pile and share all of the pens in the pile between them fairly. How many pens does each teacher get?
- On a sheet of paper or whiteboard construct the following table:

| What do I know? | What do I need to know to answer the question? | How can I find it out? |
|---|---|---|
| | | |

  Use this frame to work with pupils to unpick the question and find a route through it.
- Leave the frame with pupils to work on similar questions where a calculation needs to be carried out to find the dividend in a calculation.

### Same-day enrichment

- Tell pupils a story about a group of six children. (This story adds an extra layer of complexity, requiring at least two calculations to find the dividend.) Five of the children have bags, all of which contain an equal number of sweets. They have 570 sweets in total. One of the children drops her bag in a muddy puddle and the sweets are lost! The six children share the remaining sweets between them. How many sweets does each child get?

### Challenge and extension question

## Question 6

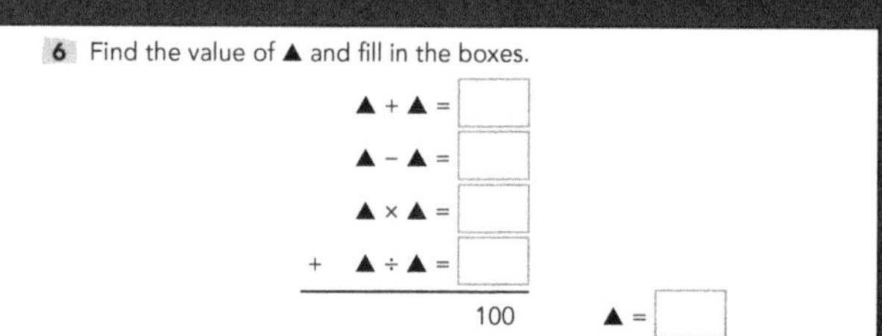

6 Find the value of ▲ and fill in the boxes.
▲ + ▲ =
▲ – ▲ =
▲ × ▲ =
+ ▲ ÷ ▲ =
100
▲ =


This question offers a complex challenge, but one in which pupils can reduce the complexity using their understanding of subtraction and division.

To support pupils in accessing the problem you might like to draw their attention to the aspects of the problem that are constant (▲ – ▲ will always be 0, and ▲ ÷ ▲ will always be 1). Do not share these with them straight away as the challenge here is finding a route through the complexity, but you might like to prompt them with suggestions or strategies.

# Unit 9.17

# Dividing a 3-digit number by a 1-digit number (2)

## Conceptual context

Building on Unit 9.16, this unit consolidates pupils' use of the column method for dividing a three-digit number by a one-digit number. It probes more deeply into the mathematics that underpins the process, while also building fluency.

It is important that the method is not simply taught as a routine and care should be taken to reinforce the structure that underpins the method through the use of manipulatives. Place value counters are particularly useful in making this structure visible, and may be referred to throughout pupils' mental calculations as a way to support. Asking pupils to 'imagine working this out with place value counters' is a prompt that may support when pupils are stuck, without having to reach for the counters themselves.

## Learning pupils will have achieved at the end of the unit

- Pupils will have developed further fluency with calculating mentally (Q1)
- Pupils will have connected multiplication and division and used this to find the greatest multiple less than a given number (Q2)
- Pupils will have used the column method for dividing a three-digit number by a one-digit number (Q3, Q4, Q5, Q6)
- Pupils will have used division to solve word problems (Q6)

### Resources

place value counters; counters; number plates; tens rods; mini whiteboards and pens; sticky notes; **Resource 3.9.17** Division – column method

### Vocabulary

multiple, divide, division, dividend, divisor, quotient, remainder

# Question 1

**1** Calculate mentally.

(a) 80 ÷ 4 = □    (b) 600 ÷ 6 = □

(c) 510 − 480 = □    (d) 39 ÷ 3 = □

(e) 900 ÷ 3 = □    (f) 60 − 37 = □

(g) 23 × 4 = □    (h) 25 × 6 = □

## What learning will pupils have achieved at the conclusion of Question 1?

- Pupils will have developed further fluency with calculating mentally.

## Activities for whole-class instruction

- Present the class with a set of calculations:
  95 ÷ 5 = □
  95 + 5 = □
  95 − 5 = □
  95 × 5 = □
  and ask them to discuss the following questions.
- Ask: *Which is the simplest calculation? Which is the most difficult? Which order would you tackle the calculations? For which of the calculations is the order important? Which, if any of the calculations, is helpful for finding 950 + 5? 950 ÷ 5?*
- Use the discussions to support pupils in making connections between the different strategies and operations, and to view the calculations flexibly rather than mechanistically resorting to one method.
- Pupils should complete Question 1 in the Practice Book

## Same-day intervention

- Identify which of the operations pupils find particularly challenging. Column division combines multiplication facts and two-digit subtraction to reach an answer, so these operations should be a focus here.
- Use manipulatives to model and work on areas that pupils need particular support with, aiming for efficient methods to calculate.

## Same-day enrichment

- Present pupils with these calculations:
  □□ + ▲ = 92
  □□ ÷ ▲ = 22
  □□ × ▲ = 352
  □□ − ▲ = 84
- Explain to pupils that □□ represents a two-digit number where both digits are the same (such as 11, 22, 33...) and ▲ represents a single-digit number.
- Ask pupils to work out the value of □ and ▲.

# Question 2

**2** What is the greatest number you can write in each box?

(a) 6 × □ < 38    (b) 5 × □ < 32    (c) 8 × □ < 85

(d) 4 × □ < 25    (e) 7 × □ < 60    (f) 3 × □ < 17

## What learning will pupils have achieved at the conclusion of Question 2?

- Pupils will have connected multiplication and division and used this to find the greatest multiple less than a given number.

## Activities for whole-class instruction

- This question revisits a structure practised in 9.11: finding the greatest multiple of a single-digit number that is less than a given value.
- In 9.11, an array supports the use of skip-counting, moving towards using knowledge of multiplication to find a solution, and you might like to reuse that whole-class task here.
- The following game gives pupils an opportunity to practise their use of multiples, and to consider the size of those multiples.
- Ask pupils to draw a set of five squares like this: □□□□□.
- Tell them that you will roll a dice, and that the number you roll will be the multiplication table you are going to work with for this round. Roll the dice and record the value on the board.
- Roll the dice again. Pupils should multiply the value by the number on the board and write their answer in one of their squares. Explain that they have to choose a square carefully because they are only able to write the numbers in ascending order in the squares. If pupils cannot fit the result in their grid, then they are out.
- For example, if your initial roll selected the 5 times table, which was followed by rolling a 6 the grid might look like this:

| | | | | |
|---|---|---|---|---|
| | | | | 30 |

Rolling a 3 next might look like this:

| | | 15 | | 30 |
|---|---|---|---|---|

Then rolling a 4 would give:

| | | 15 | 20 | 30 |
|---|---|---|---|---|

- If a 5 is now rolled, there is nowhere to place this and the pupil is out.
- The winner of the game is the last pupil who is able to place their number.
- The intention is to give pupils a context in which to practise working with multiples of a given number, and to consider the size of that multiple.
- Pupils should complete Question 2 in the Practice Book.

## Same-day intervention

- Use number plates or tens rods and explain to pupils that, using only the threes plate/rod, you want to get as close to 20 as possible.
- Ask them to predict how many threes plates/rods they will need, then count up with them to see how close their estimate was. As you count up, also mark the jumps on a number line.
- Work with pupils and draw their attention to the efficiencies of using known facts to minimise the effort needed; to take short cuts. Use the number line to record these known facts. It might be, for example, that pupils know that $5 \times 3 = 15$, and so you can make this in one jump, then consider how many more jumps are possible before reaching 20.
- Work with some more questions and encourage pupils to use the number line to calculate, then to use the tiles or rods to check their calculation.

## Same-day enrichment

- Ask pupils to fill in the blanks with the highest possible whole number (the numbers can have more than one digit).

$3 \times \square < 29$

$3 \times \square < 299$

$3 \times \square < 2999$

$3 \times \square < 29\,999$

- Ask them to describe and share strategies they are using to calculate their answer, and to explain any pattern that they notice.

# Question 3

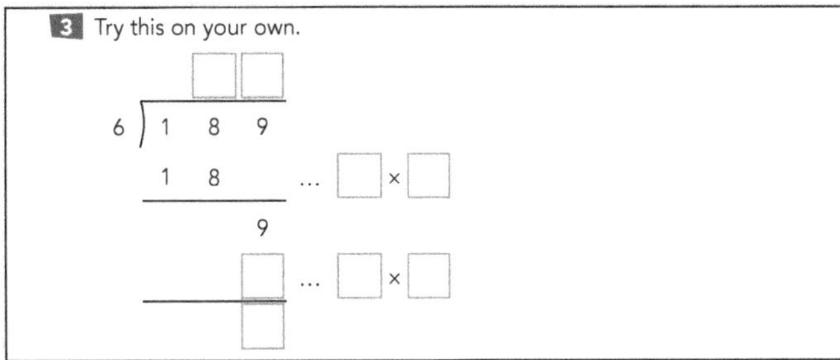


## What learning will pupils have achieved at the conclusion of Question 3?

- Pupils will have used the column method for dividing a three-digit number by a one-digit number.

## Activities for whole-class instruction

- Write a division calculation on the board, but cover over some of the digits using sticky notes or taping paper onto the board.

For example:

```
3)4 7 1
  3 0 0
  1   1
      0
    2
    2 1
      0
```

- Invite pupils to work on the problem in pairs, using mini whiteboards, then to come to the board and predict what digit is under a sticky note.
- As they reveal it, they should explain how they know and what that digit represents.
- Use this information from the class to assess where pupils are having difficulties, and which pupils you need to offer more support to during the questions.
- Repeat with a different division. You might like to ask pupils to carry out their own division calculations and cover up three or four digits for the rest of the class to work on.
- Pupils should complete Question 3 in the Practice Book.

## Same-day intervention

- Give pupils place value counters and ask them to carry out the calculations on **Resource 3.9.17** Division – column method.

**Resource 3.9.17**

Division – column method

1. $2\overline{)484}$ with quotient □42
2. $3\overline{)484}$ with quotient 16□
3. $4\overline{)712}$ with quotient □□8
4. $5\overline{)712}$ with quotient □□□

© HarperCollinsPublishers 2017

- As pupils enact the calculation with the place value counters, they should complete the boxes in the frame.

## Same-day enrichment

- Give pupils this calculation to work on. Ask them to find the digits behind each of the sticky notes.

```
  1 1 4
 )□ □ □
  6 0 0
    8 4
    6 0
    2 4
    2 4
      0
```

# Question 4

**4** First decide how many digits the quotient has, and then calculate.

(a) $3\overline{)624}$ (b) $8\overline{)936}$

(c) $2\overline{)321}$ (d) $4\overline{)5636}$

## What learning will pupils have achieved at the conclusion of Question 4?

- Pupils will have used the column method for dividing a three-digit number by a one-digit number.

## Activities for whole-class instruction

- Put pupils in pairs and tell them that one of them will be answering the question, while the other watches and checks that they are using the correct method.
- Give the calculation 747 ÷ 3 = □ and ask pupils to solve it using the column method.

  Allow time, then share ideas and discuss any problems.
- Ask pupils to see what happens with a four-digit dividend. Ask them to solve 3912 ÷ 3 = □.

  Gather responses, addressing any problems.
- Pupils should complete Question 4 in the Practice Book.

## Same-day intervention

- In this task, pupils roll a dice three times and record the numbers rolled. They then use the three digits generated to make a three-digit number and make it out of place value counters. This is their dividend.
- Give pupils a number which will act as the divisor. Ensure that the number you choose is less than the first digit of their number.
- Ask pupils to share their number into equal groups, and work with them to record the movements of the counters, using correct column notation as necessary.
- As pupils progress, ask them to not make the number using the place value counters, but to imagine the counters and just write out the column method, checking with the counters if necessary.

## Same-day enrichment

- Ask pupils to roll a dice four times and record their rolls.
- Tell them that the smallest number is the divisor, and that they should arrange the remaining digits to make a dividend of their choice.
- They should then find the quotient for their calculation, working with a partner and taking it in turns to calculate.
- As an alternative, their partner could arrange the digits to make the dividend, making it as difficult as possible!

# Question 5

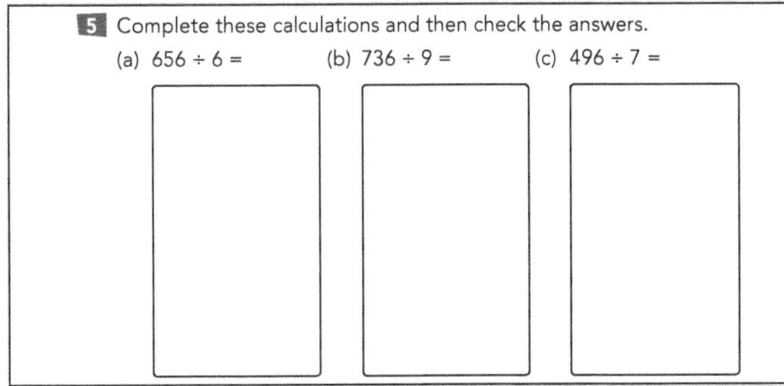
5 Complete these calculations and then check the answers.

(a) 656 ÷ 6 =    (b) 736 ÷ 9 =    (c) 496 ÷ 7 =

## What learning will pupils have achieved at the conclusion of Question 5?

- Pupils will have practised calculating a quotient using the column method.

## Activities for whole-class instruction

- Ask pupils to complete these calculations:

  648 ÷ 2 = ☐

  648 ÷ 3 = ☐

  648 ÷ 4 = ☐

  648 ÷ 5 = ☐

  648 ÷ 6 = ☐

  648 ÷ 7 = ☐
- For efficiency, you might like to ask pupils in particular sections of the room to work on just one calculation. The intention here is to give some practice at carrying out a division, but also to gather solutions to unpick some of the structure behind the notation.
- Gather the answers and point out to pupils that all of the quotients have three digits, except for the last one.
- Ask pupils to discuss in pairs why this might be. Can pupils explain that, for example 'six hundred and something' cannot be divided by seven one hundred or more times – there cannot be a hundred or more groups of seven in a number that is less than 700; so the quotient must be a two-digit number.
- Ask: *If you divide six hundred and something into seven equal groups, will there be at least 100 in each group? What about if you divided three hundred and 55 by four – will there be at least 100 in each group?*
- Challenge pupils to find any three-digit number that can be divided by a single digit that is bigger than the first of its three digits that will give a three-digit answer. Can they explain why they cannot find one?
- Pupils should complete Question 5 in the Practice Book.

## Same-day intervention

- Use place value counters or blocks to work with pupils to carry out some division calculations.
- Use a sharing image for division and place the blocks into the appropriate number of equal piles – further details for this are in the main task for unit.
- Ensure that pupils make the connection between the practical task with the manipulative and the notation being used in the calculation. If appropriate, you might like to use a sequence of calculations such as 522 ÷ 3, 523 ÷ 3 and 524 ÷ 3 and discuss with pupils why the remainder changes in the way that it does.

## Same-day enrichment

- Ask pupils to take one of the examples from Question 5 and to annotate it so that someone who does not understand the column method for division could read their notes and make sense of what they have done.

# Question 6

6 Application problems.

(a) A dragonfly eats 4200 mosquitoes in a week. How many mosquitoes does it eat each day?

Answer: ______

(b) (i) 480 toy cars were divided equally into 5 large boxes. How many toy cars were placed into each large box?

Answer: ______

(ii) If the toy cars in each large box were put into 8 small boxes equally, how many toy cars were put into each small box?

Answer: ______

## What learning will pupils have achieved at the conclusion of Question 6?

- Pupils will have practised calculating a quotient using the column method.
- Pupils will have used division to solve word problems.

## Activities for whole-class instruction

- Show pupils these calculations:

  480 ÷ 5 = ☐

  480 + 5 = ☐

  480 − 5 = ☐

  480 × 5 = ☐

  and the following questions:

  *Sadiq has £480. He has £5 more than Alf. How much money does Alf have?*

  *Sadiq's four friends also have £480 each. How much money do they have in total?*

  *Sadiq has £5 less than Lin. How much money does Lin have?*

  *Sadiq buys five pairs of roller skates. Each pair costs the same amount of money. How much does one pair of roller skates cost?*
- Ask pupils to match each calculation to a question.
- Ask pupils to describe how they know which operation to use, and use their descriptions for the division question to write another division question such as: 'Anne has 252 apples. She puts five apples into each bag. How many bags of apples will she make?'
- Ask pupils how they know which of the numbers is the divisor and which is the dividend. Ensure that, although it is true for all of the questions that they are tackling at the moment, they are not simply using the largest number as the dividend but have an understanding that the dividend is the number that is being shared, while the divisor represents the groups into which it is being shared.
- Pupils should complete Question 6 in the Practice Book.

## Same-day intervention

- Show pupils this calculation:

  $27\overline{)9\ 4\ 5}$

- Tell them that they do not need to work out the answer, but do need to help three children who are deciding what this calculation means. (The numbers are deliberately large and 'awkward' so that pupils are not focused on working out the answer.)
- Say: Tilly says that this should be read as '945 divided by 27'. Benedict says that it should be '27 divided by 945'. Elinor says that both Benedict and Tilly are correct, and that it means both of those things.
- Ask pupils to discuss who is correct and how they know.
- The purpose of this task is to provide information about the way that pupils see division, their understanding of division and any misconceptions (so that you can support them when answering worded questions), rather than to practise the process of dividing.
- Work with pupils to construct many different questions around the same division question. You might like to ask pupils to represent the division 945 ÷ 27 graphically.

## Same-day enrichment

- This question is more complex than other application problems that pupils have tackled. They should be encouraged to work through it in stages, taking one step at a time.
- Give pupils the question and ask them to work on it in pairs:

  *Sam and Cassidy are sorting out their toys. They each have four new big boxes to keep their toys safe.*

  *At the moment Sam has 7 small, scruffy boxes, each containing 12 toys.*

  *Cassidy has 5 small boxes, but she has 16 more toys in total than Sam does.*

  *They put all of their toys together in the new boxes, so that there is the same number of toys in each box.*

  *How many toys are there in one of the new boxes?*

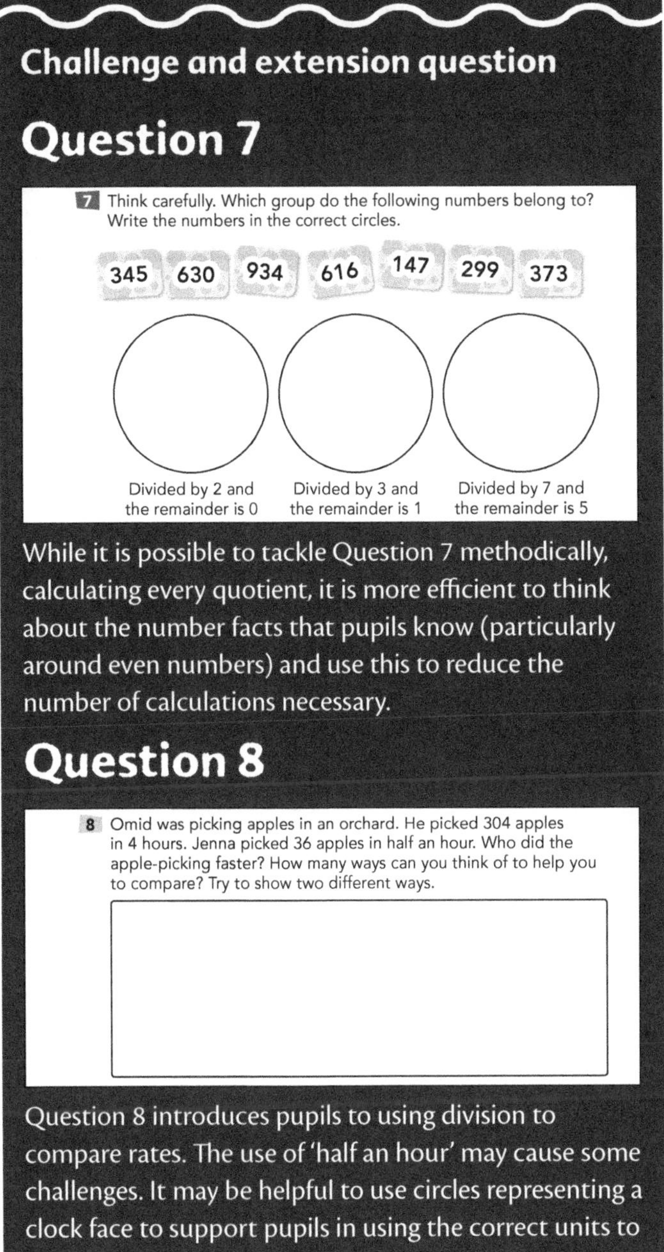

## Challenge and extension question

# Question 7

7 Think carefully. Which group do the following numbers belong to? Write the numbers in the correct circles.

345 630 934 616 147 299 373

Divided by 2 and the remainder is 0

Divided by 3 and the remainder is 1

Divided by 7 and the remainder is 5

While it is possible to tackle Question 7 methodically, calculating every quotient, it is more efficient to think about the number facts that pupils know (particularly around even numbers) and use this to reduce the number of calculations necessary.

# Question 8

8 Omid was picking apples in an orchard. He picked 304 apples in 4 hours. Jenna picked 36 apples in half an hour. Who did the apple-picking faster? How many ways can you think of to help you to compare? Try to show two different ways.

Question 8 introduces pupils to using division to compare rates. The use of 'half an hour' may cause some challenges. It may be helpful to use circles representing a clock face to support pupils in using the correct units to make the comparison.

# Unit 9.18
# Dividing a 3-digit number by a 1-digit number (3)

## Conceptual context

This unit explicitly focuses on multiplication and division as inverse operations to find unknown values and to use as a checking mechanism. The structure of the inverse relationship is visible in arrays; a 7 by 8 array, for example, might be considered as seven rows of eight counters, making a total of 56 counters, or it might be seen as 56 counters arranged into seven rows, each one eight counters long. Arrays, therefore, reveal that multiplication and division are not different things, but are the same relationship viewed from different perspectives. Pupils should understand both of these interpretations in order to deepen their understanding of the relationship between multiplication and division.

## Learning pupils will have achieved at the end of the unit

- Pupils will have used the inverse relationship between multiplication and division (Q1, Q2, Q3, Q4)
- Pupils will have reasoned, using the relationship between the size of the divisor and the dividend, to check their answer (Q3)
- Pupils will have used the image of arrays to reason mathematically about division (Q5, Q6)

### Resources

place value counters; counters; number plates; tens rods; mini whiteboards and pens; sticky notes; calculators

### Vocabulary

multiple, divide, division, dividend, divisor, quotient, remainder, inverse

# Question 1

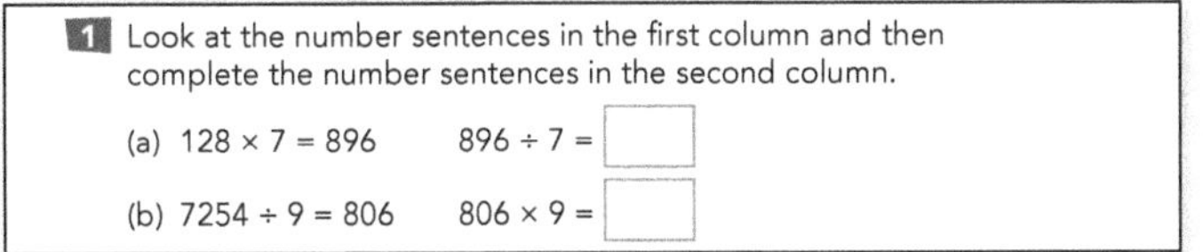
1 Look at the number sentences in the first column and then complete the number sentences in the second column.

(a) 128 × 7 = 896 896 ÷ 7 = □

(b) 7254 ÷ 9 = 806 806 × 9 = □

## What learning will pupils have achieved at the conclusion of Question 1?

- Pupils will have used the inverse relationship between multiplication and division to calculate unknown values.

## Activities for whole-class instruction

- Show pupils a simple array such as:

- Ask pupils to write on their mini whiteboards all of the associated multiplication and division facts that they know.

  Ensure that they are able to write:

  4 × 5 = 20

  5 × 4 = 20

  20 ÷ 4 = 5

  20 ÷ 5 = 4
- Select some pupils to explain what, for example, 20 ÷ 4 = 5 means in the given array.
- Now ask them to imagine a giant array that is 172 wide and 5 high. It contains 860 dots.
- Ask the class to work in pairs to write down all of the multiplication and division facts that they can about this new array.
- Again, ask pupils to explain what the different elements of the calculation mean with reference to the array. Sketch a rectangle on the board and label the sides 172 and 5 to support pupils with this.
- Ensure that pupils understand that the four facts associated with the array are different ways to express the same relationship, and that this will work with any multiplication or division calculation.
- Pupils should complete Question 1 in the Practice Book.

## Same-day intervention

- Work with pupils to identify some multiplication facts and division that they are comfortable with, for example 7 × 9 = 63.
- Use one of these facts to work on different representations with pupils, asking them to represent the fact using manipulatives – a number line, an array, a group of tens rods or number plates and any other with which they are familiar.
- Explore the way in which each of these representations can be used to represent division, and make the connections between the notation and the different representations.
- Move from this particular case to a more challenging two-digit by one-digit calculation, such as 17 × 3.
- Ask pupils to write down the three other number sentences that are linked to this and use their answers to assess whether they are confident to move forward.
- Extend to a three-digit × one-digit example and find the family of related number sentences.

## Same-day enrichment

- Ask pupils to imagine an array of 128 counters, arranged in eight columns.
- Ask them to calculate how many rows there are.
- Now ask pupils to imagine a different arrangement of 128 counters. Say: *If they were to be arranged in four columns, what would change? How about if they were to be arranged in 16 columns?*
- Ask pupils to find as many different ways of arranging the 128 counters as they can, recording each of their solutions as a division starting 128 ÷ □ = □.
- Next, pupils should list the other three members of the 'family' that is related to their division sentences. For example, for 128 ÷ 8 = 16 they should list:

  128 ÷ 16 = 8

  16 × 8 = 128

  8 × 16 = 128

## Question 2

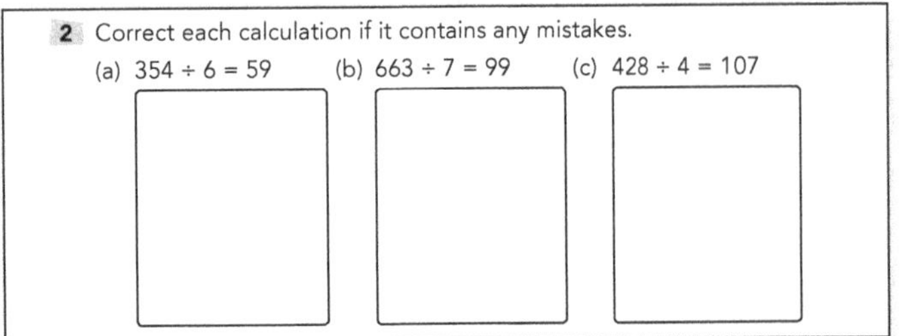
2 Correct each calculation if it contains any mistakes.

(a) 354 ÷ 6 = 59 (b) 663 ÷ 7 = 99 (c) 428 ÷ 4 = 107

### What learning will pupils have achieved at the conclusion of Question 2?

- Pupils will have used the inverse relationship between multiplication and division to check their answers.

### Activities for whole-class instruction

- This question builds on the skills practised in Question 1.
- Pupils should understand that they could use multiplication as a checking procedure to see if there is a mistake in a division sentence – that they do not actually need to divide.
- Write a division calculation on the board, but cover the dividend using paper or sticky notes, for example:

  ÷ 5 = 37
- Tell pupils that the answer under the sticky notes is one of:

  222

  322

  272
- Ask pupils to estimate which of these might be correct, then give them time to discuss and refine their answer.
- Gather some ideas, then reveal the tens digit to reduce the options.
- Again, ask pupils if this helps them to refine their estimate.
- The purpose of the task is not, in the first instance, to calculate, but to look for clues using inverse operations.
- Pupils should complete Question 2 in the Practice Book.

### Same-day intervention

- Show pupils three piles of place value counters, each containing one 100, seven 10s and one 1.
- Tell them that you have just shared some counters out into three equal piles, but have forgotten what the total value was.
- Say that you think you had 213 before you shared them, and ask pupils to discuss if this could be correct.
- Work with them and explain that it could not be the case, because there is one 100 in each pile, so the total must be more than 300.
- Choose other totals that you might have started with. Ask if it could be more than 400 or more than 600. Use pupils' ideas to discuss checking strategies for division.
- Finally (if necessary), say to pupils that you remember that it was 513, and discuss with them how you could use the multiplication to find that value.

### Same-day enrichment

- Show pupils this column calculation with sticky notes covering the dividend.

- Tell pupils that the quotient has only the digits 4, 2 and 0 once each, but not necessarily in that order.
- Ask pupils to find as many possible three-digit numbers that could be under the sticky notes that would give a quotient with no remainder.

  (One possible solution is 612, since 612 ÷ 3 = 204. Pupils can arrive at this by realising that the quotient multiplied by three has to have three digits, and use this to limit the possible solutions.)

## Question 3

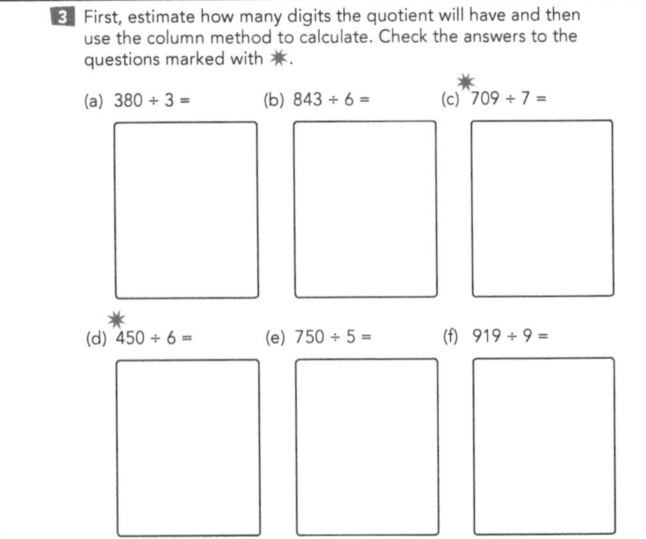
3 First, estimate how many digits the quotient will have and then use the column method to calculate. Check the answers to the questions marked with ✷.

(a) 380 ÷ 3 = (b) 843 ÷ 6 = (c) ✷ 709 ÷ 7 =

(d) ✷ 450 ÷ 6 = (e) 750 ÷ 5 = (f) 919 ÷ 9 =

### What learning will pupils have achieved at the conclusion of Question 3?

- Pupils will have used the inverse relationship between multiplication and division to check their answers.

- Pupils will have reasoned, using the relationship between the size of the divisor and the dividend, to check their answer.

## Activities for whole-class instruction

- Write on the board:

  4)3 8 7    2)3 8 7    3)3 8 7    5)3 8 7

- Ask pupils to identify, without calculating, which of the quotients will have two digits, and which will have three.
- Can pupils explain that, for example '300 and something' cannot be divided by four one hundreds or more times – there cannot be a hundred or more groups of four in a number that is less than 400 – so the quotient must be a two-digit number.
- Show that three 100 place value counters cannot be divided into four groups that have a 100 counter in each – that all the 100 counters have to be exchanged for 10s counters. Therefore, the answer will not have anything in the hundreds column – the quotient will only have two digits. This demonstration, first shown in the previous unit, might need to be repeated a few times.
- Gather pupils' responses and strategies and ask them to write on mini whiteboards a calculation where they are dividing 732 and will get a two-digit quotient. Ask them to write a division for 732 with a three-digit quotient.
- Explain to pupils that the first digit in the dividend, and its size relative to the divisor, is key to knowing the number of digits in the quotient.
- Pupils should complete Question 3 in the Practice Book.

### Same-day intervention

- Give pupils a set of calculations with three answers to choose from, for example:

  Which of these numbers could be the answer to 549 ÷ 3?

  183    93    381

- Ensure that at least one of the three options has the wrong number of digits, and use this to discuss with pupils as a strategy to eliminate incorrect answers.
- Once they have eliminated the incorrect solutions, work with pupils (using place value counters if appropriate) to check the accuracy of the final calculation.
- The intention is to build a sense of number, to give pupils strategies to consider the reasonableness of their solution, as well as to practise calculating quotients accurately.

## Same-day enrichment

- Give pupils the frame:

  □□□ ÷ □

- Tell pupils that they have to fill the boxes with four of the five digits: 2, 3, 4, 5, 6, to give a calculation where the quotient has two digits and no remainder. (One possible solution is 352 ÷ 4.)
- Ask pupils how many different arrangements they can find.
- Ask pupils to reflect on whether they checked every possible arrangement, or did they discard some? Ask how they knew which arrangements were worth trying and which were not.

# Question 4

**4** Fill in the boxes.

(a) □ × 7 = 266    (b) 9 × □ = 486

(c) □ ÷ 6 = 350    (d) 384 ÷ □ = 8

## What learning will pupils have achieved at the conclusion of Question 4?

- Flexible thinking will have been developed, exploiting the relationship between multiplication and division to reason and calculate efficiently.

## Activities for whole-class instruction

- Give a pupil a calculator and ask them to type in a two-digit number, multiply it by five and give you the result.
- When they do, tell them the number that they initially typed in (when dividing by five mentally, a useful strategy is to double the number and then divide the result by 10).
- For example, the pupil will read out from the calculator 435 and you will tell them that their number was 87 (since doubling 435 gives 870, and dividing this by 10 gives 87).
- After you have amazed pupils several times with your magic trick, explain to them that you are using an inverse and that the inverse of multiplying by five is dividing by five. By dividing their result by five you are able to find their original number.
- Play the inverse game. Tell pupils you will write an operation on the board and they must write down the inverse operation on their mini whiteboards. Write 'x 10'. Give pupils a few seconds and then say: *Show me*. Have they written '÷ 10'? Pupils should then erase and start again.

- Write '÷ 8'. Give pupils a few seconds and then say: *Show me.* Have they written 'x 8'? Repeat several times until pupils are fluent in the task.
- Write ☐ × 4 = 100. Say: *You know that the inverse of × 4 is ÷ 4. How does this help with finding the answer to this question? What is the division sentence that you should write?* Give pupils a few seconds and then say: *Show me.* Have they written '100 ÷ 4 = ☐'?

  Try these:

  ☐ × 3 = 105

  ☐ ÷ 20 = 15

  ☐ ÷ 12 = 108

  ☐ × 13 = 52
- Pupils should complete Question 4 in the Practice Book.

## Same-day intervention

- Use place value counters to model 85 × 3 = 285.
- Make three piles of 85, using the counters, and then group them together (keeping the tens as 28 tens) showing pupils that the result is 285.
- Now show the way that 285 can be shared into three equal piles, each of which has a value of 85.
- Repeat this, using the vocabulary of multiplication and division, and recording your actions for pupils using correct notation.
- Ensure that pupils are able to identify the correct inverse operation.
- Say: *I am thinking of a number and I multiply it by three. I get 375.*
- Write this down as ☐ × 3 = 375 and ask pupils what calculation they need to do to find the number you are thinking of.
- Use their answers to assess their understanding, setting further inverse operation questions as appropriate.

## Same-day enrichment

- Extend Question 4 by setting some inverse questions where the division calculation gives a remainder.
- For example, give pupils these three questions:

  *I think of a number and divide it by 5. The answer is 156, with a remainder of one.*

  ☐ ÷ 7 = 128 remainder 1

  356 ÷ ☐ = 118 remainder 2
- Pupils should set questions of their own with or without remainders for their partner to solve.

# Question 5

**5** True or false? (Put a ✓ for true and a ✗ for false in each box.)

(a) 0 divided by any non-zero number is 0. . . . . . . . . . . . . . . . . . ☐

(b) For division, ☐0☐ ÷ 4, only when the digit in the hundreds place of the dividend is 4, can the digit in the tens place of the quotient be 0. . . . . . . . . . . . . . ☐

(c) If the divisor is a 1-digit number and the dividend is a 3-digit number, with 0 in its tens place, then the number in the tens place of the quotient must be 0. . . . . . . . . . . . . . . . ☐

(d) If ● ÷ ▲ = 101 r 8, then ▲ = 9, ● = 909. . . . . . . . . . . . . . ☐

## What learning will pupils have achieved at the conclusion of Question 5?

- Pupils will have used the image of arrays to reason mathematically about division.

## Activities for whole-class instruction

- Write a calculation on the board, covering some of the digits with sticky notes, for example:

```
     7 6
  ) 3 8 1
    3 5
      3 1
      3 0
        1
```

- Ask: *How do we know, without calculating, that the divisor must be greater than 3? How do we know, without calculating, that the divisor must be 5?*
- Ask pupils to discuss together and gather their responses. Focus your feedback on the mathematics, but also on the way in which pupils explain their thinking and tell them that this is a skill that you want them to practise here.
- Now ask them to take what they have been talking about and to write their explanation on a mini whiteboard.
- Use a visualiser, or gather pupils round, to look at some of their writing and use them to show the features of a good mathematical explanation. You might now like to ask pupils to refine their own writing.
- Pupils should complete Question 5 in the Practice Book.

## Same-day intervention

- Give pupils the statement:

  *This is one way to show the calculation 121 ÷ 4 = 30 remainder 1.*

- Ask pupils to explain how this represents the calculation and to describe where each of 121, 4, 30 and the remainder of 1 can be seen in the array.
- Encourage pupils to be precise in their use of language, using 'dividend', 'divisor', 'quotient' and 'remainder' to identify each of the parts of the calculation, and ensuring that they can justify why the array represents the given number sentence.
- Now say: *Fiona says that she can write another division number sentence to fit this picture.* Ask what this might be (121 ÷ 30 = 4 remainder 1 is the most likely), how each number in the sentence is represented in the array, and how their explanation from earlier needs to be adjusted for Fiona's interpretation.

## Same-day enrichment

- Ask: *If a number is divided by 5 and has a remainder of 1, then the ones digit of the quotient must be either 1 or 6. Is this is true or false?*
- Ask pupils to discuss the statement and explain why it is true or false.
- You might like to give pupils number plates or tens rods to support their reasoning.

# Question 6

6 A school has bought 504 pots of flowers and plans to arrange them in rows. Each row must have the same number of pots. Can you design a few different ways to arrange them? Fill in the boxes and then write the number sentences.

(a) Plan 1: Put ☐ pots for each row for ☐ rows.

Number sentence: ____________

(b) Plan 2: Put ☐ pots for each row for ☐ rows.

Number sentence: ____________

(c) Plan 3: Put ☐ pots for each row for ☐ rows.

Number sentence: ____________

## What learning will pupils have achieved at the conclusion of Question 6?

- Pupils will have used the image of arrays to reason mathematically about division.

## Activities for whole-class instruction

- Show the class these four arrays:

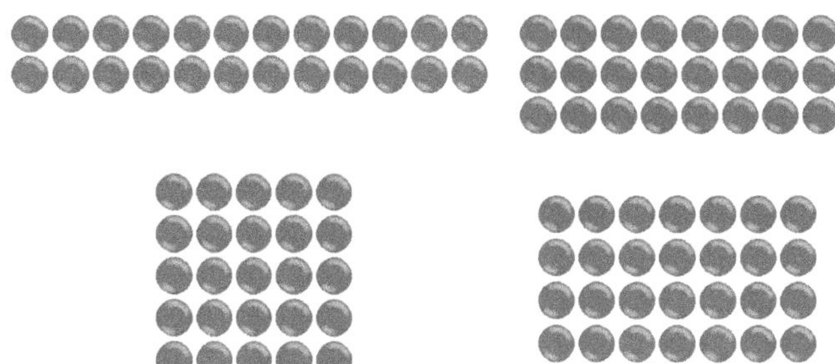

- Tell pupils that three of the arrays show the same number and ask pupils how, without counting, they could find out which is the odd one out.
- Give pupils time to discuss and then gather their responses.
- Ensure that pupils understand that the same quantity can be arranged as different arrays, representing different multiplication and division calculations. For example, the 2 by 12 array can be made by halving the 4 by 6 horizontally, and laying the two halves next to each other. The only array that cannot be transformed is the 5 by 5 square (in fact this can only be rearranged to give one other array of 1 by 25).
- Pupils should complete Question 6 in the Practice Book.

## Same-day intervention

- Give pupils 36 counters and ask them to use all of the counters to create as many arrays as they can.
- Say to pupils that, for each array, they should write two division calculations.
- Use the example, giving the divisions 36 ÷ 4 = 8 and 36 ÷ 8 = 4:

- Give pupils time to explore other possible options, discussing with them any strategies that they have to find the other arrangements more efficiently, and ensuring that the connection between the array and the calculations is made explicit.

## Same-day enrichment

- Tell pupils that there are 12 possible arrangements and ask them to use the arrangements that they have already found as a base to build on to find others.
- If, for example, they have found 3 by 168 as an option, you might ask them to investigate what happens if they decide to have six rows. The intention here is to give pupils a context in which they can explore the impact of changing one of the numbers in a multiplication or division calculation.

  (It is worth noting that there are 12 arrangements if, for example, 3 × 168 and 168 × 3 are considered as the same solution!)

## Challenge and extension question

# Question 7

**7** Two school buildings are 80 metres apart. If one pot of flowers is placed every 2 metres, how many pots of flowers are needed to cover the distance from one building to the other?

Answer: ______

This question encourages pupils to think about division and interpret the quotient in context. Pupils may find that imagining the 80 metres as a distance on a number line is a helpful strategy to access the problem.

# Unit 9.19
# Application of division

## Conceptual context

This unit provides opportunities for pupils to apply learning that they have achieved in previous units in a variety of contexts.

## Learning pupils will have achieved at the end of the unit

- Pupils will have built fluency through mentally calculating quotients (Q1)
- Pupils will have interpreted division calculations presented in words (Q2, Q3)
- Pupils will have practised explaining using mathematical language for division and reasoning (Q2, Q3)
- Pupils will have interpreted and solved problems using division (Q3)

### Resources

place value counters; counters; number plates; tens rods, mini whiteboards and pens, sticky notes

### Vocabulary

multiple, divide, division, dividend, divisor, quotient, remainder

# Question 1

**1** Calculate mentally.

(a) 17 ÷ 3 = ☐ (b) 33 ÷ 7 = ☐

(c) 43 ÷ 8 = ☐ (d) 29 ÷ 9 = ☐

(e) 52 ÷ 6 = ☐ (f) 75 ÷ 10 = ☐

(g) 25 ÷ 4 = ☐ (h) 42 ÷ 5 = ☐

## What learning will pupils have achieved at the conclusion of Question 1?

- Pupils will have built fluency through mentally calculating quotients.

## Activities for whole-class instruction

- Show pupils this 4 by 7 array:

- Ask pupils what multiplication and division calculations they can 'see' in the array (4 × 7, 7 × 4, 28 ÷ 3 and 28 ÷ 7).
- Tell pupils a story that the array might represent, for example: There are 28 children in a class. Each table has four seats around it. How many tables are needed?
- Ask: *Where in this array are the seats? Where are the children? What do the rows represent?*
- Ask pupils to write a question about another 'story' that this array might represent.
- Remind pupils that, when calculating mentally, it is often helpful to imagine an array to represent the calculation.
- Pupils should complete Question 1 in the Practice Book.

## Same-day intervention

- Using number plates or tens rods, give pupils all the 4s.
- Ask pupils to make a number as close to 25 as possible and, when they have done so, to note how many plates or rods they have used, and to record this as a number sentence. It is likely that they will use multiplication, 4 × 5 = 24 or 5× 4 = 24.
- Draw attention to the extra 1 that is needed, then ask pupils to write a number sentence to represent both the multiplication and the division that they have modelled.
- Ask pupils to use 7s to make a number as close to 30 as possible.
- Ask them to calculate how many plates/rods they will need, and which other plate they will need to use to fill any gaps. Ask them to use the plates/rods to check their answer and to write as many number sentences as they can to describe what they have just done.

## Same-day enrichment

- Give pupils the statement:

  If a number can be divided by both two and three without leaving a remainder, it can also be divided by six without leaving a remainder.
- Ask them to discuss in pairs or small groups whether the statement is always true, sometimes true or never true.
- Once pupils have decided whether it is always, sometimes or never, ask them if they can explain how they know that they are right – can they use manipulatives such as number plates, tens rods or other images (an array) to justify their answer?

# Question 2

**2** Complete the sentences.

(a) When 618 is divided by 5, the quotient is ☐ and the remainder is ☐.

(b) To see if 251 ÷ 3 = 83 r 2 is correct, you can use ☐ × ☐ + ☐ = ☐ to check.

(c) There are ☐ zeros at the end of the product of 800 × 5.

(d) In a division sentence, if both the dividend and divisor are the same, then the quotient is ☐. If the dividend and the quotient are the same, then the divisor is ☐. If the quotient is to be 0, the dividend is ☐.

## What learning will pupils have achieved at the conclusion of Question 2?

- Pupils will have interpreted division calculations presented in words.
- Pupils will have practised explaining using mathematical language for division and reasoning.

## Activities for whole-class instruction

- Draw this on the board:

  ☐☐☐ ÷ ■ = ■■ (or use coloured sticky notes/pieces of paper stuck to the board)

- The purpose is to represent a general structure for pupils to explore.
- Tell pupils that the red squares are covering the number 100, and ask them what they can tell you about the blue and green digits.
- If appropriate, use prompts such as:
  - *Can the blue be any number?*
  - *Can the blue be 1? 2? 0?*
  - *Are there any numbers that the last green digit cannot be? Are there any that the first green digit cannot be?*
- The intention is to challenge pupils to think deeply about the relationship, to see it as something to think about, not just an instruction to carry out a calculation.
- Now say that the number behind the red blocks has changed and is no longer 100.
- Ask different questions about the situation to challenge pupils. These might include:
  - *What can you say about the last red digit if the blue digit is 5?*
  - *Why can't the red number be 900?*
  - *Why can't the green number be 10?*
  - *If the green number is 22, what might the blue number be?*
- As pupils explain their thinking, draw attention to clear and precise language.
- Pupils should complete Question 2 in the Practice Book.

## Same-day intervention

- Draw this on the board:

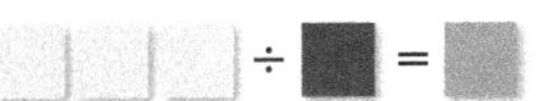

- Discuss with pupils what it represents, that it shows a three-digit number divided by a single-digit number and the result is also a single-digit number.
- Tell pupils it is not possible to find a correct solution to this without leaving a remainder.
- Work with pupils to explore the situation, trying different values in the boxes and using different representations and manipulatives to develop pupils' understanding.
- The intention of the task is to provide a context for pupils to explore the affect of changing the value of different digits in the calculation without the need to calculate a solution.

## Same-day enrichment

- Ask pupils to look at their solution to Question 2 part (b) and (c).
- They should choose one of the answers and prepare to explain how they worked out the answer. They then give a written explanation (though it will be helpful for them to explain to a partner first).
- Tell pupils that they should illustrate their explanations with pictures of the mathematics if it helps, and that they should aim their explanation at a younger pupil who does not yet fully understand division.

# Question 3

**3** Application problems.

(a) A group of pupils plan to put 140 kg of marbles into boxes. Each box can hold 6 kg. At least how many boxes are needed?

Answer: ______

(b) Two Year 3 classes go rowing. Each boat can seat 7 children. There are 29 pupils in Class One and 32 pupils in Class Two. How many boats are needed for each class if they go separately? If the classes share the boats, how many boats are needed?

Answer: ______

(c) Theo has £50 to buy some pencil boxes. Each pencil box costs £8. How many pencil boxes can he buy?

Answer: ______

(d) Ella has 147 sheets of paper. 8 sheets of paper are needed to make one exercise book.

(i) How many exercise books can she make with the 147 sheets of paper?

Answer: ______

(ii) With the remaining sheets of paper, how many more sheets are needed to make another exercise book?

Answer: ______

## What learning will pupils have achieved at the conclusion of Question 3?

- Pupils will have interpreted division calculations presented in words.
- Pupils will have practised explaining using mathematical language for division and reasoning.

## Activities for whole-class instruction

- Gather some resources and manipulatives to show pupils. You might, for example, have 40 red counters, 32 blue counters, 28 shells, three toy bears and four boxes.
- Use the resources you have gathered to ask a multiplication or division question. With the materials described you might ask:
  - *I want to put the same number of counters in each box. How many counters will I have left?*
  - *I want to give each bear seven counters. Will I have enough?*
  - *If I share the red counters equally between the bears, and the blue counters equally between the boxes, will I have more red or blue counters left over?*
- Gather pupils' responses and ask them to describe their methods. Where pupils have taken different routes to the correct solution, use their methods to discuss efficiency and accuracy with the class.
- Now ask pupils to write their own division or multiplication question that could be asked, using the materials that you have gathered. As pupils discuss and work on their questions, listen for interesting problems and discuss with class.
- Pupils should complete Question 3 in the Practice Book.

### Same-day intervention

- Use the materials that you have gathered to act out situations with pupils, then record these situations using mathematical notation. For example, share the red counters between the bears and write 40 ÷ 3 = 13 with 1 left over. Ensure that you interpret each number in the calculation as the context given.
- Now give pupils a calculation, ask them to act it out and to tell the story. You might give them 28 ÷ 4 = 7, which they could interpret as sharing 28 shells between the four boxes.
- Work with pupils to make the connections between the materials, the story and the written calculation.

## Same-day enrichment

- Give pupils this question, which adds addition layers of complexity to the application of division.

  *Sarah and Kate are making bags of sweets to sell at the school fete.*

  *Sarah has 165 sweets that she puts into bags. Each bag has three sweets. Sarah sells her bags for £4 each.*

  *Kate also has 165 sweets. She puts them into bags so that each bag has five sweets and she sells each bag for £6.*

  *Does Sarah or Kate make the most money?*
- Ask pupils to make up a similar question.

### Challenge and extension question

## Question 4

**4** A company uses 3 kilograms of fresh fish to make 1 kilogram of dried fish. How many kilograms of dried fish can it make using 750 kilograms of fresh fish?

Answer: ____________

Question 4 uses division as a way to explore a proportional relationship.

The use of manipulatives to represent the dried fish and the fresh fish, or the use of an image such as the bar model, may support pupils in getting started with the problem.

## Question 5

**5** Dylan asked Amina to work out a puzzle: 'A piece of wood is sawn into 7 pieces. It takes 5 minutes to saw each piece. How long does it take to saw all 7 pieces?'

Amina answered quickly: '5 minutes for 1 piece, of course – it takes 35 minutes to saw 7 pieces.'

'No, it takes 30 minutes!' said Dylan. Is he right? ____________

Question 5 encourages pupils to consider the practical interpretation of an application by challenging what might be their instinct on first reading the problem.

The key to solving this problem is to consider the number of cuts, rather than the number of pieces of wood being generated. Encourage pupils to use diagrams to explore and explain why Amina is not right, and also to explain what mistake she has made.

# Unit 9.20

# Finding the total price

## Conceptual context

This unit provides a context in which pupils can explore and interpret division and multiplication and, in working with 'unit price', 'quantity' and 'total price', to use this context to move towards generalising the structure of the multiplicative relationship between these variables.

When working with these real-life situations, it is important that pupils are prompted to interpret the mathematical result, returning to the context of the question and stating explicitly what their numerical solution means in that context.

## Learning pupils will have achieved at the end of the unit

- Pupils will have developed fluency with mental calculation strategies (Q1)
- Pupils will have solved multiplication and division problems in context (Q2, Q3, Q4, Q5, Q7)
- Pupils will understand and use vocabulary associated with calculating costs (Q2, Q3, Q4, Q5)
- Pupils will have used and interpreted unit price and total price (Q3, Q4, Q5)
- Pupils will have identified the relevant information to solve a problem (Q5, Q7)
- Pupils will have built fluency in representing and solving calculations (Q6)

## Resources

scissors; glue sticks; boxes of pens; place value counters; counters; number plates; tens rods; mini whiteboards and pens; sticky notes; toys and boxes; **Resource 3.9.20** Bar model costs

## Vocabulary

multiple, divide, division, dividend, divisor, quotient, remainder, unit price, quantity, total price

# Question 1

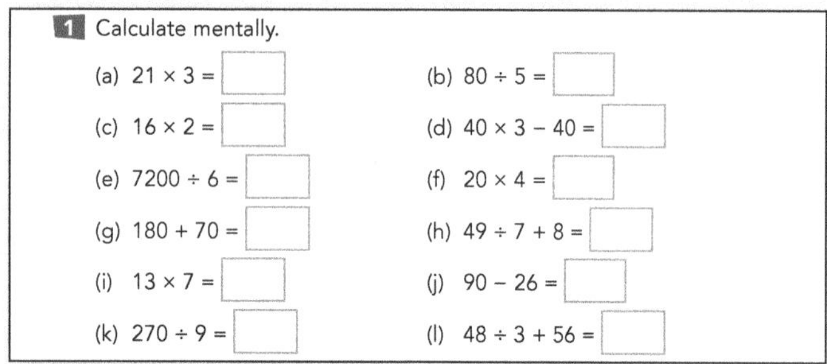

1 Calculate mentally.

(a) 21 × 3 = ☐ (b) 80 ÷ 5 = ☐

(c) 16 × 2 = ☐ (d) 40 × 3 − 40 = ☐

(e) 7200 ÷ 6 = ☐ (f) 20 × 4 = ☐

(g) 180 + 70 = ☐ (h) 49 ÷ 7 + 8 = ☐

(i) 13 × 7 = ☐ (j) 90 − 26 = ☐

(k) 270 ÷ 9 = ☐ (l) 48 ÷ 3 + 56 = ☐

## What learning will pupils have achieved at the conclusion of Question 1?

- Pupils will have developed fluency with mental calculation strategies.

## Activities for whole-class instruction

- Use sticky notes with the digits 0, 1, 2, 3, 4 and 5, and the symbols × and ÷.
- Ask pupils to write on their mini whiteboards an arrangement of some of the sticky notes so that they fit in the frame: ☐☐☐☐☐, with one note placed in each box. Explain that one of the boxes must contain either × or ÷.
- Examples might be 10 × 35, 120 × 3 or 120 ÷ 4.
- Tell them that they should first make the easiest calculation that they can think of, and gather their responses. Explore why it is easy and draw out any known facts that pupils have used. Raise pupils' awareness that using known facts is a helpful strategy when solving a problem.
- Now ask pupils to write a calculation that is as difficult as possible using the same frame. Again, discuss why this is difficult and draw out methods using known facts and other strategies.
- Pupils should complete Question 1 in the Practice Book.

### Same-day intervention

- Ask pupils to rank the calculations from Question 1 in order of difficulty, from easiest to hardest.
- Use manipulatives such as tens rods, place value counters or blocks to explore pupils' understanding of those they found difficult.
- Now ask pupils to write the most difficult division where the answer is 12.

## Same-day enrichment

- Tell pupils that each of the following calculations has had just one six removed from somewhere in the number sentence, and now they are incorrect.
- Ask where the stolen six needs to be written so that each number sentence is correct again.

13 + 135 = 271

700 − 11 = 539

201 ÷ 3 = 7

17 × 9 = 1584

# Questions 2 and 3

2 Complete the table.

| | Pencil case | Pen | Coloured pencil (in box) |
|---|---|---|---|
| Unit price (price per item) | £6 | | £9 per box |
| Quantity (number of items) | 7 | 10 | |
| Total price | | £340 | £900 |

3 Write × or ÷ in the ◯ and 'total price', 'unit price' or 'quantity' in the spaces.

(a) unit price ◯ ............ = total price

(b) total price ◯ ............ = quantity

(c) total price ◯ ............ = unit price

## What learning will pupils have achieved at the conclusion of Questions 2 and 3?

- Pupils will have solved multiplication and division problems in context.
- Pupils will have used and interpreted unit price and total price.

## Activities for whole-class instruction

- For this task, get ready the scissors, glue sticks, boxes of pens and other materials.
- Tell pupils that one pen costs 5 pence. Tell them that this is called the 'unit price', and ask them what the total cost (stress the vocabulary of 'total cost') is for three pens. What is the total cost for ten pens?
- Explain that the total cost is found by multiplying the number of items by the unit price of that item.

- Repeat this using the glue stick. Say that the unit price of a glue stick is 9 pence and ask: *How much does one glue stick cost?*
- Now ask the total cost of other quantities of glues sticks.
- Repeat again using, for example, scissors. Say that the unit price of the scissors is £1 and ask about different totals.
- Say: *I bought some pens and the total cost was 55 pence. How many pens did I buy?* Pupils should explain their answers.
- Agree that the total cost divided by the unit price gives the quantity of items bought.
- Tell pupils that you also bought some crayons, and that the total cost for 9 crayons was 54p. Ask pupils to find the unit price for a crayon, then ask: *How do you find the unit price if the total cost and quantity are known?*
- Pupils should complete Questions 2 and 3 in the Practice Book.

## Same-day intervention

- Give pupils **Resource 3.9.20** Bar model costs, which represents situations using bar models to support pupils in calculating costs.

**Resource 3.9.20**

**Bar model costs**

1. Louis buys 5 toy cars. Each car costs £2. What is the total cost of the toy cars?

| 2 | 2 | 2 | 2 | 2 |
|---|---|---|---|---|

Total cost £☐

2. Bella has £40. She spends all of her money on 5 toy dogs. How much does each toy dog cost?

£40

Each toy dog costs £☐

3. Dulcie spends £35 buying toy cars. The unit price is £7. How many toy cars does Dulcie buy?

£35

Dulcie buys ☐ toy cars.

4. A teacher buys a book for each of the children in his class. The unit price is £8 and the total cost for the teacher is £184. How many children are in the class?

£184

There are ☐ children in the class.

© HarperCollinsPublishers 2017 357

## Same-day enrichment

- Show pupils these two shopping baskets:

£6

£5

- Ask: *What is the unit cost of a toy giraffe?*
- Ask: *What is the unit cost of a toy cat?* Pupils should answer that one basket has an extra giraffe and costs £1 more, so the giraffe must be worth £1.

# Questions 4 and 5

**4** Meena bought 4 saris. Each sari costs £105.
How much did she spend in total?

Answer: ______

**5** There are 24 apples in a box. The price of each box of apples is £30. What is the total price of 3 of the boxes? How many apples are there in 8 boxes?

Answer: ______

## What learning will pupils have achieved at the conclusion of Questions 4 and 5?

- Pupils will have used multiplication to find the total price.

## Activities for whole-class instruction

- Set up items as a shop display.
- Hold up an item and say that it costs a two-digit value, for example £23.
- Ask how much four of the items would cost and ask pupils to write the number sentence on their mini whiteboards.
- Represent this calculation using a bar model.

<table>
<tr><td>£23</td><td>£23</td><td>£23</td><td>£23</td></tr>
<tr><td colspan="4">£92</td></tr>
</table>

- Explain to pupils that it is helpful to use a bar to solve problems.
- Now hold up a second item and tell pupils that it costs £35. Say that you are going to buy seven of the item.
- Ask pupils to draw a bar to represent the total cost on their mini whiteboards.
- Gather responses. Have pupils identified seven equal sections, each 'worth' £35?
- Now ask pupils to write the calculation that they would use to find the total cost of buying seven objects. Again, gather responses and make the connection between the multiplication notation, the context and the bar representation.
- Now ask pupils to calculate the total cost of seven objects on their mini whiteboards.
- Gather responses and the different methods used, discussing the efficiency and accuracy of some of the key methods.
- Pupils should complete Questions 4 and 5 in the Practice Book.

## Same-day intervention

- Work with pupils to represent questions using bar models.
- Ensure that pupils are able to represent situations from the shop that you have set up.
- Say: *I am going to buy five items* and ask pupils to draw what they can of the bar before telling them the unit price of the item. They should complete the bar model by writing this price in.
- Repeat this, focusing on representing the situation using the bar model. Only once pupils are able to draw the bar model, move on to writing number sentences for each of the bar models that you have drawn.

## Same-day enrichment

- Pupil pairs should make up questions for each other, using the outline:

  When the divisor is __, the quotient is __ and the remainder is __, what is the dividend?

  Write the number sentence: ______________________

  ______________________

  (This is modelled on the final part of Question 6 so it is familiar, but pupils will find it challenging to make up the question themselves.)

# Question 6

6 Write a number sentence for each question.

(a) What is 6 times 660?

Number sentence: ______________________

(b) How many times 6 is 660?

Number sentence: ______________________

(c) When the divisor is 8, the quotient is 402 and the remainder is 7, what is the dividend?

Number sentence: ______________________

## What learning will pupils have achieved at the conclusion of Question 6?

- Pupils will have built fluency in representing and solving calculations.

## Activities for whole-class instruction

- Show pupils this 10 by 15 array:

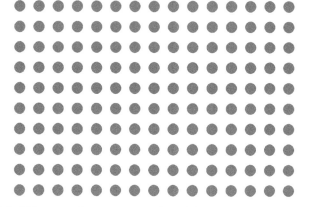

- Ask: *What number sentences does this array represent?*
- Ask: *What questions can you make up about these number sentences?* For example, 'How many tens are in 150?'
- Now ask pupils to imagine that you have two 10 by 15 arrays.
- Ask them to decide the total number of dots in the array, and discuss their strategies for calculating their result.
- Now ask them to imagine the two arrays and ask them, as before, what other questions they might ask.
- Gather their results and draw connections between the original questions with one array, and the new questions with two arrays.
- If appropriate for your pupils' current understanding, add an extra two or three dots/counters to the array and explore what impact this has on the division number sentences, adding in a remainder.
- Pupils should complete Question 6 in the Practice Book.

## Same-day intervention

- Give pupils sticky notes with the numbers 40, 8 and 2 written on, and sticky notes with the × and ÷ symbols.
- Ask pupils to use the sticky notes to write as many different number sentences as they can, placing one sticky note in each box in the frame, including a symbol for the second sticky note: □□□ = □.
- As pupils construct different number sentences, say the sentence in different ways, for example, 40 ÷ 8 = □ could be read as 'How many times eight is 40?' or 'What is 40 divided by eight?' or 'If the dividend is 40 and the divisor is eight, what is the quotient?"

## Same-day enrichment

- Give pupils a spider diagram like this:

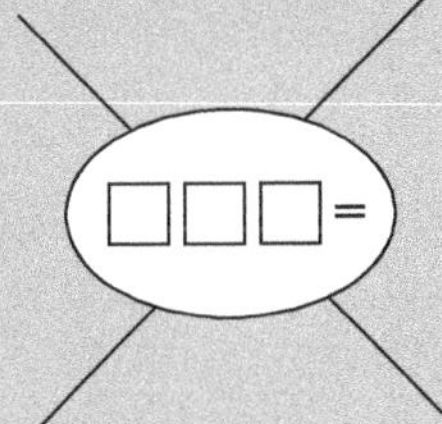

- Give pupils the sticky notes with the numbers 40, 8 and 2, and sticky notes with the × and ÷ symbols.
- Challenge pupils to arrange the sticky notes in the frame, using a symbol for the second sticky note, and to write at least four different ways to describe that number sentence at the end of the spider's 'legs'.
- Challenge pupils also to make as many spiders as they can, using the same numbers, and to think about whether the order of the sticky note matters.

# Question 7

**7** A box can hold 8 basketballs. How many boxes are needed to hold 768 basketballs?

Answer: ______

## What learning will pupils have achieved at the conclusion of Question 7?

- Pupils will have built fluency in representing and solving calculations.

## Activities for whole-class instruction

- Ask pupils to build a train that is 48 long using tens rods.
- Now explain to pupils that you want the train to be made using just one type of rod. Ask them which types of rod you definitely cannot use, or which you should use. Can pupils tell you that only factors of 48 are suitable?
- Ask: *How many 4s would be needed to make the train?* Agree that 48 ÷ 4 = □ describes the problem.
- Ask pupils to read the number sentence to you in as many different ways as they can, drawing on the work in Question 6.
- Ensure that pupils understand that this is a problem that can be solved using division, thinking of it as 'How many fours are there in 48?'
- Pupils should complete Question 7 in the Practice Book.

## Same-day intervention

- Using tens rods, ask pupils to construct two trains that are the same length. One of the trains should be made using only 4s and one should be made using only 5s.
- Ask pupils what the shortest train is that would fit these rules. Ask: *Can you find one that is over 100 long? Over 200? Can you convince me that it can be made only out of 4s and only out of 5s? How many of each rod would be needed to construct your train?*
- The intention of this task is to give pupils an opportunity to construct their own calculations, considering division as 'how many go into', rather than the sharing image.

## Same-day enrichment

- Ask: *If a car measures four metres from front to back, how many cars could be parked along a 100-metre running track if they were all just touching?*
- Tell pupils a basketball measures 25 cm across. Ask: *How long would the line of balls be if 768 basketballs were placed in a line?*
- If they need a clue, tell them to think about how many balls would measure one metre.

## Challenge and extension question

# Question 8

**8** A school has planted 12 trees along one side of the playground, from one end to the other. One tree was planted every 6 metres. How long is the playground?

Answer: ______

Question 8 encourages pupils to interpret the mathematics that they use to solve a problem. Many pupils will calculate 12 × 6 to find their solution, but using a diagram will show why this approach is incorrect.

It is important for pupils to understand that they may need to interpret the mathematical solution to a problem within a context.

# Question 9

**9** It took Leila 5 minutes to walk from the 1st tree to the 6th tree along the main path in a school playground. Which tree did she reach after 15 minutes if she walked at the same pace?

Answer: ______

Question 9 introduces the idea of rate as a context for multiplication or division.

There are many approaches that pupils might take to reach a solution, but for pupils who are finding the situation challenging, you might like to point out the connection between 5 minutes and 15 minutes, prompting a multiplicative approach to reaching a solution.

## Chapter 9 test (Practice Book 3B, pages 121–125)

| Test question number | Relevant unit | Relevant questions within unit |
|---|---|---|
| 1 | 9.1<br>9.2<br>9.10<br>9.14<br>9.15<br>9.16<br>9.17 | 2, 4<br>2, 3, 4<br>1, 2, 3<br>1<br>1<br>1<br>1 |
| 2 | 9.7<br>9.8<br>9.9<br>9.16<br>9.17 | 5<br>3<br>2,<br>4<br>4 |
| 3 | 9.6<br>9.16 | 1<br>5 |
| 4 | 9.1<br>9.9<br>9.10<br>9.14 | 6<br>5<br>4<br>6 |
| 5 | 9.1<br>9.2<br>9.4<br>9.6<br>9.18 | 2<br>2<br>1, 2<br>1, 3<br>3, 5 |
| 6 | 9.8 | 5 |
| 7 | 9.16<br>9.17<br>9.19<br>9.20 | 5<br>6<br>3<br>4, 5, 7 |
| 8 | 9.16<br>9.17<br>9.19<br>9.20 | 5<br>6<br>3<br>4, 5, 7 |
| 9 | 9.1<br>9.2<br>9.18 | 7<br>6<br>4 |
| 10 | 9.10<br>9.16 | 5<br>5 |
| 11 | 9.16 | 5 |
| 12 | 9.4<br>9.6<br>9.9 | 3<br>6<br>6 |
| 13 | No specific unit | |

# Chapter 10
# Let's practise geometry

## Chapter overview

| Area of mathematics | National Curriculum Statutory requirements for Key Stage 2 | Shanghai Maths Project reference |
|---|---|---|
| Geometry – properties of shapes | Year 3 Programme of study:<br>Pupils should be taught to: | |
| | ■ draw 2-D shapes and make 3-D shapes using modelling materials; recognise 3-D shapes in different orientations and describe them | Year 3, Unit 10.4 |
| | ■ recognise angles as a property of shape or a description of a turn | Year 3, Unit 10.1 |
| | ■ identify right angles, recognise that two right angles make a half-turn, three make three-quarters of a turn and four a complete turn; identify whether angles are greater than or less than a right angle | Year 3, Unit 10.1 |
| | ■ identify horizontal and vertical lines and pairs of perpendicular and parallel lines. | Year 3, Units 10.2, 10.3 |
| Measurement | Year 3 Programme of Study:<br>Pupils should be taught to: | |
| | ■ measure, compare, add and subtract: lengths (m/cm/mm); mass (kg/g); volume/capacity (l/ml) | Year 3, Unit 10.5 |
| | ■ measure the perimeter of simple 2-D shapes. | Year 3, Units 10.6, 10.7 |

# Unit 10.1
# Angles

## Conceptual context

Understanding what angles are and how they work is fundamental to so much of everyday life, from building a house to passing a football. This unit builds on work that pupils did in Books 1 and 2 where they learned about quarter, half, three-quarter and full turns, and related this to the number of right angles turned. In this unit pupils learn that angles are what we use to measure the turn that is needed to move one straight line onto another when they are joined together at a point. They will also have the chance to explore angles that are greater than or less than a right angle. The terms 'acute angle' and 'obtuse angle' are introduced in this unit.

## Learning pupils will have achieved at the end of the unit

- Pupils will be able to identify angles as a property of shapes or a description of a turn (Q1)
- Pupils will be able to identify right angles and know that two right angles make half a turn, three make three quarters of a turn and four make a complete turn (Q2, Q3, Q4, Q5, Q6)
- Pupils will be able to identify if angles are less than (acute) or greater than (obtuse) a right angle (Q3, Q5)

### Resources

something to measure right angles with, e.g. a set square, a square corner from a piece of cardboard or paper or a circle folded in half and half again; pictures of a selection of 2-D shapes; clock faces with moveable hands; rulers; squared paper, cardboard strips, paper fasteners; **Resource 3.10.1a** Find the angles; **Resource 3.10.1b** Angle munchers

### Vocabulary

angle, right angle, greater than, less than, half turn, acute, obtuse

# Question 1

**1** How many angles are there in each shape? Write your answers below the shapes.

(a) ☐ angles (b) ☐ angles (c) ☐ angles (d) ☐ angles

## What learning will pupils have achieved at the conclusion of Question 1?

- Pupils will be able to identify angles in 2-D shapes and know that angles are used to measure turn; that we can see angles where two straight lines meet at a point.
- Pupils will have learned that not all shapes have angles.

## Activities for whole-class instruction

Display a variety of images of 2-D shapes and ask pupils to identify the vertices. Ensure that the selection of shapes includes those that do not have vertices, such as a circle or semicircle.

*A vertex is where two straight lines meet.*

- Ask pupils to look carefully at a square and ask them to describe the angle that is formed inside the vertices. Ask: *How many can you see within the square? How about a rectangle? How about other 2-D shapes?* Explain to pupils that where two straight lines meet at a point we can see an angle.

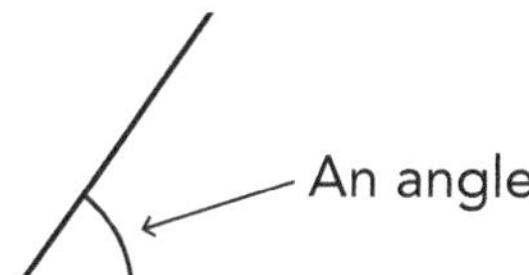


The angle **IS NOT** the space between the lines. The angle is the amount of turn that is need to move one of the lines so that it sits exactly on top of the other, when the point where they meet is the turning point. It is important that pupils experience this physically with their whole bodies by moving from facing in one direction to facing in a different direction. They have probably done this in Year 1 or 2 when learning about right angles. Now, they should move rulers or metre sticks on the desk or the floor (a fairly large-scale manipulative). They need to learn that the angle is the measure of the turn, and that angles can range from very small to a whole turn. Pupils should explore making 'small' angles and 'large' angles.

- Ask pupils to draw two straight lines that meet at a point. Label the angle. Repeat with other lines and ask pupils to indicate the angle.
- Ask pupils to draw a triangle using a ruler and pencil. Ask: *How many angles has this shape got?* Ask them to label the three angles. Repeat with other 2-D shapes as needed. Ask: *How about a circle? Does that have angles?*

*Angles are used to measure turn; we can see angles where two straight lines meet at a point.*

- Pupils should complete Question 1 in the Practice Book.

## Same-day intervention

- Give pupils a clock face and ask them to set the hands to two o'clock.

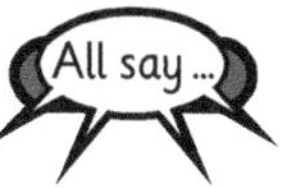


*Angles are used to measure turn; we can see angles where two straight lines meet at a point.*

- Pupils should run their finger and thumb along the inside of the hands to meet at the point so that they can feel the angle. Repeat with different times, asking pupils to show you where the angle formed by the clock hand is. Now ask pupils to identify the angles in **Resource 3.10.1a** Find the angles.

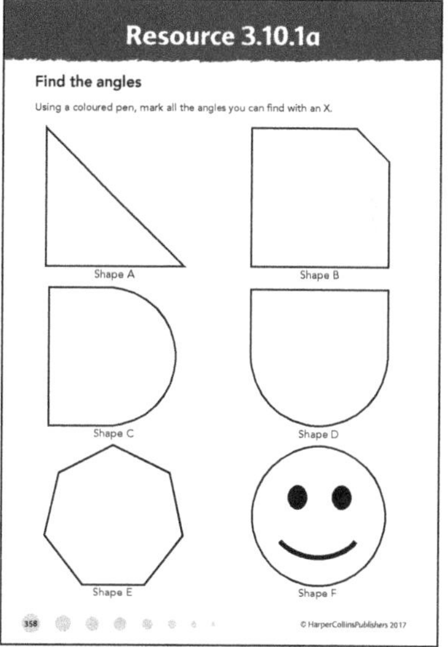

**Resource 3.10.1a**

**Find the angles**

Using a coloured pen, mark all the angles you can find with an X.

Shape A Shape B

Shape C Shape D

Shape E Shape F

© HarperCollinsPublishers 2017

## Same-day enrichment

- Ask pupils to draw a shape of their choosing. It could be a shape made up of straight lines or it could be a combination of both straight and curved lines. When complete ask pupils to swap their shapes and, using a coloured pencil, mark all the angles they can find, then return it to their partner for checking. Do they both agree that they have found all the angles?

# Question 2

2 True or false? (Put a ✓ for true and a ✗ for false in each box.)
(a) Every geometric shape must have at least one angle. . . . . ☐
(b) The wider the two sides of an angle are open, the greater the angle. . . . . ☐
(c) All right angles are equal. . . . . ☐
(d) Two right angles make a half turn. . . . . ☐

## What learning will pupils have achieved at the conclusion of Question 2?

- Pupils will have revised right angles and will be able to identify them confidently.
- Pupils will have learned that an angle is greater when the two sides are 'open wider'.
- Pupils will begin to evaluate by sight whether an angle is greater or less than a right angle.

## Activities for whole-class instruction

- Revisit previous learning (Book 2) by labelling the classroom/hall walls with the letters N, E, S, W. Ask pupils to face N(orth) and then rotate to turn and face E(ast). Ask pupils to describe the rotation they have made (quarter turn). Repeat with other rotations, including half turns, ensuring that different starting points are used and that pupils experience moving both clockwise and anticlockwise.
- Repeat the above exercise but this time replace quarter-turn moves with right angle moves and use two right angles to replace half turn moves.
- Get pupils to identify right angles within their classroom, for example the corner of a reading book, the open classroom door. List them. Ask pupils to share their findings. Ask: *Did anybody find an angle that was not a right angle?*

*Two right angles make a half turn.*

- Ask pupils to place their hands together (palm to palm). Keeping their middle fingertips touching and wrists rigid, ask them to open their hands and arms to show you a right angle. Now ask them to close them again slowly. Ask pupils to open them to show you where half a right angle would be. How about an angle that is larger than one right angle?
- Ask pupils to work with a partner: one of them shows a right angle with their hands; the other shows an angle that is less than a right angle. Ask: *Who had to open their hands the widest?*

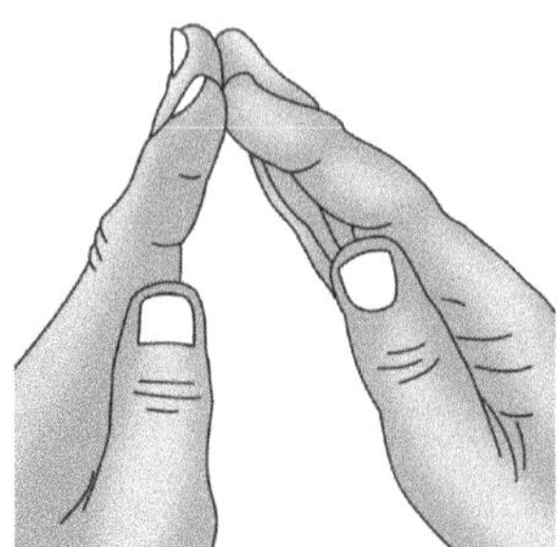

- Show pupils a large image of a 2-D shape that does not have any angles, for example a circle or oval. Ask them how many angles the shape has. Use thumbs up. Say: *Put your thumb up if you think there are three angles in this shape.* Ask: *Why do you think that?* Repeat with other numbers and zero. Ask pupils how they know there are no angles.
- Pupils should complete Question 2 in the Practice Book.

## Same-day intervention

- Give pupils two strips of cardboard, about 20 cm long and 2 cm wide that have been joined together at one end by a paper fastener so that the strips can be moved independently. Start with the strips on top of each other and ask pupils to turn the top strip to make a right angle.

*Angles are used to measure turn; we can see angles where two straight lines meet at a point.*

- Repeat with pupils forming angles greater than a right angle and angles less than a right angle. Ensure the starting point is always with the two strips together so that pupils have the concept of measurement of turn emphasised.
- Give pupils a cut out circle. Let them run their fingers along the edge. Ask: *Are there any straight lines?* Explain that not all shapes have angles because some do not have straight sides.

## Same-day enrichment

- Draw three shapes that do not have any angles. Ask: *Do you know their names? Can you find out their names?* (circle, semicircle, crescent, oval, ellipse are some they may find)

# Question 3

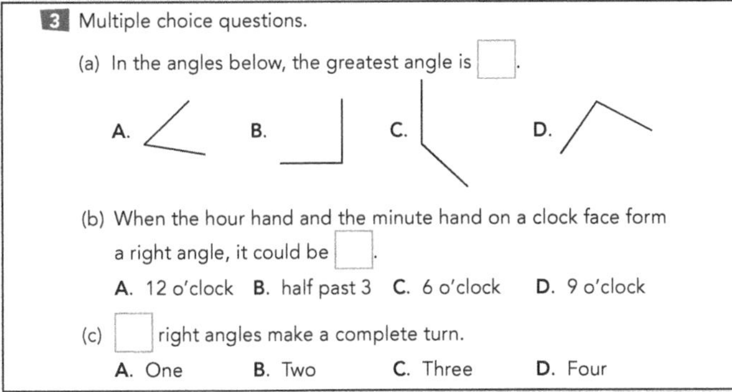

**3** Multiple choice questions.

(a) In the angles below, the greatest angle is ☐.

A. B. C. D.

(b) When the hour hand and the minute hand on a clock face form a right angle, it could be ☐.

A. 12 o'clock B. half past 3 C. 6 o'clock D. 9 o'clock

(c) ☐ right angles make a complete turn.

A. One B. Two C. Three D. Four

## What learning will pupils have achieved at the conclusion of Question 3?

- Pupils will be able to recognise right angles.
- Pupils will be able to recognise angles that are less than a right angle and greater than a right angle.
- Conceptual connections linking time, fractions and angles have been exposed (quarter turn, half turn and so on) enabling pupils to deepen their understanding across different areas of mathematics.

## Activities for whole-class instruction

- Give pupils **Resource 3.10.1b** Angle munchers.

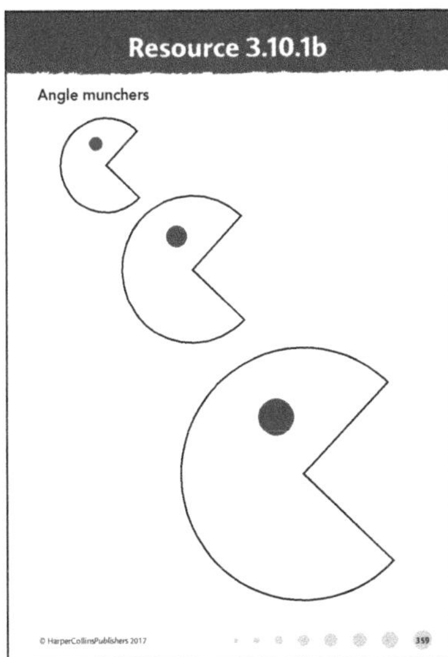


- Point to the angle munchers on **Resource 3.10.1b**. Ask: *What can you tell me about this shape?* Pupils should see that: it is three-quarters of a circle; it has a circular eye; its mouth is a right angle.
- Ask pupils to explore the classroom and find at least three items that will fit exactly into an angle muncher's mouth. Ask pupils to report back to the rest of the group. Did they find any different items? Ask: *What can we say about the items that fit into the angle muncher's mouth?*
- Get pupils to work with a partner. Ask pupils to draw five different angles, to swap their work and to use an angle muncher to decide if the angles are right angles, or smaller or greater than a right angle.
- Repeat the whole-class instruction for Question 2 by labelling the classroom/hall walls with the letters N, E, S, W and instructing pupils to make quarter turns, half turns and right angle moves. Ask pupils to describe the rotation they have made each time.
- Now label the walls of the classroom/hall 12, 3, 6, 9. Ask pupils to work with a partner. Ask Pupil A to face the 12 and Pupil B to face the 3. Ask: *How many right angles would Pupil A have to turn clockwise to be facing the same number as Pupil B?* Repeat this with different starting positions, different amounts of turn (two, three or four right angles) and both clockwise and anticlockwise.
- Ask pupils if they noticed any similarities between the quarter, half and three-quarter turns made when using amount of turn when changing direction and when facing different numbers on the clock face.
- Give pupils a clock face. Only using o'clock times, ask them to find a time when the minute hand and hour hand are at right angles to each other. Say: *Now find an o'clock time when the minute and hour hands are two right angles (half a turn) from each other.*
- Pupils should complete Question 3 in the Practice Book. Ask pupils to work with a partner, checking their answers with the angle-muncher.

## Same-day intervention

- Give pupils a clock face and ask them to set the hands to 3 o'clock. Ask them to tell you about the angle formed by the two hands. Pupils should run their finger and thumb along the inside of the hands to meet at the point so that they can feel the angle. Using another clock face ask pupils to set the hands to 10 past 3. Ask them to look at the two clocks and run their finger and thumb along the inside of the hands. What do they notice? Ask: *Which is the larger angle?* Repeat with other clock times. Now show pupils a time where the angle formed by the hands is greater than a right angle (4 o'clock) and compare how that feels with 1 o'clock. Repeat with other times. Show pupils a variety of times and ask them to tell you if the angle between the hands is a right angle, or smaller or larger than a right angle.

## Same-day enrichment

- Using a clock face, can pupils find at least five different times when the hands of the clock form a right angle? Ask: *What are these times?*

# Question 4

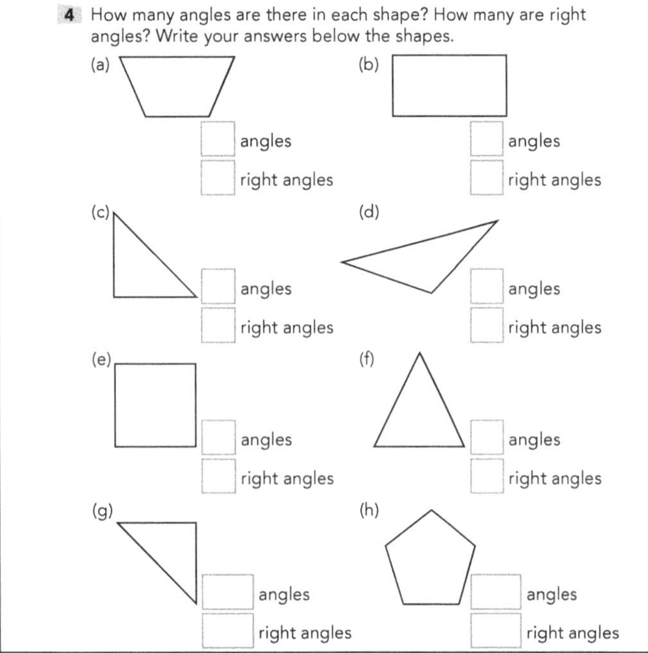

4 How many angles are there in each shape? How many are right angles? Write your answers below the shapes.
(a)
(b)
(c)
(d)
(e)
(f)
(g)
(h)
angles
right angles


## What learning will pupils have achieved at the conclusion of Question 4?

- Angles are used to measure turn; pupils will be able to see angles where two straight lines meet at a point.
- Pupils will be able to recognise angles that are: right angles, less than a right angle or greater than a right angle.

## Activities for whole-class instruction

- Ask pupils, working with a partner, to use a ruler to draw a 2-D shape. Ask them to look at each other's shapes. Ask: *How many angles does it have? How many are right angles? How many are less than or greater than right angles? Do you agree with your partner? Have you checked with an angle muncher?* Repeat with other 2-D shapes.

Look out for ... pupils who think that all polygons are regular. Ensure that you expose pupils to images of irregular as well as regular quadrilaterals, pentagons and hexagons, taking opportunities to talk about what makes them regular or irregular.

Regular polygons – all sides are the same length and angles are the same.

Irregular polygons – sides and angles are not all the same.

- Pupils should complete Question 4 in the Practice Book.

## Same-day intervention

- Ask pupils to draw two straight lines that meet at a point. Ask: *Is the angle a right angle or is it greater or less than a right angle?* Ask pupils to check using an angle muncher. Repeat this activity with different angles. Ask pupils to draw a 2-D shape, look at all the angles and predict then check whether they are right angles, or greater or less than a right angle.

## Same-day enrichment

- Ask pupils to investigate the combinations of acute, obtuse and right angles that can be used to make a quadrilateral. For example, they might try two right angles, one obtuse and one acute angle. Challenge them to find at least five different combinations.

# Question 5

5 In the grid, draw the three angles that are described below.

(a) A right angle

(b) An angle that is less than a right angle (also called 'an acute angle')

(c) An angle that is greater than a right angle (also called 'an obtuse angle')

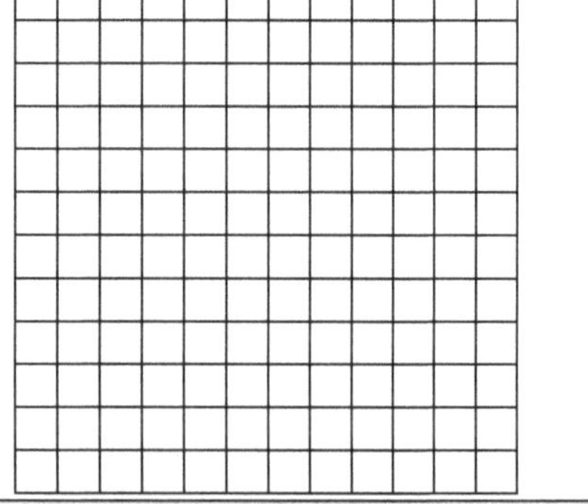

## What learning will pupils have achieved at the conclusion of Question 5?

- Pupils will be able to construct right angles, angles that are less than a right angle and angles that are greater than a right angle.
- Pupils will have learned the terms 'obtuse' and 'acute' to describe angles.

## Activities for whole-class instruction

- Ask pupils to make an 'angle maker'. Give each pupil two strips of cardboard approximately 15 cm long and 2 cm wide. At one end of the strips of cardboard they punch a hole and then join the strips together using a paper fastener, loose enough so the strips can move. Ask pupils to use the 'angle maker' to show you a right angle. Now ask them to close the strips together again. Explain that an angle smaller than a right angle is called an acute angle. Ask pupils to show you an acute angle with their 'angle maker', and another, and another.

*An angle that is smaller than a right angle is an acute angle.*

- Still using the 'angle maker', ask pupils to make an angle that is greater than a right angle but smaller than a straight line. Explain that an angle larger than a right angle but smaller than a straight line is called an obtuse angle. Ask pupils to show a different obtuse angle, then another. Get them to check each other's angles.

*An obtuse angle is bigger than a right angle but smaller than a straight line.*

- Give pupils some squared paper, a ruler/straight edge and a pencil. On the board or visualiser, show pupils how to draw right angles using the squares to help them:

- Ask them to try different positions and orientations. Repeat but with obtuse and acute angles.
- Ask pupils to work with a partner. Pupil A challenges Pupil B to draw an obtuse, acute or right angle. Pupil B draws the angle, Pupil A checks, and then they swap. Repeat five times.
- Pupils should complete Question 5 in the Practice Book.

## Same-day intervention

- Ask pupils to draw shapes with the given properties:
  1. A triangle with one right angle
  2. A quadrilateral with two right angles
  3. A triangle with an obtuse angle.
- Can pupils name the other angles in the shapes they have drawn? Ask pupils to repeat the 'All say' definitions for acute and obtuse angles as they draw the shapes.

*An angle that is smaller than a right angle is an acute angle.*

*An obtuse angle is bigger than a right angle but smaller than a straight line.*

## Same-day enrichment

- Ask pupils to investigate this statement: It is not possible to draw a five-sided shape with three obtuse and two acute angles. Ask: *Is this true or false? Can you prove it? How about three acute and two obtuse angles?*

## Challenge and extension questions

# Questions 6 and 7

**6** Use a ruler to draw a line on the shape so that it has 3 more right angles.

**7** A square has 4 angles. If one of its 4 corners is cut off, how many angles will there be in the remaining part? (You may draw squares on paper and then cut them out to help you find the answer.)

The first question enables pupils to demonstrate their understanding of right angles. Because the line they must draw to answer this question is inside the quadrilateral, two right angles will be formed at the point where the vertical line meets the horizontal line. This question is probably best trialled on paper before answering in the book. In the second question, watch out for pupils who cut diagonally from one corner to another and make two triangles.

# Unit 10.2 Identifying different types of line (1)

## Conceptual context

In this unit pupils learn about vertical and horizontal lines. Vertical lines were introduced in Book 2 when pupils found vertical line symmetry in a variety of shapes and objects; this chapter builds on that knowledge and introduces horizontal lines. It is important that from an early stage pupils identify that these are straight lines. In the next chapter, they will learn that where horizontal and vertical lines meet or cross, angles are formed.

## Learning pupils will have achieved at the end of the unit

- Pupils will be able to identify horizontal and vertical lines in their everyday life (Q1)
- Pupils will be able to explain what vertical and horizontal lines are (Q1, Q2, Q3)
- Pupils will be able to differentiate between vertical and horizontal lines (Q1, Q2, Q3)
- Pupils will develop their visualisation skills and their knowledge about lines when they apply their knowledge of quarter, half, three-quarter and full turns to mentally 'move' horizontal and vertical lines and visualise their orientation following a turn (Q4)

### Resources

metre stick; rulers/straight edges

### Vocabulary

horizontal, vertical, quarter turn, half turn, three quarter turn

# Question 1

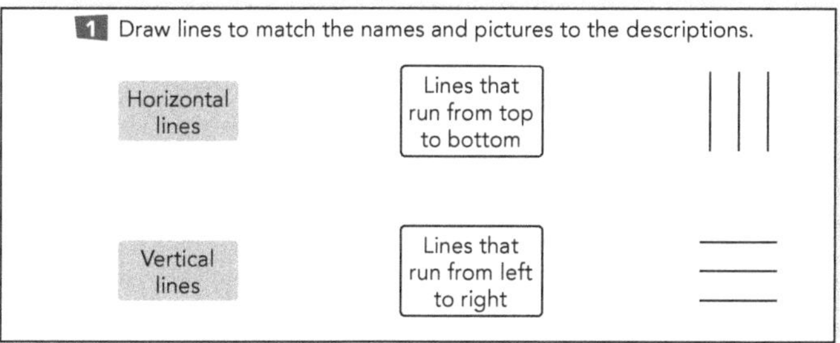
**1** Draw lines to match the names and pictures to the descriptions.

Horizontal lines

Vertical lines

Lines that run from top to bottom

Lines that run from left to right

## What learning will pupils have achieved at the conclusion of Question 1?

- Pupils will be able to differentiate between vertical and horizontal lines.

## Activities for whole-class instruction

- Ask pupils what they can remember from Book 2 about vertical symmetry. Discuss the meaning of the word 'vertical'. Show them some examples of vertical lines; demonstrate by holding a metre stick in a vertical position. Ask: *Can you see any examples of vertical lines in the classroom?*

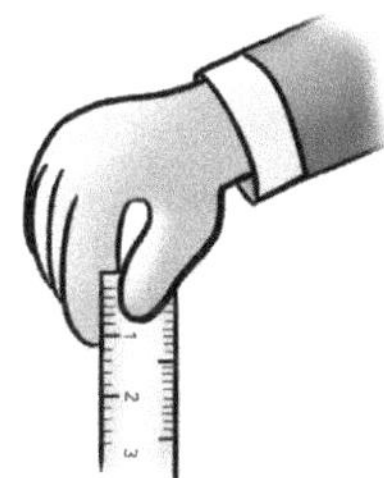

*A vertical line runs straight up and down, from top to bottom or bottom to top.*

- Now hold the metre stick horizontally. Ask pupils to describe the difference between vertical and horizontal. (One goes up and down; the other goes from side to side.) Discuss the word 'horizon' where the Earth's surface and the sky appear to meet at a straight line. If the horizon is visible from the window or playground, show it to pupils; also show them images from the internet or books. Link with the word 'horizontal'.

*A horizontal line runs straight from left to right or right to left.*

- Give pupils a worksheet with straight lines drawn in different orientations. Ask them to identify the vertical and horizontal lines and label them.
- Pupils should complete Question 1 in the Practice Book.

## Same-day intervention

- Place two rulers on a table, one horizontally and the other vertically. Invite pupils to draw an imaginary line with their finger along the horizontal ruler and ask them to repeat the word 'horizontal' as they do it. Repeat with the vertical line. Ask them to draw a vertical line on paper and label it. Repeat with a horizontal line. Finally ask them to draw a straight line that is neither horizontal nor vertical.

## Same-day enrichment

- Ask pupils to draw three 2-D shapes that have both vertical and horizontal sides. Can they name the shapes?

# Questions 2 and 3

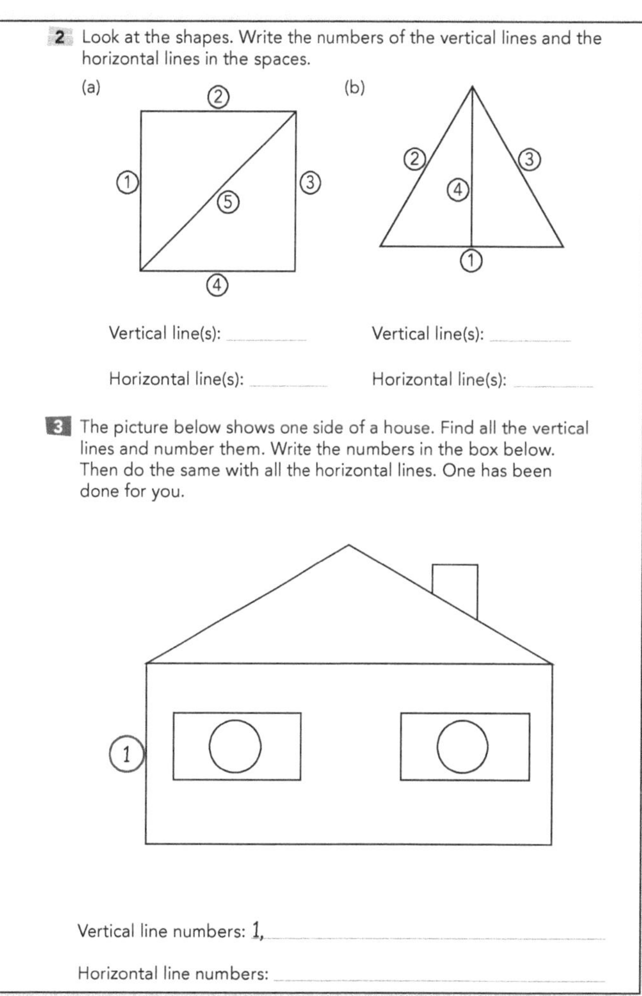
**2** Look at the shapes. Write the numbers of the vertical lines and the horizontal lines in the spaces.

(a)



Vertical line(s): ______

Horizontal line(s): ______

(b)



Vertical line(s): ______

Horizontal line(s): ______

**3** The picture below shows one side of a house. Find all the vertical lines and number them. Write the numbers in the box below. Then do the same with all the horizontal lines. One has been done for you.



Vertical line numbers: 1, ______

Horizontal line numbers: ______

## What learning will pupils have achieved at the conclusion of Questions 2 and 3?

- Pupils will be able to identify vertical and horizontal lines.

## Activities for whole-class instruction

- Ask pupils to use the 'All say' definitions for horizontal and vertical.

*A horizontal line runs straight from left to right or right to left.*

*A vertical line runs straight up and down from top to bottom or bottom to top.*

- Show pupils a diagram that includes horizontal, vertical and diagonal lines, for example a block arrow like this one:

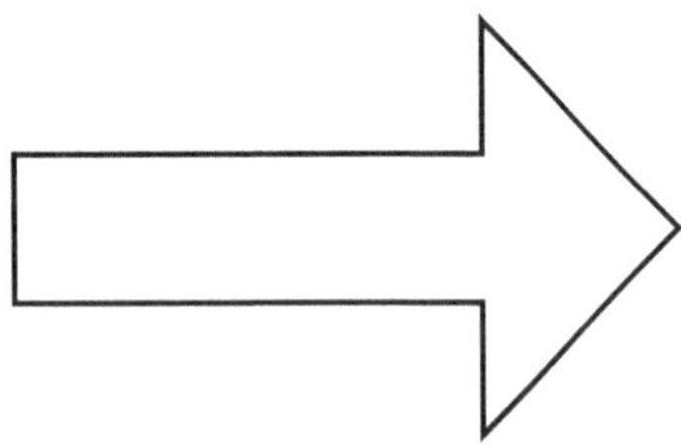

- Ask them to identify all the horizontal lines, repeating the 'All say' definition as they find them. Repeat with the vertical lines. Point to the two diagonal lines and ask: How do you know that these lines are not vertical? (Because they are not running **straight** up and down from top to bottom or bottom to top.)
- Repeat with a different example, such as:

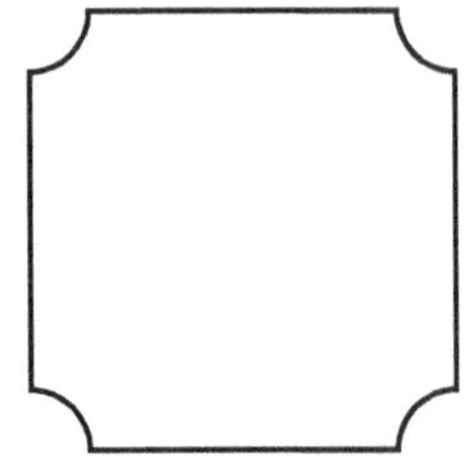

- You should point out that some of these lines are not straight lines but are curved.
- Pupils should complete Questions 2 and 3 in the Practice Book.

### Same-day intervention

- Repeat the intervention used in Question 1. Then ask pupils to draw a 2-D shape with horizontal and vertical lines and label the sides H for horizontal and V for vertical.

## Same-day enrichment

- Ask pupils to draw a triangle that has one vertical and one horizontal side. Then ask them to draw a triangle that does not have any vertical or horizontal sides.
- Challenge pupils to work with a partner. They both draw a picture, using a ruler and pencil, that is made up of only straight lines. Ask them to get their partner to find all the horizontal lines and label them H, all of the vertical lines and label them V, and all other lines and label them O. Get them to check each other's work.

# Question 4

**4** True or false? (Put a ✓ for true and a ✗ for false in each box.)

(a) After a quarter turn, a horizontal line is still a horizontal line. ☐

(b) After a half turn, a vertical line will be a horizontal line. ☐

(c) After a three quarter turn, a horizontal line will be a vertical line. ☐

(d) After a complete turn, a vertical line is still a vertical line. ☐

## What learning will pupils have achieved at the conclusion of Question 4?

- Pupils will develop their visualisation skills and their knowledge about lines when they apply their knowledge of quarter, half, three-quarter and full turns to mentally 'move' horizontal and vertical lines and visualise their orientation following a turn.

## Activities for whole-class instruction

- Ask pupils to use the 'All say' definitions for horizontal and vertical.

*A horizontal line runs straight from left to right or right to left.*

*A vertical line runs straight up and down from top to bottom or bottom to top.*

- Provide pupils with an arrow line drawn on A4 paper, like the one shown below, or ask them to draw their own.

- Ask pupils to hold their paper so that the line is a horizontal line. Check and correct as necessary, then ask them to hold it so that the line is vertical. Repeat several times. Then ask them to show you a line that is neither vertical nor horizontal.
- Now give pupils instructions and questions such as:

*Hold your paper so that your line is a vertical line.*

*Now turn it a quarter turn to the right. What type of line have you now got?*

- Repeat this several times using right and left turns, quarter, half, three-quarters and full turns.
- Ask pupils to work in pairs and give their partners similar questions. They can test their answers using the arrow line.
- Pupils should complete Question 4 in the Practice Book.

## Same-day intervention

- Ask pupils to hold the arrow line in a vertical position, run their finger up and down the edge and say:

*A vertical line runs straight up and down from top to bottom or bottom to top.*

- Repeat for horizontal.

*A horizontal line runs straight from left to right or right to left.*

- Now ask pupils to follow your instructions and tell you what type of line they have, for example say: *Show me a vertical line. Now turn it a quarter turn.* Ask: *Is it still a vertical line?* Repeat as necessary.

## Same-day enrichment

- Explain to pupils that they are going to extend the partner work from the whole class activities in Question 4 by giving their partner multi-step statements, for example: After a quarter turn clockwise and a three-quarter turn anticlockwise is your vertical line still vertical? Ask pupils to write down the instructions and work out the correct answer before testing their partner.

## Challenge and extension question

# Question 5

5 Write 2–4 examples of vertical and horizontal lines from your everyday life. (Hint: Look around your home, your classroom or the environment for ideas.)

In this question pupils write examples of horizontal and vertical lines found in everyday items.

# Unit 10.3
# Identifying different types of line (2)

## Conceptual context

In this unit, pupils are taught about parallel and perpendicular lines. Pupils learn in this chapter that when horizontal and vertical lines meet or intersect, angles are formed. This is the basis for much of the work they will undertake in geometry in later years.

## Learning pupils will have achieved at the end of the unit

- Pupils will know what perpendicular and parallel lines are (Q1)
- Pupils will be able to identify parallel and perpendicular lines in different contexts (Q2, Q3)
- Pupils will be able to apply their knowledge of horizontal and vertical lines to perpendicular and parallel lines (Q4)
- Pupils will be able to recognise perpendicular and parallel lines in their daily life (Q5)

### Resources

rulers/metre sticks; pictures of 2-D shapes; playground chalk; right-angle measurer; a real or toy ladder; **Resource 3.10.3** Parallel and perpendicular lines

### Vocabulary

horizontal, vertical, perpendicular, parallel, right angle, intersect

# Question 1

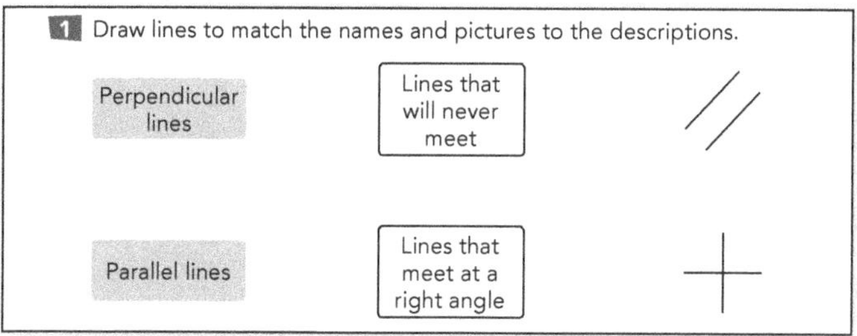

1 Draw lines to match the names and pictures to the descriptions.
Perpendicular lines
Lines that will never meet
Parallel lines
Lines that meet at a right angle


## What learning will pupils have achieved at the conclusion of Question 1?

- Pupils will know what perpendicular and parallel lines are and begin to be able to identify them.

**Parallel lines** are straight lines that are equidistant to each other along their length, so they will never meet. There are many examples in real life of parallel lines, for example: the lines in an exercise book; the 100-metre running track; swimming lanes; and the side lines on a football pitch. Parallel lines do not have to be horizontal, they can be in any orientation, as long as they are the same distance apart from each other at all opposite points along their length.

**Perpendicular lines** are formed when two straight lines meet or intersect at right angles. Again, there are many examples of these in everyday life, for example: in buildings, on the football pitch and at road junctions. As with parallel lines they can be in any orientation.

## Activities for whole-class instruction

- This activity can take place in either the playground or the classroom. Ask pupils to work with a partner and draw a line along both the long edges of a ruler/metre stick. Use chalk if working in the playground. Ask: *What do you notice about the lines?* (They are straight; they don't meet; they are the same distance apart/equidistant.) Ask pupils to extend their line using the ruler/metre stick. Ask: *Apart from having a longer line, has anything changed?* Explain to pupils that these are called parallel lines. Repeat the activity with pupils asked to place the ruler/metre stick so that it is not horizontal or vertical.

*Parallel lines are lines that will never meet.*

- Ask pupils to find examples of parallel lines in the classroom or playground. Ask them to point to them and share with the class.
- Draw an example of perpendicular lines for pupils to look at. What do they see? There are two straight lines; they cross (intersect); there are right angles where the lines meet/cross.
- Ask pupils to draw a pair of perpendicular lines. If there are examples like the one below, show the rest of the class:

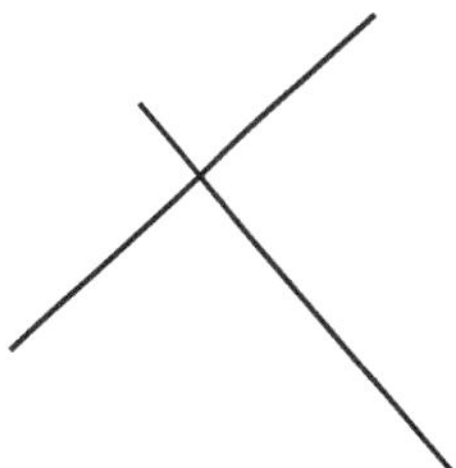

Emphasise that perpendicular lines can be in any orientation as long as they meet at right angles.

- Explain that perpendicular lines have a shared point when they cross over each other. This is called an intersection. At the point where perpendicular lines meet or cross there will be right angles. Ask: *How many right angles are there around the intersection?*

*Perpendicular lines meet or intersect at a right angle.*

- Ask pupils to find examples of perpendicular lines in the classroom or playground. Share some examples with the class.
- Pupils should complete Question 1 in the Practice Book.

## Same-day intervention

- Give pupils a ruler/metre stick and ask them to run their finger and thumb along the two long edges. Ask: *Do your fingers get closer together or do they stay the same distance apart?* Ask pupils to measure the width of the ruler/metre stick at both ends. Ask: *Is it the same?*
- Explain to pupils that straight lines that will never meet are called parallel lines.

*Parallel lines are lines that will never meet.*

- If there is a football pitch or netball court or similar marked out at school, take pupils to look at the lines drawn. Point out where two straight lines meet and make a right angle. Ask: *How many places can you find where this happens?*

- If no games pitches are marked out, give pupils the diagram of a football pitch from **Resource 3.10.3** Parallel and perpendicular lines.
- Explain that where two straight lines meet at right angles the lines are perpendicular to each other.

*Perpendicular lines meet at right angles.*

- Find perpendicular lines on sports pitches in the playground, or on images in books or on the internet.

## Same-day enrichment

- Ask pupils to draw five straight lines anywhere on a piece of paper. Say: *Using a coloured pen/pencil, add five more lines so that you now have three sets of parallel lines and two sets of perpendicular lines. Label them.*

# Question 2

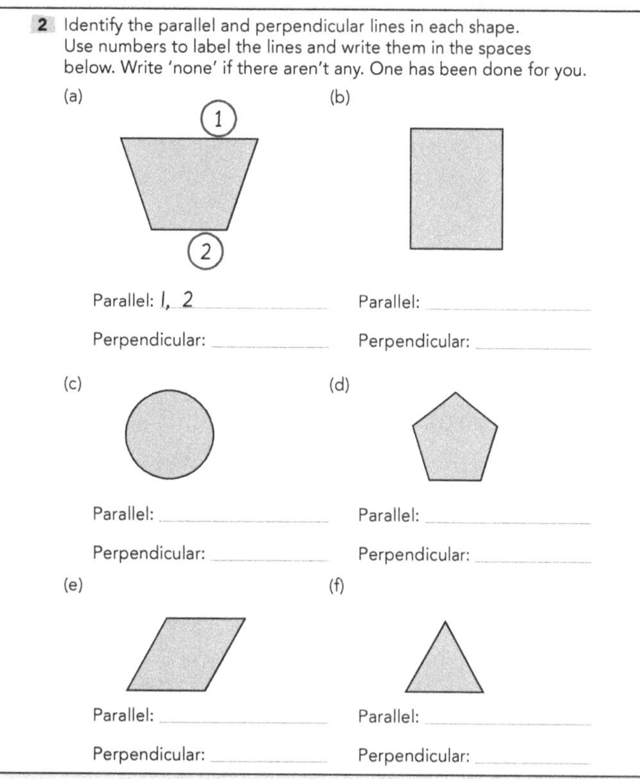

**2** Identify the parallel and perpendicular lines in each shape. Use numbers to label the lines and write them in the spaces below. Write 'none' if there aren't any. One has been done for you.

(a) ① ②

Parallel: 1, 2

Perpendicular:

(b)

Parallel:

Perpendicular:

(c)

Parallel:

Perpendicular:

(d)

Parallel:

Perpendicular:

(e)

Parallel:

Perpendicular:

(f)

Parallel:

Perpendicular:

## What learning will pupils have achieved at the conclusion of Question 2?

- Pupils will be able to identify parallel and perpendicular lines in familiar 2-D shapes.

## Activities for whole-class instruction

Recap on the definitions of perpendicular and parallel lines from Question 1 using the 'All say...' sentences.

*Parallel lines are lines that will never meet.*

*Perpendicular lines meet at right angles.*

- Give pupils squared paper and ask them to use a ruler/straight edge to draw a square. Ask them what they already know about a square. Ask: *Can you find any parallel lines? How many sets? Where are perpendicular lines?*
- Give pupils **Resource 3.10.3** Parallel and perpendicular lines.

- Ask pupils to work with a partner to identify parallel and perpendicular lines in one or more of the pictures. Ask them to compare their answers with another pair. Did they find all of them?
- Pupils should complete Question 2 in the Practice Book.

## Same-day intervention

- Give pupils a copy of the shapes found in Question 2. Ask pupils to use an 'angle muncher' (**Resource 3.10.1b**) or something that will measure a right angle (for example, the corner of a piece of A4 paper) to find any right angles in the first shape. Ask pupils to point to them and repeat after you: *Perpendicular lines meet or intersect at right angles.* Ask: *How many can you find?* (4) Now ask them to use a ruler and extend the two horizontal lines, one at a time, by drawing over the existing line and continuing it for a few more centimetres. Ask: *Are the lines getting closer together? Will they ever meet?* Ask pupils to remind you what they know about parallel lines: parallel lines are lines that will never meet. Repeat with the other shapes from Question 2.

## Same-day enrichment

- Ask pupils to investigate the following statement. Is it true: All quadrilaterals have either parallel and/or perpendicular lines. How do they know?

# Questions 3 and 4

**3** Look at the ladder and identify the types of lines shown for **a**, **b**, **c**, **d** and **e**. Write 'horizontal', 'vertical', 'parallel' or 'perpendicular' in the spaces.

(a) Lines **a** and **b** are ______ lines.

They are also ______ lines.

(b) Lines **c**, **d** and **e** are ______ lines.

They are also ______ lines.

(c) Lines **a** and **c** are ______ lines.

(d) Lines **a** and **d** are ______ lines.

(e) Lines **b** and **e** are ______ lines.

**4** True or false? (Put a ✓ for true and a ✗ for false in each box.)

(a) Two horizontal lines are parallel. ☐

(b) Two vertical lines are perpendicular to each other. ☐

(c) Two perpendicular lines will meet at a point. ☐

(d) Two lines are either parallel or perpendicular. ☐

## What learning will pupils have achieved at the conclusion of Questions 3 and 4?

- Pupils will recognise horizontal and vertical lines and be able to identify if they are parallel or perpendicular to each other.
- Pupils will know that not all lines are parallel or perpendicular to each other.

## Activities for whole-class instruction

- Remind pupils of the 'All say…' definitions for horizontal and vertical lines. Use the 'All say…' definitions and ask pupils to 'draw' the lines with their fingers as they say them.

*A vertical line runs straight up and down, from top to bottom or bottom to top.*

*A horizontal line runs straight from left to right or right to left.*

- Refer pupils back to **Resource 3.10.3** Parallel and perpendicular lines and ask them to find the picture of the railway track. Ask them to show you if they think the railway line is running horizontally or vertically by using the appropriate arm signal below:

- Address any misconceptions. What about the wooden boards under the rails? Repeat for other examples using arm signals.
- Repeat the 'All say...' definitions for parallel and perpendicular lines:

*Parallel lines are lines that will never meet.*

*Perpendicular lines meet at right angles.*

- Ask pupils to work with a partner. Can they find any examples of parallel lines on the picture of the train tracks? How about perpendicular lines? Say: *Check your findings with another pair.* Ask: *Did you find them all?*
- Ask pupils to work with a partner and choose a flag from the resource sheet. Ask them to count the perpendicular and parallel lines. Ask: *How many did you find?* Get them to check their answers with another pair. Do they agree?
- Pupils work with a partner to complete Questions 3 and 4 in the Practice Book.

## Same-day intervention

- Ask pupils to show you the window on **Resource 3.10.3**. Ask them to 'draw' with their fingers a horizontal line while saying: *A horizontal line runs straight from left to right or right to left.* Now ask pupils to show you as many horizontal lines as they can. Repeat with vertical lines, while saying: *A vertical line runs straight up and down from top to bottom or bottom to top.* If possible, show pupils a real ladder (alternatively provide a toy or model ladder) and ask them to show you examples of parallel and perpendicular lines. Change the orientation of the ladder and repeat.

## Same-day enrichment

- Look at the diagram of the football pitch on **Resource 3.10.3**. Ask pupils to imagine that a new law has been introduced that says football pitches can no longer have any parallel or perpendicular lines but any that are replaced must still be straight lines! Ask them to use a ruler to draw what the new pitch will look like.

## Challenge and extension question

# Question 5

**5** Write 2–4 examples of parallel and perpendicular lines from your everyday life. (Hint: Look around your home, your classroom or the environment for ideas.)

In this question pupils use the knowledge they have learned about parallel and perpendicular lines and apply it to everyday life, writing examples of parallel and perpendicular lines from daily life. This could be set as a school-based or home-based task, with pupils drawing pictures or taking digital photos of examples from around the school or home environment to display in the classroom.

# Unit 10.4
# Drawing 2-D shapes and making 3-D shapes

## Conceptual context

This unit builds on the work pupils did in Book 2 on knowing the names and properties of some 2-D and 3-D shapes and understanding that the faces of 3-D shapes are 2-D shapes. In this unit pupils will strengthen their knowledge about shapes by developing higher order skills in this area. Instead of recognising and identifying features, they will actually apply their knowledge to construct shapes. The unit concludes with consolidating their knowledge of the relationship between 2-D and 3-D shapes when they start to develop their understanding of how 2-D shapes fit together as the faces of 3-D shapes when they make a cube.

Until now the focus has been on regular shapes. In this unit the concept of irregular shape is introduced, which is something that is built on in later years.

## Learning pupils will have achieved at the end of the unit

- Pupils will be able to name common 2-D shapes and recognise when they are symmetrical (Q1)
- Pupils will be able to identify and name common 3-D shapes (Q1)
- Pupils will be able to accurately draw known 2-D shapes (Q2, Q3)
- Pupils will be able to construct a net for a cube (Q4)

### Resources

materials to make 3-D shapes (this could be a commercially available kit, modelling clay/sticky tack and straws, or dowelling and modelling clay/sticky tack); old cardboard boxes of varying shapes and sizes that can be flattened to make the net of the shape (remember to remove extra tabs and so on from the boxes before using them as nets); pictures of 2-D shapes; 3-D geometric shapes or pictures/posters of them; rulers; 1 cm dotted paper or 1 cm squared paper; rulers/straight edges

### Vocabulary

two-dimensional, three-dimensional, cylinder, cube, cuboid, hexagon, hexagonal, pyramid, prism, pentagon, octagon, net

# Question 1

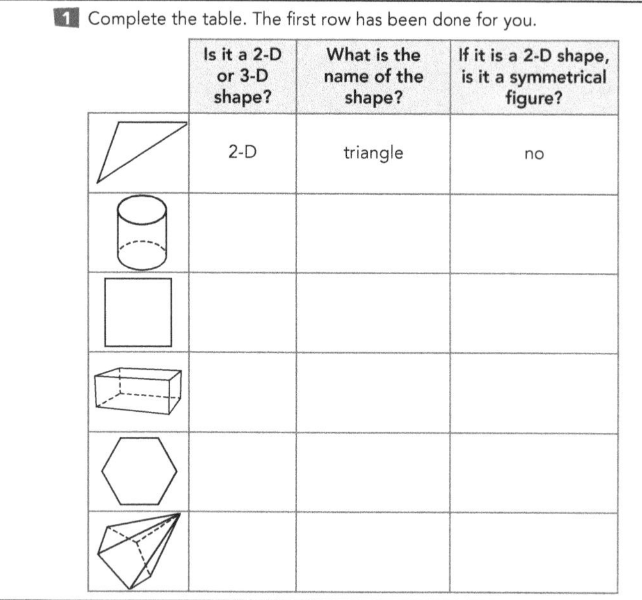

1 Complete the table. The first row has been done for you.

| | Is it a 2-D or 3-D shape? | What is the name of the shape? | If it is a 2-D shape, is it a symmetrical figure? |
|---|---|---|---|
| | 2-D | triangle | no |
| | | | |
| | | | |
| | | | |
| | | | |
| | | | |

## What learning will pupils have achieved at the conclusion of Question 1?

- Pupils will be able to recognise and name common 2-D and 3-D shapes.
- Pupils will be able to identify symmetry in 2-D shapes.

A two-dimensional shape (2-D) is a shape that only has two dimensions, width and height, but no thickness. Therefore, 2-D shapes exist only on paper or on a screen and cannot be picked up or held. It is important for pupils to know that they cannot be picked up so plastic representations of these shapes (often found in classrooms) should be avoided. Images of 2-D shapes on paper are often provided, for example when they are to be cut out for sorting activities. It is important, conceptually, that when these images are cut out, a margin of white space is left showing around the edge of the shape as shown below.

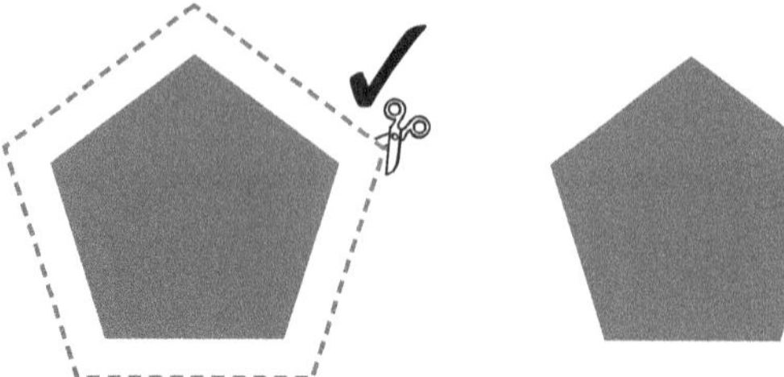

This will help to prevent the misconception being formed that a 2-D shape can be picked up because the object being manipulated is still clearly an image of the shape, not the shape itself.

For the same reason, when using pictures of 2-D and 3-D shapes it is important to consistently refer to these as 'a picture of a ...'.

## Activities for whole-class instruction

- Before starting the activity, discuss with pupils the meaning of the letter 'D' in 2-D and 3-D (dimension). Ask: *What does 2-D mean?* A 2-D shape has width and height but no thickness whereas a 3-D shape has width, height and thickness. You can pick up a 3-D shape but not a 2-D shape.
- Play '2-D or 3-D.' Explain to pupils that you are going to show them pictures of some different shapes that they have seen before in Year 1 and 2 to see if they can recognise if they are 2-D or 3-D shapes. Divide the classroom/hall into two parts, one side for 2-D shapes and the other side for 3-D shapes. Explain that you are going to show them pictures of shapes and they need to decide whether each one is a 2-D shape or a 3-D shape, and go and stand in the part of the room to match this. Make sure you include pictures of the shapes illustrated in Question 1 (triangle, cylinder, square, cuboid, hexagon and pyramid).
- Repeat the activity but change it as follows: display the names of the pictures of 2-D and 3-D shapes that you have in various parts of the classroom or in the playground. Ensure the words 'triangle', 'cylinder', 'square', 'cuboid', 'hexagon' and 'pyramid' are included. Tell pupils that hidden in your bag you have some pictures of 2-D and 3-D shapes and that when you pull a picture out of the bag you want them to go and stand by the name of the shape you are holding. Let pupils see the shape, make a choice and move to the word. Give them five seconds to move again if they think they might be wrong, then ask a pupil to give you the answer. Each pupil scores 1 point for a correct answer. Repeat several times, ensuring you use a variety of shape pictures and including ones of different sizes and different pyramids and prisms.
- Show pupils a picture of a rectangle with its vertical line of symmetry already marked on it. Ask pupils if they remember what the line is called. Fold the rectangle in half and ask them what they can tell you. Give pupils pictures of some of the 2-D shapes used in the previous activity and ask them to draw the vertical line of symmetry. Ask pupils to cut out the shapes and check their answers.
- Pupils should complete Question 1 in the Practice Book.

## Same-day intervention

- Evaluate which of the 2-D or 3-D shapes pupils are having difficulty with and focus on the properties of that shape. If it is recognising the difference between 2-D and 3-D shapes show pupils a picture of a square and give them a cube to hold. Ask: *What similarities and differences are there?* (Focus on not being able to pick up 2-D shapes.) Get pupils to sort pictorial representations of 2-D and 3-D shapes into a Carroll diagram. Refer pupils back to being able to pick up only 3-D objects and how, when looking at pictures, they need to imagine having the shapes in front of them and deciding which ones they can actually pick up.

| 2-D shapes | 3-D shapes |
|---|---|
| | |

- If pupils are having difficulties with symmetry, ask them to cut out the pictures of the 2-D shapes that they have sorted and fold them in half vertically. Ask: *Are the two halves identical?* If yes, draw the line of symmetry on the shape.

## Same-day enrichment

- Ask pupils to look at the triangle in Question 1. Establish that it is not symmetrical. Ask them to think about the statement: 'Triangles do not have vertical symmetry.' Ask: *Is it true or false?* Now ask them to investigate the statement and show examples of their findings.

# Questions 2 and 3

**2** Use a straight edge to draw these 2-D shapes.

(a) a rectangle

(b) a pentagon

(c) an octagon

**3** Use the 1 cm square dot grids to draw the shapes described.

(a) A triangle with one angle a right angle and the lengths of two of its sides 2 cm and 3 cm

(b) A hexagon with two sides parallel and the lengths of the two parallel sides 1 cm and 5 cm

## What learning will pupils have achieved at the conclusion of Questions 2 and 3?

- Pupils will know that there are regular and irregular 2-D shapes.
- Pupils will be able to draw 2-D shapes with increasing accuracy.
- Pupils will be able to draw 2-D shapes with given dimensions.

Regular 2-D shapes are shapes that have sides of the same length and all their angles are equal. Irregular shapes do not have equal sides and equal angles.

## Activities for whole-class instruction

- Give pupils some pieces of dotted paper, rulers/straight edges and pencils. Ask them to draw a square. Ask: *What do you know about a square?*
  - four sides
  - four angles
  - all sides same length
  - all angles equal – right angles

  Pupils should check each other's drawings for accuracy of measurement.

- Increase the challenge by asking pupils to draw a rectangle that has two sides of 4 cm and two sides of 2 cm. Again, get them to check for accuracy.
- Challenge pupils to draw a pentagon. Give them a few minutes and then ask if there are any problems. As pupils have not been introduced to irregular 2-D shapes, many may try to draw a regular pentagon, which is challenging. Show pupils two examples of irregular pentagons.

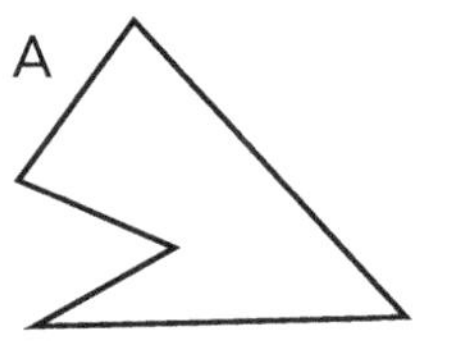


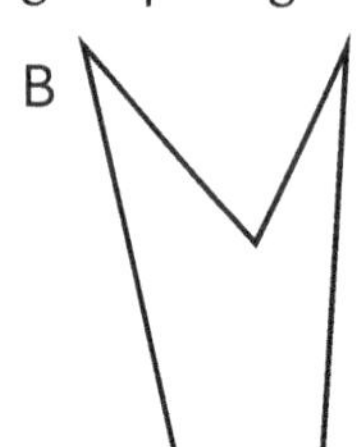


- Give pupils four choices:
  1. Hold up one finger if you think A is a pentagon.
  2. Hold up two fingers if you think B is a pentagon.
  3. Hold up three fingers if you think neither is a pentagon.
  4. Hold up four fingers if you think they are both pentagons.
- Ask pupils who held up four fingers to explain why they think they are both pentagons. Discuss with pupils that irregular shapes do not have all their sides the same length and all their angles equal. They are named by the number of sides, so any shape with five straight sides is a pentagon. Ensure that pupils understand that pentagons with all sides and angles the same are called regular pentagons, but any shape with five straight sides is also called a pentagon.

*Irregular shapes do not have all their sides the same length and all their angles equal.*

- Let pupils experiment with drawing different irregular hexagons, emphasising that the six sides must still be drawn with a ruler/straight edge.
- Before allowing pupils to try Question 3, revise the 'All say…' definition from Chapter 10.3: *Parallel lines are lines that will never meet.*
- Pupils should complete Questions 2 and 3 in the Practice Book.

## Same-day intervention

- Give pupils a piece of dotted paper, a ruler and pencil and play 'Follow the leader', with pupils giving an adult or another pupil instructions to draw different rectangles. Show pupils the shape already drawn on the paper and ask them to 'talk aloud' as they trace around the shape with their finger, for example: *The length of this line is 2 cm; there is a right angle then a vertical line of 4 cm.* Encourage the use of correct mathematical vocabulary such as right angle, parallel, perpendicular, as appropriate.

## Same-day enrichment

- Give pupils dotted paper. Challenge them to draw the following:

  a) A quadrilateral with two right angles

  b) A pentagon with one line of symmetry

  c) A quadrilateral with one pair of parallel lines

  d) A pentagon with two pairs of parallel lines

  e) A quadrilateral with no right angles.

  Examples:

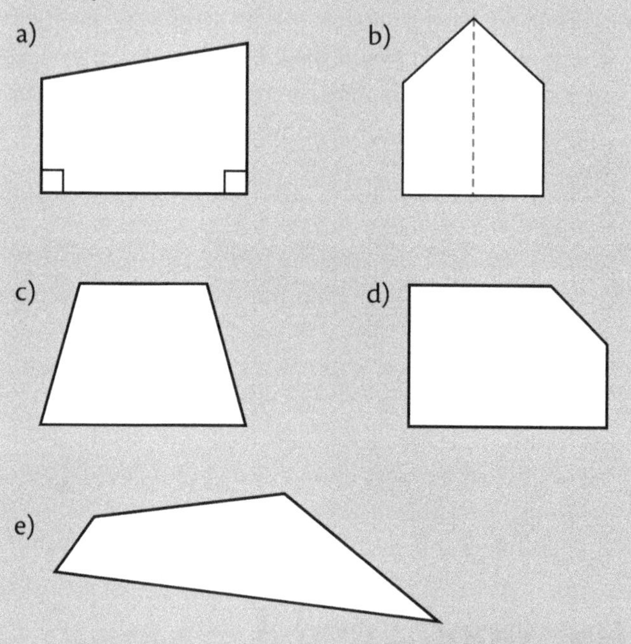


# Question 4

**4** Use square dot grid paper to draw a 2-D shape consisting of six squares as shown below (drawing not to scale). Then cut it out carefully and make a 3-D shape. What shape do you get?

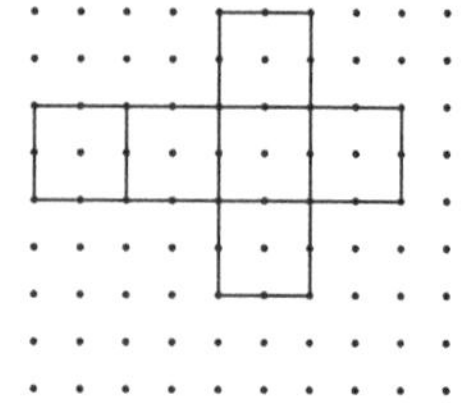

Answer: ____________________

## What learning will pupils have achieved at the conclusion of Question 4?

- Pupils will know that a cube (which is an example of a 3-D shape) can be constructed from a number of squares (which are 2-D shapes) drawn touching each other.

## Activities for whole-class instruction

- Give pupils old cardboard boxes of varying shapes and sizes and ask them to work in small groups to be prepared to tell the class the name of the shape and the properties of the shape. Ask: *What properties of a 3-D shape can you remember from Year 2?* (Faces, edges, vertices.) When the groups are ready, ask them to show their 3-D shape to the rest of the class and share their information about it. If another group have the same shape, do they agree?
- Demonstrate opening out a rectangular box and show pupils the net of the box. Ask two volunteers to show you how to 'remake' the box. Photocopy the net of the box onto card and ask pupils working in pairs to reconstruct the box. When pupils have the net of the shape, ask them to sketch it in their books and write which 3-D shape it will transform into.
- If possible, show pupils the nets of the different 3-D shapes from other boxes and ask them to predict the shape the net will make. Alternatively, the nets of different 3-D shapes could be displayed around the room for reference to help answer the next question.
- Pupils should complete Question 4 in the Practice Book.

## Same-day intervention

- Give pupils the net of a cube that has already been cut out and folded ready to be made into a cube (use card, not paper). Ask: *How many faces does it have? What shape are the faces?* Ask pupils to unfold/undo the net until it is flat. Ask: *Can you draw the net for a larger cube? Try it.*

## Same-day enrichment

- Challenge pupils to make a cube from a net that is different from the one used in Question 4 by arranging the six squares in another way. Can they find at least one more net? Ask them to cut it out and fold it to make a cube. Ask: *Did it work?*
- There are 11 possible answers to this question.

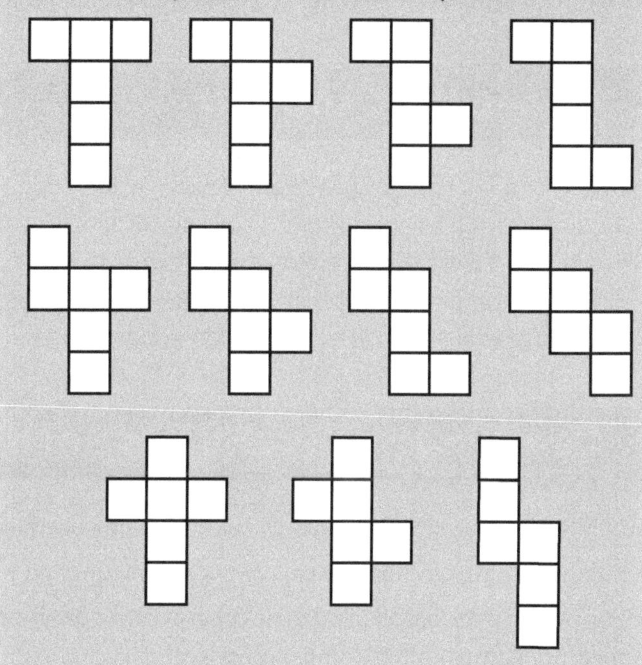

## Challenge and extension question

# Question 5

**5** Draw the 2-D shape below on a piece of paper (not necessarily to the same scale), cut it out carefully and make a 3-D shape. What shape do you get?

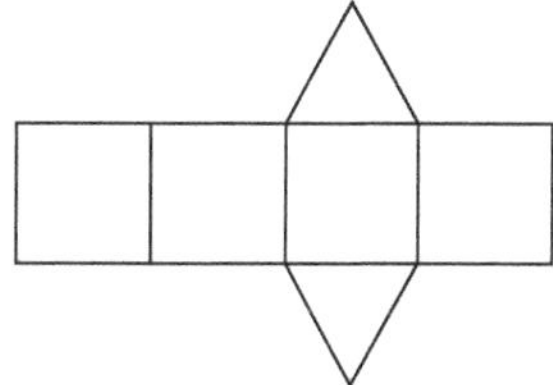

This question gives pupils the opportunity to further experiment with making 3-D shapes from a net made up of 2-D shapes. To extend this even further suggest other 3-D shapes that pupils could try to construct having made the net first. Geometric construction sets that emphasise the shape arrangement of 2-D faces to construct 3-D shapes (if available) are useful, as pupils can build the shape and then take it apart to work out how the net needs to be formed to be successful.

# Unit 10.5
# Length: metre, centimetre and millimetre

## Conceptual context

Measurement is a real life application of number. In Book 1 pupils compared lengths using the language of 'longest', 'shortest' and 'tallest'. They measured and recorded lengths in centimetres and metres. They began to develop practical skills of using a ruler and metre stick. In the second half of Chapter 10, pupils will extend their knowledge about units for measuring length by learning about millimetres and will continue to explore equivalence between different units of measurement. They will consider which unit is the most appropriate to use to measure different items.

## Learning pupils will have achieved at the end of the unit

- Pupils will have consolidated their understanding of equivalent units of length (Q1)
- Pupils will have developed a concept of millimetres and be able to measure millimetres (Q2)
- Pupils will have consolidated their concept of centimetres and metres and be more skilled at measuring in centimetres and metres (Q2)
- Pupils will have continued to make judgements about which units are appropriate to use in different situations (Q3)
- Pupils will have continued to practise comparing and ordering lengths using different units (Q4, Q5)
- Pupils will have begun to apply their understanding of length and height in order to solve problems (Q6)

### Resources

rulers; metre sticks; strips of paper; pieces of string; mixture of items from around the classroom; scissors; interlocking cubes; **Resource 3.10.5** Measuring steps

### Vocabulary

millimetre, centimetre, metre, ruler, metre stick

# Question 1

**1** Fill in the boxes.

(a) 1 m = □ cm (b) 1 cm = □ mm

(c) 1 m = □ mm (d) $\frac{1}{2}$m = □ cm

(e) 15 cm = □ mm (f) 700 cm = □ m

(g) 1 m and 30 cm = □ cm (h) 2 m and 26 cm = □ cm

(i) $\frac{3}{10}$cm = □ mm (j) 900 mm = □ cm

## What learning will pupils have achieved at the conclusion of Question 1?

- Pupils will have explored equivalent units of length.

## Activities for whole-class instruction

- Ask: *How many centimetres are equivalent to one metre?*

*One hundred centimetres is equivalent to one metre.*

- Repeat the question for two metres, four metres, and eight metres. Encourage pupils to use doubling. They can then use what they know to create other numbers of metres, for example 2 m + 6 m = 8 m. Ask pupils to write these down. Ask: *How many centimetres are equivalent to $\frac{1}{2}$ metre?* Repeat for $\frac{1}{4}$ metre, $\frac{3}{4}$ metre, different tenths and other fractions you explored in Chapter 8. Pupils should write these down.
- Ask pupils to use what they found in the above activity to add a fraction of a metre to a whole metre and convert to equivalent centimetres, for example $2\frac{1}{2}$m = 250 cm, $4\frac{1}{10}$m = 410 cm, $5\frac{2}{5}$m = 540 cm.
- Ask pupils to look at their rulers and tell you what they notice about them. They should be able to tell you about the greatest length that the ruler can measure, the centimetre marks and the numbers. What do they think the marks in between the centimetres represent? Tell them that these are millimetres. Ask: *How many millimetres are equivalent to one centimetre? Count them.*

*Ten millimetres is equivalent to one centimetre.*

- Using a large scale number line on the classroom wall for support, ask the following questions:

  *How many millimetres are in 2 cm? 3 cm? 4 cm? 5 cm? 10 cm?*

  *How many millimetres are in 20 cm? 25 cm?*

  *How many centimetres are in 1 m? 2 m? 10 m?*

  *How many centimetres are in 60 mm? 90 mm? 200 mm? 600 mm?*
- Pupils should complete Question 1 in the Practice Book.

## Same-day intervention

- Work with pupils who have difficulty converting between units of length. Focus on finding the number of millimetres that are equivalent to different centimetre lengths. Ask them to write 1 cm = 10 mm and to tell you the relationship between the two numbers, i.e. the number of millimetres is ten times greater than the number of equivalent centimetres. Review how to multiply single-digit numbers by 10 mentally and using a place value grid (and base 10 blocks if needed for understanding). Provide pupil pairs with an A3 number line 1–100. Practise converting cm to mm and mm to cm.

## Same-day enrichment

- Give pupils **Resource 3.10.5** Measuring steps and ask them to complete the questions.

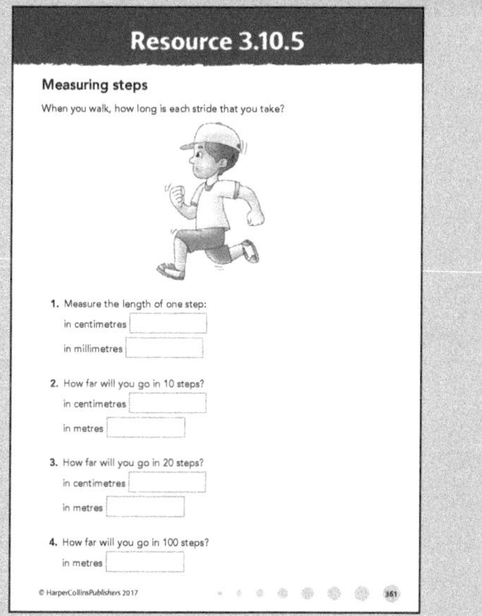

Resource 3.10.5

Measuring steps

When you walk, how long is each stride that you take?

1. Measure the length of one step:
   in centimetres □
   in millimetres □
2. How far will you go in 10 steps?
   in centimetres □
   in metres □
3. How far will you go in 20 steps?
   in centimetres □
   in metres □
4. How far will you go in 100 steps?
   in metres □

© HarperCollinsPublishers 2017 361

# Question 2

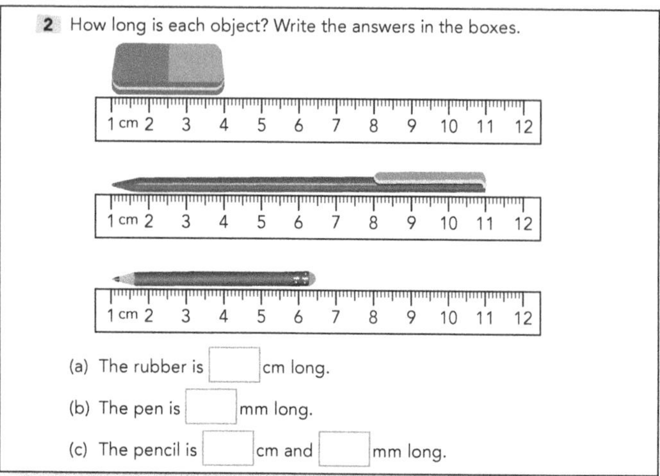

2 How long is each object? Write the answers in the boxes.

(a) The rubber is ☐ cm long.

(b) The pen is ☐ mm long.

(c) The pencil is ☐ cm and ☐ mm long.

## What learning will pupils have achieved at the conclusion of Question 2?

- Pupils will have consolidated their understanding of measuring in centimetres and begun to develop their understanding of measuring in millimetres and a mixture of centimetres and millimetres.

## Activities for whole-class instruction

- Give each pupil a ruler. Ask them to tell you all they can about their ruler, for example: there are divisions labelled with numbers that represent centimetres; there are smaller divisions between the centimetres. Can pupils tell you that these are millimetres? Ask pupils what the letters on the ruler mean. Agree that cm is the abbreviation for centimetre. Establish that the smaller divisions represent millimetres and the abbreviation for a millimetre is mm. Ask pupils to count the divisions from one centimetre to another. Agree that there are ten, which shows that there are ten millimetres in a centimetre.

*One hundred centimetres is equivalent to one metre. Ten millimetres is equivalent to one centimetre.*

- Give each pupil two strips of paper. Ask them to cut the strips into four different lengths. They should measure these to the nearest centimetre and then measure exactly in centimetres and millimetres, for example: 7 cm and 8 mm; 12 cm and 4 mm. Ask them to pass their strips to a partner who should check their measuring to see if they agree. If they do agree, pupils can stick their strips into their books and label them with the exact lengths.
- Invite pupils to demonstrate what they did to the class. Use this as an opportunity to check that they are measuring accurately.
- Give pupils four lengths of string to measure. Ask them to write these measurements down and pass these and the string to their partner to check. Invite different pupils from before to demonstrate how they measured their pieces of string. Use this as an opportunity to check that they are measuring accurately.
- Pupils should complete Question 2 in the Practice Book.

## Same-day intervention

- Work with pupils who have difficulty measuring accurately in centimetres and millimetres. Draw lines that measure an exact number of centimetres for pupils to measure. Ensure that they begin measuring from the correct starting point. When they are confident measuring in centimetres, draw lines that are whole and half centimetres in length. Discuss that if ten millimetres is equivalent to one centimetre, then five millimetres must be equivalent to half a centimetre. They should record the lengths of the lines in centimetres and millimetres, for example 6 cm and 5 mm or 65 mm.

## Same-day enrichment

- Ask pupils to find four different books. They should measure the length, width and thickness of each book. Ask them to record their measurements in two ways: centimetres and millimetres; millimetres only.

# Question 3

3 Write a suitable unit in each box.

(a) A dining table is about 80 ☐ high.

(b) A nail is about 50 ☐ long.

(c) A giraffe is about 5 ☐ tall.

(d) The length of a bus is about 10 ☐.

(e) A UK passport photo size is 45 ☐ high by 35 ☐ wide.

## What learning will pupils have achieved at the conclusion of Question 3?

- Pupils will have continued to make judgements about which units are appropriate to use in different situations.

## Activities for whole-class instruction

- Ask pupils to tell you the similarities and differences between millimetres, centimetres and metres. Ask: *Which is the longest unit? Which is the shortest? How many centimetres are equivalent to a metre? How many millimetres are equivalent to a metre?*

*One hundred centimetres is equivalent to one metre and ten millimetres is equivalent to one centimetre.*

- Discuss what would be measured in metres. Ask pupils to look around the classroom for ideas, for example: height of the window, door, whiteboard. Discuss what would be measured in centimetres. Again, ask them to look for ideas in the classroom, for example: length of an exercise book, pencil case, pencil. Discuss what would be measured in millimetres. Can they find anything in the classroom? Agree that they could measure small items, for example: the rubber at the end of a pencil, the width of a small paper clip, the nib of a pencil. Pupils were introduced to these ideas in Book 1; now they are building more sophisticated concepts about measuring.

| Items | Measurement |
|---|---|
| width of paper clip | 6 mm |
| width of pencil | 8 mm |
| length of Practice Book | $26\frac{1}{2}$ cm |
| length of pair of scissors | 16 cm |
| height of door | 2 m |
| height of whiteboard | 3 m |

- Give pairs of pupils a metre stick and rulers. Ask them to work together to find and measure two items that would be measured in metres, two that would be measured in centimetres, and two that would be measured in millimetres. They should record their results in a table.
- Ask pupils to make a list of four animals that would be measured in metres, four that would be measured in centimetres, and four that would be measured in millimetres. Share pupils' ideas.
- Pupils should complete Question 3 in the Practice Book.

### Same-day intervention

- Work with pupils with a weak sense of which units are appropriate to measure different items. Give pairs a metre stick. They place it beside the door. It should be clear that the door is longer than a metre. Explain that items that are longer than the metre stick would be measured in metres and items that are shorter than the metre stick would be measured in centimetres.
- Give pupils a metre stick and ask them to find items in the classroom that would be measured in metres and others that would be measured in centimetres. When pupils are confident identifying items that can be measured in metres and centimetres, move on to millimetres. Ask pupils to identify millimetres on their rulers. Agree that items that have very small measurements could be measured in millimetres. Ask them to think of items that can be measured in millimetres or centimetres and millimetres.

### Same-day enrichment

- Pupils make an information poster. This should include equivalent units to measure length. Ask them to work out how many millimetres are equivalent to a metre and add this to their poster. They then draw or write examples of items that would be measured in metres, centimetres and millimetres.

## Questions 4 and 5

**4** Write >, < or = in each ◯.

(a) 810 cm ◯ 8 m
(b) 7 m ◯ 75 cm
(c) 1 m ◯ 100 mm
(d) 5 cm ◯ 500 mm
(e) 6 m and 57 cm ◯ 675 cm
(f) 360 cm ◯ 3 m and 600 mm
(g) 28 m + 500 cm ◯ 33 m
(h) 1 m + 60 mm ◯ 106 cm

**5** Write the following lengths in order, from the shortest to the longest. Write < to show the order.

(a) 340cm 12m 11m 98cm 100cm 300mm

Answer: ______

(b) 50m 490mm 4m and 90cm 600cm

Answer: ______

### What learning will pupils have achieved at the conclusion of Questions 4 and 5?

- Pupils will have continued to practise comparing and ordering lengths using different units using >, < and =.

## Activities for whole-class instruction

- Recap how many centimetres are equivalent to one metre and how many millimetres are equivalent to one centimetre. Write different centimetre lengths on the board and ask pupils to convert these to metres and centimetres, for exampl, 235 cm = 2 m and 35 cm.
- Repeat for millimetres, for example 34 mm = 3 cm and 4 mm.
- Write some mixed units on the board and ask pupils to change them to centimetres, for example, 4 m 30 cm, 12 m 45 cm, 8 m 5 cm. Observe how they convert the last one. Did they remember the place holder for the tens and write 805 cm? Repeat this for millimetres, for example 2 cm 6 mm, 35 cm 9 mm, 46 cm 7 mm. Ask them to explain how they have converted.
- Draw >, < and = on the board. Ask pupils to explain what each one is with examples of how they would be used to compare lengths. Invite them to show the class by writing their ideas on the board, for example 5 mm < 2 cm, 3 m > 150 cm, 1 m = 100 cm, 20 mm = 2 cm. Give the whole class a few minutes to make up their own examples for each symbol and to share them with a partner.
- Give each pupil pair a metre stick. They should measure different items in the classroom, for example the height of their table and the height of their chair. They measure these, draw a picture of them and label with the correct measurements. They then write two statements to compare them using > and <.
- Give each pair a pile of interlocking cubes. They should make four different sized towers and order them from shortest to tallest. They measure their heights and make up comparison statements using > and <. Can they find all possibilities? They then make two equal towers, measure again and write the comparison statement to show the heights are equal.
- Write three centimetre and millimetre lengths on the board, for example 25 mm, 1 cm, 5 cm. Ask pupils to order them from longest to shortest. Ask: *How would you find out whether 25 mm is longer or shorter than 2 cm?* Discuss the conversions they would carry out. Repeat with examples using cm or mm.
- Write three metre and centimetre lengths on the board, for example 299 cm, 3 m, 1 m and 75 cm. Ask pupils to order these from least to greatest. Ask them to tell you how they would compare 299 cm with 3 m.
- Pupils should complete Questions 4 and 5 in the Practice Book.

## Same-day intervention

- Work with pupils who find it difficult to convert from one unit of measurement to another. Ask them to tell you how many centimetres are equivalent to 1 m, then 2 m and so on. Write down the equivalences. Next, ask them to tell you how many centimetres are equivalent to half a metre. Agree 50 cm. Ask them to combine the different metres and 50 cm, for example 2 m and 50 cm. They know that 2 m = 200 cm, so 2 m and 50 cm equals 250 cm. Discuss several examples with half metres, referring to them as 50 cm and half a metre interchangeably. Also include multiples of 10 cm combined with a number of metres.

## Same-day enrichment

- Give pupils a set of digit cards. Ask them to make all the possible two-digit numbers and list them. Encourage them to do this systematically. Their numbers represent numbers of metres. Ask them to take each one in turn and change them into the equivalent number of centimetres. They should rehearse their explanation for the following questions:
  - What do they need to do?
  - How do they do it?
  - Do they notice anything – any patterns or something interesting?
- Next, using the list of three-digit numbers that they have just created, pupils should write 'mm' after each one – they now have a list of measurements in millimetres. Ask them to rewrite each one as a length shown in cm and mm.

# Question 6

**6** Application problems.

(a) A ribbon is 805 cm long. It is 1 m and 5 mm longer than another ribbon. What is the length of the other ribbon?

Answer: ______

(b) A giraffe is 4 m and 50 cm tall. It is 5 times as tall as an antelope. What is the height of the antelope?

Answer: ______

## What learning will pupils have achieved at the conclusion of Question 6?

- Pupils will have developed an understanding of how to use and apply their knowledge of length and number to solve problems.

## Activities for whole-class instruction

- Tell pupils that the length of a vegetable plot was 550 cm and the owner wanted to extend it by 1 m 20 cm. Write the two lengths on the board. Ask pupils to discuss how they would find out the new length. Agree that they would add 550 cm and 1 m 20 cm. Ask: *How would you do this?* Ask them if 550 cm is equivalent to another length. Agree that it can also be written as 5 m 50 cm, which makes it easier to add 1 m 20 cm to make 6 m 70 cm. Ask more problems that involve adding length in this way, keeping the first length of 550 cm, but varying the other length (1 m 20 cm).
- Tell pupils that a piece of material was 5 m 75 cm in length. Sara cut off 265 cm to make a top. Ask pupils to discuss how they would find out how much material was left. Agree that they would subtract 265 cm from 5 m 75 cm. Ask: *How would you do this?* Agree that they could convert 5 m 75 cm to 575 cm or 265 cm to 2 m 65 cm and subtract. Encourage them to do both and check that they have the same answer of 3 m 10 cm. Ask more problems that involve subtracting length in this way. Keep the scenario and the length of the piece of material the same. Vary the amount Sara cuts off to make a top.
- Tell pupils that Rosie made a skipping rope. It was 75 cm in length. Her friend made one that was three times as long. Ask pupils how they could find out how long her friend's skipping rope was. Show this model to help pupils interpret the problem:

| Rosie's rope | 75cm | | |
|---|---|---|---|
| Friend's rope | | | |

This model shows that pupils could multiply 75 cm by 3 or add 75 cm three times. Her friend's rope would be 225 cm. Ask pupils to convert this to metres and centimetres. Ask similar problems that involve multiplication. Keep the scenario and the scale factor the same, varying the length of the rope. Then keep the length of the rope and vary the scale factor.

- Tamara had a length of ribbon that measured 3 m and 21 cm. It was three times longer than her friend's. Ask pupils how they could find the length of her friend's ribbon. Show this model to help pupils interpret the problem:

| Tamara's ribbon | | | | 3m 21cm |
|---|---|---|---|---|
| Friend's ribbon | | | | |

This model shows that pupils divide 3 m 21 cm by 3 to find the length of her friend's ribbon, which is 1 m 7 cm.

Ask similar problems that involve division. Again, keep the scenario and the scale factor the same, varying the length of the ribbon. Then keep the length of the ribbon the same and vary the scale factor.

- Pupils should complete Question 6 in the Practice Book.

### Same-day intervention

- Work with pupils who are not able to apply their understanding of length and number to solving problems. Give them counters and ask them to use these to set out the problems you give them. Tell pupils that Dan had a toy dinosaur that was 20 cm tall. Sam had one that was twice the height. They set out one counter for Dan and two underneath for Sam:

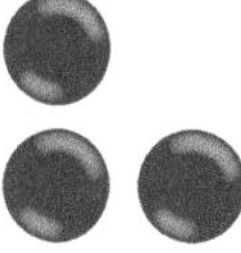

- Dan's dinosaur was 20 cm in height, so each counter represents 20 cm. Can pupils tell you that Sam's dinosaur must have a height of 20 cm + 20 cm? Repeat for different heights. When pupils are confident, move on to three times as many and then four times as many.

### Same-day enrichment

- Pupils make up their own length problems for a partner to solve. They should make up at least one for each operation.

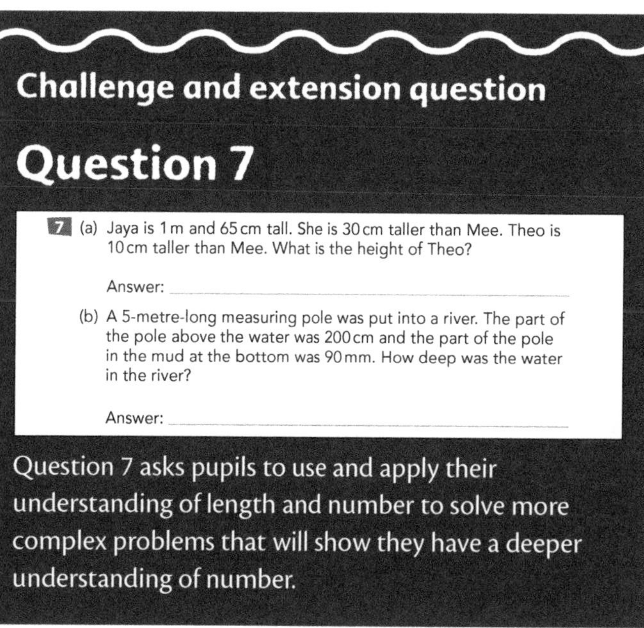

### Challenge and extension question

## Question 7

7 (a) Jaya is 1 m and 65 cm tall. She is 30 cm taller than Mee. Theo is 10 cm taller than Mee. What is the height of Theo?

Answer: ______

(b) A 5-metre-long measuring pole was put into a river. The part of the pole above the water was 200 cm and the part of the pole in the mud at the bottom was 90 mm. How deep was the water in the river?

Answer: ______

Question 7 asks pupils to use and apply their understanding of length and number to solve more complex problems that will show they have a deeper understanding of number.

# Unit 10.6
# Perimeters of simple 2-D shapes (1)

## Conceptual context

In this unit pupils explore perimeter for the first time, initially to get a sense of what a perimeter is by moving their fingers around shapes. They then count the edges of squares on grids and finally move on to measuring perimeters in units of length. Pupils need to understand that perimeters of shapes can be the same even if the shapes are different.

## Learning pupils will have achieved at the end of the unit

- Pupils will have begun to develop a concept of perimeter (Q1)
- Pupils will have begun to measure perimeter by counting sides of squares on grids (Q2)
- Pupils will have developed their measuring and calculating of perimeters by using units of length (Q3)
- Pupils will have applied their understanding of perimeter to problem solving (Q4)

### Resources

toy insect; 1 cm squared paper; plain paper; rulers; metre sticks; cubes, cuboids, triangular prisms, square-based pyramids; string

### Vocabulary

perimeter, boundary, metres, centimetres, millimetres

# Question 1

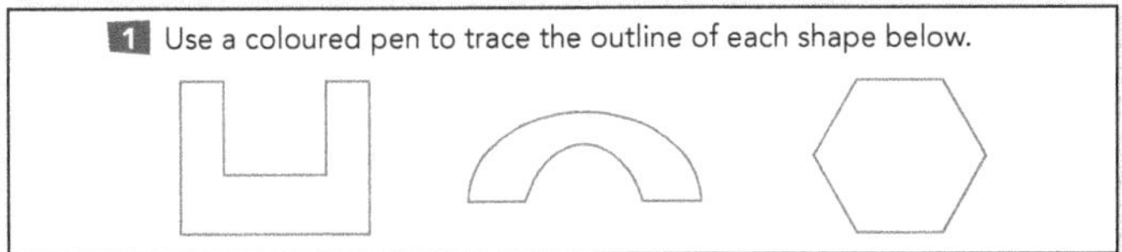

1 Use a coloured pen to trace the outline of each shape below.


## What learning will pupils have achieved at the conclusion of Question 1?

- Pupils will have begun to develop a concept of perimeter.

## Activities for whole-class instruction

- Ask pupils if they know what is meant by the word 'perimeter'. Take suggestions and establish that it is the distance around the outside of any shape that can be measured. Introduce Perry (the toy insect). Tell pupils that he likes to walk around the perimeters of different things. Demonstrate this by taking Perry for a walk around the edge of a book, explaining that the cover of the book is a rectangle and so the perimeter is the distance around the outside of the rectangle. Repeat for different objects. Invite pupils to take Perry for a walk. Ask pupils to use their Practice Book and walk their forefinger and middle finger around the edge of the rectangular cover. They then walk their fingers around the outside of other objects, identifying the shapes as they do, for example the face of a rubber, the rectangular surface of a table, the circular shape of the bottom of a mug or glass.

*Perimeter is the distance around the outside of a shape.*

- Give pairs of pupils a cube, cuboid, triangular prism, square-based pyramid and plain paper. Ask them to draw around the different faces of each 3-D shape on plain paper and label each with the name of the 2-D shape that appears. They should then use a coloured pencil or pen to trace over the perimeter of each face.
- Ask pupils to estimate which of their shapes has the longest and the shortest perimeter just by sight.
- Give them seven pieces of string. Ask them to place a piece of string around the perimeter of each shape in turn and cut it to show the length. They can then compare the pieces of string by laying them side by side. Were their estimates correct?
- Ask pupils to sketch six shapes on plain paper. These should be straight sided, curved sided and a mixture of both. Ask them to give these to a partner who should draw over their perimeters with a coloured pencil.
- Pupils should complete Question 1 in the Practice Book.

## Same-day intervention

- Work with pupils who have difficulty identifying the perimeter of simple 2-D shapes. Give pupils a cuboid that has two square faces and four rectangular faces that are not squares. Ask them to look at one of the faces and ask them to tell you what 2-D shape they can see. Ask them to trace the outside of the rectangle with their finger and say 'This is the perimeter'. Repeat for all faces. Repeat for a triangular prism and a square-based pyramid.

## Same-day enrichment

- Give pupils a length of string. Ask them to use it to make a shape and then draw around it. They should do this several times Ask: *Can you make ten different shapes with the same piece of string? What can you say about the perimeter of your shapes?* Expect them to be able to tell you that different shapes can have the same perimeter. If time allows, make a poster explaining this.

# Question 2

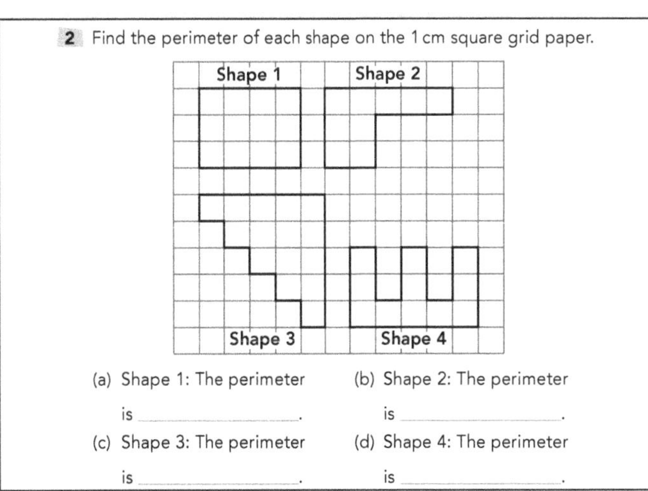

2 Find the perimeter of each shape on the 1 cm square grid paper.
Shape 1
Shape 2
Shape 3
Shape 4
(a) Shape 1: The perimeter is ______.
(b) Shape 2: The perimeter is ______.
(c) Shape 3: The perimeter is ______.
(d) Shape 4: The perimeter is ______.


## What learning will pupils have achieved at the conclusion of Question 2?

- Pupils will have developed their understanding of perimeter by counting sides of squares on grids.

## Activities for whole-class instruction

- Ask pupils to tell you all they can about the meaning of 'perimeter'. Expect them to tell you that it is the distance around a shape. Make the link between perimeter and boundary giving an example such as a flower bed. The boundary is the outside of the flower bed. Ask pupils to talk to a partner about other 'real life' boundaries that they can think of. Boundaries could include the outside edge of the floor of the classroom, a car park, a path.
- Give each pupil a piece of 1 cm squared paper. Ask them to draw a square onto it. Recap that a square must have 4 sides that are the same length. Check together that each small square on the paper measures 1 cm. Discuss how pupils can find the perimeter of any of these shapes by counting the outside edges of the squares because they know that each one measures 1 cm. Demonstrate first and then ask pupils to find the perimeter of the shape they have drawn. They record the perimeters writing them just outside their shapes, for example 10 cm. They give their results to a partner who checks to see if they agree. Repeat several times asking pupils to draw different squares and rectangles.
- Pupils should complete Question 2 in the Practice Book.

### Same-day intervention

- Work with pupils who have difficulty finding the perimeters of shapes on a grid. Draw a 3 x 3 square on 1 cm squared paper for each pupil. Ask them to use a coloured pencil to highlight each side on the outside of each square and count how many sides they have highlighted (3 on each side of the square, 12 altogether, so the perimeter is 12 cm). Repeat for other squares and rectangles.

### Same-day enrichment

- Ask pupils to draw different irregular shapes on 1 cm squared paper, similar to those in Question 2. You will need to remind pupils what is meant by irregular and regular shapes. Irregular is when the sides are **not** all the same length. They find their perimeters and record inside their shapes.

# Question 3

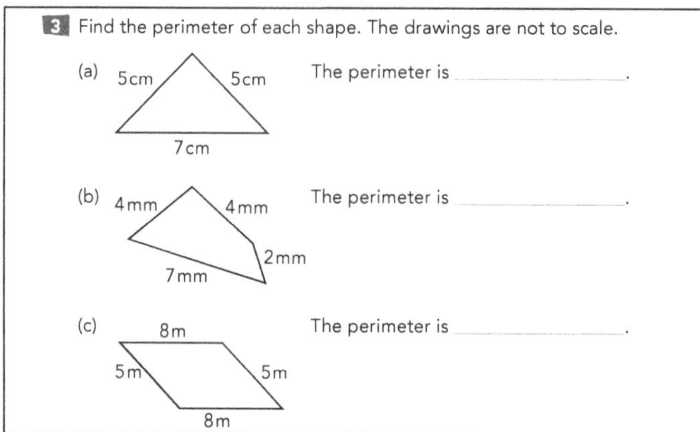

3 Find the perimeter of each shape. The drawings are not to scale.
(a) 5cm 5cm 7cm The perimeter is ______.
(b) 4mm 4mm 2mm 7mm The perimeter is ______.
(c) 8m 5m 5m 8m The perimeter is ______.


### What learning will pupils have achieved at the conclusion of Question 3?

- Pupils will have developed their measuring and calculating of perimeters by using units of length.

## Activities for whole-class instruction

- Ask pupils which units they have been using to measure length. Agree metres, centimetres and millimetres. Tell pupils that they will be using these units to measure perimeter because perimeter is a length.
- Draw a square on the board. Tell pupils that the square is not drawn to its actual size, so they need to imagine that each side is 12 cm in length. Ask them to tell you what the perimeter of the square is. Agree 48 cm. Ask how they worked this out. Who used their multiplication facts? Who used repeated addition? Repeat for other squares with different side lengths.
- Ask pupils to draw their own squares on plain paper. They then pass these to a partner, who measures one side to the nearest centimetre and then multiplies by 4 to find the perimeter.
- Draw a rectangle on the board and label it, emphasising that this had not been drawn to scale. Ask pupils how they could find its perimeter. Agree that they could double one width and double one length and then add them together, or they could add one length and width together and then double. Repeat for other rectangles.
- Ask pupils to draw their own rectangles on plain paper. They then pass these to a partner who finds the perimeter using one of the methods discussed above.

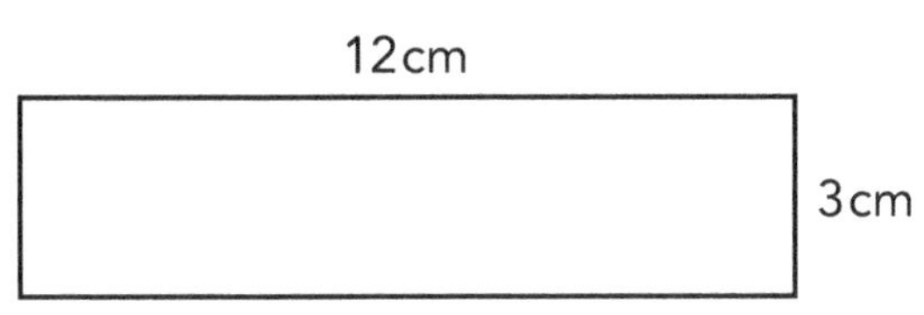


perimeter = 12cm + 12cm + 3cm + 3cm

or = 24cm + 6cm

or = 15cm × 2

- Draw an equilateral triangle on the board and label the sides in centimetres. Ask pupils to work out the perimeter. Do they multiply by 3 or add the same number three times? Discuss the fact that either is correct but it is more efficient to multiply. Repeat for other equilateral triangles.
- Ask pupils to draw their own equilateral triangles on squared paper. They then pass these to a partner, who measures one side to the nearest centimetre and then multiplies by 3 to find the perimeter.
- Remind pupils that a square is a regular quadrilateral and an equilateral triangle is a regular triangle. Draw an irregular quadrilateral on the board and label each side with a different number of metres. Ask pupils to work out the perimeter. Repeat for other irregular quadrilaterals with measurements in millimetres.
- Ask pupils to draw an irregular quadrilateral and an irregular triangle and label the length of all sides (in whole centimetres). Partners should find the perimeters.
- Pupils should complete Question 3 in the Practice Book.

## Same-day intervention

- Work with pupils who have difficulty understanding how to find the perimeter of regular shapes. Ask them to draw a 4 by 4 square on squared paper. What do they know about squares? Establish that squares have four sides, all the same length. They count the sides of the small squares that make up one side of the 4 by 4 square. Agree there are four. Can they tell you the product of 4 × 4? If not they should work out the calculation 4 + 4 + 4 + 4. Repeat for other squares. Repeat for equilateral triangles.

## Same-day enrichment

- Ask pupils to draw regular and irregular pentagons and hexagons on plain paper. They should label the dimensions and then find their perimeters.

# Question 4

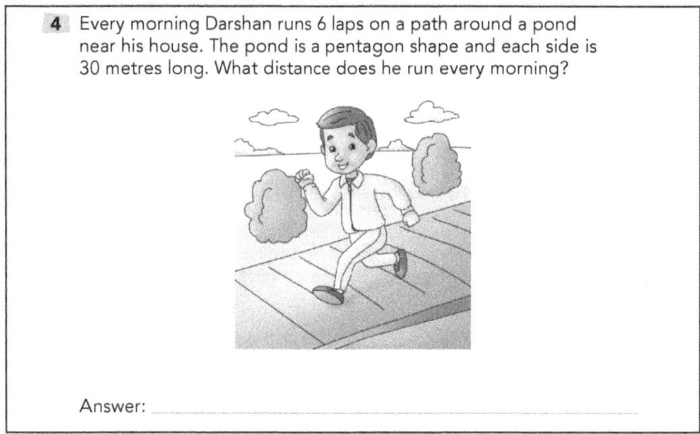
**4** Every morning Darshan runs 6 laps on a path around a pond near his house. The pond is a pentagon shape and each side is 30 metres long. What distance does he run every morning?

Answer: ______

## What learning will pupils have achieved at the conclusion of Question 4?

- Pupils will have used and applied their knowledge of perimeters to solve problems.

## Activities for whole-class instruction

- Recap what pupils have learned so far about perimeter in this unit. Agree that the perimeter is the distance around the outside of a shape. Agree that it can be measured in units of length such as millimetres, centimetres and metres.
- Draw a regular pentagon on the board. Say: *This is a pond in a garden. Each side is 200 cm in length.* Ask: *How could you find the perimeter of the pond?* Agree that 200 cm is equivalent to 2 m so they could multiply 2 m by 5 to give a perimeter of 10 m.

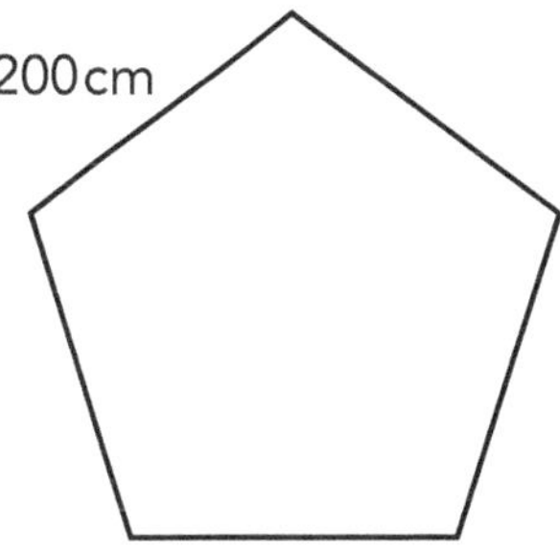


Perimeter = 200 cm × 5 or 2 m × 5 = 1000 cm or 10 m

- Say: *Sam has walked three times around the edge of the pond.* Ask them to work out how far he has walked altogether. Can they explain how they worked this out? Did they use the fact that the perimeter is 10 m and multiply that by 3?

- Ask pupils to draw a pentagon on plain paper. They should label the lengths of the sides in metres and make up a question as you did above. They ask their question to a partner.
- Draw a regular hexagon on the board. Label one side 300 cm. Say: *This represents a swimming pool.* Ask: *What is the perimeter of the swimming pool?* Discuss methods to find 300 cm multiplied by 6.
- Tell them that Samira swam around the perimeter five times. Ask: *Can you work out mentally how far Samira swam?* Can they explain, in full sentences, how they work out what 18 multiplied by 5 is? They might have:
  - partitioned 18 into 10 and 8, multiplied each by 5 and recombined the products
  - multiplied by 10 and halved the product.
- Ask pupils to draw and label the lengths of the sides of an irregular hexagon. They should make up their own question about an irregular shape for a partner to solve.
- Pupils should complete Question 4 in the Practice Book.

## Same-day intervention

- Check that pupils know that the perimeter is the distance around a shape. Draw a square and label a side 5 m. Ask a pupil to take Perry for a walk around the perimeter of the square. Say: *This is a representation of your friend's garden.* Ask: *How could you work out the perimeter of the garden?* Agree that the perimeter is 4 lots of 5 m or 5 multiplied by 4. Can they count in fives four times to find a perimeter of 20 m? Ask them how far they would travel if they walked around the perimeter of the garden twice, then three and four times.
- Repeat for other squares with different side lengths and invite different pupils to take Perry for a walk around the perimeter. Using a toy like this with a name similar to the word 'perimeter' will help pupils remember what the perimeter is.

## Same-day enrichment

- Tell pupils the perimeter of a rectangular driveway is 60 m. Ask: *Can you work out the possible lengths of the sides of the rectangle?* When they have worked these out, ask: *What might the driveway measurements be?* Point out that some possibilities are unlikely, for example 1 m by 29 m wouldn't be sensible because a car is wider than 1 m so wouldn't fit onto it.

## Challenge and extension question

# Question 5

**5** Look at the diagram. Five identical squares each with sides 1 cm in length are pieced together so that each square has at least one side touching the side of another square.

How many different arrangements are possible, not including the shape shown?

Answer: ____________

Out of all the possible arrangements of the five squares, what is the shortest perimeter?

Answer: ____________

Question 5 asks pupils to carry out a well-known pentomino problem. A pentomino is made from five squares that are placed side by side in different ways to make different shapes. There are 12 possible shapes altogether. Encourage pupils to find them all and label with the names of the shapes. Shapes cannot be translations, reflections or rotations of other shapes found. You could give them squares to manipulate. As they make their pentominoes, they should draw them. Once they have found all 12, they need to find the one with the shortest perimeter.

# Unit 10.7
# Perimeters of simple 2-D shapes (2)

## Conceptual context

Pupils will continue to strengthen their concept of perimeter, measuring and calculating in metres, centimetres and millimetres.

## Learning pupils will have achieved at the end of the unit

- Pupils will have consolidated their understanding of perimeter by calculating perimeters in m, cm and mm (Q1, Q2, Q4)
- Pupils will have consolidated their understanding of perimeter by measuring the sides of shapes and then calculating the perimeter (Q3)

### Resources

1 cm squared paper; plain paper; rulers; metre sticks

### Vocabulary

perimeter, boundary, metres, centimetres, millimetres

# Question 1

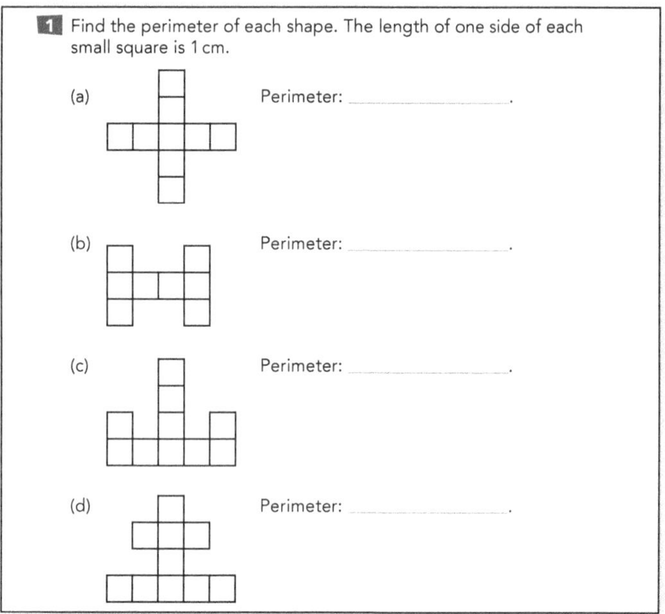

1 Find the perimeter of each shape. The length of one side of each small square is 1 cm.
(a) Perimeter: .
(b) Perimeter: .
(c) Perimeter: .
(d) Perimeter: .


## What learning will pupils have achieved at the conclusion of Question 1?

- Pupils will have calculated perimeter using 1 cm squared paper.

## Activities for whole-class instruction

- Ask pupils to tell you what is meant by perimeter and to give examples of activities that they carried out in the previous unit. Agree that the perimeter is the distance around the outside of any shape.

*Perimeter is the distance around the outside of a shape.*

- Give each pupil a sheet of 1 cm squared paper. Ask them to draw a square with sides measuring 8 cm. Recap how they can find the perimeter by counting the small squares on one side of the large square and multiplying by 4. Repeat for squares of other sizes.
- Ask pupils to draw a rectangle with a length of 12 cm and a width of 4 cm. Ask: *Can you tell me all the different ways to find the perimeter of this rectangle?* Answers may include:
  - Count the sides of the small squares.
  - Add 12 cm and 4 cm to find one width and length and then double.
  - Double 12 cm, double 4 cm and add the two sums.
- All will give the perimeter of 32 cm. Which do pupils think is the most efficient?
- Ask pupils to draw six polygons (straight-sided shapes). Encourage them to be creative and draw interesting shapes. They must ensure that their shapes follow the sides of the centimetre squares. They should then give this to a partner to work out the perimeter of each shape. Encourage them to look for efficient ways to do this.
- Pupils should complete Question 1 in the Practice Book.

## Same-day intervention

- Work with pupils who don't think of using multiplication when finding the perimeter of a regular shape. Give pupils 1 cm squared paper. Ask them to draw a square with sides of 2 cm. Discuss how to find the perimeter. Move them on from counting the sides of each square by writing a repeated addition, 2 cm + 2 cm + 2 cm + 2 cm. Ask: *How many times are there 2 cm?* Remind them that repeated addition is the same as multiplication, so the repeated addition is equivalent to 2 cm × 4. Repeat for other small squares.

## Same-day enrichment

- Ask pupils to draw irregular shapes on squared paper similar to those in the Practice Book, where efficient methods for finding the perimeter can be applied. They need to think carefully about their shapes, for example:

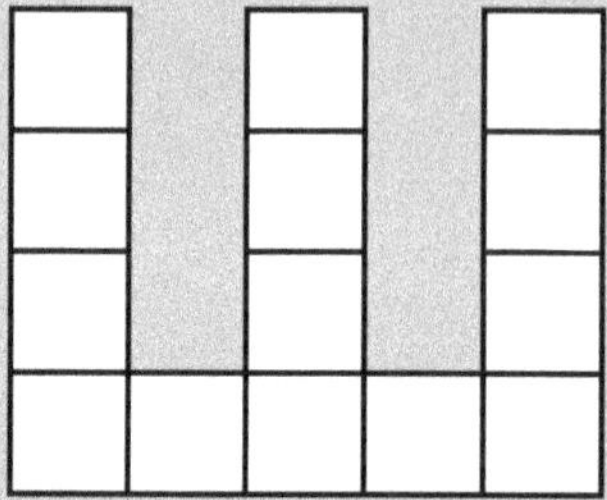

- Pupils could find the perimeter of one tower by doubling three and adding one. They then multiply that by 3 and add the remaining edges of the smaller squares of the base.

# Questions 2 and 3

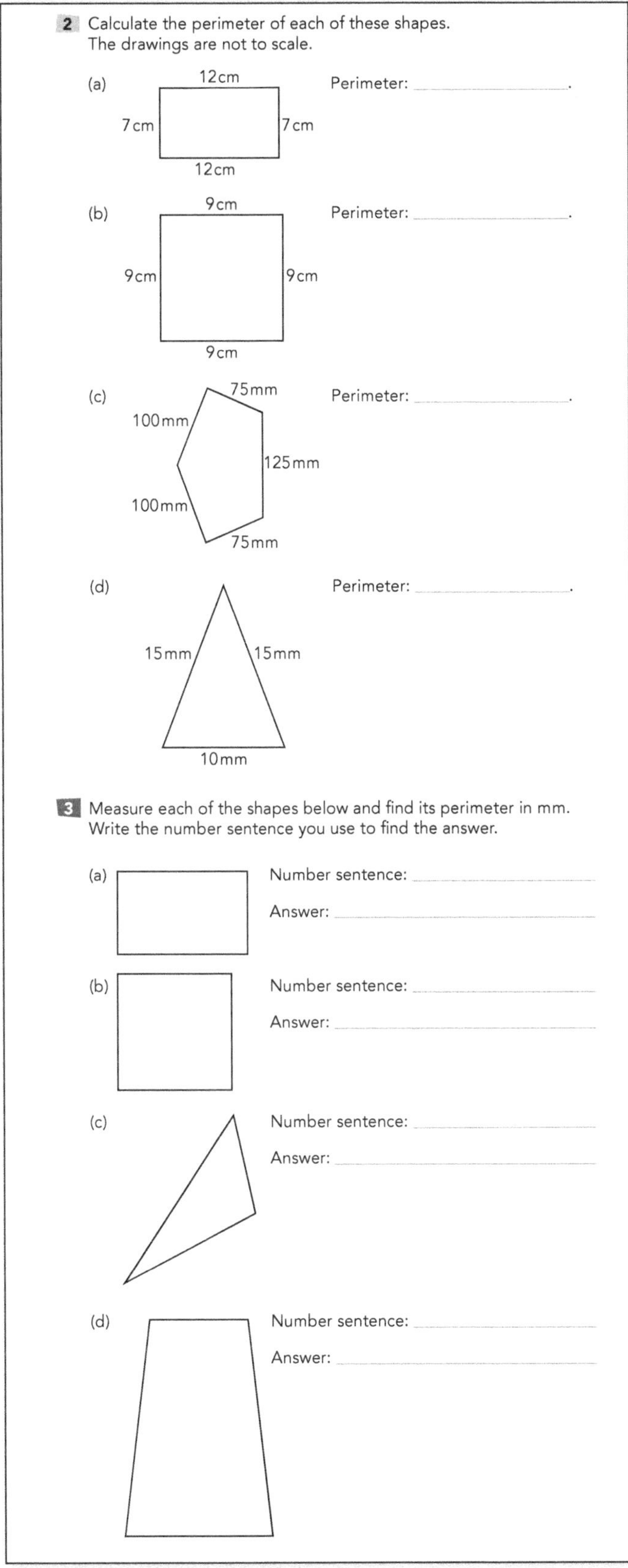


## What learning will pupils have achieved at the conclusion of Questions 2 and 3?

- Pupils will have consolidated their understanding of finding perimeters efficiently.
- Pupils will have consolidated their understanding of measuring in centimetres and millimetres.

## Activities for whole-class instruction

- Tell pupils that so far they have counted squares because they know that one side of a square measures 1 cm, and by counting squares they can tell how many centimetres the length of a side measures or how long the whole perimeter measures. Explain that now they will be working on plain paper.
- Draw a square on the board and label each side 3 cm. Ask: *How can we find the perimeter of the square?* Agree that they can add 3 cm four times or multiply 3 cm by 4. Repeat for other squares.
- Draw a rectangle on the board and label the lengths 5 cm and the widths 2 cm. Ask: *How can you find the perimeter of the rectangle?* Agree that they could add 5 cm, 2 cm, 5 cm and 2 cm. Ask: *Is there a more efficient way?* Agree that they could add 5 cm and 2 cm and then double, or double 5 cm and double 2 cm and then add the two sums. Let them use either of these two methods to find the perimeter. Establish that the perimeter is 14 cm. Ask them to convert this into millimetres. Repeat for other rectangles.
- Give pupils plain paper and ask them to draw a square and a rectangle and label the sides to show their lengths. Ask: *Do you need to label all the sides?* Ask them to give their paper to a partner, who should find the perimeters in centimetres and then convert these to millimetres. Take feedback and invite pupils to explain the methods they used to find the perimeters.
- Draw an isosceles triangle on the board and label the base 5 cm and each side 7 cm. Ask pupils how they could find the perimeter efficiently. Agree that they could double 7 cm and then add 5 cm. Establish that the perimeter is 19 cm. Ask: *What is this in millimetres?* Repeat for other isosceles triangles.
- Ask pupils to draw three of their own isosceles triangles to whole numbers of centimetres. You could give them squared paper to make this simpler. Ask them to give their drawings to their partner, who should find the perimeters in centimetres and then convert them to millimetres. Take feedback, asking pupils to explain their methods.

- Draw an irregular hexagon on the board; pairs of opposite sides should be the same length. Label the sides 10 cm, 15 cm and 20 cm.

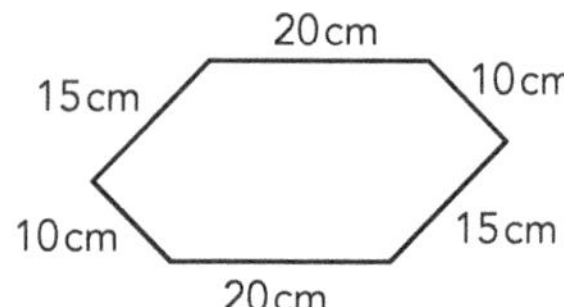


- Ask pupils to tell you how the sides of this shape could be added efficiently. Agree that they could double the length of the sides that are the same and then add the three sums. Establish that the perimeter is 90 cm. Ask: *How many millimetres is this equivalent to?*
- Ask pupils to draw their own irregular quadrilateral. They should draw two or three sides the same length. Ask them to give their drawing to their partner, who should find the perimeter in the most efficient way they can. Take feedback, asking pupils to explain their methods.
- Draw a rectangle on the board and label one of the lengths 21 mm and one of the widths 5 mm. Ask pupils to work out the perimeter using an efficient method and then convert the millimetres into centimetres and millimetres. Repeat for other rectangles. Pupils can then draw their own rectangles, which should include centimetre and millimetre measurements. Ask them to label the sides in millimetres, and then calculate their perimeters in millimetres and convert to centimetres and millimetres.
- Pupils should complete Questions 2 and 3 in the Practice Book.

## Same-day intervention

- Work with pupils who have difficulty finding efficient ways to calculate perimeters. For each pupil draw a square on plain paper with sides measuring 3 cm. Ask them to measure each side and label them. Ask them to find the perimeter by multiplying 3 cm by 4. If they find this difficult, discuss the fact that multiplication is repeated addition and let them add the sides using a numbered number line if this helps. Pupils should check by measuring the whole perimeter, marking their starting point. Repeat for other squares.

## Same-day enrichment

- Ask pupils to draw different irregular pentagons and hexagons on plain paper. They should measure the sides and ensure that two or three are the same length. They should find their perimeters in the most efficient way, and add a box close to each shape showing the perimeter in both centimetres and millimetres.

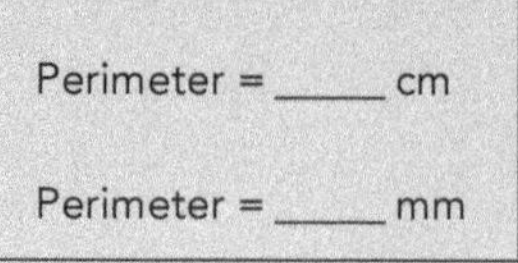


# Question 4

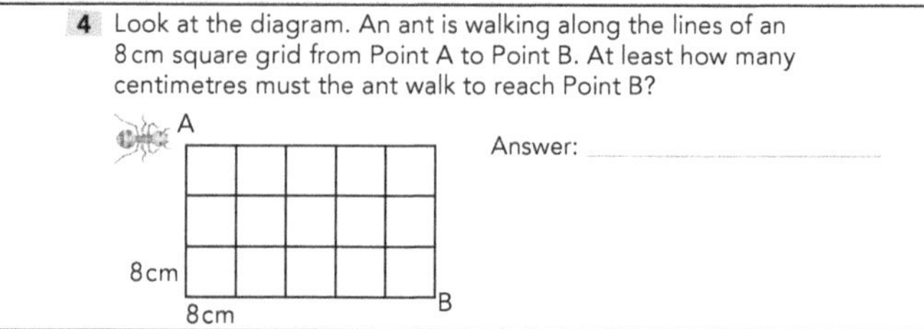

**4** Look at the diagram. An ant is walking along the lines of an 8 cm square grid from Point A to Point B. At least how many centimetres must the ant walk to reach Point B?



Answer: ______

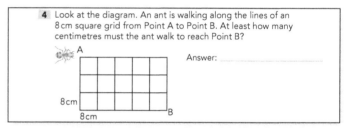

## What learning will pupils have achieved at the conclusion of Question 4?

- Pupils will have applied their understanding of how to calculate perimeters efficiently to solve problems.

## Activities for whole-class instruction

- Tell pupils that they are going to apply their understanding of perimeters to solve problems. Give each pupil a piece of squared paper. Ask them to draw a square with sides measuring 5 cm. Ask them to write A beside the top left square and B beside the bottom right square:

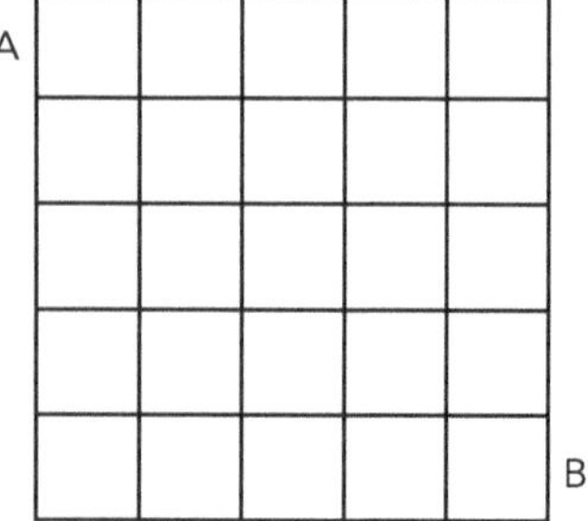


- Ask them to find the quickest way to get from A to B, moving around the outside edge. Agree that the distance is 10 cm. What do they notice about the 10 cm? Establish that this is equivalent to half the perimeter of the square, which is 20 cm. Ask them to draw a 10 cm by 5 cm rectangle. Label with A and B in the same positions again. Ask pupils to work out the distance from A to B again. What do they notice? Agree that the distance is equivalent to half the perimeter.

- Ask pupils to find and measure three other possible routes from A to B on their grids.
- Pupils should complete Question 4 in the Practice Book.

## Same-day intervention

- Work with pupils who have difficulty making the link between perimeter and half the perimeter. Give each pupil squared paper and ask them to draw a 2 cm by 2 cm square. They should be able to tell you that the perimeter is 8 cm. Tell them that finding half the perimeter is the same as finding half of any number. Can they find half of 8? If so, they can find half of 8 cm, which is 4 cm. Repeat for other perimeters, linking to halving whole numbers.

## Same-day enrichment

- Ask pupils to draw an irregular shape on plain paper. Ask them to work out the perimeter and then halve it. They should write A at one point on their shape and measure half of the perimeter and write B at that point. Ask them to give their shape to a partner, who should then find the distance from A to B.

## Challenge and extension question

# Questions 5 and 6

**5** The figure below shows a rectangle. A curve connecting A and B divides the rectangle into two shapes. Does Shape 1 have a longer perimeter? Circle 'yes' or 'no' and give your reason.

B
Shape 1
Shape 2
A

yes no

Reason: ______

**6** What is the perimeter in mm of each of the shapes below? Write the number sentence you use to find the answer.

(a) 3, 9, 7, 15, 6

(b) 20, 10, 40, 80

Number sentence: ______

Answer: ______

Number sentence: ______

Answer: ______

Question 5 asks pupils to use and apply their knowledge and understanding of perimeter to solve an investigative problem. Question 6 asks pupils to find the perimeter of compound shapes, which involves finding missing lengths.

## Chapter 10 test (Practice Book 3B, pages 150–154)

| Test question number | Relevant unit | Relevant questions within unit |
|---|---|---|
| 1 | 10.1 | 1, 2, 3, 4 |
| 2a | 10.1 | 1, 2 |
| 2b | 10.1 | 2 |
| 2c | 10.4 | 4 |
| 2d | 10.4 | 4 |
| 2e | 10.3 | 1, 4 |
| 2f | 10.3 | 1, 4 |
| 2g | 10.6 | 1 |
| 2h | 10.6 and 10.7 | General concept |
| 3 | 10.2 | 1 |
| | 10.3 | 1, 3 |
| 4 | 10.5 | 1, 4 |
| 5a | 10.1 | 3 |
| 5b | 10.7 | 2, 3 |
| 5c | 10.6 | 2 |
| | 10.7 | 1, 4 |
| 5d | 10.7 | 5 |
| 6 | 10.1 | 1, 2, 3, 4, 5 |
| 7 | 10.4 | 3 |
| 8 | 10.6 | 2 |
| | 10.7 | 1, 4 |
| 9 | 10.7 | 3 |
| 10 | 10.6 | 2 |
| | 10.7 | 1, 4 |
| 11 | 10.6 | 4 |
| | No specific unit | 1 |

# Resource 3.7.2

## Key word cards

| | | |
|---|---|---|
| minuend | subtrahend | sum |
| difference | addend | |



© HarperCollins*Publishers* 2017

# Resource 3.7.3

## Addition and subtraction cards

| | | | |
|---|---|---|---|
| 452 + 4 | 874 + 5 | 354 + 9 | 407 – 9 |
| 625 – 8 | 799 + 9 | 326 – 6 | 975 + 4 |
| 915 – 5 | 371 + 6 | 287 + 4 | 355 – 8 |
| 201 – 6 | 597 + 6 | 249 – 9 | 176 + 7 |
| 534 + 6 | 827 + 3 | 206 + 9 | 518 + 4 |
| 758 + 5 | 542 + 7 | 998 – 9 | 142 – 7 |
| 667 – 3 | 303 – 4 | 231 – 8 | 192 – 3 |
| 202 – 5 | 555 – 8 | | |

© HarperCollins*Publishers* 2017

# Resource 3.7.4

## 3-digit numbers and ones

| | | | | | |
|---|---|---|---|---|---|
| 750 + 3 | 756 – 5 | 760 – 8 | 746 + 6 | 752 – 1 | 750 – 5 |
| 749 – 8 | 751 + 1 | 752 – 7 | 744 + 8 | 758 – 4 | 747 + 6 |
| 760 – 6 | 743 + 9 | 759 – 7 | 758 – 6 | 768 + 9 | 760 – 9 |
| 761 – 7 | 748 + 4 | 750 + 6 | 747 + 7 | 755 – 5 | 744 + 6 |
| 756 – 5 | 755 – 3 | 752 + 6 | 758 – 7 | 752 + 9 | 741 + 9 |
| 748 + 9 | 757 – 5 | 751 – 9 | 747 – 5 | 764 + 3 | 751 – 7 |


© HarperCollins*Publishers* 2017

## Decision table

| | Partition everything? | Partition just the second addend? |
|---|---|---|
| Start by adding the hundreds? | A | C |
| Start by adding the ones? | B | D |

© HarperCollinsPublishers 2017

# Resource 3.7.6

## What's wrong here?

**Mistake 1**

```
  4 1 1
+ 2 3 3
-------
    1 4
```

Just added the digits

**Mistake 2**

```
  5 3 8
+ 1 2 6
-------
  6 9 1
    4
```

Right answer, wrong way round

**Mistake 3**

```
  2 5 6
+ 2 1 9
-------
  4 6 5
```

Where's the 10 (or 100)?

**Mistake 4**

```
  3 3 7
+ 4 8 2
-------
  7 1 1
  1
```

Don't forget the 100 (or the 10)!

**Mistake 5**

```
  4 1 6
+   2 0 5
---------
  4 3 6 5
```

Right question, wrong layout

**Mistake 6**

```
  8 3 7
+ 1 1 5
-------
  7 2 2
```

Mixed-up operations!



© HarperCollins*Publishers* 2017

# Resource 3.8.1

## Shape fractions

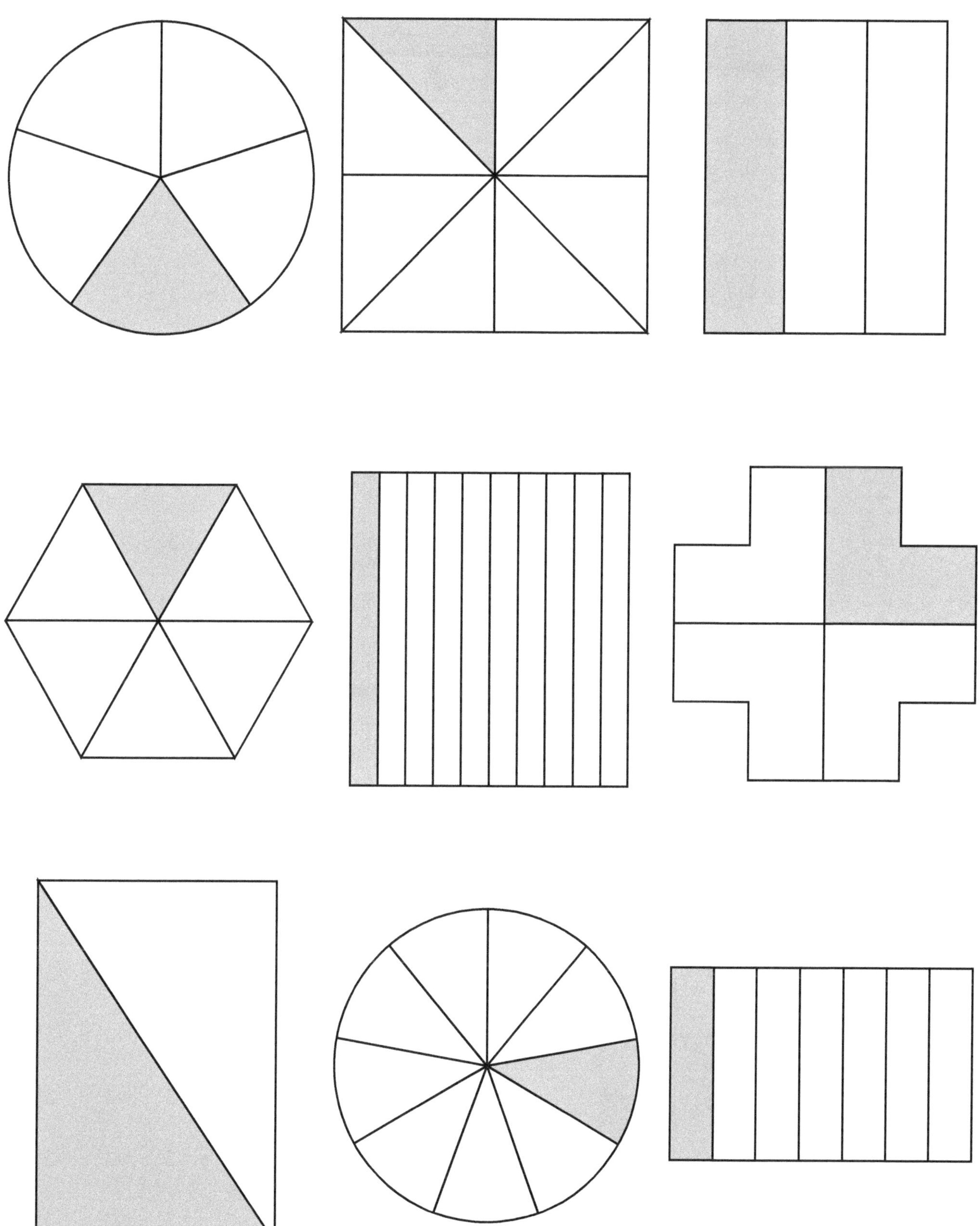

© HarperCollinsPublishers 2017

## Animal arrays

© HarperCollins*Publishers* 2017

# Resource 3.8.2b

## Shaded shapes 1

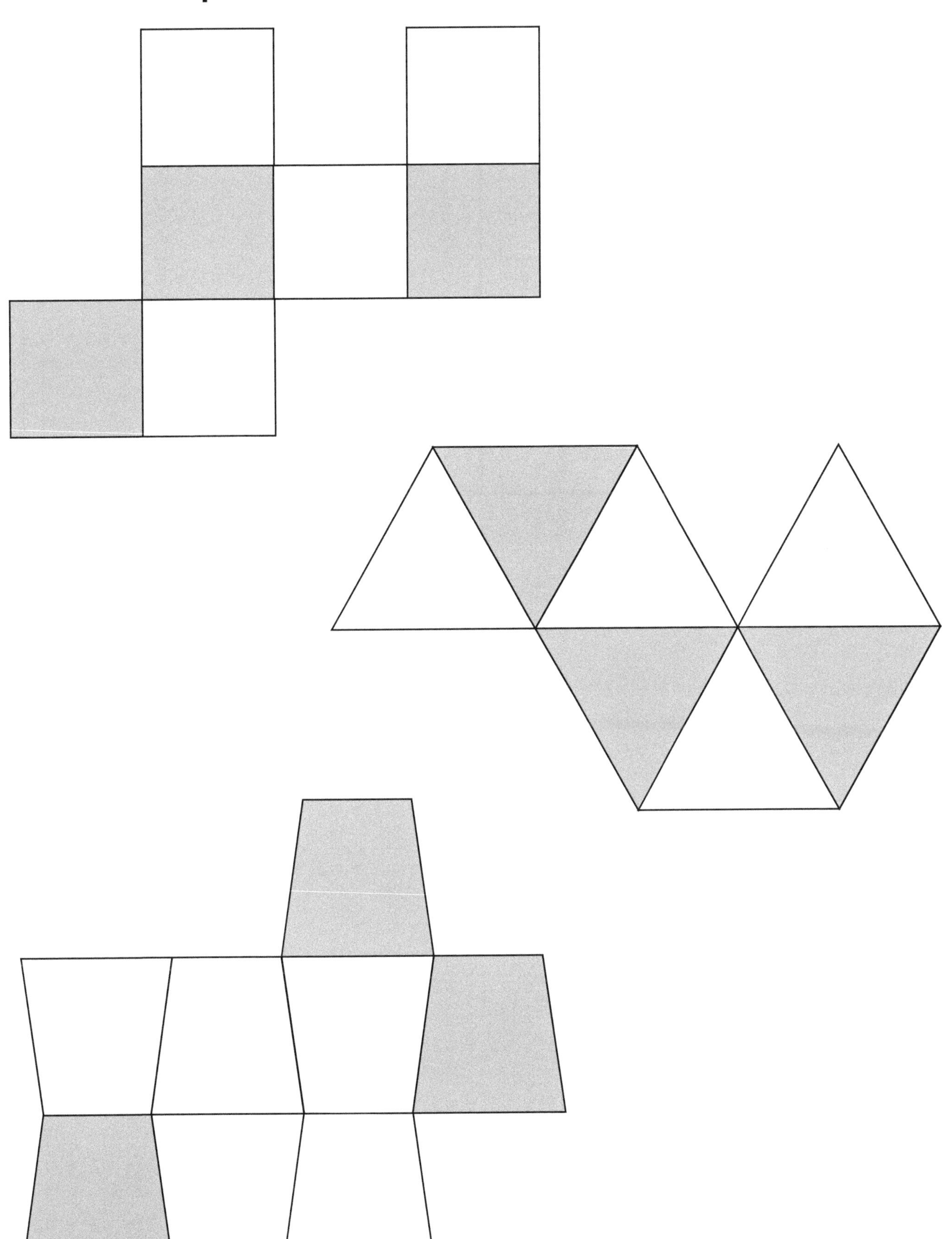

© HarperCollinsPublishers 2017

# Resource 3.8.2c

## Shaded shapes 2

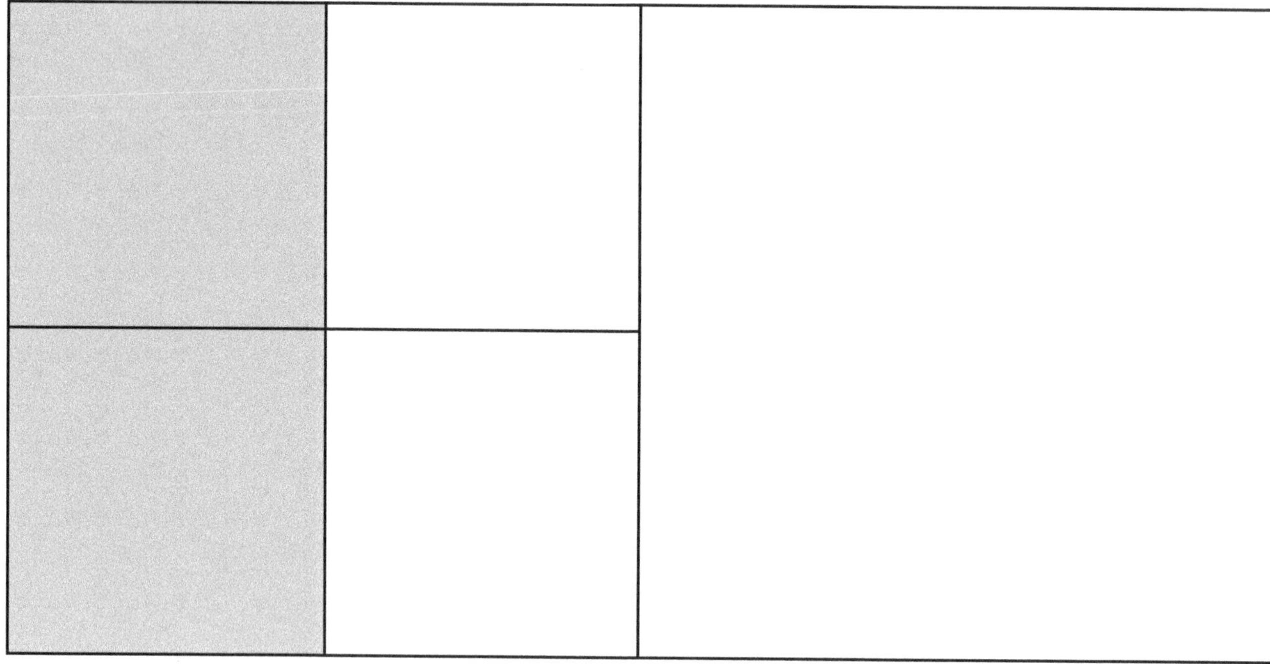



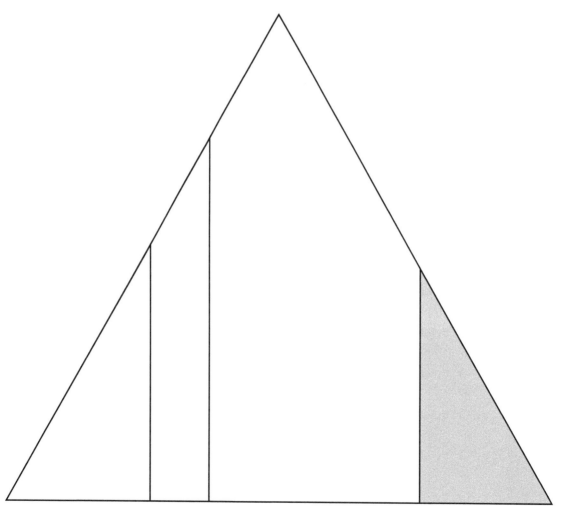

© HarperCollins*Publishers* 2017

# Resource 3.8.2d

## Odd shape out

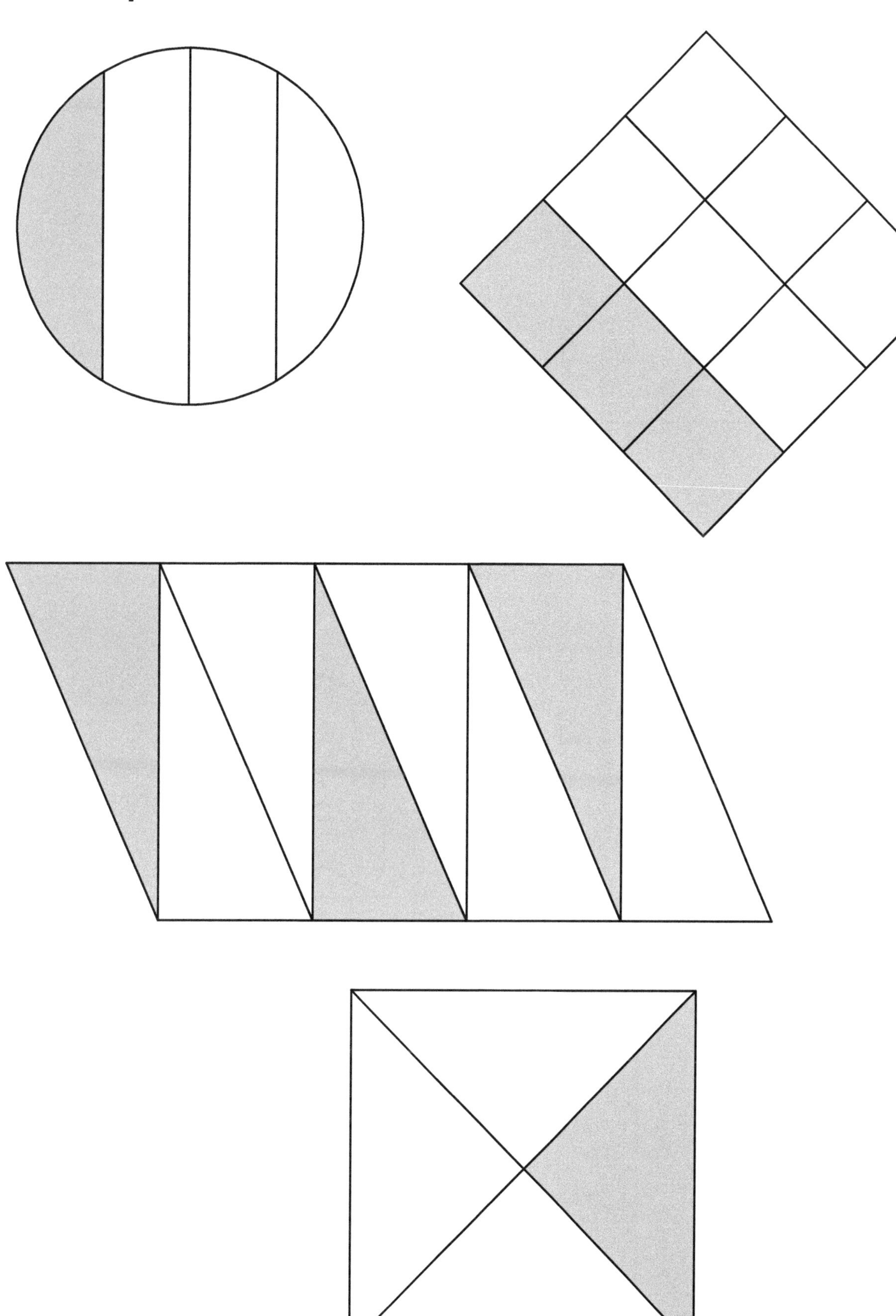

# Resource 3.8.2e

## Sorting images

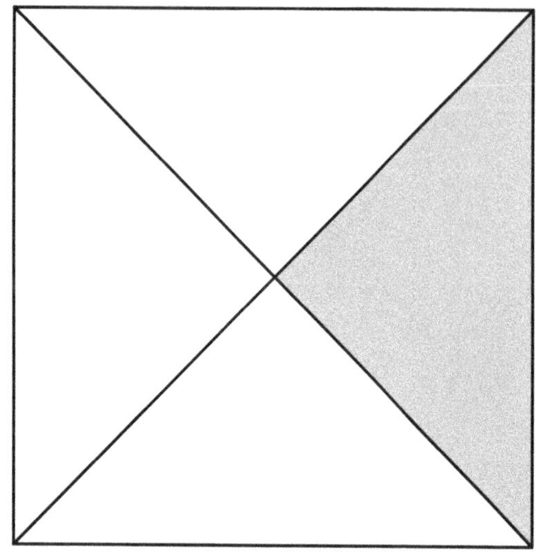
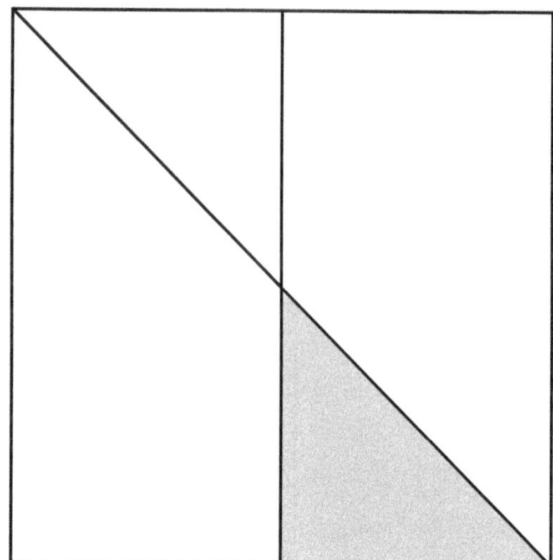
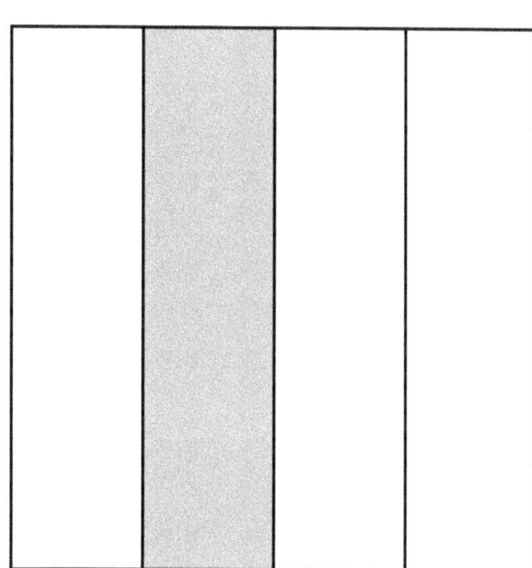
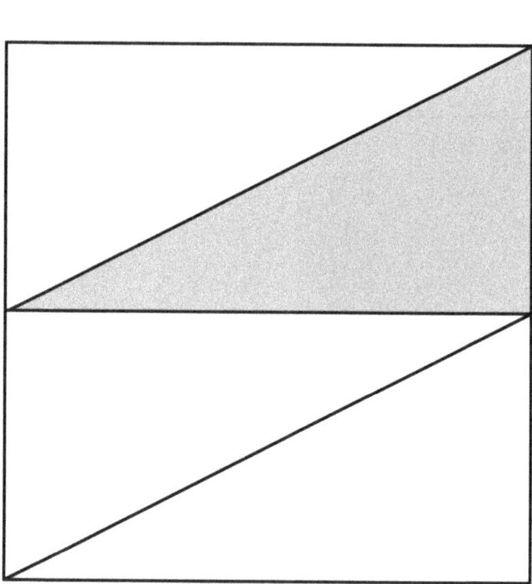

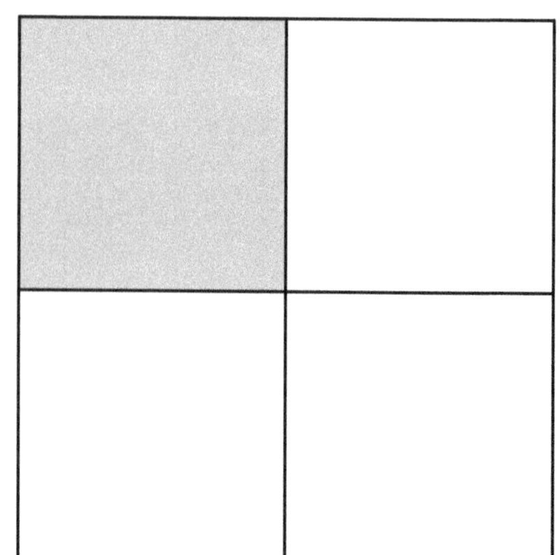

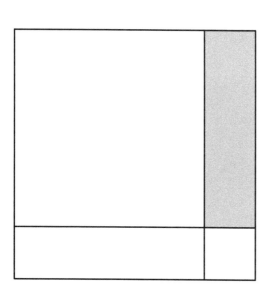

© HarperCollinsPublishers 2017

## Ordering images

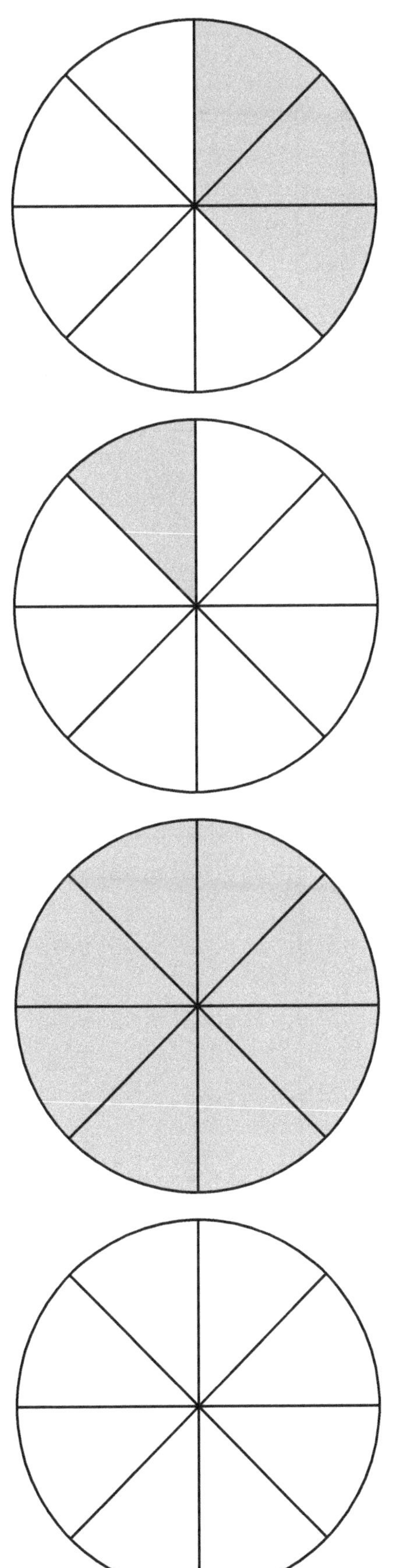

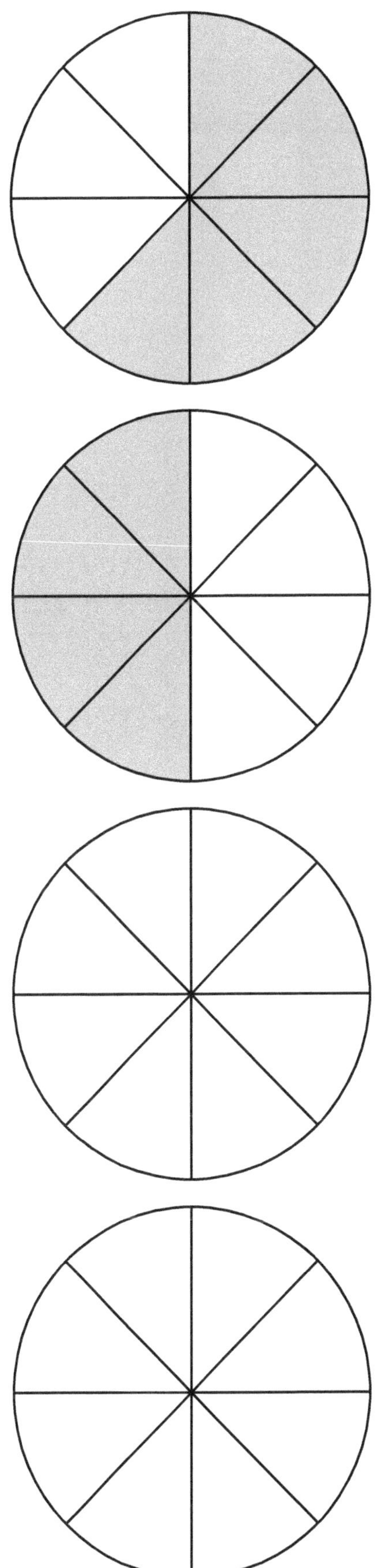

© HarperCollinsPublishers 2017

## Matching fractions

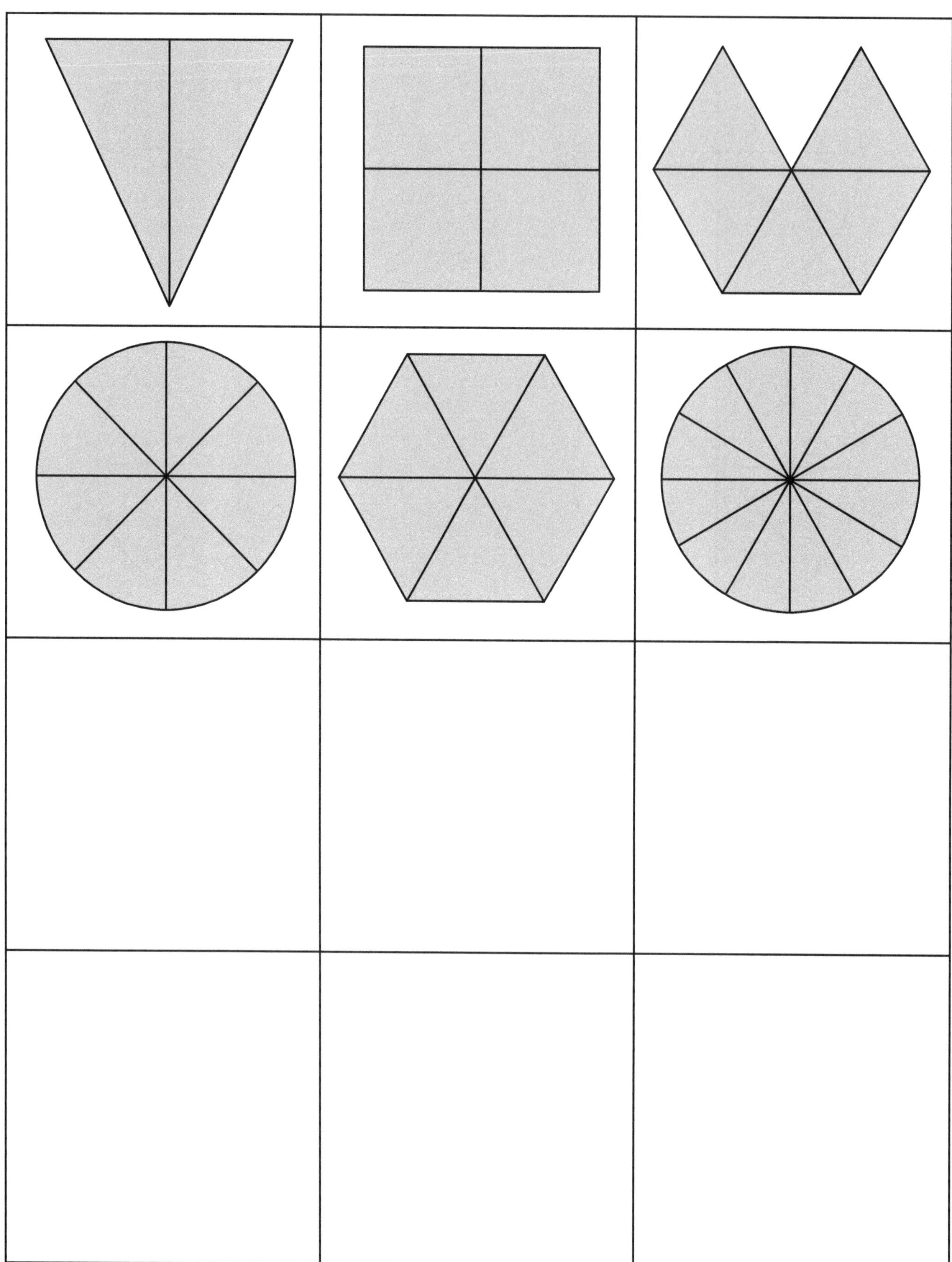



© HarperCollinsPublishers 2017

# Resource 3.8.3b

## Equivalent fractions

$\frac{1}{12}$ $\frac{1}{12}$ $\frac{1}{24}$ $\frac{1}{24}$ $\frac{1}{24}$ $\frac{1}{24}$

$\frac{1}{6}$ $\frac{1}{6}$

$\frac{1}{3}$

© HarperCollins*Publishers* 2017

# Resource 3.8.3c

## Fraction pairs

| | | | |
|---|---|---|---|
| $\frac{1}{2}$ | $\frac{6}{10}$ | $\frac{3}{4}$ | $\frac{3}{15}$ |
| $\frac{2}{3}$ | $\frac{1}{4}$ | $\frac{1}{3}$ | $\frac{1}{7}$ |
| $\frac{3}{9}$ | $\frac{8}{16}$ | $\frac{8}{8}$ | $\frac{3}{5}$ |
| $\frac{2}{14}$ | $\frac{4}{6}$ | $\frac{4}{10}$ | 1 |
| $\frac{1}{5}$ | $\frac{6}{8}$ | $\frac{3}{12}$ | $\frac{2}{5}$ |



© HarperCollins*Publishers* 2017

# Resource 3.8.4a

## Sliced eighths

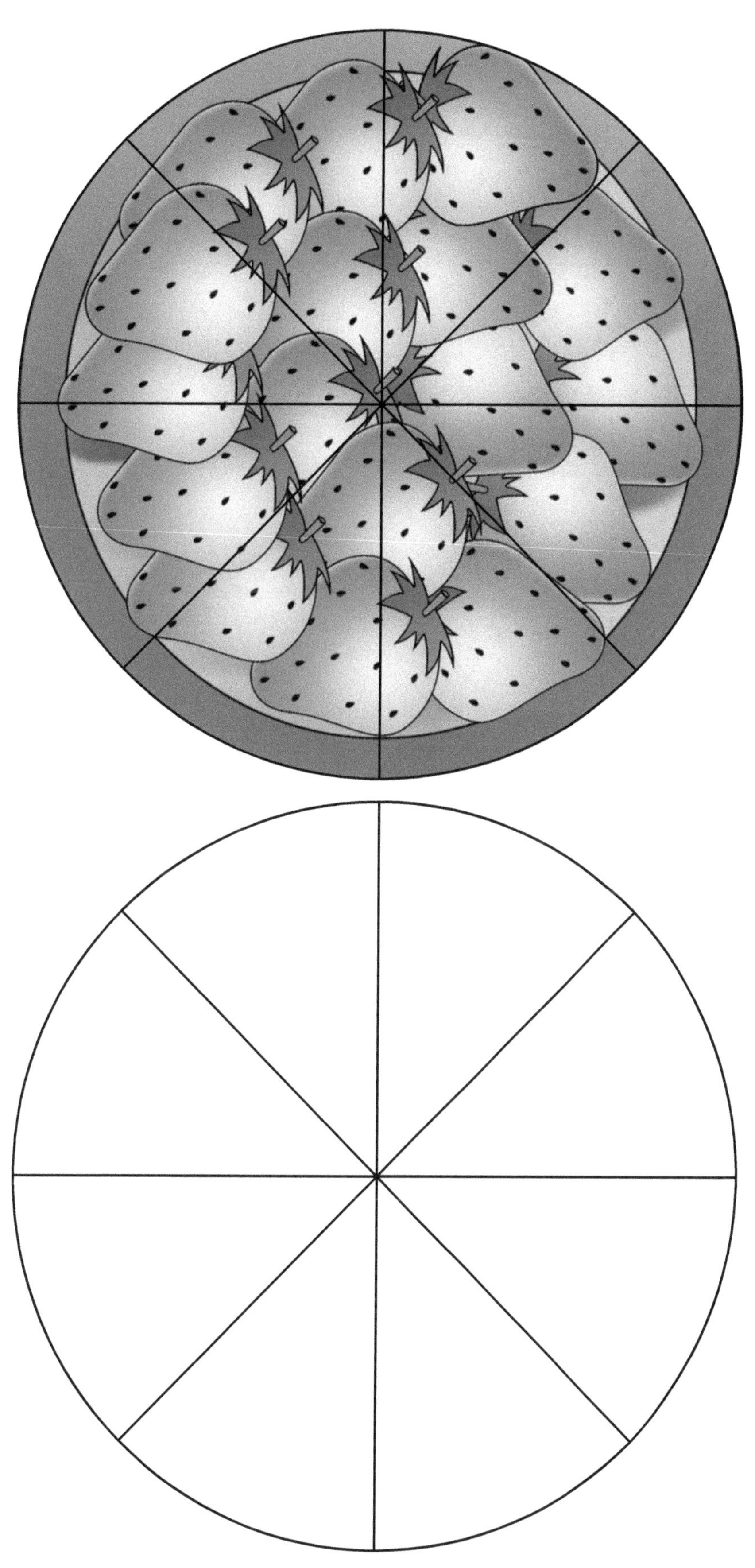

# Resource 3.8.4b

## Pie sixths

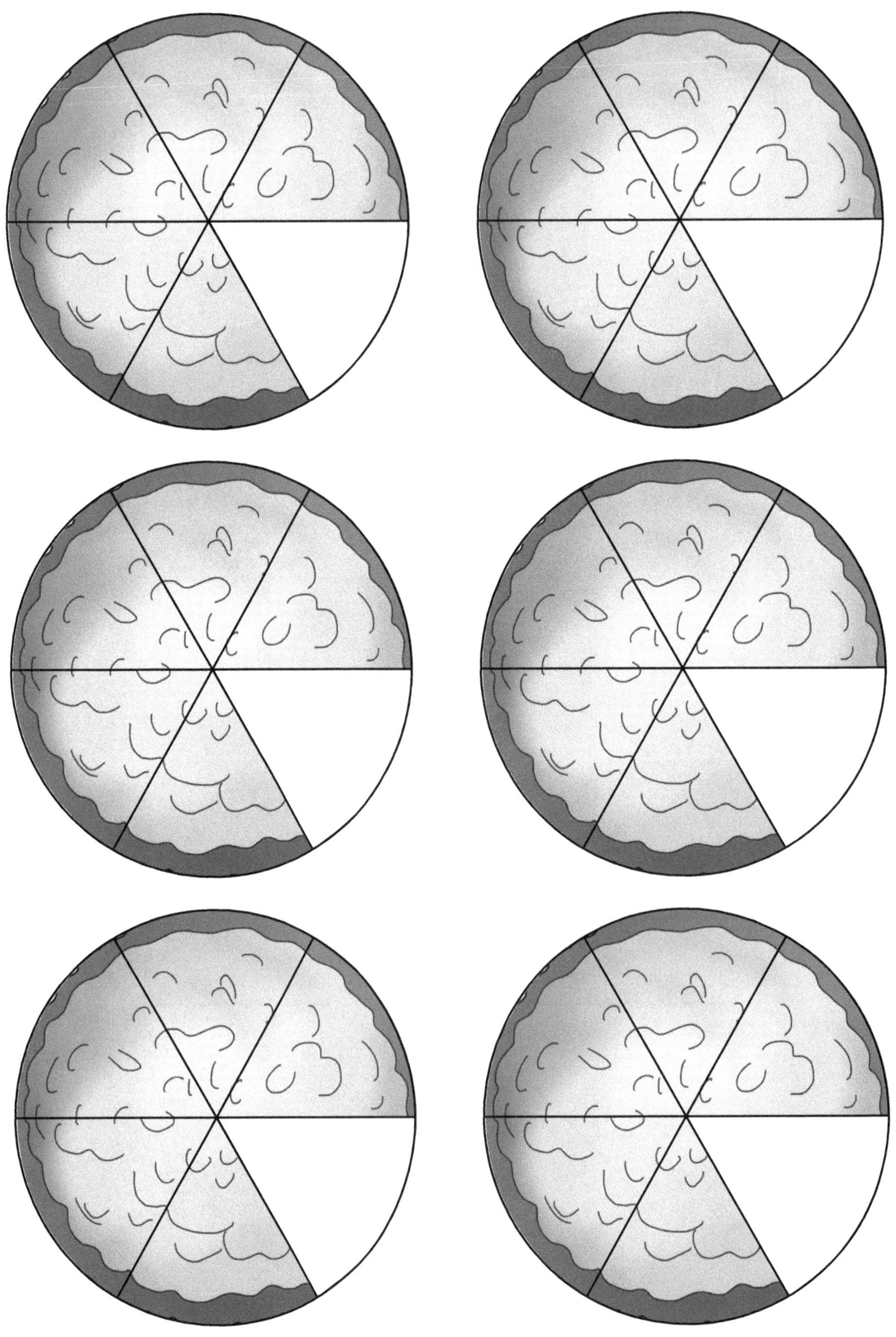



© HarperCollins*Publishers* 2017

## Parallelograms

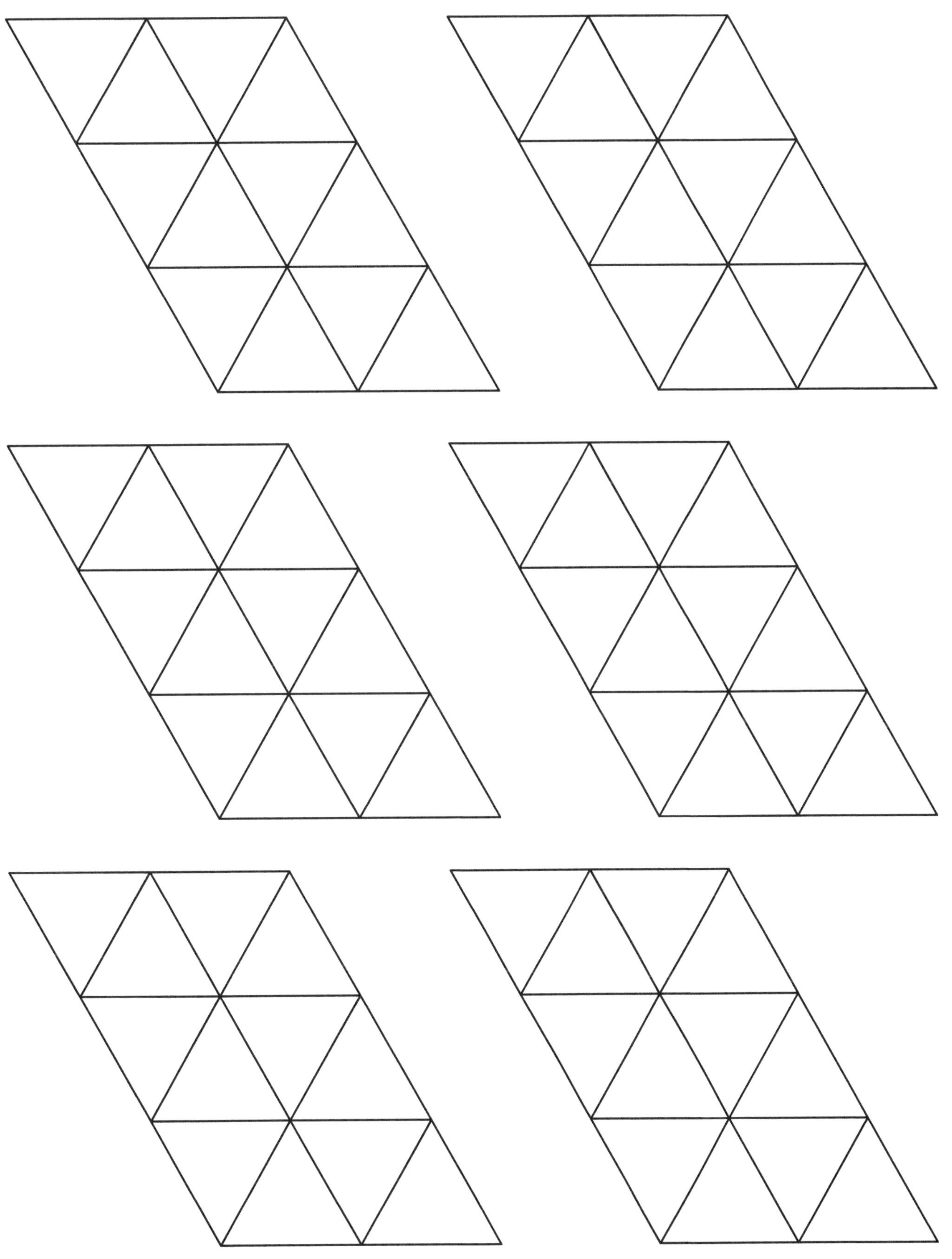

© HarperCollinsPublishers 2017

# Resource 3.8.4d

## Total fractions

| | |
|---|---|
| $\frac{1}{11}$ | $\frac{3}{11}$ |
| $\frac{5}{11}$ | $\frac{6}{11}$ |
| $\frac{4}{11}$ | $\frac{8}{11}$ |
| $\frac{7}{11}$ | $\frac{2}{11}$ |
| | |



© HarperCollins*Publishers* 2017

# Resource 3.8.4e

## Fraction towers

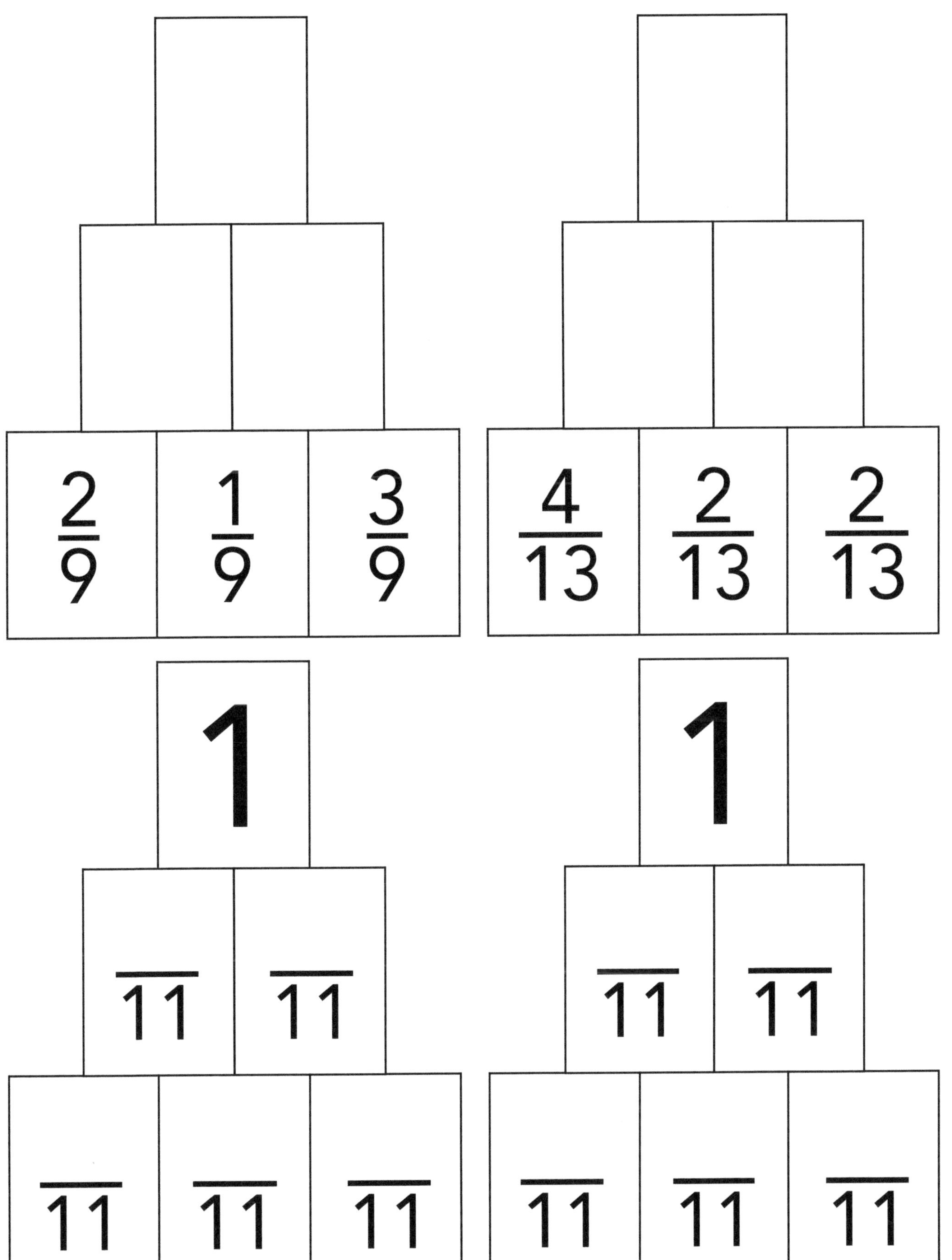


© HarperCollins*Publishers* 2017

# Resource 3.8.4f

## Comparing twelfths

© HarperCollinsPublishers 2017

# Resource 3.9.1a

## Find the largest product

1. $4 \times 6 =$ ☐
2. $3 \times 5 =$ ☐
3. $8 \times 2 =$ ☐
4. $6 \times 3 =$ ☐
5. $7 \times 4 =$ ☐
6. $9 \times 6 =$ ☐
7. $5 \times 6 =$ ☐
8. $4 \times 7 =$ ☐

| 1000 | 100 | 10 | 1 |
|---|---|---|---|
| | | | |

© HarperCollinsPublishers 2017

# Resource 3.9.1b

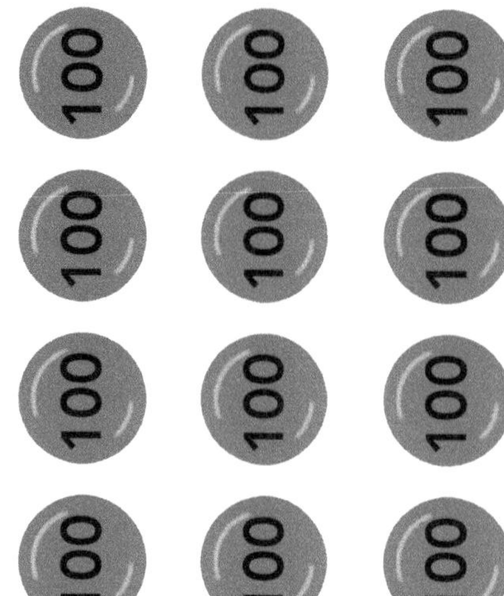


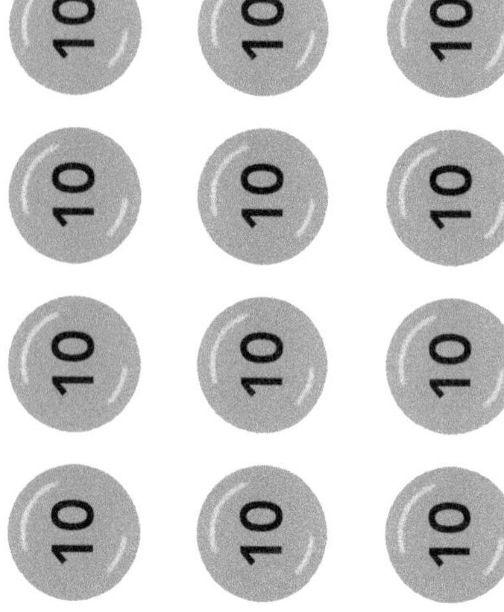


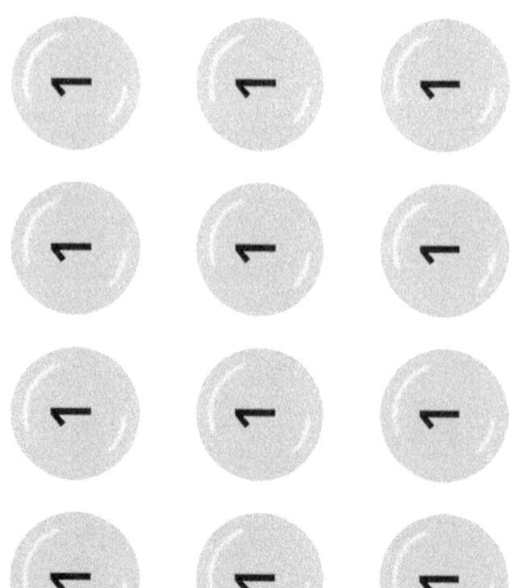






© HarperCollinsPublishers 2017

## Array multiplication

Write a multiplication sentence to match each array.

**1.**

☐ × ☐ < ☐ × ☐

**2.**

☐ × ☐ < ☐ × ☐

**3.**

☐ × ☐ < ☐ × ☐

**4.**

☐ × ☐ < ☐ × ☐

**5.** Which array is larger?

☐ × ☐ < ☐ × ☐

**6.** Which array is smaller?

☐ × ☐ < ☐ × ☐

© HarperCollins*Publishers* 2017

# Resource 3.9.2a

## Base 10, ones and tens

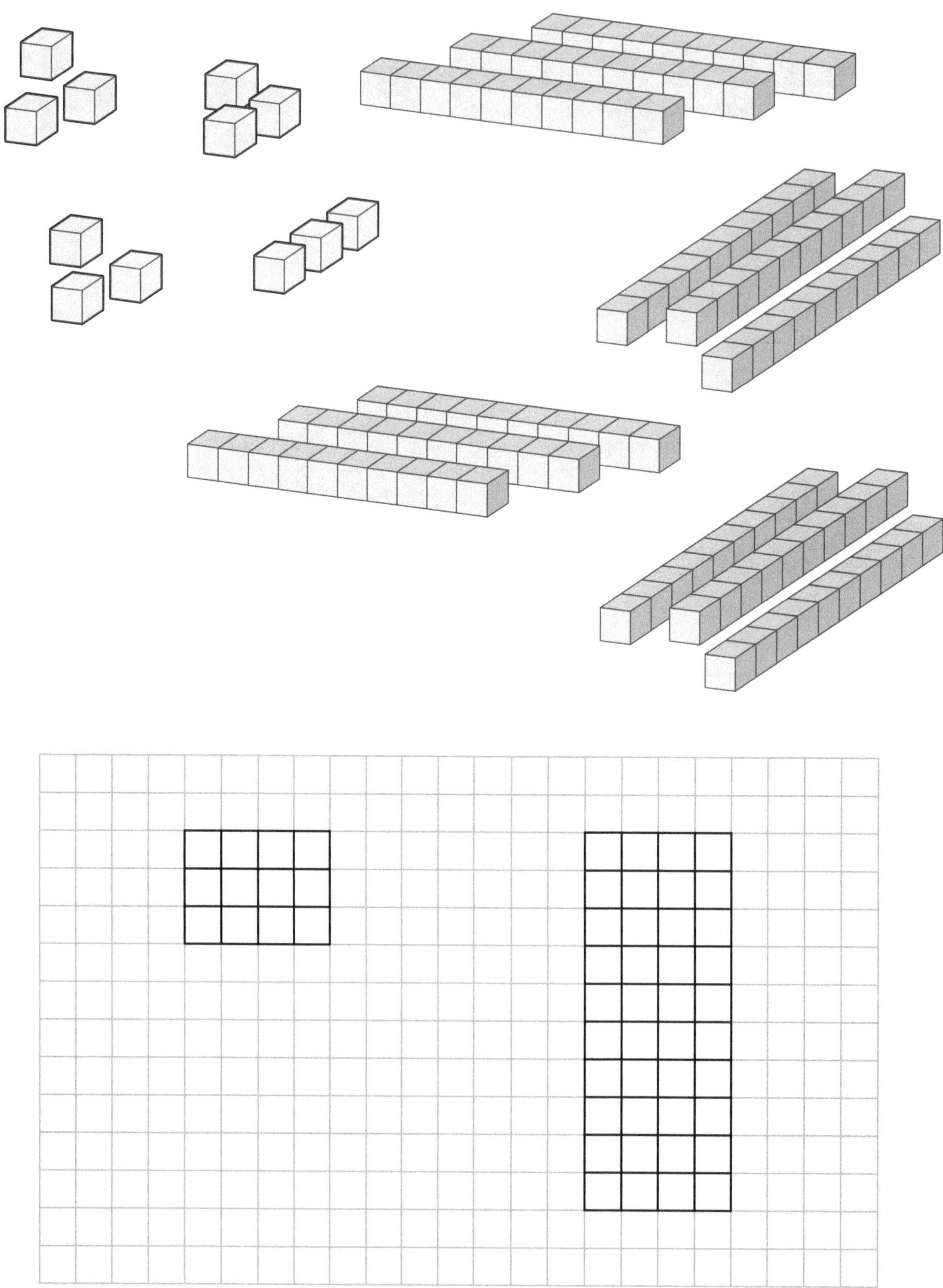



© HarperCollinsPublishers 2017

# Resource 3.9.2b

## Array

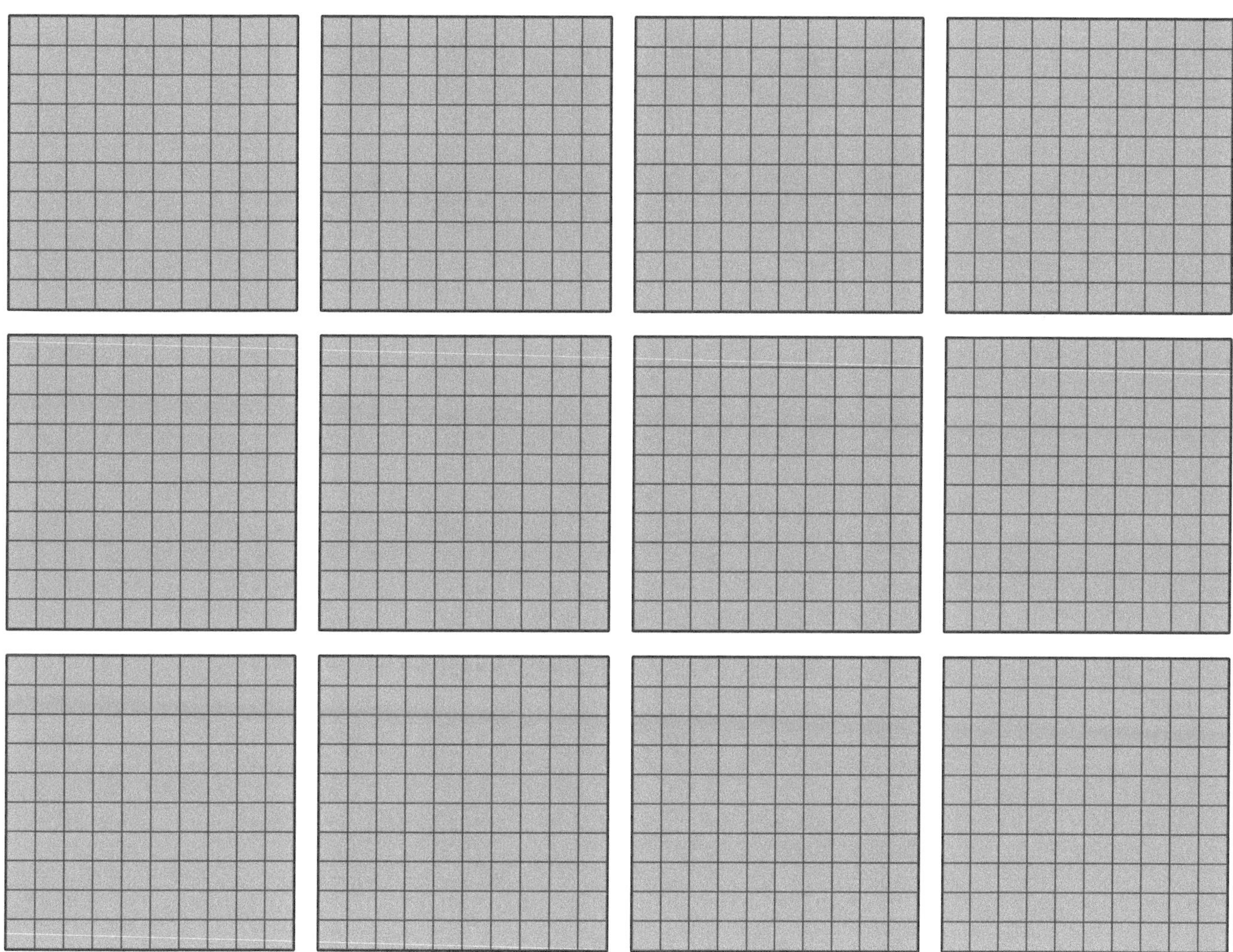

© HarperCollinsPublishers 2017

# Resource 3.9.2c

## Comparing arrays

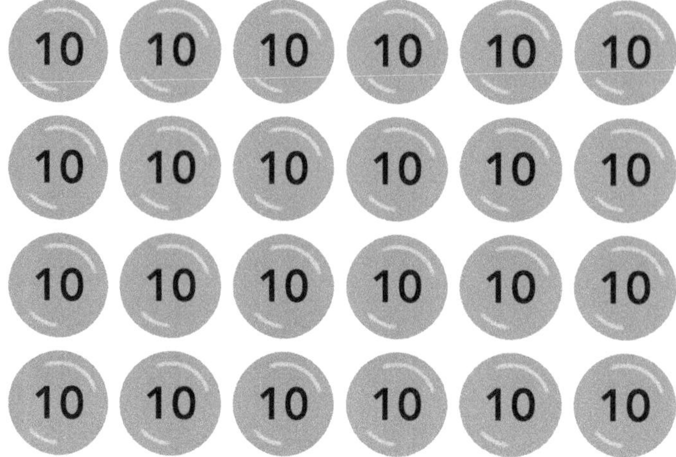

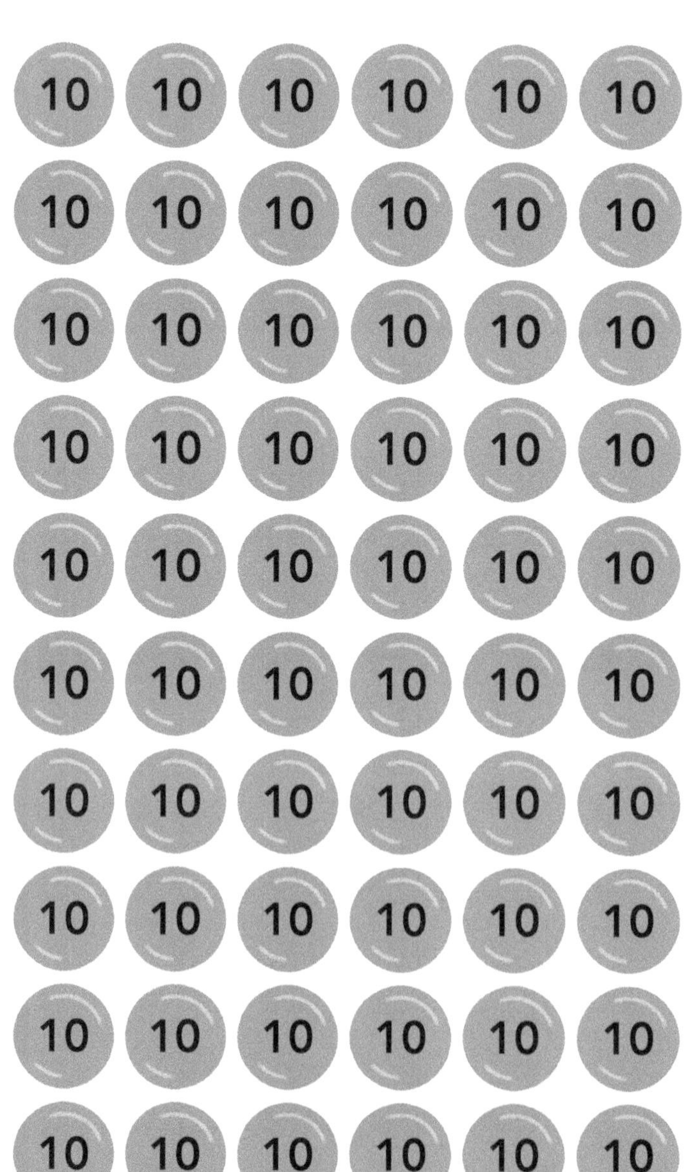



© HarperCollinsPublishers 2017

# Resource 3.9.2d

## Balancing multiplications

**1.–6.** Circle the correct multiplication sentence(s) to make each set of balances correct.

**7.–8.** Write the multiplication sentences to make these balances correct.

**1.**

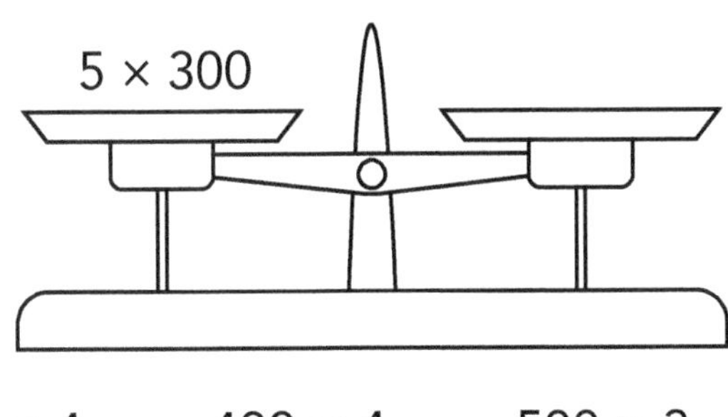


500 × 4 400 × 4 500 × 3

**2.**

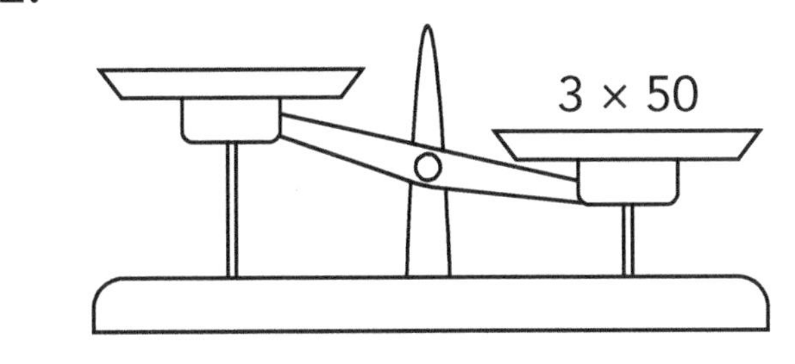


2 × 700 3 × 40 40 × 4 80 × 2

**3.**

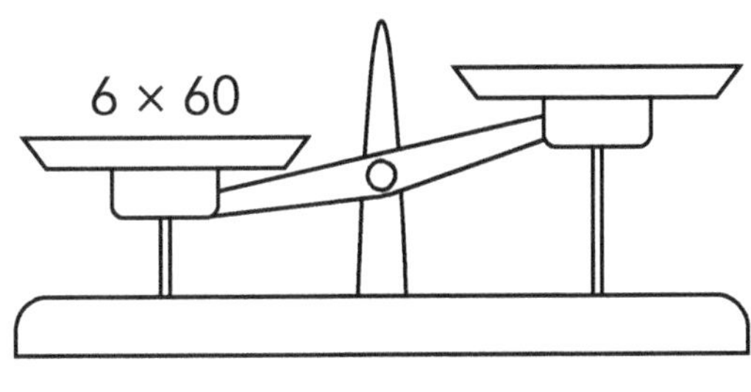


90 × 4 5 × 80 40 × 8 9 × 50

**4.**

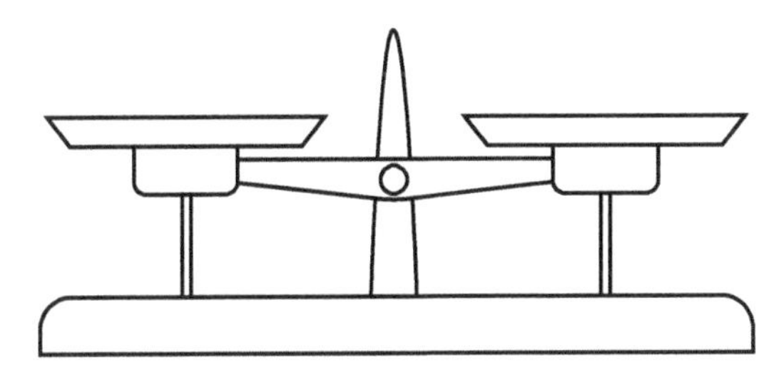

300 × 6 4 × 20 20 × 90 60 × 3

**5.**

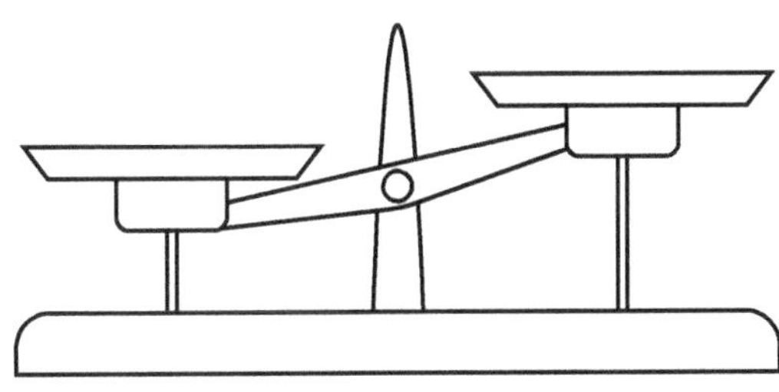

300 × 6 40 × 20 2 × 900 60 × 30

**6.**

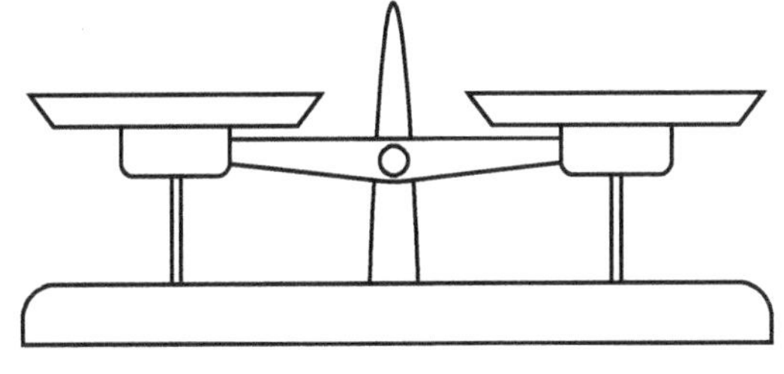

60 × 5 4 × 100 8 × 40 100 × 3

**7.**

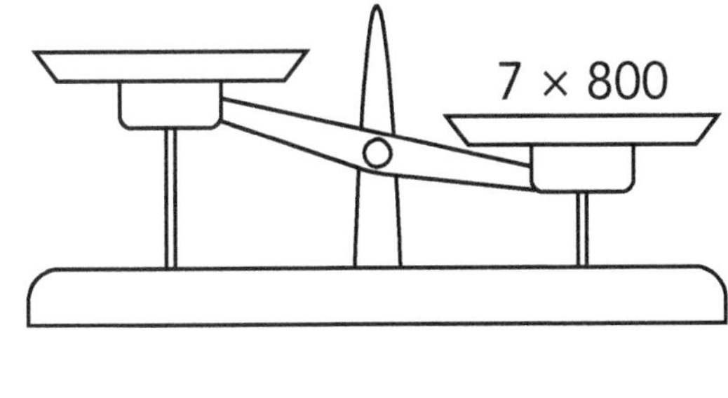


**8.**

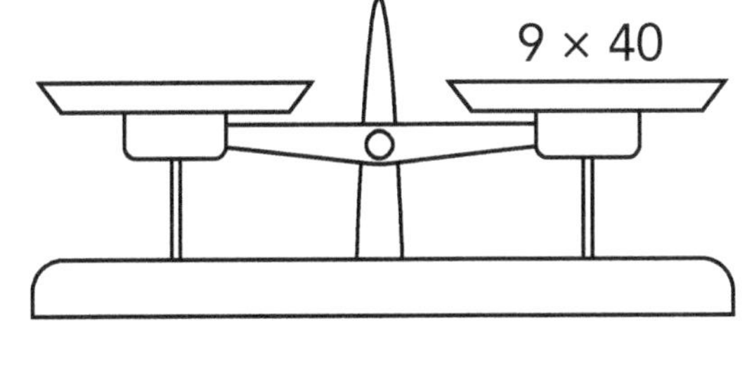


© HarperCollins*Publishers* 2017

## Changing arrays

Image 1

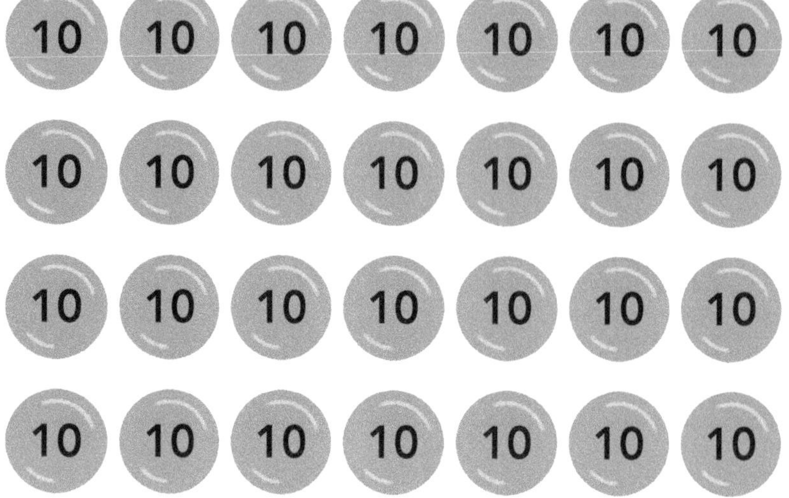


Image 2

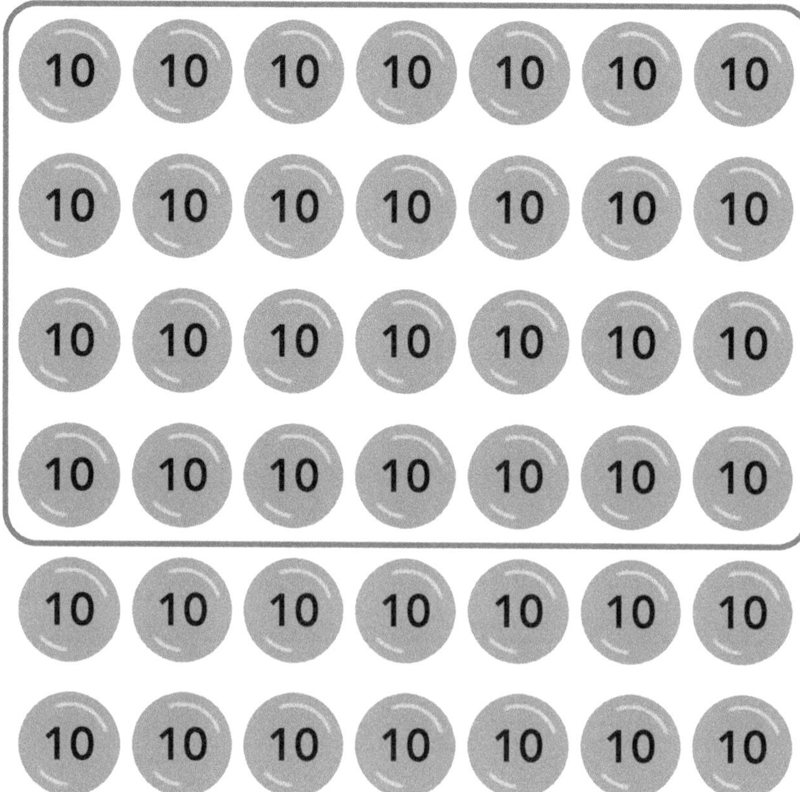



© HarperCollins*Publishers* 2017

# Multiplication problems

A shelf holds 300 books.

How many books can 7 shelves hold?

A short shelf holds 70 books.

A long shelf holds 3 times as many books.

How many books does a long shelf hold?

A small box holds 30 books.

A large box holds 7 times as many books.

How many more books are there in a large box than a small box?

$3 \times 70 =$ ☐

$7 \times 30 - 30 =$ ☐

$6 \times 30 =$ ☐

© HarperCollins*Publishers* 2017

# Resource 3.9.2g

## Problem arrays

Match each problem with an array to help you solve it. Draw a line to join each problem with its matching array.

One problem will be left over. Can you draw an array that helps solve the problem?

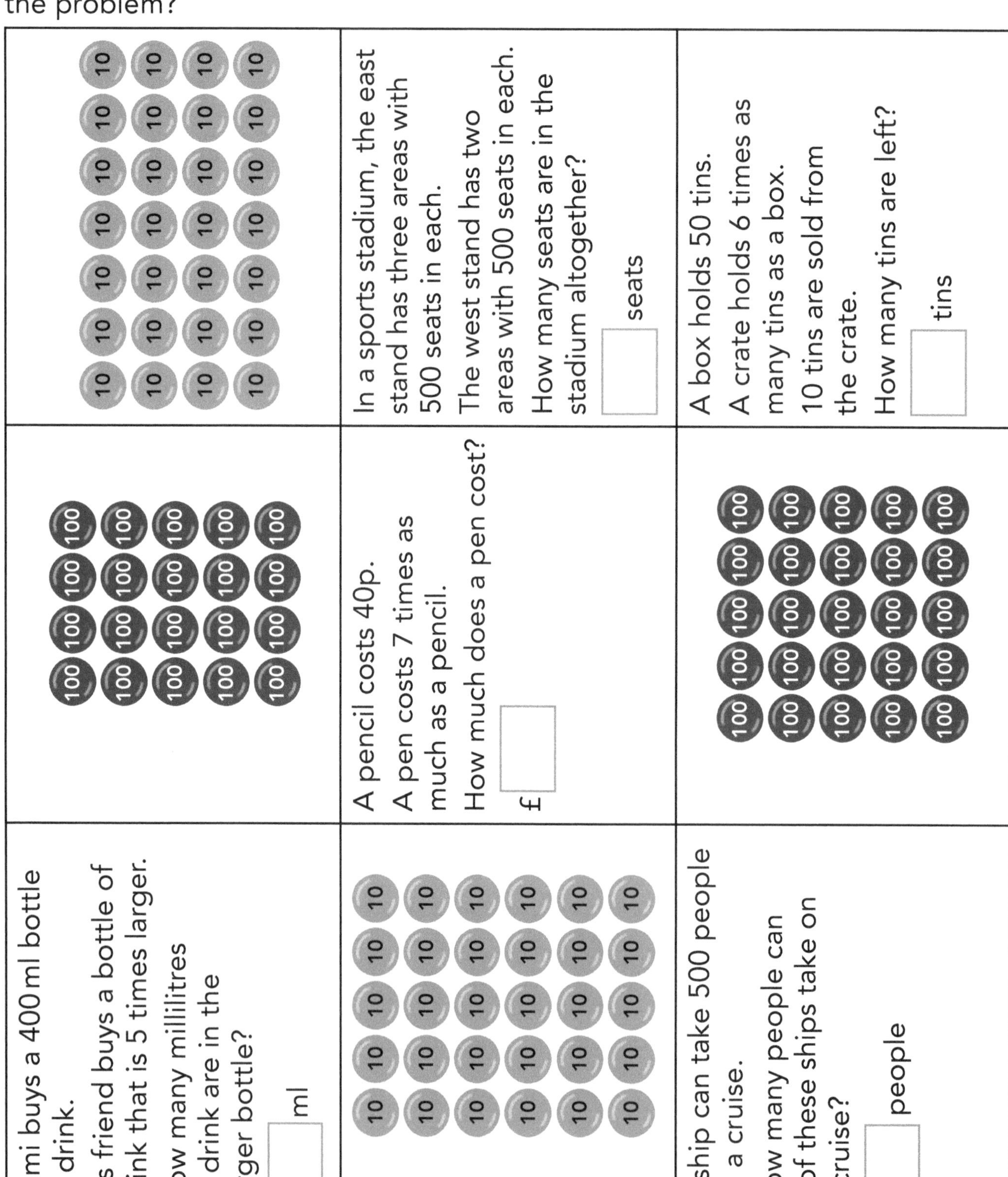




© HarperCollins*Publishers* 2017

# Resource 3.9.2h

## Writing problems

Write a problem to match each array. Think carefully about arrays 5 and 6.

| | |
|---|---|
| 1. 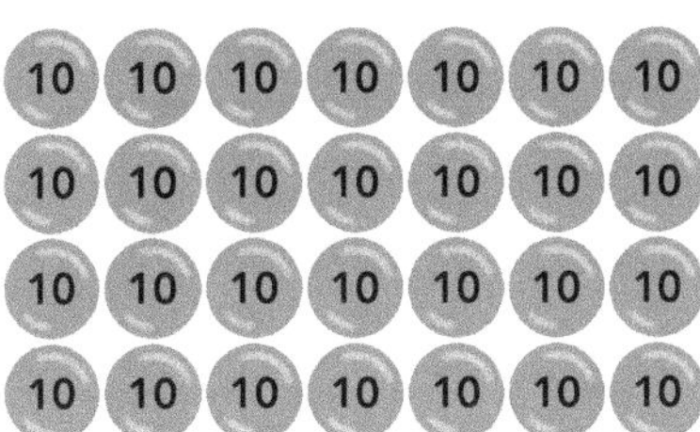 | 2. 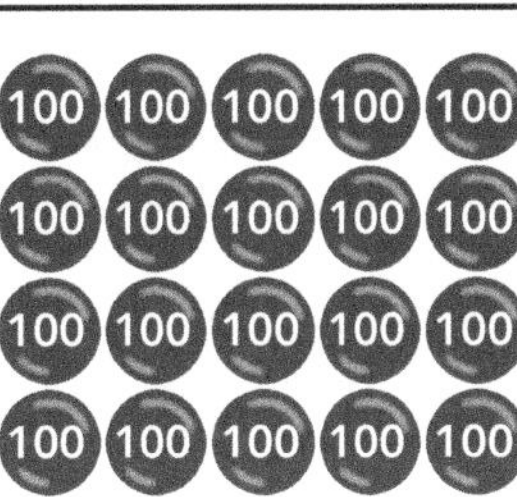 |
| 3. 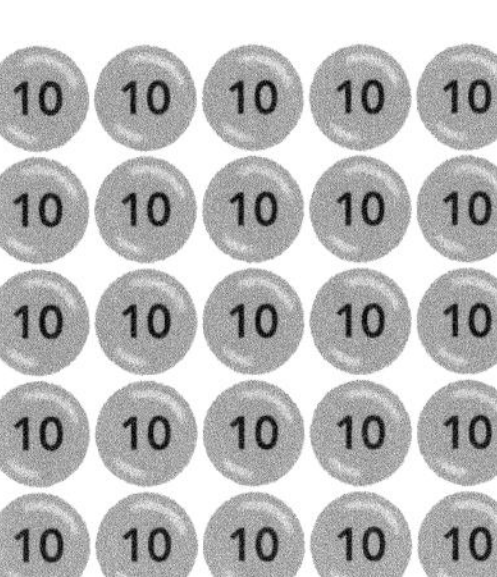 | 4.  |
| 5.  | 6. 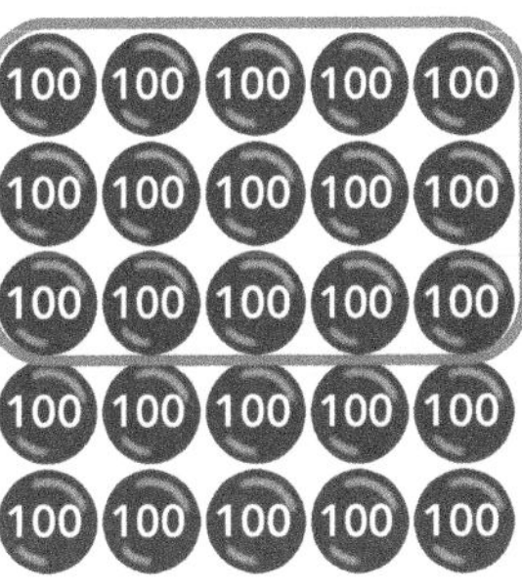 |

© HarperCollinsPublishers 2017

## Write word problems

Use facts from the number lines to help make up the following types of question.

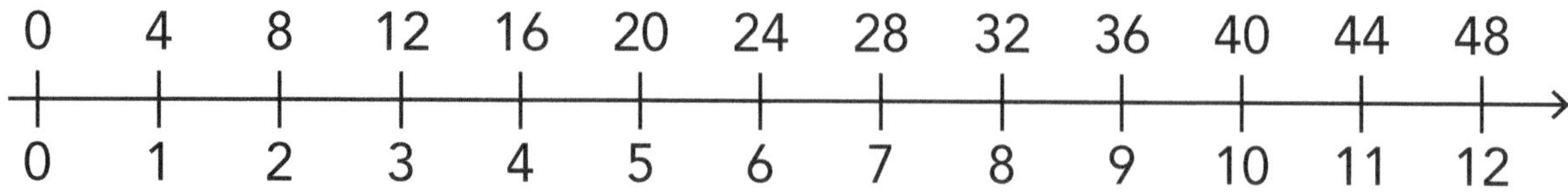


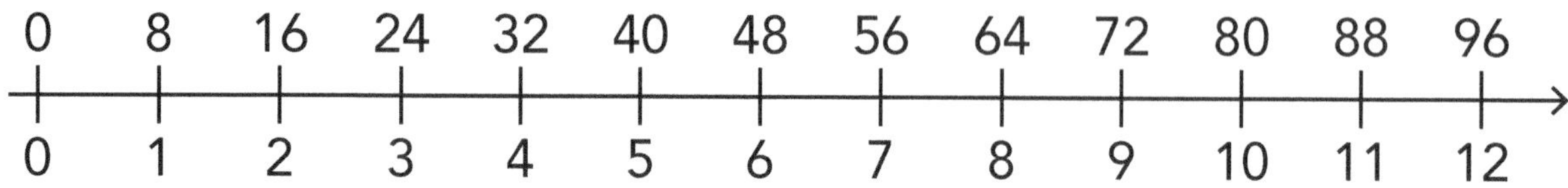


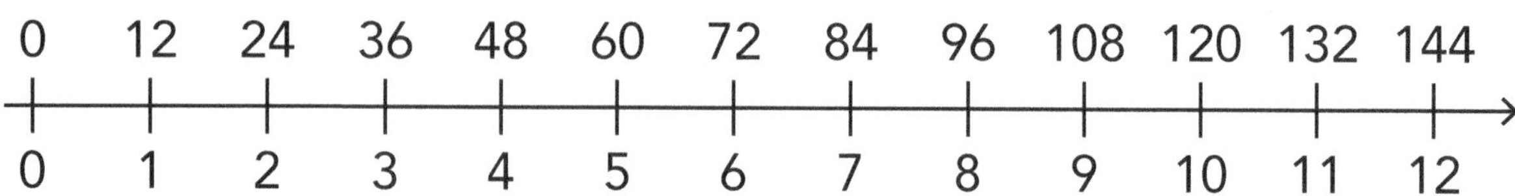


1. Write a word problem to match the fact: 6 × 12 = 72.

______________________________________________

______________________________________________

2. Write a different word problem to match a fact from the eights number line.

______________________________________________

______________________________________________

3. Write a different word problem to match a fact from the fours number line.

______________________________________________

______________________________________________


© HarperCollins*Publishers* 2017

**4.** Write a problem with two steps. Make the first step multiplication and the second step subtraction.

______________________________________________

______________________________________________

**5.** Complete this maths story with numbers of your choice:
Amy buys 7 packets of 4 stickers on the way to school.

On the way home, she buys another ☐ packets of 4 stickers.

She calculates that altogether she has ☐ × 4 = ☐ stickers.

**6.** Write a word problem for the fact: 9 × 4 = 36. Include some information in the problem that is not needed to solve it.

______________________________________________

______________________________________________

© HarperCollins*Publishers* 2017

## Multiplication sentences

© HarperCollins*Publishers* 2017

# Resource 3.9.3c

## Multiplication word problems

12 cans per box
£70 per box

12 cartons per box
£45 per box

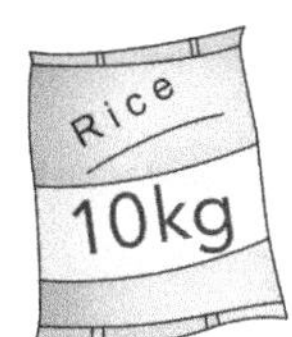


10 kilograms per sack
£50 per sack

8 cartons per box
£20 per box

| |
|---|
| 1. |
| 2. |
| 3. |
| 4. |

$20 \times 50$

$10 \times 8$

$7 \times 12$

$10 \times 70$

© HarperCollinsPublishers 2017

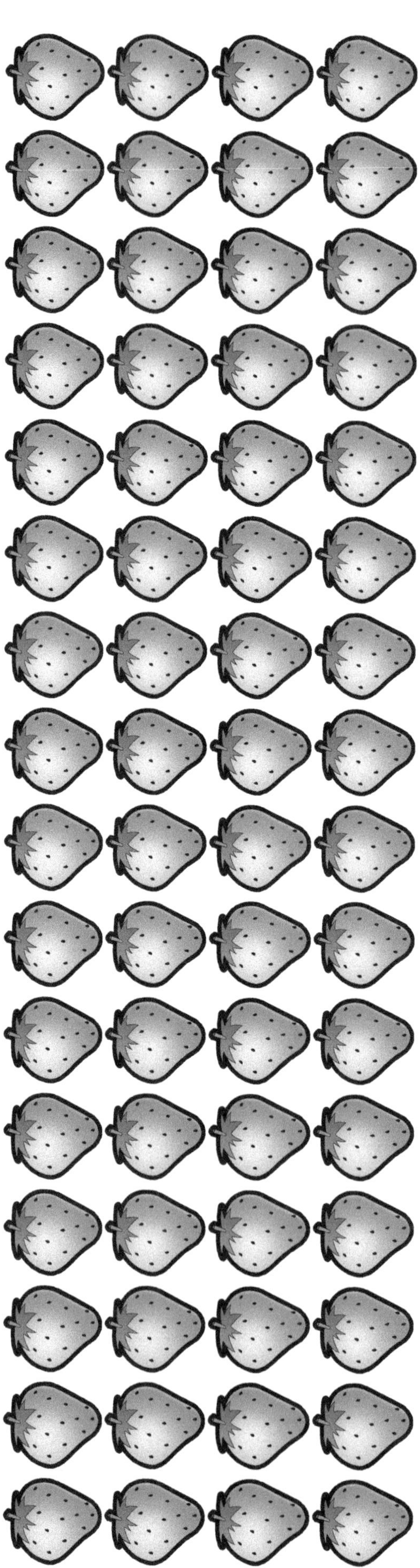

Strawberry array



© HarperCollinsPublishers 2017

## Partitioning arrays with strawberries

Annie wants to find out how many strawberries are in her picture.

1. She partitions her array and finds 9 × 5 and 8 × 5. She adds the products together.

   What is her answer? ☐

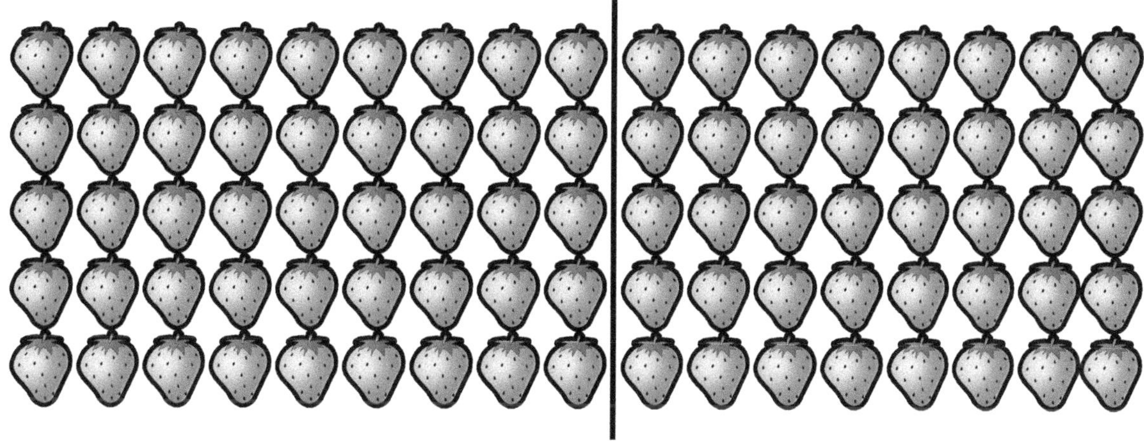

2. Explore the different ways that Annie can partition her array of strawberries and record the calculations each time.

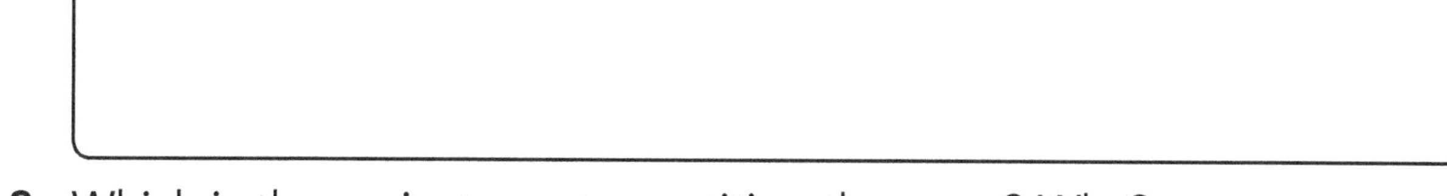

3. Which is the easiest way to partition the array? Why?

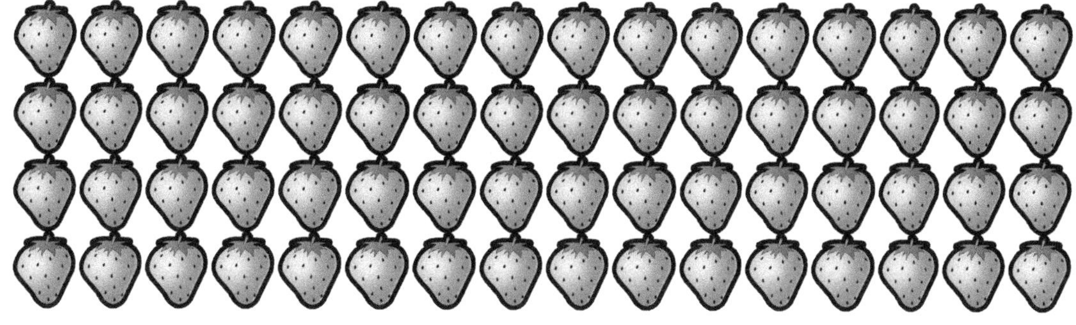

_______________________________________________

_______________________________________________

© HarperCollinsPublishers 2017

## Place value arrays

Image 1

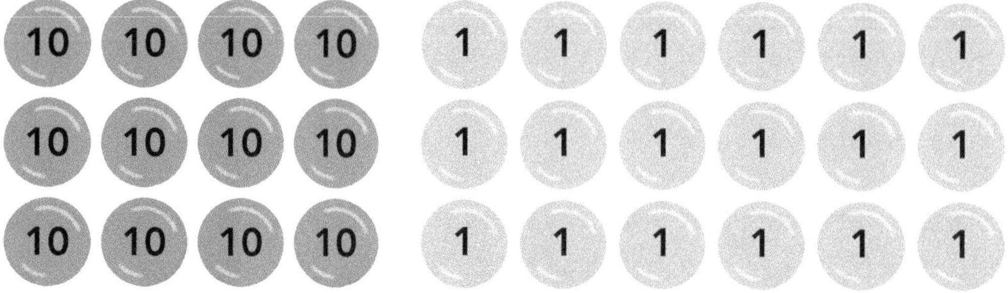


Image 2

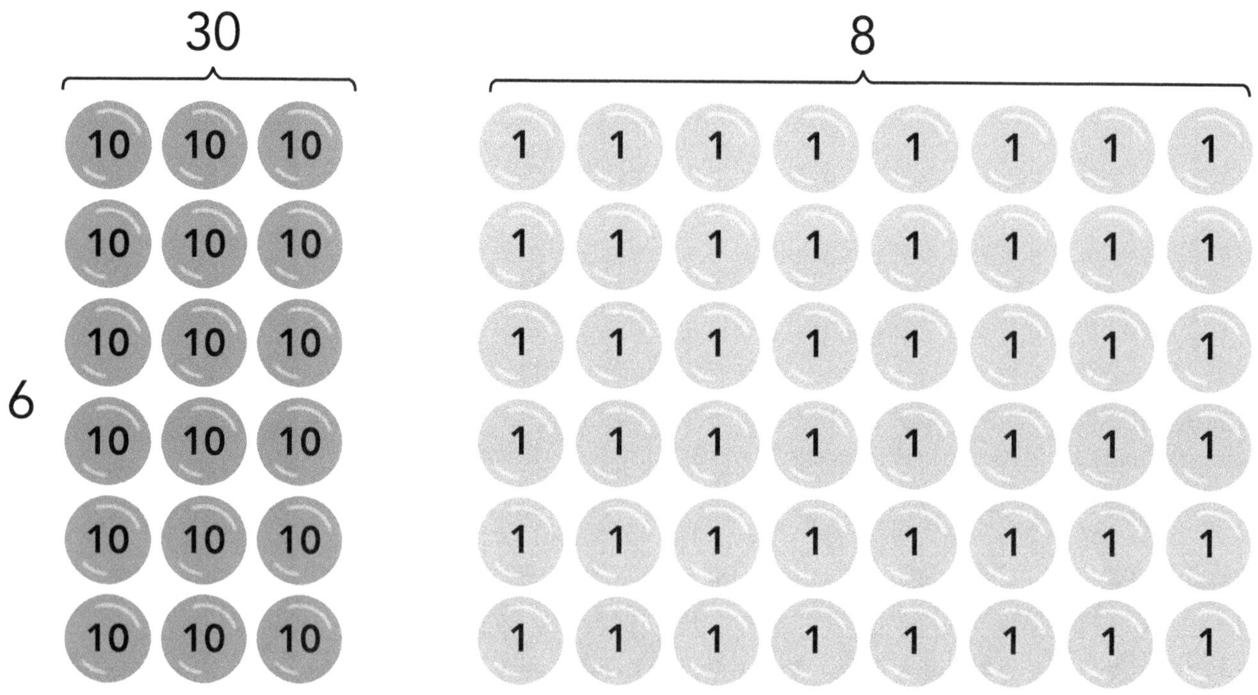



© HarperCollins*Publishers* 2017

## 2-digit × 1-digit multiplication

Choose a multiplication sentence from each grid and put them together to make a 2-digit × 1-digit multiplication.

For example, choose 50 × 4 and 6 × 4 to make 56 × 4.

Calculate the product and record the number sentences you use.

How many different products can you make?

What is the largest and smallest product you can make?

| | | |
|---|---|---|
| 4 × 40 | 50 × 4 | 8 × 50 |
| 60 × 6 | 6 × 90 | 20 × 9 |
| 80 × 7 | 9 × 40 | 70 × 3 |
| 5 × 30 | 40 × 2 | 90 × 3 |

| | | |
|---|---|---|
| 3 × 8 | 2 × 3 | 4 × 6 |
| 7 × 2 | 6 × 4 | 8 × 2 |
| 4 × 9 | 9 × 8 | 5 × 5 |
| 6 × 3 | 8 × 5 | 6 × 7 |

© HarperCollins*Publishers* 2017

# Word problem arrays

On an aeroplane, seats are arranged in rows of 3.
There are 54 rows of 3 seats on the aeroplane.
How many seats are there altogether?

A packet of stickers costs 45p.
How much will 3 packets of stickers cost?

Write your own word problem to match the array.

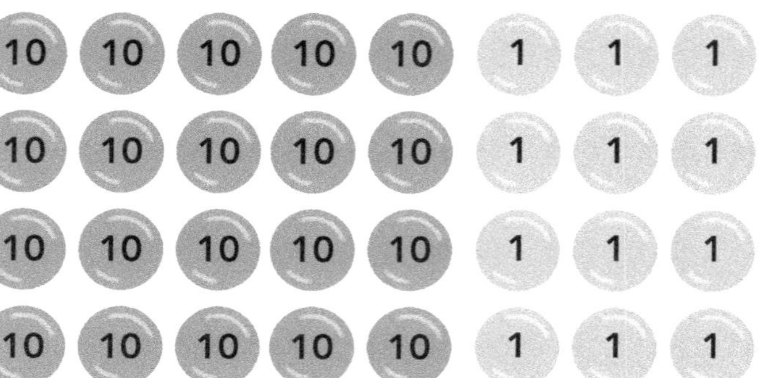

© HarperCollinsPublishers 2017

# Resource 3.9.5a

## 3-digit calculations

Use the three digits to make two different calculations. You should try to make the largest and smallest product each time.

Use a written method with partitioning for Questions 3, 4, 5 and 6.

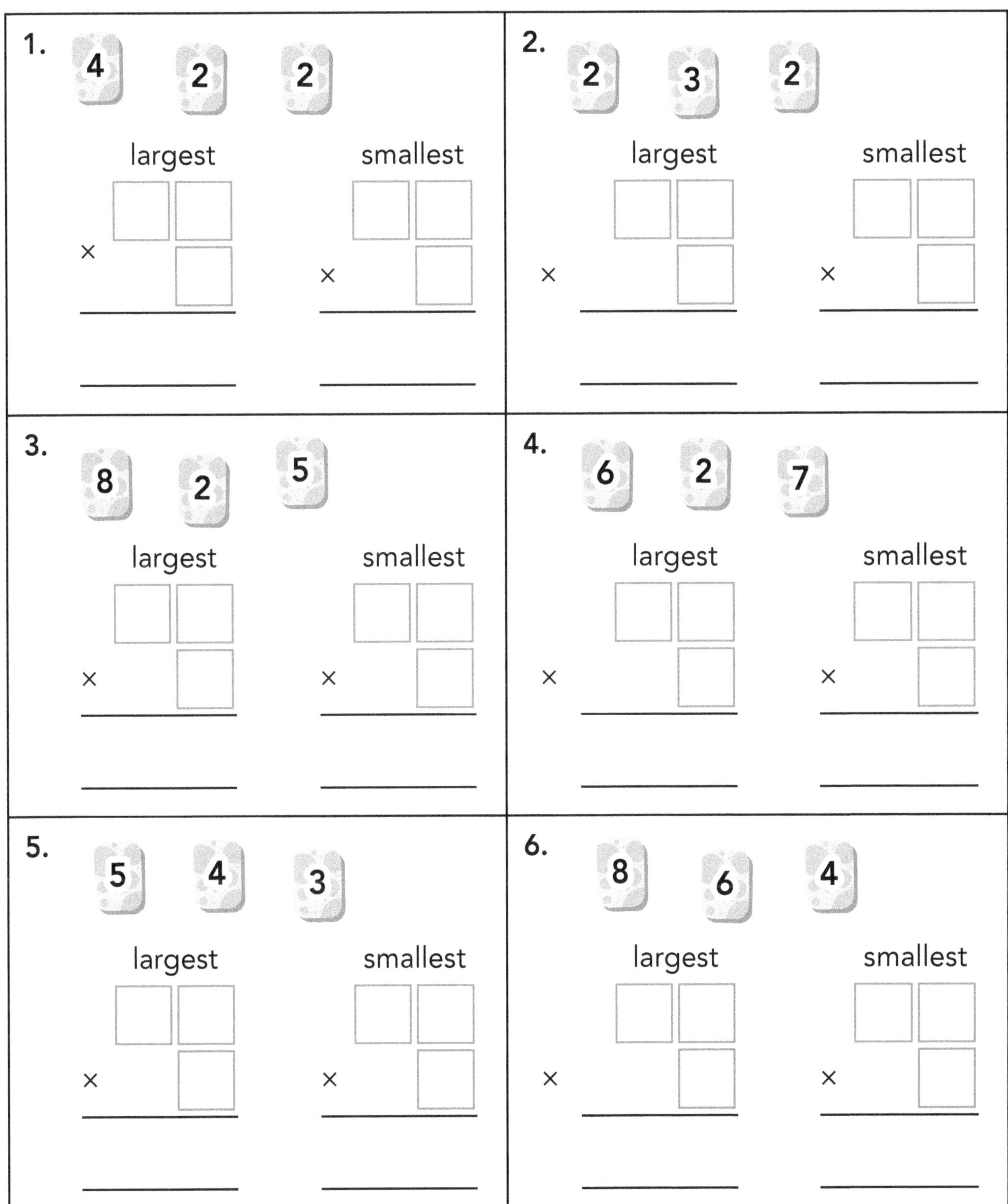


© HarperCollinsPublishers 2017

# Resource 3.9.5b

## Twice the price

How much does it cost to buy two of each of these items?
Use a written column method to calculate the cost and a mental method to check your answers.

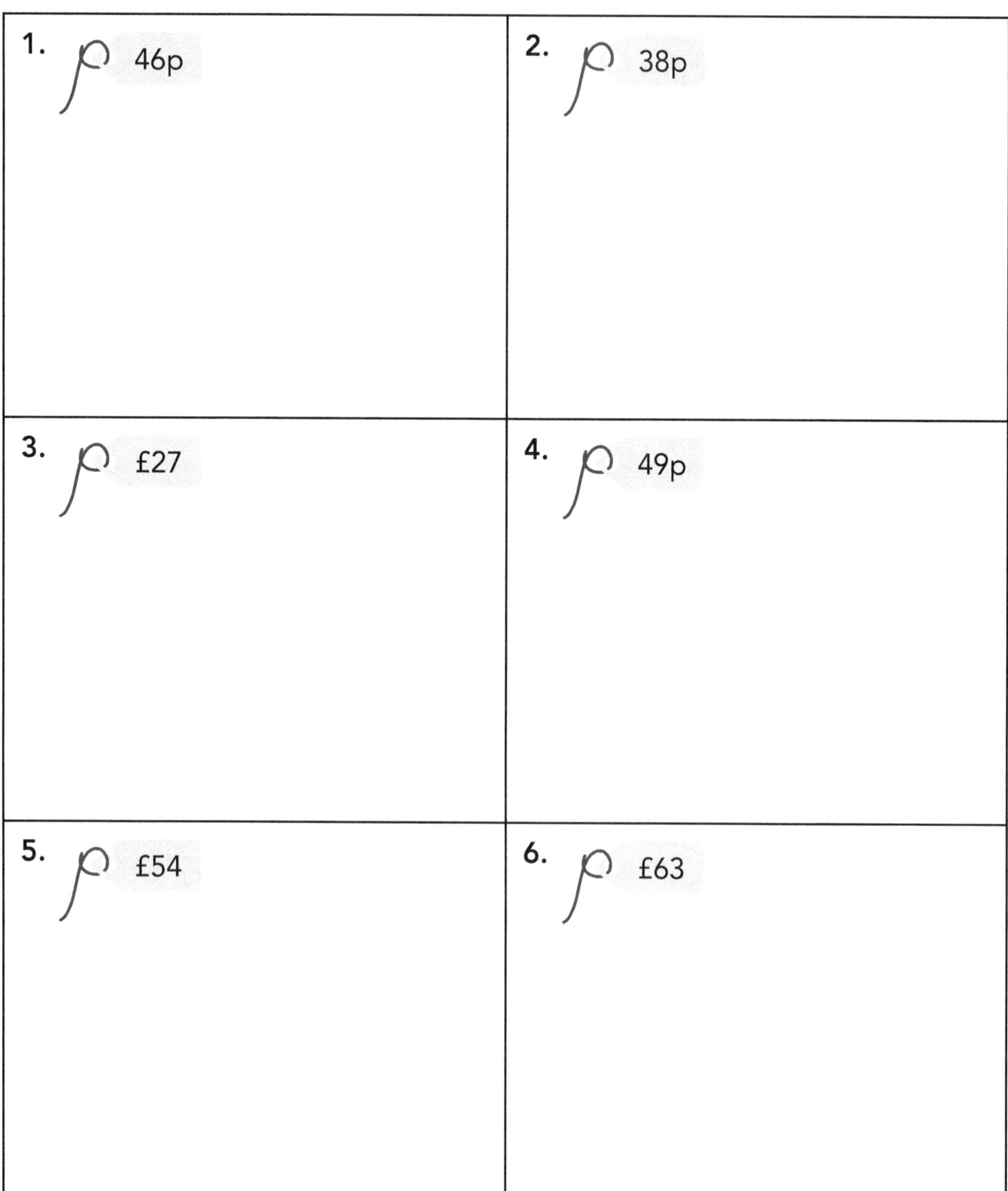

1.
46p
2.
38p
3.
£27
4.
49p
5.
£54
6.
£63



© HarperCollins*Publishers* 2017

# Resource 3.9.5c

## Missing numbers

Find the missing numbers in these multiplication calculations.
Use a mental method to check that you are correct.

| | | | |
|---|---|---|---|
| **1.** $\begin{array}{r} 7\,\square \\ \times\quad 4 \\ \hline 3\,0\,4 \\ \hline \end{array}$ | **2.** $\begin{array}{r} 6\,3 \\ \times\quad \square \\ \hline 4\,3\,1 \\ \hline \end{array}$ | **3.** $\begin{array}{r} \square\,9 \\ \times\quad 5 \\ \hline 2\,4\,0 \\ \hline \end{array}$ | **4.** $\begin{array}{r} 3\,8 \\ \times\quad \square \\ \hline 2\,4\,4 \\ \hline \end{array}$ |
| **5.** $\begin{array}{r} 6\,\square \\ \times\quad 2 \\ \hline 1\,\square\,4 \\ \hline \end{array}$ | **6.** $\begin{array}{r} \square\,5 \\ \times\quad 6 \\ \hline 1\,\square\,0 \\ \hline \end{array}$ | **7.** $\begin{array}{r} 4\,5 \\ \times\quad \square \\ \hline 4\,\square\,5 \\ \hline \end{array}$ | **8.** Make up a missing number problem for a friend to solve. |

© HarperCollinsPublishers 2017

## Multiplication methods

| | 40 | 7 |
|---|---|---|
| 6 | $6 \times 40 = 240$ | $6 \times 7 = 42$ |

$6 \times 47 = 240 + 42$

$$\begin{array}{r} 32 \\ \times \quad 3 \\ \hline \end{array}$$

10 10 10 1 1
10 10 10 1 1
10 10 10 1 1

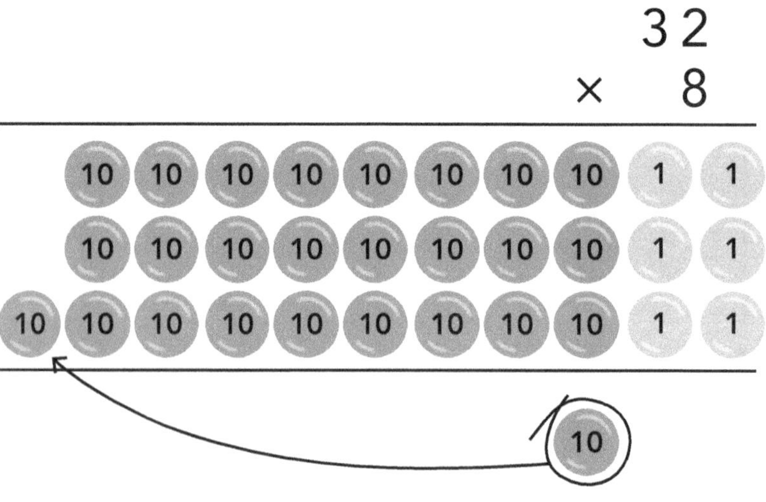


24 tens + 1 ten is 25 tens



© HarperCollins*Publishers* 2017

# Resource 3.9.6b

## Product range

Replace each triangle with one of these digits once only in order to make the calculations correct.

| 3 | 5 | 6 | 7 | 8 | 9 |
|---|---|---|---|---|---|

Remember to estimate first and then write the answer each time.

1. 48 × △ = ☐ The product is between 320 and 400.

2. △ × 63 = ☐ The product is between 180 and 210.

3. ☐ = 29 × △ The product is between 160 and 240.

4. 75 × △ = ☐ The product is between 350 and 400.

5. ☐ = △ × 65 The product is between 420 and 490.

6. △ × 84 = ☐ The product is between 480 and 540.

© HarperCollins*Publishers* 2017

# Resource 3.9.6c

## Sorting calculations

| The product is between 100 and 150. | The product is between 150 and 200. |
|---|---|
| The product is between 200 and 250. | The product is between 250 and 300. |
| The product is between 300 and 350. | The product is between 350 and 400. |
| The product is between 400 and 450. | The product is between 450 and 500. |

| | | | | | | |
|---|---|---|---|---|---|---|
| 45 × 6 | 93 × 5 | 3 × 62 | 3 × 64 | 19 × 8 | 78 × 4 | 8 × 61 |
| 6 × 75 | 34 × 3 | 55 × 6 | 47 × 4 | 57 × 3 | 9 × 55 | 72 × 3 |
| 9 × 47 | 2 × 99 | 7 × 71 | 48 × 6 | 73 × 4 | 83 × 2 | 32 × 9 |

© HarperCollinsPublishers 2017

# Resource 3.9.6d

## Shop multiplication problems

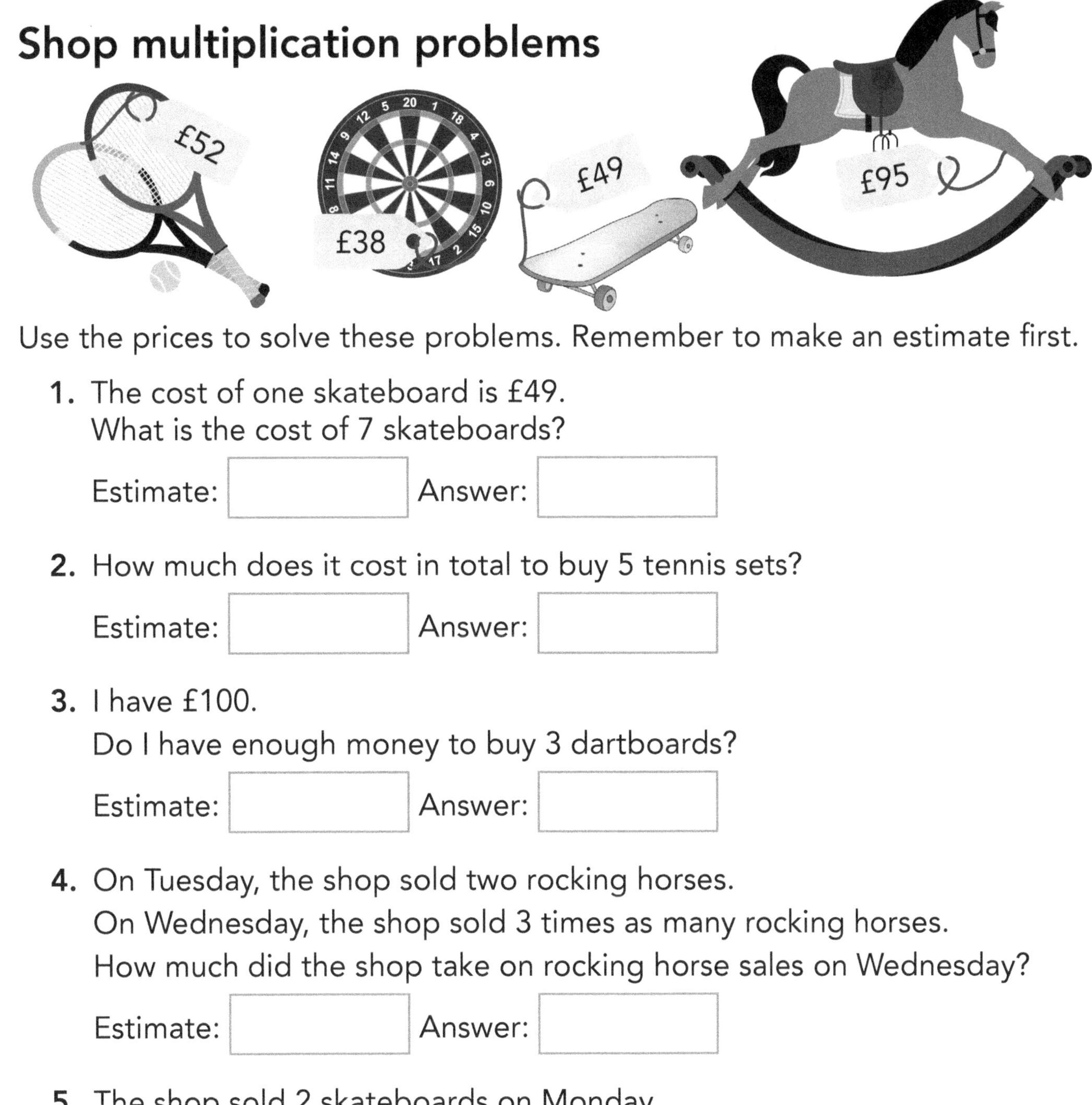


Use the prices to solve these problems. Remember to make an estimate first.

1. The cost of one skateboard is £49.
   What is the cost of 7 skateboards?

   Estimate: Answer:

2. How much does it cost in total to buy 5 tennis sets?

   Estimate: Answer:

3. I have £100.
   Do I have enough money to buy 3 dartboards?

   Estimate: Answer:

4. On Tuesday, the shop sold two rocking horses.
   On Wednesday, the shop sold 3 times as many rocking horses.
   How much did the shop take on rocking horse sales on Wednesday?

   Estimate: Answer:

5. The shop sold 2 skateboards on Monday.
   Another 3 skateboards were sold on Tuesday.
   Another 3 skateboards were sold on Wednesday.
   What was the total amount taken on skateboards on those three days?

   Estimate: Answer:

6. On Saturday, the shop sold 10 tennis sets.
   Half this number were sold on Monday.
   How much money did the shop take for tennis sets on Monday?

   Estimate: Answer:

© HarperCollins*Publishers* 2017

# Resource 3.9.7a



| | | | | |
|---|---|---|---|---|
| 12 | 3600 | 56 | 240 | 420 |
| 4200 | 54 | 2800 | 540 | 1200 |
| 560 | 42 | 120 | 280 | 360 |
| 24 | 5600 | 36 | 2400 | 28 |



© HarperCollins*Publishers* 2017

# Resource 3.9.7b

## Money multiplication

How much money is in each group of bags?

1. There are 2 coins in each bag.

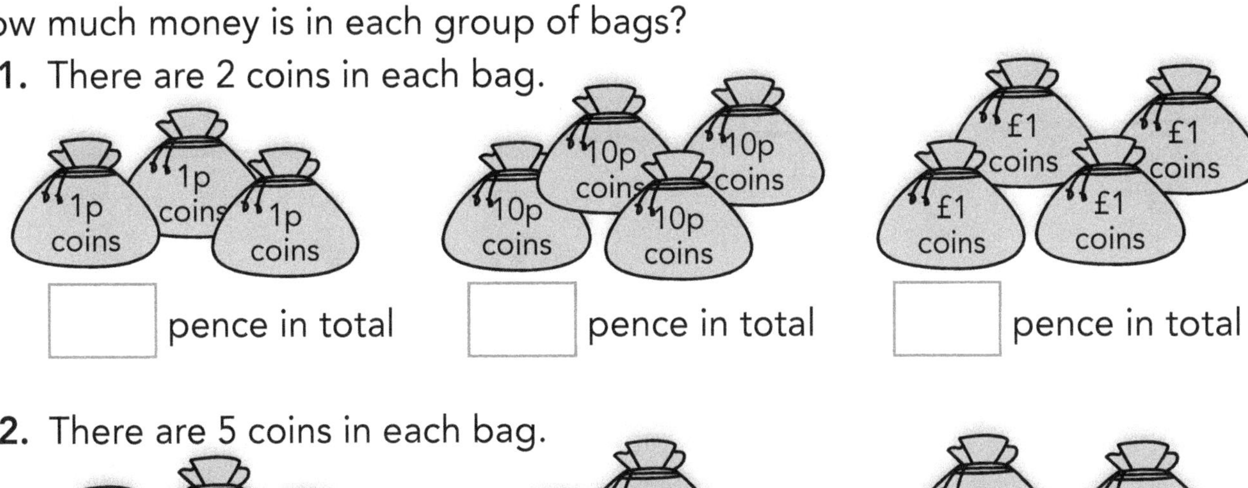


☐ pence in total ☐ pence in total ☐ pence in total

2. There are 5 coins in each bag.

☐ pence in total  ☐ pence in total  ☐ pence in total

3. There are 7 coins in each bag.

☐ pence in total  ☐ pence in total  ☐ pence in total

4. There are 6 coins in each bag.

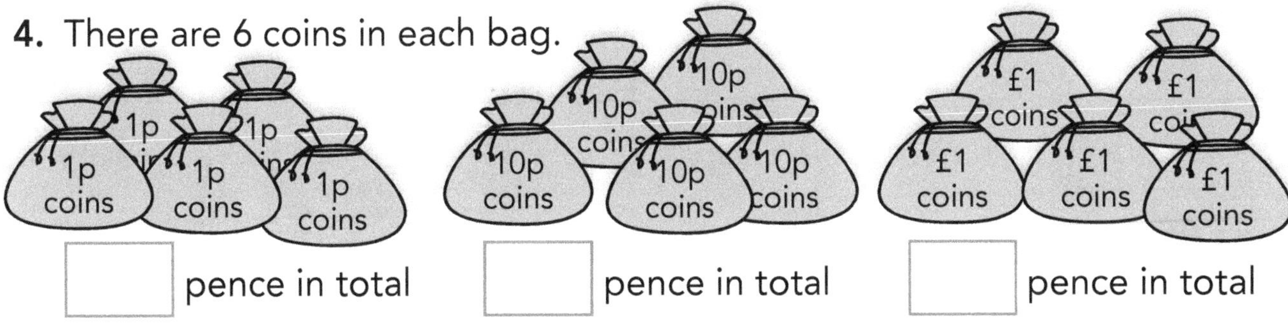


☐ pence in total ☐ pence in total ☐ pence in total

5. There are 9 coins in each bag.

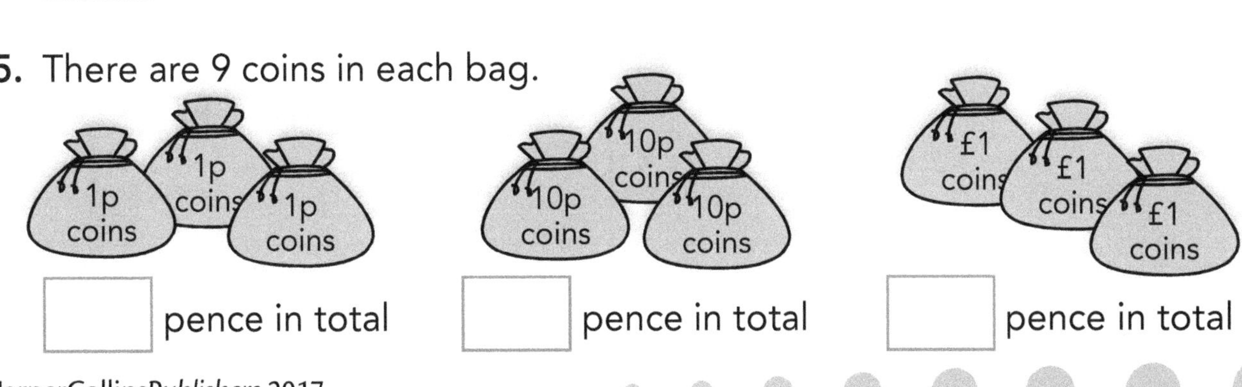


☐ pence in total ☐ pence in total ☐ pence in total

© HarperCollins*Publishers* 2017

## Finding whole numbers

How many hundreds, tens and ones can you see each time? What is the value of the whole number?

**1.**

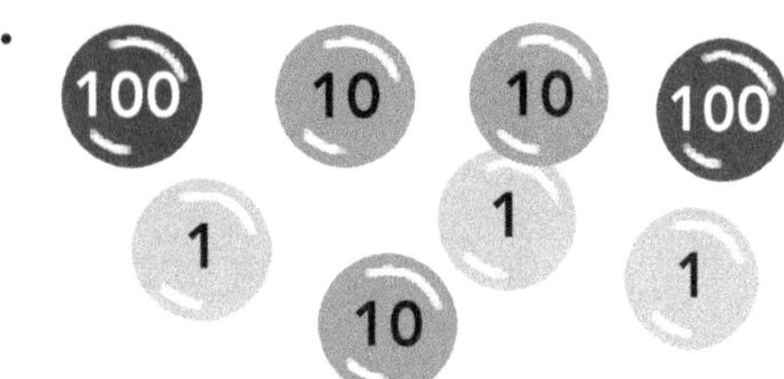

There are ☐ hundreds,

☐ tens and ☐ ones.

☐ + ☐ + ☐ = ☐

**2.**

There are ☐ hundreds,

☐ tens and ☐ ones.

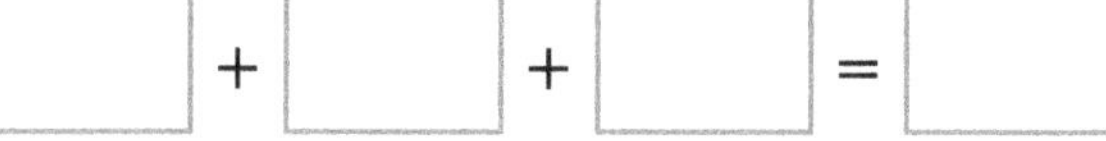

☐ + ☐ + ☐ = ☐

**3.**

There are ☐ hundreds,

☐ tens and ☐ ones.

☐ + ☐ + ☐ = ☐

**4.**

There are ☐ hundreds,

☐ tens and ☐ ones.

☐ + ☐ + ☐ = ☐

**5.**

There are ☐ hundreds,

☐ tens and ☐ ones.

☐ + ☐ + ☐ = ☐

**6.**

There are ☐ hundreds,

☐ tens and ☐ ones.

☐ + ☐ + ☐ = ☐



© HarperCollins*Publishers* 2017

# Resource 3.9.7d

## Partitioning arrays

### Image 1

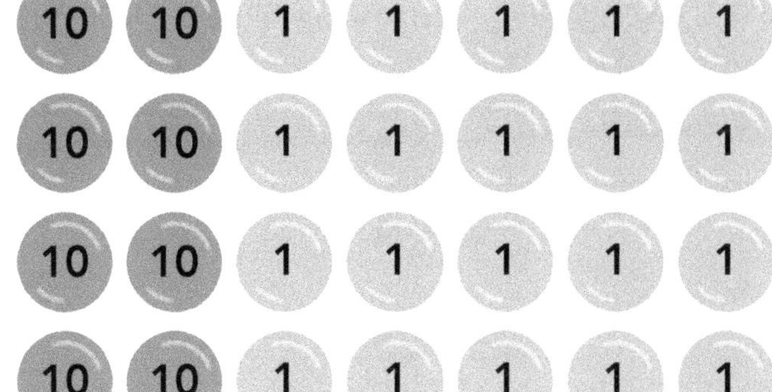


| | 20 | 5 |
|---|---|---|
| 16 | 140 (14 tens) | 35 |

### Image 2

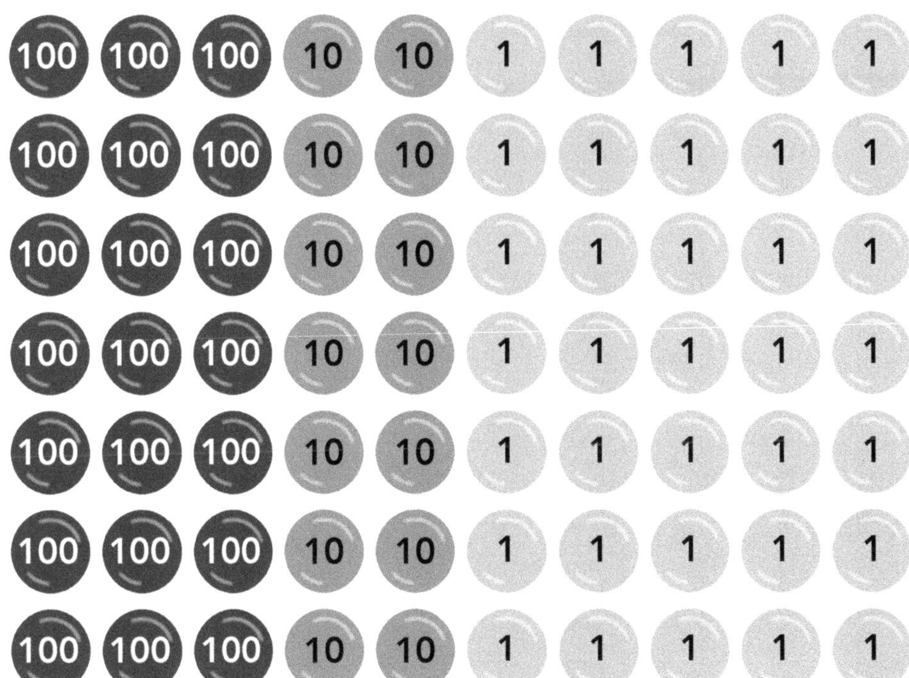


© HarperCollins*Publishers* 2017

# Resource 3.9.7e

## Finding values

Find the missing values to make these multiplications correct.

1. ☐ × 652 =

   ☐ × 600 = 4200

   ☐ × 50 = 350

   ☐ × 2 = ☐

   4200 + 350 + ☐ = ☐

2. 4 × ☐ =

   4 × ☐ = 1200

   4 × ☐ = 320

   4 × 6 = 24

   1200 + 320 + 24 = ☐

3. 491 × ☐ =

   400 × ☐ = 3600

   90 × ☐ = ☐

   1 × ☐ = 9

   3600 + ☐ + 9 = ☐

4. ☐ × 7 =

   ☐ × 7 = 5600

   ☐ × 7 = 350

   ☐ × 7 = 63

   5600 + 350 + 63 = ☐

5. ☐ × ☐ =

   ☐ × 200 = 1000

   ☐ × ☐ = 400

   ☐ × 6 = ☐

   1000 + 400 + ☐ = ☐

6. 316 × ☐ =

   300 × ☐ = 2400

   10 × ☐ = ☐

   6 × ☐ = 48

   2400 + ☐ + 48 = ☐



© HarperCollins*Publishers* 2017

# Resource 3.9.7f

## Multiplication: written methods

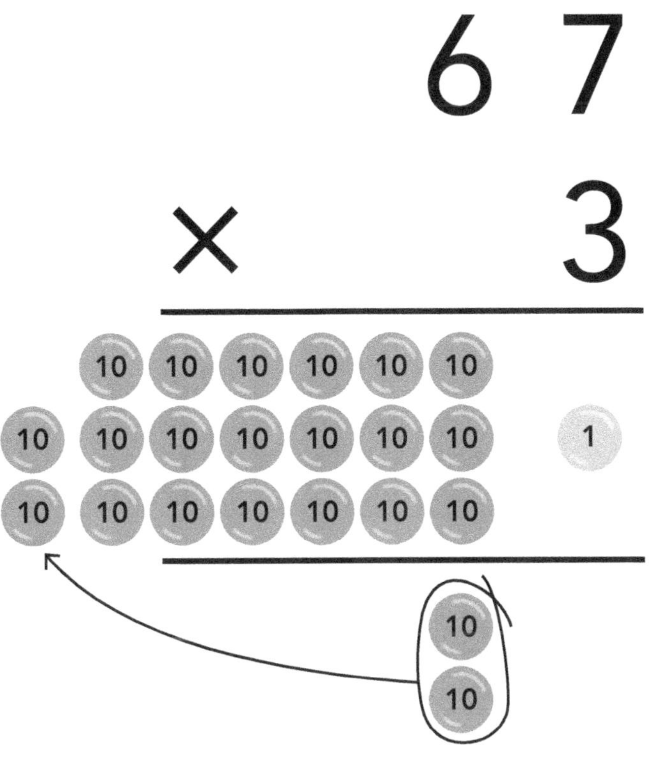


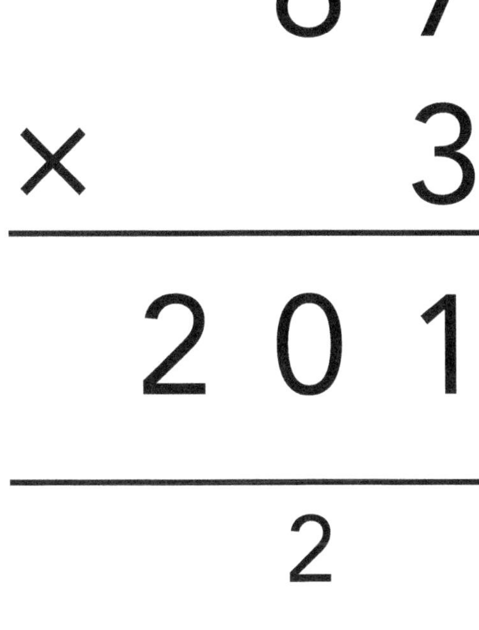


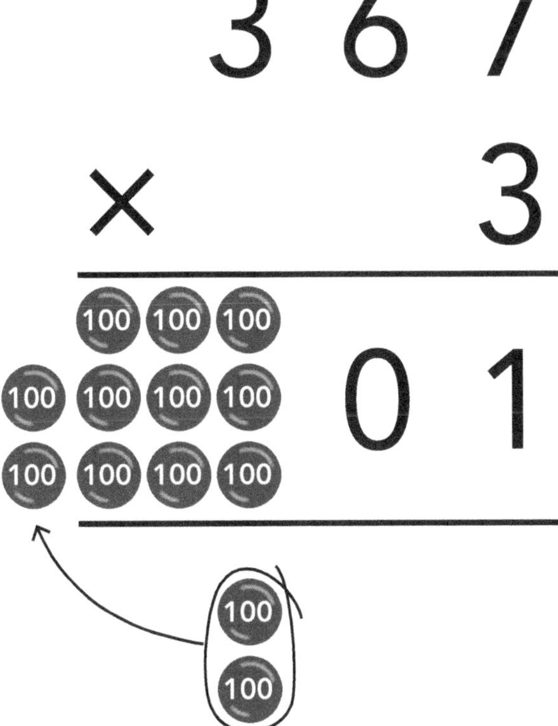


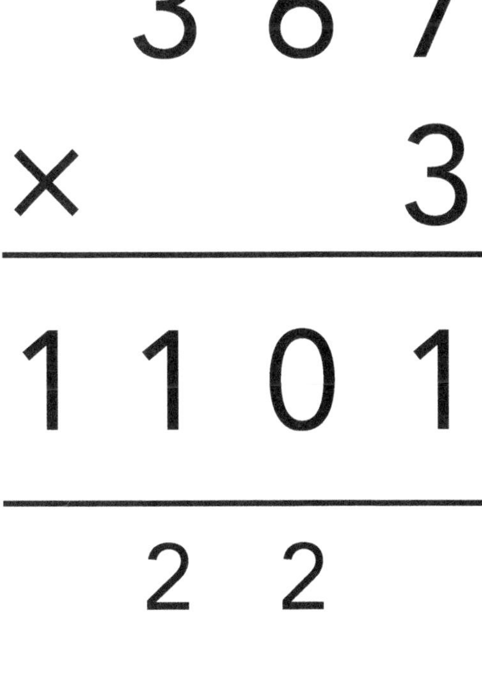


© HarperCollinsPublishers 2017

# Resource 3.9.7g

## Largest and smallest products

For each question, use the four digits to make two different calculations.
Try to make the largest and smallest product each time.
Remember to make an estimate first.

| | |
|---|---|
| 1. 4 2 5 0<br>largest □□□ × □□<br>smallest □□□ × □□ | 2. 4 3 7 2<br>largest □□□ × □□<br>smallest □□□ × □□ |
| 3. 1 2 5 8<br>largest □□□ × □□<br>smallest □□□ × □□ | 4. 6 9 2 4<br>largest □□□ × □□<br>smallest □□□ × □□ |
| 5. 3 9 3 7<br>largest □□□ × □□<br>smallest □□□ × □□ | 6. 5 6 4 0<br>largest □□□ × □□<br>smallest □□□ × □□ |


© HarperCollins*Publishers* 2017

## Total values

### Image 1

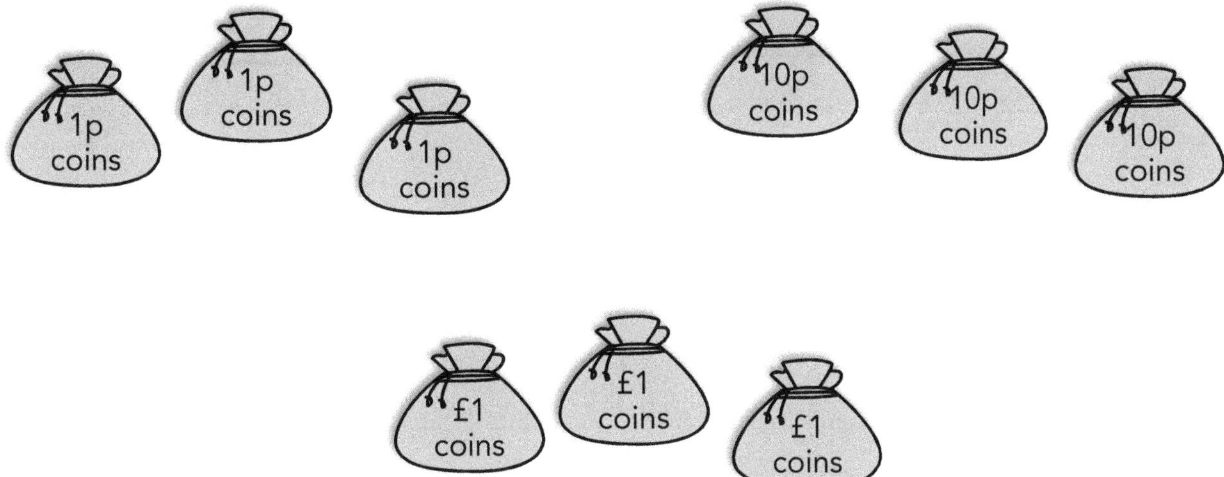


### Image 2

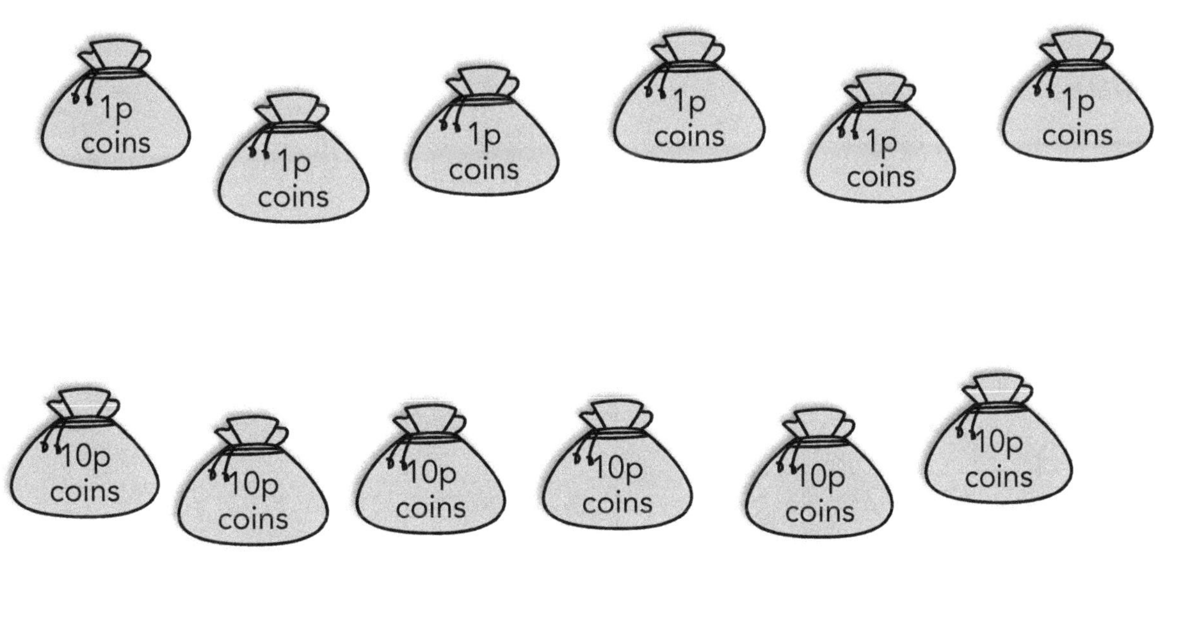

© HarperCollins*Publishers* 2017

## Money totals

Find the total value each time.

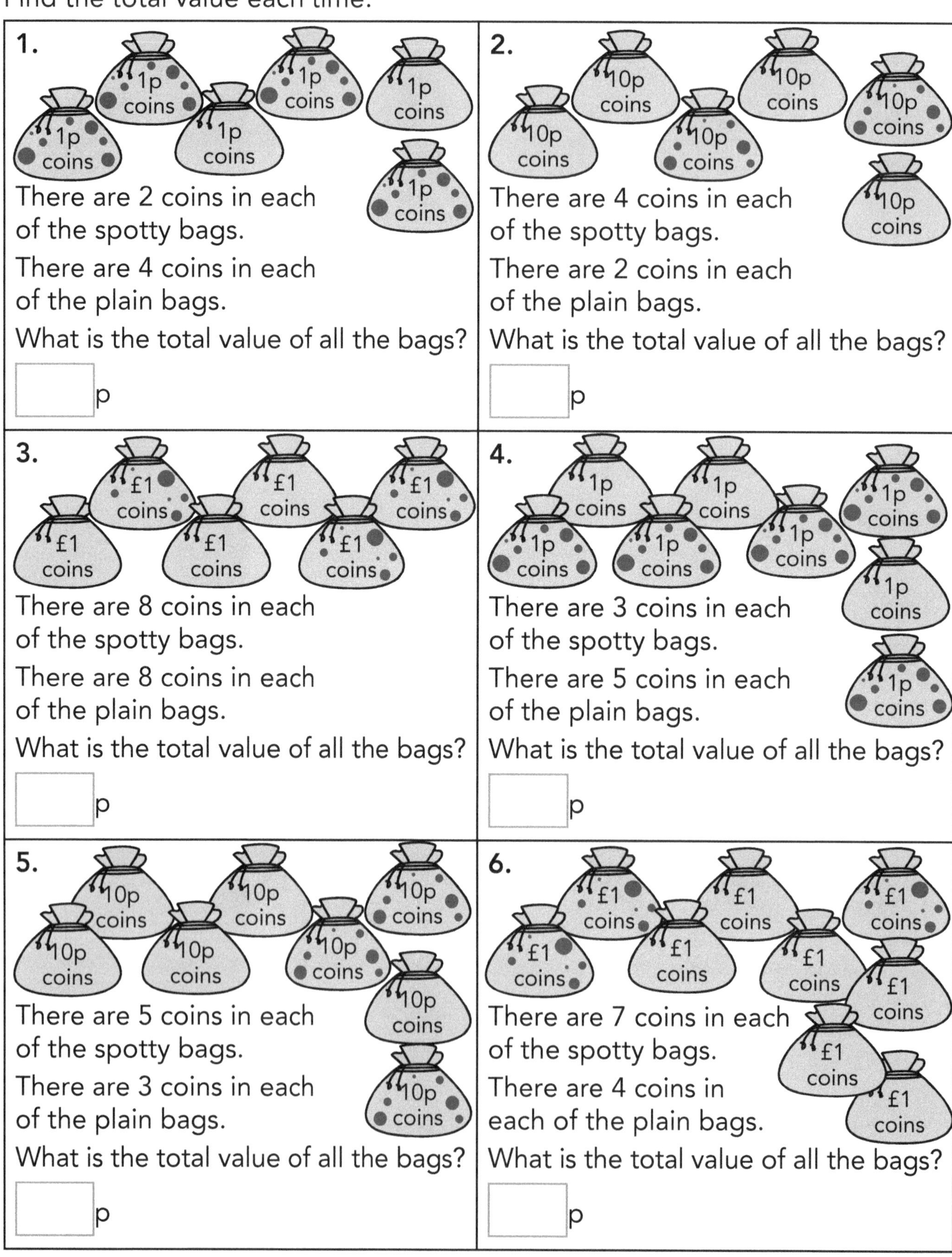

**1.** There are 2 coins in each of the spotty bags.
There are 4 coins in each of the plain bags.
What is the total value of all the bags?

☐ p

**2.** There are 4 coins in each of the spotty bags.
There are 2 coins in each of the plain bags.
What is the total value of all the bags?

☐ p

**3.** There are 8 coins in each of the spotty bags.
There are 8 coins in each of the plain bags.
What is the total value of all the bags?

☐ p

**4.** There are 3 coins in each of the spotty bags.
There are 5 coins in each of the plain bags.
What is the total value of all the bags?

☐ p

**5.** There are 5 coins in each of the spotty bags.
There are 3 coins in each of the plain bags.
What is the total value of all the bags?

☐ p

**6.** There are 7 coins in each of the spotty bags.
There are 4 coins in each of the plain bags.
What is the total value of all the bags?

☐ p


© HarperCollins*Publishers* 2017

# Resource 3.9.8c

## Matching calculations

| 230 ones × 5 | 300 ones × 8 | 5 × 25 tens | 420 ones × 3 |
|---|---|---|---|
| 42 tens × 6 | 7 × 18 tens | 23 tens × 5 | 18 tens × 2 |
| 4 × 21 tens | 42 tens × 3 | 30 tens × 8 | 420 ones × 6 |
| 180 ones × 2 | 5 × 250 ones | 180 ones × 7 | 4 × 210 ones |

© HarperCollins*Publishers* 2017

# Resource 3.9.8d

## Multiplication grid

| | | | |
|---|---|---|---|
| 302 × 4 | 2 × 2 × 10 | 3 × 10 × 7 | 6 × 300 |
| 460 × 5 | 40 × 30 | 125 × 4 | 2 × 4 × 30 |
| 40 × 7 | 247 × 3 | 200 × 5 | 5 × 5 × 10 |


© HarperCollins*Publishers* 2017

# Resource 3.9.9a

## Mental and written methods

| | | | |
|---|---|---|---|
| $47 \times 2$ | $30 \times 40$ | $3 \times 68$ | $367 \times 6$ |
| $2 \times 900$ | $5 \times 600$ | $800 \times 8$ | $72 \times 5$ |
| $592 \times 4$ | $6 \times 90$ | $28 \times 4$ | $9 \times 600$ |
| $80 \times 40$ | $508 \times 7$ | $60 \times 7$ | $400 \times 8$ |

© HarperCollins*Publishers* 2017

# Resource 3.9.9b

## Balancing multiplications

Use each of these calculations once to make all the representations correct. Write the calculations you use in the empty boxes.

900 × 7 | 6 × 72 | 701 × 8 | 255 × 4 | 84 × 5 | 40 × 70

**1.**

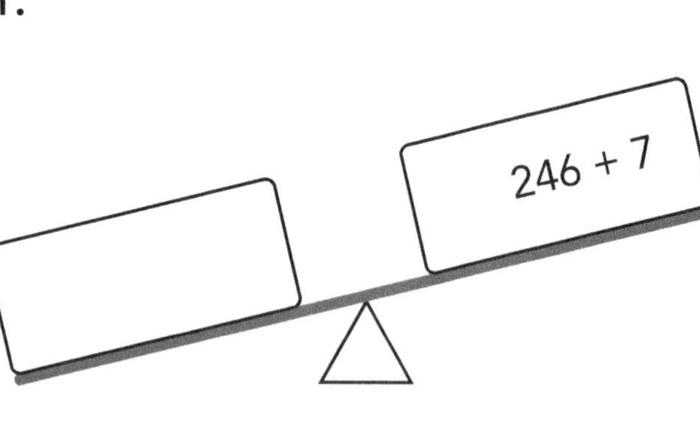


**2.**

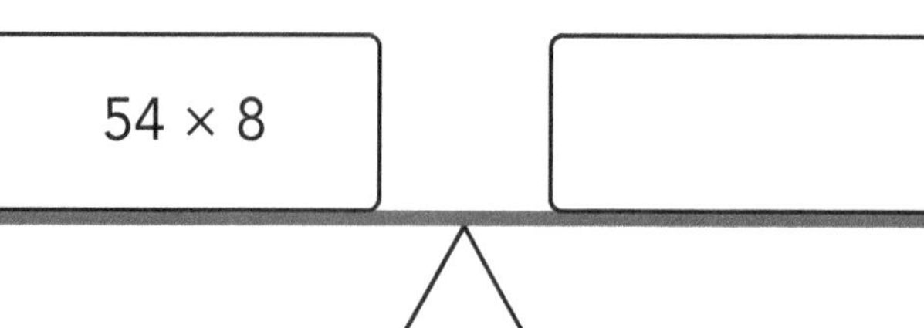


**3.**

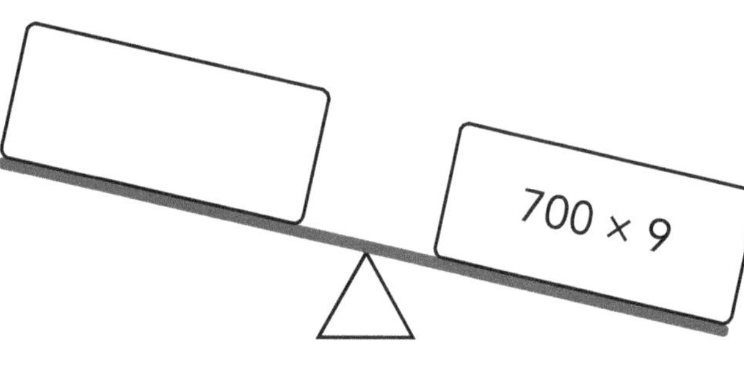


**4.**

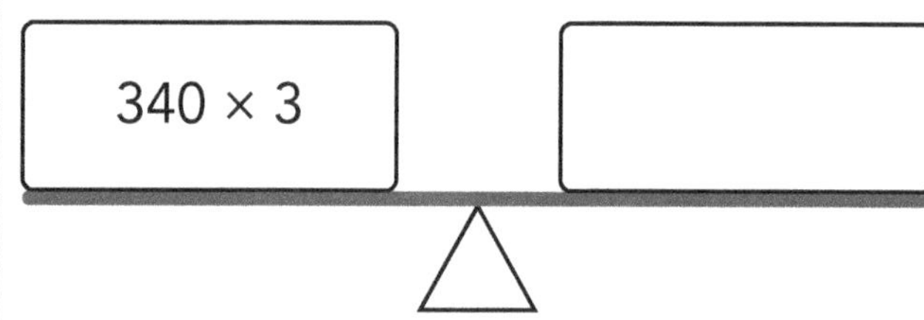


**5.**

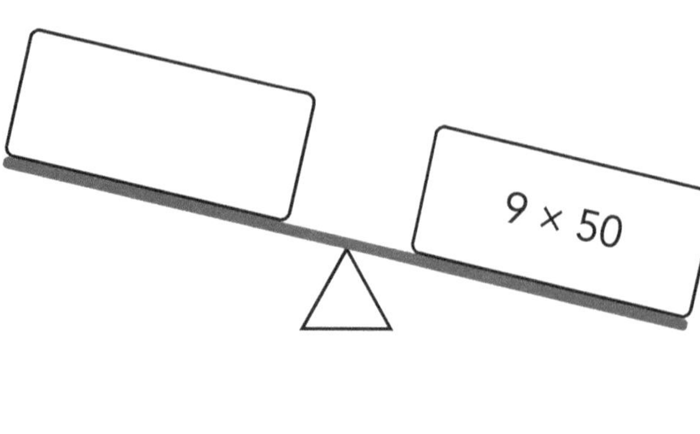


**6.**

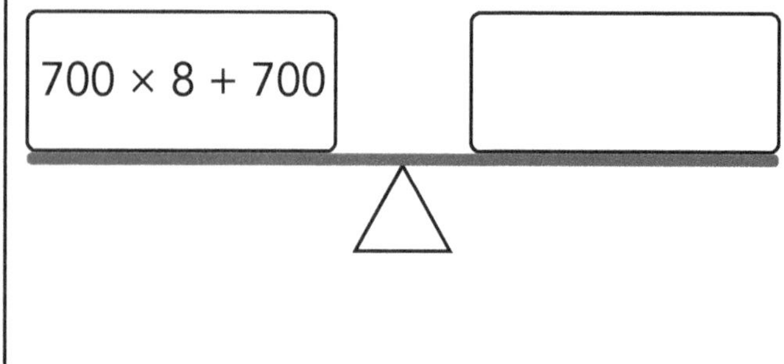



© HarperCollins*Publishers* 2017

# Resource 3.9.9c

## Making number sentences

| | | | | |
|---|---|---|---|---|
| 45 × 3 | 67 × 6 | 600 × 7 | add 99 | subtract 12 |
| 35 × 4 | 5 × 240 | 939 × 1 | add 200 | subtract 1 |
| 428 × 7 | 8 × 700 | 9 × 68 | subtract 50 | add 7 |
| 66 × 7 | 40 × 30 | 566 × 2 | add 23 | subtract 40 |

© HarperCollins*Publishers* 2017

## Relating divisions

1. 24 ÷ 6 = ☐
2. 35 ÷ 5 = ☐
3. 32 ÷ 4 = ☐
4. 18 ÷ 3 = ☐
5. 28 ÷ 7 = ☐
6. 54 ÷ 6 = ☐
7. 30 ÷ 5 = ☐
8. 28 ÷ 4 = ☐

| 1000 | 100 | 10 | 1 |
|---|---|---|---|
| | | | |



© HarperCollins*Publishers* 2017

# Resource 3.9.10b

## Multiplication and division arrays

Write two multiplication sentences and two division sentences to match each array.

1. 1 1 1 1 1
   1 1 1 1 1

☐ × ☐ = ☐ ☐ ÷ ☐ = ☐
☐ × ☐ = ☐ ☐ ÷ ☐ = ☐

2. 10 10 10 10 10
   10 10 10 10 10

☐ × ☐ = ☐ ☐ ÷ ☐ = ☐
☐ × ☐ = ☐ ☐ ÷ ☐ = ☐

3. 100 100 100 100 100
   100 100 100 100 100

☐ × ☐ = ☐ ☐ ÷ ☐ = ☐
☐ × ☐ = ☐ ☐ ÷ ☐ = ☐

4. 1 1 1 1 1
   1 1 1 1 1
   1 1 1 1 1
   1 1 1 1 1

☐ × ☐ = ☐ ☐ ÷ ☐ = ☐
☐ × ☐ = ☐ ☐ ÷ ☐ = ☐

5. 10 10 10 10 10
   10 10 10 10 10
   10 10 10 10 10
   10 10 10 10 10

☐ × ☐ = ☐ ☐ ÷ ☐ = ☐
☐ × ☐ = ☐ ☐ ÷ ☐ = ☐

6. 100 100 100 100 100
   100 100 100 100 100
   100 100 100 100 100
   100 100 100 100 100

☐ × ☐ = ☐ ☐ ÷ ☐ = ☐
☐ × ☐ = ☐ ☐ ÷ ☐ = ☐

© HarperCollins*Publishers* 2017

# Resource 3.9.10c

## Array division

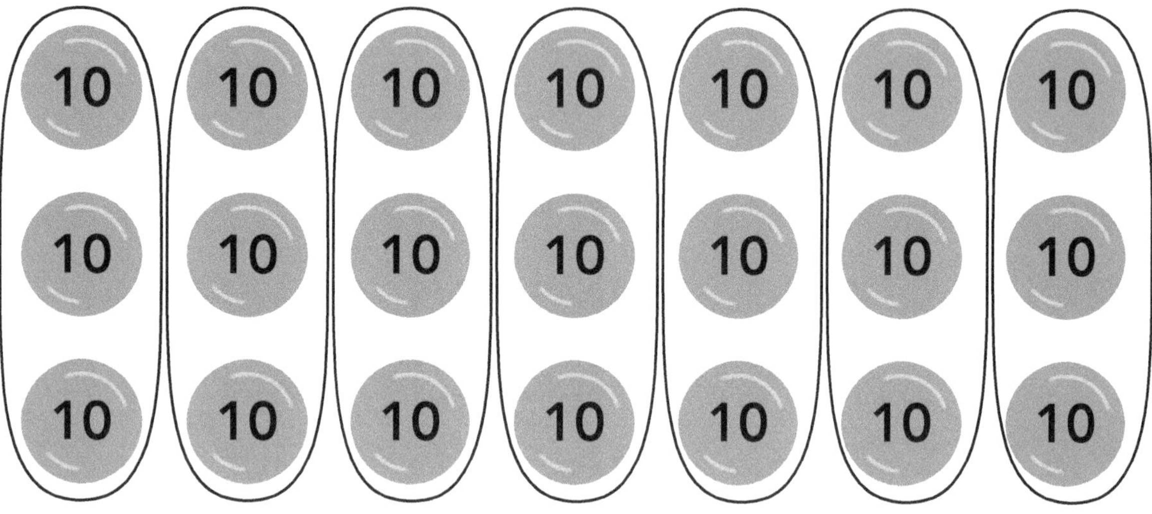


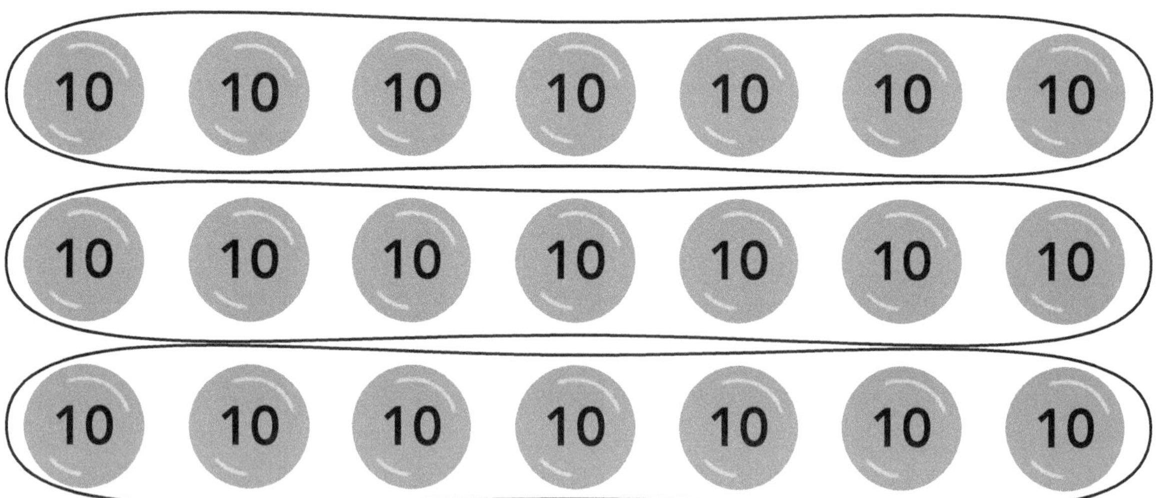




© HarperCollins*Publishers* 2017

# Resource 3.9.10d

## Division problem arrays

Write a division word problem to match each array.

**1.**

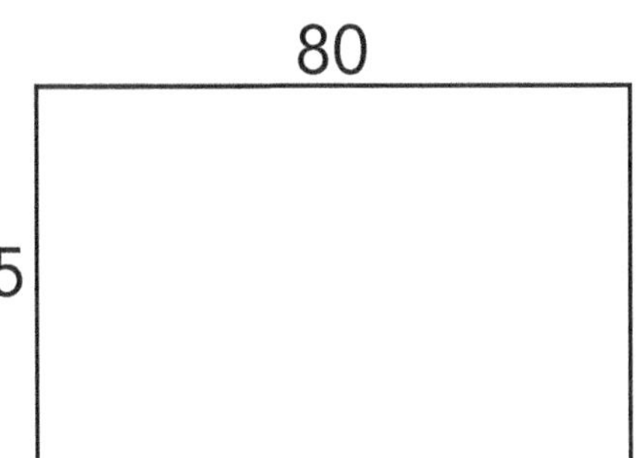


Word problem:

**2.**

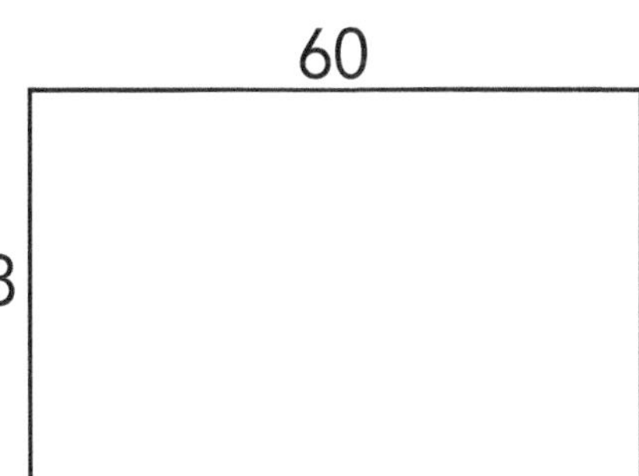


Word problem:

**3.**

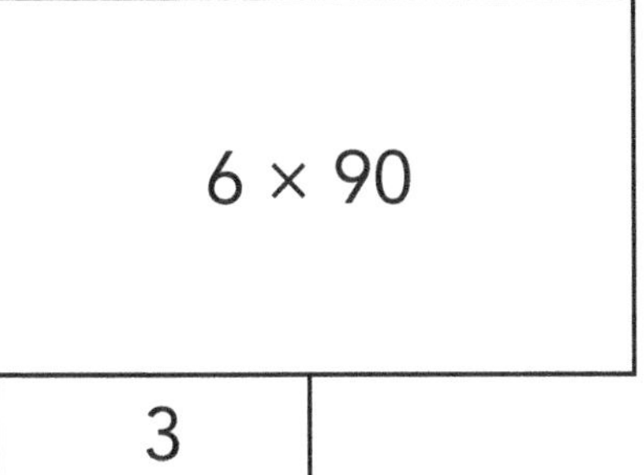


Word problem:

**4.**

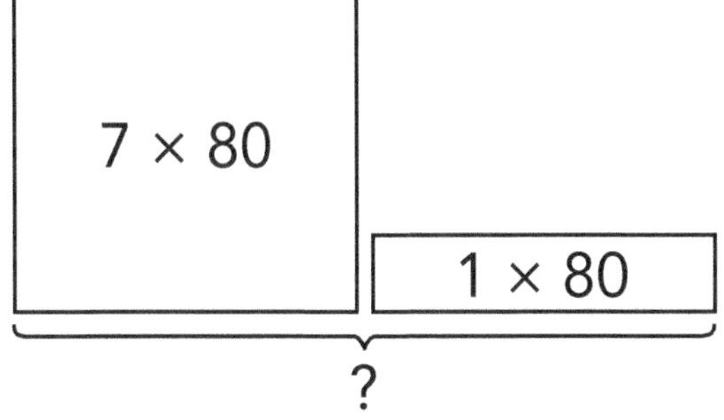


Word problem:

© HarperCollins*Publishers* 2017

# Resource 3.9.11a

## Division questions

1. 42 ÷ 9 = ☐
2. 48 ÷ 9 = ☐
3. 62 ÷ 7 = ☐
4. 69 ÷ 8 = ☐
5. 63 ÷ 7 = ☐
6. 53 ÷ 9 = ☐
7. 63 ÷ 9 = ☐
8. 43 ÷ 9 = ☐
9. 41 ÷ 9 = ☐
10. 45 ÷ 8 = ☐
11. 44 ÷ 7 = ☐
12. 60 ÷ 9 = ☐
13. 26 ÷ 9 = ☐
14. 73 ÷ 7 = ☐
15. 33 ÷ 8 = ☐
16. 46 ÷ 9 = ☐
17. 46 ÷ 7= ☐
18. 42 ÷ 9 = ☐
19. 37 ÷ 8 = ☐
20. 43 ÷ 7 = ☐
21. 24 ÷ 8 = ☐
22. 24 ÷ 9 = ☐
23. 65 ÷ 9 = ☐
24. 16 ÷ 9 = ☐
25. 46 ÷ 8 = ☐
26. 66 ÷ 9 = ☐
27. 23 ÷ 7 = ☐
28. 49 ÷ 9 = ☐
29. 42 ÷ 8 = ☐
30. 65 ÷ 7 = ☐
31. 36 ÷ 9 = ☐
32. 26 ÷ 8 = ☐
33. 33 ÷ 9 = ☐
34. 53 ÷ 8 = ☐
35. 23 ÷ 8 = ☐
36. 57 ÷ 7 = ☐
37. 28 ÷ 8 = ☐
38. 23 ÷ 9 = ☐
39. 50 ÷ 8 = ☐
40. 53 ÷ 7 = ☐
41. 13 ÷ 7 = ☐
42. 51 ÷ 8 = ☐
43. 50 ÷ 7 = ☐
44. 60 ÷ 8 = ☐
45. 43 ÷ 8 = ☐
46. 52 ÷ 8 = ☐
47. 33 ÷ 7 = ☐
48. 59 ÷ 7 = ☐
49. 56 ÷ 7 = ☐
50. 36 ÷ 7 = ☐
51. 32 ÷ 7 = ☐
52. 32 ÷ 8 = ☐



© HarperCollins*Publishers* 2017

# Resource 3.9.11b

## Sweet share

Fill in the boxes.

### Question 1

7 children share □ sweets equally. How many sweets can each child have?

□ ÷ □ = ?

Jack's solution:

7 × 10 = □

70 ÷ 7 = 10

□ – 70 = 21

21 ÷ □ = 3

10 + 3 = □

□ ÷ 7 = 13

Fatima's solution:

70 ÷ 7 = □

21 ÷ 7 = □

□ ÷ 7 = 13

### Question 2

□ children share □ sweets equally. How many sweets can each child have?

□ ÷ □ = ?

Jack's solution:

□ × 10 = 50

□ ÷ □ = 10

□ – 50 = 35

□ ÷ □ = □

35 ÷ □ = □

□ + □ = □

□ ÷ □ = □

Fatima's solution:

□ ÷ □ = 10

□ ÷ □ = 7

□ ÷ □ = 17

© HarperCollins*Publishers* 2017

# Resource 3.9.12a

## Matching divisions 1

Cut out and match the cards.

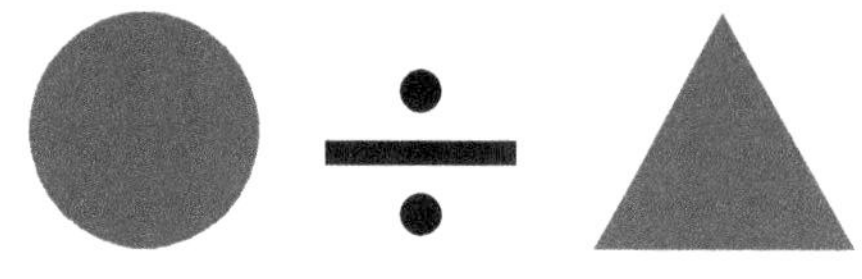

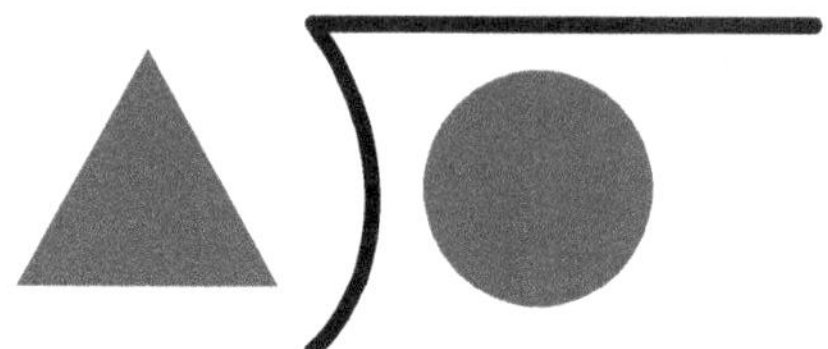

One card does not have a match.
Draw the missing card here.

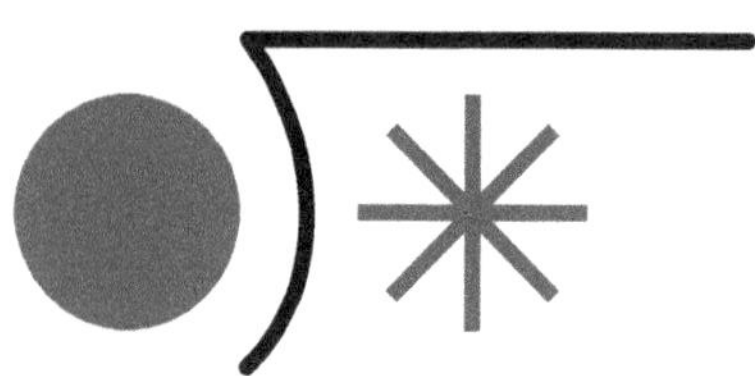



© HarperCollins*Publishers* 2017

## Matching divisions 2

Cut out and match the cards.

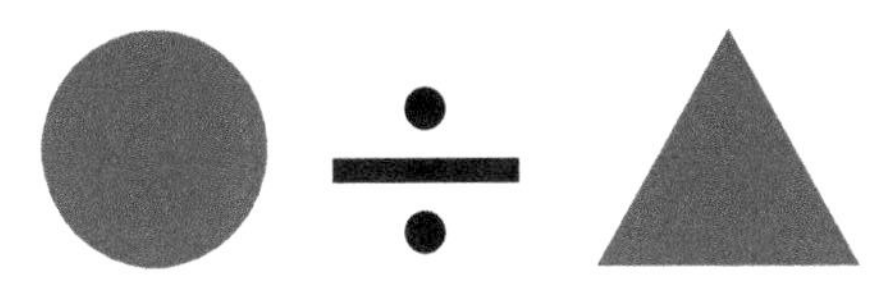

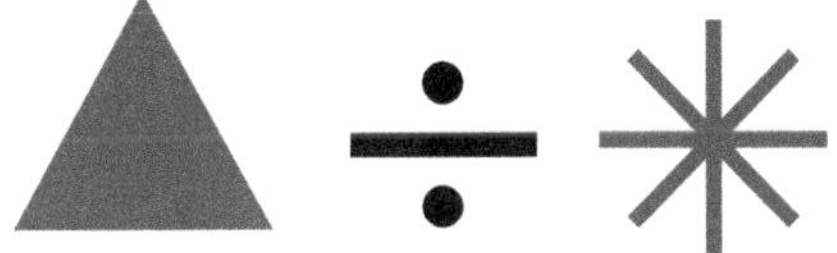

What is divided by ?

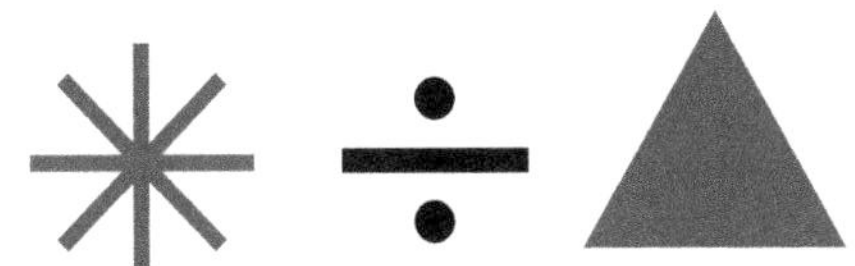

One card does not have a match.
Draw the missing card here.

What is ☐ divided by ☐?

© HarperCollinsPublishers 2017

# Resource 3.9.12c

## Division tables

Complete the table.

| Number sentence | Column method | We say: | Quotient and remainder |
|---|---|---|---|
| 57 ÷ 4 = ☐ | 4)‾‾ | | |
| | | 23 divided by 4 equals what? | |
| ☐ ÷ 3 = ☐ | | | 7 |
| | | 17 divided by ☐ equals what? | 3 remainder 2 |
| | | 23 divided by something equals 3 remainder 2 | |

Now fill in this table with questions like those above.

| Number sentence | Column method | We say: | Quotient and remainder |
|---|---|---|---|
| | | | |
| | | | |
| | | | |
| | | | |



© HarperCollins*Publishers* 2017

# Resource 3.9.12d

## Matching divisions 3

Cut out and match the cards.

| | |
|---|---|
| 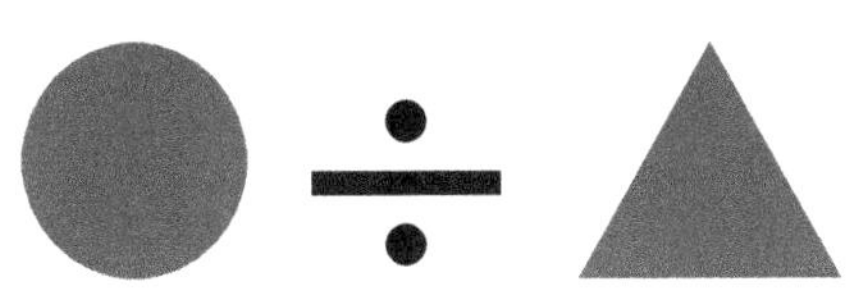 | There are ▲ sweets to be shared equally between ✳ children. How many sweets does each child get? |
| 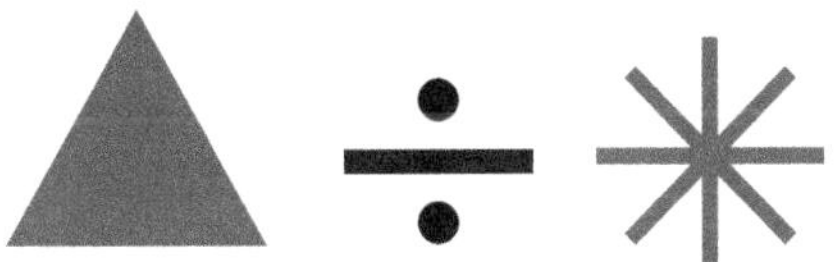 | There are ✳ sweets to be shared equally between ▲ children. How may sweets does each child get? |
|  | There are ✳ toys to be placed in boxes. Each box will hold ● toys. How many boxes are needed? |
| 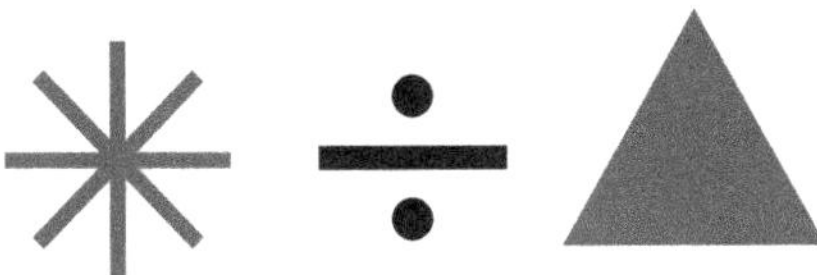 | Write your own story here. |

© HarperCollins*Publishers* 2017

# Resource 3.9.16a

## Division stories

1. 382 people are to be seated in two equal sections in a hall. How many seats are needed on each side of the hall?

   382 ÷ 2 = ☐ ÷ ☐ = ☐

   **Method 1:**

   Since 200 ÷ 2 = ☐ ÷ ☐ = ☐

   180 ÷ 2 = ☐ ÷ ☐ = ☐

   2 ÷ 2 = ☐ ÷ ☐ = ☐

   **Method 2:** Use the column method

2. 615 cakes are to be put into boxes, with 3 cakes in each box. How many boxes are needed?

   615 ÷ 3 = ☐ ÷ ☐ = ☐

   **Method 1:**

   Since ☐ ÷ ☐ = ☐

   ☐ ÷ ☐ = ☐

   ☐ ÷ ☐ = ☐

   **Method 2:** Use the column method

3. Write a story for 712 ÷ 4 = ☐

   **Method 1:**

   Since 400 ÷ 4 = ☐

   280 ÷ 4 = ☐

   32 ÷ 4 = ☐

   **Method 2:** Use the column method



© HarperCollins*Publishers* 2017

# Resource 3.9.16b

## Division odd one out

Which of these is the odd one out?

889 ÷ 7 =

860 ÷ 5 =

762 ÷ 6 =

508 ÷ 4 =

© HarperCollinsPublishers 2017

# Resource 3.9.17

## Division – column method

1.

```
   □ 4 2
2 ) 4 8 4
   4 □ □
     8 □
     □ □
       4
       4
       □
```

2.

```
   1 6 □
3 ) 4 8 4
   4 □ □
   □ □ □
   □ □ □
       4
       3
       1
```

3.

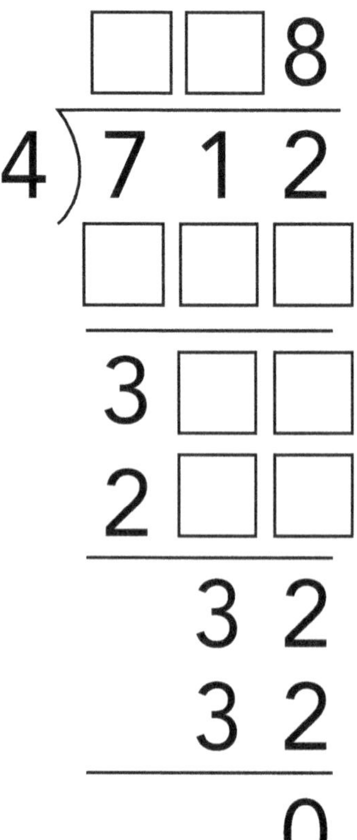


4.

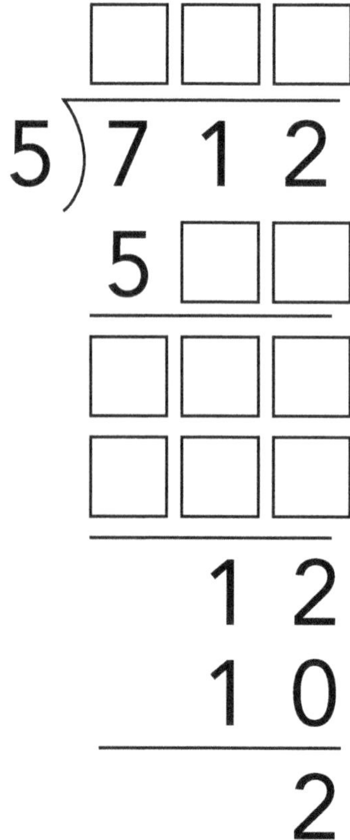




© HarperCollins*Publishers* 2017

# Resource 3.9.20

## Bar model costs

1. Louis buys 5 toy cars. Each car costs £2. What is the total cost of the toy cars?

Total cost £ ☐

2. Bella has £40. She spends all of her money on 5 toy dogs. How much does each toy dog cost?

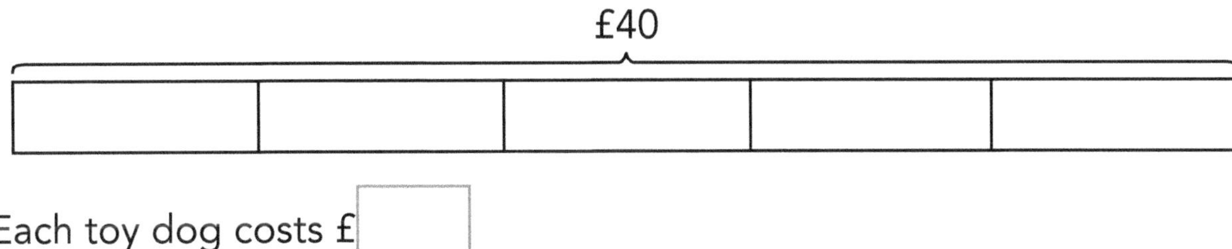


Each toy dog costs £ ☐

3. Dulcie spends £35 buying toy cars. The unit price is £7. How many toy cars does Dulcie buy?

£35

Dulcie buys ☐ toy cars.

4. A teacher buys a book for each of the children in his class. The unit price is £8 and the total cost for the teacher is £184. How many children are in the class?

£184

There are ☐ children in the class.

© HarperCollinsPublishers 2017

# Resource 3.10.1a

## Find the angles

Using a coloured pen, mark all the angles you can find with an X.

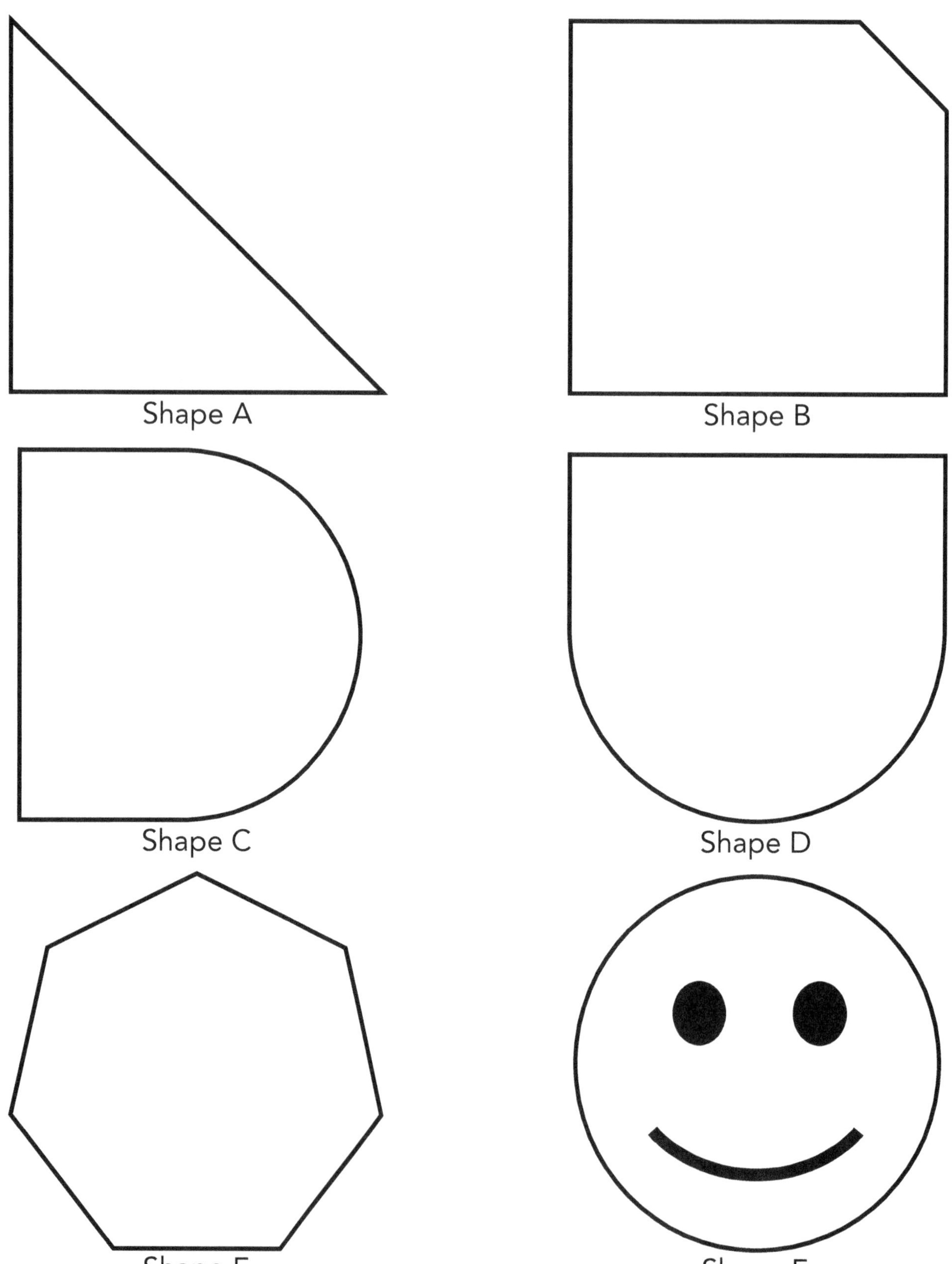




© HarperCollins*Publishers* 2017

# Resource 3.10.1b

## Angle munchers

© HarperCollinsPublishers 2017

# Resource 3.10.3

## Parallel and perpendicular lines

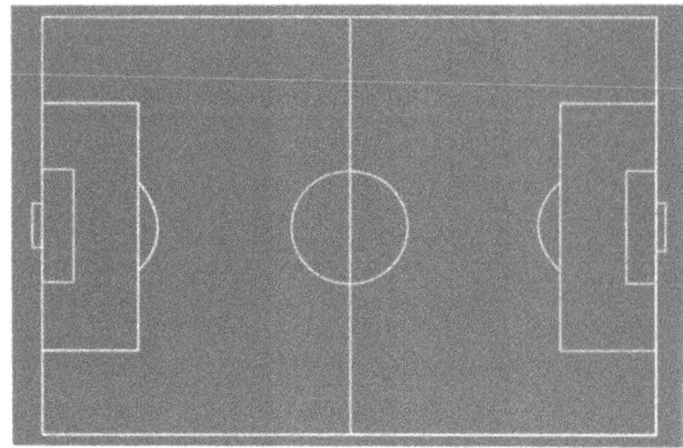

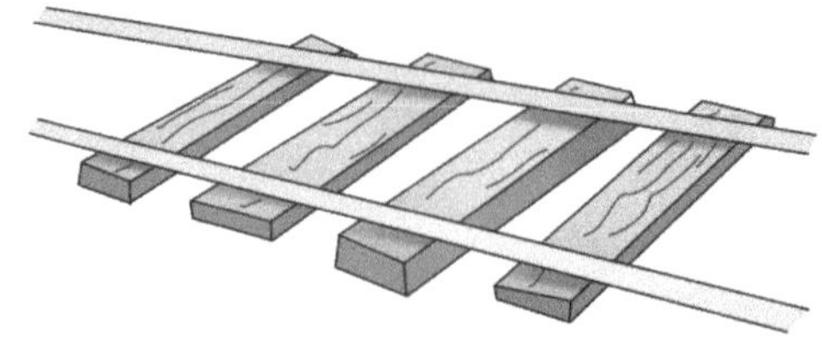

© HarperCollins*Publishers* 2017

# Resource 3.10.5

## Measuring steps

When you walk, how long is each stride that you take?

1. Measure the length of one step:

   in centimetres [ ]

   in millimetres [ ]

2. How far will you go in 10 steps?

   in centimetres [ ]

   in metres [ ]

3. How far will you go in 20 steps?

   in centimetres [ ]

   in metres [ ]

4. How far will you go in 100 steps?

   in metres [ ]

© HarperCollins*Publishers* 2017

# Answers

## Chapter 7 Addition and subtraction with 3-digit numbers

### Unit 7.1

1 **(a)** 3 2 5
**(b)** 4 5 9
**(c)** 9 3 6
**(d)** 6 4 2

2 **(a)** 700 **(b)** 600
**(c)** 300 **(d)** 600
**(e)** 900 **(f)** 500
**(g)** 100 **(h)** 400

3 **(a)** 45 2 47
**(b)** 45 2 43
**(c)** 36 12 48
**(d)** 36 12 24

4 **(a)** 19 **(b)** 190
**(c)** 37 **(d)** 370
**(e)** 43 **(f)** 430
**(g)** 86 **(h)** 860

5 **(a)** = **(b)** <
**(c)** = **(d)** <

6 **(a)** 400 – 230 = 170 (pounds)
**(b)** 530 + 380 = 910 (books)
**(c)** 200 – 180 = 20 (pounds)
**(d)** 340 + 270 = 610 (apple trees)

7 ■ is greater. It is 300 greater

### Unit 7.2

1 **(a)** 170 **(b)** 820
**(c)** 200 **(d)** 710
**(e)** 880 **(f)** 970
**(g)** 220 **(h)** 730
**(i)** 500 **(j)** 170
**(k)** 230 **(l)** 350

2 **(a)** 510 370 480 500 650 610 1000
**(b)** 80 150 220 290 260 190 160

3 **(a)** 800 400
**(b)** 330 170
**(c)** 630 290
**(d)** 1000 440

4 **(a)** 210 480 640 450
**(b)** 800 450 770 500
**(c)** 450 370 660 320
**(d)** 30 390 240 350

5 **(a)** Meera: 800 – 200 = 600 (m)
Caitlin: 800 – 250 = 550 (m)
Meera ran faster.
**(b)** 250 – 90 – 110 = 50 (apples)
**(c)** 150 + 280 + 130 = 560 (stamps)
**(d)** 30 + 80 + 160 = 270 (seats)

6 (Answers may vary) for example:

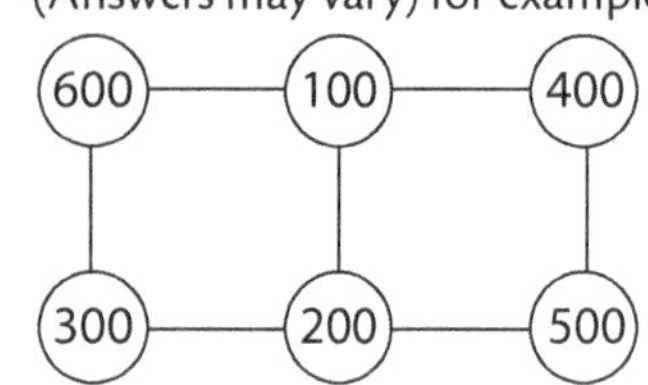


### Unit 7.3

1 **(a)** 25 **(b)** 38
**(c)** 47 **(d)** 34
**(e)** 325 **(f)** 238
**(g)** 547 **(h)** 434

2 **(a)** 334 **(b)** 108
**(c)** 320 **(d)** 111
**(e)** 219 **(f)** 241
**(g)** 444 **(h)** 600

3 **(a)** 304 **(b)** 494
**(c)** 503 **(d)** 295

4 **(a)** 401 603
**(b)** 801 907
**(c)** 195 698
**(d)** 595 497

5 **(a)** 295 **(b)** 198
**(c)** 501 **(d)** 903
**(e)** 316 **(f)** 702
**(g)** 784 **(h)** 591
**(i)** 499 **(j)** 771
**(k)** 500 **(l)** 391

6 **(a)** 234 241 249 258
**(b)** 405 400 403 397
**(c)** 695 703 694 690

7 Answers may vary

### Unit 7.4

1 **(a)** 333 **(b)** 581
**(c)** 717 **(d)** 369
**(e)** 272 **(f)** 504
**(g)** 297 **(h)** 801
**(i)** 698 **(j)** 380
**(k)** 262 **(l)** 180

2 **(a)** 6 **(b)** 5
**(c)** 4 **(d)** 1000
**(e)** 606 **(f)** 7

3 The following linked:
**(a)** 627 + 5 to 632 to 641 – 9
**(b)** 689 + 6 to 695 to 702 – 7
**(c)** 697 + 5 to 702 to 710 – 8

4 **(a)** 203 + 9 = 212 (containers)
**(b)** 132 – 5 = 127 (cm)
**(c)** 256 – 8 – 7 = 241 (TVs)
**(d)** 142 + 6 – 8 = 140 (skips)

5 **(a)** 984 + 2 = 986 or 982 + 4 = 986
**(b)** 248 – 9 = 239

### Unit 7.5

1 **(a)** 538
**(b)** 586
**(c)** 383 525
**(d)** 782 401

2 **(a)** 657 **(b)** 664
**(c)** 978 **(d)** 783

3 Answers may vary

4 **(a)** 239 + 384 = 623
**(b)** 574 + 168 = 742

5 **(a)** 3 **(b)** 4
**(c)** 3, 4

### Unit 7.6

1 **(a)** 684 **(b)** 434
**(c)** 927 **(d)** 515
**(e)** 597 **(f)** 785

2 **(a)** ✗ 614
**(b)** ✗ 504
**(c)** ✓

3 477 532 799 611 722 1000

4 **(a)** 278 + 375 = 653
**(b)** 468 + 332 = 800
**(c)** 396 + 322 = 718

5 **(a)** 312 + 268 = 580 (metres)
**(b)** 162 + 135 = 297 (pages)
**(c)** 138 + 162 = 300 (pounds)

6 781

### Unit 7.7

1 **(a)** 214
**(b)** 313
**(c)** 171 388
**(d)** 259 137

2 **(a)** 465 **(b)** 733
**(c)** 93 **(d)** 295

3 Answers may vary

4 **(a)** 429 – 290 = 139
**(b)** 695 – 348 = 347

5 The mass of 1 pack of salt: 630 – 470 = 160 (grams)
The mass of 1 pack of sugar: 470 – 160 = 310 (grams)

### Unit 7.8

1 **(a)** 156 **(b)** 41
**(c)** 76 **(d)** 168
**(e)** 332 **(f)** 29

2 (a) × 336
(b) × 82
(c) × 66

3 604 296 181 136 178 39

4 (a) 558 − 305 = 253
(b) 462 − 256 = 206
(c) 673 − 625 = 48

5 (a) 769 − 372 = 397 (kilometres)
(b) 372 − 112 = 260 (kilometres)
(c) Answers may vary

6 (a) 4 (b) 3

## Unit 7.9

1 (a) 400 (b) 220
(c) 680 (d) 73
(e) 660 (f) 550
(g) 70 (h) 590

2 530 500 660 700 710 700 350 300 500 500

3 (a) 380 380
(b) 760 759
(c) 500 498
(d) 950 948
(e) 250 256
(f) 330 334

4 (a) 600 605
(b) 800 786
(c) 700 716
(d) 900 936
(e) 200 191
(f) 100 149

5 (a) Estimate:
230 + 200 = 430 (children) 430 < 450 Yes, it is possible for Year 3 and Year 4 children to swim at the same time
(b) Estimate: 290 + 340 = 630 (trees)
340 − 290 = 50 (trees)
(c) (i) Estimate 80 + 110 = 190 (pounds) 190 < 200 She has enough money
(ii) 79 + 114 = 193 (pounds)
200 − 193 = 7 (pounds)

6 (a) 264 (b) 462

## Unit 7.10

1 (a) 610 (b) 210
(c) 640 (d) 340
(e) 150 (f) 690
(g) 910 (h) 570

2 (a) 710 700 709
(b) 1000 1000 999
(c) 520 500 522
(d) 220 200 224

3 (a) 335 (b) 336
(c) 337 (d) 338
(e) 554 (f) 555
(g) 556 (h) 557
(i) 70 (j) 69
(k) 68 (l) 67
(m) 453 (n) 452
(o) 451 (p) 450

4 (a) (i) AF CE BGH (ii) F E G
(b) (i) 389 (ii) 591
(iii) 512 (iv) 630
(v) 501 (vi) 404
(vii) 594 (viii) 538

5 (a) (Estimates may vary)
310 − 178 = 132 (metres)
(b) (Estimates may vary)
244 − 156 = 88 (metres)
(c) Answers may vary

6 Three ways:
123 + 678 = 234 + 567 = 345 + 456;
123 + 789 = 234 + 678 = 345 + 567;
234 + 789 = 345 + 678 = 456 + 567

## Chapter 7 test

1 (a) 215 (b) 162
(c) 870 (d) 220
(e) 324 (f) 295
(g) 330 (h) 218

2 (a) 255 (b) 522
(c) 109 (d) 174
(e) 147 (f) 35

3 (a) (i) 400 393
(ii) 600 588
(iii) 200 216
(iv) 200 180
(b) (i) 510 508
(ii) 390 391
(iii) 110 112
(iv) 360 364

4 (a) 402 + 148 = 550
(b) 662 − 266 = 396
(c) 800 − 482 = 318

5 (a) 560 − 388 = 172
(b) 105 − 39 = 66
(c) 288 + 109 = 397

6 337 + 368 = 705 (children)

7 700 − 678 = 22 (pounds)

8 226 − 187 = 39 (books)

9 (a) 295 + 127 = 422 (stamps)
(b) 422 − 250 = 172 (stamps)

10 (a) 215 − 36 = 179 (tonnes)
(b) 179 + 78 = 257 (tonnes)

# Chapter 8 Simple fractions and their addition and subtraction

## Unit 8.1

1 (a) $\frac{1}{2}$ (b) $\frac{1}{3}$
(c) $\frac{1}{4}$ (d) $\frac{1}{8}$
(e) $\frac{1}{10}$ (f) $\frac{4}{10}$

The unit fractions are $\frac{1}{2}$ $\frac{1}{3}$ $\frac{1}{4}$ $\frac{1}{8}$ $\frac{1}{10}$

2 (a) Three stars circled
(b) Two diamonds circled
(c) Two triangles circled
(d) Six triangles circled

3 (a) $\frac{2}{10}$ $\frac{4}{10}$ $\frac{5}{10}$ $\frac{6}{10}$ $\frac{7}{10}$ $\frac{8}{10}$ $\frac{9}{10}$
(b) $\frac{1}{10}$ $\frac{3}{10}$ $\frac{5}{10}$ $\frac{7}{10}$ $\frac{9}{10}$; $\frac{1}{10}$, $\frac{1}{10}$, 2, $\frac{9}{10}$
(c) $\frac{1}{10}$, $\frac{9}{10}$, 3, 0

4 (a) $\frac{1}{10}$ (b) $\frac{3}{10}$
(c) $\frac{2}{10}$ (d) $\frac{4}{10}$
(e) $\frac{1}{10}$ $\frac{2}{10}$ $\frac{3}{10}$ $\frac{4}{10}$

5 $\frac{1}{10}$ $\frac{1}{5}$ $\frac{1}{4}$ $\frac{3}{10}$ $\frac{1}{2}$ $\frac{7}{10}$ $\frac{9}{10}$

## Unit 8.2

1 (a) $\frac{1}{9}$ $\frac{5}{9}$ $\frac{4}{9}$
(b) $\frac{1}{4}$ $\frac{3}{4}$
(c) $\frac{1}{9}$ $\frac{1}{4}$; $\frac{5}{9}$ $\frac{4}{9}$ $\frac{3}{4}$

2 (a) $\frac{4}{9}$ (b) $\frac{2}{6}$
(c) $\frac{2}{8}$ or $\frac{1}{4}$

3 (a) ✗ (b) ✓
(c) ✓

4 (a) $\frac{1}{7}$ $\frac{4}{7}$
(b) (i) 2 (ii) 3
(iii) 6 (iv) 9

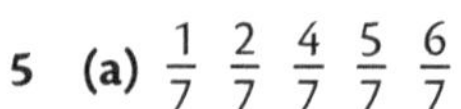



5 (a) $\frac{1}{7}$ $\frac{2}{7}$ $\frac{4}{7}$ $\frac{5}{7}$ $\frac{6}{7}$
(b) $\frac{2}{9}$ $\frac{4}{9}$ $\frac{7}{9}$ $\frac{8}{9}$ 1

6 **(a)** 4 **(b)** 6
**(c)** 8 **(d)** 12
**(e)** 18 **(f)** 24

## Unit 8.3

1 **(a) (i)** $\frac{1}{4}$ **(ii)** $\frac{4}{4}$ **(iii)** 1
**(b)** $\frac{6}{6}$

2 **(a)** $\frac{1}{2}$ or $\frac{4}{8}$
**(b)** $\frac{15}{15}$ or 1
**(c)** $\frac{2}{3}$ or $\frac{8}{12}$

3 **(a)** $\frac{10}{10}$ 1
**(b) (i)** < **(ii)** > **(iii)** =
**(c)** $\frac{4}{4}$ 1
**(d)** 2
**(e)** $\frac{4}{6}$ $\frac{1}{5}$ 1
**(f)** $\frac{5}{8}$

4 Lines drawn to link $\frac{1}{2}$ to $\frac{3}{6}$, $\frac{5}{6}$ to $\frac{10}{12}$, $\frac{2}{7}$ to $\frac{4}{14}$, $\frac{3}{5}$ to $\frac{6}{10}$, $\frac{4}{6}$ to $\frac{2}{3}$, $\frac{3}{4}$ to $\frac{9}{12}$

5 **(a)** $\frac{1}{4}$ **(b)** $\frac{3}{9}$ or $\frac{6}{18}$

6 **(a)** 6, 8
**(b)** Lily
**(c)** No, 48 is not a multiple of 5
**(d)** Answer may vary, but 48 must be divisible by the denominator of the fraction

## Unit 8.4

1 **(a)** $\frac{3}{4}$ **(b)** $\frac{5}{7}$
**(c)** $\frac{8}{8}$ 1

2 **(a)** $\frac{3}{5}$ **(b)** $\frac{4}{8}$, $\frac{1}{2}$

3 **(a)** $\frac{2}{2}$ or 1
**(b)** $\frac{6}{7}$
**(c)** $\frac{4}{4}$ or 1
**(d)** $\frac{2}{3}$
**(e)** $\frac{7}{9}$
**(f)** $\frac{5}{5}$ or 1

4 **(a)** $\frac{2}{8}$ **(b)** $\frac{1}{2}$
**(c)** 0 **(d)** $\frac{5}{7}$
**(e)** $\frac{2}{4}$ **(f)** $\frac{4}{5}$

5 **(a)** $\frac{3}{24}$ $\frac{4}{24}$ $\frac{5}{24}$
**(b)** $\frac{7}{24}$
**(c)** $\frac{12}{24}$ or $\frac{1}{2}$
**(d)** $\frac{12}{24}$ or $\frac{1}{2}$, 12 (pages)

6 **(a)** $\frac{1}{12}$ $\frac{3}{12}$ $\frac{3}{12}$ $\frac{5}{12}$
**(b)** $\frac{3}{12} + \frac{3}{12} = \frac{6}{12}$
**(c)** $\frac{3}{12} + \frac{3}{12} + \frac{5}{12} = \frac{11}{12}$
**(d)** Mum, grandma, $\frac{5}{12} - \frac{1}{12} = \frac{4}{12}$, 4

## Chapter 8 test

1 **(a)** $\frac{1}{10}$ $\frac{5}{10}$ $\frac{1}{2}$
**(b)** 2 10 15
**(c)** sixths, four sixths, $\frac{7}{8}$
**(d)** 4, 12
**(e)** bigger, bigger

2 **(a)** = **(b)** < **(c)** >

3 Lines drawn to link $\frac{2}{3}$ to $\frac{4}{6}$, $\frac{4}{5}$ to $\frac{8}{10}$, $\frac{7}{8}$ to $\frac{14}{16}$, $\frac{1}{3}$ to $\frac{3}{9}$, $\frac{7}{14}$ to $\frac{4}{8}$

4 **(a)** $\frac{1}{12}$ $\frac{1}{9}$ $\frac{3}{14}$ $\frac{1}{2}$ 1
**(b)** $\frac{2}{7}$ $\frac{4}{7}$ $\frac{5}{7}$ $\frac{6}{7}$ 1

5 **(a)** $\frac{2}{4}$ **(b)** $\frac{5}{9}$ **(c)** $\frac{10}{10}$ or 1
**(d)** $\frac{1}{3}$ **(e)** $\frac{9}{11}$ **(f)** $\frac{5}{5}$ or 1
**(g)** $\frac{4}{10}$ **(h)** 0 **(i)** $\frac{1}{8}$

6 **(a)** 14
**(b)** $\frac{3}{14}$ $\frac{4}{14}$ $\frac{7}{14}$
**(c)** $\frac{4}{14} + \frac{7}{14} = \frac{11}{14}$
**(d)** △○ $\frac{7}{14} - \frac{3}{14} = \frac{4}{14}$

7 **(a)** $\frac{3}{12}$ **(b)** $\frac{6}{12}$ or $\frac{1}{2}$ **(c)** yes

8 **(a)** $\frac{1}{4}$ **(b)** $\frac{1}{8}$ **(c)** $\frac{1}{16}$
**(d)** $\frac{1}{8}$ **(e)** $\frac{1}{8}$ **(f)** (Answers may vary)

# Chapter 9 Multiplying and dividing by a 1-digit number

## Unit 9.1

1 **(a)** 28 **(b)** 15 **(c)** 54
**(d)** 280 **(e)** 150 **(f)** 540
**(g)** 2800
**(h)** 1500
**(i)** 540

2 **(a) (i)** 240, 4 × 60 = 240
**(ii)** 1000, 5 × 200 = 1000
**(b)** 3 18 180
**(c)** 2

3 **(a)** = **(b)** > **(c)** <
**(d)** < **(e)** < **(f)** = Í

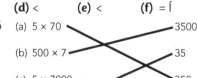

4 (a) 5 × 70 — 350
(b) 500 × 7 — 3500
(c) 5 × 7000 — 35 000
(d) 5 × 7 — 35

5 **(a)** 400 **(b)** 2
**(c)** 5 **(d)** 4

6 **(a)** 40 × 9 = 360
**(b)** 3 × 600 = 1800
**(c)** 8 × 400 + 8 = 3208

7 500 × 8 = 4000 (grams), 4000 g = 4 kg

8 50 × 8 × 2 × 3 = 2400 (pounds)

## Unit 9.2

1 **(a)** 27 **(b)** 32
**(c)** 42 **(d)** 270
**(e)** 320 **(f)** 4200
**(g)** 2700 **(h)** 320
**(i)** 4200 **(j)** 2700
**(k)** 3200 **(l)** 4200

2 **(a)** 5, 35, 3500
**(b)** 3

3 **(a)** = **(b)** =
**(c)** > **(d)** =
**(e)** > **(f)** =

4 Lines drawn from
**(a)** 5 × 80 to 400
**(b)** 500 × 8 to 4000
**(c)** 50 × 800 to 40 000
**(d)** 5 × 8 to 40 and
**(e)** 500 × 800 to 400 000

5 **(a)** C **(b)** B

6 **(a)** 400 × 4 = 1600, 400 + 1600 = 2000
**(b)** 300 × 5 = 1500 (pounds), 1500 – 300 = 1200 (pounds)

7 80, 20, 4000, 16, 160, 400, 32

## Unit 9.3

1 **(a)** 6 × 11 = 66
**(b)** 30 × 4 = 120 (pounds)
**(c)** 12 × 3 = 36 (pounds)

2 Lines drawn to match
**(a)** to 2 × 70
**(b)** to 2 × 45
**(c)** to 2 × 12
**(d)** to 4 × 10

3 **(a)** Lines drawn to match 39 × 8 to 312, 26 × 3 to 78 and 92 × 4 to 368
**(b)** 276, 138 × 2 or 92 × 3 or 69 × 4 or 23 × 12 (answers may vary)

4 Answers may vary

5 5 and 11, 6 and 10, 7 and 9, 8 and 8; 8 8

## Unit 9.4

1 10 × 6 = 60, 3 × 6 = 18, 60 + 18 = 78, 13 × 6 = 78

2 **(a)** 518 **(b)** 208
**(c)** 576 **(d)** 186
**(e)** 534 **(f)** 270

3 **(a)** 15 × 8 = 120 (children)
**(b)** 24 × 2 = 48 (children)

4 **(a)** > **(b)** <
**(c)** < **(d)** <
In each pair the calculation with the bigger 1-digit number has the bigger answer.

## Unit 9.5

1 243

2 98

3 **(a)** 248 **(b)** 64
**(c)** 85 **(d)** 357

4 **(a)** No, 14 × 4 = 56
**(b)** Yes

5 59 × 8 = 472 or 84 × 8 = 672 or 34 × 8 = 272

## Unit 9.6

1 **(a)** 20 **(b)** 30
**(c)** 53 **(d)** 53
**(e)** 61 **(f)** 41
**(g)** 52 **(h)** 3

2 **(a)** 308 **(b)** 324
**(c)** 200 **(d)** 300

3 Estimates may vary
**(a)** 343 **(b)** 450 **(c)** 704

4 **(a)** No, 99 × 9 = 891
**(b)** No, 26 × 8 = 208
**(c)** No, 68 × 5 = 340

5 Lines drawn to show 25 × 7 = 175, 56 × 4 = 224, 9 × 42 = 378 and 5 × 63 = 315

6 **(a)** 98 × 4 = 392 (pounds)
**(b)** 57 × 6 = 342 (pounds)

7 195 × 8 = 1560 or 190 × 8 = 1520

## Unit 9.7

1 **(a)** 2400 **(b)** 240
**(c)** 24 **(d)** 160
**(e)** 1600 **(f)** 16
**(g)** 6300 **(h)** 630
**(i)** 63 **(j)** 360
**(k)** 2800 **(l)** 27

2 **(b)** 427 = 400 + 20 + 7
**(c)** 987 = 900 + 80 + 7
**(d)** 634 = 600 + 30 + 4

3 3 × 316 = 948

4 **(a)** 1708 **(b)** 3804
**(c)** 1850

5 **(a)** 1197 **(b)** 837
**(c)** 1854

6 **(a)** ✓ **(b)** ×, 107 × 5 = 535
**(c)** ✓

7 **(a)** **(i)** 416 × 7 = 2912
**(ii)** 508 × 8 = 4064
**(b)** ■ = 1, ▲ = 7, ● = 2

## Unit 9.8

1 **(a)** 25 **(b)** 250
**(c)** 2500 **(d)** 10
**(e)** 100 **(f)** 1000
**(g)** 21 **(h)** 210
**(i)** 2100 **(j)** 36
**(k)** 360 **(l)** 3600

2 **(a)** 1440 **(b)** 144

3 **(a)** 780 **(b)** 4050
**(c)** 2000; 3 4

4 **(a)** 2 **(b)** 4

5 **(a)** 120 × 9 = 1080 (pages)
**(b)** 205 × 4 = 820

6 B

7 1200 2400 2400 4800; for example, when one of the numbers is doubled so is the product

## Unit 9.9

1 **(a)** 270 **(b)** 91
**(c)** 63 **(d)** 4000
**(e)** 80 **(f)** 63

2 **(a)** 294 **(b)** 804
**(c)** 3360

3 **(a)** < **(b)** >
**(c)** < **(d)** >
**(e)** > **(f)** =

4 **(a)** 4 **(b)** 3, 4
**(c)** 3 200 250

5 **(a)** 650 × 7 = 4550
**(b)** 4 × 723 = 2892
**(c)** 106 × 5 = 530
**(d)** 38 × 8 = 304

6 39 × 2 = 78 (kg)

7 18 × 9 + 42 = 204 (pages)

8 4 × 26 × 3 = 312 (books)

9 **(a)** 708 × 5 = 3540 or 728 × 5 = 3640 or 748 × 5 = 3740 or 768 × 5 = 3840 or 788 × 5 = 3940
**(b)** 190 × 4 = 760

## Unit 9.10

1 **(a)** **(i)** 2 **(ii)** 4
**(iii)** 8 **(iv)** 5
**(v)** 20 **(vi)** 40
**(vii)** 80 **(viii)** 50
**(b)** **(i)** 3 **(ii)** 4
**(iii)** 1 **(iv)** 2
**(v)** 30 **(vi)** 40
**(vii)** 10 **(viii)** 20
**(ix)** 300 **(x)** 400
**(xi)** 100 **(xii)** 200

2 **(a)** 8 **(b)** 8
**(c)** 8 **(d)** 8
**(e)** 8 **(f)** 8
**(g)** 9 **(h)** 9
**(i)** 9

3 **(a)** 8 **(b)** 30
**(c)** 6 **(d)** 20
**(e)** 50 **(f)** 7
**(g)** 90 **(h)** 2
**(i)** 4 **(j)** 5
**(k)** 5 **(l)** 9
**(m)** 6 **(n)** 7
**(o)** 7 **(p)** 5

4 (a) 270 ÷ 3 = 90
(b) 350 ÷ 50 = 7
(c) 640 ÷ 8 = 80

5 (a) 720 ÷ 9 = 80 (books)
(b) 1500 ÷ 3 = 500 (pounds)
(c) 240 × 4 + 240 = 1200 (litres)

6 ▲ = 3 ■ = 20 ● = 9

## Unit 9.11

1 (a) 4 r 1 (b) 6 r 1
(c) 5 r 2 (d) 6 r 2
(e) 6 r 1 (f) 7 r 1
(g) 9 r 3 (h) 9 r 2

2 (a) 5 (b) 6
(c) 6 (d) 6
(e) 8 (f) 8

3 (a) Minna: 50, 10, 23, 4 r 3, 14, 14 r 3
(b) Asif: 10, 4 r 3, 14 r 3

4 (a) 16, 10, 6
(b) 23, 20, 3
(c) 12, 70 ÷ 7 = 10, 14 ÷ 7 = 2
(d) 11 r 4, 70 ÷ 7 = 10, 11 ÷ 7 = 1 r 4
(e) 14 r 2, 60 ÷ 6 = 10, 26 ÷ 6 = 4 r 2

5 (a) 95 ÷ 7 = 13 r 4
(b) 75 ÷ 5 = 15
(c) 5 × 125 = 625

6 (a) 90 ÷ 6 = 15
(b) 4 × 25 = 100 (toys), 100 > 96, yes

7 (Other answers may be possible)
(a) 4 + 4 – 4 – 4 = 0
(b) (4 + 4 + 4) ÷ 4 = 3
(c) (4 + 4) ÷ (4 + 4) = 1
(d) (4 × 4 + 4) ÷ 4 = 5
(e) 4 ÷ 4 + 4 ÷ 4 = 2
(f) (4 + 4) × 4 ÷ 4 = 8

## Unit 9.12

1 (a) 3 r 2 (b) 6 r 1
(c) 7 r 7 (d) 6 r 1
(e) 8 r 3 (f) 8 r 6
(g) 5 r 3 (h) 9 r 3

2 (b) 39 (c) 13
(d) 23 (e) 31
(f) 12

3 (a) 12 (b) 32
(c) 34 (d) 25

4 (a) 39 ÷ 3 = 13
(b) 78 ÷ 6 = 13

5 (a) (35 + 53) ÷ 4 = 22 (hutches)
(b) 54 ÷ 2 = 27 (children)

6 11 ÷ 4 = 2 r 3

7 16 chocolates

## Unit 9.13

1 (a) 6 (b) 6
(c) 7 (d) 9
(e) 5 (f) 5

2 (a) 5 (b) 9 r 1
(c) 4 r 2 (d) 6 r 2
(e) 5 r 2 (f) 5 r 1
(g) 3 r 4 (h) 5 r 5

3 (a) 5 r 2 (b) 6 r 4
(c) 7 r 2 (d) 7 r 3
(e) 18 (f) 13
(g) 16 (h) 12

4 (a) 27 ÷ 3 = 9 (children)
(b) 88 ÷ 5 = 17 r 3 (balls)
(c) 78 ÷ 5 = 15 (coats) r 3 (buttons)

5 7 pencils or 14 pencils or 21 pencils or 28 pencils or 35 pencils

## Unit 9.14

1 (a) 10 (b) 20
(c) 20 (d) 100
(e) 13 (f) 24
(g) 21 (h) 2000

2 (a) 32 (b) 30 r 2
(c) 16 (d) 15 r 2

3 (a) 20 r 3 (b) 40 r 1
(c) 10 r 5 (d) 20
(e) 10 r 6 (f) 10 r 3
(g) 10 r 5 (h) 10 r 7

4 (a) 120 80 60
(b) 1000 600 500

5 (a) 400 (b) 900
(c) 2000 (d) 200
(e) 300 (f) 500

6 (a) 82 ÷ 2 = 41
(b) 900 ÷ 3 = 300
(c) 640 ÷ 2 = 320
(d) 320 ÷ 4 = 80

7 210 ÷ 3 = 70 (patches)

8 The 8th place

## Unit 9.15

1 (a) 60 (b) 360
(c) 3000 (d) 8000
(e) 23 (f) 1500
(g) 6 r 6 (h) 7000
(i) 63 (j) 210
(k) 40 (l) 400

2 (a) 14 r 2 (b) 30 r 1
(c) 18 r 2 (d) 12 r 1
(e) 16 r 1 (f) 10 r 4

3 (a) 96 ÷ 3 = 32
(b) 63 ÷ 7 = 9 (days)
(c) 96 ÷ 8 = 12 (minutes)
(d) (39 + 45) ÷ 4 = 21 (groups)
(e) 45 ÷ 5 = 9, 9 < 15, yes, the remaining jars: 15 – 9 = 6

4 31 ÷ 7 = 4 r 3 and 31 ÷ 4 = 7 r 3

5 (a) 39 ÷ 7 = 5 r 4
(b) (Answers may vary) for example: 71 ÷ 8 = 8 r 7

## Unit 9.16

1 (a) 20 (b) 50
(c) 40 (d) 200
(e) 500 (f) 400
(g) 110 (h) 210

2 149 r 1, 100, 40, 9 r 1, 149 (books), 1 left over

3 (a) 637 ÷ 3 = 212 r 1
(b) 665 ÷ 5 = 133
(c) 738 ÷ 6 = 123

4 (a) 134
(b) 122 r 2
(c) 116 r 6

5 (a) (266 – 62) ÷ 6 = 34 (apples)
(b) 100 × 4 = 400 (books) 400 ÷ 5 = 80 (books)

6 ▲ = 9

## Unit 9.17

1 (a) 20 (b) 100
(c) 30 (d) 13
(e) 300 (f) 23
(g) 92 (h) 150

2 (a) 6 (b) 6
(c) 10 (d) 6
(e) 8 (f) 5

3
```
      3 1
   ______
 6 ) 1 8 9
     1 8      ... 3 × 6
   ______
         9
         6    ... 1 × 6
   ______
         3
```

4 (a) 208 (b) 117
(c) 160 r 1 (d) 1409

5 (a) 109 r 2 (b) 81 r 7
(c) 70 r 6

6 (a) 4200 ÷ 7 = 600 (mosquitoes)
(b) (i) 480 ÷ 5 = 96 (toy cars)
(ii) 96 ÷ 8 = 12 (toy cars)

7 Divided by 2 and the remainder is 0: 630, 934, 616;
Divided by 3 and the remainder is 1: 934, 616, 373;
Divided by 7 and the remainder is 5: 299

8 Omid did it faster.
**Method I:** Omid's speed per hour: 304 ÷ 4 = 76 (apples);
Jenna's speed per hour: 36 × 2 = 72 (apples), 76 > 72;
**Method II:** Jenna picked: 36 × 2 × 4 = 288 (apples) in 4 hours;
Omid picked: 304 apples in 4 hours.
304 > 288

## Unit 9.18

1 (a) 128 (b) 7254
2 (a) 663 ÷ 7 = 94 r 5
3 (a) 126 r 2 (b) 140 r 3
(c) 101 r 2 (d) 75
(e) 150 (f) 102 r 1
4 (a) 38 (b) 54
(c) 2100 (d) 48
5 (a) ✓ (b) ✗
(c) ✗ (d) ✗
6 Answers may vary, for example,
Plan I: 18 (pots) 28 (rows)
18 × 28 = 504
Plan II: 24 (pots) 21 (rows)
24 × 21 = 504
Plan III: 36 (pots) 14 (rows)
36 × 14 = 504
7 80 ÷ 2 − 1 = 39 (pots)

## Unit 9.19

1 (a) 5 r 2 (b) 4 r 5
(c) 5 r 3 (d) 3 r 2
(e) 8 r 4 (f) 7 r 5
(g) 6 r 1 (h) 8 r 2
2 (a) 123 3 (b) 83 × 3 + 2 = 251
(c) 3 (d) 1 1 0
3 (a) 140 ÷ 6 = 23 (boxes) r 2 (kg), 23 + 1 = 24 (boxes)
(b) 29 ÷ 7 = 4 (boats) r 1 (child), 4 + 1 = 5 (boats) 32 ÷ 7 = 4 (boats) r 4 (children), 4 + 1 = 5 (boats) (29 + 32) ÷ 7 = 8 (boats) r 5 (children), 8 + 1 = 9 (boats)
(c) 50 ÷ 8 = 6 (pencil boxes) r 2 (pounds)
(d) (i) 147 ÷ 8 = 18 (exercise books) r 3 (pieces)
(ii) 8 − 3 = 5 (pieces)

4 750 ÷ 3 = 250 (kg)
5 Yes (Hint: When sawing a piece of wood into 2 pieces, it is sawed once. Thus, when sawing the wood into 7 pieces, it is sawed 6 times. (7 − 1) × 5 = 30 minutes)

## Unit 9.20

1 (a) 63 (b) 16
(c) 32 (d) 80
(e) 1200 (f) 80
(g) 250 (h) 15
(i) 91 (j) 64
(k) 30 (l) 72
2 £42 £34 100 boxes
3 (a) Unit price × Quantity = Total price
(b) Total price ÷ Unit price = Quantity
(c) Total price ÷ Quantity = Unit price
4 105 × 4 = 420 (pounds)
5 30 × 3 = 90 (pounds); 24 × 8 = 192 (apples)
6 (a) 660 × 6 = 3960
(b) 660 ÷ 6 = 110
(c) 8 × 402 + 7 = 3223
7 768 ÷ 8 = 96 (boxes)
8 (12 − 1) × 6 = 66 (metres)
9 The 16th tree

## Chapter 9 test

1 (a) 240 (b) 1600
(c) 20 (d) 101
(e) 1800 (f) 5
(g) 64 (h) 3
(i) 545 (j) 50
(k) 50 (l) 300
(m) 900 (n) 90
(o) 28 (p) 15
2 (a) 1104 (b) 130
(c) 102 r 1
3 (a) 1228 (b) 228
(c) 275
4 (a) 520 ÷ 4 = 130
(b) (38 × 4) + 99 = 251
(c) 192 × 7 + 2 = 1346
(d) 69 ÷ 3 = 23
5 (a) 240 300 300 (answers may vary)
(b) 9900
(c) 20, 12, 138, 100, 20, 6, 504
(d) tens 2
(e) 5 4
(f) 165
(g) 30
(h) 8 135
(i) 3
6 5200 pounds
7 634 ÷ 8 = 79 r 2
8 741 ÷ 9 = 82 (books) r 3 (pieces); 9 − 3 = 6 (pieces)
9 200 − 200 ÷ 5 = 160 (kg)
10 (400 − 260) ÷ 2 = 70 (flowers)
11 35 − 252 ÷ 9 = 7 (boxes)
12 24 × 4 = 96 (kg); 96 − 24 = 72 (kg)
13 9

# Chapter 10 Let's practise geometry

## Unit 10.1

1 (a) 4 (b) 6
(c) 7 (d) 5
2 (a) ✗ (b) ✓
(c) ✓ (d) ✓
3 (a) C (b) D (c) D
4 (a) 4, 0 (b) 4, 4
(c) 3, 1 (d) 3, 0
(e) 4, 4 (f) 3, 0
(g) 3, 1 (h) 5, 0
5 Drawing should show
(a) An angle of 90°
(b) An angle between 0° and 90°
(c) An angle between 90° and 180°
6 Answers may vary, for example, a vertical line from the top left vertex down to the base
7 5

## Unit 10.2

1 Lines drawn to link: 'Horizontal lines' to 'Lines that run from left to right' to the diagram with horizontal lines; 'Vertical lines' to 'Lines that run from top to bottom' to the diagram with vertical lines
2 (a) Vertical lines: 1 3;
Horizontal lines: 2 4
(b) Vertical line: 4; Horizontal line: 1
3 Correctly labelled and listed vertical and horizontal lines
4 (a) ✗ (b) ✗
(c) ✓ (d) ✓
5 Answers may vary

## Unit 10.3

1 Lines drawn to link: 'Perpendicular lines' to 'Lines that meet at a right angle' to the diagram with perpendicular lines; 'Parallel lines' to 'Lines that will never meet' to the diagram with parallel lines
2 Correctly labelled and listed parallel and perpendicular lines, and 'none' correctly shown

3 (a) vertical parallel
(b) horizontal parallel
(c) perpendicular
(d) perpendicular
(e) perpendicular

4 (a) ✓ (b) ✗
(c) ✓ (d) ✗

5 Answers may vary

## Unit 10.4

1

| | Is it a 2-D or 3-D shape? | What is the name of the shape? | If it is a 2-D shape, is it a symmetrical figure? |
|---|---|---|---|
| | 2-D | triangle | no |
| | 3-D | cylinder | |
| | 2-D | square | yes |
| | 3-D | cuboid | |
| | 2-D | hexagon | yes |
| | 3-D | pyramid | |

2 Correct drawings of any
(a) rectangle
(b) pentagon
(c) octagon

3 Correct drawings of the shapes as described (answers may vary)

4 A cube

5 A triangular prism

## Unit 10.5

1 (a) 100 (b) 10
(c) 1000 (d) 50
(e) 150 (f) 7
(g) 130 (h) 226
(i) 3 (j) 90

2 (a) 4 (b) 110
(c) 6, 4

3 (a) cm (b) mm
(c) m (d) m
(e) mm mm

4 (a) > (b) >
(c) > (d) <
(e) < (f) =
(g) = (h) =

5 (a) 300 mm < 100 cm < 340 cm < 11 m 98 cm < 12 m
(b) 490 mm < 4 m 90 cm < 600 cm < 50 m

6 (a) 7 m 45 mm
(b) 90 cm

7 (a) 145 cm or 1m 45 cm
(b) 2 m 91 cm or 291 cm

## Unit 10.6

1 Answers may vary

2 (a) 14 cm (b) 16 cm
(c) 20 cm (d) 24 cm

3 (a) 17 cm (b) 17 mm
(c) 26 m

4 900 m

5 11 ways, 10 cm

## Unit 10.7

1 (a) 20 cm (b) 18 cm
(c) 22 cm (d) 22 cm

2 (a) 38 cm (b) 36 cm
(c) 475 mm (d) 40 mm

3 (a) 110 mm (b) 112 mm
(c) 95 mm (d) 107 mm

4 64 cm

5 no; Shape 1 and Shape 2 share the same curve connecting A and B, and the other parts of their perimeters are equal because the figure is a rectangle

6 (a) 66 mm (b) 300 mm

## Chapter 10 test

1 Angles: 1 2 6 8; Right angle: 2

2 (a) ✓ (b) ✓
(c) ✓ (d) ✗
(e) ✓ (f) ✗
(g) ✓ (h) ✗

3 (a) vertical parallel
(b) horizontal parallel
(c) perpendicular
(d) perpendicular
(e) perpendicular

4 (a) 800 (b) 1000
(c) 90 (d) 5
(e) 1000 (f) 10
(g) 250 (h) 566
(i) 8 80 (j) 9

5 (a) C (b) D
(c) A (d) C

6 6

7 Correct drawings of the shapes as described (answers may vary)

8 20 m

9 (a) 128 mm
(b) 101 mm
(c) 109 mm

10 52 cm

11 1620 m

# End of year test

1 (a) 800 (b) 60
(c) 120 (d) 6
(e) 600 (f) 97
(g) 90 (h) 110
(i) 61 (j) 0
(k) 70 (l) 205

2 (a) $\frac{4}{5}$ (b) $\frac{1}{3}$
(c) $\frac{5}{6}$ (d) $\frac{8}{11}$
(e) 0 (f) $\frac{4}{7}$

3 (a) C (b) D
(c) B (d) D

4 (a) 100 1000
(b) (i) kg
(ii) seconds
(iii) pounds
(iv) days
(c) $\frac{1}{4}$
(d) 6, 8
(e) 1000, 988, 908, 857, 799
(f) 7, 27
(g) 366, 52, 2

5 (a) 739 (b) 339
(c) 409 (d) 834
(e) 992 (f) 68

6 (a) 12
(b) 2 3 5 6
(c) 1 4 7 8

7 (a) 52 m
(b) 76 m

8 (a) 180 − 125 = 55 (cm)
(b) 9 × 5 + 6 = 51 (sweets)
(c) 287 ÷ 7 = 41 (metres)
(d) 152 × 2 − 16 = 288 (girls)
(e) (i) Correctly drawn and labelled bar chart showing the data in the table
(ii) 4, 2, 6
(iii) 116
(iv) Answer may vary

# Notes

# Notes